Clio & the Crown

Clio & the Crown

THE POLITICS OF HISTORY IN MEDIEVAL AND EARLY MODERN SPAIN

RICHARD L. KAGAN

The Johns Hopkins University Press
Baltimore

This book has been brought to publication with the generous assistance of the Program for Cultural Cooperation between Spain's Ministry of Culture and United States Universities.

© 2009 The Johns Hopkins University Press
All rights reserved. Published 2009
Printed in the United States of America on acid-free paper
2 4 6 8 9 7 5 3 1

The Johns Hopkins University Press
2715 North Charles Street
Baltimore, Maryland 21218-4363
www.press.jhu.edu

ISBN-13: 978-0-8018-9294-3
ISBN-10: 0-8018-9294-5

Frontispiece: Vincente Joan Macip, *Alfonso I of Naples and V of Aragon* ("the Magnanimous"; 1396–1458), 1559. Photograph courtesy of the Museo de Bellas Artes, Zaragoza. Photographer: José Garrido. This portrait—one of several featuring the kings of Aragon—was commissioned by the town councillors (or *jurats*) of the City of Valencia and subsequently presented to the Infante don Carlos, son of Philip II, presumably to remind the young prince about his illustrious Aragonese ancestors. It depicts Alfonso (r. 1416–1458) as a ruler skilled in the arts of both war and peace. The polished black armor, matching helmet, and sword allude to Alfonso's military achievements, among them the conquest of the kingdom of Naples in 1438. The bejeweled crown underscores the king's majesty as does the inscription *Alfonsus Quintus Aragonum Rex* on the sill of the window that offers a glimpse of his realm. Macip refers to the king's literary patronage by placing the crown on top of an open manuscript book that has been identified as Antonio Beccadelli's *De dictis et factis Alphonsi Regis* (*The Sayings and Deeds of King Alfonso*), a work that Alfonso commissioned c. 1455. First published (in Castilian translation) in 1527, the book belongs to the genre of "official" history examined in the pages that follow.

Special discounts are available for bulk purchases of this book. For more information, please contact Special Sales at 410-516-6936 or specialsales@press.jhu.edu.

Library of Congress Cataloging-in-Publication Data will be found at the end of this book.

For Orest Ranum
Mentor. Colleague. Friend.

Who controls the past . . . controls the future;
who controls the present, controls the past.
GEORGE ORWELL, *1984*

CONTENTS

Preface ix
List of Abbreviations xiii

INTRODUCTION Official History   1

CHAPTER 1 Empire and History   16

CHAPTER 2 *Historia pro Persona:* Emperor Charles V   57

CHAPTER 3 *Historia pro Patria:* Philip II   94

CHAPTER 4 "His Majesty's History"   124

CHAPTER 5 Defending *Imperium*   150

CHAPTER 6 "To Mortify Our Enemies":
History and Propaganda at the Court of Philip IV   201

CHAPTER 7 Critical History or Official History?   251

CONCLUSION Rethinking Official History   290

Selected Bibliography 301
Index 335

Illustrations follow page 114.

PREFACE

This book has been long, probably too long, in the making. I first started thinking about the uses, as opposed to the idea and practice, of history back in the 1980s, when I was working on the history of Toledo, Spain's imperial city, in the era of its most famous artist, Doménikos Theotokópoulos, a.k.a. El Greco (1547–1614). My inquiries into this topic included reading histories by various Toledan scholars interested in documenting their city's past. Upon further consideration, I came to the realization that the histories had purposes other than simply preserving Toledo's historical record. I learned, for example, that the first of the histories, Pedro de Alcocer's *Historia o descripción de la imperial ciudad de Toledo* (Toledo, 1554), was specifically intended to remind Prince Philip, the future Philip II (r. 1556–1598), about the city's importance as Spain's traditional capital and to persuade him that Toledo, the *"cabeza de España"* (or "head of Spain"), was where he needed to establish his court.

As it turned out, Alcocer's arguments proved convincing. Philip, upon his return to Spain from the Netherlands in 1559, settled in the so-called Imperial City for a stay lasting almost two years. In 1561, however, apparently tired of climbing Toledo's steep hills and maneuvering the city's narrow streets, Philip moved both his capital and his court to Madrid, some forty miles to the north. The loss of the royal court prompted considerable soul-searching on the part of many Toledans. What went wrong? they asked. Some solace was provided by the repatriation of relics belonging to two of the city's early martyrs, San Eugenio and Santa Leocodia, which reinforced Toledo's traditional view of itself as Spain's spiritual capital. Additional support came from several local scholars, especially Francisco de Pisa, who wrote accounts celebrating Toledo's long and illustrious history and explaining why the imperial city still deserved to be the king's permanent residence. In the first instance these histories were intended to placate a local audience that lamented the loss of the court. Secondarily, they targeted a somewhat larger audience in Madrid in the hope of persuading the monarchy to reverse its prior decision and make Toledo Spain's capital once again.

Toledo's bid for renewed grandeur did not work, but Pisa's history and a later and more elaborate one by Pedro de Rojas, count of Mora, endure as monuments commemorating, though with questionable accuracy, Toledo's illustrious past. The two histories also prompted me to start thinking about the different ways in which cities, and then princes, put history to work. These concerns led to my "Clio and the Crown: Writing History in Habsburg Spain," which was published in 1995 in *Spain, Europe, and the Atlantic World,* a volume dedicated to John H. Elliott and one that I had the privilege of editing together with my colleague and friend Geoffrey Parker. Although I did not know it at the time, that essay served as the starting point for this book. In many ways, however, that essay and this book are worlds apart. In my "Clio and the Crown" essay, I was principally concerned with municipal history of the kind produced by Alcocer, Pisa, and other local scholars—*eruditos* in Spanish—who endeavored to insert the history of their city—it could also have been a small town, even a village—into the broader, national epic of Spain and its monarchy. In this volume, center stage goes to the royal chroniclers and the histories they wrought in honor of both country and king.

This transition from city to court—think of it as my own version of Philip II's decision to move from Toledo to Madrid—did not occur overnight. Partly it was thrust upon me by a pair of quincentennial celebrations organized by the Spanish government in honor of the death in 1598 of Philip II and the birth in 1500 of Philip's father, Emperor Charles V, Spain's first Habsburg monarch. The latter led to my essay "The Emperor and His Chroniclers," which appeared in *Carolus Imperator* (Madrid, 1999). In much revised form, this essay metamorphosed into Chapter 2 of the present volume. As for the celebrations honoring Philip II, these led to two essays—"Philip II, History, and the Cronistas del Rey," in *Philippus II Rex* (Madrid, 1998); and "Felipe II: El hombre y la imagen," in *Felipe II y el arte de su tiempo* (Madrid, 1998)—as well as a short book, *El rey recatado: Felipe II, la historia, y los cronistas del rey* (Valladolid, 2004), the published version of a lecture I had presented to the history faculty at the University of Valladolid as part of the lecture series "Catédra Felipe II." Material from these publications has found its way, again in much revised form, into Chapters 3 and 4 of the present study.

Several other chapters also have their origins in previously published pieces. Chapter 5 draws upon my essay "La historia y la crónica de las Indias durante el siglo XVII: Antonio de Herrera y Tordesillas," which appeared in *El imperio sublevado: Monarquía y naciones en España e Hispanoamérica,* edited by Victor Mínguez and Manuel Chust (Madrid, 2004). Portions of Chapter 6 represent reworkings of material from two essays: " 'Official History' at the Court of Philip II of Spain," in *Princes and Princely Culture II*, edited by M. Gosman (Boston, 2005); and "Antonio de Herrera y Tordesillas and the 'Political Turn' in the 'Official History' of Seventeenth-Century Spain," in *Les historiographes en Europe*, edited by Chantal Grell (Paris, 2006).

Support for my research and writing has come from various sources. To begin with, I am grateful to the Cátedra Fundación Banco Bilbao-Vizcaya and the Universidad Complutense de Madrid for grants that enabled me to work in Spanish archives and libraries during the 1999–2000 academic year. Further assistance came from France's Centre de Recherche Scientifique, which led to a delightful fall 2002 semester in Paris and long hours in the peaceful surrounds of the Bibliothèque Mazarine. I also appreciate the support that I have received over the years from my home institution, the Johns Hopkins University. The sabbatical leave I was awarded in 2006–2007 enabled me to complete a draft of most of the present study. That task was greatly aided by support from the School of Historical Studies at the Institute for Advanced Study in Princeton. As a member there during fall 2006, I completed most of what is now Chapters 1 and 6 of the present book.

It goes without saying that other individuals, and the institutions to which they belong, also helped to bring this study to a successful conclusion. I owe much to director José Luís Rodríguez Diego, Isabel Aguirre, and other members of the staff of the Archivo General de Simancas, along with their counterparts at the Archivo Histórico Nacional, the Biblioteca Nacional de España, the Biblioteca Real, the Instituto Valencia de Don Juan, the Archivo y Biblioteca Francisco de Zabalburú, and the Real Academia de la Historia, all in Madrid, as well as the Archivo General de las Indias in Seville. I owe a special debt of gratitude to Manolo Balmeseda, count of Puñonrostro, who kindly allowed me to work with his family archives and to explore valuable papers relating to the life and work of Antonio de Herrera y Tordesillas, one of the royal chroniclers who figures prominently in this work.

As for individuals, my memory is short, and I have certainly forgotten the names of many who, by way of passing comment or bibliographic reference, have been instrumental in helping to formulate this study. The list begins with Orest Ranum, whose seminal book *Artisans of Glory: Writers and Historical Thought in Seventeenth-Century France* (1980) served as my point of departure. Further inspiration came from John Elliott, whose expertise in Spanish and Spanish-American history is virtually unmatched; Geoffrey Parker, who, in addition to providing me with valuable archival references, kindly read portions of my manuscript; and

Fernando Bouza, a scholar who in knowledge of Spanish archives is without peer. Further assistance came from James Amelang; Xavier Gil Pujol; Fernando Marías; my brother Robert A. Kagan (thank you, Bob, for help with the Introduction); two Davids, Bell and Nirenberg, both of whom offered valuable suggestions for improving this work; Peter Arnade; Eva Botellas Ordiñas; Christina Cornette; Chantal Grell; Anthony Molho; Jean-Frédéric Schaub; Benjamin Schmidt; Jacob Soll; Gabrielle Spiegel; Bernard Vincent; Markus Völkel; and the anonymous reader who evaluated the manuscript for the Johns Hopkins University Press.

I owe a further debt to my graduate students at the Johns Hopkins University, starting with A. Katie Harris, Benjamin Ehlers, Guy Lazure, Erin Rowe, Kimberly Lynn Hossain, Carolyn Salomons, and Molly Warsh, all of whom, in one venue or another, patiently listened to me expound on the subject of "official history" and, better, offered interesting and suggestive comments in return. Andrew Devereux merits a special vote of thanks for reading an early draft of Chapter 1 in addition to helping me prepare the bibliography, as does Guy Lazure for providing me with a raft of references I had inadvertently missed. I am equally grateful to Henry Tom, executive editor of the Johns Hopkins University Press, for his foresight, comments, and support, along with my excellent copy editor, Lois R. Crum.

Finally, to Shreve, my beloved spouse, I say thank you, as always, for your patience, support, and superb editorial skills. And I guess some credit should go to Roxy, our cat, whose inability to open the front door of our house regularly dragged me away from my study and reminded me that beyond history there is life.

ABBREVIATIONS

ABZ	Archivo y Biblioteca Zabalburú, Madrid
ACC	*Las actas de las Cortes de Castilla*, 60 vols. (Madrid, 1877–1974)
ACP	Archivo de los Condes de Puñonrostro, Madrid
AGI	Archivo General de Indias, Seville
AGI IG	Archivo General de Indias, Indiferente General
AGS	Archivo General de Simancas
AGS Est	Archivo General de Simancas, Estado
AHN	Archivo Histórico Nacional, Madrid
AHN Cons	Archivo Histórico Nacional, Consejos suprimidos
AHN Inq.	Archivo Histórico Nacional, Inquisición
AHPM	Archivo Histórico de Protocolos, Madrid
AMT	Archivo Municipal, Toledo
ANT	Archivo de la Nobleza, Toledo
BAE	*Biblioteca de autores españoles*
BCC	Biblioteca Columbina y Capitular, Seville
BL	British Library
BL Add.	British Library, Additional Mss.
BL Eg.	British Library, Egerton Mss.
BNE	Biblioteca Nacional de España, Madrid
BR	Biblioteca Real, Madrid
BRAH	*Boletín de la Real Academia de la Historia*
BRME	Biblioteca del Real Montasterio de El Escorial
BUS	Biblioteca de la Universidad de Salamanca
CLC	*Cortes de los antiguos reinos de Castilla y León*, 5 vols. (Madrid, 1861–1903)

Codindias	*Colección de documentos inéditos relativo al descubrimiento, conqusita y organización de las antiguas posesiones españolas de América y Oceanía*, 42 vols. (Madrid, 1864–1884)
Codoin	*Colección de documentos inéditos para la historia de España*, 113 vols. (Madrid, 1842–1895)
HGI	Antonio de Herrera y Tordesillas, *Historia general de los hechos de los castellanos en las islas i tierra firme del mar oceano*, 3 vols. (Madrid, 1601–1615). The same work was edited by Antonio Ballesteros-Beretta (Madrid, 1934); and by Mariano Cuesta Domingo, 4 vols. (Madrid, 1991).
HGM	Antonio de Herrera y Tordesillas, *Primera [-terecera] parte de la historia general del mundo . . . del tiempo del señor rey don Felipe II, el Prudente* (Madrid, 1601–1612)
IVDJ	Instituto Valencia de Don Juan, Madrid
leg.	*legajo* (bundle)
lib.	*libro* (book)
MHE	*Memorial Histórico Español*, 48 vols. (Madrid, 1851–)
RABM	*Revista de archivos, bibliotecas, y museos*
RAH	Biblioteca de la Real Academia de la Historia (Madrid)

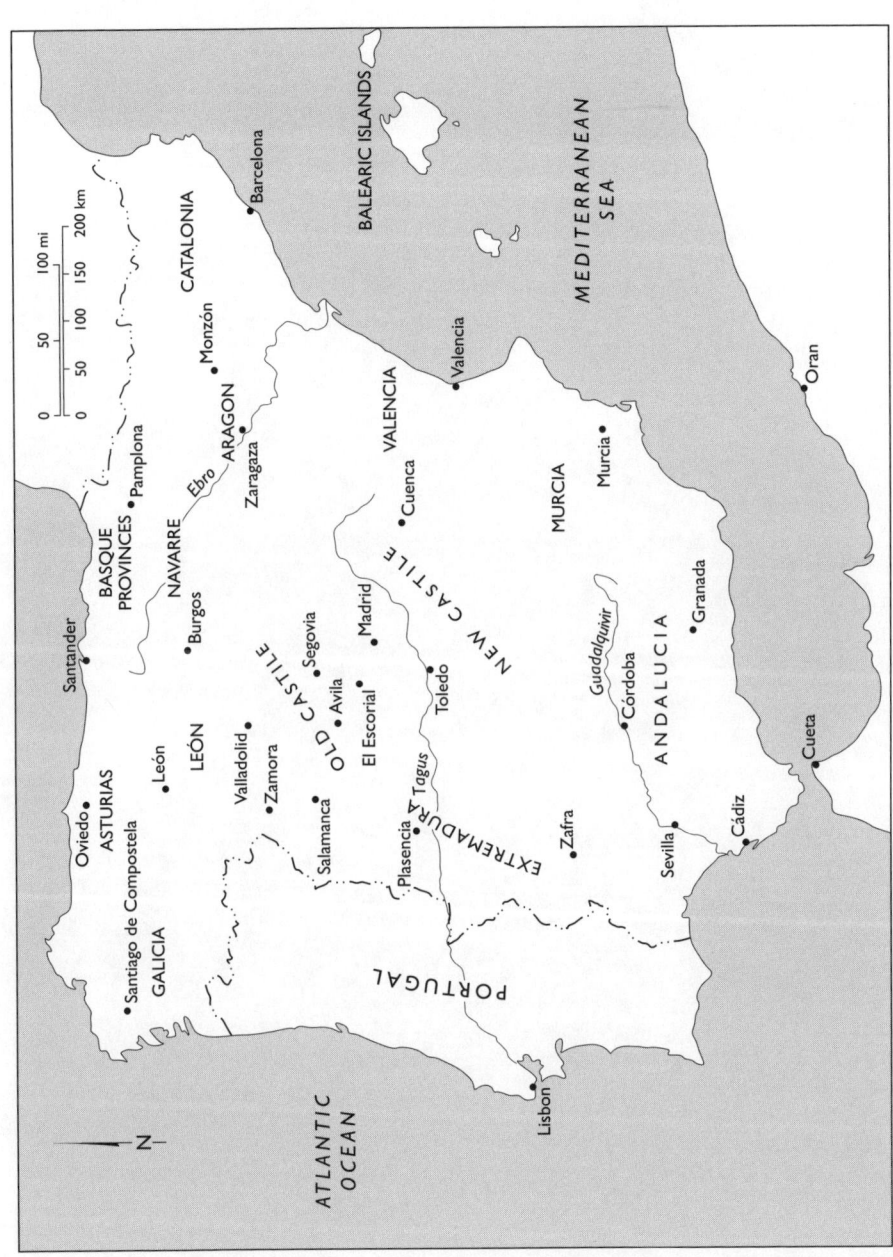

Spain under the Habsburgs

Clio & the Crown

INTRODUCTION

Official History

> Though all Historians will not . . . confesse themselves Fellowes in Lying, yet this is a true Historie, *Every Man*, and therefore every Historian, is a *Lyar*.
> —Samuel Purchas, *Microcosmus, or the Historie of Man* (1627)

> It is common experience that flatterers are the ruine of princes; and yet it is easie to shew that that princes are themselves the forgers of this, their ruine.
> —Virgilio Malvezzi, *Discourse upon Tacitus* (1642)

I begin with a short drama. The place: London. The year: 1616. The setting: not the Globe, Shakespeare's theater, but the royal residence at Whitehall. The principal characters are a king, an ambassador, a prisoner, and a book, all of whom play themselves. The king is James I, ruler of England and Scotland, their thrones newly united. The ambassador: Diego Sarmiento de Acuña, count of Gondomar, representative of King Philip III at the English court. The prisoner: Sir Walter Ralegh, businessman, courtier, explorer, historian, and, starting in 1603, inmate in the Tower of London. The book: Antonio de Herrera y Tordesillas's *History of the World in the Age of Philip II*, a work of official history that was especially commissioned to demonstrate the global reach of Spain's empire and to help document and to defend its *imperium* in the New World.

The plot line: simple, yet predictable. In March 1616 Ralegh secured his release from the Tower by promising James, then desperately in need of money, that he would lead, and largely self-finance, an expedition down the Orinoco River in Guyana. There, Ralegh claimed, lay the fabled El Dorado, a gold mine of "great importance" that would provide James all the money he needed and more. To

---

Epigraphs: Samuel Purchas, *De Microcosmus or the Historie of Man*, in *Purchas his Pilgrim* (London, 1627), 588; Malvezzi, *Discourse upon Tacitus*, 81.

justify this voyage still further, Ralegh invoked the legal doctrine of *res nullius,* or *terra nullius,* and along with it the suggestion that Guyana was a territory to which no one laid territorial claim. The explorer thus explained to James that Guyana "was something yet to be discovered or known about by anyone, the Spaniards included."[1]

The scheme was entirely far-fetched, Ralegh's way of getting out of the Tower. Moreover, since it came at a time when Spaniards were already anxious about the new British settlement at Jamestown, Virginia, Gondomar rightly regarded Ralegh's Guyana scheme as yet another threat to the territorial integrity of Spain's empire in the Americas. The ambassador, a close friend of the monarch, subsequently met with James in order to tell him that Ralegh was misinformed on two important counts: the existence of this gold mine and the idea that the area around the Orinoco was unknown to the Spaniards; in fact it harbored several Spanish settlements and formed an integral part of the Spanish empire.

But how was Gondomar able to prove this assertion? He went to his library, grabbed a book—Herrera's world history—and in another audience with the king read aloud from a chapter in which Herrera explicitly made reference to Ralegh's previous voyage to Guyana in 1595. Citing chapter and verse, Gondomar related how Ralegh had not only encountered a Spanish settlement along the banks of the Orinoco but also learned from the local residents that the gold mine he was looking for was a joke ("burlería"), the product of the Englishman's fertile imagination.[2]

In the end, Ralegh got what he wanted, permission to sail to the New World, but with the proviso, undoubtedly the result of a secret deal Gondomar worked out with James, that if he so much as injured any Spaniard or appropriated any gold that legitimately belonged to the Spanish monarch, he would be severely punished upon his return. It also seems that James purposely set up Ralegh for failure by providing Gondomar with detailed information about the expedition's itinerary and the number of ships, soldiers, and armaments it entailed.[3]

---

1. As reported in a letter of Diego Sarmiento de Acuña to Philip III, dated 2 September 1616 and reproduced in *Documentos inéditos para la historia de España,* 1:54–55.

2. Ibid. Gondomar apparently read from Herrera y Tordesillas, *Historia del mundo,* vol. 3, bk. 11, chap. 28, pp. 584–585. Note that this incident goes unreported in standard English-language accounts of Ralegh's voyages, among them Trevelyan, *Sir Walter Raleigh;* Quinn, *Set Faire for Roanoke;* Harlow, *Raleigh's Last Voyage;* and Stebbing, *Sir Walter Raleigh.*

3. Ralegh was certainly convinced that James had "set up" the expedition to result in failure. See *The Letters of Sir Walter Raleigh,* esp. letter 219, to Lady Raleigh from St. Christophers, 22 March 1618, 353–355, in which he informs his wife of the death of their son ("my braines are broken, and tis a torment for mee to write, espetially, of miserie") and says in a postscript, "there was never a poore man soe exposed to the slaughter as I was. For, being commanded upon my allegiance to sit downe, not only the countrey but the very river by which I was to enter it, to name my shipps, number my men and my artillery, this

As it turned out, the expedition proved both a political and a personal disaster, as it not only failed to find any gold but also resulted in the deaths of several Spaniards and of Ralegh's only son. Upon his return to London in 1618, Ralegh was arrested anew, imprisoned once again in the Tower of London, and, true to the deal apparently negotiated by Gondomar, executed shortly thereafter.

More than a meaningless anecdote, this little imperial drama offers rare insight into the kind of power, "soft power" in this instance, that a work of history could exert. It is also part of a larger story that historians, including even those interested in historiography, often neglect: the extent to which history can serve as an instrument of imperial policy used to document conquests, legitimate policies of expansion, justify imperial titles, and, as just witnessed, defend claims to territories. In early modern Europe, official histories similar to Herrera's were ubiquitous, because most princes employed chroniclers to write "official histories" especially designed to celebrate their victories, augment their reputations, and defend their interests and concerns.

This volume focuses on such histories with particular reference to medieval and early modern Spain, emphasizing the ways different rulers put history to work. But what is official history, and how does it differ from ordinary history? Put simply, official history is "approved" or "authorized" history, history that receives governmental sponsorship and support.[4] Official history, moreover, is generally crafted with an eye toward creating a historical record that favors the interests and concerns of the ruler—it could also be a church, a religious order, a city, a university, even a family or an individual—for whom it was originally written. In this respect, official history, like other histories, speaks to the future: it is intended to provide succeeding generations with a particular reading of the past. Equally importantly, official history addresses the present: it is often designed to court public opinion, legitimate a ruler's claim to power, or rally support for a particular political program or set of beliefs. In some instances, it serves as well to create what Stephen Orgel has called the "illusion of power,"[5] an image of princely grandeur and importance that is often overinflated but essential to a ruler's self-image as a historical actor.

---

was sent by the Spanish ambassador [Gondomar] to his master the King. The King wrote his lettres to all partes of the Indies, and espetially to the governor, Palomeque, of Guiana, Eldorado, and Trinidado."

4. For a brief discussion of official history with particular reference to early modern France, see Grell, *L'histoire entre érudtion et philosophie*, 195–219. On 195 she defines "l'histoire officielle" as an "instrument de glorification, fut dès son origine une histoire au service du prince."

5. Orgel, *The Illusion of Power*.

Defined in this way, official history is often equated with propaganda, that is, information (or misinformation) that its producers know is distorted or false. Already in the sixteenth century, one Italian observer, Girolamo Franchi di Conestaggio, described official historians such as Herrera y Tordesillas as historians who were "commissioned to lie" (*condotto a mentire*),[6] a remark that anticipated by some four hundred years Donald Kelley's recent assertion that official history, like propaganda, aims at "the willful distortion of information." Kelley's statement that "the office [of the official historian] was a polemical, not a scholarly one" also suggests that what these historians wrote is probably not worth reading, a position recently echoed by Anthony Grafton, whose dismissal of the work of official historians as "marmoreal narratives . . . as smooth and empty as modern university brochures," though memorable, is certain to upset university directors of admissions throughout the world.[7]

Both Kelley and Grafton, the high priests of early modern humanist historiography, are correct in suggesting that court historians were often second-rate characters who owed their appointment to factors such as proven loyalty to a particular ruler more than to scholarly excellence. Yet it should not be forgotten that the ranks of Europe's official chroniclers—the list includes such talented writers as Gomes Eanes de Zurara and João de Barros in Portugal, Philippe de Commines and George Chastelain in Burgundy, Pietro Bembo and Pietro Sarpi in Venice, Hugo Grotius in the Netherlands, Scipion Dupleix and Jean Racine in France, and later Voltaire, together with Juan Ginés de Sepúlveda in Castile and Jerónimo de Zurita in Aragon—were filled with top-notch scholars eager for the perquisites such offices tended to provide. Each of these historians was fully committed to Cicero's understanding of history as the *lux veritas,* or "lamp of truth," but unlike today's scholars who question the veracity of official history, they did not subscribe to the notion that truthful history is incompatible with the work of an official chronicler. For this reason few hesitated to place Clio, the famed muse of history, into the service of their respective city or prince.

It is equally an overstatement to suggest that official historians mired themselves in polemical and marmoreal narratives with neither merit nor substance. Throughout early modern Europe the boundary separating "polemical" from "scholarly" history was never well-defined, and few historians, whether official or nonofficial, wrote history free of ideological influences or polemical concerns. Open bias was almost a given, something that the Spanish theologian Melchor

---

6. Conestaggio, *Dell'unione del regno di Portogallo.* The first edition of this book dates from 1585.
7. Kelley, *The Beginning of Ideology,* 311. Grafton, *What Was History?* 235. Grafton uses the term "politic history" instead of official history.

Cano, writing in the 1540s, observed with the remark that "apart from sacred authors . . . there is no historian who has not lied about something."[8] This proposition is one that historians of Cano's era were likely to have endorsed. For these writers, the only true history was sacred history, as represented in Scripture and, secondarily, in the writings of Augustine and the other fathers of the early church. They also believed that other histories, including their own, were necessarily flawed, subject as they were to human emotions and other shortcomings. Following Thucydides, however, they also believed that truth, while never "easy to discover," might be possible so long as the historian diligently inquired into the reliability of his sources, checked and cross-checked the veracity of his evidence, and finally wrote a history that his audience found useful.[9] Yet despite such affirmations, authors of the *artes historicae*—Grafton's "artists of history"— repeatedly found it necessary to remind their fellow historians of the need to pay homage to Cicero by writing only history that adhered to the truth. Such advice was necessary because even the most high-minded and scholarly early modern historians had a nasty habit of "cherry-picking" their evidence so as to achieve a particular reading of given personage, era, or event.

I would be the first to admit that official historians, given the obligations their office, cherry-picked their evidence more often than others, and some did so with consummate skill. Rarely, however, did they willfully invent or distort the past. Like other historians, they sifted and shifted existing evidence and then tweaked it so as to produce a narrative that best served the interests of their sponsor and would impress their readers as both truthful and convincing. The official historians of early modern Europe had little in common, however, with the propagandists employed by Hitler or Stalin, many of whom knowingly engaged in the business of misinformation. Better to compare the official historians to the slick, fast-talking press officers who surround today's democratic political leaders and engage in what is colloquially known as "spin," selective but still accurate readings of the evidence relating to a particular happening or event.

In early modern Europe the semantic equivalent of spin included such terms as "light deceit" and "honest dissimulation."[10] Historians of this period also had the advantage of working within what Bernard Williams has labeled a "field of truth" that allowed for considerable slippage between what was considered to be

---

8. Melchor Cano, *De locis theologicus* (Salamanca, 1563), as cited in Franklin, *Jean Bodin and the Sixteenth-Century Revolution*, 109.

9. Thucydides' observations on history can be found at the opening (1:21–22) of his *History of the Peloponnesian War*.

10. Lipsius, *Politica*, bk. IV.14, 513. Accetto published his treatise *Della diussimulazione onesta* in 1641. For "honest dissimulation," see Villari, *Elogio della disimulazione;* and Zagorin, *Ways of Lying*.

wholly truthful (*veritas*), a term commonly defined in opposition to the mendacious statement or an outright lie, and verisimilitude (*vraisemblable* in French, *verosímil* in Spanish), a word that suggested the appearance, likelihood, or probability of truth.[11] Some official historians played this field better than others, but in general they would have agreed with Fray Juan de la Puente, a Dominican historian in the service of Philip III of Spain, who asserted that his principal obligation was to serve as the "boca de la república," or "spokesman of the state."[12]

It follows that the concepts of both truth and truthfulness employed by official historians depended, a priori, upon their personal allegiance to whatever ruler they served. In most cases, these persons were official historians because they were considered trustworthy and thus prepared to write narratives that worked to their ruler's advantage. In addition, the offices they occupied granted these historians a measure of authority that other, independent scholars often lacked. Almost by definition, therefore, readers disposed toward a particular ruler were likely to give greater weight to the narratives produced by his (or her) official historians as opposed to others. For this reason, starting already in the Middle Ages, European princes invested heavily in history, in the calculated effort first to rally their followers and second to persuade others to change their allegiances and come over to their side. In this respect, these histories served, as David Quint has defined them, as "narratives of power," instruments that rulers deployed both to defend themselves from their critics and to enhance their image and implement their will.[13]

Another way of understanding the work of official historians is to compare their narratives, as did the sixteenth-century Spanish humanist Juan Luis Vives, to the legal briefs that a lawyer prepares in support of a client.[14] Such documents offer a truthful narrative of events bearing upon an alleged violation of law, often through a selective reading of the evidence that minimizes the importance of some facts while highlighting that of others. Lawyers are also accustomed to impugning both the quality and relevance of the evidence brought forward by their opponents and insisting that their particular reading of the evidence is the one that best aligns with the truth. Official historians, or at least the ones I am concerned with, worked in similar ways, manipulating "facts" and arranging the evidence so as construct a narrative that readers would not only find convincing

---

11. Williams, *Truth and Truthfulness*, 274.
12. Puente, *Tomo primero de la conveniencia*, 2.
13. Quint, *Epic and Empire*, 45.
14. See Vives, "*De Disciplinis*," part 1, bk. 2, chap. 6, in *Obras completas*, 2:423. According to Vives, defending the reputation of one's country was the job of a lawyer, not a historian.

but accept as truthful. As in the court of law, therefore, where either a judge or the jury serves as the ultimate arbiters of the truth, when it comes to history, whether official or not, readers determine which among competing narratives best accords with the truth.[15] One difference, however, is that arguments presented by the prosecution or the plaintiff in a court of law must both convince the decision makers and satisfy what is commonly known as the "burden of proof." Otherwise, they lose the case. The outcome of histories is not nearly so immediate. Another difference is that court proceedings are generally presided over by judges with some standards for determining truth. Readers are much more diverse, as are the criteria by which they judge history. In this sense the verdict of history is far more uncertain, much harder to shape than the result in a court of law.

Thus, comparing the official historian to a lawyer is suggestive but still not quite right. Lawyers tend to be independent actors, "hired guns" who do not necessarily see eye-to-eye with the clients they represent. In contrast, official historians, more often than not, are *partis pris*, true believers, enthusiasts who are both anxious and eager to support their sponsor. For this reason, Juan de Flores, a historian in the service of the fifteenth-century Castilian monarch Isabella I (r. 1474–1504), defined his office as that of "a temporal (or earthly) evangelist" meant to render the ruler's reputation (*fama* in his language) "immortal."[16] The difference between official and nonofficial historians was neatly summarized in 1688 by Luis de Salazar y Castro, a royal chronicler in the service of King Charles II of Spain, when he contrasted a historian in his position to those who wrote "voluntarily . . . for pleasure . . . [or out of] inclination."[17]

Salazar y Castro was right. The content and character of the writings of official chronicles were generally determined by others, and in most cases their reports and narratives were closely scrutinized and subject to review. Some official historians bristled at the thought of this kind of censorship, let alone the idea of sacrificing their Ciceronian notions of historical truth to political concerns, and the chapters that follow recount the experiences of two humanists, Juan Ginés de Sepúlveda and Pedro de Valencia, who, once installed in the office of royal chroni-

---

15. For a fascinating inquiry into the manner in which audiences are the arbiters of truthfulness, see Williams, *Truth and Truthfulness*.

16. Cited in Agnew, *"Evangelista temporal,"* 11–47. Fernández de Oviedo, one of the first to chronicle Spain's conquests in the Indies, also likened the office of royal chronicler to that of an evangelist in his *Libro de la cámara real del príncipe Don Juan*, 174, where he writes: "Oficio es de evangelista, e conviene que este es persona que tema a Dios, por que ha de tratar en cosas muy importantes, e develas dezir, no tanto arrimándose a la eloquencia e ornamento retórico, quanto a la puridad e valor de la verdad, llanamente e sin rodeos no abundancia de palabras, puese que son memorias que han de durar mas que los reyes e vida del príncipe a quien sirven."

17. Salazar y Castro, *Advertencias históricas*, 156.

cler, found it difficult to reconcile their personal notions of scholarly integrity with political exigencies and other constraints.[18] Others had little difficulty dealing with such restrictions. They also welcomed the benefits attached to the offices of court chronicler: a regular salary, lodging, publication subsidies, privileged access to important state papers, and a modicum of prestige. These and other perquisites assured that individuals who aspired to these positions were rarely in short supply. Thus in 1621, when King Philip IV publicly announced that a position of court chronicler was vacant and invited interested candidates to submit their résumés, almost a dozen individuals put in for the job, among them Spain's most famous playwright, Lope de Vega (1562–1635), who was desperate to secure the perks attached to the office of *cronista del rey*.[19] Had Lope's bid proved successful, Spain's famed Siglo de Oro, its Golden Century for both literature and the arts, would likely have lost much of its luster. From this perspective, it is better that the position went to another scholar.[20]

Spain did not invent official history, of course, nor were its rulers the only ones bent on using history for political ends. Power has always expressed itself through narratives intended to offer rulers ways of justifying their actions, excoriating their enemies, and trumpeting their achievements for the benefit of future generations. In this respect, kingship and history go hand in hand. Some of the first traces of official history can be found in the wall inscriptions by victorious Assyrian rulers in the second millennium BCE, in clay tablets that recorded the annals of deeds of early Hittite rulers such as Tudalhiya I, Arnuwanda I, and Suppiluliuma I, and in hieroglyphs that successive Egyptian pharaohs had painted on the walls of Karnak and other temples scattered up and down the valley of the Nile.[21] Similarly, Cyrus, the Persian ruler, turned to the Greek scholar Xenophon to write his official history, whereas Livy, as J. B. Bury recognized, was "a Court historian . . . [whose] work fitted into the system of the political ideals of the Emperor."[22] The historians who worked for the rulers of Byzantium served a similar purpose, as did the various chroniclers attached to Emperor Charlemagne and other medieval monarchs, virtually all of whom sponsored self-serving chronicles designed to augment their authority and legitimate their rule. Initially, these chronicles were the

18. For another early modern example of an official historian who refused to bend the truth, see Johannesson, "The Renaissance of the Goths," 207–209, which relates how Olaus Petri had second thoughts about the history that the Swedish monarch Gustavus Vasa had ordered him to write.
19. Papers relating to this *concurso* are located in AGS: Cámara de Castilla, leg. 1111, n. 17. These are published, albeit somewhat inaccurately, in García Oro and Portela Silva, "Felipe III y sus cronistas," 1:255–279.
20. For an account of this competition, see the Conclusion.
21. Bryce, *The Kingdom of the Hittites*, 124–125, 129, 150–151.
22. Bury, *The Ancient Greek Historians*, 226.

work of chancery officers, royal secretaries, and other members of the princely household, but in the course of the fifteenth century specialized offices with such titles as *historiographe de roi, Historiograaf, Hofhistoriker, cronista-mor,* and *cronista del rey* emerged.[23] Impetus for the creation for these and similar offices derived in the first instance from the spread of Renaissance ideas about the importance of earthly or temporal achievement that, especially when translated into the conflictive world of dynastic politics, made reputation into a key component of kingship, something that no ruler could do without. One of the first Renaissance princes to learn this lesson was the Aragonese ruler Alfonso I, "the Magnanimous" (r. 1442–1468), who enlisted the services of Lorenzo Valla and other noted humanists to fashion a series of chronicles in which he and his father were to play starring roles.[24] Another was Francesco Sforza, a *condottiere* who came out of nowhere in 1447 to become ruler of Milan despite opposition from many of the city's older, more established patrician families. Sforza soon had his secretariat prepare a history glorifying both his genealogy and his personal record of accomplishment; his purpose was partly to sway public opinion in his favor and partly to solidify his reputation for posterity.[25]

Yet another fifteenth-century ruler who played the history game with consummate skill was Alfonso V of Portugal (r. 1448–1481). In 1467, on the heels of an expedition to Ceuta, Alfonso appointed his personal librarian, Gomes Eanes de Zurara (ca. 1410–1474), to the new office of *cronista-mor*. He then sent him to Africa to help the chronicler get a better sense of the region's topography and to write an eyewitness account celebrating the role of the monarchy in the Portuguese conquest of Guinea and other parts of that continent's northern and western coast. After receiving a preliminary report from Zurara, Alfonso—one eye trained on his future, the other on that of his family—wrote the following reply: "It is not without reason that men of your profession should be prized and honored, for next after the Princes and captains who achieve deeds worth remembering, they that record them, when those are dead, deserve much praise. What would have become of the deeds of Rome if Livy had not written them? What of Alexander's without a Quintus Curtius, of those of Troy without a Homer, of

---

23. The institutionalization of history is examined in Guenée, *Histoire et culture historique;* and Guenée, *Politique et histoire au Moyen Age.* See also Völkel, *Geschichtes-schreibung,* 217–218.

24. I refer to Bartolomeo Facio, *De rebus gestis ab Alphonso I* (1456); Antonio Beccadelli, a.k.a Panormita, *De dictis et factis Aphonsi regi* (1455); and Lorenzo Valla, *Historarum Ferdinandi Regis Aragoniae* (1446). For these commissions, see the introduction to Valla, *Historia de Fernando de Aragón;* Bartolomeo Facio, *Rerum gestarum Alfonsi regis libri*, edited by Daniella Pietragalli (Alessandria, 2004); and Ianziti, *Humanistic Historiography under the Sforzas,* 142–143.

25. This commission resulted in Lodrosio Crivelli's *De vita rebusque gestis Francesci Sfortiae* (1461–1463). See Ianziti, *Humanistic Historiography under the Sforzas,* 6.

Caesar's without a Lucan? . . . Many there are who devote themselves to the exercise of arms, but few to the art of oratory."[26]

As already seen, Alfonso was hardly the only fifteenth-century ruler to think this way. The kings of France had two kinds of chroniclers, the *historiographe de France*, a true officer of the Crown, and those who were given the more honorific title of *historiographe de roi*, which essentially qualified them for a pension granted to historians approved by the Crown.[27] And as we shall see in the case of Spain's Catholic Monarchs Ferdinand and Isabella, official chroniclers became even more important after the introduction of printing, with the possibility that whatever these chroniclers wrote could reach readers far and wide.[28] The sixteenth century in this respect represented a high-water mark for official history, a time when virtually all churches, cities, and rulers retained the services of chroniclers they could call their own. One notable holdout was the British monarchy, which stayed off the bandwagon of official history until 1608, when James I persuaded William Camden to write a Latin history of his predecessor, Elizabeth I.[29] But this monarch also wanted his own historian, and in 1615 he negotiated with Parliament in the hope of persuading it to approve the appointment of Thomas Dempster, a Scotsman who was to write a new history of Great Britain that, among other things, would prove that James's mother, Mary Stuart, was not the murderess described by the rabidly anti-Catholic George Buchanan in his history of Scotland.[30] In the end, this appointment had to wait, and not until 1661 did Charles II finally persuade Parliament to install James Howell as England's first Historiographer Royal.[31]

The princes of Europe were not alone in their desire to transform history into a servant of the state.[32] Chinese emperors, starting in the Han Dynasty (206 BCE–220 CE), maintained two official chroniclers, one to record their actions and another to record their words, and the so-called "veritable records" they compiled

---

26. As cited in Edgar Prestage, *Chronicles of Fernão Lopes and Gomes Eannes de Zurara* (Watford, UK, 1928), 167.

27. For these offices, see François Fossier, "A propos du titre d'historiographe sous l'ancien régime," *Revue d'histoire moderne et contemporaine* 33 (1985): 361–417. See also Christian Jouhaud, *Les pouvoirs de la littérature* (Paris, 2000).

28. On this theme, see *Les princes et l'histoire du XIVe au XVIIIe siècle*; Grell, *Les historiographes en Europe*; and Völkel, *Geschichtes-schreibung*.

29. Camden was apparently the king's third choice, as he had previously asked the French historian Jacques-Auguste de Thou as well as his librarian, Patrick Young, to write this account. See Trevor-Roper, *Queen Elizabeth's First Historian*; and Woolf, *The Idea of History in Early Stuart England*, esp. 110–119.

30. See Stenhouse, "Thomas Dempster."

31. See Denys Hay, "The Historiographers Royal in England and Scotland"; and Saslow, "Dryden as Historiographer Royal."

32. Comines's influential history was translated into Spanish by Juan de Vitrián and published as Comines, *Las memorias de los hechos y empresas*.

constitute one of the basic building blocks of Chinese historical studies today.[33] Subsequently, T'ang rulers centralized the writing of court annals and diaries into a special "Historiographical Office" whose members (*shih-kuan*) were responsible for compiling a "National History" and also expected to provide the emperor with advice on matters entailing issues of historical precedent.[34] This office, continued into the Ming period, exists today in the shape of the quasi-official Qing History Project sponsored by the Chinese People's University and histories of the Communist era in Chinese history sponsored by the Party History Office in Beijing.[35]

Similarly, Ottoman sultans, starting in the mid-sixteenth century, created a special office [*Sehnameçi*] for the purpose of writing official accounts of their military victories and other achievements.[36] Mughal emperors did the same; Akbar (1542–1605) at one point in his reign specifically commissioned Abu el Fazl "to write with the pen of sincerity the account of the glorious events and of our ever-increasing victories."[37] Official chroniclers in the guise of sculptors who carved intricate glyphs recording a ruler's achievements also figured in the courts of Maya rulers in Central America during the classic and postclassic period. And according to one scholar, in times of war victorious Mayan kings habitually executed the historians attached to the court of their vanquished foes or, at the very least, amputated their fingers in order to assure that they could no longer practice their trade.[38]

To my knowledge, few other rulers were quite as ruthless as the Maya in their efforts to secure a favorable reading of their achievements, but if this practice actually occurred, it sprang from the widespread notion that controlling the past was essential to controlling the future, or at least the future's understanding of a particular ruler or regime. Any history offering an interpretation that differed substantially from one's own was necessarily branded a calumny, a fabrication, a fable that had to be either censored or suppressed; and whenever this action proved impossible, the offending account had to be answered with a counter-history offering a supposedly more "truthful" rendition of the past.

It goes almost without saying that the totalitarian regimes of Europe's twen-

---

33. For an introduction to the history of Chinese official history, see Beasley and Pulleyblank, *Historians of China and Japan;* and Wilkinson, *Chinese History,* 471–526. For a sampling of one of these early histories, see Qian, *Records of the Grand Historian: Qing Dynasty.*
34. On this office, see Twitchett, *The Writing of Official History under the T'ang,* 5–30.
35. I am grateful to my colleague William A. Rowe for this information.
36. See Woodhead, "An Experiment in Official Historiography."
37. See Rashed, "The Treatment of History by Muslim Historians," 143. Abul Faza completed this history, *Akbar Namah,* in 1593.
38. See Johnston, "Broken Fingers," 373–381.

tieth century played this history game with consummate if often quite brutal skill. I have vivid recollections of some of the tactics used by the Spanish dictator Francisco Franco—manipulation of the mass media; the orchestration of school curricula and textbooks; and the purposeful construction, using forced labor, of artificial "sites of memory"—in the hope that his particular vision of his country's history would prevail.[39]

Earlier rulers attempted to do much the same, albeit with far fewer tools at their disposal. Starting in ancient Assyria, kings regularly chipped away at the "marmoreal" portraits and inscriptions left by their enemies, while simultaneously threatening with genital mutilation anyone cheeky enough to deface the kings' statues.[40] Rituals of *damnatio memoriae* can be also be found in ancient Egypt, where pharaohs expunged the memory of rulers they did not approve by effacing their lapidary inscriptions and replacing them with hieroglyphs of their own.[41] Such practices were institutionalized by the Romans: the Senate voted more than once to obliterate all physical traces (coins, statues, monuments, and so forth) of emperors judged to have dishonored the *civitas romana*.[42] But the one ancient ruler who probably went the furthest to make certain his reading of the historical record would prevail was Shih Huang Ti (r. 221–210 BCE), the great Qin emperor who famously ordered the burial, supposedly alive, of Confucian scholars opposed to his rule and the wholesale destruction of all histories housed in the imperial archives save those by scholars sympathetic to the Qin.[43] Right or wrong, the emperor's actions were successful to the extent that, starting in the first century, they have remained a source of headaches for historians seeking to document the circumstances that contributed to the rise of the Qin.[44] But Shih Huang Ti also established something of a precedent. Although he did not go so far as to bury any scholar opposed to Manchu rule, Emperor Qianlong (1736–1795) instructed his officials in 1774 to "put to flames" any wood block or printed sheet containing

---

39. This topic is developed in Boyd, *Historia Patria*.

40. One such admonition, dating from the twenty-fourth century BCE, reads: "Whosoever should deface my statue and put his name on it and say it is my statue, let Emil, the lord of this statue and Shamasg tear out his genitals and drain out his semen. Let them not give him any heir." For this curse, see Bahrani, "Assault and Abduction," 374. I owe this reference to the kindness of Paul Dinero.

41. For more on these practices, see Assman, *The Mind of Egypt*, esp. 226, on efforts to expunge the memory of Akhenaten (r. 1352–1338 BCE); Bochi, "Death by Drama"; and Yoyette, "Le martelage des noms royaux éthiopiens par Psammétique II." I owe these references to the kindness of my Johns Hopkins colleagues Betsy Bryan and Richard Jasnow.

42. The ritual of *damnatio memoriae* figures centrally in Flowers, *The Art of Forgetting*.

43. The incident, known as the "The Burning of the Books and the Burial of Scholars," is recorded in Qian, *The Records of the Grand Historian*, chap. 6.

44. As the Taliban's recent destruction of the Bamiyan Buddhas in western Afghanistan readily suggests, hard-fisted attempts to destroy or at least tamper with the historical record still occur today. On the destruction of these statues, see Flood, "Between Cult and Culture."

language that was critical of his dynasty, on the grounds that "heterodox opinions must be quashed that later generations may not be influenced."[45]

In the course of this study, we shall encounter similar attempts to alter the historical record through physical intimidation (Chapter 1), the willful destruction or seizure of both manuscripts and books (Chapters 3, 4, and 5), diplomatic negotiations expressly designed to force authors to rewrite their histories (Chapter 2), and deliberate attempts to rewrite older histories to suit new political aims (Chapters 1, 5, and 7), as well as efforts to restrict the writing of history to authorized historians appointed by the Crown (Chapters 6 and 7). I also document several instances in which Spain's Habsburg monarchy, inspired by sixteenth-century notions of "perfect history" that equated historical veracity with documentary proof, restricted access to important state papers to historians in their employ (Chapters 3, 4, and 5). In hindsight, the policy seems not only foolish but also short-sighted, since these monarchs were generally powerless to control the writing of history outside their domains. But in the short run, it enabled the Crown's official historians to argue that their narratives were "truthful," that is, based on documentary evidence, while others were based solely on ideology.

Viewed from this perspective, official history is best interpreted as an investment that offered a hedge against a future fraught with uncertainty and doubt. To protect themselves and their reputation, successive generations of rulers purchased shares in this offering. As we shall see, in a few instances these investments paid off. As the incident involving Ralegh cited at the outset of this Introduction suggests, history served to chase English adventurers out of the land of El Dorado and, by extension, to defend Spain's imperium over large swaths of the New World. We shall also see that toward the end of the fifteenth century, the investment of Queen Isabella of Castile in a series of official chroniclers enabled the memory of her providential succession to enter, almost without dispute, into Spain's historical record. Even today some die-hard supporters are working to persuade the Vatican to proclaim her a saint.

In other instances, rulers learned that the costs of writing histories far outweighed the returns; they discovered that memory was something impossible to orchestrate or control. In the seventeenth century, for example, Philip IV, together with his energetic minister, the count-duke of Olivares, hired a cluster of chroniclers ("hired pens" in the language of the famous Spanish writer Baltasar Gra-

---

45. As cited in Brook, "Censorship in Eighteenth-Century China," 177. Qianlong issued this decree in conjunction with his efforts to create a vast imperial library. Apparently the search for relevant materials discovered some items labeled "seditious books." I would like to thank Geoffrey Parker for bringing Brook's fascinating article to my attention.

cián), but much to their disappointment, this investment yielded only meager returns in the court of public opinion. Censorship could silence individual historians. It might even curtail the circulation of certain books, but otherwise it could do little to erase historical memory of either individuals or groups.

In a recent brilliant study, David Lowenthal likened the past to a foreign country, one with which the historian-cum-time-traveler can never become truly familiar.[46] In this study I envision the past as something more akin to an overpopulated country brimming with so many histories that it was beyond anyone's capacity, even that of powerful rulers, to exercise effective, let alone lasting, governance or control. In the end, therefore, this volume, in addition to exploring the ways in which different rulers put history to work and the contribution of official history to the practice of history, illustrates the futility, even for the powerful, of shaping history forever.

What follows is an account of official history in Spain from the Middle Ages until the middle of the eighteenth century, when the kingdom's Bourbon rulers incorporated all existing positions of royal chronicler into the newly established Royal Academy of History, and finally up to the start of the nineteenth century, when, on the brink of the moment when the monarchy's American possessions achieved independence, the academy abandoned its effort to write the general history of the Spanish New World. Although I make reference to official chroniclers in the kingdom of Aragon, the emphasis is primarily on that of Castile, especially during the Habsburg era (1516–1700), during which successive rulers, following the example of the last Trastamara rulers, Ferdinand of Aragon and Isabella of Castile, attempted to harness the writing of history to the interests of the state. Different rulers used history in different ways, however, and one of my themes is the apparent tension between personalized, king-centered history, or what I call *historia pro persona,* and *historia pro patria,* a broader, somewhat more Livy-esque narrative centered on the achievements of the kingdom as a whole.

Rulers also differed with respect to the particular kind of history that they sought to embrace. In the Middle Ages, most were content with straightforward chronicles, written in the vernacular, which offered a narrative of their accomplishments, or *gestae.* Starting in the fifteenth century, with the start of the Renaissance, humanist history, written in Latin, adorned with a variety of rhetorical tropes and infused with examples designed to provide moral instruction and

---

46. Lowenthal, *The Past Is a Foreign Country.*

political advice, came into vogue, forcing rulers to make decisions about the particular brand of history their chroniclers were going to write. But whatever brand of history they chose, successive rulers instructed their chroniclers to emphasize the sacred character of monarchy together with the notion that their actions, no matter how Machiavellian, had received divine sanction and support.

Another of the monarchy's concerns was the history of the discovery and conquest of the New World, the region that, already in the sixteenth century, served as the fulcrum around which the fate of Spain's global empire revolved. Starting in 1571, Philip II assigned this history to a special officer known as the *cronista mayor de las Indias*. Although it dealt with only one chapter in Spain's national epic, the history of the Indies was of key importance; it was related directly to the issue of imperium and the manner in which Spain's rulers managed to justify the conquest and acquisition of distant lands. Aragonese and Castilian rulers had grappled with this same issue during the course of the Reconquest, the term now used for the efforts of Christian rulers during the course of the Middle Ages to retake those portions of Iberia that, starting in 711 CE, had been conquered by Muslims from North Africa and the Middle East. Imperium was also at issue when, starting in the fifteenth century, Castilians ventured into the Atlantic, first taking possession of the Canaries and then, following Columbus's momentous voyage of 1492, much of the New World. In the end, efforts to write the history of Spain's imperium in the Americas remained woefully incomplete. If they achieved nothing else, however, Antonio de Herrera y Tordesillas's contributions to this chronicle figured among the factors that precipitated Sir Walter Ralegh's untimely death.

Together, the following chapters offer a detailed look at the differing ways in which five centuries of Spanish kings put history to work. They also explore the ideas of these rulers about history, along with the different ways in which such ideas influenced the kinds of histories that their official chroniclers wrote. Yet this survey is not intended as a comprehensive account of Spanish historiography within the period I cover. The last such book, by the Spanish scholar Benito Sánchez Alonso, was published in three volumes between 1941 and 1950.[47] It desperately needs a replacement, but such an enterprise lies beyond my scope.

47. Sánchez Alonso, *Historia de la historoiografía española*. More recent is *Historia de la historiografía española*, edited by Andrés-Gallego, but this volume of essays is far from comprehensive.

CHAPTER ONE

Empire and History

> Of all the many achievements of great kings and lords in the past, nothing remains, not even of the buildings they erected, nor of the deeds they did—except what we read of them. However great they may be, their buildings fall and are silent, but what is written of their deeds does not fall, and is never silent.
>
> —Fernando del Pulgar

"Language has always been the companion of empire."[1] This memorable and oft-quoted phrase, included in the prologue of Antonio de Nebrija's *Gramática Castellana* of 1492, proved prophetic. In the months and years that followed, language for the Spanish monarchy became a tool of conquest, helping its missionaries and conquistadors to consolidate political power, spread the Catholic faith, and unify its nascent empire in the New World.

Yet Nebrija (1444–1522) was no visionary. A humanist schooled in the classics, he fully appreciated the extent to which Latin had served the Romans as a kind of imperial glue. Nebrija's confidence, therefore, was palpable when he advised Queen Isabella, Castile's reigning monarch: "After Your Highness takes under her yoke many barbarian towns and nations with strange tongues, and with the conquering of them, they will need to receive the laws that the conqueror puts on the conquered and with those, our language."[2]

Nebrija's pride in his native language speaks directly to his patriotic instincts—he was native to a small town near Seville—and his ardent support for Spain and its culture. Because he was a philologist and a grammarian, history, especially that

---

Epigraph: Pulgar, *Letras*, 153, as translated in *Isabel la Católica, Queen of Castile: Critical Essays*, 264.
1. Nebrija, *Gramática de la lengua castellana*, 13. Nebrija's ideas about the relationship between language and power came from Lorenzo Valla, *Elegantiae*, one of that author's most influential works, where, with reference to Latin, he would have read: "Ibi nanque Romanum imperium est, ubicunque Romana lingua dominatur" (wherever the Roman language [Latin] is, there, too, is Roman power [*imperium*]). See Valla, *Opera Omnia*, 1:4. I am grateful to my editor, Henry Tom, for this reference.
2. Nebrija, *Gramática de la lengua castellana*, 16.

of Roman Spain, also fell within his ken, and in 1499, while serving as professor of rhetoric at the University of Salamanca, he published a short survey of Spanish antiquities, *Antigüedades de España*, in response to a similar book, *De Rebus Hispaniae* (1493), by the Sicilian scholar Lucio Marineo Sículo, another member of the arts faculty at Salamanca.³ Nebrija hated Sículo, so much that he reportedly refused to walk on the same street as his Sicilian colleague. Given his nationalist sentiments, he also believed that Spain's ancient history was far too important a subject to be entrusted to foreigners such as Sículo. "I do not consider it quite safe to rely on foreigners for historical truth," Nebrija observed, "and least of all on Italians who call us barbarians and peasants and insult us with derogatory epithets."⁴ It is not clear what Sículo had written or said to spark such animosity, although his *De Rebus* had emphasized Spain's debt to the Romans by Latinizing the place name of virtually every town that he mentioned. In contrast, Nebrija referred to these same places in the vernacular with an eye toward demonstrating the antiquity of Spanish culture together with its independence from Rome.⁵

Nebrija's interest in promoting Spain's history did not end with antiquity. Anxious to cultivate ties with Isabella's consort, Ferdinand of Aragon, he lobbied for the permission to write a biography of Ferdinand's father, Juan II of Aragon. He was disappointed to learn that the king had given this commission to Sículo following the Sicilian's move from Salamanca to the court of the Catholic Monarchs in 1497.⁶ Nebrija's opportunity to serve Ferdinand finally came in 1509, when the king, in his capacity as regent of Castile, asked him to write a Latin history of his reign, a commission that the humanist could hardly refuse. The king also flattered Nebrija by naming him to the lucrative office of royal chronicler (cronista del rey), a position he had long desired and one that enabled him to refer himself as "chronicler by royal wish of the history of Spain and of the Spanish."⁷ Ferdinand's decision to appoint Nebrija, arguably Spain's most cele-

---

3. Nebrija wrote this treatise, dedicated to Queen Isabella, in the vernacular. See Tate, "Nebrija, historiador."
4. As cited in Rummel, "Marineo Sículo," 717. For Nebrija's criticisms of foreign scholars, see Maestre Maestre, "La divinatio in scribende historia de Nebrija."
5. The rivalry between these two humanists is briefly discussed in Maestre Maestre, "La divinatio in scribende historia de Nebrija."
6. The commission to Marineo Sículo resulted in *De rebus gestis a Joanes II rege*, a work he completed in 1509 but did not publish until 1530 as part of the revised edition of his *De rebus hispaniae*. See Ramos Santana, "Una biografía desconocida de Lucio Marineo Sículo."
7. Nebrija, in *Guerra de Granada*, 27. While serving as chronicler, Nebrija wrote *Rerum a Ferdinando et Elisabe Hispanorum felicissimus Regibus gestarum decades due*, a history based on an existing vernacular chronicle written by Fernando del Pulgar (d. 1492), another chronicler in the queen's employ. He also wrote *De bello navaraiense*, a chronicle based on Luis Correa's account of Ferdinand's invasion and conquest of the kingdom of Navarre. For these chronicles, see Nebrija, *Guerra de Granada*; Nebrija historiador; Nebrija, *Historia de la guerra de Navarra*; and Sánchez Alonso, "Nebrija, historiador."

brated scholar, to the office of royal chronicler, together with Nebrija's decision to accept the nomination, indicates the importance that the Catholic Monarchs accorded to the writing of history. It also shows the prestige these rulers attached to the office of cronista del rey, a position that figured centrally in their efforts to promote an official history of their accomplishments and, more broadly, those of both Spain and its people.

In recent years these and related topics in Spanish medieval historiography have been addressed by specialists, and this chapter, which offers a broad-brushed introduction to the role and function of official history in medieval Spain, is heavily indebted to their research.[8] In the main, however, the work on Spanish medieval historiography has been done by literary scholars interested in matters of style and presentation. In contrast, I am primarily interested in the way monarchs made use of history to promote their personal ambitions and dynastic agendas. I also examine the manner in which history-writing, like language, became the "companion of empire" in sixteenth- and seventeenth-century Spain.

Official History in an Imperial Guise: Castile

For all of the importance Isabella and Ferdinand attached to the writing of history, they were by no means the first Spanish monarchs to sponsor the writing of chronicles aimed at justifying conquest and territorial expansion of the royal domain. Already in the ninth century, the Christian kings of Asturias began to sponsor chronicles touting their military victories and other accomplishments. Redacted in Latin, these chronicles tended to be the work of ecclesiastics close to the king. They also emphasized royal contributions to what later became known as the Reconquest, the epic struggle to reclaim and restore Hispania, the unified Christian kingdom that was associated with the Visigoths and ended with the Muslim invasion of Spain in 711 CE.

As then understood, Hispania was more myth than reality, a historical fiction created by the celebrated scholar Isidore of Seville (560–636). Sometime between 619 and 624, Isidore finished his *Historia Gothorum Wandalorum Sueborum*, a brief but triumphant history of the Visigoths that traced their origins back to Japheth, son of Noah, and described the many victories these northern wanderers

---

8. I refer here to such scholars as Diego Catalan, Alan Deyermond, Peter J. Linehan, Georges Martin, and Robert Tate, whose works are cited throughout this chapter. A useful, although now somewhat dated, introduction to this historiographical literature may be found in Deyermond, *Historical literature in medieval Iberia*. See also Georges Martin, *Histoires de l'Espagne médiévale* (Paris, 1997).

won against Rome. Isidore also highlighted the accomplishments of the Visigoths in Spain, underscoring their military prowess, their conversion from Arian Christianity to that of the Roman Church, and finally their success in creating a powerful yet just regime. Introducing this history was a prologue, a *laudes,* describing the natural abundance and riches that rendered Spain "the glory and ornament of the world, the most illustrious part of the earth, in which the glorious fecundity and Getic [Gothic] people rejoices much and abundantly flourishes."[9]

Isidore's Gothic paradise was not destined to last. At the start of the eighth century, the Visigothic kingdom, weakened internally by a combination of inept leadership and factional feuds and overpowered by invading Muslim armies, collapsed, practically overnight. Yet even as the Muslims endeavored to create what later emerged as the powerful and prosperous caliphate of *al-Andalus,* copies of Isidore's *Historia Gothorum,* circulating in manuscript, became a source for both history and myth in Asturias and other parts of northern Spain that remained under Christian rule. Starting in the ninth century, the kings of Asturias, following Isidore, claimed direct descent from the Visigoths via the legendary Pelagius (or Pelayo), son of the last Visigothic king.[10] They also credited Pelayo with defeating a Muslim army at the battle of Covadonga, a victory later dated to 722 and viewed as the symbolic beginning of what later became known as the *reconquista,* or Reconquest of Spain. Stories surrounding the "loss of Spain" to the Muslims and the subsequent victories of Pelayo and his successors quickly became the Iberian equivalent of the tales of England's King Arthur and France's Roland, providing centuries of traveling minstrels and troubadours a seemingly endless font of stories for rhymes, stories, and songs—the famous *romances,* along with a string of chronicles among which the twelfth-century *Crónica de Alfonso VII* was by far the most influential. In this chronicle Pelayo appears as a chivalric champion itching to restore not only the "well-being of Spain and the army of the Gothic people" but also the "church of God."[11]

Yet these same stories, whatever their ludic value, also served political ends, offering the kings of Asturias, and their successors in León and in Castile, various ways to legitimate their rule. By the eleventh century, the kings of León, claiming direct descent from Pelayo, asserted that it was their God-given duty to recon-

9. Isidore of Seville, *History of the Goths,* 1.
10. Some chronicles identify Pelayo as the son of Duke Fafila, who was of the Gothic royal lineage. Others assert that he married into the Gothic royal lineage. In this way the chroniclers could avoid the negative characterization that would come with being the son of the king who lost Hispania. I owe this observation to Andrew Devereux.
11. As cited in *Conquerors and Chronicles,* 165.

stitute the *imperium gothicorum* and restore Christianity to the Hispania that Isidore had so eloquently described. Alfonso VI (1065–1109), king of León and Castile, styled himself "imperator Hispaniae," following his conquest of the Muslim *taifa* kingdom of Toledo in 1085, only to be trumped by Alfonso VII (1126–1157), who, in a special ceremony held at León in 1135, had himself crowned "emperor of all the Spains" (*imperator totius Hispaniae*) in the expectation that dominion over the whole peninsula, the Hispania of old, would soon be his. In this context, the *Historia gothorum* was much more than a source of information and delight. It also became, following Polybius's pragmatic notion of history, a guide to action, as the restoration of Isidore's paradisiacal Hispania, coupled with armed forays against the Muslims who had destroyed it, became the measure by which monarchs were judged.

Isidore's history also created a historiographical template that, starting with the ninth-century *Crónica de Alfonso III,* structured a series of chronicles associated with later rulers of both León and Castile.[12] This template had two distinguishing features. One was a nostalgic vision of Hispania—united, prosperous, and above all, Christian—that awaited recovery and restoration through heroic royal action. The second was a record of Gothic accomplishment and success that rested, as Isidore had written, more on "force rather than prayers."[13] It follows that these early royal chronicles (essentially, the only type of history-writing then practiced in Castile) made military prowess into the benchmark of royal achievement and success. Such prowess could be achieved in "just wars" defending the kingdom against Christian aggressors—Bernardo del Carpio's defeat of the French hero Roland at the eighth-century battle of Roncevalles quickly became the stuff of legend—but even more honorably in "divine wars" directed against the infidels, that is, Muslims, and the conquest of territories they had usurped.[14] This same historiographical template also accounts for the "imperial" dimension of chronicle-writing in early medieval Castile, with "imperial" defined as the establishment of *señorío* (jurisdiction, in the sense of *dominium* or authority) or *imperium* (sovereignty) over lands occupied by Muslims. As we shall see, this "imperial" template proved remarkably durable, lasting well into the seventeenth century and influencing both the character and the content of histories associated with successive monarchs in Aragon and Castile.

12. See *Crónica de Alfonso III.* For the influence of Isidore's "gothic" thesis upon later Spanish rulers, see Hillgarth, "Spanish Historiography and Iberian Reality."
13. Isidore of Seville, *History of the Goths,* 32.
14. Cartagena specifically linked the terms "guerra divinal" and "guerra de Dios" to wars fought "contra los infieles" and in "ensalçamiento de la Fe cathólica" in a speech delivered at the Council of Basle in 1423. See Cartagena, "Discurso de . . . ," 221.

Consider, for example, the thirteenth century, arguably the high-water mark of both "imperial" aspiration and "imperial" history in medieval Spain. The first part of this century witnessed the conquest of vast stretches of southern Spain by Ferdinand III, king of Castile and León (r. 1217–1252), and the conquest of Valencia by King Jaume I (r. 1213–1276) of Aragon. These victories effectively doubled the size of the territories under Christian rule while reducing those controlled by Muslim rulers to the peninsula's southernmost regions around Granada. Rapid territorial expansion caused innumerable administrative problems; both monarchs had difficulties integrating these new regions, with large Muslim populations, into their domains. But the aspirations of both monarchs were seemingly limitless. Jaume celebrated his conquests in the form of a semiautobiographical chronicle, *Libre dels feits* (or *Book of Deeds*), in which he appears as Spain's savior and does little to disguise his appetite for further conquests abroad. Similarly, Ferdinand III wanted far more than a kingdom. He dreamed of empire, one that entailed imperium over the entire peninsula, including the Muslim *taifas* (or "party kingdoms") in Andalucia and possibly Tingitana, the North African province formerly controlled by Visigoths. Sharing these aspirations was Ferdinand's son and successor, Alfonso X (1224–1284), a ruler known for his admiration of both Alfonso VI, "emperor of the Spains," and Wamba, the seventh-century Visigothic king who, according to Alfonso, "ruled from sea to sea, including Tangier, the city in Africa, extending his rule as far as the Rhone."[15] But Alfonso's imperial aspirations, unlike those of his predecessors, did not end with the conquest of Spain. Early in his reign he made plans to invade North Africa. He also dreamed of becoming Holy Roman Emperor, King of the Romans, and in doing so effect a *translatio imperii* from Germany to Spain. In the end these aspirations came to naught.[16]

Even so, imperial dreams rapidly translated into imperial histories centered around the idea of reconquest. In Castile, the first was Lucas de Tuy's *Chronicon Mundi* (completed ca. 1236), a world history commissioned by Ferdinand III's mother, Berenguela, (1180–1246), wife of King Afonso IX of León, around 1229.[17] The second, a much more influential history, was Rodrigo Ximénez de Rada's

---

15. As cited in O'Callaghan, *The Learned King*, 149. Alfonso's interest in Wamba was such that he ordered Wamba's body transferred from a small town in northern Spain to Toledo, where it could better serve as an icon of the imperial regime to which he aspired.

16. For the imperial aspirations of Alfonso X, see Socarrás, *Alfonso X of Castile;* and Salvador Martínez, *Alfonso X, el Sabio,* 135–160.

17. See Lucae Tudensis, *Chronicon mundi*. The text is translated into Spanish as Lucas, Obispo de Tuy, *Crónica de España*. For Lucas de Tuy, see the various studies devoted to his life and work published in *Cahiers de Linguistique et Civilisation Hispaniques Médiévals* 24 (2001); Rodrigo Ximénez de Rada is the subject of various essays appearing in vol. 26 (2003) of the same journal. Ximénez de Rada's history is available in Spanish as *Historia de los hechos de España*. A general introduction to these chronicles may be found in O'Callaghan, *The Latin Chronicles of the Kings of Castile*.

Historia de rebus Hispaniae, a work personally commissioned by Ferdinand III following his momentous conquest of Córdoba, the traditional capital of al-Andalus, in 1236. Ximénez de Rada, archbishop of Toledo, who was among the monarchy's strongest supporters, wrote this history largely to support Ferdinand's efforts to strengthen the institution of kingship in Castile. Accordingly, the narrative centered upon the deeds (or *fechos*) of Castile's rulers and their determination to restore the Hispania lost to the Moors. Within this narrative, Ferdinand merited special attention. Ximénez de Rada described him as the "direct descendant of Spain's first inhabitants," the monarch whose victories brought with them imperium, again in the sense of sovereignty, over all but a small corner of Spain.[18]

The Alfonsine Chronicles

Imperial themes were even more pronounced in a series of histories sponsored by Alfonso X. Though politically inept as a ruler, Alfonso's patronage of scholars earned him the sobriquet of "the learned" or "wise" following his death in 1284. At a time when many of Europe's kings were illiterate and cared little for learning, Alfonso's interests ran the gamut from astronomy and mathematics to language and law. He also surrounded himself with men of learning and organized them in the *majlis* tradition of Spain's Muslim rulers into a series of specialized workshops: one devoted to astronomy and cosmography, another to music and the arts, still another to jurisprudence and law. There was also a *taller historiográfico,* a historical workshop or *scriptorium,* comparable in some respects to that of the Abbey of Saint-Denis, outside of Paris, where, starting around 1230, groups of monks composed, illuminated, and assembled the *Grandes chroniques de France.*[19] The organization of Alfonso's historical workshop (located, in all probability, in Seville) was somewhat similar, if not more advanced, since it entailed a division of labor involving a wide range of specialized officials. They included *ayuntadores,* whose task was to link one text to another; *trasladores,* responsible for the translation into Castilian of both Arabic and Latin texts; *capituladores,* who composed chapter titles and marginalia; and an "escrevidor de las estorias" or "writer of histories," a position occupied at one point by the Franciscan polymath Juan Gil

18. Ximénez de Rada, *Historia de los hechos de España,* 57.
19. For Alfonso X's "taller de las estorias," see Catalan, *De la silva textual al taller historiográfica Alfonsí;* and Fernández-Ordoñez, *Alfonso X el Sabio,* 61–82. See also Martin, "Alphonse X et le pouvoir historiographique." The bibliography on Alfonso X's historical patronage includes Fraker, *The Shape of History;* and Dyer, "Alfonsine Historiography." For the French chronicles, see Spiegel, *The Chronicle Tradition of Saint-Denis.*

de Zamora, who also served as a tutor for the king's son and heir, Sancho IV "the Brave."[20]

The day-to-day activities of this workshop are not fully documented, but starting around 1270, its members embarked on two major historical projects. One was the *Estoria de Espanna* (also known as the *Primera crónica general de España*), a national history comparable to the *Grandes chroniques* or Geoffrey of Monmouth's *History of Great Britain*. Following Ximénez de Rada, this history looked back to Spain's mythical founder, Tubal, and the "deeds that occurred in times past."[21] It also sought to include "those happening in the times in which we now live, including those of Moors, Christians, and even the Jews,"[22] language consistent with Alfonso's dream of becoming the emperor of all the peoples—and religions—of Spain. Unfortunately for Alfonso, his workshop was not quite up to the task, and by the time of his death in 1284, its members had not advanced the narrative beyond the sixth century CE.

The workshop's other project, even more ambitious than the first, was a world history, or *General estoria*, which envisioned Spain's history as sacred history and sought to demonstrate that the kings of Castile and León represented the end of history, the last in a line of divinely assisted rulers who had created an universal monarchy, exercising dominion over other peoples and kings. As originally planned, this history was to begin with the Hebrews, whose deeds were reflected in the book of Genesis, which Alfonso's translators parsed and then rendered into Castilian. Later sections were to recount the accomplishments of the Persians, the Greeks, the Macedonians, the Romans, and finally the kings of Castile and León, who were to be represented as rulers with a God-given mission to advance Christianity to the ends of the earth. According to all reports, Alfonso was more deeply involved in this history than in the *Estoria de Espanna*. Even so, the members of his workshop succeeded only in writing a narrative that ended in the first century BCE and the birth of the Virgin Mary.

These two histories, well known to specialists, are important in several respects. One is their use of the vernacular as opposed to Latin, the language previously employed by Ximénez de Rada and Lucas de Tuy. According to Gabrielle Spiegel, vernacular history in France emerged, starting toward the end of the

---

20. For these officials, see Menéndez Pidal, "Cómo trabajaron las escuelas alfonsíes"; and Alfonso X, *Primera crónica general*, 1:xvii. Related titles include Dyer, "Alfonsine Historiography"; Frank Tang, "De 'sterke' koning"; and Castro, "Las ideas políticas y la formación del príncipe."

21. Alfonso X, *Primera crónica general*, 1:4.

22. Ibid., 2:653.

twelfth century, as a "historiography of resistance," the offshoot of aristocratic patrons in search of a "sense of social worth and political legitimacy" vis-à-vis the ever-more-powerful Capetian monarchy.[23] But Spain, Castile in particular, was different. Here the rise of vernacular history had less to do with the nobility than with Alfonso X's determination to enhance his royal authority and his efforts to make Castilian (i.e., Spanish) the official language of both administration and law. His empire, like that of Rome or of the Greeks, required its own language, and in this respect Alfonso anticipated by several centuries the advice that Nebrija offered to the Catholic Monarchs in 1492. Henceforward, Spain's official history was a vernacular history, a celebration of the imperium to which its rulers aspired.

Another point of difference between Alfonsine historiography and that of the Capetians was the king's personal involvement in the activities of his historiographical workshop. The monastery of Saint-Denis enjoyed such a close relationship with the Capetians that the *Grandes chroniques* are generally viewed as the "official" history of the medieval kings of France even though the monks responsible for the chronicles generally did not occupy positions at the royal court. In comparison, Alfonso X assumed responsibility for Spain's history in ways that his French contemporary Louis IX, "Saint Louis," did not. To be sure, Alfonso was no *roi historiographe*, comparable in any respect to his chronicle-writing contemporary and imperial rival Jaume I, but he deliberately sought to have himself represented as a monarch who immersed himself in the activities of his historical workshop, as the prologue to the *General estoria* readily suggests: "After having ordered many documents and many histories of old deeds to be gathered together, I chose the best and most truthful, intending to make this book. And I ordered that it was to include all of the important deeds, including those from the histories of the Bible as well as others that happened in the world since the time of its creation until our own day."[24] Similarly, the prologue of the *Estoria de Espanna* conveys the image of a monarch deeply interested in the writing of history: "We Alfonso, King of Castile . . . by the grace of God, order the gathering of the books of history that relate anything about the deeds of Spain . . . from the time of Noah until those of our own day. And this we do because we want to make known the beginnings of the Spanish people and of those peoples who invaded it from outside."[25]

If these statements are at all accurate, and most specialists believe they are, they

---

23. Spiegel, *Romancing the Past*, 94.
24. Alfonso X El Sabio, *General Estoria, Primera Parte*, 1:6. For Alfonso's participation in the preparation of this history, see ibid., 1:xli–xlii.
25. *Primera crónica general*, 1:4.

also suggest that Alfonso was intimately involved in the composition and overall design of the histories his workshop produced. The anonymous authors of the *General estoria* described the king's "authorship" in the following way: "The king makes the book not because he writes it with his own hands, but because he creates its rationale, organizes and plans it, and then shows the way in which it should be made, and from this is written what the king commands; for this reason we say that the king makes the book. For the same reason, although we say that the king builds a palace or some other structure, it is not that he does it with his own hands, but because he orders it built and gives the necessary instructions."[26]

Whatever the exact extent of Alfonso's involvement in the activities of his workshop, his sponsorship of these histories should not be attributed to a disinterested love of history for history's sake. Instead, it was ideological, part of an overall scheme to enhance the power and prestige of the monarchy vis-à-vis Castile's fractious and often rebellious nobility. This program had various parts, the most important of which was Alfonso's attempt to introduce Roman law and legal procedure in an effort to increase the importance of royal as opposed to seigneurial courts.[27] He also sought to elevate the prestige of the monarchy by having himself represented as the kingdom's natural lord ("señor natural"), a position that his famous legal compilation known as *Siete Partidas* defined as an absolute ruler whose power derived from God. At the same time, the *Partidas* conjured up the concept of monarchy as a corporate entity in which the king represented the head and the soul of the body politic, the people (or *pueblo*) constituting its lesser parts. The relationship between king and people thus became something of a contractual arrangement, with the king having the responsibility, as the nominal head, to provide justice, promote religion, and defend the integrity of the realm. Another of the king's obligations was to expand the size of his dominions, and starting in the thirteenth century, Castilian rulers customarily took an oath requiring them to reconquer the territories the Visigoths had surrendered to the Muslims.[28] In exchange, the *pueblo* pledged submission and service. Yet this reciprocal arrangement, according to the *Partidas*, also underscored the divine nature of royal sovereignty, since it denied the people the right of rebellion, even during those times when the king failed to fulfill his God-given obligations. God, and God alone, possessed the right to punish rulers who proved corrupt, impious, or

---

26. Ibid., 2:393.
27. For these reforms, see González Jiménez, *Alfonso X*.
28. For one example of such an oath, see *Gran Crónica de Alfonso XI*, 1:44, where it is written that "en el comienço de su rreynado le avía dado Dios a conquerir la tierra de los moros enemigos de la fe católica." For more on these oaths, see Ruiz, "Unsacred Monarchy," 123.

unjust.[29] This line of juridical reasoning takes on special significance because Alfonso had to contend with a noble uprising that included the participation of his own son Sancho at the moment when the *Partidas* were nearing completion.

Alfonso's legal compilations are probably the best guides to his ideas about kingship, but the theme of imperium also pervades the histories he sponsored during the course of his reign. The narrative of the *General estoria* centers on the succession of a series of earthly powers (*reinados*) and culminates in that of Spain, a nation destined to achieve universal dominion and, in so doing, eliminate the enemies of God. In contrast, the principal subject in the *Estoria de Espanna* was, as the book's original title suggests, "los fechos d'Espanna," or "deeds of Spain."[30] For Alfonso, these deeds were royal deeds, and in keeping with the didacticism characteristic of medieval historiography, they were intended to serve as examples to help guide and educate future kings. More immediately, Alfonso hoped that the *Estoria* might add to his luster by reminding the Castilian nobility that the monarchy, starting with Pelayo, was essential to the ongoing struggle to liberate Spain from the Moors. The book's prologue therefore suggests that Alfonso had this history written "so that the beginnings of the Spains [sic] might be known . . . [and] how the Christians later began to recover the land . . . and afterward how God re-united her, and which kings won the land as far as the Mediterranean Sea."[31] Accordingly, the *Estoria* eschewed the *laudes* that opened the histories of both Isidore and Lucas de Tuy and began instead with two short chapters devoted to the repopulation of the world following the flood before moving on to the *fechos* of Tubal, Spain's first king, those of the legendary Hercules, and those of King Hispan, who is referred to as the "sennor de Espanna," presumably to conjure up the peninsula's supposed jurisdictional unity in ancient times. In keeping, moreover, with Alfonso's particular interest in empire, the narrative accorded particular attention to Roman Spain, especially under Julius Caesar, who is described as "the emperor and ruler of all the earth," a title that Alfonso evidently wanted for himself.[32] Later sections focus on the *fechos* of Spain's Visigothic rulers, of the invincible Pelayo, and of rulers engaged in the struggle against the Moors.[33]

This last part of the chronicle dates from the reign of Alfonso's son Sancho IV (r. 1284–1295), but the emphasis is still upon the *fechos* of the king. Sancho, however, possibly as a way of appeasing noblemen opposed to his rule, endeav-

---

29. For the idea of kingship in medieval Castile, see Maravall, "El concepto de monarquía."
30. *Primera crónica general*, 1:4.
31. Cited in González-Casanoves, *Imperial Histories*, 47.
32. *Primera crónica general*, 1:95.
33. Ibid., 1:231.

ored to transform what had been an exclusively king-centered history into a broader national history (or *historia pro patria*) by incorporating into the narrative the stories of such popular heroes as Fernan González, the knight who became the first count of Castile, and Ruy Díaz de Vivar, a.k.a. El Cid, the warrior whose exploits as related in the *romances* were already legendary. Yet in keeping with Alfonso's original agenda, these latter additions did little to weaken the linkage between monarchy and imperium, a theme that surfaces at the very end of the chronicle, where Ferdinand III appears as a ruler whose virtue and piety led not only to victory on the battlefield but also to dominion over Spain itself. Ferdinand also appears as a ruler who embodies all the qualities necessary for good kingship, a veritable "mirror of princes," whose deeds future rulers would do well to emulate, as the following conversation between Ferdinand and his son is clearly meant to suggest: "Señor, [says the king] I leave you all of the land, from the sea to here, that the Moors took from King Rodrigo. All of it falls under your rule—part by conquest, part by tributary right. If you are able to protect and maintain all this land I have given you, you are as a good a king as I am, and if you conquer more, you are better than me; and if you lose any, you are not as good as me."[34] The conversation is imagined, but its imperial exordium, urging new conquests, is consistent with the oath pledging further conquests expected of each Castilian monarch at the outset of his or her reign. That it was written during the reign of Sancho IV further suggests that despite Alfonso X's many failings as a ruler, his chronicles successfully bequeathed to his heirs his imperial ideas.

The Rise of Official History

From a historiographical perspective, the two centuries bracketed by the death of Alfonso X (1284) and the accession of the Catholic Monarchs (1474) are commonly regarded as an era in which the interests of Castile's monarchs narrowed. Alfonso's broader concerns, epitomized by the "general chronicles," gave ground to individualized "royal" chronicles (*historia pro persona*) focused on the achievements of a single reign.[35] Evidence that this view of late medieval Spanish historiography is true is that Alfonso X's immediate successors abandoned the *General estoria*, whose purpose, as noted above, was to set Spanish history upon a wider stage. However, even as *historia pro persona* came to the fore, few rulers lost sight of the *Estoria de Espanna*, which, circulating in manuscript, quickly assumed, in

34. Ibid., 2:772–773.
35. See Gómez Redondo, *Historia de la prosa medieval castellana, 1225–1291*.

Castile at least, the status of a national epic that privileged themes of both empire and conquest.

An early sign of the importance of the *Estoria* was the determination of Alfonso's son Sancho IV (r. 1284–1295) to update the narrative through the addition of one hundred chapters devoted to the conquests of Ferdinand III, a monarch who, as noted above, had come to epitomize the ideals of Castilian kingship. In addition, the fact that Sancho's scribes, evidently using materials already gathered by Alfonso's workshop, managed to complete that portion of the history by 1289 suggests something of the urgency that Sancho accorded this project.[36]

Further additions to the *Estoria* soon followed, again in the form of chronicles narrowly focused on the *fechos* of individual monarchs. Starting around 1344, for example, Alfonso XI (1312–1350) had his chancellor, Fernán Sánchez de Valladolid, write three such chronicles, each focused on his immediate predecessors, and another focused on Alfonso himself.[37] Castile's Trastamara rulers, starting with Enrique III (1390–1406), sponsored similar chronicles, whereas Juan I (1405–1454) institutionalized this kind of king-centered chronicle by creating the position of cronista del rey,[38] a court officer whose primary task was to record and then write about the deeds of the reigning monarch as opposed to those of previous rulers. The idea of a general *Estoria de Espanna* still existed; each of these individual royal chronicles was conceived as an addition to what had been written before. But whereas in France the abbey of St. Denis assumed the responsibility of integrating individual royal chronicles into the general chronicle, the *Grandes chroniques,* Castile's rulers did little to create anything that resembled a comprehensive general history of the kingdom.

Yet it is worth remembering that Castile's apparent drift from general to particular history, or from *historia pro patria* to *historia pro persona,* was far from unique. As Bernard Guenée has argued, Europe's historical culture in the early Middle Ages was fluid and flexible, in the sense that the past was open and still relatively unknown.[39] As such, it was susceptible to "invention," that is, the creation of legendary or near-legendary figures such as King Arthur, Pharamond, the Trojan who founded the French monarchy, and in the case of Castile, Tubal, Hispan, Pelayo, and others. Gradually, however, this open historical culture began to close, and by the thirteenth century the great national chronicles, as represented

---

36. For Sancho IV's contributions to the general history, see Gómez Redondo, "La construcción del modelo de la crónica real."
37. See note 47.
38. On this office, see Bermejo Cabrero, "Origines del oficio de cronista real."
39. Guenée, *Histoire et culture historique.*

by Geoffrey of Monmouth's *Historia Regum Britanniae,* France's *Gesta gentis Francorum,* and Alfonso X's *Estoria de Espanna,* were mostly in place. Blanks remained, and these had to be filled, but, starting in France about 1260 with the redaction of the *Grandes chroniques,* there occurred a shift, especially in princely circles, away from sweeping general histories toward royal histories intended to document the *gestae* of a particular ruler. History of this kind was not hagiography; nor was it biography, comparable, say, to Einhard's ninth-century "life" of Charlemagne; nor was it strictly panegyric similar to the *Vita Ludovici Regis* that the abbot Suger wrote in the twelfth century in behalf of Louis VI of France. It was rather, again following Spiegel, "king-centered history," or history focused on the deeds and sometimes even the words of a particular ruler.[40]

In Castile, however, the move away from *historia pro partria* toward *historia pro persona,* or chronicles focused on the achievements of individual monarchs, also had its roots in a political culture that was becoming increasingly fractured and divided. It is difficult to pinpoint the precise moment when this development began, but it accompanied the civil wars that broke out during the later part of the thirteenth century when Sancho IV, son of Alfonso X, led an aristocratic revolt that challenged the legitimacy of his father's rule. From then until almost the very end of the fifteenth century and the *pax hispanica* created by the Catholic Monarchs in the wake of their victory over Granada, Castile's political history was a history of competing *bandos.* These were factions that coalesced around the households of individual nobles—warlords in today's political language—vying for power and influence over the monarchy or, as actually happened in 1369 (see below), usurping monarchical power for themselves. In such an atmosphere, warfare and politically motivated violence was the order of the day, and in an effort to transform themselves into charismatic leaders, kings and warlords alike surrounded themselves with both lawyers and churchmen prepared to celebrate their achievements, generally in the form of king-centered chronicles that were only loosely connected to the wider story of the Reconquest itself. Changes in Castile's political culture thus served to determine the manner in which history—secular history in this instance—was both written and conceived.

Other changes were also under way, and in many ways the emergence of king-centered history belongs to what Barbara Shapiro has called the "culture of fact."[41]

---

40. Spiegel, *The Chronicle Tradition of Saint-Denis,* 47.
41. Much of this paragraph, as well as the term "culture of fact" derives from Shapiro, *A Culture of Fact.* Recent studies suggest that the notion of establishing "truth" on the basis of written documents was evident in judicial practices in Castile and León in the twelfth century, or before the introduction of Roman law. See Alfonso Antón, "Judicial Rhetoric and Political Legitimation in Medieval León-Castile."

In Europe, the origins of this culture can be traced to the twelfth century and the gradual spread of judicial procedures based on Roman law, which, in Castile at least, were codified in the *Siete Partidas,* the great legal compendium compiled under the direction of Alfonso X. These procedures privileged proofs based on "facts," preferably in the form of a written document; "facts" could also derive from oral testimony of a reliable individual, especially one who was an eyewitness to a particular occurrence. Once assembled, the facts could serve as the basis of legal judgment.

Transposed into history, the emergent culture of fact privileged the writing of contemporary or at least nearly contemporary history, since ordinarily it was recent events that could be verified on the basis of facts derived either from eyewitness testimony—ideally that of the historian himself—or written documents. It is no coincidence, therefore, that king-centered history in France emerged in the era immediately following the creation of permanent royal archives. These archives were repositories of facts relevant to the monarchy and constituted a font of raw material that the monks of Saint-Denis could incorporate into the *Grandes chroniques.* Much the same happened in Aragon, where starting shortly after Pedro III's reorganization of the monarchy's archives at the end of the thirteenth century, one of his officials, Bernat Desclot, wrote a chronicle (in Catalan) documenting this king's many achievements; another, Ramón Muntaner, wrote about the recent history of the counts of Barcelona, the dynasty to which Pedro belonged.[42] Similar developments took place in Castile, where the first king-centered histories were the work of notaries, secretaries, and chancellery officials who enjoyed privileged access to what were referred to as the "libros de la cámara real," the "books of the royal chamber."[43] These books offered would-be chroniclers the raw material needed to document the achievements of a particular king.

To be honest, what a fourteenth-century chronicler regarded as fact-filled history had little in common with what today's historians understand as objective history, or history that is nominally based on the patient accumulation of evidence, careful consideration of the relative weight and reliability of the sources surrounding a particular happening or event, and a self-conscious commitment to create a disinterested narrative that appears to be both balanced and fair.[44] Chroniclers of the fourteenth and fifteenth centuries, especially the ones I am concerned with here, approached their subjects with different objectives in mind.

---

42. I refer here to Desclot, *Crónica;* and Muntaner, *Crónica.*
43. *Crónica del rey don Alfonso X,* edited by Cayetano Rosell, *BAE* (Madrid, 1875), 66:3.
44. The idea of objective history can be approached through Novick, *That Noble Dream.* See also Appleby, Hunt, and Jacob, *Telling the Truth about History.*

To begin with, their methodology was objective only to the extent that their accounts were based on "facts," that is, reliable, eyewitness testimony or written evidence in the form of documents, as opposed to rumor, hearsay, or legend. The use of such "facts" allowed chroniclers to present themselves as the equivalent to what Marcial Detienne, with reference to poets in ancient Greece, described as "masters of truth."[45] Yet truth was malleable to the extent that it depended on authors, as opposed to audiences; the "facts" employed were subject to manipulation, and for the most part chroniclers proved skillful in presenting them—spinning them, in today's political lexicon—in ways expressly designed to provide an accurate yet ideologically slanted understanding of the past. At the same time, these chroniclers, taking their cue from Cicero's idea that truth and persuasiveness went hand-in-hand, understood that history as a discipline was a branch of rhetoric and that its importance derived primarily from the ability of its author to persuade his audience that his argument was not only convincing but true. It was therefore incumbent on chroniclers to muster sufficient evidence to construct a convincing narrative and then organize that narrative in ways that would prove entertaining. In addition, chroniclers were increasingly expected to add to the weight of their narratives through the inclusion of aphoristic *exemplae* offering a range of both moral and political advice as well as invented speeches of the kind Thucydides had employed in his *History of the Peloponnesian Wars* in order to provide evidence of the thinking and motivations underscoring the actions of his principal characters. What all this meant was that the writing of history was increasingly seen as a work of artifice, one that required the chronicler to organize facts in ways that best suited his particular interests and concerns.

The fourteenth-century Castilian historian who best epitomizes both the changes in Castile's political culture and those in the chronicler's craft is Fernán Sánchez de Valladolid (1325–?), author of a series of royal chronicles commissioned by Alfonso XI (1312–1350).[46] His biography remains somewhat sketchy, but Sánchez de Valladolid, a jurist or *letrado* by training, was among the king's closest and most trusted advisers. He also served in several offices—*notario mayor* and *canciller mayor*—that afforded him regular access to the "facts" housed in the royal archives. He was therefore ideally positioned to write the history of Alfonso XI.[47]

45. Detienne, *Les maîtres de la verité*.
46. These included *crónicas* of Alfonso X, Sancho IV, and Fernando I [i.e., IV], all of which are included in *Crónicas de los reyes de Castilla*. Alfonso XI's own chronicle is also included in that volume. This chronicle subsequently served as the starting point for the *Gran Crónica de Alfonso XI*, which was completed ca. 1376.
47. For the place of Sánchez de Valladolid in the political program of Alfonso XI, see Estepa, "The Strengthening of Royal Power"; and Linehan, *History and the Historians of Medieval Spain*.

But what kind of history would he write? Sánchez de Valladolid's understanding of history was decidedly different from that of the historians associated with Alfonso X. In the thirteenth century, the "writer of histories" was an anonymous figure charged with organizing the sources previously assembled by other, subaltern members of the king's historical workshop.[48] In comparison, Sánchez de Valladolid self-consciously identified himself in his chronicles with such descriptors as "this writer" (*el escrevidor*), "this historian" (*el estoriador*), or "the writer of these events" (*el que escrivió estos fechos*). In this way he regularly inserted himself into his chronicle, presumably as a reminder that history, far from being an autonomous process—"one damn thing after another"—or even a train of events providentially ordained from above, was something that required the active intervention of a chronicler, in this instance the hand of *el escrevidor*.[49] It follows that Sánchez de Valladolid understood that the writing of history entailed far more than the mere compilation of sources. Rather it was a matter of making choices—*fazer departmientos* in his language[50]—a process that seemed to involve selecting the relevant sources and organizing them in a particular way, or more specifically, in accordance with what he termed a *razonamiento*, a word best translated as ideology or point of view.[51]

A better appreciation of how Sánchez de Valladolid wrote history can be obtained by comparing the prologue to Alfonso X's *Estoria de Espanna* with the one found at the beginning of Sánchez's *Chronicle of Alfonso X*, the first of the many chronicles he was commissioned to write. The former emphasized that the *Estoria*, in the tradition of Livy's *historia pro patria*, would include "all the deeds that occurred [in Spain], from the time of Noah until those of our own day."[52] The latter simply noted, "It is fitting that the deeds of kings, who hold God's place on earth, be found in writing, particularly those of the kings of Castile and León, who through the law of God and the increase of the Catholic Faith took up many tasks and exposed themselves to grave dangers in battles with the Moors, driving them

---

48. The duties assigned to the "writer of histories" are likely to have resembled those of the monks in Saint-Denis who, starting in twelfth century, identified themselves as *cronographus Francorum regis*, a title suggesting that they were to organize the sources prepared by other, lesser members of the *scriptorium*.

49. See, for example, *Crónica del rey don Alfonso X*, chap. 58, p. 47; and the *Crónica de Alfonso XI*, as cited in *Crónicas de los reyes de Castilla*, chap. 51, p. 204. My argument here derives from Gómez Redondo, "Historiografía medieval."

50. *Gran Crónica de Alfonso XI*, xxx. The idea of making "departmientos" also appears in the earlier *Crónica del rey Alfonso XI*. See *Crónicas de los reyes de Castilla*, chap. 42, p. 200.

51. See Gómez Redondo, "De la crónica general a la real."

52. *Primera crónica general*, 1:4.

out of Spain."⁵³ The difference between "all the deeds" of Spain and "it is fitting that the deeds of kings" may appear subtle, but it signaled a shift away from *historia pro patria* toward *historia pro persona*, that is, from the general to the particular. Equally importantly, it suggested that the *escrevidor* actually had the power to determine which deeds would be included in the history he was about to relate. In keeping with this idea, the *escrevidor* in Sánchez de Valladolid's chronicle of Alfonso X interrupts the narrative to remind the reader—or, as was probably more likely, the listener, since these texts were generally meant to be read aloud— that he privileged some deeds, notably those of the king, over others, including those of nobles and lesser types. "It is appropriate," he writes, "that the deeds that are done by greater men be written before those that are done by lesser men."⁵⁴ The *escrevidor* also reminds his readers-cum-listeners that the history before them is one whose contents the chronicler, for reasons of his own, selected.

The chronicler's newfound mastery over the narrative is particularly evident in the chapter devoted to Alfonso X's imperial aspirations and his meeting with the pope. Here *el escrevidor* notes that he purposely omitted certain events related to this journey "because what he did and how things transpired where he went the chronicler did not know."⁵⁵ It is likely that Sánchez de Valladolid skipped over the details of this trip in order to avoid the embarrassment of having to explain Alfonso's failure to become Holy Roman Emperor, but whatever his motivations, his selective use of "facts" bears witness to the rise of what I have defined as "official" history and the emergence of chroniclers prepared to shape the past in accordance with a set of predetermined *razonamientos* or ideas.

Sánchez de Valladolid's reliance upon *razonamientos* of his own choosing ap-

---

53. My translation follows the *Chronicle of Alfonso X*, translated by Shelby Thacker and José Escobar, 25–26. The complete prologue reads: "It is fitting that the deeds of kings, who hold God's place on earth, be found in writing, particularly those of the kings of Castile and León, who through the law of God and the increase of the Catholic Faith took up many tasks and exposed themselves to grave dangers in battles with the Moors, driving them out of Spain. Therefore, the most high and honorable and blessed Alfonso [XI], by the grace of God, King of Castile, León, Toledo..., desiring that the feats of the kings who were before him be found in writing, ordered the old history and chronicles inspected. He found written in the chronicles of the books of his royal chamber the deeds of the kings who were in times past: Visigothic kings up to King Rodrigo, and from the reign of King Pelayo, who was the first King of León, until the death of King Fernando [III], who conquered Seville and Cordoba.... [But] many things happened in the time of the kings who lived after that King Fernando that were not recorded in the chronicles; therefore, King Alfonso, called the Conqueror, realizing that these deeds were forgotten, in order to make known all the things that happened during the reign of his great-grandfather, King Alfonso X, and during the time of his son King Sancho IV, the Valiant, and of his father, King Fernando III, ordered them to be written in this book so that those yet to come may know how things happened in the days of the aforementioned kings."
54. *Chronicle of Alfonso X*, chap. 42, p. 139.
55. Ibid., chap. 59, p. 195.

pears in his other chronicles, most spectacularly in the *Gran crónica de Alfonso XI*, a work that was completed some fifteen years after Alfonso's death.[56] Written in large measure as a response to Juan Manuel, a disgruntled nobleman who was the supposed author of a chronicle (*Libro de tres razones*) critical of the king, the *Gran crónica* relied on the playbook of ideal kingship to highlight the many benefits that Alfonso had brought to Castile. Accordingly, Sánchez de Valladolid juxtaposed order with chaos, equating the former with the king's personal rule, the latter with the era immediately preceding Alfonso's coming of age. This era, which coincided with the minority of both Alfonso and his predecessor, Fernando IV, was not an especially peaceful moment in Castile's history, but in order to dramatize the importance of what Alfonso had done for his kingdom, the *escrevidor* resorted to a series of stock literary tropes and characterized it as an era of wanton disorder when "no man dared to travel along the roads unless armed and accompanied by others, in order to be able to fend off the bandits."[57] Miraculously, everything changed for the better as soon as Alfonso assumed personal control of the kingdom in 1313.

The *escrevidor's* next move was to dredge up the traditional image of the Castilian monarch as a champion of faith. He relates how Alfonso, only age fourteen, stood up before his courtiers and swore to "conquer the land of the Moors, enemies of the faith." The narrative continues by showing how Alfonso made good on this oath by successfully besieging Olivera, a Muslim enclave near Seville.[58] More victories soon follow, and the chronicle ends on a suitably triumphant note: Alfonso's conquest of the port town of Algeciras in 1344.

But perhaps the ultimate challenge facing Sánchez de Valladolid as he prepared the *Gran crónica* was to craft an image of Alfonso as an ideal monarch—a new Pelayo, or even a Ferdinand III—whose manifold virtues, piety, prudence, generosity, valor, and more, future rulers would do well to emulate. It follows that the *escrevidor* represents him as a just monarch who, in addition to uniting a troubled kingdom, fights for "the service of God and the increase of the Holy Catholic faith."[59]

The next court chronicler to write this kind of history was Pedro López de Ayala (1332–1407), unquestionably the most famous historian in fourteenth-century Castile. Whereas Sánchez de Valladolid aimed at transforming Alfonso XI into an

---

56. See *Gran Crónica de Alfonso XI*, 1:162, for the date of its completion. The chronicle was first printed in 1787 at the initiative of the Real Academia de la Historia.
57. Ibid., 1:369.
58. Ibid. 2:414.
59. Ibid., 2:441.

ideal ruler, López de Ayala, taking his cues from Suetonius and other Roman historians, attempted to do something quite different: create the image of a king who was so nasty that he could use it to justify his vassals' efforts to effect the equivalent of what would be called "regime change" today. The monarch in question was Pedro I (1334–1369), a ruler whom López de Ayala artfully labeled "the cruel" so as to legitimate his murder by Enrique de Trastamara, the leader of the aristocratic faction to which Ayala belonged.

López de Ayala's chronicles span the period from 1344 through 1395, and for some scholars, their classicizing tone marks the beginning of humanist history in Castile. This may be exaggerating, because Ayala never wrote in Latin, but he was among the first Spanish noblemen to be schooled in the classics, and his interest in cultivating the arts of both peace and war—*armas y letras* in Castilian—made him a prototype of what Castiglione later characterized as a Renaissance gentleman. López de Ayala also epitomized the Renaissance ideal of the *vita activa e civile* in that he was a nobleman who put himself in the service of his prince, eventually occupying the position of royal chancellor (*canciller mayor*), the office previously held by Sánchez de Valladolid and one that necessarily granted him access to the papers needed to confect his chronicles.[60]

Yet in view of Ayala's background as a high noble, his historical sensibilities were quite different from those of a *letrado* such as Sánchez de Valladolid. The latter's interest in history derived principally from the law, the former's from history, philosophy, and literature. López de Ayala was also a poet, the author of an important treatise on falconry (*Libro de la caza de los aves*), and the translator (into Castilian) of Boethius's philosophical treatises and several books of Livy's Roman history.[61] These humanistic concerns furthered López de Ayala's appreciation of history as a branch of rhetoric, together with an understanding of the discipline's power to shape and to mold public opinion.

In addition, López de Ayala conceived of history as a mixture of two different genres: *historia pro patria* and *historia pro persona*. That he was mindful of the kingdom's larger history is evident in the prologue of his chronicle, where he asserts that his only purpose in writing was to add to the *Estoria* the "deeds of the kings of Spain" by recapitulating those of Pedro I, Enrique II, Juan I, and Enrique III. López de Ayala further informed the one he called his "reader" (*el*

---

60. López de Ayala is best approached through Súarez Fernández, *El canciller Pedro López de Ayala*.
61. See López de Ayala, *Las Décadas de Tito Livio*. His most famous poems are those found in his *Rimados de Palacio* (Rhymes of the Palace), a satirical collection of poems he reportedly began in a Portuguese prison following his capture, after fighting alongside King Juan I, at the battle of Albujarrota (1385).

leedor) that the history he was about to relate was a "true report" based on events that he had personally witnessed (*lo que ví*) and on testimonials obtained from individuals "worthy of trust."[62]

Yet for all of this Ciceronian insistence on truth, López de Ayala's history was partisan history purposely written to justify Enrique de Trastamara's succession to the crown of Castile as Enrique II. It was factual to the extent that he drew from his personal experiences as a courtier, and in keeping with his understanding of the persuasive power of rhetoric, he sprinkled his narrative with snippets of conversation that added to the drama and immediacy of the events being related. These in turn gave López de Ayala's writings an "I was there" quality that earlier chronicles and histories often lacked. This rhetorical strategy was particularly evident in his account of the death of Pedro I, where he relates how Enrique repeated the phrase, "I am your enemy, I am your enemy" before dispatching Pedro with his sword.[63] A tragic moment—regicides always are—but by injecting Enrique's words in the narrative, López de Ayala added demonstrably to the drama of one of the key turning points in the history of medieval Castile.

The fact that López de Ayala wrote for the winning side in the struggle between Pedro and Enrique can also be credited with the transformation of Pedro I into Pedro "the Cruel," the name by which he is still known today. Pedro was no saint, but López de Ayala succeeded in portraying him as a Castilian Nero, a tyrant who ordered the death of anyone he suspected of disloyalty, including his own brother, his aunt, and other courtiers. The chronicler did this partly to justify his own decision to switch his allegiance from Pedro's faction to that of Enrique, but his wholly negative image served also to legitimate the beginnings of Trastamara rule. López de Ayala clearly understood, *pace* the *Siete Partidas,* that only God had the right to remove tyrants, and this knowledge surely accounted for his decision, in the chapter recounting Pedro's murderous actions, to quote the prophet Daniel ("Now the kings will learn, and be punished for all they have done in this world") to assure his readers that Pedro's death was divinely ordained.[64]

The elegance of López de Ayala's style and his superb eye for detail make him one of the finest prose writers in late medieval Castile. He also understood that eyewitness testimony accorded history a degree of credibility that other kinds of

---

62. *Crónicas de los reyes de Castilla,* 66:399, 406. This prologue also announces that the history will be divided into chapters but will also include a table of contents (*tabla*) so as to enable *el leedor* to find exactly what he wants.
63. Ibid., 66:592. The Spanish reads: "Yo so[y] su enemigo, Yo so[y] su enemigo."
64. Ibid., 66:593.

evidence did not. But what ultimately served to render his narrative all the more convincing was his decision to side with the noble faction that came out on top. López de Ayala was never officially designated a royal chronicler, but from the outset his chronicles served the first Trastamara rulers as "narratives of power" intended both to legitimate their origins and highlight those achievements, especially their efforts to promote justice and to further the cause of the Reconquest, that would help them broaden their following and consolidate their rule. The next step was for these rulers to institutionalize the writing of history by creating new offices of royal chronicler, but, as we shall now see, this was a development that prompted other rival groups in Castilian society to appoint chroniclers of their own.

The Sea of Histories

One window into this kind of tit-for-tat history comes in the form of a seemingly minor confrontation that took place in the city of Segovia during the fall of 1467. One of the principals was Diego Enríquez del Castillo, a cleric who, in his role as the personal chaplain of Henry IV (r. 1454–1474), became one of this monarch's most loyal and trusted advisers. Starting in 1460, Castillo also served in the office of cronista del rey. In the mid-fifteenth century the responsibilities attached to the office of royal chronicler were still ill-defined, but given that Enríquez del Castillo defined historians as "judges of fame and the preachers of honor," he believed that his chief responsibility as the king's "loyal chronicler" was to provide "lasting fame" (*perdurable fama*) to noteworthy achievements, among them the construction of churches and monasteries; notable acts of justice, charity, and piety; and the defense of religion as measured by military victories over the Muslims. At the same time Enríquez del Castillo engaged in a bit of interdisciplinary wrangling—or what later became known in artistic circles as the *paragone*—by noting that commemoration of this sort was better done with the "pen" than "the painter's brush, the silversmith's hammer, or the sculptor's stone."[65]

From Castillo's pen came one of the few fifteenth-century chronicles to offer a wholly positive portrait of Henry IV, a ruler otherwise considered as the paragon of weak and ineffective kingship. Following López de Ayala's example, Castillo stuck close to Henry. He regularly accompanied the king on his travels and occasionally went with him into battle, as in 1467 when he got caught up in the

65. Enríquez del Castillo, *Crónica de Enrique IV*, 130–132.

battle of Olmedo, which pitted forces loyal to Henry against a rebel army supporting the king's younger brother, Prince Alfonso. The battle itself was something of a standoff, neither side winning a clear-cut victory, but Castillo was there, taking notes that he later transcribed into "secret notebooks"—his chronicle?—suggesting that the king's army had in fact won the day. Castillo kept these papers together with his other belongings at his house in Segovia. One evening a group of men he described as "traitors, partisans of Alfonso," forcibly broke into the house, treated him "dishonestly," and "robbed me of everything, including portions of the king's chronicle which I had written and organized." Despite this setback, Castillo eventually managed to complete his chronicle but included an apology attributing his sketchy account of the first part of Henry's reign to the robbery and loss of his papers.[66]

So far, this is Castillo's side of the story. But there is a second version, which comes from the pen of another royal chronicler, Alonso de Palencia (1423–1492). Initially, Palencia supported Henry, who in 1456 had appointed him to the post of Latin secretary and subsequently to that of cronista del rey. Palencia and the king soon parted ways, and after a number of years Palencia joined the noble faction supporting Alfonso.[67] This faction sought to depose Henry IV and replace him with Alfonso, but the game plan changed with Alfonso's untimely death in 1468. The rebel faction subsequently pressured Henry IV into designating his sister Isabella, as opposed to his daughter Juana, as his legitimate heir. As these events unfolded, Palencia worked on a chronicle, written in Latin, which was not only critical of Henry but insisted that Castillo's account of the battle fought at Olmedo was wholly incorrect. In Palencia's telling, Olmedo was a clear-cut victory for Alfonso, partly because Henry, out of cowardice, fled the fray *in media res*.

Palencia also offered an account of the seizure of Castillo's papers that differed from Castillo's. Referring to Castillo as "his adversaries' chronicler" (*cronista de los contrarios*), Palencia reported that two noblemen loyal to Alfonso did in fact enter the chaplain's house, found his notebooks, and subsequently brought them, together with Castillo, to Alfonso's court. There the archbishop of Toledo, one of Alfonso's chief supporters, read Castillo's account of Olmedo and determined that it was filled with "lies," an opinion seconded by several other courtiers who, based on their own experience, claimed that Castillo's account of the battle was filled with "clear and totally unfounded nonsense." At this juncture Palencia reported that Alfonso wanted to execute Castillo but relented after it was pointed

---

66. For the seizure of Castillo's papers, see Foronda, "Le prince, le palais et la ville."
67. For Palencia's biography, see Paz y Melia, *El cronista Alonso de Palencia;* and the introduction to Palencia, *Gesta Hispaniensia*.

out that he was a cleric. Castillo was released but without his papers, which remained in the possession of the rebels.⁶⁸

This incident is one that rarely figures in standard accounts of the reign of Henry IV, but it underscores the value that rulers, and would-be rulers, attached to chronicles of the kind kept by Castillo and Palencia. As noted the Introduction, it has been suggested that victorious Mayan rulers made a practice of cutting off the fingers of the chroniclers retained by their defeated rivals, evidently for the purpose of appropriating the past, or at least the inscription and memory of that past, for their own. On occasion, these same chroniclers were put to death. In Castillo's case, Alfonso's instincts, or at least those of Cardinal Mendoza, seemingly matched those of the Maya; under the circumstances, Castillo, although forced to relinquish his manuscript, was lucky to escape with his life—and all of his fingers intact.

The arguments used by the rebels to justify the seizure of Castillo's notebooks are not entirely clear, although another fifteenth-century chronicler, Fernán Pérez de Guzmán (1377–1460) understood the rebels' rationale. A humanist in the service of the Mendoza, a powerful grandee family allied with Prince Alfonso, Pérez de Guzmán is best known for his *Generaciones y semblanzas*, a kind of advice book drafted ca. 1450, in which he worried openly about the pernicious influence of chroniclers who wrote in the service of one faction or another:

> Often it happens that the chronicles and histories that tell of powerful kings, notable princes, and great cities are regarded with suspicion and doubt. Little faith is put into their veracity for two particular reasons, among others. First, because some of those who undertake the writing and commentary of ancient matters are shameless men who would rather relate what is bizarre and extraordinary than what is true and exact, in the belief their story will be regarded as inconsequential if they do not tell of things that are bigger-than-life, even if those things are more worthy of awe than of credulity.⁶⁹

Pérez de Guzmán directed these remarks at the *Crónica Sarracena*, a fourteenth-century work criticized for the manner—more "romance" than "history" according to another fifteenth-century critic of this same work—in which its author, Pedro de Corral, dealt with the Muslim invasion of 711. Yet Pérez de Guzmán was equally concerned about the reliability of contemporary chronicles such as the one by Castillo. Consequently, he recommended that, following Roman prece-

---

68. Palencia, *Crónica de Enrique IV*, década 1, bk. 10, chap.1, p. 232.
69. My translation follows Pérez de Guzmán, *Pen Portraits*, 3. For the original, see Fernán Pérez de Guzmán, *Generaciones y Semblanzas*, edited by J. Domínguez Bordona (Madrid, 1924), 1.

dent, rulers should not only censor the work of chroniclers who write about them but also punish "corrupt and mendacious writers who give fame and renown to those who do not deserve it, and take away from those who had accomplished deeds worthy of mention."[70]

At the heart of these suggestions was the idea of *fama*, or glory, earthly reputation or renown. The importance of *fama* dates back, of course, to antiquity, to Homer and Herodotus as well as to Cicero and other Roman authors for whom glory constituted one of the essential building blocks of the Republic: "The leading men of state must be fed in glory."[71] Yet the ancients also distinguished between true or lasting glory, which was considered a virtue inasmuch as it brought honor not to just to an individual but to all of society, and false glory, or vainglory, which smacked of ambition and selfishly individualistic aims. Early Christian writers were decidedly less enthusiastic about any notion of earthly glory, noting its passing nature—*Sic transit gloria mundi*—in comparison with the everlasting eternal glory associated with salvation. Yet for all of the criticism levied by centuries of Christian writers, *fama* stubbornly refused to slip away. It played a crucial role, especially in chivalric circles, during the Middle Ages, and Renaissance writers regularly accorded the acquisition of worldly glory new importance and respect. Ambition, the single-minded pursuit of *fama*, won universal disapproval, but few humanists dared challenge the proposition that individuals who performed noble and virtuous deeds for the benefit of their city, country, or prince, or even more importantly, for God, merited *fama*. As Pérez de Guzmán observed, "a good reputation . . . is the true reward for those who performed good and virtuous deeds."[72]

But how was *fama*, once achieved, to be preserved? No surprise that chroniclers, given the nature of their profession, opted for written narratives. As noted earlier, Enríquez de Castillo affirmed that commemoration was better done with the "pen" than "the painter's brush, the silversmith's hammer, or the sculptor's stone."[73] According to this logic, memory, which was seen as ephemeral, required other, more plastic media to be preserved. Portraits might help, but these were regarded as accessible to only a few, whereas sculpture and architecture, as the shards of ancient sculptures and the ruins of Rome's monuments readily at-

---

70. Pérez de Guzmán, *Pen Portraits*, 3–4.
71. Cicero, *Republic* v:vii. The classic study of *fama* is that of Lida de Malkiel, *La idea de la fama*, but it can be supplemented with Fenster and Smail, *Fama*.
72. Pérez de Guzmán, *Pen Portraits*, 30.
73. Enríquez del Castillo, *Crónica de Enrique IV*, 130–132.

tested, were destined to crumble. Only history, written history, could perdure; hence the importance attached to chronicles of the kind that Castillo wrote.

But if humanist writers were unanimous in supporting the importance of history for commemorative ends, there remained the question of the person (or persons) to whom this all-important task should be entrusted. Pérez de Guzmán's recipe was simple: keep history out of the hands of "corrupt and mendacious writers" lest evil be rewarded and good penalized. Fair enough, but the next hurdle was to decide who was a "mendacious" writer as opposed to ones who were worthy of trust. This problem, at least for Alfonso, Cardinal Mendoza, and the other individuals involved in the seizure of Enríquez de Castillo's papers, was essentially moot, as they had already decided that Henry IV's chronicle should be entrusted to the historian (in this instance Palencia) who was most sympathetic to their cause. Otherwise, Alfonso's future, his *fama*, might be at risk.

I have gone on at length about the incident involving Castillo's papers because it neatly illustrates the importance that contemporaries attached to the court chronicles that Castillo and his rival Palencia produced. How and why these chronicles had become so important is still not entirely understood, but the contributing factors were several, starting with the rise of literacy among noblemen, who, following the example of López de Ayala, embraced the "arms and letters" ideal, and the attendant introduction of humanist values into the peninsula. Put simply, Castile's political culture increasingly privileged both culture and learning, a development that not only expanded the audience for chronicles but enhanced their importance and utility as well. Castile's complicated, fractious, and often turbulent political dynamic also figured in this development. Starting in the reign of Juan II (1406–1454), Castile entered into a protracted period of feuding and civil war as a series of aristocratic factions (*bandos*) competed for influence over monarchs who were perceived as indecisive or weak. Initially, these struggles revolved around Alvaro de Luna, Juan II's controversial favorite, but they grew to a crescendo during the reign of Henry IV, when rival *bandos*, one supporting Henry, the other his brother Alfonso and then Isabella, seemingly divided the kingdom in half. For the most part, these battles were fought with sword and lance. But pens were also pressed into service, with the leaders of each *bando* engaging the services of chroniclers prepared to write less in the spirit of disinterested "witnesses" than of partisan "judges" whose narratives were designed both to denigrate those of their rivals and to add to the legitimacy of their particular cause.

From this perspective, Enríquez de Castillo's chronicle was just one of a growing swell or proliferation of chronicles that created a veritable *mare magnum* of competing, often quite contradictory accounts of both recent and current events.[74] This sea of histories first emerged during the reign of Juan II, whose own chronicle, as it survives, is a composite of various authors, each representing a different faction and point of view: Alvar García de Santa María (1370–1460), known for his sympathy toward Alvaro de Luna;[75] Pedro Carrillo Huete, the royal falconer;[76] Juan de Mena, who was probably rewarded with the title of cronista del rey in order to enhance the authority of his contributions to the chronicle; and Pérez de Guzmán, who, in keeping with his reputed hostility for Alvaro de Luna, "cut and suppressed parts of it [the chronicle] in conformity with his own opinions."[77] According to one later observer, each of these chroniclers "wrote what they wanted and believed in," as opposed to redacting what actually occurred.[78]

This sea of competing chronicles achieved its maximum depth during the fractious reign of Henry IV. His reign is also important because it marks, in Castile at least, the appearance of chronicles written by individuals living at considerable remove from the royal court. One such chronicler was Pedro de Escavias, a supporter of Henry IV who worked on his *Reportorio de principes de España* while serving as an *alcaide* (castle warden) in the small Andalusian town of Andújar. As history, the *Reportorio* was little more than a potboiler, one of many summary histories that recapitulated many of the arguments put forward in Alfonso X's *Estoria de España*.[79] The *Reportorio* fits this mold precisely, as it begins with Tubal and then races through the Middle Ages before ending with a brief but wholly laudatory pen portrait of Henry IV. Good history the *Reportorio* is definitely not. Its importance lies in the fact that it was the work of a provincial who had a stake in the factional in-fighting that characterized Henry's reign but was otherwise distant from it. Why Escavias decided to embark on such a history is not

---

74. My notion of a "sea of histories" derives from the work of the fourteenth-century Dominican scholar Giovanni Colonna, whose *Mare historiarum*, a universal history, was translated rapidly into Spanish. Meanwhile, Colonna's *De viris illustribus,* a collection of biographies of famous men, served as a model for many similar works in fifteenth-century Spain. See *Mar de historias* and Braxton Ross, *Giovanni Colonna*, 538–539.

75. García de Santa María wrote the first part of the king's chronicle, documenting the years between 1406 and 1420, but then, for reasons still to be discovered, the project passed into the hands of other writers, presumably with the approval of King Ferdinand.

76. Carrillo de Huete, *Crónica del halconero de Juan II.*

77. *Crónica de Juan II*, 68:273–275, with an introduction by Lorenzo Galíndez de Carvajal.

78. Ibid., 273.

79. These capsule histories include the *Sumario de los reyes de Castilla*, attributed to Juan Rodríguez de Cuenca, chief steward (or *despensero mayor*) of Queen Leonor, the first wife of Juan I (see Rodríguez de Cuenca, *Sumario de los reyes de Castilla)* and the *Atalaya de las Crónicas,* by Alfonso Martínez de Toledo, Arcipreste de Talavera, supposedly written at the request of Juan II in 1444. Other such histories, written in Latin, include Alfonso de Cartagena, *Anacephaleosis: Liber genealogiae regum Hispanie* (ca. 1456); and Rodrigo Sánchez de Arevalo, *Compendiosa historia Hispánica* (1470).

entirely clear, but he demonstrated his allegiance to Henry with the lament that in comparison with past centuries, when Castilians rallied around their rulers to fight Muslims and to advance the cause of religion, he lived during an era when "loyalty was forgotten" and "robberies, scandals, disorders" threatened to destroy the very kingdom whose history he had traced.[80]

Escavias's passion is real, but it is nothing compared with that of chroniclers such as Enríquez del Castillo and Alonso de Palencia, who were directly party to the political fray that divided Castile into two warring camps. Of the two, Palencia is by far the better known. He was a humanist by both training and inclination, and his first love was the history of Roman Spain, just then a topic of growing interest and scholarly concern. By his own account, Palencia worked for ten years on a (now lost) volume dedicated to the "antiquity of the Spanish people." In addition, he planned a more comprehensive general history of Spain, written in Latin, that was to be modeled on Livy's Roman history and which he hoped would provide Spain with a humanistic history similar to those that his contemporaries Flavio Biondo and Robert Gaguin had written for Italy and France, respectively.[81] As a court officer, however—remember that, starting in 1456, he occupied the offices of Latin secretary and royal chronicler—Palencia found himself inexorably drawn into the vortex of Castile's partisan politics, as his decision to abandon Henry IV and side with the *bando* supporting the king's younger brother readily suggests. Palencia was also an eyewitness to the seizure of Castillo's chronicle, an incident that apparently convinced him that, in addition to antiquity, he needed to write about "our own times" (*de nuestro tiempo*) and to do so in Latin, the language of learning; Latin would theoretically grant his chronicle greater authority than the vernacular chronicles written by Castillo, Escavias, and other chroniclers on the opposing side. The result was Palencia's *Gesta Hispaniensia* ("deeds or events of Spain"), a Livy-esque work he divided into decades and started around 1474, when he was already a member of the Isabelline camp. Small wonder then that Palencia was fully prepared to condemn Henry IV's chroniclers, including Castillo in particular, as "fabricators of lies ... bribed historians, known as chroniclers, who pretend to leave behind everlasting literary monuments of meritorious deeds" but who do so in such exaggerated fashion that "it is not only ridiculous but sad."[82]

80. Escavias, *Reportorio de Principes de España*. For Escavias's biography, see Avalle-Arce, *El Cronista Pedro de Escavias*. Also attributed to Escavias is *Hechos del condestable don Miguel Lúcas de Iranzo*.
81. I refer here to Flavio Biondo, *Italia ilustrata* (Rome, 1474); and Robert Gaguin, *Compendium de origine et gestis francorum* (Paris, 1497).
82. Palencia, *Crónica de Enrique IV*, 1:xlv. For Palencia's career, see Paz y Melia, *El cronista Alonso de Palencia*; and the introduction to Palencia, *Gesta Hispaniensia*.

Palencia's reliance on eyewitness testimony together with the elegance of his style served to establish his chronicle as the most accurate and authoritative history of the reign of Henry IV. In the words of a later royal chronicler, it was nothing less than a "fountain of pure water" in an otherwise mendacious sea of competing chronicles.[83] Adding to the authority and supposed truthfulness and purity of Palencia's account was that he, like López de Ayala before him, wrote for the winning side. His portrayal of Henry IV, for example, was pure invective; Palencia went so far as to belittle the king's physical appearance, noting that "he looked ferocious, almost like a lion, frightening everyone who looked at him," mocking his flattened, "monkey-like nose," and describing his "indecent dress and sloppy shoes." Enríquez del Castillo praised Henry for clemency and piety. Palencia emphasized Henry's temper, penchant for cruelty, and lack of faith, noting specifically that Henry once dismissed church documents as "ridiculous parchments." He further undermined the king's image and authority by underscoring his friendship with "low and indecent" types—read both Jews and *conversos*—his interest in Moorish customs, and, perhaps most importantly, his lack of interest in pursuing the touchstone of Castilian kingship: the fight against the Moors. "From the time he was a child until reaching a mature age," wrote Palencia, "[Henry IV] has not done any feat of arms." Palencia even represented Henry as an out-and-out coward, one "more interested in contemplating the city [of Granada] than in besieging it."[84]

All this was character assassination, a concerted effort to destroy Henry's *fama* and, simultaneously, increase that of Isabella, whose personal qualities Palencia presented as the polar opposite of Henry's. Palencia also wanted to demonstrate that Isabella, Henry's half-sister, as opposed to Juana, his daughter, was the king's only legitimate successor. Palencia managed this by representing Henry not only as impotent but also as so lascivious that he allowed one of his courtiers, Juan Beltrán de la Cueva, to consummate his marriage to Juana of Portugal. Palencia could thus maintain that Juana, whom he famously referred to as "la beltraneja" [daughter of Beltrán] was illegitimate, an argument that enabled him to declare Isabella as Castile's rightful queen. And if this was not enough to legitimate the Isabelline cause, he claimed that the events leading to her succession were part of a divine plan meant to usher in a period a period of peace and prosperity that would enable the kingdom's rulers to return to their God-given destiny of defending and extending the Christian faith.

---

83. Cited in Palencia, *Crónica de Enrique IV*, 1:li.
84. Palencia, *Crónica de Enrique IV, década* 1, bk. 1, chap. 2, p. 11; and bk. 3, chap. 1, pp. 59–60.

A fascinating story, but probably wrong. Most of today's scholars are convinced that Juana, notwithstanding Palencia's assertions to the contrary, was not *la beltraneja* but rather the legitimate offspring of Henry IV. Thus the supposed purity of Palencia's account of Henry as opposed to Castillo's is somewhat moot. In effect, they wrote as competing chroniclers, manipulating "facts" and tweaking evidence in order to legitimate the particular faction whose cause they supported. But history, to repeat the old chestnut, belongs to the winners, and when Isabella, once queen, reappointed Palencia as her royal chronicler, she effectively authorized his chronicle as the official history of the events leading up to her succession. It follows that while Castillo's chronicle was all but forgotten, Palencia's became a model, and probably a source, for others interested in writing chronicles in Isabella's behalf.

The most important of these pro-Isabelline chroniclers was Diego de Valera (1412–1488), another nobleman who, having embraced the "arms and letters" ideal, embarked on a literary career that entailed the writing of poetry and treatises on nobility and kingship.[85] Residing in the Andalusian port city of Puerto de Santa María, Valera also wrote history in the form of several chronicles, notably one known as the *Crónica abreviada de España*, which was supposedly written at Isabella's command and then published, with royal assistance, in 1482, making it the first vernacular history of Spain ever to appear in the form of a printed book.[86]

Valera's idea, like Palencia's, was to demonstrate the role of Providence in granting Isabella accession to "the monarchy of all the Spains." Taking his cue from Isidore, Valera opened the *Crónica abreviada* with a geographical description meant to inform the queen about the nature of the realm over which she ruled, and he followed this with a capsule history of Castile that ended with the death of Isabel's father, Juan II. All this was but a prelude for a detailed chronicle of the reign of Henry IV in which the king appeared as a tyrant whose personal failings became the principal source of the kingdom's many disorders. Next came a chronicle of Ferdinand and Isabella casting the two monarchs in the role of saviors who managed to put an end to the "corrupt and abominable customs" their predecessor had engendered. Compared, however, to Palencia, Valera was especially keen to return to the imperial theme found in earlier Castilian chronicles. He did so by highlighting the monarchs' determination to "make war against the Moors,

---

85. For Valera's biography, see the introduction to Valera, *Crónica de los Reyes Católicos*. His chronicles of the reign of Henry IV include *Crónica anónima de Enrique IV de Castilla;* and *Memorial de diversas hazañas*.

86. The first printed history of Spain was Rodrigo Sánchez de Arevalo's *Compendiosa historia Hispanica* (Rome, 1470), a work that was principally addressed to Italian humanists who were otherwise ignorant of both Spain and its history. See Tate, *Ensayos*, 74–104.

to decrease the enemies of our Holy Faith, and to take from them land they have usurped."[87] He was equally enthusiastic about Ferdinand and Isabella's interest in conquering new territories and in converting pagans, notably the indigenous peoples of the Canary Islands, or "canarios," to Christianity. For Valera, in short, history, with the attendant idea of conquest, was firmly in the monarchs' camp.

The Catholic Monarchs

We are now back to the reign of the Catholic Monarchs, Ferdinand and Isabella (1474–1516), where this chapter began. Their interest in publishing Valera's chronicle represents the beginning of a new era in Spanish historiography. Printing, introduced into Spain as early as 1474, created new possibilities for image-making that Ferdinand and Isabella, who were among the first European rulers to adopt this new technology, seem to have immediately grasped. The monarchs' interest in exploiting the new medium for political ends began in 1476 during that year's meeting of the Cortes, held in the town of Madrigal de las Altas Torres, a small fortified enclave in Old Castile. As the participants gathered, Isabella named a chronicler, Juan de Flores, to record the proceedings, and Flores's record of what was decided during the course of the meeting was subsequently printed in the form of a broadside. The queen did the same in 1480 at the Cortes of Toledo, although on that occasion the commission to publish the *Leyes hechas en las Cortes de Toledo* went to Diego de Valera, then serving as a royal scribe.[88] The rationale underpinning both publications was fundamentally propagandistic: they were intended to represent the monarchs as lawgivers, another test of the Castilian kingship, and in doing so weaken noble factions still opposed to their rule.[89]

History was also integral to the monarchy's growing propaganda machine, and the publication of Valera's chronicle, reprinted on no fewer than eight occasions between 1482 and 1500, reflected a new historiographical policy that was only fully implemented following the conquest of Granada in 1492 and Columbus's successful return from the New World.[90] Central to this policy was the

---

87. Valera, *Crónica de los Reyes Católicos*, 108.
88. This pamphlet was printed in Salamanca in 1484. See Haebler, *Bibliografía ibérica*, 167.
89. Isabella's reputation as a "lawgiver" was largely deserved, as she sponsored the publication of a series of legal compilations, including Alfonso Díaz de Montalvo's *Ordenanzas reales de castilla* (1484); *Cuadernos de las leyes nuevas de la hermandad: Cuaderno de Alcabalas* (1484); *Siete Partidas* (1491); *Libro de la bulas y pragmáticas* (1503), etc. Ferdinand was responsible for others, including the *Furs de valencia* (1482); *Constitucions fets en la segunda cort de Barcelona* (1493); and the *Leyes de Toro* (1505). See Carrasco Manchado, "Discurso político y propaganda."
90. Valera to Ferdinand, 19 May 1483, as translated by Boruchoff in "Historiography with License,"

increase in the importance accorded to the office of cronista del rey. To begin with, Isabella raised the annual salary of the office from a measly 25,000 to 40,000 *maravedís*, a figure that doubled to 80,000 *maravedís* when in 1509 King Ferdinand, acting in his capacity of regent of Castile, named Nebrija royal chronicler. In yet another effort to enhance her chroniclers' importance, Isabella presented this office only to individuals who already formed part of her personal entourage, serving either as chaplains or as secretaries.[91] The chroniclers' prestige also derived from their role as experts to whom the monarchs could turn whenever they needed advice on historical matters. Ferdinand, for example, did just this in 1474 after he learned about the manner in which his wife, Isabella, had assumed power in Castile following the death of King Henry IV. On 24 December 1474, in her first public showing following her proclamation as queen, Isabella elected to enter the city of Zamora in a procession headed by a page holding an erect sword, a symbol of royal authority and justice and one that Ferdinand understandably associated exclusively with males. Surprised and seemingly troubled by the ceremony, Ferdinand wrote to Alonso de Palencia, Isabella's chronicler, as well as to a jurist, for advice. "You who read so many histories," he wrote, "tell me whether there is any precedent for any Queen to march in procession with a sword, a symbol of the threat of punishment for her vassals."[92] Their answer is not recorded, but presumably it was no, inasmuch as that ceremony had previously been a male prerogative.

Isabella's ceremonial pretensions aside, when it came to royal chroniclers, the queen's instructions were clear and precise. Juan de Flores's letter of appointment specified that he was "responsible for our chronicle and to write, discover [*declarar*], copy, and organize all the papers relating to it."[93] On this score, it is worth noting that Isabella's historiographical agenda differed from her husband's in being predicated on her need to establish the legitimacy of her succession in the teeth of lingering aristocratic opposition to her rule. It follows that the royal chroniclers closest to Isabella (Flores, Valera, Fernando del Pulgar, and finally

---

278n55. First published in Seville by Alfonso del Puerto in 1482, Valera's chronicles was reprinted in at least eight editions before 1500. See Haebler, *Bibliografía ibérica*.

91. Given these preferences, the queen rebuffed the efforts of one of Henry IV's chroniclers, Enríquez de Castillo, to serve her in a similar capacity. One of the queen's secretaries, Alonso de Avila, brusquely informed Castillo that to pay him anything would "disorder the [royal] household and put it into confusion . . . as if everybody in her royal service has the right to be a chronicler." Castillo's response to this insult was to write directly to the queen, noting, somewhat menacingly, that if she failed to appoint him as chronicler, it would lead to the "destruction" of her *fama* which otherwise "could, in his hands, be rendered immortal." On this incident, see Paz y Melia, *El cronista Alonso de Palencia*, xlvi.

92. Cited in Paz y Melia, *El cronista Alonso de Palencia*, xix.

93. Cited in Bermejo Cabrero, "Orgines del oficio de cronista real," 408.

Andrés Bernáldez, the famous "cura de Los Palacios") wrote in Castilian rather than Latin so as to reach as large a domestic audience as possible. These same chroniclers tended also to favor Isabella as opposed to Ferdinand; this bias is especially evident in Flores's chronicle, which dates from around 1480 and survives only in fragments. In it Flores defines his office as that of "a temporal [or earthly] evangelist" meant to render the ruler's *fama* "immortal."[94] And in addition to emphasizing the queen's divinely mandated succession and manifold virtues—courage, justice, modesty, piety—Flores offered a ringing defense of female rulership in an effort to silence certain nobles whose opposition to Isabella was grounded, at least in part, on gender. In his view, Isabella ruled "like a powerful man" (*como esforçado varon*), and in an invented speech that anticipated Elizabeth I's famous Tilbury address ("I may be a woman, but I have the heart and stomach of a king") by over a century, he quotes her as saying: "It may be that women lack the discretion to know things and the strength to stand up to others, perhaps even the language to express themselves properly, but I have discovered that we have the eyes to see."[95]

Presumably Isabella approved of such adulation, since it was totally in line with the kind of *historia pro persona* expected of chroniclers who, in keeping with the title of their office, cronista del rey, were essentially her personal servants and subject to her whim. Ferdinand had his own chroniclers, as well as his own ideas about how history was to be written. For one thing, unlike Isabella, he did not have to contend with the issue of illegitimate rulership; he was the rightful and uncontested heir of his father, Juan II of Aragon. However, he did have to deal with the Diputación, the institution that watched over the *furs*, certain laws and liberties that every Aragonese monarch, at the start of his reign, swore to uphold. Over time, the Diputación, as the representative of some of the most powerful families in Aragon, used its powers to restrain the development of royal absolutism in that kingdom, much to the chagrin of its monarchs, many of whom looked to history as a means of augmenting the monarchy's power and prestige. Already in the fourteenth century, Ferdinand's predecessor, Pedro IV (1336–1387), commissioned the monks attached to several Catalan monasteries to gather the materials he needed to create a chronicle designed to support the royal prerogative vis-à-vis the *furs*.[96] A century later, Ferdinand attempted something similar by order-

---

94. My argument here follows that of Agnew, "*Evangelista temporal.*" See also Gwara, "The Identity of Juan de Flores."

95. *Crónica incompleta*, 239. For more on the manner in which Isabella's chroniclers depicted the queen's "manly strength," see Boruchoff, "Historiography with License," 283.

96. For this commission, see the introduction to Pedro IV, *The Chronicle of San Juan de la Peña*.

ing his royal archivist, Pere Miguel Carbonell (1434–1517), to refashion existing Aragonese chronicles into a new one intended to preserve the "memory of the deeds of the kings of Aragon, our predecessors."[97] Ferdinand also responded to the Diputación's expressed interest in a "reliable, general history [of Aragon]" by having his "cronista mayor," Fray Gauberto Fabricio de Vagad, write the *Crónica de Aragón*, which was first printed in 1499. Ferdinand's historical preferences also emerged in the commission he offered to the Italian humanist Lucio Marineo Sículo to write a history of his father, Juan II, and then to have it printed as part of this same author's *Chronicle of the Kings of Aragon*, a work that was first printed in Latin (1509) and subsequently (1524) in the vernacular.[98]

But perhaps the most famous, and certainly the most controversial, of Ferdinand's historical commissions was that offered by Bernardino de Carvajal, his ambassador in Rome, to another Italian humanist, Giovanni Nanni (a.k.a Annius of Viterbo), to document the early history of Spain's ruling house. This commission led to Nanni's infamous *Commentaries*, a history of antiquity based on the supposedly long-lost but actually forged texts by Berosus, Manetheo, Metasthenes, and other ancient authors.[99] Published in Rome in 1498 and dedicated to both Ferdinand and Isabella, Nanni's book provided the Catholic Monarchs what they had previously lacked: a king list that spanned the dark ages separating the time of Tubal and Hispan from the arrivals of the Romans. Though quickly recognized by some scholars as a work of forgery (see below, Chapter 2), Nanni's list allowed Ferdinand to claim that the Spanish monarchy was far older than that of his arch rivals, the Valois kings of France.[100]

But whatever the differences between the two historical traditions that Ferdinand and Isabella brought with them at the time of their marriage, over time the Catholic Monarchs forged a common historiographical program with one fundamental aim: to represent themselves as rulers with a divine mandate to unite Hispania and defeat the enemies of the Church—in Iberia, then Africa, and following Columbus's momentous voyage, Asia as well. Toward this end they

97. This commission resulted in Carbonell's *Cròniques d'Espanya*, which was completed about the time of Ferdinand's death but not printed until 1547. The quote is from Carbonell, *Cròniques d'Espanya*, 172. In addition to the chronicle by Desclot, Carbonell was instructed to revise one by Pere Tomich. Cf. Tomich, *Histories e conquestes dels reys d'Arago*.

98. See above, note 3. Marineo Sículo modeled his biography of Juan II on the one that the famed Florentine humanist Lorenzo Valla had written for Ferdinand I of Aragon, father of Alfonso V, "the Magnanimous."

99. Annius and his *Commentaria per opera diversorum auctorum de antiquitatibus loquentium* are best approached though Anthony Grafton, "Traditions of Invention and Invention of Traditions in Renaissance Italy: Annius of Viterbo," in Grafton's *Defenders of the Text*, 76–103; and his recent *What Was History?*

100. Andrés de Uztárroz and Dormer, *Progresos de la historia de Aragón*, 68–69.

assembled a team of chroniclers, both official and semiofficial, seemingly to take advantage of the differing interests and literary styles of the two rulers. Other fifteenth-century rulers, including the dukes of Burgundy, the Sforza in Milan, and the Medici in Florence, also surrounded themselves with chroniclers for propagandistic purposes, but Ferdinand and Isabella went one step further by assigning different chroniclers what were in effect overlapping tasks.[101] The basic idea: introduce a bit of rivalry into the writing of history, take advantage of the chroniclers' competitive instincts, and ultimately achieve the best product.[102] In addition, the chroniclers they favored were appointed to the office of cronista del rey and granted other rewards, whereas those who either failed to complete their assignments or fell out of favor customarily found themselves on the street. Just this happened, for example, to Alonso de Palencia in 1480, when he arrived in Toledo with the understanding that as Isabella's chronicler he was to record the proceedings of the Cortes about to gather in that city. Palencia soon discovered that his commission had been withdrawn, and within a few months he was essentially out of a job. Though allowed to retain his salary as royal chronicler, he was stripped of the title, which was given to Isabella's secretary, Fernando del Pulgar. Strictly speaking, therefore, Palencia was unemployed at the time he completed the fourth and last of his *decades*, which dealt with the reign of Ferdinand and Isabella.

Another of the monarchs' tactics was to keep their chroniclers on a fairly tight leash, something that Pulgar learned shortly after he replaced Palencia as the queen's favorite chronicler. A talented and well-educated commoner of *converso* background, Pulgar (1430–1492) initially sided with Henry IV, but in 1474 he switched his allegiances and moved into Isabella's camp. He subsequently became the queen's personal secretary, a member of the royal council, and starting in 1482, cronista del rey. At this point Pulgar began work on his *Claros varones de Castilla* (1486), a collection of pen portraits of those clerics and noblemen who had supported the Isabelline cause, together with what became the most detailed vernacular chronicle of the monarchs' war against the Muslim kingdom of Granada.[103] The agenda of this chronicle, which combined elements of *historia pro persona* with *historia pro patria*, was complex: to prove that the queen was divinely

---

101. These court chroniclers can be approached through Ianziti, *Humanistic Historiography under the Sforzas*; and Tate, "The Official Chronicler in the Fifteenth Century."

102. For the retrospective complaints about the Catholic Monarchs' practice of pitting one chronicler against the other, see Carrillo Castillo, *Naturaleza e imperio*. 50–51.

103. Pulgar, *Claros varones de Castilla*; and Pulgar, *Crónica de los Reyes Católicos*.

inspired, that her campaign was a "just war" against an enemy whose possession of Granada was both "tyrannical and unlawful,"[104] and to represent the war as the closing chapter in the long saga of the monarchy's efforts to restore the Hispania lost in 711 to the Moors. What is interesting is that in writing this chronicle, Pulgar was rarely accorded much slack, as a letter he wrote to Isabella appears to suggest. It reads: "I will go to Your Highness in accordance with the order you have sent me, and I will bring what is written to this point, so that you can have it examined."[105]

Examined? by whom? The answer is not entirely clear, but by the 1490s, and most probably before, the Catholic Monarchs created what was tantamount to an updated version of Alfonso X's historiographical workshop, designed both to coordinate and to control the work of their various chroniclers. The activities of their workshop are not well documented. Even its membership remains vague. But its purpose was to review, discuss, and then edit the work of individual chroniclers with an eye toward publication. One of the workshop's first and arguably most important products was the letter announcing Christopher Columbus's discoveries in the Indies. Columbus had first drafted this letter—addressed to Luis de Santangel, treasurer of Aragon—aboard ship in the mid-Atlantic on his return from the Caribbean. The original has never been found, and it is known only through the printed version, published in Basel in Latin in 1493. In recent years, however, several Spanish scholars have convincingly demonstrated that the printed version of Columbus's letter was one of two—and possibly more—versions of the same letter, both prepared by the monarchs' secretariat after the mariner's arrival in Barcelona in October 1493. In the two known versions of the letter, the concluding paragraph varies considerably. The printed version concluded by announcing the benefits of Columbus's discoveries for the Church. It reads as follows:

> Therefore let the king and queen, the princes and their most fortunate kingdoms, and all other countries of Christendom give thanks to our Lord and Saviour Jesus Christ, who has bestowed upon us so great a victory and gift. Let religious processions be solemnized; let sacred festivals be given; let the churches be covered with festive garlands. Let Christ rejoice on earth, as he rejoices in heaven, when he foresees coming to salvation so many souls of people hitherto lost. Let us be glad

---

104. Pulgar, *Crónica de los Reyes Católicos*, part 3, chap. 112, p. 492.
105. Cited in Boruchoff, "Historiography with License," 259n58. See also Pulgar, *Crónica de los Reyes Católicos*, lxi.

also, as well on account of the exaltation of our faith, as on account of the increase of our temporal affairs, of which not only Spain, but universal Christendom will be partaker.

In the other, Columbus addressed Ferdinand's imperial aspirations by announcing that he expected that the monarchy could use the riches derived from his discoveries to finance the conquest of Jerusalem.[106] The process by which the monarchs decided to print the first rather than the second version of this all-important letter remains unknown, but the final result was tantamount to "history by committee," a work of consensus and one whose content was determined largely by political concerns.[107]

The attention accorded to Columbus's letter, given its historical importance, may have been exceptional, but there is also evidence to suggest that Ferdinand and Isabella regularly scrutinized other documents before they were sent to the printer's shop. Of particular concern were the news sheets or *relaciones* announcing important military victories and other important events, virtually all of which were carefully edited before publication. One such news sheet was Gonzalo de Ayora's letter reporting on the conquest of the North African enclave of Mazalquivir in 1505. In this letter, subsequently printed for wide distribution, Ayora, one of Ferdinand's official chroniclers, represented this battle as a great triumph, a "victory for God and the church." He also echoed Cato the Younger by suggesting that Mazalquivir was a necessary outpost for both the "conquest of Africa and security of Spain." Ayora also affirmed that, owing to this victory, "all of Africa can be conquered with little resistance owing to the great disorders of the Moors."[108]

Studies of Ayora are few, but he was a learned soldier, originally from Córdoba. Appointed cronista del rey by Ferdinand in 1504, he was soon instructed to prepare a chronicle, in both Latin and Castilian, of the monarchy's accomplishments starting in 1492, the year in which Pulgar's chronicle ended. This chronicle, if ever written, is lost, although Ayora was evidently working on it when he "wrote" the letter reporting on Mazalquivir. The same chronicle apparently included a detailed narrative of Ferdinand's conquest of the Kingdom of Navarre. One of Ayora's surviving letters indicates he had completed this chronicle in 1514 but then forwarded it to the king for inspection, correction, and review. Unfortu-

---

106. *Libro copiador del Cristóbal Colon*. The first study to call attention to the existence of variant editions of Columbus's letter was Ramos Pérez, *La primera noticia de América*.
107. See Ruiz García, "El poder de la escritura," 284–287; and Hernández González, *El taller historiográfico*.
108. *Codoin* 47:555. Ayora was appointed cronista del rey in 1504.

nately, it is now lost, a victim, it seems, of Ayora's decision in 1519 to join in the antimonarchical uprising known as the Revolt of the Comunidades.[109]

Another history, also lost, that received similar scrutiny was Hernando de Ribera's verse chronicle of the conquest of Granada. Lorenzo Galíndez de Carvajal, Ferdinand's secretary, reports that the king met more than once with Ribera to go over what he had written. He further observed that Ribera read parts of this history aloud at "His Highness's table," where it was openly discussed and then "approved or revised . . . in accordance with the truth of what had happened."[110]

The attention Ribera's manuscript received further attests to the importance that Isabella and Ferdinand attached to the writing of history, especially that related to their own achievements. On this score, the Catholic Monarchs left little to chance, carefully orchestrating the work of their chroniclers, rewarding their favorites with offices and other gifts, and dismissing or ignoring the work of those they did not approve. And though they never openly stated it as such, their overall aim was to create a single composite history of their accomplishments that was meant to appear in both Latin and the vernacular.

The individual chosen to oversee this task was Ferdinand's Latin secretary, Lorenzo Galíndez de Carvajal (1472–1528), who, starting in 1509, was especially commissioned to "correct and emend" the many and sometimes conflicting chronicles of Ferdinand's reign, as well as those of his predecessors.[111] With this appointment, Carvajal assumed the role of what one later chronicler described as "censor and judge" of chronicles pertaining to the House of Trastamara, and it was a job he took seriously.[112] It turns out that Carvajal had his own ideas about

---

109. Ibid., 47:535–557. For Ferdinand's review of Ayora's writings, see Ayora, "Cartas de Gonzalo de Ayora," 73, letter of 22 September 1512. The only biography of Ayora is Cat, *Essai sur la vie*. See also Carrillo Castillo, *Naturaleza e imperio*, 45–48.

110. Hernando Ribera cited in Cátedra, *La historiografía en verso en la época de los Reyes Católicos*, 32. The incident was first recorded by the chronicler Lorenzo Galíndez de Carvajal, who writes: "y en la verdad, según muchas veces yo oí al Rey Católico, aquello decía él que era lo cierto; porque en pasando algún hecho o acto digno de escribir, lo ponía en coplas y se leía en la mesa de su Alteza, donde estaban los que en lo hacer se habían hallado, e lo aprobaban o corregían, según en la verdad había pasado." Following this discussion, Carvajal reports that the count went out looking for Rivera's manuscript in a monastery and "casi que por fuerza la sacó e quitó lo que quiso, y . . . la crónica no quedó tan cumplida, no en la sinceridad que Rivera la escribió." See Galíndez de Carvajal, "Memorial y registro breve de los lugares," 244.

111. Galíndez de Carvajal, "Prefación en la crónica del rey don Juan el Segundo," 254. For Carvajal, see Ruiz Povedano, "El Doctor Lorenzo Galíndez de Carvajal"; and "Vida y obra del doctor D. Lorenzo Galíndez de Carvajal."

112. Zurita, *Correción y enmienda de las crónicas de Pedro I*, prologue, where Zurita writes: "El doctor Lorenzo Galíndez de Carvajal, postreramente en tiempo del Rey Católico, se hizo censor y juez para enmendar los escritos de los cronistas que fueron de los reyes, Juan el Segundo y Enrique su hijo, que por letras y autoridad lo podía muy bien ser."

what royal chronicles should be like, and once he got hold of the chronicles in question—many had been kept for security in the king's private chambers—he not only organized them sequentially but also rewrote them in ways specifically designed to create a more uniform narrative style and to remove from the texts material he judged superfluous and which detracted, as he put it, from the truth. Ostensibly, Carvajal made these changes to create what he considered a dignified chronicle that would provide future generations with *exemplae* ("grandes doctrinas" in his language) about governance and kingship.[113] Yet his underlying rationale was propagandistic to the extent that he was determined in the first instance to legitimate Isabella's succession to the Crown of Castile and, second, to represent Ferdinand and Isabella as monarchs who, with God's assistance, had rescued the kingdom from the "tyrannies" resulting from the "negligence" and corruption of their predecessors.[114]

As "judge and censor," Carvajal handled different chronicles in different ways. He did relatively little, for example, with those of López de Ayala, an author he respected. But he intervened quite heavily in those relating to Enrique III and Juan II, stitching together the work of five different chroniclers so as to create a continuous narrative.[115] He did the same with the multiple and often conflicting chronicles covering the reign of Henry IV, and as he worked on the *Crónica de Enríque IV*, he admitted to having merged material gleaned from Enríquez de Castillo, Palencia, and Valera into a more unified "history and narrative." Yet in making these changes, Carvajal felt obliged to reassure his readers, "I did not take the liberty of removing or adding anything to what these historians wrote, but only what was prolix and superfluous and what is commonly known to have been written with an excess of passion."[116]

Carvajal was even more interventionist when he arrived at the chronicles about the Catholic Monarchs. Different authors—he specifically mentioned Pulgar, Tristán da Silva, Juan de Flores, Hernando de Ribera, Palencia, Ayora, and Martire—had written portions of this chronicle, but whatever the merits of their individual

---

113. Galíndez de Carvajal, "Prefación en la crónica del rey don Juan el Segundo," 274.
114. Ibid. For Carvajal as editor, see the introduction to Galíndez de Carvajal, *Memorial o registro breve*, where (p. xi) Carretero Zamora observes that Carvajal's task was "[el] re-escribir la historia del pasado inmediato, adaptándola a las necesidades políticas del presente."
115. Galíndez de Carvajal, "Prefación en la crónica del rey don Juan el Segundo," 273. See also *Crónicas de los reyes de Castilla*, 66:698, where Carvajal explains his efforts to "re-organize" the various chronicles relating to the reign of Enrique III and Juan II in the name of truth and the defense of the *patria*. He justified this intervention by citing Guido de Colupina's translation of the "historia troyana" from Greek into Latin.
116. Torres Fontes, *Estudios sobre la "Crónica de Enrique IV,"* 71.

contributions, these differed in substance, language, and style. They also lacked continuity and thus detracted from what Carvajal believed was the magnitude of the monarchs' many deeds. He therefore set out to weave these chronicles into a single, more unified whole and seemingly began work on this project by crafting a chronology of the two monarchs that began in 1468 and ended with the death of Ferdinand in 1516. His next step was to rework Pulgar's account of the war against Granada in the belief that the original was a "brief summary, lacking in details" and, more importantly, one that failed to do justice to such "glorious" princes as Ferdinand and Isabella. Carvajal was equally critical of what he called Pulgar's "vain rhetoric," by which he meant the chronicler's habit of larding his narrative with superfluous orations—"embellishments" in Pulgar's language—and also of Pulgar's failure to take note of the contributions of individual captains who had participated in the campaign.[117] So out came Carvajal's quill, and when, in 1565, Pulgar's chronicle was finally printed, it owed as much to the editor as to the original author.[118]

It was much the same with Nebrija's Latin translation of this same account. In undertaking this project, Nebrija aimed at far more than a straightforward translation. He also sought to transform Pulgar's vernacular account of the conquest of Granada into a grand Latin epic comparable to the one that celebrated Caesar's conquest of Gaul. In contrast, Carvajal was more interested in placing Ferdinand and Isabella's individual successes within the broader national context of the Reconquest of Spain, and it was probably his decision, rather than Nebrija's, to include in the text such comments as that the two monarchs fought "as much for glory as for total union of the reign—*imperio*."[119]

Such changes reflected Ferdinand's interest in a chronicle that linked his personal triumphs with the broader history of Spain itself. But they also conformed to Carvajal's notion of what a royal chronicle should be: a seamless, well-organized narrative that combined *historia pro persona* with *historia pro patria* as a way to dignify the institution of monarchy and to demonstrate its continuing commitment to the service of God, both on the battlefield and off. This, in Carvajal's view, was a history worth telling, or as he subsequently informed Ferdinand's fabled successor, Emperor Charles V, a history that would redound to the "Glory

117. Galíndez de Carvajal, "Memorial y registro breve," 240.
118. Pulgar's chronicle, attributed to Nebrija and dedicated to King Philip II, was first printed as *Chronica de los muy altos y eslcarecidos reyes catolicos don Fernando y doña Ysabel de gloriosa memoria . . . compuesta por el Maestro Antonio de Nebrixa . . .* (Valladolid, 1565).
119. Nebrija, *Guerra de Granada*, 2:21. Nebrija's chronicle was first printed in 1547, at the initiative of his son Sancho. See Tate, "Sancho de Nebrija y su antología historiográfica."

of God, the splendor and fame of your Royal Name, and the advantage of all of the subjects of your many kingdoms."[120]

Yet Carvajal's legacy went further than this. As Ferdinand's last and possibly most trusted chronicler, he sought to give shape not only to a reign but to a tradition, and for this purpose he embarked on his own, supposedly more authoritative, history of Ferdinand and Isabella that represented these monarchs as the rulers who set Spain on the path to greatness by ending the "chaos" and "corruption" associated with their predecessor, Henry IV.[121] As he wrote this history, though, Carvajal tinkered with the past so as create a future, in this instance one worthy of the monarchy's first Habsburg ruler, Charles V. He also did it in the expectation that it would provide the emperor with a better understanding of the kingdom he was about to inherit. In this respect Carvajal's history was Charles's history, one deeply imbued with the traditional Castilian idea that the true measure of a monarch was the extent to which he fought, like a crusader, to further the Christian faith.

120. Galíndez de Carvajal, "Prefación en la crónica del rey don Juan el Segundo," 274.
121. Torres Fontes, *Estudios sobre la "Crónica de Enrique IV,"* 19. Carvajal's chronicle of the reign of the Catholic Monarchs remained in manuscript until 1787. It is available as Galíndez de Carvajal, "Anales breves del reinado de los Reyes Católicos," 236.

CHAPTER TWO

Historia pro Persona
Emperor Charles V

Animo! Get on with your work. It is shameful that the deeds, so glorious, of our kings are forgotten. History is partly to blame; also the neglect of our historians.

—Ramiro Núñez de Guzmán (1533)

Kings and great princes should have not just one, but many historians.

—Gonzalo Fernández de Oviedo (1555)

In June 1550, traveling aboard ship on the River Rhine, the emperor Charles V began writing his memoirs with help of his aide-de-camp, Guillaume van Mâle. It was unusual for a sixteenth-century monarch to engage in this kind of autobiographical writing, but by no means unprecedented. Before him, Charles had the example of several Roman emperors' writings, notably Julius Caesar's *Commentaries*, the *Res gestae* of Augustus, and the *Meditations* of Marcus Aurelius. From the Spanish Middle Ages there was also the thirteenth-century Aragonese monarch Jaume I (1213–1276), otherwise known as "the Conquerer," whose partly autobiographical *Llibre dels fets* narrated his many deeds and achievements. Charles also knew that his own paternal grandfather, Emperor Maxmilian I, in addition to dictating his autobiography, *Historia Frederici et Maximiliani*, to one of his aides, had written two semiautobiographical romances, the *Theuerdank*, in verse, and the *Weisskunig*, in prose.[1] Even so, Charles embarked upon his mem-

---

Epigraphs: Ramiro Núñez de Guzmán to Juan Ginés de Sepúlveda, 19 October 1533, in *Epistolario de Juan Ginés de Sepúlveda*, 106; Gonzalo Fernández de Oviedo, "Batalla I, Quinquágena III, diálogo XIX," as cited in Carrillo Castillo, *Naturaleza e imperio*, 50.

1. Maximilian's autobiographical writings represented an exercise in what German literary scholars have called *Selbstilisierung*. See Wade, "The Education of the Prince."

oirs with considerable misgivings, as he indicated two years later in a letter to his son Philip II:

> This history is the one I wrote in romance, when we were traveling on the Rhine and which I finished in Augsburg. It is not written in the way I would wish, and God knows that I did not do it out of vanity, and if anyone should take offense at it, my excuse is that it was done more out of ignorance than out of maliciousness. God is accustomed to get angry for similar reasons, but I hope that he would not turn against me for what I have done. I would understand it if he did; Heaven knows, I have given reason to do so on other occasions. But I pray to Him to temper his anger, and release me from punishment even though he sees me at work. I was ready to burn everything, but if God is pleased to give me life, I swear that I will write [my history] in a manner that will not do him a disservice, and in order to avoid all danger of losing it, I send it to you, so that you can keep it locked up, and not opened until . . .[2]

Why Charles ended this letter in midsentence remains a mystery, but his decision to keep his memoirs a secret speaks directly to the emperor's reservations about the writing project in which he was engaged. Memoirs represented a form of autobiography, and in the sixteenth century autobiography was a literary genre still regarded, especially by churchmen, with considerable suspicion.[3] For many, it smacked of vanity, a deadly sin, and for this reason Teresa de Jesús and other divines, both male and female, were frequently reluctant to write their autobiographies, even when urged to do so by their spiritual advisers. Charles, it seems, harbored similar doubts about writing memoirs. Still working on them in his retirement retreat at the Jeronymite monastery at Yuste, in Extremadura, he evidently felt the need to justify his actions when he granted an audience to the famed Jesuit father Francisco de Borja. As later reported by another Jesuit, Charles asked Borja: "Do you think any hint of vanity is involved when a man sets out to write about his deeds?" Borja's answer is not known, but Charles, anxious to avoid all suspicion of vanity, added that "when he began writing his history, he was motivated neither by glory nor vanity but simply the idea of knowing the truth because the historians of our times that he had read had managed to obscure it, either out of ignorance or as a result of their particular aims and desires."[4]

---

2. Cited in Morel-Fatio, *Historiographie de Charles-Quint*, 184.
3. For doubts about the propriety of writing autobiography in early modern Europe, see Amelang, *Flight of Icarus*, introduction.
4. Ribadeneyra, *Vida de San Francisco de Borja*, vol. 2, chap. 18, fol. 109v. For a slightly different version of this interview, see Sandoval, *Historia de la vida y hechos del emperador Carlos V*, 3:504.

In view of Charles's reservations about a project known to carry certain spiritual risks, how was it that the emperor, after having commissioned no fewer than six historians to write an "imperial chronicle" of his reign, found it necessary to write memoirs justifying his actions and defending his policies? And how did these memoirs, his particular interpretation of *historia pro persona,* relate to the historical concerns of his individual dominions, many of which gravitated toward national chronicles, *historia pro patria,* reminiscent of those sponsored by King Alfonso X for Castile? What follows is an attempt to answer these questions and in doing so shed some light on the way in which the emperor put history to work.[5]

Charles V and Official History

Charles V's interest in and knowledge of history began at an early age. Raised by his aunt Archduchess Margaret of Burgundy at her court in Malines in Flanders, Charles had a series of tutors, among them the clergyman Adrian Floriszoon (later Pope Adrian VI), who hoped that the future emperor would acquire a love of letters and learn something of Latin as well.[6] But the young prince, encouraged by the Flemish nobleman Guillaume de Croy, Lord of Chièvres, grew up with a marked preference for "arms" and "horses" as opposed to books. Chièvres, moreover, had no love for Latin, and when it came to reading history suggested that Charles read works in either French or Spanish so that he could learn more about "the deeds of his ancestors in peace and in war,"[7] especially those of his illustrious Burgundian forebears Philip the Good and Charles the Bold. Willem Snouckaert van Schouweberg, who later served as the emperor's librarian in Brussels, claims that Charles actually learned how to read by leafing through the pages of George Chastelain's chronicle of Philip the Good and Olivier de la Marche's *mémoires* of the chivalric exploits of Charles the Bold. He was apparently also familiar with *Le chevalier délibéré,* the same author's poetic tribute to Charles the Bold.[8] Otherwise, his education focused on becoming a knight: "fights, jousts, ball games and

---

5. This chapter is heavily indebted to those scholars, starting with the great French *hispaniste* Alfred Morel-Fatio, whose early-twentieth-century research on the historians and historiography of Charles V remain indispensable. I have also benefitted from the work of another French scholar, Augustín Redondo, together with various Spaniards who have also written about this aspect of Charles's reign, notably Manuel Fernández Álvarez and Baltasar Cuart Moner, both of the University of Salamanca. Of key importance are the following works: Redondo, *Antonio de Guevara;* Fernández Álvarez, "Las 'memorias' de Carlos V"; Cuart Moner's "Estudio histórico," 1:xxv–cxxi; and his "La historiografía áulica en la primera mitad del siglo xvi."
6. Sandoval, *Historia de la vida y hechos del emperador Carlos V,* 1:19.
7. Ibid.
8. See Henri Pirenne, *Histoire de Belgique* (Brussels, 1948–1952), 3:82, as cited in Redondo, *Antonio de Guevara,* 305.

hunting, and everything else that makes one agile and readies the body for fighting and war."⁹

In 1516, shortly before Charles inherited the kingdoms of Castile and León, Desiderius Erasmus made one last-ditch effort to turn Charles toward classical learning. In his treatise *Institutio Principis christiani*, written for and especially dedicated to Charles, Erasmus suggested that the young prince immerse himself in the works of such classical authors as Aristotle, Cicero, and Plato. He also suggested that he read history. "A great fund of wisdom may be gathered from the reading of histories," wrote Erasmus, and he specifically recommended that Charles engage such authors as Caesar, Livy, and Plutarch. Yet he also warned Charles that he did not necessarily have to believe everything he read in these "pagan" books. "History," wrote Erasmus, was "dangerous" because it could easily tantalize the prince with the exploits of such legendary figures as Achilles, Xerxes, Cyrus, Darius, and Caesar, individuals who could easily stir up unwanted ambitions in a young reader. For Erasmus, therefore, ancient history was to be "read with discretion," and Charles should be taught only "to imitate the best of the best."¹⁰

We do not know what impression, if any, Erasmus's suggestions had upon Charles, although among the books the young ruler reportedly took with him on his first trip to Spain in 1516 was Livy's *History of Rome*, Enguerrand de Monstrelet's chronicle of the "cruel civil wars between the houses of Orleans and Burgundy,"¹¹ and another book on the "conquest of Jerusalem," possibly Raimundus des Agiles's history of Geoffrey de Bouillon and the First Crusade.¹² Somewhat later the Venetian writer Francisco di Sansovino reported that the emperor's reading included Castiglione's *Book of the Courtier*, Machiavelli's *Discourses* and *The Prince*, and Polybius's *History of Rome*, but none of these titles figured among the books that Charles had with him during his last years in retirement at the monastery at Yuste. His library there consisted of such books as Boethius's *Life of Constantine*, Olivier de la Marche's *Chevalier délibéré*, Caesar's *Commentaries*, and the first volume of Florián de Ocampo's *Crónica general de España*, a publication Charles helped to support.¹³ What Charles made of these histories remains unknown.

---

9. Sandoval, *Historia de la vida y hechos del emperador Carlos V*, 1: 19.
10. Erasmus, *Education of a Christian Prince*, 200–201.
11. Editions of Enguerrand de Monstrelet's *chronique*, which covered the period from 1400 to 1444, appeared in 1500, 1503, 1512, and 1518. It is not clear which one Charles possessed, but depending on the edition, it was published together with other chronicles by Pierre Desrey and Jean Froissart.
12. See Clavería, *Le Chevalier Délibéré*, 68.
13. For the emperor's books at Yuste, see Cardenas y Vicent, *Carlos de Habsburgo en Yuste*. Erasmus's influence on Charles V in political matters is examined by Mesnard, "L'expérience politique de Charles Quint." See also Gonzalo Sánchez-Molero, *El César y los libros*.

What is certain is that by the age of eighteen Charles already understood the unique role history had afforded him and the many opportunities—and challenges—that lay ahead. The prince's political education can be said to have begun in 1507 when at age seven he first addressed the States General of the Netherlands (the speech was written by Chièvres). In 1515 Chièvres took him on a tour of the various provinces of the Netherlands to be sworn in as sovereign ruler, and then in 1518 Charles, again in Chièvres's company, journeyed to Spain in order to meet his new subjects in Castile and Aragón. Charles soon learned more about what was expected of him from Mercurino Arborio di Gattinara (1465–1530), the Savoyard adviser he appointed as his grand chancellor in 1518. A lawyer and a humanist, Gattinara was a keen proponent of empire and crafted for Charles the idea of an universal world monarchy along with that of an united Christendom that would, in eschatological terms, prefigure the second coming of Christ. "Sire," wrote Gattinara, in an oft quoted phrase, "God has been merciful to you; he has raised you above all kings and princes of Christendom to a power such as no sovereign has enjoyed since your ancestor Charles the Great. He has set you on the way towards world monarchy, towards the uniting of all Christendom under a single shepherd."[14] A similar message came from Luigi Marliani (d. 1521), the Italian humanist and physician who designed Charles's famous heraldic device: the Pillars of Hercules inscribed with the term *Plus Ultra*. The pillars represented the Straits of the Gibraltar, the supposed limits of Herculean realm. *Plus ultra*, "even further," suggested that Charles, the new Hercules, was destined to carry his empire beyond the legendary pillars to Africa, to Asia, and the world beyond, America included.[15] For his advisers, therefore, Charles's reputation resided in empire, and this was a concept that the young ruler seemingly embraced as his own when he was elected king of the Romans at Aachen in 1520.

Yet a good reputation required more, much more, than a heraldic device and military victories, and it was precisely to enhance the emperor's *fama* that his advisers created what amounted to Europe's largest and most elaborate publicity machine outside the Vatican. That machine, recently the subject of an important essay by Peter Burke, literally stage-managed virtually every aspect of Charles's life, up to and including the shape of his beard (square in Germany, pointed in Italy); his hairstyle (cut short, in the Roman style, following his imperial election in 1520); the style and color of his clothes; and the design of his armor (preferably polished black and engraved). Little was left to chance. Charles's handlers even

---

14. Brandi, *The Emperor Charles V*, 112.
15. On Charles's device, see Rosenthal, "*Plus Ultra, Non Plus Ultra*"; and his "The Invention of the Columnar Device."

made certain to "prewash" (and presumably dry) the feet of the twelve paupers that the emperor stooped to clean on Maundy Thursday in an annual ritual symbolizing his humility. In addition, they engaged the services of a small army of speech-writers and publicists, architects and artists, archivists and librarians, print-makers and publishers, all paid to promote Charles's image in various media and to enhance—one might say manufacture or create—what one of his advisers defined as his "imperial reputation."[16]

History's role in this enterprise must not be underestimated. Today we are captivated by the emperor's likeness as preserved in portraits by Bernard van Orley or by Titian and impressed by the size and scope of the rounded, neoclassical palace designed in the emperor's behalf by the Spanish architect Pedro Machuca, erected in the middle of the Alhambra, and emblazoned with the inscription "Semper Augustus Pius Felix Invictissimus" (always august, pious, successful, unconquered). Yet in the sixteenth century there was a lively scholarly debate about which medium—the choices tended to be painting, architecture, sculpture, and written history—was the best means to preserve one's reputation for posterity. Some writers opted for painting, others for architecture, still others for history, among them the Spanish chronicler Fernando del Pulgar, cited at the outset of Chapter 1. Yet another vote for history came from the Italian historian Paolo Giovio, who wrote at length about the emperor's deeds and claimed that "the memorial of [written] triumph [was] more durable than marble sculptures."[17] As we shall see, these were arguments that the emperor adopted as his own.

The first suggestion that such a "memorial" was pending came from Chièvres, who, in a casual remark to a French ambassador in 1519, expressed his interest "to make a chronicle of his . . . master."[18] Little is known about the kind of chronicle Chièvres envisioned, although it is likely to have been in the vernacular, possibly something akin to the court chronicles that Chastelain and De la Marche had written in behalf of the dukes of Burgundy. Chastelain's account offered a detailed, eyewitness account of Philip the Good's achievements, on and off the field of battle, emphasizing the duke's personal qualities—virtue, nobility, courage—and abiding commitment to the service of God and the Church.[19]

Gattinara envisioned a more elevated humanist history, written in Latin, pre-

16. Juan Pardo de Tavera, Archbishop of Toledo, as cited in Burke, "Presenting and Representing Charles V," 393.
17. As quoted in Zimmerman, "The Publication of Paolo Giovio's Histories," 56.
18. Gachard, *La bibliothèque-nationale de Paris*, 2:65, as cited in Redondo, *Antonio de Guevara*, 305.
19. Michael Zingel, "Les princes et l'histoire: L'example des ducs Valois de Bourgogne," in Grell, *Les princes et l'histoire du XVIe au XVIIIe siècle*, 205–220. See also Chastellain, *Oeuvres de Georges Chastellain*, 6:244.

sumably one that transformed Charles into a ideal ruler whose *res gestae* could provide useful lessons or *exemplae* for generations to come. In keeping with his own universalist ideas, Gattinara probably sought a history that promoted a more classical image of Charles as the "last descendant of Aeneas," a ruler destined, like the Romans before him, to possess *imperium sine fine*, albeit in a Christian guise.[20]

Charles's own views on this subject are difficult to pin down, partly because they evolved over time. But judging from the individuals he appointed as his official chroniclers, he hedged his bets, opting initially for the kind of humanist history envisioned by Gattinara but later demonstrating a growing preference for vernacular history of a chivalric sort. Otherwise, Charles evinced less interest in the medium than the message; his primary concern was, as another of his advisers had allowed, to obtain a history that "both clarifies and glorifies both reputation and renown." But acquiring such a history, even for a ruler as powerful Charles, Europe's new Hercules, proved more difficult than either he or his advisers first imagined.

Historia pro Patria, Historia pro Persona

In March, 1520, just at the end of his first and rather tumultuous visit to Spain, Charles V received a letter from Fray Gonzalo de Arredondo, a monk attached to the Benedictine monastery of San Pedro de Arlanza in Old Castile. Arredondo had recently begun work on a revised and updated version of Alfonso X's *Estoria de Espanna* and suggested that the king could support this project by appointing him to the office of royal chronicler. Charles responded with a encouraging letter, urging Arredondo to continue to "organize, write, abbreviate" this chronicle as he saw fit.[21] In addition, Charles suggested that Arredondo consider writing a complementary work on Spanish "antiquities," evidently another subject that had captured the young monarch's attention.

Arredondo's interest in revising the *Estoria de Espanna* was but part of a wider effort to update Spain's national chronicle. Starting in 1523, the Cortes of Castile urged Charles to sponsor a new, authoritative, printed edition or *recopilación* of the *Estoria* together with editions of other older chronicles relating the history of both Castile and its monarchy. "It is right," the Cortes stated, "that the truth about

---

20. Charles's mythic genealogy is the subject of Tanner, *The Last Descendant of Aeneas*.
21. For more on Arredondo, see García Oro and Portua Silva, *La monarquía y los libros*, 61–62, 176–177. A royal order dated 10 March 1520 instructed Arredondo: "ordenar, y conponer y abreviar la crónica de España."

past things be known; this is not possible in other, private books [manuscripts?] that are being read."²² This petition, together with Arredondo's proposed history, reflects the kingdom's interest in *historia pro patria,* which would set forth not only Spain's ancient history but, more particularly, the history of the Reconquest. The historical interests of Charles's Aragonese subjects moved along similar lines, and the same can be said of his vassals in Naples, Burgundy, and other parts of his many realms, many of whom clamored for histories celebrating their particular achievements and, equally importantly, their place in the wider history of Christendom itself.

But *historia pro patria* was one thing, *historia pro persona* another, and the former did not fit neatly into Gattinara's supranational vision of the *monarchia* of Charles V.²³ Nor did *historia pro patria* much interest Charles, whose own historical preferences, following the autobiographical concerns of his paternal grandfather Maximilian I, ran toward his own history together with the ongoing discovery and conquest of the Indies, a topic that neatly dovetailed into the imperial agenda Gattinara had laid out for the young ruler. All this helps to explain why Charles, while expressing interest in Arredondo's projects, stopped short of offering him any financial assistance, let alone the office he sought. Charles's interest in his own history also accounts for his failure to support the publication of Alfonso X's *Estoria de Espanna* (this history was printed, but at the initiative of a private bookseller in 1543) or even accede to repeated requests from the Cortes of Castile asking him to appoint a chronicler who would not only prepare this history for publication but bring it up to date.²⁴ Charles in fact only gave in to the wishes of the Cortes in 1539, when he finally appointed Florián de Ocampo, one of Nebrija's disciples, to the office of royal chronicler with specific instructions to prepare a printed edition of the "crónica de España."²⁵ Until then, the only history that truly fascinated Charles was his own.

The tensions between these two modes of history writing, *pro persona* and *pro patria,* are also evident in a document especially prepared for Charles by the aging royal councillor Lorenzo Galíndez de Carvajal (1472–1527) around 1525. Acting in his capacity as "judge and censor" of Castile's older chroniclers, Carvajal was a strong advocate of *historia pro patria* as opposed to histories narrowly focused on a

---

22. *CLC* 4:382.
23. For Gattinara's concept of empire, see Headley, "The Habsburg World Empire."
24. Cf. Ocampo, *Las cuatros partes enteras de la Crónica de España.* The book was published at the expense of Juan de Spinola, a book dealer in Medina del Campo. See Samson, "Florián de Ocampo." The Cortes presented the king with petitions to update this work in 1523, 1525, 1528, and again in 1538. See Kagan, "Clio and the Crown," 77.
25. For this commission, see Bustos Guadaño, "La crónica del Ocampo."

ruler's individual *gestes*. He recognized the temptation of the latter, however, and reminded the young monarch that "a good reputation [*fama*] . . . is the true prize and reward of the living." Carvajal also conceived of reputation in temporal terms. *Fama* was a word that spoke to the future, especially the way in which later generations would be presented with and thus ultimately remember an individual's deeds and achievements. History and reputation were therefore inextricably linked, or as Carvajal expressed it: "History both clarifies and glorifies both reputation and renown." Accordingly, he advised Charles V to pay particular attention to the ways in which his history was written.[26]

In offering such advice, Carvajal was suggesting that Charles should definitely have a history that represented his interests and concerns, yet he recognized the many pitfalls this kind of history entailed. Historians, he informed Charles, were only human; personal and scholarly considerations often clouded their judgment. Some were prone to enhance and embellish their histories with superfluous rhetorical flourishes that obscured history's main purpose, which, as he saw it, was not only to be truthful, in the sense of factually accurate, but also to convey moral as well as political advice. "History's role," Carvajal stated, "is like that of a mirror, to put in front of the eyes understanding of past good and evil, so that those in the future can imitate good and avoid evil." He also advised Charles to watch out for historians whose only aim was to please and flatter the patrons for whom they wrote. Court historians, he noted, were especially susceptible to this practice because "the chronicles commissioned by kings and princes are written both to please and praise them and also out of fear of angering them; as a result their authors write more than they should and write what they think will be flattering, at the expense of the truth of the event they are writing about."[27]

Yet for all the dangers that official history entailed, Carvajal insisted that Charles could not ignore it. In his view only court historians could be trusted to write chronicles that were historically accurate. At the same time, these chroniclers had to be chosen with care: they had to be "discreet and wise"; capable of writing "in a beautiful and elegant style, because good form honors and enriches the subject at hand"; and not be allowed to write on the basis of secondhand information. Rather, the chroniclers had to be eyewitnesses to the events they narrated or, failing this, must rely exclusively upon the testimony of individuals

---

26. Galíndez de Carvajal, in *Crónicas de los reyes de Castilla*, 2:1. Galíndez de Carvajal made these remarks in his introduction to Pérez de Guzmán's *Generaciones y semblanzas*. See Pérez de Guzmán, *Generaciones, semblanzas*, in *Crónicas de los reyes de Castilla*, BAE 68:697–698. He offered similar observations in the *proemio* of his *Anales breves del reinado de los Reyes Católicos*, 18:237.

27. Galíndez de Carvajal, "La chrónica y hechos acontecidos," 70.

"worthy of faith and who have seen the events first-hand." Chroniclers, moreover, needed to be free to write what they understood as the truth, "without fear of reprisal" because "the office of chronicler, like that of a witness or scribe, is not to judge and to gloss the deeds, but only to record them as they occurred."[28] Finally, Carvajal recommended that Charles, if his desire for a wholly truthful account of his achievements was sincere, should not expect to have his history published during his lifetime.

In proffering this advice, Carvajal drew directly upon the work of the fifteenth-century chronicler Hernan Pérez de Guzmán, whose writings he was editing. Carvajal's arguments concerning the pitfalls of contemporary history also anticipated those found in Jean Bodin's *Methodus ad facilem historiarum cognitionum*, first published in 1565.[29] It is also tempting to think that when, in the 1550s, the emperor left instructions to keep his memoirs secret, he remembered Carvajal's advice. Juan Ginés de Sepúlveda, another of the emperor's chroniclers, suggests that Charles resisted the temptation of having his history published during his lifetime. Sepúlveda visited Charles in 1557 at Yuste and offered to show Charles parts of a history that he was writing about him. The emperor apparently brushed off the historian with the words: "It is scarcely pleasing to me to read or hear what is written about me. Let other people read this when I am dead."[30]

Is Sepúlveda's account of the emperor's modesty accurate? Or simply part of his effort to mask what other contemporaries described as the emperor's "cupidity for glory?"[31] No easy answer to these questions exists, but existing evidence suggests that Charles was far more interested in his own history than that of Castile, Aragon, and other parts of his empire.[32] The one exception was the history of the Indies, a subject for which Charles first expressed his support in 1520 (see below) when he named Peter Martyr (Pietro Martire d'Anghiera), a specialist in "things of the Indies," to the office of cronista del rey.

---

28. *Crónicas de los reyes de Castilla*, 2:1.
29. For the risks that writing contemporary history entailed, see Chapter 3.
30. As reported in Sepúlveda, *Historia de Carlos V*, bk. 30, chap. 31: "en absoluto no es grato leer u oir lo que de mí se escribe; que lo lean otros, cuando haya muerto; tú, si quieres saber algo de mí, pregunta, que yo no negaré a respoderte." I follow the translation offered by Zimmerman, "The Publication of Paolo Giovio's Histories," 71.
31. Ibid., 85.
32. In his pioneering account of Charles V's retirement at Yuste, the Belgian historian Louis-Prosper Gachard claimed that the emperor instructed one of his attendants, Juan Vázquez de Molina, to publish not only Sepúlveda's manuscript but also portions of a general history of Spain by Florián de Ocampo, a royal chronicler he had appointed to update and revise Alfonso X's *Estoria general*. Molina was only able to comply with half of the emperor's wish. Philip II assisted with the publication of Ocampo's history, but for reasons explained in Chapter 3, he was not only reluctant to publish his father's history but equally determined to prevent Charles's *memoires* from ever seeing the light of day. Cf. Gachard, *Retraite et mort de Charles-Quint*, 1:310.

The Imperial Chronicle

As it developed, Charles's "imperial" chronicle was something beyond the capacities of any one individual. It was conceived, instead, as a collective or collaborative enterprise, a kind of historical *bricolage* that involved input from various officials in addition to the chronicler, each with different, though occasionally overlapping, tasks. These officials included secretaries such as Pedro Girón and Jean de Vandenesse, who traveled with the emperor and kept detailed records of his every move. Assisting them was the emperor's comrade-in-arms, Luís de Avila y Zúñiga (d. 1573), who, starting in 1530s, regularly accompanied Charles into battle and wrote eyewitness accounts of what occurred.[33] Further assistance came from the equivalent of today's war correspondents, many of whom were "embedded" with imperial troops and reported on what they saw.[34] There were also speechwriters, archivists, and librarians, each of whom helped not only to craft Charles's image but to preserve the documents and other papers that the emperor's chroniclers needed to write his history.

Coordination and direction of this historical enterprise fell initially to Gattinara, the imperial chancellor, and Charles's aunt Margaret of Austria. Acting in her capacity of regent of the Low Countries, Margaret handled much of the emperor's publicity in the north of Europe, arranging at one point (1529) to have the well-known German humanist Heinrich Cornelius Agrippa (1486?–1535) appointed as her archivist and official historian (*historiographis*) so that he could write panegyrics in her and Charles's behalf.[35] The deaths of both Margaret and Gattinara in 1530 temporarily brought this publicity machine to a halt, but it restarted with help from Mary of Burgundy (1505–1558), Margaret's replacement as regent in the Netherlands (1530–1555), and Antoine Perrenot de Granvelle (1517–1586), the Flemish cleric who emerged as one of the emperor's principal advisers during the latter part of his reign. Together Mary and Granvelle orches-

---

33. See González Palencia, *Don Luis de Zúñiga y Avila*.

34. Among the reporters who covered the emperor's assault on the fortress of Halk-el-Oued (a.k.a. La Goletta) in Tunis in 1535 were his secretary, Antoine de Perrenin, the Franciscan writer Alonso de Sanabria, Hernando de Vega, and Guillaume de Montoche. Perrenin's original French account of the battle was subsequently published as *Commentarius expeditionis Tunetane* (Basel? 1560?). Vega's "Noticia de lo que paso en Africa con Hrdo de Vega" is located in the BRME: Ms. U-II-3. For other accounts, see Voigt, *Die Geschichtschreibung über den Zug Karls V gegen Tunis*.

35. Published somewhat belatedly in 1535, Agrippa's account (*De duplice coronatione Caroli V Romanorum Imperatoris apud Bononiam, historiola*) of this momentous event was relatively brief, but as he explained in the preface, it would still redound to "Charles's glory," which, as he put it, "is impossible to exaggerate." For background, see Antonio Bernárdez, *Enrique Cornelio Agripa: Filósofo, astrónomo, y cronista de Carlos V; traducción al castellano de' Historia de la doble coronación del emperador en Bolonia (en latin)* (Madrid, 1934); and Marc van der Poel, *Cornelius Agrippa: The Humanist Theologian and His Declamations* (Leyden, 1997), 41.

trated the great publicity campaign mounted in the emperor's behalf following his decisive victory over the Schmalkaldic league at Mühlberg (1547), and in 1549 they conducted another campaign to suppress negative publicity relating to the emperor that had surfaced in France. Of particular interest here is Mary's letter instructing the imperial ambassador in Paris to do what he could to prevent circulation of a book, *Paragon de la verité*, that she considered "scandalous and seditious . . . and defamatory of My Lord, the Emperor." She also suggested that the ambassador find "other means and examples to publicize his [the emperor's] life and good and saintly works."[36] Apparently, these "other means" included the important artistic commissions offered at that moment to Titian for the famous equestrian portrait of Charles at the battle of Mühlberg, to the Milanese sculptor Leone Leoni for a bronze statue of Charles suppressing heresy, and the publication in 1548 of Avila y Zúñiga's *Commentarios de . . . la guerra de Alemania hecha de Carlos V*, a book that was immediately translated into Italian, French, English, German, and Latin and which represented Charles as a new and improved version of the great medieval emperor Charlemagne. By this date, however, Charles was also acting as his own publicity agent, as his decision to write his memoirs, starting in 1550, readily suggests.

The Emperor's Humanists

In keeping with the emperor's universal aims, the chroniclers assigned to write what was referred to as "nuestra coronica" (our chronicle) hailed from various parts of his empire, although the office they occupied, that of cronista del rey, was loosely attached to the Royal Council of Castile. Its salary, set at eighty thousand *maravedís*, was fairly substantial and in theory provided its occupant the freedom to write without having to seek other sources of support. Obligations were minimal: four months' annual residence at court in addition to the preparation, theoretically every December, of an account of notable happenings that had transpired during the previous calendar year. These writings, once assembled, were intended to be the raw materials for a comprehensive imperial chronicle surveying the whole of the emperor's reign.

Most importantly, at least for its incumbent, the office of royal chronicler carried with it notable prestige, rendering it a much-sought-after post. Gonzalo Fernández de Oviedo, echoing the fifteenth-century chronicler Juan de Flores, likened the office to that of an "evangelist" with the responsibility of memorializ-

---

36. Letter dated Brussels, 28 February 1549. See *Papiers d'état du Cardenal de Granvelle*, 411.

ing for eternity glories and honors that would otherwise fade with time. Fernández de Oviedo also believed that only royal chroniclers, paid out of the royal purse, could be trusted to write about royalty "with the truth and clarity that is required"; other historians writing about the monarchy generally did so "with bad intention, to criticize . . . without any affection whatsoever nor love."[37]

Yet this office, as Fernández de Oviedo soon learned, was not for everyone, nor even necessarily reserved for established historians such as himself. A royal chronicler was a royal officer first and a historian second, and it was essential for would-be chroniclers to have a close personal relationship with either the ruler's key advisers or, preferably, the ruler himself. Without such connections, these appointments were almost impossible to obtain. Gonzalo de Arredondo, the Benedictine scholar, discovered as much in 1520, when Charles decided to appoint Peter Martyr to the office of cronista del rey.[38] Martyr not only had the advantage of being a respected expert in the "cosas de las Indias," a topic of particular interest to Charles, but was also a close friend of his fellow Lombard Mercurino Gattinara. In addition, Martyr shared Gattinara's messianic vision of Charles as an emperor whose destiny was to rule the world, and Martyr had expressed his thoughts on this topic in the 1516 edition of his *De orbe novo*, the first published the history of the New World. In the dedication, pointedly addressed to Charles, Martyr observed that while God had reserved the discovery of the Indies for Charles's maternal grandparents, Ferdinand and Isabella, he left it to Charles to reap the benefits of this New World and use its wealth for further conquests: "From here, young and honored King, they will extract all that you will need for the world to obey you."[39]

As for Fernández de Oviedo (1478–1557), his bid for the office of royal chronicler began in 1524 when he personally presented the emperor with a copy of his *De la historia natural de las Indias*, a short book also known as the *Sumario* that drew from his personal experiences in the Caribbean. Oviedo envisioned this book as a corrective to Martyr's *De orbe novo*, which he dismissed as a work of fiction, in large part because its author had never visited the Indies or witnessed the events about which he wrote. Oviedo expected that the *Sumario* would lead to an appointment as royal chronicler following Martyr's death, which occurred the

---

37. Fernández de Oviedo, *Libro de la cámara real del príncipe don Juan*, 174.
38. Appointed on 5 March 1520, Martyr filled the position of royal chronicler vacated by Gonzalo de Ayora following this chronicler's decision to join the Revolt of the Comunidades in 1519. Ayora was subsequently arrested, deprived of his office, and ordered into exile. For Ayora's career as a historian, see Cat, *Essai sur la vie*. Martyr's life is examined in Ramón Alba, "Pedro Mártir de Anglería: Su vida y obra," in Mártir de Anglería, *Décadas del Nuevo Mundo*, i–xxxvii.
39. Mártir de Anglería, *Décadas*, 6.

following year. But the position, together with Martyr's papers, went to Fray Antonio de Guevara, an accomplished humanist scholar who enjoyed a close personal relationship with the emperor and other members of his court. Oviedo renewed his campaign for the office of chronicler in 1532 when he presented the empress Isabella with his *Catálago de los reyes de España*, a genealogical treatise he had begun as early as 1505.[40] Again he failed to obtain the office he sought, although on this occasion he did not go away empty-handed. The emperor, having learned that Oviedo was writing a larger history of the New World, offered him a small subsidy, a salary, and other assistance.[41] Three years later Oviedo published the first part of his *Historia general y natural de las Indias*, the first comprehensive treatment of Spanish accomplishments in the New World. But the office of royal chronicler continued to elude him, partly as a result of his contentious personality, partly because of the opposition of his sworn enemy the Dominican friar Bartolomé de las Casas, who was about to embark on his own history of the New World.[42]

Oviedo's bid for this position was further complicated by the emperor's habit of reserving the office of royal chronicler for individuals prepared to write his personal history. The only official chronicler exempted from this obligation was Florián de Ocampo, but Ocampo's appointment was something of an exception and occurred only after the Castilian Cortes, in a tactic clearly designed to pique the emperor's interest, represented the "crónica de España" as a dynastic chronicle that would help preserve the memory of the emperor's Castilian ancestors. Even then the salary allocated for Ocampo, forty thousand *maravedís*, was exactly half that assigned to the chroniclers writing Charles's personal history.

The first chronicler Charles specifically assigned to "our chronicle" was the Dominican friar Bernardo de Gentile, who was named cronista del rey on 8 August 1523, filling the vacancy created by the death of Antonio de Nebrija the previous year. A native of Sicily but residing in Salamanca at the time of this ap-

---

40. Oviedo's *Catálogo* subsequently found its way into the library of San Lorenzo del Escorial, where it remains (Ms. H-I-7) today. It was part of a larger work that eventually included, in addition to the royal genealogies, others pertaining to the great noble houses of Castile. The best introduction to Oviedo's career is Carrillo Castillo, *Naturaleza e imperio*, 31–107.

41. Scholars persist in confusing this commission with an appointment as cronista del rey, an office that Oviedo, much to his disappointment, never received. See, for example, Myers, *Fernández de Oviedo's Chronicle of America*, 19.

42. Although the office of cronista del rey eluded Oviedo, the emperor referred to him as "nuestro coronista de yndias" in a letter dated Nordlingen, 20 March 1547. See Pérez Pastor, "Cronistas del emperador Carlos V," 422. In this letter, the emperor, having learned that Oviedo had recently completed a revised and expanded version of his history, instructed the Council of the Indies to have it sent out for review in order to determine whether it ought to be published. Las Casas's *Historia de las Indias* remained in manuscript until 1875.

pointment, Gentile was not much of a historian, although he had written a short panegyric honoring the near-legendary figure of Gonzalo Fernández de Córdoba (1453–1515), the "Gran Capitan" whose stunning victories against Charles VIII of France in southern Italy at the start of the sixteenth century had assured that Naples and Sicily would remain part of the emperor's inheritance.[43] More importantly, Gentile was a friend of Gattinara, and it was apparently this connection that landed him the position of cronista del rey.[44]

Once in office, Gentile proved a disappointment. In 1525 Charles V was residing temporarily in Madrid when news arrived of the imperial army's stunning victory over French forces at Pavia together with the startling announcement that his arch rival, Francis I, had been taken captive and was being brought to Spain. Pavia represented the first notable military victory of the emperor's reign, and to make the most of the event, Gattinara shifted the imperial publicity machine into high gear, first by commissioning several commemorative paintings, including one by the noted Flemish artist Bernard van Orley, and then by ordering the emperor's Latin secretary, Alfonso de Valdés, to write an official report describing Pavia as a "miraculous victory" prefiguring Charles's determination to lead a crusade that would finally release Jerusalem and the Holy Sepulchre from the grip of Islam.[45] Gentile's sole contribution to this publicity campaign was a short Latin panegyric, *Carmen ad Carolum quintum Caesarum*, based entirely on Valdés's *relación*.[46] Otherwise, he proved incapable of writing the imperial chronicle that Gattinara had envisioned. Gentile was therefore soon shunted off to a bishopric in Sardinia and required to relinquish the office of royal chronicler.

By the time Gentile vacated this office, in October 1526, Charles had already engaged the noted humanist Fray Antonio de Guevara (1480–1536) to write the chronicle he sought. At the time Guevara was living in Bologna, busy with what became his famous *Libro áureo de Marco Aurelio y Relox de Príncipes* (first published in 1529), a "mirror of princes" based loosely on the autobiographical reflections of this famous Roman emperor and a work that he originally envisioned as an advice book for Charles. Guevara in this respect resembled the "wise and

43. A copy of Gentile's panegyric, *De rebus gestis Ferdinandi di Cordoba*, has yet to be located. See Peña y Camara, "Un cronista desconocido de Carlos V," 540.
44. Gentile's knowledge of Italian history must also have appealed to Gattinara, who firmly believed that Italy "would forever be the seat of empire." See Headley, "Rhetoric and Reality," 242.
45. The report was printed as *Relación de las nuevas de Italia*. See Valdés, *Relación de las nuevas de Italia*. Valdés provided a detailed list of the individual captains who had contributed to the victory, among them Hernando de Avalos, marques de Pescara, whose achievement was also later celebrated in a Latin poem by the famous Italian poet Ludovico Ariosto. See Headley, "Rhetoric and Reality," 265.
46. Gentile, *Carmen ad Carolum quintum Caesarum*. The panegyric depicted the "divine Charles" as a great Christian emperor whose triumphs were destined to bring peace, justice, and religion to the entire globe.

discreet man" that Carvajal had recommended to Charles as an ideal chronicler. Also working in Guevara's favor was his lineage: he was the son of Diego de Guevara, another of Charles's most trusted advisers. Even more importantly, he had previously proven his loyalty to Charles during the Revolt of the Comunidades when he championed the monarchy's cause and subsequently was rewarded with the office of royal preacher. Guevara, in sum, possessed virtually all of the credentials—family background, experience at court, fidelity to the Crown, and intellectual skills—that the office of royal chronicler demanded.

In his letter of appointment, Charles instructed Guevara to write "nuestra coronica," a term that suggested that he was to write about the emperor's *res gestae*. Furthermore, he was expected to do so on the basis of *relaciones* or news sheets similar to the one Valdés had written about Pavia and of documents and other materials provided by the emperor's secretaries, along with input from informants located outside Spain itself. Guevara also asked for and received the emperor's permission to consult the papers of his predecessor, Peter Martyr, together with those of Galíndez de Carvajal. These and other communications are indicative of the energy that Guevara invested in the chronicle, and in a letter addressed to the emperor in 1529, Guevara expressed not only his enthusiasm for his office—"I am his chronicler"—but the pleasure he derived from writing the emperor's history.[47]

But whatever the extent of his commitment to this history, other obligations, including his appointment (in 1529) as bishop of the Andalusian city of Guadix, soon intervened. Guevara remained in Andalusia, tending his flock, until 1535, when the emperor ordered him to return to court and, in keeping with his obligations as royal chronicler, to accompany him on the military expedition that Charles was preparing to launch against Tunis, an important Muslim stronghold in North Africa. As the official chronicler of this expedition, and as administrator of the campaign's mobile hospital, Guevara traveled alongside the emperor for a little over a year, from Spain to Tunis (and victory), then Sicily, Naples, and Rome.

At this juncture, Guevara pulled back from writing the emperor's history for reasons that are still not entirely clear. For one thing, he had a lot on his plate, including the administration of yet another diocese—Charles had appointed him bishop of Mondoñedo in 1537—and the completion of his famous advice book, *Menosprecio del corte y alabanza de aldea*, which he sent off to his printer in 1539. Pragmatic considerations also intervened, especially after 1541, when Guevara moved to Mondoñedo, a somewhat isolated town in Galicia, in order to reside in

---

47. Redondo, *Antonio de Guevara*, 208.

his diocese. Although part of his salary as royal chronicler was specifically earmarked to pay for eyewitness reports prepared by individuals in the emperor's immediate entourage, once in Mondoñedo Guevara found it difficult to get the information he needed to continue with the emperor's history.[48] Then too there is the possibility that Guevara's initial enthusiasm for this project waned as he learned that the history would require him to replace Cicero's "lux veritas" with one that enabled him to avoid mention of such infamous events as the brutal Sack of Rome by imperial troops in 1527. What is certain is that Guevara left this history *in media res*, even though he continued to refer to himself as emperor's chronicler until his death in 1545. At this point a copy of his unfinished chronicle passed to the royal cosmographer, Alonso de Santa Cruz, who subsequently used it to write his own, semiofficial chronicle of the emperor's achievements. Santa Cruz finished the chronicle in 1551, but it was immediately confiscated on the orders of Prince Philip, the future Philip II (see below) and placed in the royal archives for safekeeping. At the start of the seventeenth century, Fray Prudencio de Sandoval, another royal chronicler, drew upon Guevara's work to write his own, monumental history of the emperor, but at this point whatever was left of Guevara's chronicle disappeared.[49]

Guevara's apparent decision to stop work on the imperial chronicle represented an important setback both for the emperor and for his advisers, but Charles lost no time in seeking a replacement, turning first to the Italian historian Paolo Giovio, who was part of the papal entourage in Rome. No friend of Spain, Giovio (1483–1553) had once watched Spanish troops pillage his home in Como; in 1527 he had also observed some of the brutalities committed by Spanish and imperial soldiers during the Sack of Rome. However, Giovio had enormous admiration for the emperor, once describing him as a "summit of a man" (*cima l'huomo*) even though Charles stood no taller than about five feet six. Such admiration stemmed from Giovio's belief that Charles was the only ruler capable of uniting the fractious republics and principalities of northern Italy against the French. Giovio's vision of Charles as Italy's savior accorded perfectly with the image that Charles himself sought to project, notably in a speech made before the Aragonese Cortes on the eve of his departure for Genova in 1529. Here he announced, "It is not my intention to go to Italy to tyrannize its peoples, or to displace its noblemen, or to seize any states, or to enrich myself with money, because these and similar actions are more the work of tyrants than pious princes. . . . If I have gone to war and supported

---

48. Ibid., 307, for Guevara's payments, starting in 1538, to outside informants.
49. For Guevara's manuscript, see Jones, "Fragments of Antonio de Guevara's Lost Chronicle." Santa Cruz's chronicle is available as Santa Cruz, *Crónica del Emperador Carlos V*.

armies, my reasons for doing so have not been to take anything from anyone, but simply to defend and protect what is mine."[50]

Giovio's first encounter with the emperor took place in 1530, at the time of Charles's coronation in Bologna. Giovio was already working on what later became his *History of Our Times*, a lengthy current-events history focused on Italy that was published in two hefty volumes in 1550 and 1552.[51] The emperor, in an apparent bid to retain his services, awarded Giovio a patent of nobility and granted him permission to add his personal device, the Pillars of Hercules, and the inscription *plus ultra* to his family's coat of arms. Giovio returned the favor by dedicating to the emperor his *Commentaries on the Turks* (published 1532), in which he congratulated Charles for his victory over the Ottomans at Vienna in 1529 and praised "the sincerity of his faith and grandeur of spirit."[52] Charles was impressed, so much so that he even flirted with the idea of creating a new office of "imperial chronicler," with Giovio in mind. However, when the two next met, again in Bologna, in 1532, the encounter did not go well, allegedly because Giovio, who had a reputation for avarice, angered Charles when he offered to write his history in exchange for a "lame mule," his euphemism for some kind of gift or reward.[53] Charles's response to such effrontery was a letter stating that "if Giovio imagines that because he writes history, he will prompt me to give him what I have already promised him, he is mistaken. It is precisely because he writes history that he has nothing to hope for from me."[54]

Whatever happened in Bologna in 1532, Charles and Giovio met again in Naples in November 1535, following the emperor's triumphant return from Tunis. Throughout that campaign, which had taken place over the previous summer, Giovio received regular battle reports from various imperial commanders[55] and upon meeting the emperor, asked him for his own reflections on the victory. Giovio subsequently informed a friend, "His Majesty recounted, and partly at my interrogation, many fine things about the taking of Goletta which pertain to the histories, and I persuade myself that the history . . . will please him greatly."[56]

---

50. Santa Cruz, *Crónica del Emperador Carlos V*, 2:456–457.
51. I refer to Giovio, *Historiarum sui temporis*. The work was immediately published in Italian translation and appeared in other European languages shortly thereafter.
52. Giovio, *Commentario de le cose de' Turchi*. The treatise was first published in 1532.
53. Giovio's reputation for covetousness colored his reputation as a historian for centuries. See, for example, Wheare, *Order and method of Reading Histories*, 126: "He [Giovio] was too violent both in his love and hatred, and because he was a lover of money, he was a slave to it in the very writing of history."
54. My translation follows that in Morel-Fatio, *Historiographie de Charles-Quint*, 108. The incident was originally reported by Sepúlveda in his *Historia de Carlos V* (bk. 30, chap. 33).
55. Giovio's chief informant was the imperial commander, the Marquis of Vasto.
56. Letter of 12 December 1535 to Carpi as translated in Zimmerman, "The Publication of Paolo Giovio's Histories," 54. La Golette was the name of the Muslim fortress in Tunis.

However, Giovio again asked for but was refused a subsidy, prompting another letter in which he reported: "It appears to me that flattery would please him [the emperor], but if he wants it on parchment, I shall first have to ride a lame mule. Otherwise, I shall leave the task to a friar *noviter* stamped *coronista* [that is, Guevara], of His Majesty, who writes in Spanish and refectory Latin."[57]

These complaints suggest that Giovio had succeeded once again in offending Charles, who, still in Italy, immediately started a search for another chronicler. The person he selected on this occasion was Juan Ginés de Sepúlveda (1490–1573), a well-known Spanish humanist whom he had met on several previous occasions and met again in Rome just after the Tunis campaign.[58] Sepúlveda's scholarly reputation rested chiefly on his translations of Aristotle from Greek into Latin, but the work that seems to have caught the emperor's eye was his *Exhortation to War against the Turks* (1529), a pamphlet that appealed to Charles's universalist ambitions by describing him as a providentially sanctioned *imperator* destined to liberate Jerusalem and add "all the remaining lands of the earth . . . to the power of and most holy religion of Christians."[59] Sepúlveda subsequently demonstrated his support for Charles's imperialist leanings in *De bello Africa* (1535), a treatise ostensibly intended to celebrate the imperial victory at Tunis but which represented the emperor as Christianity's savior. This was the kind of publicity that Charles savored, and on 15 April 1536 he appointed Sepúlveda cronista del rey. Two months later, Sepúlveda, bursting with pride, wrote to a friend commenting on this appointment, albeit in a way that masked the emperor's personal interest in the history he had been commissioned to write: "I have been included in the list of the [emperor's] servants and ordered to follow his court and not to leave it, given the requirements of the job, which is that I should write about his deeds, as well as those carried out under his command, and not because Charles is immodest (*ambicioso*), because he is indifferent to honors. But, according to the tradition of his ancestors, it is appropriate for the kings of Spain to have learned men who can write, truthfully and diligently, about the history of his reign."[60]

In keeping with the obligations of his new office, Sepúlveda traveled with the emperor for several months and returned with him to Spain in October 1536, by

---

57. Ibid., 55. Letter of 28 December 1535.

58. According to the emperor's seventeenth-century biographer Prudencio de Sandoval, Giovio "no era muy amigo de españoles." See Sandoval, *Historia de . . . Carlos V*, 1:95. For more on Giovio, see Zimmerman, *Paolo Giovio*.

59. As cited in Headley, "The Habsburg World Empire," 67. Sepúlveda apparently wrote this pamphlet to rally support for the emperor at the moment when the armies of the Turkish sultan, Suleiman, were threatening the city of Vienna.

60. *Epistolarum libri septem* (Salamanca, 1557), bk. 1, letter 11, as cited in Cuart Moner, "Juan Ginés de Sepúlveda," 3:353.

which time he started what became his *Historiarum de rebus gestis Carolus V.* Initially, the writing went smoothly, and in 1539 Sepúlveda asked for permission to leave the royal court in order to reside in an "isolated place" where he could better concentrate upon his history. He requested another leave the following year, again noting that he would be able to write with "more relaxation and repose . . . in any village or spot located away from the court."[61] Sepúlveda was working on a number of projects, including his *Democrates segundus,* a controversial defense of the Spanish right of conquest in the New World, but the *Historiarum* seemingly occupied much of his time.[62]

But not for long. As early as 1540, Sepúlveda informed one friend that while he continued to work on the emperor's history, his translations of Aristotle were far more pressing, "severiores" in his language.[63] In addition, Sepúlveda's prolonged absences from court meant that he found it difficult to obtain the firsthand information needed to document his history. Consequently, and in keeping with Cicero's precept that a historian should "not incur falsehood" nor "hide the truth," he instructed one of his servants, Pedro Martín, to travel with the emperor, keep track of his activities, and then forward him reports that could incorporate into the history.[64] Even then he lacked the information he needed, and in 1552, residing in his native Córdoba, Sepúlveda confessed that "for some time now I do not know what either the Emperor nor his brother, Fernando, are doing."[65]

Additional distractions were Sepúlveda's ongoing debate with Las Casas over the juridical status of America's natives and his efforts to get his controversial treatise *De justi belli causis apud Indios,* which defended Spain's right to extract forced labor from America's natives, into print. After Las Casas opposed its publication, Sepúlveda appealed to the emperor, who, in an order issued in Nördlingen, offered his chronicler permission to print the treatise on the grounds that it "established the just causes of the war and especially of the conquest of the Indies."[66] But this debate continued, and it apparently consumed so much of Sepúlveda's time that in 1552 he received a letter from Prince Philip accusing him of neglecting the duties attached to his office of royal chronicler. Sepúlveda responded by assuring the prince that, despite his prolonged absence from court, he was continuing to work on the emperor's history and thus still merited his salary as chronicler. Yet other evidence suggests that Sepúlveda, having changed his

61. For these petitions, see Losada, *Juan Ginés de Sepúlveda,* 497–498.
62. Rodríguez Peregrina, "Juan Ginés de Sepúlveda."
63. Cited in Cuart Moner, "Juan Ginés de Sepúlveda," 3:353.
64. Ibid., 3:360.
65. Ibid., 3:360, letter of 14 February 1552 to Luís de Carvajal.
66. For the document, see Pérez Pastor, "Cronistas del emperador Carlos V," 420.

opinion of the emperor, was in fact neglecting the chronicle he had been commissioned to write.[67]

As Baltasar Cuart has argued, Sepúlveda had originally accepted the office of royal chronicler because he thought of the emperor, as his early panegyrics allowed, as a great Christian champion who was wholly committed to the idea of an united Christendom. He therefore perceived of writing the emperor's history as a noble task, a thoroughly humanistic enterprise that would not require him to be either a "liar" or an "adulator."[68] Increasingly, however, Sepúlveda, like Giovio before him, came to the recognition that the emperor's political agenda was becoming ever more personal and directed principally to advancing the dynastic and territorial interests of the Habsburgs as opposed to the defense of religion. How then could he, like the good humanist he was, continue a chronicle to which he was no longer fully committed?

Sepúlveda's working drafts have disappeared, and the only existing manuscript of his history of Charles V dates from the eighteenth century. It is difficult, therefore, to follow the evolution of Sepúlveda's thinking about Charles, although one letter, addressed to Cardinal Reginald Pole in 1555, suggests that he was decidedly less enthusiastic about the history he was writing than when he began it in 1536. "History," wrote Sepúlveda, "is not exactly my favorite pastime, as it prevents me from dedicating more time to those activities and studies to which ... I have devoted my life; these are the ones for which I truly feel affection."[69] Despite these reservations, Sepúlveda did not abandon the history completely. He also remained on good terms with the emperor, as his above-mentioned visit to Yuste in 1557 and his efforts to show Charles his manuscript might suggest. Yet he continued to have misgivings about the chronicle, as suggested by a letter written in 1560, almost four years after the emperor's death, to an old friend from Bologna, Diego de Neila. Sepúlveda had previously sent Neila portions of his chronicle for review, but upon reading them, Neila advised Sepúlveda not to circulate the manuscript or even attempt to publish it during his lifetime. Sepúlveda agreed: "I approve and accept your suggestion, so filled with prudence and good sense, and I will obey all of your recommendations." Unfortunately, the correspondence ends there, but from another letter it is clear that Sepúlveda had essentially lost interest in writing a chronicle that bordered on flattery.[70]

---

67. Losada, *Juan Ginés de Sepúlveda*, 308.
68. Cuart Moner, "Juan Ginés de Sepúlveda," 3:355.
69. *Epistolario de Juan Ginés de Sepúlveda*, 216–217.
70. Written to Diego de Neila, the letter, edited and translated by B. Cuart Moner and J. Costa, is published in Sepúlveda, *Historia de Carlos V*, libros 1–5, in *Obras completas*, 1:xvii–xxiii.

Sepúlveda's humanistic commitment was admirable, but it also explains why the final version of this history—Sepúlveda apparently completed it in about 1563 but continued to tinker with the manuscript until his death in 1573—had relatively little to say about the emperor's *res gestae*.[71] To be sure, it included a wholly positive assessment of the emperor's achievement, absolving him, for example, of any responsibility for the infamous Sack of Rome. At the same time Sepúlveda succeeded in subtly transforming what began as the personal chronicle of the emperor into a broader history of Spain in the era of Charles V, moving in other words from *historia pro persona* into the realm of *historia pro patria*, a subject that Italy's humanist scholars traditionally regarded as both noble and worthwhile. He announced this change in the opening chapter of book 1 with the statement: "I am going to write the history of the deeds realized in our times by Charles, king of Spain, and also Roman Emperor, together with those done by the Spaniards."[72] That he followed this announcement with a *laudatio hispaniae* as opposed to the emperor's genealogy or even a pen portrait of Charles is equally telling, as it suggests that in writing this history—remember that he dawdled—Sepúlveda distanced himself from the person of the emperor in order to concentrate on Spain's growing preponderance in world affairs, a topic he also addressed in *De rebus hispanorum gestis ad novum orbem*, a book that emphasized "the deeds of the Spaniards in the New World."[73] This change in direction also reflected the historical preferences of Philip II, whose interest in *historia pro persona*, as opposed to *historia pro patria*, was practically nil.

It therefore seems reasonable to conclude that Sepúlveda, in an effort to please the new monarch, reworked his history of the emperor so that it could better serve as a counterweight to histories by such Italian authors as Galeazzo Capello and Marco Guazzo,[74] as well as John Sleidan's *Commentaries on Government and Religion in the Age of Charles*,[75] none of which had anything positive to say either about

---

71. RAH: Ms. 9/112, fol. 209, Sepúlveda to Martín Pérez de Guzmán, dated 8 March 1563, in which he announces that his history of Charles V is almost finished but that he will revise it should new information arrive. This letter is published in Losada, *Juan Ginés de Sepúlveda*, 178; and in Sepúlveda, *Obras completas*, vol. 11, part 2, p. 385.

72. Sepúlveda, *Historia de Carlos V*, libros 1–5, in *Obras completas*, 1:3. For propagandistic elements in this history, see Pozuelo Calero, "Propaganda y crítica."

73. First published in 1780 under the auspices of Real Academia de la History (see Chapter 7), Sepúlveda's *De Rebus Hispanorum Gestis Ad Novum Orbem* is now available in both Latin and Spanish, in his *Obras completas*, vol. 11, *Del Nuevo Mundo*, edited and translated by Luis Rivero García (Pozoblanco, 2005).

74. I refer here to Capello, *De rebus nuper in Italia gestis*, which covered wars in Italy between 1521 and 1530. Another history critical of Charles was Guazzo, *Historie*.

75. Although Sleidan's pro-Protestant *De statu Religionis & Republicæ, Carolo Quinto Cæsare, Commentarii* was not published until 1555, portions of the text were circulating in manuscript form as early as 1545. In this work Sleidan professed loyalty to the emperor but was outspoken in his criticism of the

Spaniards or about Spain. Even then, Sepúlveda's history of the emperor failed to meet with Philip's approval. Refusing to sanction its publication, he left the manuscript to molder in royal archives until it was rescued by the Royal Academy of History, edited, and finally published in 1780 as part of that institution's effort (see below, Chapter 7) to recover lost chapters in Spain's glorious history.

The Vernacular Turn: Busto and Mexía

As history, Sepúlveda's account of the emperor is a truly remarkable achievement, one that demonstrates the writer's determination to free himself from the constraints that official history imposed. For the emperor, however, Sepúlveda's failure to complete this history in a timely fashion represented a notable setback, especially as his determination to secure a chronicle of his achievements seemingly increased in direct proportion to his advancing age and deteriorating health. A key turning point occurred in 1542, the year that marked the beginning of his war against the Protestant princes of the Schmalkaldic League. The emperor recognized that victory might restore unity to Christendom, whereas defeat was likely to lead to its lasting separation into two separate and warring religious camps. He also understood that, in view of his gout and other infirmities, this campaign was likely to be the last upon which he would ever embark. He was therefore determined to find a historian prepared to chronicle its progress.

The first sign of the emperor's eagerness to appoint a new chronicler surfaced in 1543 when he encountered, almost by chance, his old nemesis Paolo Giovio in the northern Italian town of Bussetto. Our knowledge of this encounter comes from Giovio, who reports that the emperor practically begged him to write a history of the campaign: "Take up pen your pen, Giovio, and hasten to write what I have already done, because this moving of arms will truly set before you a new and great labor."[76]

This conversation is likely to be apocryphal, but if the emperor tendered such an offer, and it seems likely he did, Giovio refused, since by this date his opinion of the emperor was decidedly less positive than it had been when they first met in 1530 or even in 1535, in the wake of the campaign against Tunis. In his private correspondence, Giovio regularly expressed disappointment in the emperor's policies, informing his friends that the emperor "dissimulated" and that his true

---

Spaniards, noting at the start of his history what he called their "designs on this, our empire." For Sleidan and his history, see Vogelstein, *Johann Sleidan's Commentaries;* and Kelley, "Johann Sleidan and the Origins of History as a Profession."

76. As translated in Zimmerman, "The Publication of Paolo Giovio's Histories," 56.

intention was not to unite Christendom against the Turks but rather to proclaim himself king of Milan (until then, Charles was only the duke of Milan), dominate the other "Italian princes," become "emperor of all Italy," and ultimately put an end to the "liberty and health of Italy."[77] Giovio was exaggerating, although he was right to believe that the emperor's political agenda had changed so that his dynastic concerns were as important as those of protecting the Church. But whatever the emperor's motives, the incident reflected the urgency with which the emperor, his eyes firmly set on posterity, looked for yet another chronicler to defend his reputation.

The chronicler to whom the emperor eventually turned was Dr. Bernabé de Busto, a clergyman from Extremadura who was serving as a royal chaplain in Madrid. Why Busto was chosen is not entirely clear, since he was more of a grammarian and a philologist than a historian.[78] On the other hand, he was a known quantity, after having been appointed to served as Latin tutor to Prince Philip.[79] Equally importantly, Busto, despite his humanist background, was prepared to write the emperor's history in the vernacular as opposed to Latin. I have yet to locate any document explaining the vernacular turn in the emperor's historical preferences, but it appears that, by the time of Busto's appointment as royal chronicler in 1546, Charles had determined that his imperial chronicle could be redacted in Spanish, a language in which he had become proficient and one that, *pace* Nebrija, also served as the "language of empire." Put simply, Latin was out, Spanish in, as Charles had decided to replace Gattinara's notion of humanist history with a vernacular chronicle modeled on those of his Burgundian ancestors and close to the kind of history originally recommended to him by Chièvres in 1519. Busto was therefore freed from many of the strictures that writing humanist history imposed, among them the need to pepper the narrative with elaborate rhetorical flourishes and *exemplae* meant to give it intellectual heft.

It follows that Busto's assignment was far less problematic than that of Charles's humanist chroniclers. They had instructions to write a comprehensive history of the emperor's accomplishments in both peace and war, whereas Busto's

---

77. For Giovio's changing opinion of Charles, see Zimmerman, *Paolo Giovio*, 159, 186. Giovio's comment about "la libertà e salute de Italia" may be found in his letter of 21 January 1542 to Vicente Fedelli, in Giovio, *Lettere*, 1:331. See also Paolo Giovio, *La Prima [e segunda parte] dell' istorie de suo tempo* (Florence, 1551), bk. 31, chap. 3, where he worries about Italy losing its "old honor and liberty"; and bk. 39, chap. 5, where he comments on the "dissimulation of the emperor." For one Spaniard's criticism of Giovio, especially his critical account of Spanish troops serving in Italy, see Jiménez de Quesada, *El Antijovio*.

78. For an introduction to Busto, see García Fuentes, "Bernabé de Busto."

79. Busto's publications included a Spanish translation of Erasmus's *Institutes for a Christian Prince* as well as *Introductiones gramáticas*.

assignment was only to write about Charles's exploits on the field of battle; and starting in 1547, the emperor granted him permission to absent himself from court for six months out of every year in order concentrate on his chronicle.[80] Busto assembled various reports on the emperor's earlier campaigns in Italy, Germany, and North Africa but devoted most of his attention to the ongoing Schmalkaldic War. The Protestant princes who constituted the Schmalkaldic League had as their official historian Johannes Sleidan, whose task was to defend the Protestant cause. Busto, in contrast, was to write the same history from the emperor's perspective, and he did so by gathering reports provided by soldiers who accompanied the emperor on campaigns.[81] He subsequently used these and other sources to compile two histories—*España y la conquista germanica del Emp Cath. Carlo Maximo* and *Historia de Carlos V en Alemania alto y bajo*—both of which took the form of annals emphasizing the emperor's exploits, both on the battlefield and off.[82] Neither was especially original nor inspired, but they seem to have approximated the way in which Charles wanted to be remembered as he entered the twilight of his reign.

Yet another sign of the importance that the emperor accorded vernacular history was his naming Pedro Mexía (1497–1551) to the office of royal chronicler. The appointment was extraordinary inasmuch as Charles already had two chroniclers, Sepúlveda and Busto, writing his imperial chronicle and a third, Ocampo, working on Spain's general history. A Sevillian by birth, Mexía had entered Charles's service in 1538, when he was appointed royal cosmographer in Seville's House of Trade. He subsequently exploited the prerogatives of this office to write on a variety of subjects, few of which had anything to do with his work as a cosmographer. But Mexía had his sights trained on becoming a royal chronicler and toward this end wrote his *Historia imperial y caesarea*, which traced the history of the imperial dignity from the time of Julius Caesar to that of Charles's grandfather Maximilian I.[83] Dedicated to Charles, this history flattered the emperor by announcing that Charles had finally effected the long-awaited *translatio imperii*, or transfer of the imperial dignity from Germany to Spain. Mexía also used this work

80. For this permission, see Pérez Pastor, "Cronistas del emperador Carlos V," 426.
81. His sources included Avila y Zúñiga, *Comentarios*; and Salazar, *Coronica*.
82. For Busto, see Morel-Fatio, *Historiographie de Charles-Quint*, 86–87. His history of the emperor's German campaigns is published as *Geschichte des Schmalkaldischen Krieges*. Several manuscripts, including "España e conquista germanica del Emp Cath. Carlo Maxximo" and "Dos cuadernos de Historia de Carlos V en Alemania alto y bajo" also survive. See BRME: Ms. L-I-6, fols. 112–199 and fol. 206ff.
83. Immediately before his appointment, Mexía also published his *Silva de varia lección*, a miscellany dedicated to Charles and purposely designed to highlight both the range and the extent of his knowledge, as well as his *Coloquios*. See Castro Diaz, *Los "Coloquios" de Pedro Mexía*. See also Costes, "Pedro Mexía"; and Mexía, *Historia del Emperador Carlos V*.

to announce that a ruler as illustrious as Charles V merited his own history; but, with a bit of false modesty, Mexía claimed that he lacked the ability to undertake such a work.[84] As it turned out, Mexía was lying, since he had already begun work on his *Historia del Emperador Carlos V* when, in July 1548, Charles named him to the office he sought, even granting him license to live in Seville instead of at the royal court.[85]

The timing of this appointment was no accident. It was part of the publicity campaign mounted to capitalize on the emperor's victory at Mühlberg in April 1547. The victory was of greater symbolic than political importance: it dismantled the Schmalkaldic League but did little to weaken the overall Protestant position in Germany and nothing to unite the divided Christendom. Charles's ambassador in Venice, Juan Hurtado de Mendoza, admitted the limited value of Mühlberg when, in a letter directed to Prince Philip, he reported that the victory "will add more to the fame of His Majesty than to the benefit of Christendom, which remains in a perilous state."[86] Even so, Hurtado de Mendoza, acting in conjunction with Mary of Burgundy and Cardinal Granvelle, sought to make the most of the victory with a grandiose publicity campaign. As noted briefly above, this campaign was a true multimedia affair, involving a set of nine tapestries commemorating the emperor's victory at Tunis in 1535; a book of engravings (by Martin vans Heemskerck) celebrating Tunis as well as the emperor's other victories; a Latin pamphlet highlighting the emperor's continuing determination to defend Christendom against the forces of Islam; Leone Leoni's bronze statue of Charles suppressing heresy; and Titian's equestrian portrait of the emperor at Mühlberg, a commission arranged by Juan Hurtado de Mendoza, as a series of his letters, now in Simancas, make clear.[87]

History's role in this campaign was expressed first by Avila y Zúñiga's *Commentaries on . . . the war in Germany by Charles V,* published (initially in Italian) in

---

84. For a recent assessment of Mexía's historical vision, see J. G. A. Pocock, *Barbarism and Religion* (Cambridge, 2003), 3:239–257.

85. For the document entitling Mexía to reside in Seville, see Pérez Pastor, "Cronistas del emperador Carlos V," 427.

86. AGS Est: leg. 11.318, letter dated Venice, 20 November 1547.

87. More is to be learned about Juan Hurtado de Mendoza's activities in the emperor's behalf, but he was involved in the publication of the engraved portrait of the emperor by the Venetian artist Anea Vico (later copied by Titian), as well as the biography-cum-hagiography of the emperor written by Alfonso de Ulloa and published in Venice in 1561. For Hurtado de Mendoza, see Checa Cremades, *Carlos V,* 260. The pamphlet in question is Juan Cristóval Calvete de Estrella's *De Aphrodosio expugnato quod vulgo Aphricam vocant, Commentarius* (Antwerp, 1551). It was allegedly commissioned by the emperor after he received news of the defeat of Ottoman fleet at Mahdia, in North Africa, in October 1550. See Sánchez-Molero, "Juan Christóval Calvete de Estrella," in Calvete de Estrella, *El felicíssimo viaje,* xxxii.

Venice with help from Hurtado de Mendoza. Modeled on Caesar's account of the conquest of Gaul, the *Commentaries* represented Charles as the new Caesar, albeit a Christian one. In addition, Avila made a point of comparing Charles's victories to those of Caesar and even mimicked the famous words that Caesar proclaimed to the Roman Senate following his victory at Zela in 46 BCE by ending his account of Charles's victory at Mühlberg with the quote "Vine y vi y Dios venció" (I came, I saw, and God conquered), a phrase designed both to emphasize the emperor's modesty and to cast the victory in providential terms. Avila also represented Charles as a new and improved version of the great medieval emperor Charlemagne and, with specific reference to their efforts to conquer Germany, offered the observation that Charles had accomplished in ninety days what took Charlemagne almost a lifetime. As history, Avila's chronicle was, as Cardinal Granvelle remarked, "impassioned" in that it openly boasted of the "grandeur of this [the emperor's] war," but the emperor loved it and is even said to have remarked that "Alexander's achievements surpassed mine, but he was less fortunate [than me] in his chronicler."[88] In other words, it appears that Avila y Zúñiga's avowedly adulatory *Commentaries* was exactly the kind of history he craved.

That Mexía was prepared to write history in a similar vein accounts for his appointment as royal chronicler. Sepúlveda, as noted earlier, found it difficult to compromise his humanistic notion of historical truth, but Mexía had few qualms about writing panegyric masquerading as history. Sepúlveda's reluctance to write this kind of official history also helps to explain why he began his history of Charles V with a geographical description of Spain. Mexía, in contrast, opened his *Historia del Emperador* with the emperor's genealogy, according particular attention to his illustrious grandparents, both maternal and paternal, and including a reference to Charles as a new David especially chosen by God to expand his kingdoms and defend the Catholic faith.[89] He also emphasized Charles's most memorable accomplishments, notably his defeat of the Comunidades, the great victory at Pavia, and the imperial coronation in Bologna, an event that Sepúlveda had all but ignored. As for the Sack of Rome by mutinous imperial troops in 1527,

---

88. Ávila y Zúñiga, *Comentarios*, fol. 43, where Avila, following a comparison made to him in a letter written by Paolo Giovio, also noted that while it took Charlemagne thirty-three years to conquer Savoy, the emperor accomplished the same feat in less than three months. For the "apasionado" nature of Avila's history, see Antoine Perrenot de Granville's letter of 5 November 1558, cited in Fernández Álvarez, "Las 'memorias' de Carlos V," 714–716. For Avila's relationship to Giovio, see Morel-Fatio, *Historiographie de Charles-Quint*, 112.

89. Mexía, *Historia del Emperador Carlos V*, bk. 1, chap. 2, p. 19, for Charles as a new David.

an incident widely attributed to the emperor himself, Mexiá did nothing to disguise the enormity of the event—"The entire city was robbed and sacked, together with every house and church as well"—but endeavored to rescue the emperor's reputation by attributing it to the "secret wishes" of God and the "obstinacy" of Pope Clement V. The emperor, he wrote, "neither wanted nor ordered it, nor even imagined that such a thing might have occurred," and upon learning about what had occurred took immediate steps to ensure the safety of His Holiness.[90]

As Mexiá related these and other notable events, he claimed that he differed from other historians—was he thinking possibly of Guevara?—in that he had no interest in "using words to enrich and aggrandize the descriptions of battles and combats simply to entertain and delight the reader and to make his history more agreeable." With this phrasing Mexiá rejected the rhetorical devices that other humanist historians used to "embellish" their narratives and opted instead for what he referred to as a "naked" style and "a comprehensive brevity," albeit one that still allowed for "[a description] of all of the principal deeds."[91] In this case, the "deeds" concerned only Charles, and in order to stick to this subject Mexiá further announced that he would not write about either Hernan Cortés or the conquest of Mexico, "the story of which . . . I leave for the chronicler who has a special interest and particular expertise in things of the Indies."[92] Finally, striking a patriotic note, Mexiá, writing in the vernacular, openly declared that the ultimate purpose of history was to glorify what he described as the "public weal of my country [*patria* = Seville] and nation."[93]

Despite such promises, Mexiá's health prevented him completing the task on which he had embarked. As it was, in less than three years he managed to compose a narrative encompassing the first twelve years of Charles's reign. Compared to the accomplishments of Guevara and Sepúlveda, Mexiá's output was prodigious. The *Historia* was not particularly original, however, a deficiency that Mexiá was openly prepared to admit. Yet he, like Avila, evidently wrote the kind of history that Charles craved, and his unexpected death in 1551 provided Charles with another reason to continue the memoirs on which he had started to work only a few months before.[94]

---

90. Ibid., bk. 4, chap. 4, p. 466.
91. Ibid., bk. 4, chap. 2, p. 446.
92. Ibid., bk. 1, chap. 17, p. 113. The chronicler to whom Mexiá referred was either Fernández de Oviedo or Francisco López de Gomara.
93. Ibid., lxvi. The citation is from the *proemio* of Pedro Mexiá, *Historia imperial y cesária* (Seville, 1545).
94. Cited in López de Gómara, *Annals of the Emperor Charles V*, xlvii.

The Memoirs

One of the earliest reference to the "memoirs" of Charles V appears in Ludovico Dolce, *Vita dell'invitiss. e gloriosiss. imperador Carlos Quinto* (Venice, 1561), one of the first (unauthorized) biographies of the emperor to appear in print. According to Dolce, "it is said that he [Charles V], imitating Julius Caesar, composed [in French] some beautiful commentaries of the things he had done."[95] Unfortunately, the version of the memoirs mentioned by Dolce has been lost, and the only surviving copy is one dated 1620 and written in Portuguese. It is therefore difficult to determine the extent to which these memoirs (now also available in Spanish translation) approximate those the emperor wrote. Yet as the only surviving copy, this text offers at least some idea of what Charles wanted his history to be.[96]

As a historical document, the memoirs occupy some ninety-two manuscript pages and cover the period from 1513 to 1550. Within this framework, the 1520s and 1530s receive relatively little attention in comparison with the decade of the 1540s, which occupies more than half of the document. As for content, the memoirs have little to say about Charles himself, offering few insights into either his character or his motivations. In other words, Charles's memoirs are not the kind of introspective memoirs offered by Marcus Aurelius in his *Meditations*. Neither are Charles's memoirs confessions in the sense of a soul-searching, first-person narrative designed to seek divine forgiveness, that is, a work resembling the famous *Confessions* of Saint Augustine. Rather than use either Augustine or Marcus Aurelius as his model, the emperor chose Julius Caesar, an author whose *Commentaries* he had read as a boy and had with him again during his retirement at Yuste. And Charles, imitating Caesar, wrote in the third person. Why he did so is not entirely clear, but it may have been out of the conviction that his achievements were comparable to Caesar's. Alternatively, he may have used the third person as a means of distancing himself from his text and thus avoiding any semblance of writing an autobiography. Whatever the emperor's ultimate rationale, the royal "we" never enters into the narrative. Instead the memoirs are presented as if they were written by a chronicler who was an eyewitness to the events being recounted: "His Majesty did this," "the emperor did that." Eyewitness writing of this sort was, as Carvajal had suggested, the sine qua non of good history, and in this respect the memoirs were structured so as to convince the

---

95. Quoted in Morel-Fatio, *Historiographie de Charles-Quint*, 157.
96. For the Castilian translation, see *Corpus documental de Carlos V*, 4:485–567. For another early reference to these memoirs, see Sánchez-Molero, *El César y los libros*, 360.

reader of their accuracy. It thus appears that Charles, with his eye firmly fixed on his future reputation, wrote his memoirs simply to defend the righteousness of his actions and, like Caesar before him, to present his particular notion of historical truth.

But if this was Charles's purpose, the memoirs are disappointing, one might even say dull; they offer few insights into Charles as a ruler, let alone the inner workings of his reign. Personal and family matters—his marriage to Isabella of Portugal, the birth of Philip II—are mentioned only in passing, although he does linger over the death of the empress in 1539, an event that clearly caused him considerable grief.[97] Nor does Charles have much to say about matters of policy, the character of the many individuals (popes, kings, princes) he encountered, or even the outcome of his deeds. The memoirs in this respect have little in common with modern autobiography, with its characteristic emphasis on inner feelings and questions of personality.

Rather, in writing or, at the very least, dictating these memoirs, Charles sought first and foremost to compose his own version of a "mirror of princes," a genre to which he had been introduced as a child. The idea was to cast himself as a model ruler who, despite the multiple responsibilities of his imperial office, dutifully attended to his subjects' many needs. Toward this end Charles recounted his endless journeys among his far-flung possessions, carefully enumerating the times he crossed the Mediterranean to visit either Italy or Spain as well as the occasions on which he convoked meetings of representative assemblies—Cortes, Diets, Estates, and so forth—in different lands. The other image he sought to convey was that of himself as a "Christian prince" who endeavored not only to unite Christendom but also to defend it with his wars against "heresies in Germany" and the Infidel in the form of both Barbarossa and the Turk.[98] Consequently, he paid particular attention to his expedition against Tunis in 1535, a victory he regarded as a personal triumph but one that Giovio, in part 2 of his *History of Our Times,* recounted in ways that so embarrassed the emperor that he attempted to censor this section of Giovio's book.[99]

In fact, the correspondence relating to this incident offers an unusual window into the highly personalized nature of the emperor's historical concerns at the time he was working on his memoirs. According to one report, Charles was "so concerned for the immortality of his deeds that not a day passes that he does not

97. Morel-Fatio, *Historiographie de Charles-Quint,* 223.
98. Ibid., 191.
99. Ibid., 209.

write with his own hand two or three hours along with Guillaume van Mâle," the private secretary known to have assisted Charles with his memoirs.[100] In this instance, the emperor's concern for his "immortality" was such that he also wrote to Cosimo II de' Medici, Grand Duke of Tuscany, under whose auspices Giovio's history was to be published and who, for political reasons of his own, sought to remain on good terms with the emperor. The ensuing negotiations quickly mushroomed into a complicated three-way affair involving the author (Giovio), desperate to get his history into print; the grand duke and his representative at the emperor's court; and Charles and his advisers, especially Cardinal Granvelle and Luis de Avila y Zúñiga, his aide-de-camp.

The negotiations started in July 1550, when, at the grand duke's suggestion, Giovio sent a copy of his manuscript to Granvelle with instructions to show it to the emperor. Giovio also wrote to the emperor, noting that he was sending him that part of his "universal history" that related to Tunis "in order it that it may be perused and revised by Your Majesty before I send it along with the books to the press . . . to change, add, and diminish as seems best to Your Majesty."[101] The emperor subsequently gave Giovio's manuscript to Avila y Zúñiga, who had accompanied him to Tunis. Avila then wrote to Giovio, pointing out errors and offering suggestions as to how the account might be emended or changed. Meanwhile, the Florentine ambassador informed the grand duke that Avila's report on the manuscript was "secretly commissioned by His Majesty, who is so eager for glory he has looked very much askance at this history, because it appears to him that Giovio has detracted from his figure and from the truth and because His Majesty thinks that Giovio in his other writings has treated him worse to please France." Avila then complained directly to Cosimo, informing him that he should "make certain to correct [Giovio's] errors and not consent to publication" until the necessary changes were made.[102] Cosimo subsequently pressured Giovio to accommodate the emperor's wishes, and Giovio followed up by informing Avila that he was prepared to revise his text, "with the light of truth" ("con la luce

---

100. The Florentine ambassador, Sgr. Forli, as quoted in Zimmerman, "The Publication of Paolo Giovio's Histories," 71. At the time, Van Mâle had previously assisted in various projects relating to the construction of the emperor's image, including the famous tapestries celebrating the conquest of Tunis in 1535. These were initially designed by the Flemish artist Jan Cornelisz Vermeyen, who had actually accompanied Charles on this crusade, and then later woven by Willem de Pannemaker, starting in 1548. For these tapestries, see Horn, *Jan Cornelisz Vermeyen*, 1:15, 75n157; and *Lettres sur la vie intérieure de Charles V*.

101. Zimmerman, "The Publication of Giovio's History," 62. Giovio had previously informed Granvelle that he was sending the manuscript to Charles "in order that it may be emended and perfumed according to his taste."

102. Ibid., 65.

della verità") and do so "without art and without interest" ("senza arte e senza parte").[103] Understandably, both Avila and Granvelle remained skeptical of Giovio's intentions, prompting Cosimo's agent to write: "In substance, they want the deeds of the emperor to be celebrated more than they are, and not only do they lament the description of Tunis, but also the published first volume in which, as they say, Giovio continually seeks to belittle the achievements of His Majesty, or else narrate them tepidly." At this point, Avila asked Cosimo once again to make certain that Giovio introduced the changes he asked for, underscoring the emperor's particular interest in making certain that "name and glory are not obfuscated in the mists of passion."[104] Finally, Giovio agreed to make certain factual adjustments in his text, but he doggedly resisted Avila's efforts to magnify the battle's importance and especially to exaggerate the extent to which the emperor was personally responsible for the conquest of La Goletta, the Muslim fortress at Tunis. Avila especially wanted Giovio to emphasize the emperor's selfless courage and the manner in which he had exposed himself to danger, whereas, according to Giovio, Charles had remained somewhat aloof from the action while other captains, notably the marquis of Pescara, had plunged right in. On this point Giovio stood his ground, refusing to surrender to what he called the emperor's "cupidity for glory";[105] with Cosimo's support, his history was published the following year with only a few of the changes that Avila had suggested.

These negotiations are important because, at the broadest level, they indicate the extent to which history-writing in the mid-sixteenth century had ventured into the political realm. As it made this journey, history, especially that which concerned contemporary or near-contemporary events, shed its slavish devotion to Cicero and his notion of history as "lux veritas" and adopted instead Quintillian's concept of historical narrative as a rhetorical exercise whose purpose was to persuade more than instruct.[106] As we have seen, Galíndez de Carjaval had warned the emperor about the dangers of this kind of history, and a half century later Bodin did the same in his *Methodus* when he observed that historians who wrote about present-day affairs generally did so with "emotion" owing to the difficulty of writing openly and honestly about living personages, "lest the report should injure the name of someone or damage his reputation."[107] In making this observation, Bodin was undoubtedly thinking about Giovio, about whom he had little

---

103. Ibid., 67.
104. Ibid., 68, 72.
105. Ibid., 55.
106. Quintilian, *Institutio Oratoria*, bk. IV.ii.21.
107. As translated in Bodin, *Method for the Easy Comprehension of History*, 46.

positive to report, although he might have also mentioned any one of a number of other sixteenth-century historians—Francesco Guicciardini, Johannes Sleidan, Benedetto Varchi, for example—who, as he put it, were "orators" first and historians second, or writers whose narratives were especially crafted to defend particular agendas, both spiritual and secular.[108]

In this respect, the negotiations between Giovio and the emperor and, to a lesser degree, Cosimo belonged to a wider sixteenth-century debate about the meaning and direction of history itself. This was a moment in which most historians, as Montaigne allowed, occupied the middle ground between "simple historians," defined as those whose wrote straightforward annals devoid of interpretation, and "outstanding historians," that minority of historians with the "capacity to choose what is worth knowing and then interpret it." "Those in between," Montaigne observed,

> ... spoil everything for us. They want to chew our morsels for us; they give themselves the right to judge, and consequently to slant history to their fancy; for once the judgement leans to one side, one cannot help turning and twisting the narrative to that bias. They undertake to choose the things worth knowing, and often conceal from us a given word, a given private action, that would instruct us better; they omit as incredible the things they do not understand, and perhaps also some things because they do not know how to say them in good Latin or French. Let them boldly display their eloquence and their reasonings, let them judge all they like; but let them also leave us the wherewithal to judge after them, and not alter or arrange by their abridgements and selection anything of the substance of the matter, but pass it on to us pure and entire in all its dimensions.[109]

Giovio, from the emperor's perspective, was among these "in-between" historians. So too were Avila y Zúñiga, Mexía, and seemingly all of the other chroniclers he had engaged. It follows that the emperor's negotiations with Giovio were as much about substance—the facts of what actually transpired in Tunis—as about style, that is, the particular manner in which the facts were presented. Thus, when Giovio's book finally appeared, Charles seemed to have no choice except to continue with his memoirs and provide future readers with an image of himself as a crusader with the "courage" to end the "disorder" his "enemies," that is, Lutherans and their supporters, had caused. In this sense, the emperor who actually appears in the memoirs combined the attributes of an idealized chivalric ruler—

---

108. Ibid., 45.
109. Montaigne, "Of Books," in *Complete Works*, 2:303.

the kind of ruler Charles had read about as a boy—and the Christian *imperator* that Gattinara and Charles's other publicists had sought to create.

As he worked on these memoirs, and there are indications that he did so right up until the moment of his death, Charles was fully aware of the spiritual dangers that the enterprise in "Renaissance self-fashioning" entailed. Consequently, he instructed his successor, Philip II, not to publish the manuscript until some future date—unfortunately, the emperor failed to specify exactly when. But whatever the precise nature of the emperor's instructions, Philip, upon learning of his father's death in September 1558, moved quickly to confiscate all existing copies of the memoirs; apparently several had been made. Thus in 1561 when Philip learned that Guillaume van Mâle had taken a copy of the memoirs with him to Flanders and written a history based on the manuscript, he immediately ordered it seized on the grounds that "it could be that in it he introduced untruthful things and others unworthy of the person he is writing about."[110] In the end, only the Portuguese copy of Charles's memoirs survived, and this manuscript, hidden in the archives, did not surface until 1862, after its discovery in Paris by the Flemish scholar Kervyn de Lettenhove. For all intents and purposes, therefore, Charles's image of himself as a bold crusader and a chivalric knight was one that only a few individuals, over the course of three centuries, ever managed to see.[111]

Toward an Official Biography

One final note. Even as Charles worked on his memoirs, he had still not totally abandoned the idea of an imperial chronicle. Indeed, in what proved to be a last-ditch effort to reach this elusive goal, in 1555 the ailing emperor appointed Dr. Juan Páez de Castro to the office of royal chronicler vacated by Mexía in 1551. Páez de Castro, a philologist and a bibliophile, was the author of "Of the Things Needed to Write History," a treatise that outlined a plan for a general history of Spain that included "the life of Your Majesty with all of its grandeur," and one that he planned to write "with all of the skill my abilities allow."[112] Charles thus hoped that Páez de Castro would succeed where others had failed; yet once again, the emperor was too optimistic. Páez de Castro liked to read about history, not write it,

---

110. See Morel-Fatio, *Historiographie de Charles-Quint*, 166, citing a letter of 17 February 1561 from Philip II to Cardinal Granvelle, originally published in *Papiers d'état del Cardinal Granvelle*, 6:273.
111. For the fascinating history of the memoirs, see Morel-Fatio, *Historiographie de Charles-Quint*, 157–180. This volume includes Morel-Fatio's translation of the memoirs from Portuguese into French, the language in which they were originally composed.
112. Páez de Castro, "De las cosas nescesarias para escribir la historia," 29:34.

and when it came to actually setting pen on paper, he managed little more than a few preliminary notes.

But another key question remains: how to explain the failure of Páez de Castro, together with all of Charles's other chroniclers, to complete their assignment? Were they simply inept? Like Sepúlveda, the wrong men for the job? Or, as is more likely the case, writers who were cognizant of Galíndez de Carvajal's admonition that official chroniclers should not be expected to publish their works when their patrons were still alive? If the latter is true, it may well explain why Charles never lived to see the imperial chronicle he sought.

In the end, therefore, Charles was, to cite Baltasar Cuart, an "emperor without chroniclers."[113] The emperor's official historians, both Italian and Spanish, had failed him, and ultimately it was left to other historians to write the imperial chronicle he sought. The first to attempt such a work was the Italian humanist Giovanni Michele Bruto, but his *De rebus Carolus V Caesare Romanorum imperatore gestis* (Antwerp, 1555) was little more than a brief *laudatio* highlighting the emperor's personal virtues.[114] Next came Willem Snouckhaert's *De republica, vita, moribus, gestis, fama, religione sanctitate, Imperatoris, Caesaris, Augusti, Quinti, Caroli, Maximi, Monarchae libri septem* (Ghent, 1559), a short book whose grandiose title masked the fact that it offered little more than a series of anecdotes relating to the emperor's career.[115]

Much more complete—and commercially successful—was Alfonso de Ulloa's *Vita dell' invitissimo imperator Carlo V* (Venice, 1560). Ulloa (ca. 1530–?) was a Spaniard who, after having served as secretary to one of Charles's ambassadors in Venice, elected to remain in the island city and earn his living by translating into Italian various works of Spanish literature.[116] This background explains why the *Vita* was less an original work of scholarship than a distillation of bits and pieces of information gathered from other authors, notably Giovio, Guevara, and Mexía.[117] Despite this shortcoming, Ulloa gave his readers a comprehensive biohistory that combined what he called a "brief" but "truthful" narrative of the

---

113. Cuart Moner, "Estudio histórico," 1:xxxv.
114. Not mentioned by Morel-Fatio, a copy of this pamphlet, dedicated to Prince Philip, may be found in the James Ford Bell Library of the University of Minnesota, Minneapolis, where it is bound in a volume that includes a copy of an equally rare pamphlet, *Rerum a Carolo V Caesare Augusto in Africa bello gestarum Commentarii* (Antwerp, 1555), an anonymous account of the emperor's expedition to Tunis.
115. Snouckhaert wrote this work in an effort to restore his reputation after being forced to resign his office of councillor-ordinary of the State of Holland. For more on Snouckhaert's political machinations, see Tracy, *Holland under Habsburg Rule*, 182–190.
116. See Arróniz, "Alfonso de Ulloa."
117. For Ulloa, see Morel-Fatio, *Historiographie de Charles-Quint*, 123–144; and Cochrane, *Historians and Historiography*, 316–318. In addition to his biography of Charles, Ulloa published biographies of the emperor Ferdinand I, Ferrante Gonzaga, governor of Milan, together with a *Historia di' Europa* (1570).

major events of the emperor's reign with an overtly hagiographical description of Charles's "nature." In this format the book sold rather well, appearing in no fewer than four Italian editions between 1560 and 1575. By 1573 it had also been translated into Castilian, but that version of the *Vita*, owing possibly to the opposition of Philip II (see below) failed to appear in print.

By 1573 there also appeared, again in Italian, two other biographies of Charles V. The first, already mentioned, was Ludovico Dolce's life of the emperor, published initially in Venice in 1561. Dolce (1508–1568) was a famous Venetian man of letters known for his work on art theory as well as other works on the nature of language, love, and women. He had also translated into Italian various historical works, among them Mexía's *Hiustora imperial e caesarea*, which appeared in 1561. Yet Dolce, a "populizer," did not pretend to write original history, and in his biography of the emperor he did no more than provide a short, reworked, and easy-to-digest version of the *Vita* Ulloa had published the previous year. Less history than encomium, Dolce's history was important only for the fact that his biography was the first to take note of the emperor's memoirs.[118]

The other Italian biography of Charles was *Il simolacro di Carlo quinto imperadore* (Venice, 1567), the work of Francesco Sansovino (1521–1583), natural son of the noted Venetian sculptor and architect Jacopo Sansovino. Like Dolce before him, Sansovino was a wide-ranging scholar whose history of the Turks, published in 1568, seems to account for his interest in Charles.[119] *Il simolacro*, however, was less history than hagiography and, like Snouckhaert's earlier work, amounted to little more than a miscellany of anecdotes relating to the emperor's personal life, including his reading habits (Sansovino claimed that the Charles's favorite authors were Castiglione, Machiavelli, and Polybius), rather than a detailed survey of his reign. Accordingly, the book did little to promote wider understanding of Charles's place in history.

In the meantime, Philip II proved reluctant to support publication of any history relating to his father.[120] As a result, the manuscripts by Mexía and Sepúlveda, together with those of other Spanish chroniclers, notably Alonso de Santa Cruz and Francisco López de Gómara,[121] who had written histories of Charles V, languished in the archives until the early seventeenth century, when they were

---

118. For Dolce, see Cochrane, *Historians and Historiography*, 409; and Grendler, "Francesco Sansovino," 171. Dolce's biography was reprinted twice in 1561 and again in 1567.
119. I refer to Francesco Sansovino, *Dell' historia universale*. See Grendler, "Francesco Sansovino," esp. p. 171, where he discusses Sansovino's biography of the emperor.
120. See Chapter 3 for Philip's historical preferences.
121. I refer to Alonso de Santa Cruz, *Crónica del Emperador Carlos V*, which was completed ca. 1551 and covered the era from 1500 to 1550 (see above, note 49); and López de Gómara, *Anales del emperador Carlos V*, which was not published (in English) until 1912 (see above, note 91).

finally resuscitated by another royal chronicler, Fray Prudencio de Sandoval, and incorporated into his *Historia de la vida y hechos del Emperador Carlos V*, the first truly official history of the emperor to appear in print (see Chapter 5). Philip II's refusal to sanction the publication of these histories, let alone his father's memoirs, is still not totally understood, although it is likely to have been connected to his own somewhat inflated understanding of his father's achievements, coupled with the sense that none of the chroniclers who wrote about the emperor did so in ways he approved. It stemmed in this respect from Philip's own understanding of history, which, as the next chapter explores, was predicated more on *historia pro patria* than the more personalized *historia pro persona* that the emperor had consistently embraced.

CHAPTER THREE

Historia pro Patria
Philip II

The road to truth is straight, never winding.
—Maffeo Barberini, the future Urban VIII (1607)

On 13 September 1598, only hours after learning about the death of Philip II, Francesco Soranzo, the Venetian ambassador at the Spanish court, wrote to inform the Doge and Senate of the momentous news. "The king is dead," the dispatch began. "His Majesty expired at the Escorial this morning at daybreak, after having received all of the sacraments of the church with every sign of devotion, piety, and religion." Soranzo then proceeded to list Philip's numerous accomplishments: his many victories ("He has acquired more by sitting still, by negotiations, by diplomacy, than his father did by armies and by war") as well as his many defeats. Soranzo also provided a short sketch of Philip's character, specifically noting that he "hated vanity, and therefore never allowed his life to be written."[1]

The idea that Philip had refused to commission a biography is one that quickly entered the mythology of the deceased king. Already in 1621, Baltasar Porreño observed that Philip II's "modesty was such, that he never wanted to have a chronicler."[2] Much more recently, a best-selling biography of Philip reiterated this idea with the assertion, "Philip II refused to let his life be written during his lifetime. He thereby saved himself from adulators, whom he hated. But he left the field wide open to his detractors."[3]

Epigraph: As cited in Soman, "Press, Pulpit, and Censorship in France," 462.
1. Public Record Office, Great Britain, *Calendar of State Papers and Manuscripts*, 9:342–343. The original reads: "Non ha mai voluto, che si scriva la sua vita." Archivio di Stato di Venezia: Senato, Dispacci Spagna, filza 30n58. I am grateful to Luca Mola for supplying a copy of Soranzo's original dispatch.
2. Porreño, *Dichos y hechos*, 110. The same idea appeared in Nieremberg, *En la corona virtuosa*, 259: "[Felipe] no quería tener coronista."
3. Kamen, *Philip of Spain*, xi.

But is this observation correct? Was Philip, out of modesty, as adverse to the writing of his biography as generally supposed? No easy answer to these questions exists, partly because of confusion about the meaning of biography, especially as that genre was understood in the time of Philip II. A biography emphasized what Plutarch, contemplating the life of Alexander the Great, had referred to as *ethos,* a term that referred to an individual's character and personality. Biography in this sense supposed a retrospective assessment of Alexander as a moral being. Yet Plutarch also understood that biography could be history, the equivalent of *praexis,* the Greek word for action and thus a term that, again with reference to Alexander, called for a narration of the Macedonian monarch's deeds and accomplishments together with those of his associates and followers.[4]

It follows that biography and history were traditionally understood as two separate genres, each of them illuminating different, albeit complementary, aspects of an individual's life. Such was the position of Giovanni Antonio Viperano (1535–1610), a Jesuit scholar for whom narrative history, as defined in his *De scribenda historia* (1569), was fundamentally different from biography, whose task was "to rescue deeds of great men from oblivion and the damage of time."[5] Soranzo used a similar definition when he wrote that Philip "refused to let his life be written." The Venetian ambassador said nothing about history, a genre that Philip warmly embraced.

To learn more about the king's interest in history and, more generally, the place of history at his court, this chapter examines Philip's patronage of chroniclers and historians, in particular those he honored with the title of royal chronicler. The work of these chroniclers suggests that Philip was, as Soranzo correctly observed, suspicious of biography. His attitude toward history, however, a considerably more complex view, was one that evolved in the course of his reign. As a young man Philip distanced himself from any history that touched, even indirectly, on his "life," and in doing so explicitly rejected the kind of self-serving *historia pro persona* his father had embraced. Instead the young monarch opted for *historia pro patria,* particularly as it related to Hispania and its constituent parts. With age, these preferences changed. Biography remained out of the question, but gradually Philip warmed to the notion of an "official" history that defended his policies and, most importantly, Spain's right to imperium in the both the Old World and the New.

---

4. My understanding of Plutarch on this point follows Wallace-Hadrill, *Suetonius,* 8.
5. Cited in Weinberg, *History of Literary Criticism in the Italian Renaissance,* 1:297.

History for a King

To understand the complexity as well as the diversity of Philip II's historical interests, a good place to start is two memoranda prepared by Dr. Juan Páez de Castro, the last of the royal chroniclers named by Charles V.[6] Upon receiving this appointment, in September 1555, Páez de Castro (d. 1570) wrote his *Método para escribir la historia*, a treatise that emphasized the importance of history for monarchs. It also outlined in general terms a comprehensive history of Spain, suggesting that this history continued up to the present, and he included both maps and a detailed geographical survey of the Iberian peninsula.[7]

In a second memorandum, dating from around 1556 and addressed to Philip II, Páez de Castro expanded on the *Método* and laid out a blueprint for a multifaceted historiographical program worthy of the new king.[8] The program's showpiece was a new royal library designed to serve as a museum of the monarchy and as a repository for documents, maps, and other materials that could be used to write Spain's general history. This library, to be constructed in Valladolid, was to incorporate three large rooms. The first, to be decorated with portraits of distinguished scholars, was the library proper, housing books both ancient and modern. The second approximated a *cabinet des curiosités* filled with "maps and city views," scientific instruments, antiquities, "marvelous natural things," genealogies of monarchs, and portraits of famous people, among them Columbus and Cortés. The third room, "the most secret part" of the proposed library, was an archive housing state papers and treaties, royal testaments, and account books recording the expenses of the royal household. Striking a more personal note, Páez de Castro also conceived of this archive as the perfect place for keeping "the commentaries that your ancestors wrote about themselves as well those that Your Majesty will eventually write."[9]

Philip II's response to these suggestions has yet to be found, but his subsequent actions point to his wholehearted endorsement of Páez de Castro's ideas, with certain changes. The royal library planned for Valladolid, for example, meta-

---

6. For the circumstances surrounding Páez de Castro's appointment, see Morel-Fatio, *Historiographie de Charles-Quint*, 87–88.

7. The text is published as Páez de Castro, "De las cosas necesarias para escribir historia."

8. Páez de Castro still awaits his biographer, even though much of his correspondence survives. See, for example, Andrés, "31 Cartas inéditas de Juan Páez de Castro." Páez de Castro does, however, figure in Pablo Fernández Albadalejo, "'Materia' de España y 'edificio' de historiografía: Algunas consideraciones sobre le década de 1540," in *Materia de España*, by Fernández Albadalejo, 41–64.

9. See Páez de Castro, "Memorial." The memorial is briefly discussed in Checa Cremades, *Felipe II*, 377–378, and his "Significado del proyecto archivístico de Felipe II," in *Imágenes históricos de Felipe II*, 183–196.

morphosed into the one incorporated into El Escorial monastery, a building whose planning and construction began in 1564. Meanwhile, the proposed secret archive took the form of the royal archive at Simancas, a repository established by the emperor but one that Philip totally reorganized in 1567, partly for the purpose of providing historians with the materials necessary to write "true and precise memories" of the past.[10] Similar thinking underscored the king's decision to create, starting in 1575, a new archival repository in Barcelona (now the Archive of the Crown of Aragon) along with the archive of documents and papal privileges concerning the Spanish monarchy that Philip, in 1558, decided to establish in the Spanish embassy in Rome.[11] Philip also adopted Páez de Castro's interest in city views when in 1561 he brought the noted Flemish view painter Anton van de Wyngaerde to Spain and commissioned him to prepare views of the kingdom's principal cities and towns. Large-scale versions of these views were subsequently placed on display in the Pardo, a royal hunting lodge situated on the outskirts of Madrid. Still others found their way into Madrid's Alcázar, the royal palace that doubled as the seat of government, starting in 1561.[12] The chronicler's influence can also be detected in several of Philip's geographical projects, including the *Relaciones Geográficas*, the geographical questionnaires that Philip, starting in 1575, sent to royal officials both in Spain and in the New World, as well as the so-called *Escorial Atlas*, a small portfolio of maps of the Iberian peninsula executed during the 1570s by an international team of cartographers headed by Pedro de Esquivel.[13] A connection also exists between the chronicler's recommendations and the collections of both maps and scientific instruments that Philip II assembled at El Escorial together with the portrait gallery he installed at the Pardo palace starting in 1563.[14]

Páez de Castro's formative role in the development of the cultural and scientific agenda of Philip II has rarely been recognized, but for all of his successes, the

---

10. Royal cédula, dated 14 March 1567, as cited in Rodríguez de Diego, *Instrucción para el gobierno*. For more on the history of Simancas, the work of Rodríguez de Diego, its current director, is invaluable. See especially his "La formación del Archivo de Simancas"; and his "Un archivo no solo para el rey: Significado social del proyecto simanquino en el siglo xvi," in Martínez Millán, *Felipe II (1527–1598)*, 4:463–475, which includes references to his other publications on the archive's history; see also the introduction to Plaza, *Archivo General de Simancas*.

11. For the archive in Rome, see López de Toro, *Epístolas de Juan Verzosa*, xxv; Rodríguez de Diego, *Instrucción para el gobierno*, 52; García Hernán, "La iglesia de Santiago de los Españoles en Roma"; and Verzosa, *Anales*, xlii–xliii. Philip II originally decided to establish this archive in 1558. For more on archives in the sixteenth century, see Bouza Álvarez, *Del escribano a la biblioteca*, 71–93.

12. For this commission, see Kagan, *Spanish Cities of the Golden Age*; and Kagan, "Philip II and the Art of the Cityscape."

13. For an introduction to these projects, see Parker, "Maps and Ministers."

14. For this gallery, see Kusche, *Retratos y retratadores*, 163–178. See also Civil, "Culture et histoire"; and Joanna Woodhall, "His Majesty's Most Majestic Room."

chronicler's suggestion that the king write "commentaries" fell on deaf ears. By using the term "commentaries," then broadly defined as a kind of personalized gloss on history, Páez de Castro was referring to Julius Caesar's self-serving account of the conquest of Gaul and, more immediately, to the *memorias* of Charles V. In the sixteenth century, memoirs represented a form of autobiography, a genre that ecclesiastics likened to *vanitas,* a deadly sin. Writing in the early seventeenth century, Luis Cabrera de Córdoba referred to this current of criticism in his book *De historia* (1611), where he urged great princes to write their own histories but recognized that many were likely to consider such a practice an "ajena ocupación," which translates roughly as "something for others [to write]."[15]

As noted earlier, Charles V confronted this very issue during his interview with Francisco de Borja but managed to justify writing his memoirs on the grounds of political expediency. Even then, Charles had reservations about the propriety of what he was doing, and these undoubtedly account for his instructions to his son to keep the *memorias* secret following his death. Philip did just this, promptly rounding up every copy of the *memorias* he could find.[16]

While religious sensibilities figured in Philip II's reservations about memoirs, his doubts about autobiography and biography had other causes too. One stemmed from his elevated notion of royal dignity, which he apparently first came to appreciate in 1543, when the emperor decided to do away with older Castilian etiquettes and protocols governing Philip's household and replace them with others imported from Burgundy, a changeover that served mainly to isolate Philip inside an elaborate ceremonial cocoon. Over the years, these etiquettes transformed Philip into what has been called a "hidden king," a *rey oculto,* who kept himself out of the limelight and limited his public appearances to important religious spectacles that enhanced the sacred, as opposed to the more corporeal, aspect of the royal person. Philip's reticence about appearing too human helps also to explain why he endeavored to keep his personal papers private, as in 1573 when he directed the principal royal officer (*corregidor*) in Toledo to go to the archives of the city's archepiscopal palace and collect all of the letters he had written as a child to his former tutor Juan Martínez de Siliceo on the grounds that it was "not convenient that these letters circulate about, out of decency and respect."[17] It is not clear what these papers contained, but Philip

---

15. Cabrera de Córdoba, *De historia,* 19.
16. Morel-Fatio, *Historiographie de Charles-Quint,* 166.
17. RAH: Billetes de Antonio Gracián, fol. 231r, 25 November 1573, cited in Bouza Álvarez, "Monarchie en lettres d'imprimerie," 209.

evidently feared that they might reveal secrets that in the wrong hands might prove embarrassing.

Similar reasoning accounts for Philip's reluctance to sanction any history that touched upon his reign. He did this first by rejecting suggestions that chroniclers be appointed to document his actions and record his speeches, something his father had scrupulously done. In 1548, for example, Philip's Latin tutor, Juan Cristóbal Calvete de Estrella (1526–1593), took it upon himself to record the prince's every move during the course of his upcoming journey to Italy, Germany, and the Netherlands. Other officials in the prince's entourage did much the same, but this practice of daily chronicling ended shortly after Philip took possession of the monarchy following his father's abdication in 1556.[18] The new king, moreover, also rejected one churchman's suggestion that he "emulate the example of Christ, who had named four chroniclers to narrate his achievements for didactic reasons as well as for eternity."[19] Historians who offered to write the king's history were also rebuffed, among them Calvete de Estrella, who in 1570 promised to write at the close of each year "a Latin chronicle of the year's noteworthy events";[20] Juan de Verzosa, whose Latin annals of the first decade of Philip's reign, a project apparently undertaken at the initiative of Juan de Zúñiga, the Spanish ambassador to the Vatican, remained unpublished;[21] Uberto Foglietta (1518–1581), a Genoese scholar seeking to write a history on "the ancient and modern affairs of Spain";[22] and Wigle (or Vigilius) van Aytta (1507–1577), the Frisian nobleman who presided over Philip's privy council in the Netherlands and who had written a history of the early years of the Dutch revolt.[23] The king's refusal to allow pub-

---

18. For these chronicles, see Calvete de Estrella's *El felicíssimo viaje*, xxxii–xxxiii. The other chronicles detailing Prince Philip's journeys outside Spain include Álvarez, *Relation du beau voyage*; Muñoz, *Viaje de Felipe II a Inglaterra*; and Vandenesse, *Journal des voyages du Philippe II*, vols. 2, 4.
19. Navarra, *Diálogos para la eternidad del alma*, iv.
20. This letter is cited in Díaz Gito, "Un epigrama y una carta del humanista Calvete de Estrella." See also Calvete de Estrella, *De rebus indicis de Calvete de Estrella*, xxxvi; Gonzalo Sánchez-Molero, introduction to *El felicíssimo viaje*, by Calvete de Estrella, xliv; and Díaz Gito, "Un epigrama y una carta," 1135–1342.
21. Verzosa's comments may be found in López de Toro, *Epístolas de Juan Verzosa*, 268, 271. For a recent edition of Verzosa's epistles, see Verzosa, *Epístolas*. For the *Annalium liber primus*, see Verzosa, *Anales*. In his introduction to that volume, José María Maestre Maestre corrects my erroneous suggestion (see my "Philip II, History, and the Cronistas del Rey") that Philip II was personally responsible for the failure of Verzosa's annals to appear in print.
22. AGS Est: 918, no. 78, Luis de Requeséns to Antonio Pérez, 12 March 1578. I owe this reference to the courtesy of Michael Levin. For details, see his *Agents of Empire*. In 1558 Cardinal Granvelle contacted Foglietta about the possibility of writing a history of the emperor's wars in Germany. See Fernández Álvarez, "Las 'memorias' de Carlos V," 709–715. Foglietta went on to publish a history of his native Genoa, a history of the Turks, and *De ratione scribendae historiae*, his contribution to the *ars historicae* genre. He awaits detailed study as a historian, although his *De ratione* may be approached through Grafton, *What Was History?* 42–44.
23. See Aytta, *Mémoires de Viglius et d'Hoperus*, 1–158, where the text of Viglius's *Philippo Secundo*

lication of this latter history is particularly surprising because van Aytta was one of the few Dutch leaders who remained loyal to Spain after the rebellion began in 1566.

Philip's reservations about any history that smacked of biography even affected the work of his own royal chroniclers, including his former history tutor, Juan Ginés de Sepúlveda. In 1560 Sepúlveda, having tired of the emperor's history, set out to write one of Philip II, without official authorization.[24] The king did nothing to provide Sepúlveda with access to the papers and reports he needed to write this history, essentially leaving the chronicler, then residing in Córdoba, to fend for himself. Undeterred, Sepúlveda forged ahead by cobbling a few secondhand sources together with a few documents he had collected when the emperor was still alive. In this manner he managed to write three rather thinly documented books of *De Rebus Gestis Philippi, Regis Hispaniae*, which covered the period from 1556 to 1564. The king did not have the slightest interest in this chronicle, however, and in 1573, upon learning of Sepúlveda's death, arranged to have his papers and manuscripts bundled up and brought to Madrid. The shipment included, apart from his own history, the manuscript history of the emperor and *De Rebus Hispanorum Gestis Ad Novum Orbem*, Sepúlveda's unfinished survey of Spanish accomplishments in the New World. The royal confessor, Fray Bernardo de Fresneda, welcomed the arrival of these manuscripts and urgently recommended their publication on the grounds that these histories would help defend the reputation of the monarchy against the calumnies of Bartolomé de la Casas (Fresneda was referring to Las Casas's vitriolic *Brevísima relación de la destrucción de las indias*, first published in 1552). The king's response is not recorded, but he apparently rejected Fresneda's advice and, in doing so, effectively squashed publication of all of Sepúlveda's work.[25]

At first glance, this incident lends credence to the argument that an elevated sense of personal modesty prevented Philip from sanctioning the publication of any history that touched upon his life. Yet this argument ignores Philip II's ongoing determination to promote his *majestas* through architecture, portraiture, sculpture, commemorative medals, and other media.[26] It appears, therefore, that factors other than personality figured in Philip's reluctance to have his history

---

Rege Oratio appears both in French and in Latin. I am grateful to Geoffrey Parker for bringing this work to my attention.

24. See Losada, *Juan Ginés de Sepúlveda*, 502–503.

25. IVDJ: Envio 44, fol. 147r, document of 18 May 1573. Sepúlveda's history of Philip II and his history of the New World are now available, in both Latin and Spanish, in Sepúlveda, *Obras Completas*, vols. 11 and 4, respectively.

26. Bouza Álvarez, "La majestad de Felipe II."

written. Borja's admonition to his father about the spiritual dangers of memoirs undoubtedly accounts for Philip's refusal to write the "commentaries" of the kind that Páez de Castro had suggested, but history was a different matter. Sepúlveda's narrative, for example, had little to say about the king's personal life. Rather, it followed the standard humanist formula of emphasizing the particularly heroic or noteworthy events over which the young monarch had presided: the Spanish victory over the French at St. Quentin in 1559, the Inquisition's efforts to suppress Lutheranism in Castile, and various maritime expeditions directed against Turkish forces in the Mediterranean. From this perspective, Sepúlveda did little to compromise Philip's modesty. But his comments concerning the actions and experiences of living individuals seemingly violated Philip's understanding of what good history was about. Ironically, this was an understanding that Sepúlveda, as Philip's history tutor, had helped to instill.

Philip's introduction to history, like his father's, began at an early age, probably around thirteen or fourteen, when Charles appointed a trio of humanists—Juan Calvete de Estrella, Honorato Juan, and, starting in 1542, Sepúlveda—to guide the prince's education. But whereas Charles had been encouraged to read chivalric history, mostly in French, Philip's tutors organized a graduated reading program that took advantage of the prince's ability to read Latin and was principally designed to prepare the prince for the challenges of rulership.[27] Toward this end they encouraged him to begin by reading history, starting with the classics (works by Livy, Lucio Floro, Pliny, and Polybius were already in the prince's private library by 1541) and then continuing with such later works as Froissart's chronicles (albeit in Latin), Bartolomeo Platina's *Vitae pontificum* (Lives of the popes), and Johannes Cuspinianus's newly published history of the Roman emperors, *De caesaribus atque imperatoribus romanis*.[28] In 1547, just as Philip was about to leave Spain on a trip to Italy and the Low Countries, Sepúlveda specifically recommended that the prince, then age twenty-one, read, again in Latin, "histories of ancient Greece and Rome" on the grounds that these histories—presumably he was referring to Livy, Sallust, Tacitus, Polybius, and Thucydides—would teach Philip invaluable lessons in prudence and thus how to become a better king. Sepúlveda also suggested that the prince read Aristotle's *Politics*, a work he considered particularly useful for "governing cities and kingdoms."[29]

27. Philip was introduced to Latin at the age of eight by the royal chronicler Fray Bernardo de Gentile.
28. The best account of Philip's education remains March, *Niñez y juventud de Felipe II*, but important new information is available in Gonzalo Sánchez-Molero, *El aprendizaje cortesano de Felipe II*, as well as his *El erasmismo y la educación de Felipe II*.
29. For Sepúlveda's reading suggestions, see Losada, *Juan Ginés de Sepúlveda*, 572–574.

Such recommendations reflected Sepúlveda's own, somewhat Ciceronian understanding of history as *magistra vitae,* a discipline whose purpose was to convey useful moral and political advice. They were also in keeping with the humanistic idea that history required an objective, disinterested approach to the past, something that was considered next to impossible when historians were asked to write about living persons and recent events. Sepúlveda, in his capacity as royal chronicler, vacillated on this issue, but when it came to teaching the future Philip II about history, he was more in line with Jean Bodin, whose *Method on the Art of History* advised that historians seeking to write "truthful" history concentrate on that of earlier ages as opposed to their own day. Luís Cabrera de Córdoba, the first Spanish historian to write about Philip II, offered similar advice: "Writing about today's things is dangerous and difficult, because of the many irritations it sparks, some of which result from affection for friends, others from hatred for enemies, all of which leads to perturbations, which tend to be blind, impede right judgement, and prevent one from seeing what is honest, and from maintaining equity and neutrality."[30]

Philip's own historical preferences are difficult to judge, but the prince and his humanist tutors did not always see eye to eye, especially when it came to works written in the vernacular and relating specifically to the history of Spain. In 1543, for example, the prince ordered his tutors to purchase a copy of Florián de Ocampo's newly available chronicle of Spain's early history. Over time Philip also developed a particular interest in Spain's medieval history, especially as it related to the Reconquest, yet there is little to suggest that he had much affinity for histories of "today's things" even though he once ordered his tutors to get him a copy of the *relación* recounting the captivity and subsequent hair-raising adventures of Alvar Núñez Cabeza de Vaca in North America.[31]

Philip II's own thoughts on the matter of contemporary history remain elusive, but some inkling of his doubts about histories of "today's things" can be found in a letter that Páez de Castro wrote to his friend and fellow historian Jerónimo de Zurita in 1569. As noted earlier, Páez de Castro was planning to write a general history of Philip's reign but envisioned this work as less of a "monarchical" history than a "universal" history, words that suggest a broad-based history that respected the king's aversion to biography.[32] Páez de Castro met on several

---

30. Cabrera de Córdoba, *De historia,* 73.
31. For this request, see Gonzalo Sánchez-Molero, *El erasmismo y la educación de Felipe II,* 523.
32. BRME: Ms. & III, 10, "Apuntes históricos del Dr. Páez de Castro," fol. 144, in which the chronicler informs Diego Hurtado de Mendoza, the Spanish ambassador in Rome, that the history he was contemplating was to be "mas universal q monarquica."

occasions with Philip to discuss the history, but the king, while expressing some interest in the project, did little to provide his chronicler with access to the documents he needed to write it, as Páez de Castro, exasperated, explains:

> As for this history, I have talked with His Majesty as well as his ministers, and in this no one can fault me. His Majesty understands that I should not write this history on the basis of letters from soldiers, nor from what is talked about in the town squares, but solely upon the basis of approved and authenticated sources. But if His Majesty wants me to write about him with the necessary weight and authority, reason suggests that he should provide me with the sources I require. And so I asked him to show me what the emperor wrote about his reasons for going to war, especially in Germany, and he replied that he would be happy to do so and that I speak with [Antonio de] Eraso [a royal secretary] about it. This I did, but to no effect. More recently, Doctor Velasco told me that he would help me obtain state papers belonging to His Majesty and that he would arrange to get me the permission to visit the archive of Simancas, arguing that this was important for many reasons, among them the need for His Majesty's chroniclers to consult the relevant papers. I wrote to ... Cardinal [Espinosa, president of the Royal Council] about this ... but until now these efforts have not yielded any fruit. I, sir, do not believe it would be a bad strategy to have such material at hand unless I wanted my history to be a thing of invention. If permitted to consult documents and established authors, I will be able to achieve a lot, giving substance to the body of the history that I propose to write. But if the papers of the Council of State and other instructions are not in my possession, this history will be a body without a soul. But enough of this, because it pains me to talk about such an important subject, and have it result in something defective.[33]

The quote underscores Philip's understanding of history as a humanistic endeavor, or at least one that approximated what François Baudoin and other sixteenth-century writers defined as "historia integra," or "perfect history."[34] Perfection was achieved when historians included in their narratives *examplae* designed to offer their readers sound moral advice. Perfect history had also to be truthful history to the extent that it was factually verifiable and rested on a solid documentary base as opposed to street gossip and "reports from soldiers," that is, the kind of mendacious history associated with such writers as Paolo Giovio.

Philip II's apparent refusal to allow Páez de Castro's access to the royal archive at Simancas in search of this kind of truth is revealing. Perfect history, as the

---

33. Andrés de Uztárroz and Dormer, *Progesos de la historia de Aragon*, 557, letter dated Quer, 30 January 1569.
34. On perfect history, see Huppert, *The Idea of Perfect History*.

authors of most *artes historicae* allowed, was nigh unto impossible if it examined current or even recent events. It appears, therefore, that Philip, to borrow Cabrera de Córdoba's language, was perturbed, possibly even irritated, by the thought of having one of his own chroniclers even attempt to write his own history.

The irony here is that Páez de Castro was largely responsible for the king's decision to revamp the archive at Simancas. As it happened, Philip II conceived of Simancas as the storehouse of the monarchy's most important papers, a place where its history could be preserved in perpetuity. In practice, the archive was officially closed to historians and other researchers, although in 1567 the king made an exception when he personally granted Jerónimo de Zurita (see below) the privilege of working in Simancas, solely for the purpose of consulting materials relating to Aragon's remote past. In contrast, the king made certain that no one other than his chief archivist, Diego de Ayala, had access to more recent papers, and even then the archive housed certain boxes of documents to which only the monarch had the key.[35] All this suggests that the king's refusal to grant Páez de Castro access to the documents he requested was in line with his personal conception of Simancas as a repository for future historians as opposed to those interested in writing about his personal achievements or even the events of his reign. Philip's chroniclers would therefore necessarily have to avoid "today's things" and concentrate instead on yesterday's, especially those related to the various Iberian kingdoms over which he ruled.[36]

Historia pro Patria: La Crónica General de España

Apart from his youthful purchase of Ocampo's chronicle, the first recorded instance of Philip's interest in Spain's history, or what can be defined as *historia pro patria*, occurred in 1547 at the Cortes de Aragón, then gathered in the town of Monzón. Acting as a stand-in for his father, who was absent in Germany, the prince listened to a petition requesting the appointment of a chronicler who could write a history of Aragon. Patriotic concerns had occasioned this petition, among them the appearance, in 1541, of the first volume of Florián de Ocampo's *Los primeros cuatro libros de la Crónica General de España*, a work that members of the Aragonese Diputación considered prejudicial to their own interests inasmuch

---

35. In a letter dated 16 January 1569, Diego de Ayala, the royal archivist at Simancas, complained that he could not gain access to the papers contained in certain chests because "His Majesty has the key." AGS: Secretaria, leg. 5, 4.

36. Writing in the 1620s, the royal secretary Antonio de Mendoza observed that Philip II disdained any history that touched upon "lo arcano del palacio." Cf. BL Eg, Ms. 2061, fol. 73v.

as it emphasized Castile's history, not their own. At the time, only two verifiably "Aragonese" general histories were readily available: Gauberto Fabricio de Vagad's late-fifteenth-century *Crónica de Aragón* and Lucio Marineo Sículo's handsomely illustrated *Crónica de los reyes de Aragón*.[37] But these and other more specialized histories, including Pere Antoni Beuter's *History of Valencia*, were deemed inadequate because they failed to deal with the Middle Ages and the origins of the laws and privileges that served as the basis of the Aragonese polity as opposed to that of Castile.[38] The petition avoided these issues, but Philip still agreed to appoint a new chronicler and authorize a search for what the Aragonese authorities defined as "a person with expertise and experience with chronicles and histories, a native of Aragon, and one who would be responsible for writing, compiling, and ordering all of the notable events of the Aragon, both past and present, just as in other kingdoms [that is, Castile]."[39]

That person was Jerónimo de Zurita (1511–1580), an Aragonese humanist with interests in both history and antiquities who was then serving as a secretary of the Inquisition. Once appointed, in 1548, Zurita began work on his monumental *Anales de la Corona de Aragón*, the first volume of which appeared in 1563, another in 1577, and a third in 1578. Together they narrated Aragonese history from 711 to the start of the reign of Ferdinand II, the Catholic.[40] Though he wrote in the vernacular, Zurita modeled the *Anales* on Livy's Roman history, paying particular attention to the heroic actions of its monarchs, notably Jaume I, "the Conquerer," who was credited with liberating the kingdom from the grip of Islam. He also dwelled at length on the twelfth-century "Laws of Sobrarbe," which established the basis for the kingdom's legal regime.

Critics applauded Zurita for his erudition and sound historical judgment and welcomed his decision to begin the narrative in 711 CE, a choice that enabled him to avoid the pitfalls of writing about Spain's earliest history, most of which, owing to the lack of the documentation, belonged to the realm of both legend and myth. Ocampo had made this mistake in the *Crónica General;* his decision to draw upon Annius de Viterbo's list of Spain's mythical kings led to no end of criticism in Spain's humanist circles.[41] Zurita, in contrast, emphasized Aragonese contribu-

37. See Chapter 1, note 98.
38. I refer to Beuter, *Primera part de la historia de Valencia*. Beuter subsequently published this volume in Castilian translation (1546) and added a second part, also in Castilian, in 1551.
39. My translation is based on the transcription published in Andrés de Uztárroz and Dormer, *Progresos de la historia de Aragón*, 63–64. This work was first published in 1680.
40. Various seventeenth-century Aragonese historians continued the *Anales*, bringing it forward to the end of the reign of Ferdinand the Catholic. See below, Chapter 5.
41. Especially noteworthy is the criticism Ocampo received from Hernán Núñez de Guzmán, professor of rhetoric at the University of Salamanca. In a series of letters addressed to Zurita, Núñez

tions to the Reconquest, a topic of special interest to Philip II.[42] Yet when the first volume of the *Anales* appeared, in 1563, a number of Castilian scholars sought to prevent its circulation on the grounds that Zurita "writes like an Aragonese who, when it comes to writing about matters touching upon Castile, does so critically and in prejudice of the kingdom's honor."[43] Zurita's admirers, however, far outnumbered his detractors. Most importantly, he had the support of the king, who is known to have read the first part of the *Anales*, "enjoying everything," as he traveled to Monzón in order to preside over a meeting of the Cortes of Aragon held in 1564.[44] Philip subsequently rewarded Zurita by appointing him to the office of royal secretary, a position he retained until his death in 1580.

As Philip's reaction to the *Anales* suggests, the king seemed to know exactly what kind of history he liked. His humanist tutors had steered him toward the classics and other works written in Latin. Over time, however, Philip developed a taste for vernacular histories, preferably those dealing with the history of Christianity in Spain along with that of the Reconquest, which symbolized the beginning of Spain's—and his own—epic struggle against Islam, together with the idea of resurrecting the Gothic Hispania lost to the Moors. Several of Philip's secretaries commented upon the king's interest in reading the chronicles of Alfonso X and of Juan II, but they also referred to his difficulties in reading these histories in manuscript, inasmuch as Philip's paleographical training and his understanding of different historical genres left much to be desired. One of the secretaries, Antonio Gracián, informed Zurita, "The king wants to see the *gestas* of the King don Alfonso [X]; His Majesty then asked me what *gestas* were, and I told him that they were like old chivalric tales; he then wanted to see if this were so." A few weeks later, again with reference to this particular chronicle, Gracián reported: "On the day he departed from Móstoles [a town near Madrid], His Majesty told me that he would like to see this book [written] in a clear hand that he could read."[45]

---

faulted Ocampo for his decision to write in the vernacular, his dubious remarks about Tubal's presence in Spain, and the suggestion that Spaniards were responsible for the foundation of the city of Rome. This correspondence is published in Beltrán de Heredia, *Cartulario*, 3:94–116.

42. See RAH: Salazar y Castro: Ms. 9/112, fol. 5, letter of Prince Philip to Zurita, 21 May 1553, in which he asks the chronicler to visit archives in Baca and Barcelona to find certain documents relating to "el augmento y conservación del real patrimonio y recuperación de las ... cosas enajenadas."

43. Zurita's chief critic was Alonso de Santa Cruz, the royal cosmographer. See RAH: Salazar de Castro: Ms. 9/112, fol. 77. For more on the controversy sparked by the *Anales*, see Uztárroz and Dormer, *Progresos de la historia de Aragón*, 154, 161; and Enrique Flórez's introduction to the 1791 edition of the *Coronica general de España*.

44. On 18 November 1564, the royal chronicler Ambrosio de Morales informed Zurita that "estara el rey N. S. leyendolos [sus anales] en Monzón, y aprobándolo tanto." Cited in Uztárroz and Dormer, *Progresos de la historia de Aragón*, 167.

45. Letters of 10 January and 11 February 1574, transcribed in Uztárroz and Dormer, *Progresos de la historia de Aragón*, 590.

The lack of legible copies of these and other older chronicles undoubtedly contributed to Philip's readiness to patronize the work of scholars prepared to edit these chronicles and get them into print.

Though never spelled out in any detail, what Philip wanted was a comprehensive general (or national) history of a kind comparable to those of France, England, and other European states. Alfonso X had sponsored this kind of history in the form of the *Estoria de Espanna*, but it had never appeared in print, partly because its annalistic format impressed sixteenth-century readers as woefully antiquated. In fifteenth-century Italy, humanist scholars had embraced a new kind of history, written in Latin, which put a premium on such matters as eloquence, presentation, and style. Following Thucydides, humanists tended also to lard their histories with invented speeches designed to provide special insights into the character of the people about whom they wrote. They also structured their narratives around particularly heroic or noteworthy events, each of which was to serve as an *exemplum* of proper or improper behavior. The overriding purpose of these national histories, however, was to promote patriotic sentiment and pride. "The true historian's duty," wrote Leonardo Bruni, author of the *Historiarum Florentini Populi* (1449) "is to reshape the sources and to further the prestige of the fatherland."[46]

Historians of other Italian republics and principalities quickly followed suit, and by the end of the fifteenth century the vogue for patriotic history had spread far and wide; by the early sixteenth century many of these histories were already in print.[47] Charles IX of France (r. 1560–1574), for example, could point with pride to Paolo Emilio's *De rebus gestis Francorum* (Paris, 1516–1539), a survey of French history from Pharamond, the legendary founder of France, through to the reign of Charles VIII and the start of his own Valois dynasty. Charles could also boast about the French translation of this history, *Histoire générale des rois de France* (Paris, 1576), which was prepared by the *historiographe royal*, Bernard Girard du Haillan.[48] As for Philip's great nemesis Elizabeth I, she possessed printed versions, in both Latin and the vernacular, of Geoffrey of Monmouth's older *History of the Kings of Britain* as well as Polydore Vergil's humanistic *Anglicae historiae* of Great Britain published in 1534. Although Vergil was Italian and his history, like Monmouth's before it, mixed fiction with fact, it still offered the queen a lengthy genealogy together with a record of royal accomplishment to which she

---

46. As cited in Ianziti, "Bruni on Writing History," 380.
47. For these histories, see *Les princes et l'histoire du XIVe au XVIIIe siècle*.
48. For French official history in the sixteenth century, see Chantalle Grell, "Les historiographes en France XVIe–XVIIIe siècles," in *Les historiographes en Europe*, 127–156.

could easily refer. The same was true of the Vasa kings of Sweden, thanks to the appearance in 1554 of Johannes Magnus's *Historia de omnibus Gothorum Sueonumque regibus*, a broad survey used by King Gustav I in his efforts to wrest Scania (the southernmost part of Sweden) from Danish control. The Danish monarchy responded first with a short treatise (published in 1561) refuting both Magnus's history and his (from their perspective) unfounded territorial claims, and then later with a full-blown history, *Synposis Historiarum Danicarum*, written by the Danish royal historiographer C. C. Lyschander and published in 1622.[49] This kind of national or patriotic history was not limited to kings. Many of Europe's minor princes acquired similar works, including the Catholic dukes of Bavaria, who in 1517 commissioned their official historian, Johannes Aventinus (1477–1534), to prepare a Latin history designed not only to document their illustrious past but also to demonstrate, with the help of a map, their claims to a Bavaria far larger than the one they presently ruled. Aventinus published a condensed vernacular version of this history in 1522 and finished his *Annalium Boiorum* the following year, but its publication was delayed until 1554 because of the author's arrest on charges of Protestantism in 1528.[50]

In comparison, Philip II, arguably the world's most powerful ruler in the mid-sixteenth century, did not possess any single work of history that did justice to his kingdom's illustrious past. In 1545 Sancho de Nebrija, son of the famous humanist, printed (in Granada) a historical miscellany that included such older works as Ximénez de Rada's *Historia gótica* and Sánchez de Arevalo's *Compendiosa histórica hispánica*, which dated from ca. 1470, along with his father's Latin history of the reign of Ferdinand and Isabella, but none of these works measured up to Philip II's notion of general history.[51] Nor did the more recent Latin histories of Spain by the Flemish scholar Joannes Vaseaus (1552) and the Catalan Francisco Tarafa (1553), both of which were short compendia that ended in the eleventh century, or just as the Reconquista was gathering steam.[52] What Philip wanted was a far more comprehensive, vernacular history of Spain modeled on the one

---

49. See Skovgaard-Petersen, "The Literary Feud between Denmark and Sweden." The Danish monarchy responded to these territorial claims in a treatise (published in 1561) refuting Magnus's history and later in a full-blown history, *Synopsis Historiarum Danicarum* (1622), written by the Danish royal historiographer C. C. Lyschander.

50. My understanding of Aventinus (born Johann Turmair) and his work derives principally from Strauss, *Historian in a Age of Crisis*.

51. For this miscellany, see Tate, "Sancho de Nebrija y su antología historiográfica."

52. I refer to Johannes Vaseus [né Jean Vassé], *Chronicon Rerum Memorabilium Hispaniae*; and Francesc [or Francisco] Tarafa, *De origine ac rebus gestis Regum Hispaniae*. Lorenzo de Padilla (1485–1540), a scholar much influenced by Annius de Viterbo, had also written a general history, *Libro de las antigüedades de España* but it remained in manuscript until 1669. For these histories, see Tate, "The Re-Writing of the Historical Past"; and García Carcel, *La construcción de las historias de España*.

that Nebrija had suggested to Philip's grandparents Ferdinand and Isabella. He consequently opened a search for a historian prepared to continue Ocampo's chronicle, which, even after the addition of a fifth book, ended somewhat abruptly in 210 BCE at the start of the Punic Wars.

The historian selected for this all-important task was the Cordoban cleric, humanist, and antiquarian Ambrosio de Morales (1513–1591). A protonationalist through and through, Morales regarded this chronicle as a patriotic duty and also one that, by his own admission, he had dreamed about since boyhood and the awakening of his interest "in writing about the history and antiquities of Spain." Morales's taste for these subjects came partly from his uncle Fernán Pérez de Oliva, a humanist who taught him both Latin and Greek, although it may also have been related to his decision as a young friar to cut off "his virile members," an act of self-mutilation and self-purification that left him, by his own account, "as smooth as the palm of a hand." Later, Morales's devotion to the subject was total, and as a professor of rhetoric at the University of Alcalá de Henares, he outfitted his house with antique inscriptions in an effort to inspire students to learn more about the past. "They want to know more about them [the inscriptions] and what they mean," he proudly wrote.[53]

As for a general chronicle, Morales reportedly became convinced of the need for such a work in 1560 when, temporarily residing in Toledo, he listened to an Italian ambassador complain that "the Spaniards . . . have not yet written about either their antiquities or the rest of their history."[54] The incident may be apocryphal, but in 1563 Morales petitioned the Cortes of Castile to appoint him "coronista del reino," an honorary position for which he asked for no remuneration except the opportunity to "serve the kingdom." One member of the Cortes opposed the appointment, alleging that Morales was a "grammarian" lacking "experience" in matters of history, but his colleagues elected to grant Morales the title he sought.[55]

The king soon followed this appointment with one of his own. In 1569 he offered Morales the position of cronista del rey *ad honorem* (without salary) but with the understanding that he would finance Morales's effort to continue the

---

53. AGS: Casas y Sitios Reales, leg. 258, fol. 243. For Morales's biography, see the introduction by Enrique Flórez to Morales, *Viage santo*; and Sánchez Madrid, *Arqueología y humanismo*. Pérez de Oliva began, but never completed, a history of Columbus. See Pérez de Oliva, *Historia de la inuención de las Yndias*, 39–126; Olschki, "Hernan Perez de Oliva's 'Ystoria de Colon,'" and Ruiz Pérez, *Fernán Pérez de Oliva*.

54. Morales, *La coronica general de España*, 3–31.

55. ACC: 2:251–253. The office of "cronista del reino" was purely honorary and carried no salary, but Guadalajara's representative to the Cortes, Pedro Suárez de Alarcon, opposed Morales's appointment on the grounds that he was a "gramático sin experiencia" in historical matters.

general history that Ocampo had begun.[56] Morales said yes and soon began to tackle this assignment head on. He soon learned, however, that his obligations as royal chronicler, even an honorary one, entailed far more than the writing of history. He was asked to serve, for example, as a royal censor and to review books for the Royal Council of Castile, the agency entrusted with the power to issue licenses for publication within the confines of the Kingdom of Castile. Philip also looked to Morales for advice on a variety of historical issues and in 1566 even asked him for his thoughts on the decorative scheme of the new royal monastery then under construction as El Escorial. Morales responded with the suggestion that the building could be made into a giant teaching machine if its doorways were inscribed with "good quotations from Holy Scripture, from the Church Fathers, from a [monastic] rule or some other pointed phrase that would speak to, warn and advise those who enter and pass through them." "This," he added, "would be a fine ornament, as it would transform dead stones into live ones . . . [since inscriptions] are like books that are perpetually open, to be read at any time and to teach at every moment."[57]

Another of Morales's responsibilities was to gather books and manuscripts for the new royal library that Philip, following Páez de Castro's suggestion, hoped to incorporate into El Escorial. As early as 1566, Morales presented the monarch with a document specifying which books and manuscripts the library ought to contain.[58] Once he became chronicler, many of the items destined for this collection passed through Morales's hands, and as it happened, he often had to find the items himself. In 1570, for example, having learned about Páez de Castro's death, Philip II sent Morales on a "literary voyage" to the chronicler's home in the village of Quer (Guadalajara) with instructions to inventory his papers and forward his valuable collection of Greek, Latin, and Arabic manuscripts to the Escorial library.[59] Two years later Morales went off on yet another literary voyage to the north of Spain, where he was supposed to locate and inventory old manuscripts and relics in monastic libraries, determine which of these ought to be sent to El Escorial, and also collect materials relating to the life and works of St. Isidore of

56. On this appointment, see Alvar Ezquerra, "Sobre la historiografía castellana," 96. In a letter dated 31 May 1566, Morales expressly noted, in response to a query from a royal secretary: "Yo no soy capellan de S.M. como V.M. me la haze de mandarme poner, sino su cronista." See AGS: Casas y Sitios Reales, leg. 258, fol. 240.

57. AGS: CSR, leg. 258, fol. 243. Letter dated Alcalá de Henares, 20 September 1566.

58. Ibid., fols. 225–246, "Apuntamientos de Ambrosio de Morales. . . ."

59. BL Add. 10, 248, consulta dated Córdoba, 20 April 1570, ordering Morales and Dr. Gasca, a royal councillor, to go to Páez de Castro's residence in the Monastery of San Bartolomé de Lupiana and "hagaís inventariar ante escribano todos los papeles tocante a la dicha coronica" and also have Morales inventory his "buena librería" and determine which books, if any, should go to El Escorial.

Seville.[60] Similar voyages soon followed: one to Plasencia in 1575, where Morales was to inspect the Greek and Latin manuscripts that belonged to the city's bishop, Pedro Ponce de León; and another to Córdoba, where he was to report on "incidents and events" relating to the discovery of certain bones pertaining to the "holy martyrs of Córdoba."[61] Along the way, Morales was also expected to identify old cartularies and privileges having to do with the royal patrimony that ought to be deposited for safekeeping in Simancas.

These literary voyages provide insights into Philip II's interest in finding new sources to document Spain's sacred history, especially as it related to the nation's conversion to Christianity, the lives of its early martyrs and saints, church councils, and the like. At the same time, they offered Morales the opportunity to gather the materials necessary to advance the general history he was so eager to write. He began this work by publishing, in 1574, a history of Roman Spain (see below) that was followed in 1575 by *Antigüedades de las ciudades de España*, an archaeological-cum-geographical treatise that used coins, medals, and lapidary inscriptions and other artifacts to pinpoint the location of towns, roads, and other monuments built by the Romans during their time in Spain. Modeling the *Antigüedades* in part upon Flavio Biondo's fifteenth-century Latin treatises on Italy in the time of the Romans, Morales deliberately elected to write it in Spanish, a language in which he, as well as Nebrija, took enormous pride. Morales regarded the book as a response to the Italians who had criticized the Spaniards for failing to write about their "antiquities." Recently it has been discovered that Morales marketed this book quite aggressively and compensated for his lack of an official salary by personally distributing copies to various booksellers in and around in Madrid and collecting royalties in return.[62] But Morales's interest in this history was probably less pecuniary than patriotic, since his overarching aim was to write the kind of history he believed that Spain, his *patria*, deserved.

Assisting Morales in this enterprise were various antiquarians who shared his historical concerns. The activities of these *anticuarios* still await detailed study, but together they comprised a small but active Spanish "republic of letters," one whose members maintained close ties to the rest of Europe, especially Italy and the Low Countries. Charter members included Morales's uncle Fernán Pérez de

60. The journey is recorded in the volume *Viage santo*. For Philip II's personal interest in this journey, see ABZ: leg. 148, fol. 51, consulta of 9 November 1572, in which the king asks Morales to provide him, in person, a full report on what he discovered during his "peregrinación" to Asturias. For more on this journey, see Edouard, "Enquête hagiographique"; and Lazure, "Possessing the Sacred."
61. This journey is mentioned in ABZ: leg. 148, fol. 54, consulta of 23 February 1573, in which the king approves of Morales's "ida a Plasencia." See also BNE: Ms. 5732, fols. 49–50, letter of Tamayo de Vargas, 18 August 1639.
62. De la Campa della Gavela and Montero Reguera, "El mundo del libro."

Oliva, as well as Diego Hurtado de Mendoza, Pedro Chacón, and Juan de Verzosa, all of whom lived for a time in Rome. Also on the roster were Antonio Agustín, the Aragonese scholar known for his pioneering numismatic research; Benito Arías Montano, the famed biblical scholar who served as Philip II's librarian at El Escorial; and two Andalusian antiquarians, Juan Fernández Franco and Gonzalo Argote de Molina, both of whom shared Morales's interest in the history of Bética, the Latin name for southern Spain.[63] Morales corresponded with these and other like-minded scholars, along with Sepúlveda and Zurita, and together they helped the royal chronicler to prepare not only the *Antigüedades* but also the history of Roman Spain that he included in his 1574 addition to the *Crónica general* that Ocampo had begun. Rarely read today, this chronicle, *La coronica general de España*, was an especially noteworthy achievement; it accomplished what a number of fifteenth-century historians, including Nebrija, had envisioned but, lacking the kind of archaeological and epigraphic evidence at Morales's disposal, were unable to complete.

Yet for all of the *coronica*'s importance, Morales was not altogether happy with what he had achieved. In the preface he informed readers, "As a Spaniard, I celebrate everything about Spain" but apologized that what he had written "was more about Rome than Spain" because "we do not have information about the things that happened in Spain during these ancient times that comes from histories written by Spaniards but only those written by the Romans. Thus, this history is not about the things of Spain . . . but about the things the Romans did in it."[64] All this is certainly true. But Morales deserves credit for having compiled a detailed narrative of Roman Spain and also one that focused in good humanist fashion on important matters of governance and war. He further succeeded in highlighting the Spanishness of Hispania through his decision to dedicate several chapters to some of the key founding myths of Catholic Spain, among them James the Apostle's mission to the country in 37 CE followed by his burial in the city that later became known as Santiago de Compostela. In these chapters, Morales demonstrated his awareness of the latest trends in antiquarian scholarship with his willingness to question the verisimilitude of sources relating

---

63. Spain's "republic of letters" in the sixteenth century awaits detailed study, but it may be approached through Lazure, "To Dare Fame"; and Coroleu, "Humanismo en España." The history of antiquarian research in early modern Spain remains to be written, but the subject may be approached through Gimeno Pascual, *Historia de la investigación epigráfica;* and Sánchez Madrid, *Arqueología y humanismo.* The connections between Spanish antiquarians and their Italian counterparts may be approached through Stenhouse, *Reading Inscriptions,* and Elliott van Liere, "'Shared Studies Foster Friendship.'"

64. Morales, *La coronica general de España,* 4v–5.

to Santiago that previous scholars had accepted as authentic. However, as Kate Elliott van Liere has recently argued,⁶⁵ Morales did little to question of the validity of the myths surrounding Santiago's presence in Spain. Rather, following the Council of Trent's 1546 decree on sacred books, which reasserted the authority of tradition alongside of Scripture, he suggested that there was no reason for any self-respecting Spaniard to doubt received opinion about Santiago, or, as he put it, "That which is received in all of Spain, now becomes so well established that it would not be advisable to insist on the contrary."⁶⁶ As we shall see, the papal secretary Cesare Baronio soon questioned the validity of historical proofs that rested solely on the strength of tradition, but for a patriot such as Morales, such arguments carried little weight. For this same reason he devoted an entire book (book 10) to another of his favorite topics: the martyrs and saints whose lives in his view served to "ennoble" Spain.

Morales's patriotism was even more evident in the next installment of the chronicle, published in 1577. Its subject was Spain of the Visigoths, a subject that, starting in the Middle Ages, played a formative role in the monarchy's history. Drawing upon his own research and earlier histories by Orosius, Isidore, Ximénez de Rada, and the medieval Muslim historian al-Rasis, Morales celebrated the "sovereign glory of the Goths," emphasizing how the Visigoths struggled to create a politically and spiritually homogeneous state following King Recarred's conversion from Arian to Roman Christianity in 589.⁶⁷ The volume ended with the so-called destruction of Spain occasioned by Arab conquest in 711, although Morales optimistically assured his readers that Christianity survived the Muslim onslaught in the north of Spain under the leadership of Pelayo, the king he described as a direct ancestor of Philip II. As for the rest of the peninsula, Morales observed that "many ancient Spaniards of Roman heritage," known today as Mozarabs, continued to practice their religion, even in Córdoba, "the Moors' capital and court." To document these assertions, Morales pointed to various archaeological discoveries, including Christian tombstones he had unearthed.⁶⁸

Morales was also ahead of his times in his use of demography to support his findings about Christianity's survival, noting that Muslims were far too few "to

---

65. Elliott van Liere, "The Missionary and the Moorslayer," 542.
66. Ibid.
67. I refer to Morales, *Los otros dos libros* [books 11 and 12] *de la coronica general*. Book 11 explored the history of early Christian martyrs in Spain, book 12 the history of the Goths. Starting with the Alcalá de Henares of 1578, these books were customarily bound together with the first five books of the chronicle by Ocampo.
68. Morales, *La coronica general de España*, bk. 10, 214–215.

populate everything, let alone work the land." In making such assertions, Morales avoided the issue of conversion, let alone the possibility that any of the stalwart "ancient Spaniards" he had written about could ever have become renegades. Rather, he stuck closely to idea of continuity and the idea that Spain remained fundamentally Christian even during the time of the *moros,* a theme that figured centrally in his next installment of the chronicle, published in 1586.[69]

This volume, Morales's last, examined Spain's history from the eighth to the eleventh century and ended with the death of King Bermudo III of León in 1037. This period marked the heyday of al-Andalus, but as Morales admitted, he had no desire "to narrate events during the time of the Moors," a bias that enabled him to ignore the accomplishments of Abd-al-Rahman III, the greatest of Spain's Muslim rulers, together with the entire history of the caliphate at Córdoba.[70] He focused instead on the early years of the Reconquest, emphasizing the conquests of Pelayo and his followers in Asturias, León, and Castile but avoiding the counts of Barcelona and the early kings of Aragon, subjects well covered by Zurita in his *Anales* and ones that Morales, as a Castilian patriot, deliberately decided to ignore.

For Morales, however, the Reconquest was little more than a series of individual royal *gestes*. In the sixteenth century this kind of king-centered history was somewhat old-fashioned, but it apparently appealed to Philip II, who, as noted earlier, delighted in reading about the victories of his ancestors in their battles against the Moors. One can only speculate, but reading about these victories may well have stiffened the king's resolve to emulate his ancestors and champion the cause of the Roman Church against the Ottomans in the Mediterranean and the south of Europe as well as against Protestants in the north.

What is certain is that the king took enormous satisfaction in Morales's achievement; and in the expectation that his aging chronicler would be able to write yet another installment of the *crónica,* he rewarded him with a monastic office worth thirteen thousand *reales* a year. According to Gabriel de Zayas, another of Philip's many secretaries, this sum represented "pearls" for the impoverished chronicler in addition to offering him the "peace" needed to continue his histories.[71] Yet in 1583, the year in which these pearls arrived, Morales was too old to do anything to advance the chronicle. Thus, at his death in 1591, Spain's general history, particularly that of the Reconquest, was far from complete.

69. I refer to Morales, *Los cinco libros postreros de la coronica general*. Note that this volume is generally cataloged under Ocampo's name.

70. Ibid., prologue.

71. BUS: Ms. 2657, consulta to Philip II, 156. Zayas also suggested that the position of cronista del rey would help assuage "His Majesty's conscience," inasmuch as Morales had been serving as chronicler in a purely honorary capacity without pay.

Gallery

Anonymous. *Alfonso X of Castile*. El Escorial Library; Foto Oronoz. A patron of learning and the arts, Alfonso X, king of Castile and León (1221–1284), commissioned one of the first "general" histories of Spain and its monarchy. This history helped to create a model of kingship based on territorial conquest and the defense of the Catholic Church.

Anonymous. *Ferdinand of Aragon and Isabella of Castile*. Foto Oronoz. Ferdinand (r. 1479–1516) and Isabella (r. 1474–1504), generally known as the Catholic Monarchs, were among the first European rulers who made use of the printing press for propagandistic aims. They also employed a team of chroniclers whose task was to magnify the importance of the monarchs' achievements in both war and peace.

Titian, *Charles V on Horseback*. Museo de Prado, Madrid; Foto Oronoz. Titian portrays Emperor Charles V (r. 1516–1556) as a Christian knight. The portrait formed part of the propaganda campaign organized by the emperor's advisers in the wake of his victory over Germany's Protestant princes at Mühlberg in 1548.

Antonis Mor, *Philip II of Spain*. Museo de Bellas Artes, Bilbao, Spain; Foto Oronoz. Early in his reign, Philip II (1556–1598) ordered his chroniclers to write about the history of ancient and medieval Spain. Later, and especially in the wake of the defeat of the Spanish Armada in 1588, his historical interests turned to more contemporary subjects and he commissioned a series of histories designed to enhance both his and Spain's reputations as historical actors.

Archivo General de Simancas, Simancas, Spain. Foto Oronoz. Created by Charles V in 1544 and subsequently reorganized by Philip II, the royal archive at Simancas served as a repository for important state papers. Not opened to the public until 1836, Simancas was a "secret" archive accessible to only a handful of authorized royal officials. Even royal chroniclers needed to obtain special permission in order to access the documents it housed.

Anonymous, *Diego Sarmiento de Acuña, Conde de Gondomar*. Foto Oronoz. An amateur historian in his own right, Gondomar (1567–1626) recommended that the Spanish monarchy exercise strict control over the writing and publishing of history. He believed that it should deploy history as an instrument of diplomacy and statecraft, and he put this policy into action while serving as the Spanish ambassador in London.

Anonymous, *Pedro de Valencia, Coronista*. Foto Oronoz. A humanist by training and inclination, Pedro de Valencia (1555–1620) was one of the few royal chroniclers who was reluctant to write the kind of self-serving history that monarchs often demanded. He was appointed to the office of "general chronicler" by Philip III but failed to deliver and, as a result, almost lost his job.

Juan Bautista Maino, *Surrender of Bahía*, ca. 1633. Museo del Prado, Madrid; Foto Oronoz. Maino's depiction of the Spanish victory at Bahía in 1625 was one of a series of battle paintings that decorated the walls of the Hall of Realms in Madrid's Buen Retiro Palace. Philip IV and the count-duke of Olivares (both featured in the tapestry within the painting) used both art and history to glorify the monarchy as well as to win support for their foreign and domestic policies. Olivares also believed that history was a weapon that could be used to "mortify" Spain's enemies.

Antonio de Carnicero, *Pedro Rodríguez de Campomanes*. Foto Oronoz. As president of Madrid's Royal Academy of History, Campomanes (1723–1802) embraced the Enlightenment idea of "scientific" history. He was challenged by other royal officials who believed that histories should primarily serve patriotic ends.

Frontispiece to Antonio de Herrera y Tordesillas, *Descripción de las indias occidentales* (Madrid, 1601). Photograph courtesy of the Library of Congress. Herrera y Tordesillas's geographical description of the Indies served as the introduction to his general history of the Spanish New World. A likeness of the author appears in the medallion at the lower left. The frontispiece also included a map of the Americas, a representation of an Aztec temple, and depictions of various Aztec gods.

Frontispiece to Antonio de Herrera y Tordesillas, *Historia general de los hechos de los castellanos* (Madrid, 1601), decade I. Photograph courtesy of the John Carter Brown Library at Brown University, Providence, Rhode Island. Each of the seven "decades" of Herrera's history of the Indies opened with a frontispiece that summarized, in pictorial form, the narrative to follow. This frontispiece included, in addition to medallion portraits of Ferdinand and Isabella (at the top), and Christopher Columbus and his brother Bartolomé (at the bottom), a series of vignettes relating to Columbus's voyage of 1492, the discovery the "island of the Lacayos" (Hispaniola), the foundation of the Spanish settlement called La Navidad, and various battles that ensued.

At this juncture, one royal official, palpably upset by what he described as "the inopportuneness and never finishing of the historians," advised the king to entrust the history to a committee or junta composed of two or three scholars and one soldier. Such a junta, he claimed, could complete the history "in a very short time and without much expense for His Majesty."[72] But the king, an early critic of history by committee, thought differently and rejected the idea of such a junta as not only cumbersome but expensive. In 1592, however, he did agree to appoint Esteban de Garibay y Zamalloa (1533–1599) to the office of chronicler vacated by Morales for the purpose of advancing the *crónica general*.

Basque by origin, Garibay was an ambitious, hard-working historian who in 1571 had published, at his own expense, an important history of Spain. This was the *Compendio historial de todas las historias de los reinos de España*, a comprehensive survey that began with Tubal, the kingdom's mythic founder, and ended with the conquest of Granada.[73] As suggested by its title, the *Compendio* was less an original work of scholarship than a reworking of existing older chronicles, yet Páez de Castro, acting in his capacity as censor for the Royal Council of Castile, described it as "the most comprehensive that has been written to date; reading it will be very useful and pleasurable for all nations" and enthusiastically recommended its publication.[74] Soon afterward Garibay wrote to the president of the Royal Council, explaining that he had written "the history of our own Spanish nation" in order to provide a full account of its "glorious triumphs and in both worlds, the old and the new." Patriotism, in this case more Spanish than narrowly Basque, also led Garibay to boast that every Spaniard would find in these triumphs examples that were far more useful and enlightening than those taken from the histories of "foreign things," which, in his view, were often "quite odious." In other words, what Garibay was doing—or at least thought he was doing—in the *Compendio* was constructing a nation by creating a common history, which would not only help to define Spaniards vis-à-vis citizens of other nations but also give them a heritage around which they could rally. Garibay sought to do this by writing what he called a "general and universal history of Spain" that drew upon the "particular" histories of Castile, Aragon, and the other kingdoms that made up the Spanish monarchy. This task, he admitted, was

---

72. ABZ: carpeta 159, fol. 107, memorandum of Juan López de Velasco, "Que Su Mag. deve mandar escrevir su historia." Ironically, López de Velasco, who was briefly cronista mayor de las Indias, never wrote much history himself. See Chapter 5.

73. Garibay y Zamalloa, *Los XL libros*. For a brief biography of Garibay, see Moya, *Esteban de Garibay*, together with his introduction to Garibay, *Discurso de mi vida*.

74. IVDJ: envio 44, fol. 146. Garibay to Espinosa, 25 III 1567. Páez de Castro's evaluation, "Sobre el compendio universal," is dated Quer, 10 March 1567.

enormous, one that required him to be highly selective; it was similar to that of a florist who, in making a "garland or crown of flowers, does not pick all of the flowers that nature produces, but only those best suited for beauty and decoration."[75] Garibay, who was never overly modest, also boasted that his book represented nothing less than the "summary and compendium of the all the histories and most notable things of all of the reigns that comprise Spain."[76]

In effect, this is what Garibay, starting in the 1560s, managed to achieve. After a lengthy introduction that ended with the Arab invasion of Hispania, Garibay divided the *Compendio historial* into a series of separate and essentially parallel narratives, each devoted to one of Spain's constituent parts: León, Castile, Aragon, Navarre, and even Portugal. Especially innovative was his decision to devote one section to "the Moorish kings of Spain, especially Córdoba" and another to the "Moorish kings of Granada," subjects that Morales had studiously avoided. In this respect, Garibay was somewhat ahead of his times. Furthermore, he believed that his all-inclusive approach would enable all Spaniards, regardless of *patria*, to identify with a common, supranational past.

More immediately, Garibay hoped to parlay the book into an appointment as cronista del rey, an office for which he had petitioned unsuccessfully on several occasions.[77] He was persistent, and in 1592 he asked for the appointment "without pay," a request that apparently caught Philip's most senior councillors, members of what was called the Junta Grande, by surprise. The junta hesitated, arguing that Garibay wanted the office only to enhance his personal credentials and "to give more authority to his works."[78] One junta member, Cristóbal de Moura, a Portuguese nobleman also serving on the Council of State, was even more skeptical, as he had recently criticized Garibay's *Compendio* for its failure to unite the separate histories of Spain's various kingdoms into a single harmonious narrative.[79] In the end a compromise was reached. Garibay got the appointment, *ad*

---

75. Garibay y Zamalloa, *Los cuarenta libros*, 14.
76. IVDJ: envio 44, fol. 146.
77. Garibay petitioned (unsuccessfully) for this office in 1571, 1574, 1576, and 1585. In 1576, however, the king, recognizing that none of his other chroniclers had worked harder or published more than Garibay, appointed him to the office of *aposentador* in the royal palace, a position worth about one thousand ducats a year. Additional grants followed (see ABZ: carpeta 160n62). However, he was not formally installed in the office of cronista del rey until 16 April 1592, following the death of Ambrosio de Morales. See RAH: Colección Pellicer, Ms. 9/4067, consulta dated 8 July 1571; and Pérez Pastor, *Bibliografía madrileña*, 3:375–376.
78. ABZ: Ms. Altamira, 160n54. La Junta en Madrid, consulta of 30 January 1592.
79. ABZ: leg. 148/16 [1588?] The consulta reads: "Y aproposito de la coronica q quiere sacar a luz, q no dubdo sera muy buena, creo que seria bien encargarle que mire si se podria hazer una continuada de todas las de España q andan divididas, en forma de compendio, que si no me engaño seria de grande estima y ya que Ambrosio por su edad no lo pudiese emprender, importaría mucho, tracarlo quien o tiene mejor entendido que ninguno de los q viven y con susentarle los scrivientes que huviesse

honorem, evidently because certain members of the junta decided he was the best person to organize what they envisioned as a history of Philip II (see below). The general history, however, was by no means forgotten, and it was about this time that the Royal Council of Castile, acting in its role as watchdog of all publications in the kingdom, authorized publication of Juan de Mariana's *Historia de rebus hispaniae*, a book that offered precisely the kind of synthetic history that Moura, and presumably Philip, both sought.

Juan de Mariana and the *Historia General*

For Philip II, the publication in 1592 of Mariana's *Historia*, although not totally unexpected, came as something of a surprise. He apparently learned about the book in 1586, when Mariana first requested a publication subsidy. On this occasion the king said no, evidently because he had previously commissioned Mariana to prepare an edition of the works of Isidore of Seville but Mariana had failed to complete it. Mariana was therefore advised to finish with Isidore and not to ask for any support until that task was done.[80] At this point, communication between Mariana and the monarch all but stopped, although the king is likely to have been kept apprised of Mariana's work via García de Loaysa Girón (1541–1599), the Toledan cleric who served as his principal adviser on ecclesiastical matters and, starting in 1585, as the tutor of his son, the future Philip III.[81] An accomplished scholar in his own right, Loaysa was Mariana's most loyal patron, not only helping to subsidize the initial publication of *De rebus* in 1592 but also persuading him to write *De rege et regis institutione*, a treatise that he had conceived as a textbook to help the prince learn about the practice of kingship.[82]

Mariana's history was a monumental achievement, one that seemingly developed out of his interests in the early history of the Spanish church. Patriotic concerns loomed equally important; as Mariana tells it, he first thought of the history while traveling in "foreign nations." Like other travelers, both present and

---

menester, se le facilitaria mucho, pues el agora no tiene otra mucha ocupacion. Mandarlo mirar VM y avisarme de su voluntad."

80. See Cirot, *Mariana historien*, 35n1.

81. Loaysa, an influential cleric about whom more is to be learned, may be approached through Braun, "Conscience, Counsel, and Theocracy at the Spanish Habsburg Court." It should be noted that he assembled in Toledo an important (and still almost unstudied) *contubernium* of scholars, Mariana among them, who studied the history of both Spanish culture and the early Spanish church with a particular emphasis on documenting Toledo's right to claim the title of Spain's primatial see. For its membership, see Chapter 7.

82. See Mariana, *De rege et regis institione libri III*. For the printing of *De rebus*, see Rodríguez de Gracia, "Contratos de impresión."

past, he discovered his national identity while living abroad. In Mariana's case, his travels took him first to Rome, where he taught theology at the Jesuits' Colegio Romano; Loreto, famous for its Marian shrine; Messina; and finally to Paris, where in addition to earning a doctorate in theology, he discovered Paolo Emilio's *De rebus gestis Francorum*, a possible model for his own history of Spain. But whatever the precise source of his inspiration, that Spain had no Latin history comparable to Emilio's was enough to convince the Jesuit to write about "our [Spain's] things; the start of, then the ways, in which it achieved the grandeur it has today."[83]

Writing this history, Mariana's aims were many. To begin with, he sought to meld "the secular accomplishments of the monarchy" with "the ecclesiastical accomplishments of the church" and also lay the foundation for a more comprehensive ecclesiastical history of Spain that he planned but never managed to write. He also was eager to craft a national history that would transcend the individual histories of the peninsula's kingdoms, that is, the particular brand of *historia pro patria* that Zurita had fashioned for his native Aragon. Mariana's aspirations were different. "We are not content," he wrote, "with relating the deeds of any one kingdom, but those of every part of Spain."[84] Yet, he informed one early critic of his work: "I never pretended to write a history of Spain nor to write about all its particulars, which would mean never finishing. Rather I wanted to organize and render in Latin all that others have written, as materials for a larger fabric that I wanted to make."[85]

In the end, Mariana succeeded where Garibay did not. In his *Compendio* Garibay dealt separately with each of Spain's many kingdoms, mainly by devoting separate books to each. Mariana envisioned Spain's history in more holistic—call them national or supranational—terms. As a theologian, moreover, he envisioned Spain's history in sacred terms, embracing an era of sin, symbolized by the personal failings of Rodreric, the last Visiogthic king; punishment, in the guise of the Muslim invasion and occupation of Iberia; and finally redemption as the nation's monarchs united in their struggle to restore Iberia to Christendom. Mariana also perceived this history, somewhat teleologically, as the equivalent of Spain's long march toward greatness, which began with the Reconquest; arrived midway at unity, symbolized by the marriage of Ferdinand and Isabella and

---

83. Mariana, *Historia general de España*, prologue, 1:li.
84. Ibid., 1:li.
85. Mariana to Lupercio Leonardo de Argensola, Toledo, 23 August 1602, in Leonardo de Argensola, *Obras*, 1:395.

subsequently by Philip II's acquisition of the kingdom of Portugal in 1580; and ended with dominion on a global stage.

In keeping with this broad, grandiose vision of Spain's road to greatness, Mariana endeavored to integrate into almost every chapter events that occurred in Castile, Aragon, and the other parts of Hispania. Generally, Castile enjoyed pride of place in the narrative, but Mariana, clearly aware of the significance of Philip II's annexation of Portugal in 1580, sought to integrate that kingdom's history into the larger history of Spain. He did the same with Aragon, partly on account of his sympathy for the way Aragon's laws and privileges preserved individual liberties and helped keep tyranny at bay (in *De rege*, which was originally conceived as a companion to the history, Mariana suggested that subjects had a legitimate right to overthrow and even kill monarchs deemed to be tyrants).[86] Yet Mariana's overarching aim was to write a *historia pro patria* that offered the unequivocal evidence needed to explain Spain's path to glory.

In a landmark study of Mariana first published in 1904, the French scholar Georges Cirot wrote that Mariana's primary aim in this history was to create a "conscience nationale," a term roughly equivalent to what Maurice Halbwachs later called "collective memory."[87] This concept is now understood as one of the essential building blocks of nationhood. Yet nation-building was not Mariana's primary concern. From his perspective, Spain, or Hispania, already existed, both as a geographical unit, as described in the opening pages of his history, and as a political entity resembling what Benedict Anderson defines as an "imagined community," one with common interests transcending those of its constituent parts.[88] Mariana, moreover, defined this community in messianic terms. "Its [Spain's] path and design," he wrote, was to "conquer foreign kingdoms and peoples," albeit in the name of the church.[89] He subsequently reiterated this message in his discussion of Ferdinand and Isabella, monarchs he credited with bringing "good government" to Spain but, more importantly, setting Spain on the path toward "empire and grandeur."[90]

The extent to which Mariana explicitly tailored this imperial message for the king's benefit is not altogether clear, although Philip II does make a dramatic appearance at the end of the section Mariana devoted to Visigothic Spain. Like Morales before him, Mariana trumpeted the Visigoths' many achievements, em-

---

86. Mariana's political thought is best approached through Braun, *Juan de Mariana;* together with Lewy, *Constitutionalism and Statecraft.*
87. Cirot, *Mariana historien,* 333. See Halbwachs, *On Collective Memory.*
88. Anderson, *Imagined Communities.*
89. Mariana, *Historia general de España,* vol. 2: bk. 26, chap. 1, p. 240.
90. Ibid., p. 241.

phasizing how Recarred's conversion to Roman Christianity firmly placed Spain in Heaven's camp. "Divine providence," wrote Mariana, "looked after Recarred's affairs," both militarily and politically.[91] Similarly, Spain's "loss" to the Muslims was part of Heaven's grand design, done purposely so that Spain, like phoenix, would rise from the "ashes" to become a "new and holy Spain, stronger and more powerful than ever before, a refuge, column, and support of the Catholic religion and one composed of all its parts . . . , able to extend its empire, as we now see, to the most remote parts of both east and west." Then, in good humanistic fashion, Mariana brought this argument to a dramatic climax by introducing Philip II into the narrative and applauding him for having annexed Portugal to Spain and subjecting the entire peninsula to the rule of "one scepter and lord." Having dismissed the defeat of the Spanish Armada in 1588 as little more than a temporary setback, Mariana concluded that this new, unified Spain "is beginning to frighten, as never before, the wrongdoers along with the enemies of Christ."[92]

When the *Historia* first appeared, in 1592, it was far from a commercial success. Sales were hurt both by the book's high price and by the simple fact it was in Latin, a language relatively few Spaniards had mastered. One early reader also suggested that Mariana could improve the history, which originally ended with the conquest of Granada in 1492, by bringing the story forward to the death of King Ferdinand in 1516, an addition that necessarily required a discussion of Spain's conquests in the Americas and the beginnings of Habsburg rule. Mariana agreed and introduced the new sections into the expanded Latin edition of the history published in 1595,[93] which then served as the basis for the Spanish translation, which appeared in 1601.

But whatever its original defects—and there were more—the *Historia* received a warm reception at the royal court, where Mariana's image of Spain as a mighty colossus seemed to help dispel some of the gloom, or what Pedro de Ribadeneyra called the "disillusionment" or *desengaño*, that descended on Madrid following the Armada's defeat.[94] Loaysa, Mariana's friend and supporter, was so impressed with the history that he suggested that Prince Philip read it as part of his education, and there is probably some truth in the story that Philip II, in keeping with his preference for vernacular history, personally encouraged Mariana to translate it into Castilian. Mariana did just this, finishing what later became *Historia general*

---

91. Ibid., vol. 1, bk. 5, chap. 14, p. 146.
92. Ibid., vol. 1, bk. 6, chap. 27, p. 188.
93. See García Hernán, "Construcción de las historias de España." For the early publishing history of *De rebus*, see Rodríguez de Gracia, "Contratos de impresión," 60–75.
94. One of the first expressions of the *desengaño* may be found in the work of the Jesuit Pedro de Ribadeneyra, especially his "Carta . . . sobre las causas de la pérdida de la Armada."

de España relatively quickly, and certainly before January 1596, when he successfully petitioned the monarch for a subvention to help defray printing costs.[95] Even so, the book's publication did not occur until 1601; the delay can be partly attributed to the costs of publication, but also to such factors as the death of Philip II in September 1598, Jesuit reservations about allowing members of that order to publish histories that did not fit neatly into the category of sacred history, or *historia sacra*, and Mariana's decidedly rocky relationship with the duke of Lerma, the all-powerful favorite of the new monarch, Philip III.[96]

Despite this delay, and possibly because of it, the vernacular *Historia general* sold rather briskly, with copies quickly turning up in Lima and Mexico City, and was reprinted on several occasions. Its popularity was such that it inspired a number of knockoffs, short compendia whose authors, pillaging Mariana's history, sought to cash in on some of the Jesuit's success.[97] Yet Mariana's history continued to sell, appearing in no fewer than sixteen editions between 1601 and 1784, by which time it had become standard reading in provincial towns and cities scattered across Spain.

Success did not necessarily mean perfection, and from the outset Mariana's critics made themselves heard. Antonio de Herrera y Tordesillas, another of Philip II's royal chroniclers, respected Mariana's erudition and the elegance of his prose but described parts of the history as "pure conjecture," notably the section devoted to Spain's early kings, much of which derived from the inventions of Annius of Viterbo. Herrera also criticized Mariana for having failed to do the archival work necessary "to reveal all of the truth, which is the soul of history."[98] Here, too, Herrera was correct. Those portions of the book that addressed the early history of the Spanish church were somewhat original, but Mariana mainly relied on information gleaned from other chroniclers, often without checking his facts, as he candidly acknowledged in a letter addressed to Pablo Ferrer, a fellow Jesuit residing in Portugal. "The truth is," he confessed, "that I did not pretend to write Spain's history but rather to organize [*poner en estilo*] that which others had written. I was content to follow them without verifying all of the details, for

---

95. For this subsidy, see Mariana's letter to the king, dated Toledo, 1 June 1596, in which he thanks the king for "la ayuda y limosna" that enabled him to publish the history. See Cirot, "Quelques lettres de Mariana," 9.

96. Mariana's problems with Lerma can be traced to his strident criticism of royal favorites in *De rege*, first published in 1599. For Jesuit publication policies, see below, Chapter 7, the section titled "*Novatores*, the 'False Chronicles,' and the Rebirth Of National History."

97. The first knockoff was Manuel Correia Montenegro's *Historia de los reyes, señorias y emperadores de España* (1608). For others, see Cirot, *Mariana historien*, 263.

98. BNE: Ms. 5781, fol. 130. For the reception of Mariana's history, see Cirot, *Mariana historien*; and Soons, *Juan de Mariana*, 23–46.

otherwise I might have never finished."⁹⁹ One of these "others" happened to be Garibay, Mariana's principal source for Portugal and one that, as he later acknowledged, led to "several mistakes." There were other criticisms as well. These ranged from pointing out errors of fact, as when the constable of Castile, Pedro Fernández de Velasco, and his secretary, Pedro Mantuano, criticized Mariana for his faulty knowledge of Spanish geography, to questioning Mariana's loyalty to the monarchy about which he wrote, as the royal secretary, Antonio de Mendoza, did.¹⁰⁰

Some of the most insightful comments about the history came from Mariana himself. In 1609 he found himself in the middle of a criminal trial arising from the unauthorized publication in 1603 of *De monetae mutatione*, a treatise critical of Philip III's decision to devalue the popular copper coin known as the *vellón*. Mariana regarded the devaluation as detrimental to the interests of the "republic" and classified it as an act of tyranny—this from an author whose position on regicide had already sparked considerable debate.¹⁰¹ Arrested and imprisoned on charges of lèse majesté, Mariana as part of his defense reflected on the history and what he thought it had achieved. "[His Majesty Philip II] wanted it [the history] very much, since no chronicler of previous kings had been capable of writing it, and if any one had, we do not know anything about it.... They say it compares well to those of other nations.... I could say more, but will refrain from doing so out of modesty."¹⁰² At the same time, Mariana acknowledged his errors. "If I am not mistaken, the book has been rather well-received. There are criticisms, but the book addresses most of the most illustrious things of Spain, and so honors the nation. I recognize that I have not been able to please everyone, causing some feelings [*sentimentos*] to be hurt, and for these I sincerely apologize."¹⁰³

In offering these remarks, Mariana did not specify the individuals whose

---

99. Cirot, *Mariana historien*, appendix 5, document 9, Mariana to Paulo Ferrer, dated Toledo, 24 June 1596.

100. For the Mariana-Mantuano dispute, see González Palencia, "Polémica"; and AHN Cons: leg. 24,341, exp. 27a. Mariana did his best to stay out of this particular dispute. Cf. BL Add.: 10,248, fol. 19, letter dated 19 July 1616, where he comments: "El libro que ha escrito contra Mantuano yo no le visto ni tampoco el libro de Mantuano; no he querido meteme en estas cosas." For Mendoza's comments, see Mendoza, "Tratado de los titulos y grandes de España," fol. 73v, where he notes (Mariana's) "ruin intención y mal afecto a lo Real y lo noble y a la nación española." The Jesuit general Claudio Aquaviva is also reported to having expressed dissatisfaction with Mariana's remarks about the Borja, the family to which Francisco de Borja, one of the founding fathers of the Society of Jesus, belonged.

101. Mariana's treatise on devaluation was a true cause célèbre discussed in the highest reaches of the Spanish government as well as in Rome. See Cirot, "Quelques letteres de Mariana," 1–15, esp. 12–24 for relevant documents; as well as BNE: Ms. 2919, "Proceso contra P. Mariana"; and Ms. 12,179, "Consultas originales del Estado," fols. 138r–v, 141r.

102. See BNE: Ms. 2819, fol. 113v. Mariana offered these remarks in 1609, as part of his trial over the publication of his controversial treatise in Germany in which he criticized the tax policies of Philip III.

103. Ibid., 114.

sentimentos had been bruised. He also ignored those critics who complained about the history's failure to address "cosas modernas," or events occurring after the death of King Ferdinand in 1516.[104] Mariana had already updated the book once, and he did so again in 1623 when, at the request of King Philip IV, he added a short summary that covered the years between 1516 and 1621.[105] However, he did not examine this period's history in any detail so as not to step on anyone's toes and also to avoid the pitfalls associated with writing about current and recent events.

Mariana's original decision to end the narrative in 1492 possibly reflected his understanding of Philip II's well-known dislike for histories that examined "today's things." But what Mariana could not possibly have known in 1591, when he first asked permission to publish the history, is that Philip's long-standing reservations about "today's things" was beginning to change. For three decades *historia pro patria* was the only history on Philip's plate, but now the aging monarch made room for histories—official histories—expressly designed to defend not only his policies but also his reputation as a historical actor. How this turnabout happened, and its implications for Spain's future rulers, is addressed in the next chapter.

---

104. Note, however, that Mariana was totally *engagé* with respect to such contemporary issues as currency reform, gambling, the education of Philip III, etc. For his treatises on these subjects, see his *Obras completas*, vol. 2.

105. For Philip IV's interest in this new edition, see Chapter 6. The circumstances surrounding the 1623 edition of Mariana's history, published in a print run of 4,500 copies, are explored in Morena Gallego, "Juan de Mariana ante la imprenta," 122–124.

CHAPTER FOUR

"His Majesty's History"

> Narrations of past events [are] useful for political deliberations.
> —Justus Lipsius

> Truth for us nowadays is not what it is, but what others can be brought to accept.
> —Michel de Montaigne

In 1589 Justus Lipsius and Giovanni Botero lived almost at opposite ends of Europe, Lipsius in Leiden, Botero in Turin. Lipsius was a borderline Calvinist, almost a *politique*, although one who was reconciled to the Roman Church in a matter of years, Botero a Jesuit with orthodox Catholic beliefs. Despite these differences, the two shared similar political ideas, as both were practically charter members of a philosophical movement known now as Christian reason of state. This movement began in reaction to Machiavelli and what was perceived as his essentially amoral, thoroughly unchristian approach to the business of state. Christian reason of state endeavored to reconcile Machiavelli's notion of power politics with the fundamental precepts of the Christian religion, especially charity, virtue, temperance, and prudence. A powerful prince, according to this line of thought, could still be a Christian prince, so long as he (or she) was motivated less by self-interest than by the good of the commonwealth over which he (or she) ruled.

Lipsius (1547–1606) was a Flemish political philosopher whose Neo-Stoic ideas found a wide audience in Spain. As a young man Lipsius served as secretary to Cardinal Granvelle, long-time adviser to Philip II. Later he toyed with Cal-

---

Epigraphs: Lipsius, *Politica*, 1.19 (p. 259); Michel de Montaigne, *Du Démentir*, in *Essais*, bk. 2, chap. 18, edited by Pierre Villey (Paris, 1992), accessed through The Montaigne Project, www.lib.uchicago.edu/efts/ARTFL/projects/montaigne.

vinism but was reconciled to the Catholic Church in 1591, was subsequently appointed to a professorship in Louvain, and in 1596 was made Philip II's royal historiographer in the Netherlands, a largely honorific office but one with considerable prestige. As a scholar Lipsius was best known for editions of Seneca and Tacitus, but his *Sixe Books of Politickes, or Civil Discourse,* a collection of political maxims culled from the ancients, quickly became a best seller. First published in Latin in 1589, it was especially influential in Spanish ruling circles; Bernardino de Mendoza, Philip II's former ambassador in London and Paris, translated it into Spanish following his return to Madrid in 1590.[1] In this handbook, Lipsius offered suggestions on how powerful princes such as Philip II could best preserve their power and authority and especially conserve the integrity of their kingdoms in the teeth of rebellion and civil war. Moreover, Lipsius considered it essential for princes to have "a good report" in terms of reputation. He also emphasized the importance of leaving behind a "good memorie." His recommendation to princes: "Have alwaies before thine eyes the honor of thy posteritie," and also have "worthy wits to record the historie of thy time."[2]

Botero offered similar recommendations in his influential treatise on statecraft, *Ragion di stato,* first published (in Italian) in 1589. A Jesuit attached to the court of the dukes of Savoy, Botero (1544–1617) enjoyed close connections to the Spanish court through Catalina Miquela, Philip II's eldest daughter, the wife of duke Carlo Emanuale I.[3] Like Lipsius, Botero was particularly interested in ways that princes might increase their power and enhance their reputation without recourse to some of the amoral subterfuges advocated in *The Prince.* Toward this end, the *Ragion* offered numerous suggestions, including the need for powerful princes to sponsor a "finely-written history which is read by everyone and goes all over the world." He further observed that "a ruler should also ensure that his wars and campaigns are recorded in writing; thus his own deeds will be celebrated . . . as well as those of the commanders and soldiers who have distinguished themselves by their deeds." And still on the subject of history, he recommended that "since the prince alone has full knowledge of the reasons and circumstances of his undertakings and their outcome, history should preferably be written by him, or at least some one who is supported by the prince with his authority, value, and money; otherwise it will be of little value."[4]

1. For Mendoza, see Cabañas Agrela, *Bernardino de Mendoza.*
2. Lipsius, *Sixe Books of Politickes,* 40.
3. Bireley, *The Counter Reformation Prince.*
4. As cited in Botero, *The Reason of State,* bk. 9, pp. 190–191.

Following these general precepts, Botero offered examples of rulers who had effectively used history in this way, that is, as an instrument of state. One was Charlemagne; another the "King of Siam," possibly the famed thirteenth-century ruler Rama Tibodi, "who, in an effort to inspire his vassals to bear themselves well in war, ordered the deeds of the valorous written in a book and then read to him." As for modern rulers who had made effective use of history, Botero applauded the kings of Portugal, noting specifically that "their achievements have been chronicled by more than one in both the Portuguese and Latin languages." In contrast, Botero emphasized that "the Castilians have failed . . . [in the writing of history], for although they have accomplished feats worthy of the Greeks and Macedonians, crossing great seas, discovering islands and continents, subjugating many countries, and, in sum, acquiring a new world, they have never had these deeds recorded by men worthy of the theme."[5]

It is difficult to determine whether Philip II actually read the *Ragion di stato*, although Antonio de Herrera y Tordesillas, whose Spanish edition of this treatise appeared in 1594, reportedly began his translation at the king's personal request. But even if Philip had not read Botero, and it is unlikely that he did, several of his most influential councillors quickly absorbed many of its lessons, marking the start of what Xavier Gil Pujol has aptly called "the generation that read Botero," although it should also be said that this same generation read Lipsius as well.[6] But these Spaniards were not alone. Botero's and Lipsius's call for histories relating directly to the political needs of princes reverberated across much of Europe and served as an important catalyst for what is often known as "politic history," a subject addressed in Chapter 6.

In Spain, one of the first to call for this kind of history was Juan López de Velasco, then serving in the double office of *cronista y cosmógrafo mayor de las Indias*. Writing around 1591, Velasco advised the king to sponsor the writing of his own history, or what we might call a biography. He warned of the dangers of allowing the king's history to be written by foreigners, especially those ill-disposed toward Spain. In addition, he conceived of this history as something Philip could, and should, use to protect his reputation. In keeping, moreover, with the Lipsian notion of "light deceit," he further suggested that the author of this history might find it necessary to suppress certain information that was not in the monarchy's best interest. "In effect," Velasco wrote, "there are things that history, as it should, can and must be silent about. This [history] is a suitable means for discrediting

---

5. Ibid., 190.
6. For Spanish interest in Botero, see Gil Pujol, "Las fuerzas del rey." Translation from Lipsius in Lipsius, *Sixe Books of Politickes*, 40.

and undoing false rumors by manifesting the truth, while also leaving unwritten others that might not be advisable to be known."[7]

"That might not be advisable to be known" smacked of Machiavelli and his "pernicious" doctrine of "reason of state." It also suggested that Philip integrate dissimulation, another suspicious practice, into the management of his monarchy's affairs. Yet López de Velasco, who is otherwise not known for his political views, went even further: he suggested that the king resort to the subterfuge of publicly announcing the writing of such a history while secretly ordering it not to be written. However, should Philip elect to proceed with this history, he strongly recommended that the history be published both in Castilian and in Latin so that it could reach an audience outside Spain itself.

López de Velasco was not the only royal official urging Philip II to promote an official history of his reign. In 1592 the powerful committee known as the Junta Grande (and, more sinisterly, as the Junta de Noche, or Junta of the Night)—its members included Juan de Idiáquez, Cristóbal de Moura, and the count of Chinchón—made a similar recommendation:

> The time has come for Your Majesty to consider how necessary it is, both for your royal service and the truth of recent important happenings and events as well as those occurring today, for these things to be written about carefully in a history, based on truthful reports derived from the papers belonging to the ministers through whose hands most of this business has passed. This information should then be communicated to the person or persons selected to write this history. All this should be done slowly and with the careful attention it deserves, knowing that Your Majesty will be well-served if it is written properly.[8]

In offering such advice, the junta's members were fully cognizant of the many challenges confronting the monarchy, both at home and abroad. To begin with, the king was aging; Philip turned sixty in 1587. More importantly, the king's health was increasingly precarious, and as recently as 1585 he had been so ill that many feared he would die. Compounding this problem was the monarchy's perceived weakness. The war against the Dutch rebels in the Netherlands, begun in 1566, had deteriorated into a long and increasingly costly war of attrition. Victory was nowhere in sight, especially following the loss of the Armada in 1588. News from the Indies was hardly better, as the Council of the Indies debated how to prevent repetition of the damaging raids commanded by Drake against Spain's

---

7. ABZ: Altamira Ms. D 107, 2v. My translation follows that of Portuondo, "Secret Science," 200.
8. ABZ: carpeta 160n54, consulta, 30 January 1592. This the same document in which Philip agreed to appoint Garibay cronista del rey.

Caribbean ports during the summer and fall of 1587. The monarchy remained a colossus, but seemingly one with feet of clay, unable to defend itself, whether at home or in the New World.

The junta members also offered their recommendation for a new official history with the knowledge that the king's personal reputation was under direct and sustained attack from various enemies, both foreign and domestic. The first to mount such an attack, at least publicly, was William, prince of Orange, the Dutch nobleman whose support for the Dutch rebels led Philip II to declare him an outlaw and order his death. Orange responded in kind. His famous *Apologie*, written in 1580 and published the following year, compared the Spanish monarch to the emperor Tiberius, the archetypical tyrant accused of having murdered members of his own family for political gain. Orange thus implicated Philip in the deaths of both his French wife, Elisabeth de Valois, and his "own son and heir," don Carlos. He also criticized Philip for both personal failings—adultery and illegitimate children—and political shortcomings, notably his failure to respect the laws and privileges of the Low Countries, all in an effort to convince "the kings and rulers of the Christian world" of the illegality of Philip's actions against him.[9]

The impact of Orange's accusations was immediate. Translated into several languages and reprinted in various versions, the *Apologie* circulated widely throughout Europe, especially in Protestant areas, where it acted as a catalyst, sparking dozens of other libels and polemics that defamed Philip and Spaniards in general. It also led to more serious works, among them Louis Mayerne de Tourquet's *Histoire general de l'Espagne*, which was published in Paris in 1587. The work of a Huguenot staunchly opposed to Philip II's intervention in the French Wars of Religion, this history formed part of the growing body of anti-Spanish literature that has come to be known as the Black Legend. It follows that Mayerne, far from trumpeting the monarch's successes, claimed that Philip was little more than a bloodthirsty monarch guilty of unspeakable crimes.[10]

Criticism of Philip also mounted back at home, as his seemingly endless wars

9. William of Orange, *Apologie*, 44, where Philip is referred to as "an incestuous King, the slayer of his son, and the murderer of his wife." This rumor is attributed both to Louis de Foix, a French engineer in the service of Isabella de Valois, and to Pierre de Bourdielle, seigneur de Brantôme, who, during his stay at the Spanish court in 1564–1565, described Philip as a Machiavellian fanatic, a monarch prepared to sacrifice everything, his own son included, for the interests of the Catholic Church. Brantôme's diatribe against Philip was not published until 1651, however. See Brantôme, *Oeuvres complètes*, 71–99. Most modern scholars believe that Philip never committed the murders attributed to him by Mayerne, but the mystery surrounding the death of don Carlos has been rekindled by the appearance of Moreno Espinosa, *Don Carlos*. The abundant literature on the Black Legend may be approached through Maltby, *The Black Legend in England*; and García Carcel, *La leyenda negra*.

10. See Mayerne, *General Historie of Spain*, 1286.

in the north of Europe drained Castile's economy of much-needed resources, including gold and silver, which was arriving in record amounts from the mines in Mexico and Peru. To make up for the shortfall, Philip raised taxes, provoking additional complaints. Already in 1580 one prominent Jesuit, in a private letter sent to the inquisitor general, expressed alarm that many of the king's vassals were "embittered, discontented and upset with His Majesty."[11] In the decade that followed, the number of such individuals multiplied as a succession of street prophets openly asserted that Philip was personally responsible for the kingdom's multiple problems, both at home and abroad. The defeat of the Invincible Armada in 1588, followed by Drake's raids in Galicia and in Portugal the succeeding year, made it even easier for critics to represent Philip as old and weak, a monarch so feeble that he was unable to look after the welfare of his vassals, let alone defend them against armed attack.[12] Philip's reputation probably hit bottom in 1591, a year marked by antitax riots in both Avila and Madrid, as well as the so-called "alteraciones de Aragón," a more serious upheaval triggered by the arrest of Philip's fugitive secretary, Antonio Pérez, in Zaragoza. As is well known, Pérez subsequently escaped to France, where he published his *Relaciones,* a scurrilous, anti-Philippine polemic that served to further undermine Philip's reputation as a historical actor.[13]

Under the circumstances, with both the king's person and his policies at risk, his future reputation, his *fama,* in jeopardy, and the distinct possibility that his "memory" would be the work of his enemies, the Junta Grande had in effect advised Philip that the time had come for him to bolster his "report" by means of a history dedicated to the events of "his time." It is also clear that, without saying so directly, members of the junta saw this history as a strategic necessity at a moment when the kingdom's honor and reputation was under attack.

The first indication that Philip II heeded such advice comes in the form of a letter written in 1599 by Antonio de Herrera y Tordesillas, a historian then serving as cronista mayor de las Indias, the official chronicler of Spain's empire in the New World. The letter records an interview Herrera had in 1585 with Juan de Idiáquez, one of Philip II's closest advisers.[14] In that year Herrera was an aspiring historian in the service of Vespasiano Gonzaga Colonna, Philip's former viceroy

---

11. Pedro de Ribadeneyra to Gaspar de Quiroga, 16 February 1580, as cited in Kamen, *Philip of Spain,* 159.

12. For more on the criticisms of Philip II during the 1580s and 1590s, see my *Lucrecia's Dreams.* See also Domínguez Ortiz, "Un testimonio de protesta social."

13. Pérez, *Relaciones y Cartas.* Copies of Pérez's *Relaciones* quickly arrived in Spain and by the start of the seventeenth century were circulating quite freely in Salamanca and other cities.

14. Antonio de Herrera to don Bernardino de Avellaneda, 22 November 1599. The letter is reproduced in Bouza Álvarez, "Para no olvidar y para hacerlo," 162–163.

in Valencia, and extremely anxious for royal patronage. He recounts how Idiáquez commissioned him to write a "life of His Majesty" but within certain predetermined limits. For one thing, the councillor told him that the king was so "circumspect" that he did not want a "life," that is, a biography. Instead, Idiáquez suggested that Herrera undertake a "general history of the world," and start it in 1559, the year in which Philip concluded a peace treaty with France and began his personal reign in Spain. This kind of history, the councillor explained, was necessary because a number of foreign scholars—he was probably thinking of the Venetian historians Giovanni Battista Adriani and Pietro Giustiniani—had already published histories that did little to promote Spanish interests and, even worse, contained "gossip [that could be used by] rivals of His Majesty and our nation."[15]

The extent to which Philip II involved himself in this project remains uncertain, although, in another letter, also dating from 1599, Herrera reported: "His Majesty ordered me to investigate how one might write about his glorious life, and, after having discussed various possibilities, modesty suggested that it should take the form of a general history of the world, the first part of which would begin in the year 1559 and continue through 1585."[16]

Herrera fails to indicate when this conversation took place, but it can probably be dated to around 1592–1593, when Idiáquez and several of Philip's other counselors were discussing the kind of history that Philip might be persuaded to accept. What is certain is that by 1594 Philip II had not only accepted his councillors' advice about history but had actually begun to do something about it, implementing what was in effect a full-fledged program of history-writing that matched a series of new and increasingly aggressive military efforts intended to preserve the integrity of his empire.

To be honest, this change in policy did not occur overnight. As early as 1571, the king had authorized López de Velasco to begin collecting the materials necessary to write a new, authoritative account of Spain's history in the Indies (see Chapter 5) in an effort to defend the monarchy's record in the New World. Next came his decision to support efforts to write a history of Portugal that legitimated his claims to the kingdom he annexed following the deaths of King Sebastian in 1578 and, two years later, of his successor, Cardinal Enrique. Philip's lawyers argued that he

---

15. The text of the letter is printed ibid., 162. Herrera y Tordesillas was probably thinking of Pietro Giustiniani, *Rerum Venetarum anb urbe condita historia* (Venice, 1560); and Adriani, *Istorie de'suoi tempi*.
16. Letter of 20 April 1600, Herrera to Archduke Albert of Austria, cited in Morel-Fatio, "El cronista Antonio de Herrera," 55–57.

was the rightful heir to that kingdom because his mother, Isabel, was Portuguese. Mindful, however, that Portuguese law, following French practice, customarily excluded descent through the female line, they also claimed that a pledge once made by King Manuel of Portugal paved the way for Philip's eventual succession.[17] Opposition came from the Portuguese pretender, Dom Antonio, prior of Crato, who asserted that the throne was legitimately his, but Philip, backed by a large army, pressed his cause, taking personal possession of the kingdom as Philip I at the Cortes of Tomar in 1581. Dom Antonio initially took refuge in the Azores and subsequently in England, where, with the help of Elizabeth I, he continued to cause trouble for Philip while his supporters continued to write legal treatises attesting to the illegitimacy of Philip's succession.

Philip's lawyers responded in kind, but it was undoubtedly Cristóbal de Moura, the king's personal emissary in Lisbon, who suggested that what the king really needed was a full-fledged history documenting the legitimacy of his succession.[18] Another catalyst for this history was the publication in 1585 of Girolamo Franchi di Conestaggio's *Dell' unione del regno di Portogallo alla corona di Castiglia*.[19] Conestaggio was an independent-minded Genoese historian and a self-proclaimed enemy of "official" history, or what he referred to as "the corrupt writing of the Historiographers."[20] In practice, Conestaggio was not quite the independent observer than he pretended to be, but his history offered a fairly objective account of the manner in which Philip II of Spain became Philip I of Portugal. It suggested, quite rightly, that the annexation had less to do with a legitimate right of succession than with a series of adroit political maneuvers entailing the use of bribery, intimidation, and brute military force, that is, realpolitik worthy of Machiavelli and a style of statecraft that the Catholic Monarch supposedly eschewed. Conestaggio also observed that large segments of the Portuguese population—he especially singled out the women of Lisbon—were "in their hearts" opposed to Spanish rule. On this and related issues, Conestaggio got it right, but this kind of history did not sit well in either Lisbon or Madrid, and Philip, acting upon Moura's advice, responded

17. For this pledge, see Bouza Álvarez, *Portugal no tempo dos Filipes*, 42–48.
18. John H. Elliott has described the Habsburg monarchy as a "composite" monarchy consisting of various kingdoms (Castile, Portugal, Aragon, Naples, Mexico, Peru, etc.), each owing fealty to a single ruler. See Elliott, "A Europe of Composite Monarchies."
19. Conestaggio's history was reprinted (in Italian) in 1589 and again in 1592. It was also translated into French (1596), English (1600), German (1589), and Latin (1603). Luis de Bavia translated it into Spanish in 1610, albeit with changes and emendations that allowed it to pass the king's censors.
20. Citations from Conestaggio, *The Historie of the Uniting of the Kingdom of Portugal to the Crowne of Castile*, 1; and *Dell'unione del regno di Portogallo alla Corona d Castiglia* (Florence, 1642), "al lettore." The only biographical study of Conestaggio that I am aware of is Manuppella, "Girolamo de Franchi Conestaggio." I owe this last reference to the kindness of Fernando Bouza.

with a decree ordering the seizure of this history and prohibiting its circulation in both Portugal and Spain.[21]

Rarely were such confiscations effective, and Moura, well attuned to the political currents in Portugal, understood them for what they were: half measures that would do little to squelch the circulation of potentially subversive ideas. Better to counter these histories with other, "finely-written" histories that would help get Philip's message across. This historical counteroffensive officially began in 1591 when Philip appointed João Bautista Lavanha (1550–1624) *cosmógrafo-mór* of Portugal. Tradition required the cosmógrafo-mór to prepare maps and charts related to the Portuguese *estado da India,* a responsibility for which Lavanha, who was known for his expertise in cartography and mathematics, was ideally equipped. On this occasion, Lavanha's first commission was to prepare a "book of description and history of His Majesty's kingdoms and estates as well as a genealogy of its princes and kings," up to and including Philip I, that is, the king himself.[22] Lavanha completed the genealogy—it exists in the form of several elaborately engraved and printed genealogical "trees" housed in Madrid's National Library—along with several maps, including a detailed "description" of the Kingdom of Portugal, but the history, if ever finished, is now lost.

Philip II's interest in Portuguese history—or, to be more correct, that of his monarchy—did not end with Lavanha. In 1592, the same year in which Mariana's history first appeared, he ordered Francisco de Andrade (ca. 1535–1614), *cronista-mor* in Portugal, to write the chronicles of "dom João [III], dom Sebastian, and dom Enrique," that is, his immediate predecessors on the Portuguese throne.[23] Here too the idea was to strengthen the legitimacy of his claims to the kingdom and demonstrate that Philip II, as Philip I, represented continuity as opposed to dramatic change. The king also commissioned another Portuguese scholar, Duarte Núñes de Lião (1530–1606) to write what became his *Primeira parte das chronicas dos reis de Portugal,* yet another history designed to support the legitimacy of his actions.[24] Another Portuguese historian to receive Philip's support was Frei Bernardo de Brito (1569–1617), whose *Monarchia Lusitana* was prompted, or so Brito claimed, by Juan de Mariana's failure to deal adequately with Portugal's

---

21. Philip II considered giving Conestaggio's history to the Jesuit scholar Giovanni Antonio Viperano for possible emendation and revision, but this plan was dropped upon the advice of Cristóbal de Moura, who warned that "los estilos son como los gestos, y se conoscería luego la diferencia." See ABZ: carpeta 148, fols. 16 and 21, consulta dated 19 September 1589.

22. See BNE: Ms. 11588, for Lavanha's genealogical study of Philip II. For more on Lavanha and his work for the Spanish monarchy, see Kagan, "*Arcana Imperii*."

23. Andrada, *Crónica de D. João III,* xxvi.

24. Núñes de Lião completed this volume, in 1596, but because the subsidy he had asked for, though granted, never arrived, the book was not printed until 1774.

"cousas antiguas" in his general history of Spain.²⁵ Brito, a monk attached to the Benedictine monastery at Alcobaças, published the first part of this history in 1597 and sent a copy to Philip for review. Brito's emphasis on Portuguese antiquity—he began the survey with Adam and Eve—appealed to Philip's personal interest in antiquities but, more importantly, to his notion of himself as Rex Hispaniae, King of the Spains. Philip wrote to Brito ordering him to continue his work, and then to the abbot of Alcobaças asking that Brito be given license to do so. The king's interest in this project also accounts for Brito's subsequent appointment to the office of *cronista-mor* in 1599.²⁶

Yet for all of Philip's efforts to defend himself on the Lusitanian front, still lacking was the comprehensive history his advisers had suggested. Preliminary plans for such a history began as early as 1585, as Herrera's above-mentioned letter suggests. Further steps were taken in 1588, when Philip II issued a new set of ordinances governing the internal operations of the royal archive in Simancas. These ordinances stipulated that Diego de Ayala, the royal archivist, was to prepare a "report on memorable and curious events" ("relación de cosas memorables y curiosas") based on what he found as he inventoried new materials entering into the collection.²⁷ To assist Ayala with this compendium, the king instructed the secretaries attached to the councils of state and of war to supply him, every December, with brief accounts of the important events that had transpired in the course of the preceding year. Yet another indication of the king's growing interest in his own history was his decision, in 1587, to appoint his former tutor Juan Cristóbal Calvete de Estrella to the newly created position of "Latin chronicler," evidently for the purpose of writing annals of a kind that Calvete had previously suggested in 1570; his offer, however, was turned down.²⁸ But now the calculus had changed. Pushed by his councillors, notably Idiáquez and Moura, Philip turned to Calvete with an eye toward reaching an international audience increasingly skeptical about King Philip's policies and designs. Ideally, annals, written in Latin, might help turn this situation around, but Calvete, age sixty-one and ailing, was unable to accept the assignment. Consequently, Idiáquez and Chinchón began a search for another chronicler with the credentials, and the energy, to produce the kind of "finely-written history" recommended by Botero.

Their first candidate was Esteban de Garibay, cronista del rey as of January

---

25. Philip II's letter to Brito, dated 3 April 1597, is included in the front matter in Brito, *Monarchia Lusitana*, vol. 2.

26. Once in this office, Brito published *Elogio dos Reis de Portugal* and the second volume of *Monarchia Lusitana*.

27. Rodríguez de Diego, *Instrucción para el gobierno*, 105.

28. For this appointment, see *Crónicas del Peru*, 164:cxi.

1592. Shortly thereafter, Idiáquez and Chinchón asked Garibay to draft an outline for a planned history of the king. Garibay's *Memorias* notes that he met with the two councillors on 22 September 1593 in Moura's chambers in the Alcázar, Madrid's royal palace:

> Meeting very secretly in the chambers of don Cristóbal, the two councillors told me that I should prepare a document outlining the best way in which His Majesty's history might be written. At the time, I responded with two suggestions. One was a single volume history organized in the commonly accepted and popular annalistic style, that would proceed year by year, starting with that of his birth. The other was a four volume work, in which the first dealt with matters pertaining to Spain; the second for those of the Indies; the third for Flanders and the fourth for Italy. Señor don Cristóbal preferred the second, and they both instructed me to prepare a written outline by the time His Majesty either went to the Pardo [one of Philip's palaces] or came here to Madrid.[29]

What happened next is not entirely clear. On the one hand, according to Idiáquez, the king "heartily approved it [the outline] and was very content." On the other hand, the promised follow-up meeting never occurred. Garibay's *Memorias* indicates that he expected to meet again with Idiáquez and Moura for further discussions. "I waited for the day when I would meet with both of these gentlemen so that together we could review my papers." That day never came. "On account of their being so busy," Garibay writes, "the day kept on being postponed," leading him to admit that Idiáquez and Moura "had, in effect, buried" the project.[30]

But it was not the outline that was buried, but Garibay, at least metaphorically, because the two councillors selected another individual to write the history that Garibay had outlined. As for Garibay, he was essentially relegated to the sidelines and given other projects to occupy his time. The first smacked of make-work, since it entailed little more than the preparation of inscriptions to accompany a series of royal portraits that Philip II had commissioned for the throne room in the royal palace in Segovia. His task: write labels identifying all of the monarchs, giving their regnal dates. Somewhat more challenging was the order to prepare a genealogy of Spain's royal house, a commission that resulted in Garibay's *Illustraciones genealógicas de los Cathólicos reyes de las Españas, y de los Christianíssimos de Francia, y de los Emperadores de Constantinopla, hasta el Cathólico Rey nuestro señor*

---

29. Garibay, *Memorias*, 587–588. A copy of the traça was included among the papers Garibay left behind at his death in 1599. See Antolín, "Inventario de los papeles," 26.

30. Garibay, *Memorias*, 588.

Don Philipe el II, y sus sereníssimos hijos.[31] The orotund title masks the volume's underlying political purpose, which was to represent Philip II as the legitimate descendant of both Charlemagne and the first Christian emperor, Constantine the Great.[32] More immediately, it was intended to provide the historical ammunition necessary to justify Philip II's intervention in France's Wars of Religion and his continuing efforts to depose Henry IV.[33] The genealogy in this respect complemented the actual history of Philip II, which, much to Garibay's regret, was already well under way.

Antonio de Herrera y Tordesillas

The individual entrusted with this history was Antonio de Herrera y Tordesillas (1549–1625), a fledgling historian who just happened to be Juan de Idiáquez's protégé. Herrera proved an excellent choice. A native of Cuellar, a sheep-raising town in the heart of Old Castile, Herrera belonged to an Old Christian family known for its loyalty to the monarch; his grandfather Rodrigo de Tordesillas had been murdered by the *comunero* rebels in Segovia in 1520. Schooled initially in Cuellar, probably in the town's famed municipal college, Herrera furthered his education by traveling to Italy, probably in the company of the lord of Cuellar, Gabriel de la Cueva, duke of Albuquerque, who assumed the office of captain-general and governor of Milan in 1563. Once in Italy, Herrera entered the service of Vespasiano Gonzaga Colonna (1532–1591), a cultured Italian *condottiere* who spent much of his life in the service of Philip II, first as the prince's page of honor, later as a captain fighting alongside the duke of Alba in Naples, and subsequently as viceroy in Navarre (1571–1574) and Valencia (1574–1578) before retiring to Sabionetta, a "new" town (near Mantua) that he built as a model of Renaissance urban planning and design. Exactly how and when Herrera met up with Gonzaga is not

---

31. ABZ: carpeta 160, fol. 54. For Garibay's work in Segovia, see Fernando Collar de Cáceres, introduction to Garibay, *Letreros e insignias reales*, the facsimile of the original 1593 edition. Before publishing this work, Garibay was probably aware of Dr. Antonio Gomez, a professor at Salamanca, who had been working on a "genealogy of the House of Austria" since the early 1580s. Gomez's interest in the subject stemmed from Philip's claims to the Kingdom of Portugal. He was also able to establish, as did Garibay, that Philip's ancestors included Constantine the Great as well as several members of Rome's Colonna family. See ABZ: carpeta 242, fol. 58, Dr. Antonio Gomez, letter dated 4 July 1584.

32. For a list of these genealogies, and Garibay's other papers, see Antolín, "Inventario de los papeles." For Garibay's interest in genealogies, see the critical comments of Antonio de Herrera y Tordesillas cited in Bouza Álvarez, "Guardar papeles," 8. For Garibay's own thoughts about his work as royal chronicler, see his *Memorias*. This work is also available as Garibay y Zamalloa, *Discursos de mi vida*.

33. See Moya, "Garibay, historiador vasco," esp. 173–174, where Garibay appears to have met personally with Philip II to examine these genealogies and discuss the legitimacy of the king's rights to the French throne.

documented, but his firsthand knowledge of Italy, and Sabionetta in particular, suggests that he did so sometime before Gonzaga's journey to Madrid in 1569.[34]

In 1571, now serving as Gonzaga's secretary, Herrera went with Gonzaga to Navarre, where he helped the viceroy with the fortification of Pamplona, accompanied him on at least one secret mission to France, and, carrying certain information to Madrid, once met with Philip II on Gonzaga's behalf. Herrera's experience alongside Gonzaga in Valencia was equally varied: he was quickly embroiled in matters of coastal defense, royal policy involving the *moriscos,* and prickly negotiations with the *jurats* (city councillors) over questions of fraud and governmental reform. Following the Italian's return to Italy, Herrera remained in Gonzaga's employ as his agent at court, a position that offered an introduction to several members of the king's inner circle, Idiáquez in particular.

By 1585, the year of his reported meeting with Idiáquez, Herrera was already writing history, a career for which he seemed ideally suited, given his considerable linguistic skills (knowledge of Latin, French, English, Italian, and Portuguese), administrative experience in matters of both governance and war, and interest in writing about current events. Herrera initially demonstrated his aptitude for this kind of history in his *Cinco libros de la historia de Portugal y la conquista de las islas de los Azores,* a narrative he wrote ca. 1585 in response to dangerous "false histories"—he clearly was thinking of Conestaggio—of this important event. Published belatedly in 1591, this history closely resembled the kind of "official" history that Philip's ministers envisioned in their memorandum of 1592, since Herrera not only defended the legitimacy of Philip's claims to Portugal but offered a triumphal account of the kingdom's annexation that played down the idea of conquest and emphasized the "universal content" that accompanied the king's arrival in Lisbon.[35] Ironically, much of the material Herrera incorporated into his history came directly from the historian he sought to refute: Conestaggio. But he presented it, à la Botero, in ways expressly designed to defend and enhance, rather than tarnish, Philip's reputation. A later critic faulted Herrera for having plagiarized Conestaggio, accusing him of "removing all the good from the Genoese, and taking way from his elegance and ordered style [*policia*]."[36] In any case, Herrera's straightforward, unadorned prose appealed to a king known for his sober

---

34. Herrera's biography remains sketchy. Apart from the information presented in this and the next chapter, he is best approached through Antonio Ballesteros-Beretta's introduction to Antonio de Herrera y Tordesillas, *Historia general de los hechos de los castellanos en las islas i tierra firme del mar oceano* (Madrid, 1934); and the capsule biography included in Cuesta Domingo, *Antonio de Herrera y su obra,* 40–46. See also Pérez Pastor, *Noticias y documentos,* 1:144–148.

35. Herrera y Tordesillas, *Cinco libros de la historia de Portugal,* bk. 4, p. 151.

36. Cabrera de Córdoba, *Historia de Felipe II,* 3:1142.

style and avoidance of what one of his officials called "superfluous things."[37] At the same time, however, Philip remained deeply interested in anything that served to enhance his "authority," and this is precisely what Herrera had set out to achieve.

Herrera did much the same in his next book, a history that examined events in England and Scotland during the era of Mary Stuart, Queen of Scots (1553–1588). This blatantly partisan work was another counterhistory, one meant in this case to challenge George Buchanan's recent *Rerum Scoticarum Historia*, a rabidly anti-Catholic work that cast Mary, Queen of Scots, as a wrathful tyrant determined to impose Roman Catholicism on an unwilling kingdom in violation of the people's wishes and rights.[38] Herrera responded by describing Buchanan as "a great heretic . . . and the falsest, most lying historian in the world."[39] He also maintained that his own history would reveal the "truth" about Mary's history and how this honest, pious queen was mistreated and then brutally executed by Elizabeth I. For Herrera, Elizabeth was a "monster," a ruler whose "diabolic fervor" made her the modern, female equivalent of Diomedes, king of Thrace, who taught his horses to eat human flesh but who was eventually vanquished by Hercules. Herrera reconfigured this myth into contemporary politics by proclaiming: "This Hercules will be the invincible Philip II, king of Spain."[40]

Published in the wake of the Armada's defeat, such pronouncements were mostly hot air, but by invoking King's Philip's God-given right to invade England and free its people from the yoke of a cruel and impious tyrant, Herrera invoked the time-honored image of Spain's monarchs as champions of the faith, a message tailored to win the favor of both the king and his councillors. Adding further to his credentials was his translation of Botero's *Ragion de stato* and of a polemical French pamphlet advising that the only way to deal with heretics was through "force." It further suggested that the future of Catholicism in France was at risk unless Philip II intervened militarily to prevent the accession of Henry of Navarre to the French throne.[41]

---

37. See AGI: Secretaria: leg. 5, 1, 18, letter of Diego de Ayala, 15 September 1567, which hints at both his and the king's preference for "lo necesario" as opposed to "cosas superfluas." Ayala was head of the royal archive in Simancas.

38. Buchanan's *Rerum Scoticarum Historia* was initially published (in London) in 1582. It is worth noting that Buchanan's antipathy toward Roman Catholicism came partly from his arrest by the Portuguese Inquisition in Coimbra in 1550 and subsequent imprisonment in a Benedictine monastery in Lisbon. Released in 1551, he left Portugal the following year.

39. Herrera y Tordesillas, *Historia de lo sucedido en Escocia y Inglaterra*, prologue. Herrera pointedly dedicated this book to the count of Chinchón, a powerful member of Philip's Council of State.

40. Ibid., 171.

41. Herrera's translation of this polemic, supposedly sent by English Catholics to their brethren in France, was published as *Advertencias que los catolicos de Inglaterra escrivieron a los Católicos de Francia, tocantes a las presentes reboluciones, y cerco de Paris*.

The translation of the pamphlet served as a prelude to Herrera's next book: a full-fledged history of the French wars of religion, which he completed around 1596, claiming that the king had specifically ordered him to write it.[42] Herrera's history of these wars was none too original, as it was based mainly on secondhand sources.[43] But he went out of his way to flatter Philip II as "the first prince of Christendom" and offered an extended defense of the king's decision to intervene in the conflict, with the claim that he had done so only reluctantly and because of his "sincere and zealous wish to protect the Catholic religion."[44] Herrera offered similar arguments in his other histories (these included works on Milan [1598], Turkey [1598], and Flanders [1600])[45] and then in his impressive general history of the Indies, a protracted defense of Spain's imperium in the New World that Philip II personally encouraged him to write (see Chapter 5).[46] Herrera's finger, it seems, was in every historical pie. One can get a sense of what he was up to, and how he was thought of, from the following memorandum, part of Herrera's bid for the office of cronista mayor de las Indias, dating from 1596:

> He [Herrera] translated [Minadoi's] *History of Persia*, wrote one about Scotland, and translated what the English Catholics wrote to the French, "*Açote de los políticos y el cerco de Paris*," [Botero's] *Reason of State*; he wrote the *History of Portugal* and has written a general history that covers twenty-seven years of the current time—a work commissioned by the Council of Castile; he is also known to have finished writing about the French civil war from 1585 until the end of 1594 that proves that Your Majesty assisted the Catholics only in order to protect the faith.[47]

---

42. Herrera y Tordesillas, *Historia de los sucesos de Francia*, prologue, where Herrera writes: "He [the king] ordered me to write about happenings in France." The monarchy purposely delayed publication and distribution of this book for two years so as not to alienate Henry IV in the wake of the Peace of Vervins, the treaty that ended hostilities between the two kingdoms. See Morel-Fatio, "El cronista Antonio de Herrera," 55–57.

43. For the early years of this conflict, Herrera seemingly relied on Mendoza, *Comentarios de don Bernardino de Mendoza*. Other sources may have included Laval's virulent anti-Protestant history, *L'historical des rois non-catholiques*; and Guadalajara, *Historia de la rebelión y guerras de Flandes*.

44. Herrera y Tordesillas, *Historia de los sucesos de Francia*, prologue and 353.

45. Titles include Herrera y Tordesillas, *Información en hecho y relación de lo que pasó a Milan*; Minadoi, *Historia de la guerra entre Turcos y Persianos* (a translation by Herrera); and *Comentarios de las alteraciones de Flandes*.

46. I refer to Herrera y Tordesillas, *HGI*. See the 1991 edition by Mariano Cuesta Domingo. A document dated 12 February 1596 describing this book is printed in Vicente Maroto and Piñeiro, *Aspectos de la ciencia aplicada*, 131–132.

47. AGI IG: leg. 743, fol. 209, consulta of 12 February 1596. The other candidates for this post were Esteban de Garibay and Lupercio Leonardo de Argensola, an Aragonese poet and historian then working on a history of the Molucas. The consulta indicated that the king was to select the candidate he preferred, granting him an annual salary of 400 ducats. Philip II selected Herrera, albeit with the provision, scribbled in his own hand, "dexando lo q tiene por el aposento, sino lo ha dexado ya."

The last line says it all. Small wonder then that Garibay was "buried" and his outline of the king's history given to Herrera; Herrera was precisely the kind of official historian that members of the Junta Grande had recommended to the king.

How to Write the History of Philip II?

As this memorandum suggests, by 1596 Herrera was busy with several histories, including one referred to as the "general history that covers twenty-seven years of the current time," roughly the opening decades of King Philip's reign. As it developed, however, this history owed much to Garibay and to the outline, or *traça*, he was asked to prepare. This document merits close attention because it not only allows us to "deconstruct" the history that Herrera was about to write but offers, in remarkable detail, fascinating insights into the thought and planning that went into an official history of this sort.

The traça opened with an exordium, "The principal utility of history," in which Garibay, in an effort to persuade the king of the importance of history, emphasized that

> Each of the world's monarchies, kingdoms, and republics, especially those governed with prudence and good laws, tries to perpetuate its praiseworthy deeds. They do so through history, as it, given the fragility of memory, is the most durable means of preserving a record of these events both for the example and instruction of future centuries, and as reward for those who, owing to their virtue, have done them. They do so [write these histories] in recognition that lessons of history are important both for good government and for the conduct of human affairs, because without such histories, people live in darkness and perpetual ignorance, and because history is the witness of time, life of the memory, teacher of human life, and messenger of antiquity, as Cicero says in the book of *De oratore*, affirming that those who ignore the past will forever remain as a child. This same author rightly affirms that just as iron is necessary for war, history is essential for governance, because memory of past events is knowledge for those yet to come.[48]

Expanding on this theme, Garibay noted how one churchman—Giovio, perhaps?—persuaded Charles V that it was necessary to record "in perpetual memory the glories of the deeds he had done." Echoing both Lipsius and Botero, he then

---

48. The entire text of the traça is available in the appendix of Kagan, *El Rey Recatado*.

wrote that princes had a particular responsibility not to leave their "illustrious deeds... hidden in obscurity." Next, using words tailored specifically to appeal to Philip's modesty and to help him overcome his reservations about history, Garibay asserted that "he who desires divine glory, should not despise human glory, which is both a testimonial and a reward for his illustrious deeds, since the authority of history has always been regarded as venerable and sacrosanct. Sallust, the classical Roman historian, argued this point very well in the prologue of his work, noting that man's life is brief, but as he is superior to other animals, he should make certain that it does not pass in silence."

The next section, getting down to details, addressed the "composition of this history." Here Garibay anticipated Cabrera de Córdoba's notion of "legitimate and perfect history" by insisting that Philip's history should be based solely upon original documents because only these "contain the purity of truth."[49] But Garibay also recognized that "truth" in history was a relative matter and that different nations would necessarily have different interpretations of the causes of war, rebellion, and other important events. This recognition accounts for his next recommendation: "that, with assistance from the Inquisitor General, histories written by secretaries of the kingdoms and provinces of the apostates be brought here and read, in order to better respond to their calumnies and evil objections." He was especially interested in reading those written by Dutch rebels, "because enemies inside one's house are far worse than those outside it." In other words, Philip's official historian should be given the opportunity to review what other historians, the avowed enemies of the monarchy, had written. By definition, histories written by heretics were "calumnies," whereas Philip's history, drawing upon the king's own papers, necessarily lined up with the facts.

The traça next outlines the "notable things" this history was to address. Arranged chronologically—Garibay's word is "epilogamente"—starting in 1527, the year of Philip's birth, this year-by-year outline ends in 1574, although elsewhere the document states that the account of the reign was to continue until "this year, 1593," a discrepancy that is left unexplained. The "notable things" consist of the usual round of royal births, marriages, and deaths, both Spanish and foreign; the election of emperors and popes; wars, treaties, important discoveries; and the like. Before 1558, most of these "things" deal with Charles V, and references to Philip are few. The year 1527 corresponds to "His Majesty's birth and baptism," 1528 to "the oath of fealty to His Majesty as heir and prince." Philip then disappears, reappearing in 1543 with references to such events as "The beginning of

---

49. Cabrera de Córdoba, *De historia*, 28.

His Majesty's regency in these kingdoms" and "His Majesty's first marriage, with the princess Doña María, infanta de Portugal." After 1559, the year in which Philip assumed full control of the monarchy, the traça deals primarily with Philip, but the emphasis, probably out deference to the king's reservations about biography, is less on his "life" than upon the great events corresponding to his reign. The short entries for 1567 are fairly typical of the rest. They include

> the duke of Alba's trip with the Army of Flanders;
> Señor Don Juan de Austria, general of the Mediterranean Sea;
> the birth of the Señora infanta Doña Catalina;
> the imprisonment of Mary, Queen of Scots, by her vassals; and
> Queen Elizabeth of England's public rupture of the peace.

One rationale for including such a broad spectrum of information was, as Garibay later explained, that "many will be interested, and quite rightly so, in the history of the greatest king in the world, especially his family members and other relatives." Clearly, he was planning a history meant to appeal not just to Castile but to the king's subjects in other parts of the monarchy, including Aragon, Portugal, Flanders, and other regions.

What follows is perhaps the most interesting part of the traça. Here Garibay explains that this history can be written in one of two ways. The first option is to write it in strict chronological fashion, starting in 1527. Such an organization, he explains, "is the most common and used by authors from a variety of different nations and places," as well as the one most readers would prefer, providing them with both "satisfaction and delight." The second option is to divide the history into "four tomes or parts, corresponding to the four principal parts" of the monarchy: Spain, Italy, Flanders, and the East and West Indies." Such an organization, Garibay asserted, would be necessarily "longer" because it would inevitably entail some overlap and repetition, but as he explained, if written in this way "the work will be more agreeable to each nation, as each will find there its own distinct and separate part, and for everyone it will be universally easier either to read or hear, as they go to the part that they like the most." According to Garibay, this second option was more unusual—more "extraordinaria" in his language—and also one that would require "more work." However, in a reference pointing to Philip's participation in the project, he suggested that the king himself should decide which option he preferred: "His Majesty should elect the one that pleases him the most."

Whichever organization Philip selected—and ultimately, he chose option two —Garibay recognized that the history would be divided into books, then chapters, and finally into paragraphs accompanied by explanatory marginal notes. Then, again depending on which of the two options "His Majesty decides to chose," every chapter would include a section on "material relating to the governance of the kingdoms, as this will be of great importance for the instruction and understanding of future centuries," and another on military issues, "since arms are the way of exercising reason and justice against tyrants, and usurpers who take what is not their own." An obvious lacuna here was material relating to church history, a lacuna that is all the more surprising given the importance that Philip accorded to matters of faith. Garibay drew attention to the monarch's attention to religion in other parts of the projected history (see below), but in keeping with the general tenets of humanist historiography, as he envisioned it, Philip's history was to focus on matters of both governance and war.

After these generalities, Garibay got down to specifics. Following an introductory section devoted to the emperor, he wanted Philip's history to begin with a detailed physical description of Philip, "describing, quite literally, the physiognomy of his face and body, along with his great virtues, internal and external actions, and done as rapidly yet as substantially as possible." In addition, he wanted to include an engraved portrait of Philip, arguing that histories that include such images are read "with greater affection and attention" than those that do not. With these recommendations, Garibay revealed his hand: his notion of Philip's history was teetering on the edge of biography. Furthermore, in keeping with the humanist concept of history as a didactic genre, he wanted to include a list of Philip's virtues in order to represent him as the ideal prince. The list is lengthy but hardly original; many of the virtues Garibay associates with Philip are identical with those outlined in "mirrors of princes." Thus, in an effort to demonstrate Philip's piety, he includes such items as

—"his singular and admirable constancy . . . in the conservation, defense, and augmentation of the Holy Catholic Faith" and
—"his admirable determination to expurgate errors [of faith] from his kingdoms, by always supporting and assisting the Holy and General Council of the Inquisition."

Then, in an effort to represent Philip as a monarch who attended to the needs of his vassals, Garibay underscored the following:

—"his continual and indefatigable dedication to the dispatch of the affairs of state";
—"his perpetual attention to distributive justice, and to the affairs of his coun-

cils, from the supreme Council of State to the lowliest court or governorship, from the most worthy individuals to . . ."; and
—"his exemplary temperance, and royal meekness, gracefully granting audiences to his subjects as well as foreigners."

Next came Philip's personal attributes, many of which were little more than literary topoi. This list includes:

—"his royal liberality";
—"in private chambers . . . religion and silence [reigned] . . . as in a most secluded monastic life"; and
—"his great temperance in dress, his extraordinary sobriety in eating and drinking."

More original and somewhat more particular to Philip was Garibay's decision to include in this somewhat standard catalog of princely virtues the king's "public works," among them

—"his enormous determination . . . to rid his kingdoms of old and ugly buildings and to replace them with architecture done with art and perfection, as is evident in the house of Saint Lorenzo el real, and the other buildings that derive from it [here the traça lists various palaces, hunting lodges, etc.]";
—"the new fortification he has had constructed in Spain, such as the very beautiful citadel of Pamplona [this item was almost certainly added by Herrera]";
—"the reconstruction of the beautiful and agreeable plaza of Valladolid, after it was destroyed by fire. . . . It has no equal in the rest of Europe"; and
—"the notable present augmentation of the *villa* of Madrid, which has served for thirty-two years as his royal court, and which he has made into one of the great cities of Spain."

Garibay concludes that together, "these attributes, all of which derive from His Majesty's royal person . . . [offer] irrefutable witnesses to the truth, and have nothing to do with affection, adulation, or artifice, and thus render manifest to the readers the integrity of the author's full integrity."

Yet for all the emphasis on "royal person," Garibay was fully aware, given the monarch's antipathy to biography, that this history needed to be *historia pro patria* in the broadest sense of the term. It would therefore require multiple actors, individuals representative of the kingdom as a whole: archbishops and bishops, the presidents and members of the royal councils, viceroys and ambassadors, and those deputies of the Cortes who "with great willingness" had provided the king with the money necessary "for his many extraordinary expenditures in defense of the Holy Faith." Garibay's definition of the kingdom even extended to "distinguished men of letters," along with "famous professors," an addition that would draw attention to Philip as a *rey sabio* or patron of learning. Nevertheless, Garibay wanted the emphasis in this part of the history to be reserved, in traditional fashion, for "famous noblemen and valiant captains, and others who profess arms, and who, through both wise counsel and great deeds, zeal, magnanimity, and constancy, serve their king, and in doing so exemplify that notable refrain, 'For your law, and for your king, and for yourself, you shall die' ('Por tu ley, y por tu Rey, y por lo tuyo morirás')." He then added, in what is perhaps the most evocative prose in the entire document, that the section on the military affairs was to include references to defeats as well as victories: "Here the fortuitous events. Here the adverse ones. Here the vicissitudes and inconstancies of human affairs. Here the clash of arms. Here the rivalries among generous souls, who put honors before their lives. Here the truces and cease-fires. Here the return to war. Here the peace, its conditions, and the persons who made them." "This kind of material," Garibay concluded, "will ultimately be the most copious and longest of the entire work, because its argument is much, much more important than all the rest." As we shall see, Herrera, in writing the history that grew out of this traça, took this particular recommendation seriously, cognizant, no doubt, of Philip's continuing reservations about history itself.

Historia General del mundo . . . en la época de Felipe II, el prudente . . .

As noted, the memorandum recommending Herrera for the office of cronista mayor de las Indias indicated that by 1596 he had already completed the first twenty-seven years of a history of Philip's reign. By 1598 he managed to bring the story forward to 1580, and it was in December of that year, three months after the king's death, that the royal council of Castile granted him the license he needed to publish this history, which appeared in three hefty volumes starting in 1601.[50]

This history, as its title suggests, was less biography than history. It also differed in several important respects from the history previously outlined by Garibay, whose initial plan conceived of a narrative beginning with the year of Philip's birth, 1527. Herrera omitted Philip's early years and began his history in 1554,

---

50. Antonio de Herrera y Tordesillas, *HGM*, part 1. Subsequent installments appeared in 1606 and in 1612.

when the prince journeyed to England to marry Mary Tudor and was proclaimed king of England. "From this point on," Herrera informed his readers, "I will begin to write what happened in the world since this prince assumed the title of king."[51]

The geographical scope of Herrera's history also differed from the one the traça outlined. Garibay's proposed that the history examine the four major parts of the Spanish monarchy: Spain, Italy, Flanders, and the Indies, whereas Herrera's history was, as announced in the title, to be a "general history," a term synonymous with universal or world history. Herrera's conception of world history, however, was decidedly different from that of his nemesis, Sir Walter Ralegh, who organized his *Historie of the World* (1614) in chronological order and aimed at demonstrating the guiding hand of Providence in human affairs.[52] In contrast, Herrera's starting point was geography, and in keeping with the vast expanses of Philip's empire, his world history aimed at recounting events that occurred in Asia, Africa, Europe, and America during the course of King Philip's reign. Herrera in this respect reached far beyond the boundaries of the Spanish monarchy, but in order to write such a history, he opted for the first, and evidently the easier, of Garibay's organizational options, that is, a history written as a single, continuous narrative. Herrera thus divided the *Historia general* into books, each dedicated to an individual year. The books were then divided into chapters focused on a particular geographical region: Spain, England, France, Flanders, Germany, Poland, Muscovy, Turkey, and, further afield, the Indies, both east and west. This global span allowed Herrera to boast that he was the "first Spaniard to write a general history of the world."[53]

Working on such a broad canvas, Herrera's world history—together with later iterations of this genre—was necessarily superficial and derivative, because he garnered much of his information from such works as Giovanni Botero's *Le relationi vniversali* (1595) together with various books on the history of China and Ottoman Turkey.[54] Yet in an effort to provide readers with greater insight into

---

51. *HGM*, 1:5.

52. I refer to Walter Ralegh, *Historie of the World* (London, 1614). Raleigh had finished only the first part of this history when he was executed in 1618.

53. *HGM*, vol. 2, dedicatory letter, dated 25 February 1606, to Juan de Zúñiga, count of Miranda. Had he been less vain, Herrera might have referred to Isidore of Seville's *Etymologies* or Román, *Repúblicas del Mundo*, a work whose chronological and geographical scope surpassed that of the *Historia general*. Although it fails to make note of Herrera's history, world histories of his era may be approached through Subrahmanyam, "On World Historians in the Sixteenth Century."

54. Apart from Botero, it is likely that Herrera's sources included Campana, *Compendio histórico* (1597); González de Mendoza's *Historia . . . de China*; and Giovanni Tommaso Minadoi's *Historia della gverra*. With respect to Campana, it appears that this author based his *Vita del . . . Filippo Secondo di Austria* on Herrera's world history.

events of particular importance, Herrera regularly interrupted his broad-brushed, somewhat annalistic narrative to include the equivalent of a "particular history," that is, monographic accounts of certain events that he conceived of as signal moments, or turning points, in Philip's reign. Among them were the Piemontese war between France and Spain that culminated with Spanish victory at St. Quentin in 1556, the Battle of Lepanto in 1571, the revolt of the Granadine Moriscos (1567–1569), Spain's conquest of Portugal (1580–1581), the Invincible Armada (1588), Antonio Pérez and the Aragonese rebellion (1590–1591), and in the last chapter of the third volume, the king's final moments on earth in September 1598. Furthermore, as the subjects of these minihistories suggests, Herrera tended to give his global history something of a tilt toward events and personalities in Spain itself. Here the emphasis was, as Garibay's traça suggested, upon those individuals who had distinguished themselves for their service to the monarchy, either in war—the duke of Alba merited particular attention as the ideal captain-general—or in government.

Whatever the book's strengths and weaknesses, Herrera's decision to present Philip's history in global terms was commensurate with the monarch's doubts about the appropriateness of the project as a whole. On the one hand, it allowed Herrera to draw attention away from Philip's person, clearly an emphasis that the king would have vetoed. On the other, it allowed Herrera to represent Philip as the fulcrum of his age, the monarch around whom the world revolved, both literally and figuratively. It follows that Herrera, in his effort to separate Philip's history from his biography, dropped Garibay's suggestion that the narrative begin with a detailed physical description of the king and the idea of including a portrait of Philip in his text. The king, in fact, appears only as a somewhat disembodied "royal person" except in the final chapter, which was written long after Philip's death. There Herrera referred to the king's "extraordinary humanity" and "incomparable humility," but otherwise he avoided mentioned of the many virtues—piety, constancy, study, moderation—Garibay had previously associated with Philip.

Another way of looking at Herrera's decision to steer clear of biography would be to examine the *Historia general* from the perspective of the well-known medieval doctrine of the "king's two bodies," the first being the king's earthly body, the second the mystical or political body. Viewed in this way, Philip "the man" scarcely appears in the *Historia general*. The emphasis is rather upon his "political body" as represented by his "royal majesty,"[55] a strategy evidently designed to

---

55. *HGM*, 3:286. For this concept, see Ernst H. Kantorowicz, *The King's Two Bodies: A Study in Medieval Political Theology* (Princeton, NJ, 1957).

appeal to Philip's sensibilities but also one that permitted Herrera to make occasional, albeit rather abstract, references to Philip as an ideal king: a true Catholic monarch ("rey católico") who defends what he believes is the One True Faith in the pursuit of both "peace and tranquility."[56] The king also appears as a ruler whose support for such projects as Giovanni Battista Antonelli's 1566 attempt to navigate the Tagus River from Toledo to Lisbon and open the heart of Castile to oceanic trade reflected his "grandeur of spirit and interest in his subjects' welfare." He is also a prince "inclined to follow the opinion of his councillors" as well as one whose actions depended more on "law" than personal whim ("alvedrio").[57]

Herrera's efforts to portray Philip solely in terms of his "political body" also fit with his decision to refer to the king in the book's title as "the prudent," the name by which Philip II is still known today. Herrera had originally suggested the use of this sobriquet for Philip in a memorandum he prepared for Philip III shortly after his father's death. The others he suggested—"the religious," "the composed," "the good," "the honest," "the just," "the devout," "the modest"—were apt, but in differing ways they referred more to the king's personal attributes, that is, his earthly body. In contrast, "the prudent" fit with Lipsius's (and Mariana's) definition of prudence as the highest and most dignified of the cardinal virtues. It also served, for princes at least, as a symbol of good governance and just rule. In this respect, the choice of "el prudente" was wholly consistent with Herrera's efforts to avoid Philip's "life" and put "royal majesty" in its place.

Herrera's emphasis on the broad political and religious dimensions of Philip's reign is also important because it reveals something about the way in which Philip himself wanted his history to be written. Evidence for this assertion comes from a letter that Herrera addressed to the governor of the Spanish Netherlands, Archduke Albert of Austria, complaining about some of the problems surrounding the publication of his history of recent events in France.[58] Herrera also touched upon the forthcoming publication of the *Historia general*, specifically making note of the conversation he had had with Philip II about the project in 1585. On that occasion, Herrera informed the archduke, "His Majesty ordered me that I should consider writing about his glorious life, and after several exchanges, it seemed in keeping with modesty that I should do so in form of a general history of the world that began in 1559 and ended in 1585.[59] If Herrera's recollections are correct, Philip not only took an early interest in this history but also determined

56. *HGM*, 1:253.
57. *HGM*, 3:71, 286.
58. See note 42.
59. Herrera as cited in Morel-Fatio, "El cronista Antonio de Herrera," 55–57.

that it would quite different from the king-centered *historia pro persona* so favored by his father. Rather, it was to be a work consistent with *historia pro patria*, like the broader national chronicles he had long encouraged his earlier chroniclers to write. Herrera does not say so directly, but in many respects the *Historia general* represented a continuation of Alfonso X's efforts to set Spain's national achievements—the *fechos de Espanna*—on a global, truly imperial scale. It follows that Herrera dedicated the *Historia general* not to the person of the monarch but to the "glory of this nation," with nation defined less in terms of territory than as an abstract spiritual entity whose members had united to defend the Catholic faith. Herrera expressed similar sentiments deep in the third and final volume of this massive work, which only appeared in 1612. There he claimed that he especially enjoyed writing this history because it offered him "the opportunity to devote so much space to the Spanish nation, because when I see what foreign historians say about it, besides the fact that they rarely agree among themselves, they tend to magnify the importance of their own but treat those of the Spaniards only half-heartedly, highlighting their failures, either because of lack of information, or some other reason."[60] At this point, Herrera changes his train of thought, although he clearly meant to say that the foreign historians were motivated by hostility to the Spaniards' religion, jealousy of their power, or some combination of the two.

In making this statement, Herrera was clearly expressing some of his own deeply felt patriotism, a patriotism that oscillated regularly between Castile and Spain. In his history of Portugal, for example, he proudly announced "I am a Castilian," and in his other histories he often claimed that he wrote in defense of the reputation of the "Castilian nation." Yet, as already noted, Herrera also wrote in defense of "Spain," a term he equated with the monarchy and the empire over which it ruled. Herrera's apparent ambivalence about this issue, that is, the tension between Castile, narrowly construed, and Spain and the broader monarchy, is apparent throughout his work. But were such thoughts, such ambivalences, exclusively Herrera's? Or can they also serve as tunnels into the mind of the circumspect king, clues to the way in which Philip II justified the many histories that he apparently enjoined Herrera to write? The answers to these questions are difficult, but it appears that Philip, for reasons connected either to his own sense of modesty or, at the very least, to a strategy that would allow him to avoid accusations of *vanitas*, had collapsed the line separating *historia pro persona* from *historia pro patria*, in effect linking his personal reputation to that of the united

60. HGM, 1:722.

Hispania over which he ruled. In this respect, Herrera's world history fulfilled Alfonso X's original goal of setting Spain's imperium on a truly global stage. It would, of course, be left to Philip's descendants, the later Habsburgs, to defend that imperium and maintain it intact, but in the meantime, Herrera y Tordesillas had other assignments, starting with the official history of the Indies that Philip had personally commissioned him to write.

CHAPTER FIVE

Defending *Imperium*

> The historian's job is not to make either gold or silver, but to work it and polish it, narrating events in a clear, organized manner.... The historian's proper task ... is to decide where his history is to begin, then those things he will address, and those he will suppress.... Secrecy has its advantages, especially for those who govern.
> —Antonio de Herrera y Tordesillas

On or around May 24, 1596, having had just learned of his appointment as cronista mayor de las Indias, an office dedicated to writing the history of Spain's empire in the Indies, Antonio de Herrera y Tordesillas made the two-day trek from Madrid to San Lorenzo de El Escorial in order to meet with Spain's aging monarch, Philip II. The previous chronicler, Juan López de Velasco, who doubled as royal cosmographer of the Indies, had done little to advance this history, and it was apparently to encourage Herrera to get on with this assignment that the king summoned his new chronicler to El Escorial. As later reported by Herrera, in the course of their conversation the king offered the following remark: "Juan López [de Velasco, the previous chronicler] was not able to attend to this history [of the Indies] because he was preoccupied with navigational [geographical?] matters. You will do it, and make certain to demonstrate that the Catholic Kings [Spain's monarchs] have complied with the bull of the Pope [Alexander VI], also that this nation is much defamed by foreigners with cruelty and avarice as result of omissions by its governors. You must investigate this, always making certain to tell the truth."[1]

If this statement is at all an accurate reflection of what Philip actually said, as

---

Epigraph: Antonio de Herrera y Tordesillas, "Discurso sobre los provechos de la historia que cosa es y de quantas maneras, del officio del historiador y de como se ha de inquirir la fe y verdad de la historia y como ha de escribir," BNE: Ms. 3011, fols. 142, 147; *HGI* 3:230 (decade V, bk. 3, chap. 4).

1. AGI IG, leg. 752. See also Herrera y Tordesillas, *Historia general* (1991), 3:604 (decade VI, bk. 3, chap. 19), where Herrera notes that Philip I "me mandó escribir esta General Historia."

opposed to what Herrera later wrote, the king had a clear and succinct idea about the kind of history he wanted his new chronicler to write: nothing, it seems, about the customs and practices of America's natives, although these were topics that Herrera did in fact address. Instead, Philip envisioned a straightforward political narrative that would clear the Spanish monarchy of responsibility for any abuses that had occurred during the conquest and settlement of the Indies. This history would also emphasize that the monarchy had fulfilled all the obligations imposed by the Alexandrine Bulls of Donation, which had granted dominion over the Indies to the Catholic Monarchs with the proviso that they attend to the conversion of its inhabitants to Christianity. Finally, the king charged Herrera to write only the truth, which, as then understood, meant offering the documentary proofs necessary to demonstrate that the charges foreigners (read Protestants like Richard Hakluyt and Theodore de Bry) had leveled against Spain were unjustified, unsubstantiated, and patently false. Herrera, in short, was to write a history expressly designed to defend Spain's, and the monarchy's, imperium in the New World.

The Cronista Mayor de las Indias

Created by royal decree in October 1571, the office Herrera assumed required its incumbent to write the "general history of all of its provinces [in the Indies] as well as the particular histories of individual ones with the greatest precision and truth that is possible."[2] It was further stipulated that this chronicler had to do more than provide an annalistic account of happenings in the New World. Rather, in keeping with the work of such influential historians as Francesco Guicciardini and the dictates of the *ars historicae* genre, he was also to reflect on the causes of events and the motives underlying individual actions and include, for didactic reasons, *exemplae* of various sorts. Finally, the cronista mayor had to write a comprehensive history, one that incorporated both the natural history of the Indies and its "moral" (or human) history with special emphasis upon Spain's progress in "civilizing" the Indies in terms of both government and religion.

It happened that at the moment when this office was created, the idea that Spaniards had done anything positive in the Indies was a matter of international dispute. Spain's title to the Indies rested on the Bulls of Donation, which were

---

2. *Recopilación de leyes*, vol. 1, título 12, fol. 318, "Del coronista mayor de las Indias." The classic study of the history of this office is Carbia, *La crónica oficial de las Indias Occidentales*. An excellent discussion of the task of the cosmógrafo/cronista mayor de las Indias may be found in Portuondo, "Secret Science."

granted by Pope Alexander VI to Ferdinand and Isabella in 1493. Modeled on those previously awarded to the kings of Portugal following their "discoveries" in Africa, these bulls, starting with *Inter caetera,* granted the monarchy sovereignty (imperium) over the Indies providing that it attend to the conversion of its natives to Christianity. This concession proved controversial. John III of Portugal challenged it on the grounds that the parts of the Indies the papacy had granted to Spain encroached on those that were legitimately his, a complaint that led in 1494 to the famous Line of Demarcation, which effectively granted Portugal sovereignty over what is now Brazil and granted the rest of the Americas, north and south, to Spain. Europe's other powers, especially England and France, also contested this division and demonstrated their dissatisfaction by sending their own expeditions off on voyages of discovery and exploration to the New World. A half century later Protestants challenged Spain's monopoly on the grounds that the Bulls of Donation were, *ab initio,* illegitimate. They also maintained that Spain's record of cruelty toward America's natives deprived the Spaniards of whatever titles to the Indies they possessed by right of conquest and discovery. Such, for example, was the position of Richard Hakluyt (the elder), one of the first advocates of an English empire in North America, who expressed his views on the subject in his "Discourse on Western Planting," a treatise that he prepared to enjoin Queen Elizabeth I to embark on the creation of colonies in North America. By the late sixteenth century, the Dutch, then in open revolt against Spain, employed similar arguments to justify their trading voyages to the Americas, soon adding, with help from the great legal scholar Hugo Grotius, others predicated on the doctrine of "open seas."

Yet the challenge to Spain's title to the Americas was by no means limited to its Atlantic rivals or to debates over the legitimacy of the papal bulls of donation. Equally pressing was the question of whether sovereignty (imperium) carried with it certain property rights (*dominium rerum*), notably the right to exploit the region's land and natural resources, together with the labor of its inhabitants. As Anthony Pagden and others have explained, the debate over this issue began early in the sixteenth century but heated up during the 1540s after the Salamanca theologian Francisco Vitoria and his pupil Melchor Cano questioned the papacy's right to grant the Spanish monarchy temporal jurisdiction over the Indies, let alone the power to dispossess its inhabitants, whom they defined as "natural lords" of their land.[3] Juan Ginés de Sepúlveda, the emperor's chronicler, re-

---

3. Anthony Pagden, "Dispossessing the Barbarian: Rights and Property in Spanish America," in his *Spanish Imperialism,* 13–36.

sponded to Vitoria in his treatise *Democrates segundus,* where he vigorously defended the papal donation together with the monarchy's rights to expropriate the natives, defined as "natural slaves," and consequently make use of their labor.

Closely related to this controversy was another spawned by the *encomiendas,* the legal instruments that granted the labor services of a specified number of natives to individual conquistadors. Starting already in the 1490s, the grants led to untold abuses as individual *encomenderos* (holders of encomiendas) treated the natives as slaves. The debate over these abuses began in 1511, when Antonio de Montesinos, a Dominican friar resident in Hispaniola, preached about the immorality of the encomienda in a church filled with encomenderos. It gathered steam during the 1530s as Fray Bartolomé de Las Casas, a former conquistador who became the self-proclaimed champion of native rights, condemned the institution in ever more forceful terms. As part of this debate, Las Casas drafted his *Brevísima relación de la destrucción de las Indias* (*Short Account of the Destruction of the Indies*), a fiery polemic meant to enlighten the monarchy about the "excesses" that encomiendas had engendered and to portray the encomenderos as a bunch of murderous thugs who, as he put it, had become "so anaesthetized to human suffering by their own greed and ambition that they had ceased to be men in any meaningful sense of the term."[4] Thanks to Las Casas, the New Laws of the Indies, promulgated in 1542, did place some curbs on the encomiendas, although the restrictions were partially rescinded in 1545 following revolts by outraged encomenderos in both New Spain and Peru. But Las Casas continued to press the issue, arranging to have the *Brevísima* and its relentless catalog of Spanish atrocities in the New World printed, albeit clandestinely and without an official license, in Seville in 1552.

Adding to the monarchy's difficulties was the failure of existing histories of the Indies to contradict Las Casas or even demonstrate that the monarchy was in compliance with *Inter caetera* and the other Alexandrine bulls. Peter Martyr, the first of Spain's royal chroniclers to write about the New World, only raised the subject of Spanish efforts to convert natives to Christianity in the final chapter of *De orbe novo* (printed posthumously in 1530), and then only in passing.[5] Nor did Martyr do anything to hide his disappointment with those Spaniards who had treated the natives in particularly cruel or harsh ways.[6] The chronicler's openness

---

4. Casas, *A Short Account,* 3.
5. See Mártir de Anglería, *Décadas,* 540, where he makes passing reference to the conversion of the natives following the 1524 arrival in New Spain of eight Franciscan missionaries.
6. Martyr was especially critical of Juan de Ayora, one of the captains who accompanied Pedro Arías Dávila to Central America in 1514: "[Era] más codicioso de oro que de hacer bien las cosas o de merecer alabanza. Aprovechando ocasión contra los caciques, despojó a muchos, y contra derecho y justicia; les

on this issue suggested that Las Casas was more right than wrong.⁷ In addition, with statements such as "It was gold they kept watch for, gold they constantly pursued," Martyr conveyed the impression that the Spaniards were far less interested in religion than in riches and enabled such later Protestant readers as Hakluyt to opine that Spain's record in the Indies was little more than a narrative of "avarice, ambition, butchery, rapine, debauchery, their cruelty towards defenseless and harmless peoples."⁸

Gonzalo Fernández de Oviedo's *Historia General y Natural de las Indias* (1535–1550) was read in much the same way. As noted earlier, Oviedo began this history in the expectation that it would help pave the way to the office of royal chronicler, a position he craved. Such an appointment seemed around the corner when, in 1532, the emperor granted him a small subsidy to continue with his history, together with access to official correspondence relating to the Indies. Oviedo subsequently used this privilege to proclaim that his history, which was based partly upon his personal experiences and other eyewitness accounts, was far more "authoritative" than other "historiales" motivated primarily by "passions," which "did not deserve to be heard"—a not altogether transparent reference to Martyr's *De orbe novo*.⁹

An enormously complicated work that Oviedo wrote, rewrote, expanded, and revised over the course of almost thirty years, the *Historia general* defies easy description. Given his failure to secure an official appointment as royal chronicler or financial support in the form of a subsidy, Oviedo had difficulty getting his history into print.¹⁰ The first part, which essentially dealt with Hispaniola and the Caribbean, came off the presses of the famous Sevillian printer Juan Cromberger in 1535. The book's publication was a stupendous achievement, since it was arguably the first history of the Indies by an author who could rightfully claim to have been an eyewitness to many of the events that he narrated. It was also the first history of the Indies written in Castilian, a language that Oviedo, echoing Nebrija, celebrated as "the best of the vulgar languages" and a vehicle that would do justice to what he proudly described in one letter as "an honorable history, one that is

---

sacó oro y les trató cruelmente, según cuentan." Ibid., 242. Ayora's brother Gonzalo was a royal chronicler in King Ferdinand's employ.

7. Ibid., 197.

8. Hakluyt, *Dedication of Peter Martyr*, 1:364. Hakluyt was referring to Richard Eden's English translation of Martyrs's *Decades*, published in 1552.

9. Fernández de Oviedo, *Historia general*, 118:319. Oviedo made equally critical remarks about Martyr in his memoirs. See *Las memorias de Gonzalo Fernández de Oviedo*, 1:301.

10. The complicated organization and publishing history of the *Historia general* is best examined in Carrillo Castillo, "The *Historia general y natural de las Indias*." See also Carrillo Castillo, *Naturaleza e imperio*.

much desired all over the world and very worthy of being known."[11] In addition, Oviedo offered some of the first reliable descriptions of New World flora and fauna, together with details about native customs and religious practices. Small wonder, then, that the French cosmographer André Thevet had nothing but admiration for the *Historia general* and praised its author for having rendered "the conquest easy [to grasp]."[12]

Yet Oviedo had his own critics, none more vitriolic than Las Casas, who claimed that the *Historia general* contained "as many lies as pages." Las Casas's criticisms derived both from personal differences between the two writers and from Oviedo's determination to represent the conquest of the Indies as the culmination of "Spain's glorious chronicle," an epic of unalloyed triumph that far surpassed any of those attributed to the ancient Romans or Greeks.[13] Las Casas also disparaged Oviedo's credentials as a historian, criticizing, for example, his "presumption and arrogance in thinking that he knew anything when he had no inkling of Latin even though he cites authorities in that language."[14] Also at issue was Oviedo's decision, announced in the book's preface, that his history would not discuss any topic related to *gobernación,* that is, the administration and governance of the New World. Why Oviedo made this announcement is not entirely clear, but at the very least it provided him with an excuse to avoid such hot-button issues as the encomiendas along with the countless abuses that Las Casas attributed to the encomenderos, of whom Oviedo was one.

This decision did not serve Oviedo well, especially in Spain, where, in addition to Las Casas, other chroniclers were also engaged in writing the history of the New World. To begin with, Oviedo's studious avoidance of *gobernación* meant that the *Historia general* made no reference to the monarchy's ongoing efforts to rein in the excesses of the conquistadors and bring order, justice, and religion to the New World; this silence did not sit well with Las Casas's allies on the Council of the Indies, the governing body especially created by Charles V to oversee the governance of his dominions in the New World. Neither did the council take to Oviedo's habit of repeatedly referring to America's natives as "barbarians, "savages," and "wild beasts"; these were terms totally at odds with its own efforts to

---

11. Fernández de Oviedo, *Historia general,* 117:10. My translation follows that of G. F. Dille; cf. Fernández de Oviedo, *Writing from the Edge of the World,* 21. For Oviedo's letter to La Gasca dated 3 January 1550, see Carrillo Castillo, "The *Historia general y natural de las Indias,*" 328.

12. André Thevet, *Cosmographie universelle* (1575), as cited in Pagden, *Lords of all the World,* 32.

13. For Oviedo's comparisons between the Spanish and the ancient empires, the Romans in particular, see Lupher, *Romans in a New World,* 19–31.

14. My translation follows that of G. F. Dille in Fernández de Oviedo, *Writing from the Edge of the World,* 21. As Dille points out, Las Casas ordinarily wrote in Latin but, following Oviedo's example, elected to write his *Historia de las Indias* in the vernacular.

support Francisco de Vitoria's contention that America's natives were human beings entitled to all of the protections offered by natural law. On one level Oviedo understood that these issues, especially that of Spanish mistreatment of the Indians, were far too important to be ignored, but he massaged them with arguments borrowed from Juan Ginés de Sepúlveda, the leading apologist for Spain's empire in the New World. The *Historia general* thus blamed the Indians for their own sufferings, especially for their "crimes and abominable customs and rites."[15]

If Oviedo believed that his position on this and related issues would improve his standing at court, possibly leading to an appointment as cronista del rey, he was clearly mistaken. For one thing, he misjudged the extent to which the emperor, together with the Council of the Indies, had accepted the fundamental logic of Las Casas's arguments, especially those relating to the evils that encomiendas had spawned. That acceptance led, in 1542, to the New Laws of the Indies, a code expressly intended to protect native rights. Four years later, it figured directly in the council's decision to deny Oviedo the license he needed to publish the second part of the *Historia general*, which focused on Venezuela and New Spain. The council soon reversed this decision but, once again, failed to provide Oviedo any kind of financial assistance to help with the publication of a work that, in revised form, had mushroomed in both size and complexity. At this point, publication of the *Historia general* ground to a halt. Oviedo, who had been residing in Spain since 1546, left a copy of his manuscript with a friend in Seville before returning to Hispaniola. Subsequently, he made one last-ditch attempt to print the whole of his history, but his efforts resulted only in a truncated (and unillustrated) edition that included revisions of part 1 of the history and portions of part 2.

Historians have written at length about the reasons for Oviedo's failure to print the whole of parts 2 and 3 (part 3 was to deal with both the Philippines and Peru) of his history—a complete (although unillustrated) version did not appear until 1851. Traditionally, blame for the book's delayed publication has gone to Las Casas, his personal vendetta against Oviedo, and his success in convincing the Council of the Indies that Oviedo's history of the Indies was fundamentally flawed owing to its failure to condemn the encomenderos and the sufferings they caused. There is certainly some justification in this argument, inasmuch as the council was definitely in sympathy with Las Casas on this issue and mindful of Oviedo's decision to ignore the topic of *gobernación*. More recently, Jesús Carrillo has suggested that while Las Casas was important in determining the outcome of

---

15. Fernández de Oviedo, *Historia general*, 117:111, proemio to bk. 3.

Oviedo's book, financial considerations played their part too, since Oviedo failed to secure the money necessary to get his book into print.

What is forgotten in this discussion is the extent to which Prince Philip and his ideas about history are likely to have delayed the publication of an expanded version of Oviedo's book. To begin with, we know that Oviedo, in making his revisions, had labored diligently to incorporate updated geographical information pertaining to the Indies. In addition to maps and charts by his own hand, he included (in part 2, book 21) a detailed description of the entire Atlantic coast, from Labrador in the north to the Straits of Magellan in the south, and (in part 3) a wholly original account of the Pacific coast of South America that was based partly upon his own experience and partly on maps and charts he had obtained from cosmographers and pilots attached to Seville's House of Trade. As the *proemio* to part 3 of the history makes clear, Oviedo took pride in these descriptions; he considered them important both for the advancement of knowledge concerning the Indies and for helping to satisfy Emperor Charles V's interest in New World geography.[16] Yet as he made these additions, Oviedo was seemingly unaware that the historical and geographical interests of Prince Philip were far different from those of his father. Nor did he recognize that, starting already in the 1550s, Philip, together with the Council of the Indies, had already begun to classify detailed geographical information pertaining to the Indies as state secrets best kept under lock and key (for more on this policy, see below, "Juan López de Velasco"). Precise documentation is lacking, but growing awareness of the potential risks contained in the dissemination of knowledge relating to the Indies, coupled with this failure to address the issues Las Casas had raised, seemingly joined forces to doom publication of a complete version Oviedo's revised manuscript, especially those sections (part 2, book 21, and part 3) that contained what was considered sensitive geographical information. It was thought better for the Council of the Indies to take control of Oviedo's manuscripts and to support other New World chroniclers whose histories the monarchy could promote as its own. So it was that in November 1563 the Council of the Indies ordered Antonio Gascó, the inquisitor who had been watching over Oviedo's papers in Seville since 1549, to remit to Madrid "the manuscripts of Gonzalo Fernández de Oviedo . . . that relate to the Indies."[17]

---

16. Ibid., 120:336–338. Oviedo's description of the Pacific coast of South America appears in the chapters that follow. A complete illustrated edition of the *Historia general* remains an important desideratum, but in Myers, *Fernández de Oviedo's Chronicle of America*, one can get a sense of some of the cartographic material that Oviedo included. See also Turner, "Forgotten Treasure from the Indies."

17. In 1549, before returning to the Indies, Oviedo left a copy of the completed manuscript with Andrés Gasco, an inquisitor in Seville, for review. In 1563 Gasco was ordered to submit this manuscript

The imbroglio triggered by Oviedo's manuscripts proved something of an embarrassment, but it did little to prevent the Council of the Indies from remaining on the lookout for other chroniclers prepared to defend the legitimacy of the monarchy's presence in the New World. One such individual was Francisco López de Gómara (1512–1572), a humanist-trained clergyman who, starting in 1541, served as both the chaplain and the secretary of Hernán Cortés. Using information derived from his employer and other veterans of the conquest of Mexico, Gómara began work on the *Historia general de las Indias y conquista de México* well before Cortés's death in 1547. He subsequently continued the history with support from the conquistador's son Martín Cortés, who evidently expected that Gómara's history, which was to include an encomium of his father, would convince the emperor to restore certain privileges that he had granted his father at the time of conquest but later revoked. Gómara did tailor his history to puff up the accomplishments of Cortés (see below). Gómara had his own ambitions, however, and a recently discovered letter he directed to Cardinal Granvelle indicates that he expected his history to receive official recognition and lead to an appointment as "coronista de las Indias" and a regular salary.[18]

The extent to which Gómara's aspirations to become royal chronicler colored the content of his history remain unknown, but they do help to explain his efforts to legitimate the monarchy's presence in the New World on spiritual grounds, a topic that Oviedo had pointedly failed to address. Gómara moved this topic to the very beginning of his *Historia general*, which opens with the famous sentence announcing that the discovery of America was the most important event in world history since the death of Christ. And in contrast with Oviedo, who avoided the subject of evangelization, Gómara emphasized that Spain's discovery and conquest of the Indies was but part of a providential plan to further the spread of Christianity. He substantiated this assertion by reproducing (in Spanish translation) the complete text of *Inter caetera* and devoting several pages to the missionary activities of the Franciscans in New Spain in an effort to prove that the monarchy, notwithstanding the complaints of Las Casas and other critics, was fully in compliance with the requirements of this bull.[19]

If Gómara's search for the office of royal chronicler colored the contents of his

---

to the Council of the Indies in Madrid. He did not do so, however, until 1566. For this incident, see Wagner, "Legajos y otras aficiones del inquisidor Andrés Gascó," 160.

18. Gómara to Cardinal Granvelle, 20 November 1552. Gómara also had the marquis of Oaxaca, Martín Cortés, the conquistador's son, write to the cardinal in support of this request. See *Avisos de la Biblioteca Real de Madrid*. For the place of Cortés in Gómara's history, see Carman, "The Voices of the Conquerer."

19. López de Gómara, *Historia de la conquista*, 484–486.

history, his plan, like those of others who harbored similar ambitions, quickly went awry. First printed in 1551, the *Historia general* was a phenomenal commercial success, appearing in nine editions in less than two years. However, the book provoked controversy from the start. One sore point was the manner in which Gómara lionized Cortés, his former employer, at the expense of Francisco Pizarro, conqueror of Peru. A close look at Gómara's text reveals that he organized the history in Manichean terms, casting Cortés as the good conquistador—the noble knight fighting "a good and just war,"[20] the eloquent orator who lectured his soldiers on the evils of idolatry and human sacrifice, the prudent captain who tried, though unsuccessfully, to prevent his soldiers from torturing Cuauhtémoc as they searched for Aztec gold—and Pizarro, who appears as an unlettered captain, just as greedy and avaricious as his men, as the bad. Similarly, Gómara, again in keeping with his efforts to rescue the honors the emperor formerly invested on Cortés, represented the conquest of Mexico as a noble battle, fought with bravery against a courageous and worthy foe, and depicted that of Peru, starting with Pizarro's one-sided victory at Cajamarca, as little more than an ambush that deteriorated rapidly into a wildcat search for treasure and gold. "Never," observed Gómara, commenting on the search of Pizarro's army for Inca gold, "had soldiers enriched themselves so much, and in so short a time, and with so little danger [to themselves]."[21]

Today we know that Gómara's account of what happened at Cajamarca is essentially correct, but at the time soldiers who fought alongside Pizarro took it as an insult, and at least one of them openly criticized Gómara for having misrepresented what happened at that battle.[22] From the Crown's perspective, however, the principal shortcoming of Gómara's history, the one that almost certainly explains why he failed to obtain the office he sought, was his decidedly dark account of the civil wars that erupted in Peru starting in 1536. In Gómara's telling, Peru was violent and chaotic, a world dominated by "evil and avarice," a place where men killed "with justice and without justice, and simply to get rich."[23] Again, we now know that Gómara's description conforms with what today's historians tell us about the murderous state of Peru during the 1540s and 1550s, but at the time it

---

20. López de Gómara, *Historia general*, 2:58.
21. Ibid., 1:177.
22. For this incident, see Garcilaso de la Vega in *Royal Commentaries of the Incas*, 2:1206. Gómara defended himself by claiming that the fault in this instance lay with those soldiers who had provided him with biased accounts. The soldier replied that "a historian's judgement was intended precisely for such cases, and he should either not get his reports from such people, or not write at length without considering at length, so as not to defame those who deserve all honor and praise in his writings."
23. López de Gómara, *Historia general*, 1:277.

was diametrically opposed to the rosier view of the Indies that both the monarchy and the Council of the Indies sought to convey. More directly, it prompted Pedro de la Gasca, one of the royal officials the emperor had dispatched to end the violence in Peru, to complain that Gómara, lacking accurate information, had published a "deceitful" account of what had transpired in Peru.[24] These complaints subsequently figured in the royal order, issued by Prince Philip in November 1553, prohibiting further sale and distribution of Gómara's book.[25] Even then, Gómara's history appeared in two clandestine editions, and these illegal printings, together with the unlicensed publication of Las Casas's *Brevísima* in 1552, contributed to yet another royal decree, promulgated in 1556, ordering printers in both Spain and the Indies not to publish, and booksellers not to distribute or sell, any book dealing with "cossas de las nuestras Indias" unless first inspected and approved by the Council of the Indies.[26]

These measures underscore the inability of the Habsburg monarchy to control the manner in which its history, in this case that of its accomplishments in the New World, was to be read. But as Philip II soon discovered, this particular problem soon went from bad to worse. The clandestine editions of Gómara's history and the *Brevísima* had taught Prince Philip an important lesson: the inability of his administration to prevent publication of books it did not approve within the territorial confines of his realm. On top of this he learned that he was completely powerless to prevent the publication of such works in regions beyond his control. Consider, for example, the publication record of Gómara's history. Though banned in Spain, the *Historia general*, starting with its appearance in Italian in 1556, quickly became an international best seller, with ten editions published in Italian, nine in French, and two in English in the sixteenth century alone. By 1600 Gómara's history was so widely read that it served, almost by default, as the official history of the Spanish New World.[27] At the same time, it was a history that Philip, despite all his power, was unable to suppress.

Even more worrisome for Philip was the runaway success of the *Brevísima*. Following its clandestine publication in Seville in 1552, the treatise appeared in Dutch translation (in 1568) and subsequently in French, German, Latin, and English. Today's readers are prepared to engage the *Brevísima* as an imaginative

24. *Documentos relativos a Pedro de la Gasca*, 1:68, reproduces the text of a letter dated Palencia, 23 July 1553, that La Gasca wrote to Guillermo Mallinco, in which he remarked that "otras cosas también hay en Gómara engaño, por haberle mal informado."
25. For possible reasons for this ban, see Bataillon, "Hernán Cortés." For a recent analysis of this controversy, see Lupher, *Romans in a New World*.
26. Philip II promulgated this decree on 21 September 1556. It was reissued in 1560, suggesting it had had little effect. See León Pinelo, *Recopilación de las Indias*, 1:329.
27. For these editions, see López de Gómara, *Historia general*, 1:xiii.

and impassioned polemic that used the standard rhetorical devices of hyperbole and repetition to argue an important point, but in the sixteenth century this treatise, coming as it did from the pen of a Spanish friar with personal experience in the Indies, had the ring of accuracy because it appeared as a true, faithful eyewitness account of events in the New World. In the hands of Spain's enemies, especially the Dutch, the *Brevísima* morphed into a powerful weapon, one that provided just the ammunition they needed: first, it served to document the failure of Spain's monarchy to live up to the dictates of the Alexandrine bulls, and second, it helped them drum up support for their nascent revolt against Philip II by suggesting that their countrymen would soon suffer from the kind of cruelties that Spaniards had wreaked upon the Amerindians.[28] The influence of the *Brevísima* was even felt in far-off Peru, where one cleric, writing in 1573, warned that books by Las Casas were already in "the hands of nations who are enemies of the Church, and all of them defame the Christian nation, and among the Christians, the Spaniards as cruel thieves and tyrants who have usurped and claimed lands they have no right to possess."[29]

As this cleric rightly surmised, the *Brevísima* had opened the historiographical equivalent of Pandora's box, inspiring writers ill-disposed to Spain's monarchy to write their own, generally negative histories of Spain's record in the New World.[30] Among the first to do so was the Venetian merchant Girolamo Benzoni (1519–c. 1570), whose *Historia del Mondo Nuovo* pointedly emphasized Spain's lackluster attempts at conversion.[31] Initially published in 1565, Benzoni's history, translated into numerous languages, was a key text in the emergence of the famous Black Legend and the facile description of Spaniards as a people prone to cruelty, religious bigotry, and hate.[32] Hard on its heels was Nicolas Le Challeux's *Discours de l'histoire de la Floride* (1566), a book whose wholly sensationalist account of Spain's destruction of a Huguenot colony in Florida appears to have been lifted directly from the pages of Las Casas.

Put simply, with histories like those of Benzoni and Le Challeux enjoying wide circulation, and the *Brevísima* rapidly etching its way into Europe's *imaginaire*, Philip II's ministers determined that the king needed a new and authoritative history, a counterhistory, that would not only legitimate the monarchy's title to the

28. For the place of Las Casas in Dutch propaganda, see Schmidt, *Innocence Abroad*.
29. This letter, dated 17 March 1573, is printed in *Codoin* 13:425–469. See esp. 439–443.
30. See, for example, Richard Hakluyt's "preface to the reader" in his *Principal Navigations*, where he refers to the "fame-thirsty and gold-thirsty mindes" of both the Spanish and Portuguese. Cited in Hakluyt, *Original Writings and Correspondence*, 1:436.
31. For its publishing history, see the introduction to Benzoni, *La historia del nuevo mundo*.
32. I refer to Theodore De Bry, *Collectionem peregrinationum in Indiam* (Frankfurt, 1590), a compilation completed (by De Bry's son) in 1601.

Americas but also establish that the accounts by Benzoni, Le Challeux, and other like-minded authors were slanderous accounts lacking any basis in fact.[33] The first of Philip's ministers to make such a recommendation was Juan de Ovando, a cleric who assumed the office of president of the Council of the Indies in 1571. Philip's initial reaction to the prospect of supporting such a history was almost predictable, since at this moment he still harbored doubts about the need, and indeed the propriety, of any history relating to "cosas de nuestro tiempo." But in October 1571, in conjunction with his efforts to reform the governance of the Indies, Ovando succeeded in convincing Philip that good government required not only good history but also full command over the geographical information the Council of the Indies needed to do its job. He thus recommended that the king create a new office, to be known as the *cronista y cosmógrafo mayor de las Indias,* whose incumbent, in addition to safeguarding the relevant geographical data, would write about the "important and memorable deeds" of Spaniards in the New World.[34] On this occasion the king acquiesced, but in light of his checkered experience with other historians, he remained reluctant to give the new cosmographer-cum-chronicler the freedom to work independently and to write whatever he wished. Thus, the royal decree announcing the creation of this office stipulated that the resulting history would be a collective enterprise involving the chronicler, the official responsible for fabricating the history; a historical "commissary" to be selected from among the members of the Council of the Indies and whose job was to censor and review whatever the new chronicler wrote; and finally the Council of the Indies, whose members were empowered to determine whether the completed chronicle actually merited publication. The arrangement was cumbersome, destined almost to fail, yet also one that underscored the importance that Philip II accorded to the history of Spain's accomplishments in the New World.

Juan López de Velasco

The first to be named to the double office of cronista y cosmógrafo mayor de las Indias was Juan López de Velasco (1530–1598). A humanist by training, Velasco first evinced an interest in the Americas in 1560, when he published a Castilian grammar meant to help missionaries in their ongoing efforts to catechize the

---

33. A possible model for this history was Alejo Fernández's *Virgen de los Mareantes,* an "official" painting that visualized the creation of Spain in wholly Christian terms. Executed ca. 1538, this painting hung in the chapel of Seville's Casa de Contratación. Cf. Philips, "Visualizing *Imperium.*"
34. Cited in Casas, *Historia de las Indias,* lii.

region's indigenous inhabitants.³⁵ More importantly, he had served as Juan de Ovando's personal secretary since the early 1560s, and starting in 1567 he not only had helped Ovando with the official inspection (or *visita*) of the activities of the Council of the Indies but also had drafted several reports about the way in which the Indies were being managed. In the end, however, the key to his appointment as chronicler-cum-cosmographer was his close personal relationship with Philip II. For reasons not immediately apparent in the documents, Velasco had succeeded in gaining the monarch's trust.

Velasco's first assignment was to collect and organize existing materials, both geographical and historical, relating to the New World. This roundup was partly predicated on the need to assemble materials that Velasco would require for the history and description of the Indies that he was commissioned to write, but it also was connected to Philip II's habit of restricting circulation of any information pertaining to the Indies that might prove prejudicial to the interests of the Crown. Paranoia? Perhaps. But Philip's determination to keep a lid on the Indies had its roots in administrative practices that dated back to the fifteenth century and the efforts of both Spanish and Portuguese rulers to regard maps, charts, and other navigational materials as *arcana imperii*, state secrets best stored in a locked box or, at the very least, what Peter Martyr once referred to as "la cartera de los secretos," or the "notebook of secrets."³⁶ In this instance, the documentary roundup began in 1573, when Philip II learned that unpublished portions of Pedro Cieza de León's history of Peru were in the possession of an inquisitor in Seville. Cieza had published the first part of this history in 1553, and it was feared, quite rightly, that his other manuscripts, one of which dealt with civil wars in Peru, might prove an embarrassment to the Crown. Philip consequently ordered royal officials to take possession of these papers and forward them to the Council of the Indies with "diligence and speed."³⁷

Similar reasoning accounts for the decision in 1575 to order the sequestering of all of books and papers belonging to Fray Bernardino de Sahagún, the Franciscan friar who had gathered a wealth of information about the religious rites and practices of the natives in New Spain. At the time, Sahagún had practically finished his *History of the Things of New Spain*, but the king, along with Velasco,

---

35. I refer to López de Velasco, *Ortografía y pronunciación castellana*. For more on Velasco as a humanist, see Redondo, "Exaltación de España"; and Berthe, "Juan López de Velasco." See also Portuondo, *Secret Science*, 142–171.
36. Mártir de Anglería, *Décadas*, 41. For more on this policy of secrecy as it applied to the Indies, see Baudot, *Utopia and History in Mexico*, 505–518; Kagan, *Urban Images of the Hispanic World*, 74–76; and Kagan, "Arcana Imperii."
37. For the council's confiscation of Cieza's papers, see Cieza de León, *Obras completas*, 1, 39, 50–52.

worried that publication of this manuscript might serve to reacquaint natives with practices that the missionaries were attempting to suppress. Therefore the king ordered his viceroy to seize all of Sahagún's papers and forward them as quickly as possible to Spain for safekeeping in the library of the Escorial.

Next on the king's—and Velasco's—hit list of potentially subversive papers were the unpublished works of Las Casas, especially the friar's *Historia general del Nuevo Mundo*, which, not surprisingly, included a critique of Spanish treatment of natives in the Indies. In 1559, almost seven years before his death in 1566, Las Casas deposited the manuscript of this history, together with his other papers, in Valladolid's Colegio de San Gregorio, a Dominican house. He also wrote a will instructing the executors of his will not to allow any "secular person" access to the history for "forty years," at which time they had permission to publish it "for the glory of God and the manifestation of truth." For twenty years Las Casas's manuscripts remained undisturbed, but in 1579, as part of the general crackdown on information pertaining to the Americas, Philip II issued a decree ordering the cronista mayor "to keep secret the books of Las Casas" and to have these "books" brought to Madrid and handed over to the Council of the Indies for safekeeping.[38]

More difficult to explain is why Philip accorded similar treatment to the papers of his own chronicler, Juan Ginés de Sepúlveda, one of the staunchest defenders of Spain's empire in the New World. Following Sepúlveda's death in Córdoba in 1573, the king ordered his papers, including the manuscript of his important New World history, *De Rebus Hispanorum Gestis Ad Novum Orbem*, to be brought to Madrid. The history was far from complete, as it ended with the capture of Tenochtitlan in 1521, but Sepúlveda, echoing ideas previously expressed in his *Democrates alter*, had peppered the narrative with arguments supporting his contention that the natives' idolatry, human sacrifices, and other sins constituted violations of natural law, thus legitimating the Spanish conquest of the New World. Similarly, Sepúlveda's history emphasized the humanitarianism of the Spaniards and the determined efforts of their "friars and priests" to "civilize" the natives and to convert them to Christianity.[39] Such arguments were precisely those one would have expected to find in an official history of the Spanish New World. For this reason, the royal confessor Fray Bernardo de Fresneda urged Philip to authorize the printing of this history on the grounds that it would help to refute the charges brought against Spain by Las Casas and other authors. The king, however, thought otherwise and ordered that this history, together with

---

38. Kagan, "Arcana Imperii," 58.

39. Sepúlveda, *Obras completas*, vol. 11, *Del Nuevo Mundo*, translated by Luis Rivero García, bk. 2.6, p. 68.

Sepúlveda's manuscripts, be forwarded to the Council of the Indies for safekeeping. Presumably, Philip had determined that it would be better to incorporate Sepúlveda's arguments into the general history he had entrusted to his cronista mayor than to publish them on their own.[40]

The idea of granting the cronista mayor sole jurisdiction over the history of the Americas reflected the statist mentality that had pervaded Spain's New World empire since the time of Columbus. This monopoly also accounts for the reluctance of the monarchy to sanction the publication of any New World history that did not flow directly from López de Velasco's quill. Typical was the treatment accorded Pedro Sarmiento de Gamboa's *Historia de las Incas,* a history specifically commissioned by the Spanish viceroy Francisco de Toledo, shortly after his arrival in Lima in 1572. At the time the only other available history of pre-Hispanic Peru was Pedro Cieza de León's *Crónica de Peru,* first published in 1553. Influenced by Las Casas, Cieza, an eyewitness to the violence associated with civil wars that erupted in Peru following its conquest in 1533–1534, was openly sympathetic toward the Incas, describing them as benevolent rulers who had successfully established a peaceful, ordered community throughout the Andean world. In contrast, Sarmiento wrote his history with specific instructions to depict the Incas as usurpers and tyrants who had "oppressed" the natives over whom they ruled. He consequently emphasized the cruelty and tyranny of the Incas and their barbaric customs, and, following Sepúlveda, he concluded that, because of their sins, Inca rulers had violated the law of nature and could therefore legitimately be deprived of their sovereignty over Peru. Sarmiento presented his completed manuscript to Toledo in February 1572, at which point the viceroy, in an effort to enhance its authority, ordered an interpreter to read it aloud, in Quechua, to twelve native leaders "so that they together could determine whether it conformed to the truth as they know it and if anything in it should be revised and corrected." After listening to the interpreter for three days, the caciques gave the history a glowing review and certified its veracity, as did four conquistadors whom Toledo had also asked to read the manuscript. Toledo then forwarded the manuscript, together with several genealogical trees and certain pictures (*lienzos*) depicting important events in Inca history, to the Council of the Indies and recommended its publication on the grounds that it would help "to refute the other false and lying books that have circulated in these parts, and to explain the truth, not only to our people but to foreign nations as well."[41] What happened next is not entirely clear, but the

---

40. IVDJ: Envio 44, fol. 147r, document of 18 May 1573.
41. See Levillier, *Francisco de Toledo,* 1:155–159; and Steffen, "Anotaciones a la historia," iv.

council, in addition to denying Sarmiento the approval he sought, confiscated the manuscript and gave it to López de Velasco for inspection.[42]

In this respect, Velasco's role as cronista mayor mimicked that of Lorenzo Galíndez de Carvajal, the royal chronicler who had previously served as the "judge and censor" of chronicles relating to the reign of Ferdinand and Isabella. Velasco's main job as a judge was to organize and review all manuscripts pertaining to the Indies, extract from them whatever information he deemed valuable, and then regurgitate this material into the general history he was commissioned to write. At the same time, his other office, that of cosmógrafo mayor de las Indias, required him to exercise similar oversight over the hundreds of maps and sea charts that had been prepared under the auspices of the Casa de Contratación, the institution responsible for supervising trade and navigation with the Indies.[43] At the time, many of these maps were in private hands, and López de Velasco endeavored to collect as many as possible, among them those recently prepared in Mexico under the auspices of Francisco Hernández, the royal physician who had been sent to New Spain on a special mission to gather information about the region's geography and natural history. Once in Madrid, these maps, together with Hernández's other papers, including his famous drawings of Mexican flora, were deposited for safekeeping in the new royal library in the Escorial.[44]

Among López de Velasco's many responsibilities, his most important—and lasting—accomplishment was an ambitious survey intended to produce the raw material, both geographical and historical, that was later to be condensed and incorporated into the general history. This project, known as the Relaciones Geográficas, got under way in 1572, when Council of the Indies notified its viceroys and governors that in order to "conserve the memory of the things of the Indies," an officer (Velasco) had been appointed to "collect the relevant sources and to write a history of the New World." The council's letters also instructed these officials to contact their subordinates about "any history, commentaries, and accounts of discoveries, conquests, expeditions, wars, peace treaties or alliances ... from the time of the discovery up to the present" and have them sent, together with any other maps or descriptions, to Madrid.[45]

---

42. The Crown's policy of confiscating chronicles relating to the Indies is explored in Freide, "La censura española."

43. Bustamante, "El conocimiento como necesidad de estado."

44. For Hernández, see his *Mexican Treasury*. See also Varey, Chrabrán, and Weiner, *Searching for the Secrets of Nature*; and López Piñero, *El Códice Pomar*.

45. *Codoin*, 1:361–362: Real Despacho del Consejo Indias a Martín Enríquez, Virrey de Nueva España, San Lorenzo el Real, 17 August 1572. In this letter Philip II informs the viceroy that in order to

From Velasco's perspective, geographical information of this kind constituted an essential part of the general history, but even as he began work on the project, he doubted that Philip II, given the monarch's reservations about contemporary history, was fully prepared to see such a work through to publication. Velasco's worries first surfaced in a letter he directed to Francisco Cervantes de Salazar, the official chronicler of Mexico City, in 1573. There he questioned whether "His Majesty will care to have one [a history] written or published. I do not see how."[46] As it turned out, Velasco's suspicion was merited. In 1581, after reviewing some of the papers Velasco had collected for the Relaciones project, Philip II, in keeping with his efforts to keep the Indies away from prying eyes, ordered the Council of the Indies "to gather them up and put them in a locked trunk, where, should the occasion arise, they could be consulted and then returned to their proper place."[47] In addition, the king was instrumental in blocking publication of some of Velasco's own work, notably his *Geografía y descripción universal de las Indias*. Velasco wrote this treatise, complete with maps, in the hope that it might serve as a kind of administrative manual to assist in the governance of the New World; in 1574 he submitted a draft to the Council of the Indies in order to receive the *licencia* (permission) required for publication. The council reviewed the manuscript and recommended that Velasco remove from the book materials relevant to the voyages of the French and the English in North America (presumably because information of this kind might give the impression that the monarchy was not doing enough to protect its monopoly over the Indies), together with his comments about the deleterious effect of climate upon *criollos*, the new term referring to persons of Spanish descent who were born in the New World. Velasco proceeded with the prescribed revisions, but ultimately this treatise and another that addressed the still-controversial Line of Demarcation marking the division between the Spanish Indies and the Portuguese Indies, ran afoul of Philip II's policy of keeping the Indies under wraps. In 1582, therefore, the king issued an order instructing that this manuscript be reserved for the exclusive use of the Council of the Indies "on account of the inconveniences that might arise if the work circulates among many hands."[48]

---

protect the memory of "things in the Indies," he has appointed an official to "recopilarlas y hacer historia dellas." He then orders the viceroy to contact anyone in his district who possesses "alguna historia, comentarios o relaciones de alguno de los descuibrimientos, conquistas entradas, guerras ó facciones de paz y de guerra que en esas provincias ó en parte dellas hobiere habido desde su descubrimeinto hasta los tiempos presentes." The king also asks for accounts of native customs and maps and instructs him to send both the originals and copies to Madrid.

46. *Cartas recibidas de España*, 107–110.
47. See Vicente Maroto and Esteban Piñero, *Aspectos de la ciencia aplicada*, 435–436.
48. Cited in Freide, "La censura española," 60. Velasco's *Geografía* was first printed in 1894, when it

This decision, a personal setback for Velasco, helps to explain why he began to pester the monarch for other appointments and grouse about his salary even though he was earning substantially more than the king's other chroniclers.[49] Yet for all these complaints, Velasco proved to be a consummate bureaucrat, dutifully carrying out the responsibilities attached to his office, especially that of censor, a task that required him to serve as a kind of historical watchdog guarding against the circulation of any book or manuscript that might possibly tarnish the monarchy's reputation. One such work was Fray Jerónimo Román's *Repúblicas del mundo* (1575), a precocious exercise in comparative government that included a section devoted to the Aztec "republic" or state.[50] An Augustinian friar much influenced by Las Casas, Román (1535–1595) incorporated into his account of the Aztecs a brief history of the Spanish conquest of Mexico that differed markedly from the much more triumphal account by López de Gómara, who had interpreted the invasion as a just war, nobly fought for legitimate ends. Román offered a somewhat grisly narrative that attributed the death of many Indians to "the avarice of the Spaniards." In addition, he pointedly criticized Cortés for his brutal treatment of Moctezuma and especially the conqueror's decision to torture Moctezuma's successor, Cuauhtémoc, in an effort to force him to reveal the location of the Aztecs' hidden treasures. According to Román, this act was "the most evil and most cruel thing any man had ever done in the world, and as a result I insert it here for the memory of future generations." Such comments were wholly understandable in light of the brutality known to have accompanied the conquest of Mexico, but they did not please Velasco, nor the Council of the Indies, which criticized the book on the grounds that it "dishonored the first conquistadors" and "cast doubt on the [legitimacy] of [the monarchy's] dominion [in the New World]."[51] At this point, the Inquisition stepped in and expurgated the book, literally inking out those portions that were deemed offensive.[52]

Velasco's own attitudes toward official history may be gleaned from a docu-

---

was finally published under the auspices of the Real Academia de la Historia. The best modern edition is López de Velasco, *Geografía* (1971). These reports, it seems, were not for prying eyes. Rather, they were to be treated as *arcana imperii* and relegated to what Peter Martyr had previously referred to as "la cartera de secretos" relating to the New World.

49. Velasco's salary was a respectable 100,000 mrs per year, plus an additional 50,000 for expenses. The base salary of the king's cronistas del rey was only 80,000 mrs.

50. For Román, see Villarroel, *Fray Jerónimo Román*. Román was appointed "cronista general del orden de San Agustín" in 1573 in recognition of his *Chronica dela orden de los Ermitaños*. Like the other historians of Spain's religious orders, he requires further study.

51. Freide, "La censura española," 61–62.

52. Meanwhile Román, after removing the offending passages, went ahead with a new, revised edition, which finally appeared in 1595. The book's checkered history is the subject of Adorno, "Censorship and Its Evasion"; and her "Sobre censura y su evasión."

ment in which he argued against the publication of a history of Peru's civil wars attributed to Diego Fernández de Palencia, a Spanish official who sported the title "historiador y cronista de Perú."[53] In his report on this manuscript, Velasco observed that the book accurately portrayed "the disloyalty of certain town councils, royal officials, and other persons." However, he was reluctant to recommend the book's publication on the grounds that a "published and approved history" would open old wounds, provoke unnecessary conflicts ("desasosiegos"), and more generally prove "an embarrassment for the monarchy" ("incómodo para el estado"). Better therefore to put Palencia's history aside for safekeeping, all in the name of "reason of state" (this is my phrase, not his).[54] Velasco also observed that histories of former times ("historias antiguas") generally did not require as scrupulous censorship as those relating to "present, given the dangers of making errors and offending someone." Reputation (*fama*), he added, is both "uncertain and precarious," and he therefore requested that the Council of the Indies, in its deliberations over Palencia's manuscript, not reveal his opinion "to any of the individuals" involved.[55]

Further evidence of Velasco's (and the council's) openly statist view of history can be found in the *censura* of Fray Pedro de Aguado's *Recopilación historial*, a history of the conquest of New Granada (roughly, today's Columbia and Venezuela) that was submitted to the Council of the Indies for approval in 1581. Like Román before him, Aguado wrote in a Lascasian mode and did not hesitate to point out the failings of individual conquistadors, let alone the darker side of the Spanish enterprise in the New World. History of this kind was definitely not what Velasco wanted to read, and it was apparently at his instructions that the secretary of the Council of the Indies introduced substantial changes in Aguado's text in order to ready it for publication. Fortunately, Aguado's original manuscript survives, albeit in censored form, in the archives of Madrid's Royal Academy of History, and it reveals the extent to which the friar's account was doctored to make it conform with the dictates of official history. For example, the censors removed from the manuscript entire chapters documenting the governing institutions and religion of the region's natives. Also deleted were sections relating to the natives' near nudity and seemingly brazen sexual habits. As for the activities of Spaniards

---

53. Palencia was given this title by Andrés Hurtado de Mendoza, viceroy of Peru from 1556 to 1561.
54. Freide, "La censura española," 65. He subsequently recommended that the manuscript be returned to the audiencia in Lima to be reviewed by "persons of confidence" who could determine "what is poorly written or false."
55. Cited in *Crónicas de Perú*, 164, lxxxii. Following Velasco's report, the Council of the Indies ordered an immediate halt to the book's publication and ordered the confiscation of the fifteen hundred copies of Palencia's book that had already been printed. The book was not reprinted until 1876.

in New Granada, and in keeping with Philip II's decree, promulgated in 1573, to remove the word "conquest" from Spain's imperial lexicon, every time the censor of Aguado's manuscript encountered such words as "conquistar" (to conquer), "conquista" (conquest), and "guerra" (war), they were deleted and replaced with "pacificar" (to pacify), "poblar" (to settle), "entrada" (expedition), or "jornada" (journey), terms that were far more neutral, even benign.[56] Excised too were the names of rebellious Spaniards, among them the notorious Lope de Aguirre, Werner Herzog's "wrath of god." The censors also endeavored to replace such words as "rebellion" and "treasonous act" with the far weaker term of "motín," or mutiny. The idea, in short, was to smooth out the rough edges, massage the narrative, and refashion history in ways that not only enhanced the monarchy's reputation as a historical actor but also helped to both justify and legitimate Spain's military actions in the New World.[57]

At the same time Velasco had little patience with other historians who dared to write about subjects he considered his own. One was Juan Calvete de Estrella, Philip's former Latin tutor, who, during his tenure as a professor of law at the University of Salamanca, had written *De rebus indicis,* a history centered on Pedro de la Gasca, the royal official who in the course of the 1560s successfully managed to end the bloody civil wars that had disrupted life in Peru for almost a generation. Calvete petitioned the Council of the Indies for the permission he needed to publish this work, but according to a letter dated 20 May 1582, Velasco and another royal chronicler [possibly Ambrosio de Morales] joined forces to deny him this license on the grounds that only the royal chroniclers had the right to publish histories of the New World, let alone anything relating directly to the history of Philip II. "All this," Calvete wrote, "is envy, and since neither of these chroniclers can write Latin history with the necessary purity and elegance that is required, they do not want anyone else to do it." Calvete was probably right, and though he later managed to get around this road block by persuading the king to appoint him to the office of "Latin chronicler" in 1587, Velasco still managed to keep *De rebus indicis* out of print.[58]

Velasco in this respect was a monopolist, one who successfully deployed the prerogatives attached to the office of cronista mayor to block the publication of

---

56. For the decree removing the term "conquest" from Spain's imperial lexicon, see Hanke, *Spanish Struggle for Justice,* 131. Xavier Gil Pujol kindly brought this reference to my attention.

57. The Council of the Indies's ban on the use of the word "conquest" should be understood in relation to the "Controversy of the Indies," especially the legal arguments posed by the Spanish theologian Francisco de Vitoria, who, in lectures known as *De Indis,* had questioned the legitimacy of Spain's "just war" in the Americas. See Vitoria, *Political Writings.*

58. For this incident, see *Crónicas de Perú,* 164:cix–cx.

histories he did not approve. Together with other official chroniclers, however, he did little to advance his own. As noted above, Velasco seemingly lost interest in this history around 1582, the year in which Philip II squelched publication of his book on geography. Petitions claiming that the combined office of cronista-cosmógrafo mayor de las Indias was not in line with his temperament (*inclinación*) soon followed.[59] He also volunteered to write a biography of the king, asked to be appointed tutor for Prince Philip (the future Philip III), and immersed himself in projects that ranged from the reform of Madrid's primary schools to the editing of the collective works of Isidore of Seville, all of which served as excuses for his failure to write the history he had been assigned. In 1591 the Council of the Indies, taking note of Velasco's lack of progress, attributed it primarily to the incompatibility of the offices of cronista mayor and cosmógrafo mayor. Consequently, after Velasco relinquished the post and assumed a new and more lucrative position in the royal exchequer, the council elected to separate the two offices, curiously recommending the appointment of a mathematician, Dr. Juan Arías de Loyola, to the newly independent position of cronista mayor while appointing Pedro Ambrosio de Onderíz to that of cosmógrafo mayor.[60] Not surprisingly, Arías de Loyola took no more interest in the general history than Velasco had, but it took another five years before the Council of the Indies located someone who was genuinely committed to this project. That was Antonio de Herrera y Tordesillas, who, after having been vetted by the council and then by the king, was offered, and immediately accepted, the office of cronista mayor de las Indias in 1596 (incidentally, this was the same year in which Lord Burghley suggested to William Camden that he write what was tantamount to an "official" history of Queen Elizabeth I).[61]

"For the glory of this nation"

Once in this office, Herrera moved aggressively to strengthen its power and prerogatives, which had eroded during the end of Velasco's tenure as cronista mayor and the five years Arías de Loyola served in this office. Both, for example, neglected to enforce the requirement that authors writing about Americas submit their manuscripts to the cronista mayor, a *lapsus* that seemingly explains why the Jesuit missionary José de Acosta was able to publish his *Historia natural y moral de*

---

59. Portuondo, *Secret Science*, 152.
60. For this division, see AGI IG, leg. 743, fol. 203., consulta of 12 February 1595. The first person appointed as cosmógrafo mayor was Lic. Pedro de Onderiz.
61. Trevor-Roper, *Queen Elizabeth's First Historian*, 10.

las Indias in 1590 with a license from the Council of Castile as opposed to that of the Indies. This loophole was quickly closed, and in 1597 the Council of the Indies, apparently at Herrera's insistence, asked the king to inform the Council of Castile that the authority to publish books "dealing with matters concerning the Indies" was the exclusive prerogative of the Council of the Indies.[62] It was also in 1597 that Herrera learned that the famous author Lope de Vega had recently published *La Dragontea*, an epic poem that recounted Drake's failed raid on the Panamanian port of Portobelo, without bothering to solicit the authorization of the Council of the Indies.[63] Herrera not only alerted the council about this illegal publication but added that Lope had willfully misrepresented this history by attributing the successful defense of Portobelo to the wrong man.[64] The council subsequently informed the king, who in turn ordered authorities to prohibit the poem's further sale, seize those copies already in print, and forward them to Madrid. Herrera's next move came in 1599, when, using the example of Lope's poem, he persuaded the new monarch, Philip III (1598–1621), to strengthen the law requiring the Council of the Indies to review, prior to publication, any history that touched upon the history of the New World.[65]

In the meantime, Herrera plunged headlong into the general history of the Indies that his predecessors as *cronista mayor* were unable to write. Working at breakneck speed, he produced the first volume of *Historia general de los hechos de los castellanos en las islas i tierra firme del mar oceáno* (also called the *Décadas* because of its Livy-esque division into decades) in 1601 and a second volume in 1615. Together these tomes surveyed Spanish exploits in the New World from 1492 until 1554, the year marking the end of the civil wars in Peru, and it is clear that Herrera had planned to continue his narrative, but he got into trouble with the monarchy, as is explained below.

Designed as a comprehensive survey of Spanish exploits in the Indies, the *Historia general* resembles the kind of marmorealized narrative that Anthony

62. The text of their memorandum, "Sobre la censura que ha de tener los libros que se imprimen sobre cosas de Indias," is available in *Catálogo de consultas*, 2:374. I am grateful to María Portuondo for bringing this document to my attention.

63. Lope was able to skirt the law requiring permission to publish by having the poem printed in Valencia, where the laws of the kingdom of Castile did not apply.

64. For this incident, see AGI IG, leg. 762, fol. 227 See also Wright, "Epic and Archive"; her *Pilgrimage to Patronage*, 24–51; Jameson, "Lope de Vega's *La Dragontea*; and Sánchez Jiménez, "Muy contrario a la verdad." Herrera's problem with *La Dragontea* began with Lope's decision to downplay the role of Alonso de Sotomayor, the lieutenant governor of Portobelo, in the city's defense. Instead, he trumpeted that of Diego Suárez de Amaya, alcalde mayor of the nearby town of Nombre de Dios. Herrera was right. Sotomayor was the actually the first to advise the audiencia of Panama about Drake's impending attack.

65. AGI IG, leg. 227, consulta dated 13 March 1599. The text of this directive is published in Revelló, *El libro*, xxv.

Grafton has associated with the official history genre: it is a plodding, tiresome, somewhat uninspired work that has done little to enhance Herrera's reputation as a historian. Over the centuries, in fact, Herrera has come to be regarded as little more than a hack who borrowed freely from the unpublished work of other chroniclers. At the same time, it is probably unfair to label him a plagiarist (as some critics have done), if only because Herrera, in his position as cronista mayor, was expected to write a general history that, starting with Velasco, was never expected to be a single-author work. It was designed as a collective or collaborative project, the work of an office, rather than an individual. The office's first task was to collect and then organize the primary materials necessary for such a history. Only then was the actual writing to begin. It follows that Herrera was obliged to utilize as source material all of the papers accumulated by the office of cronista mayor, in order to guarantee the "great accuracy and truth" of the history he was required to write. No matter that Herrera was not an eyewitness to the events about which he wrote. His sources, he claimed, were authoritative to the extent that they included state papers housed in the personal apartments of Philip II or in the possession of the Council of the Indies, along with a host of unpublished manuscripts by such eyewitness authors as Pedro Cieza de León, Fray Toribio de Motolinia, Las Casas, Pascual de Andagoya, Bernal Díaz del Castillo, and more.[66] On this basis Herrera could rightfully claim that his history was superior to those written by others who lacked access to these all-important papers. Finally, to counter critics who alleged that his history lacked authority because he had never visited the Indies, Herrera pointed to Tacitus, claiming that this widely respected historian was able to write authoritatively about events in Africa, Germany, and the Levant without leaving Rome.[67] He further claimed, probably with reference to Oviedo, that even those historians who had been to the Indies had not been everywhere nor witnessed all of the events about which they wrote.[68]

Little is known about how Herrera actually fashioned this history, but like many other historians of his generation (the roster includes such notables as J. A. De Thou in France and Francis Bacon in England), Herrera was less interested in

---

66. See *HGI*, 3:604–605 (decade VI, bk. 3, chap. 19), for Herrera's list of some of the sources he employed. He notes that Philip II ordered him to consult papers in the possession of Pedro de Ledesma, secretary of the Council of the Indies. In addition to reports by the first bishop of México, Zumárraga, and Diego Muñoz de Camargo's *relación* of Tlaxcala, Herrera mentioned others sent specifically by viceroys Antonio de Mendoza and Francisco de Toledo "a fin de hacer historia." Herrera's modern editor, Mariano Cuesta Domingo, offers another list of sources in *HGI*, 1:57–80.

67. *HGI*, 3:605.

68. *HGI*, 4:5 (letter to don Luis de Velasco, president of the Council of the Indies, at the beginning of decade V).

discovering new "facts" than in rearranging and reinterpreting old ones in ways that served political ends. He can also be characterized as a historian who, following Francesco Guicciardini, viewed history as primarily the work of men rather than God.[69] From his perspective, divine intervention had clearly helped steer Spain on the path to empire, but history for Herrera consisted mainly of human actions, and he firmly believed that his primary obligation as cronista mayor was to write a history that would perpetuate the memory of the "important and memorable deeds" of those individuals who collaborated in discovery and conquest of the New World.[70] At the same time, Herrera understood that some of these individuals had committed deeds of unspeakable cruelty that he, as a historian, could not ignore. Citing Lipsius, he thus asserted that one of the responsibilities that fell to him as cronista mayor was to "honor the good and to vituperate the bad."[71] Yet the chief problem confronting Herrera was to craft a history that placed a wholly positive spin on Spain's record of achievement in the New World. To resolve this dilemma, he essentially adopted the same method he had previously employed in his histories of Portugal, England, and France, namely to cherry-pick his evidence and select only those "facts" necessary to prove his central assertion that the good Spain had achieved in the Indies far outweighed the bad.

Additional insight into Herrera's working method comes from his notes to Francisco Cervantes de Salazar's *Crónica de Nueva España*, a text that he used to write decade III of his history, which dealt mainly with Cortés and the conquest of Mexico. Cervantes de Salazar was a Toledan humanist who had emigrated to New Spain around 1550 and soon became one of the first professors attached to the university that was founded in Mexico City in 1536. He was also named that city's official chronicler, and it was in this capacity that he wrote what is now considered an important chronicle of the conquest of New Spain. Yet this book—another victim of Philip II's policy of secrecy—remained in manuscript; eventually it found its way to Madrid, where Herrera encountered it in the archive maintained by the Council of the Indies.

Herrera's marginalia in the surviving manuscript, currently housed in Spain's

---

69. For this "political" history in England, see Levy, *Tudor Historical Thought*, 237–285. Also useful is Brian Vickers's introduction to *The History of the Reign of Henry VII*, by Bacon.

70. In the preface to the first volume of the *Historia general*, Herrera criticized Giovanni Battista Ramusio for having ridiculed the efforts of Spanish authors to "escribir los nombres y patria de los que sirivieron en las cosas de las Indias" in the *proemio* of the third volume of his *Navigatione e viaggi*, a popular collection of travel narratives. Herrera attributed Ramusio's criticisms to "envy." See *HGI*, 1:129, letter to Lic. Pablo de Laguna, president of the Council of Indies, dated Valladolid, 15 October 1601.

71. *HGI*, 1:129.

National Library in Madrid, suggest that he did much more than simply copy verbatim those sections he wished to incorporate into the *Historia general*. Rather, he engaged in a critical dialogue with Salazar's text, correcting its grammar and spelling as he read along, crossing out individual words and phrases and substituting others, and occasionally even crossing out whole paragraphs that he found distasteful. Some of these alterations were purely stylistic, as when he replaced the adjectival phrase "tan pujante" with "poderoso";[72] this change was in keeping with Herrera's preference for "estillo llano," the plain, unadorned prose he favored for works of history. Other alterations reflected his—and Philip II's—efforts to put a good face on conquest, such as replacing the verb "to conquer" with "to pacify" (as in "provincias que quedan por pacificar" for "provincias que quedan por conquistar").[73] Still other changes stemmed from his patriotic instincts, among them his decision to replace Cervantes de Salazar's term "españoles," with "castellanos," a change consistent with Herrera's use of *castellanos* in the title of the *Historia general*.[74] Finally, Herrera grappled with Cervantes de Salazar on matters of interpretation and even criticized him for believing that the name New Spain derived from its topographical resemblance to Old Spain.[75] More serious was the note suggesting that Cervantes de Salazar was wrong to think that that the friars believed they could convert the natives without help from or the protection of soldiers. For Herrera, this was "engaño," or deceitful, and his marginal note indicated that he considered soldiers crucial to Spanish evangelical efforts in the New World.[76]

If the care and attention Herrera paid to Cervantes de Salazar's manuscript is at all indicative of the manner in which he read and used other authors, Herrera appears less a plagiarist, as his critics have suggested, than a judicious historian who selected his sources with consummate care. Also worth noting are his efforts to cite his sources by name. Herrera understood that he was writing about events he had never witnessed and individuals he had never met, but by citing his sources, he was in effect demonstrating his reliance on eyewitness evidence and emphasizing the authority and reliability of his account.

Yet for all this insistence on historical accuracy, Herrera could never see beyond his responsibilities as cronista mayor. From the outset his understanding of

---

72. BNE: Ms. 2011, fol. 83v.
73. Ibid., fol. 416. In the same vein, Herrera (for example, on fol. 192), changed such phrases as "indios punidos" into "indios castigados," which sounded less harsh.
74. Ibid., fol. 104.
75. Ibid., fol. 7v. On this point, Herrera's reaction was harsh—"en todo esto se engaña"—and belied the fact that he never set foot in Mexico.
76. Ibid., fol. 136.

history was colored by his loyalty to the monarchy, and as he wrote this history he did so mainly with an eye toward mounting a defense against writers critical of the monarchy's imperium in the New World. Nowhere is this clearer than in Herrera's preface to the first volume of the *Historia general:* "Some writers, against the neutrality that history requires, have tried to obscure the piety, courage, and constancy of spirit that the Castilian nation has demonstrated in the discovery, pacification and settlement of territories that are so many and so new. Also, in their efforts to obscure the importance of these accomplishments, [these same writers] have represented these deeds as cruelties . . . while ignoring the good that many did to achieve God's respect."[77] Herrera's purpose, therefore, was simple: craft a narrative that utilized firsthand evidence to legitimate Spain's title to the Indies, record those deeds worthy of memory, and, in keeping with the instructions Philip II had personally given him during their meeting at El Escorial, tell the truth about the nature of Spain's accomplishments in the New World.

As ambitious and as far-reaching as this agenda appears, Herrera did not hesitate to address the dark side of Spain's conquest of the New World. Like Martyr before him, he included accounts of certain captains known to have treated the natives in a particularly cruel or inhuman way; the list included Juan de Ayora, Pedrarías Dávila, and Nuño Beltrán de Guzmán, the brutal conqueror of the western region of New Spain later known as New Galicia.[78] Yet Herrera's decision to present these individuals as *exemplae* of wrongdoing was wholly strategic and designed, as it were, to put Spain's critics off balance. He thus positioned himself midway between the outspoken critics of empire and those who gave it their unvarnished support. Choosing his words carefully, and following the example of the censors who had doctored Aguado's manuscript, he generally refrained from using such aggressive terms as "conquista" or "conquistar" but chose blander, more palatable terms such as "pacificar" and "poblar." And whereas Jerónimo Román had been so bold as to condemn Cortés for having tortured Cuauhetémoc, Herrera, in his version of this same event, defended Cortés as a just and noble leader and made it appear as if the decision to torture the Aztec leader was the fault of unnamed soldiers who, driven by avarice, had acted against the wishes of their captain.[79]

As for those writers who, starting with Las Casas, had alleged that the Crown had done not nearly enough to protect natives and prevent their use as slaves,

---

77. *HGI*, 1:257. The prologue is dated Valladolid, 20 October 1601.
78. For Juan de Ayora and Pedrarías Dávila, see *HGI*, 2: decade II. For Nuño de Guzmán, see *HGI*, 3:512 (decade VI, bk. 1, chap. 9).
79. *HGI*, 2:300–301 (decade III, bk. 2, chap. 8).

Herrera approached this issue through the selective use of *exemplae*. He addressed the dark side of the conquest by recounting the deeds of those individuals who acted in unnecessarily cruel or murderous ways. He then counterbalanced these individual acts of cruelty and corruption with the monarchy's efforts to bring the evildoers to justice, and both tactics served to exemplify the monarchy's lofty determination to establish order and government throughout the New World.

To drive this point home, as well as to make a larger point, Herrera reminded his readers that many of the Spaniards who first ventured to the Indies were "soldiers" accustomed to "liberty" as opposed to the rule of law, or what he defined as the "harmony and concert" of government.[80] Even then, he admitted that many of the governors and other officials sent to the Indies were easily corrupted—"they were men, not angels"—and their "arrogance and avarice" were difficult for the monarchy to control. "In a new republic," he once admitted, "[the Crown] was unable to remedy [such ills] very quickly."[81] For Herrera, however, the shortcomings of individual Spaniards, though difficult to eradicate, did not detract from the monarchy's commitment to "good government," both temporal and spiritual. And in order to refute critics who alleged otherwise, he incorporated into the narrative, almost on a year-by-year basis, summary transcriptions of royal orders and instructions that were issued with "good government in mind." In addition, he included in the history the entire text of the New Laws of the Indies and commented that these were intended for the "benefit of the Indians."[82] He also went out of his way to applaud those officials who labored to construct what he defined as a "republic"—in the sense of *res publica*, or law-based government— in the New World. And as if to emphasize the lengths to which the monarchy had gone to bring good governance to the Indies, he opened his history with a lengthy (but incredibly boring) catalog of the officials and institutions that governed the Indies, together with a list of the dioceses whose bishops were responsible for the spiritual welfare of its natives. These lists also represented Herrera's efforts to separate his history, the official *Historia general de las Indias*, from similar works, especially that of Fernández de Oviedo, who, as noted above, had studiously avoided the topic of "gobernación."

80. *HGI*, 4:539 (decade VIII, bk. 7, chap. 1).
81. *HGI*, 3:765 (decade VI, bk. 9, chap. 7). For Herrera's comment about angels, see BUS: Ms. 2168, fol. 77.
82. *HGI*, 4:158–162 (decade VII, bk. 6, chap. 5). See also *HGI* 2:400–401 (decade III, bk. 4, chap. 12) for Charles V's concern with the "predicación y conversión de los indios"; 2:611–620 (decade III, bk. 10, chaps. 7–10), where he lists the decrees promulgated by the monarchy in 1526; 2:705 (decade IV, bk. 3, chap. 3), where he discusses the 1528 instructions sent to Cortés regarding "la conservación y buen tratamiento de los indios"; and 4:535 (decade VII, bk. 6, chap. 7), on the decrees concerning "el buen gobierno espiritual y temporal de las Indias" promulgated in 1550.

Yet Herrera's overriding purpose—remember again the oral instructions given to him by Philip II—was to write a history to document the monarchy's complete and utter compliance with the papal bulls of donation, specifically the requirement to attend to the spiritual needs of the natives inhabiting the lands over which the papacy had granted Castile's rulers temporal dominion. Herrera outlined his position on this issue in a letter directed to King Philip III, where he confessed: "My principal goal in writing the *Historia general de las Indias,* which I was instructed to write, was to demonstrate the interest and desire that the Catholic Monarchs, your antecessors, and Your Highness, have and still have in complying with the Papal Bull [of donation] and establishing both spiritual and temporal order (*policia*) in all earnestness and at great cost to the royal treasury and with great effort on the part of the king's advisors, all this to document the deceit of foreign nations who have not done anything similar except to extract profits from the Indies."[83]

It follows that the eight decades that comprised the *Historia general* are best read as an extended defense of Spain's empire in the New World. Because he was neither a jurist or a theologian, Herrera avoided detailed discussion of the thornier intellectual issues raised by the "controversy of the Indies" and simply claimed, using an argument previously articulated by Ginés de Sepúlveda, that the "law of nations ("el derecho de las gentes") had legitimated Spain's conquest of the New World. He also asserted that the monarchy's *principado*—his word for imperium— depended on a combination of "razón natural," a term best defined as logic or common sense, and what he called the "rules of divine, natural, and human law."[84]

Having dealt—briefly—with these issues, Herrera pushed ahead with his narrative, emphasizing the monarchy's determination, starting with the orders given to the "first discoverer" by Ferdinand and Isabella, to attend to the natives' conversion to Christianity and to a "Christian way of life."[85] This line of argument began in the opening geographical section or "description of the Indies," where Herrera, in keeping with his interest in the topic of "gobernación," emphasized the monarchy's efforts to build churches, hospitals, and schools in the natives' behalf.[86] He also addressed the question of indigenous rights by noting that natives,

83. ACP: Caja 91, letter of 6 November 1601.
84. *HGI,* 1:312 (decade I, bk. 2, chap. 4).
85. *HGI,* 1:224.
86. Herrera based this "description" on Juan López de Velasco's still-unpublished *Geografía y descripción universal de las Indias.* See above, note 48. It also included sixteen maps representing different parts of the Indies, including the Caribbean, New Spain, Central America, Peru, and Chile. While not especially detailed, these were the first maps of the Indies that the Spanish monarchy allowed to be

like the king's other vassals, had the "libertad" to dispose of their property, organize their own markets, and retain their old customs, except, of course, in matters of religion. Nor did Herrera shy away from the thorny issue of slavery. Here he admitted that the early years of the conquest had occasioned the unlawful enslavement of natives; but with reference to New Spain, he added that this practice disappeared after 1531, the year marked by the creation of a new royal *audiencia* (or high court) in New Spain and the arrival of a new royal governor, Bishop Sebastián Ramírez de Fuenleal. For Herrera, both Ramírez de Fuenleal and the *audiencia* he headed were synonymous with royal justice, together with the monarchy's determination to curb the individual abuses that had contributed to the unwarranted enslavement of natives in previous years.[87]

This theme, the contrast between private interest, as represented by a handful of abusive conquistadors and local officials, and the public good, symbolized by the royal laws and ordinances promoting "good government," is the fulcrum around which the whole of the *Historia general* revolves. Herrera returned to this topic again and again, regularly praising the monarchy for its determination to bring abusive Spaniards to justice while celebrating its efforts to spread the "divine cult."[88] Although ecclesiastical history was not his primary concern, a missionary ideal infused the whole of the narrative, and rarely did Herrera miss an opportunity to juxtapose a chapter describing the "old" pre-Hispanic customs of the natives with one recounting their conversion to Christianity.

Typical were the chapters he dedicated to the natives of Michoacán, in western New Spain. This section, based on his reading of Fray Bernardino de Sahagún's still-unpublished account of New Spain, opened with a description of the natives' traditional religious practices and ended with another describing, in glowing terms, their existence under the Spaniards. Michoacán, Herrera boasted, had not only a cathedral but more than fifty parish churches. It was also home to an active and dedicated clergy, trained in native languages, who, living in native villages (*estancias*) "preach, confess, and teach with *cartillas* and in schools." He then used this information to assert, contradicting those writers who claimed that the monarchy had failed to attend to its pastoral duties, that the natives in Michoacán "had

---

printed. They also help to explain why foreign publishers, especially Michaek Colijn in Amsterdam translated Herrera's description and published it independently of the rest of the *Historia general*. For these translations, see Cuesta Domingo, *Antonio de Herrera y su obra*, 74–76.

87. *HGI*, 1:236–237. The new audiencia did in fact ban the enslavement of natives in 1532, the year after the arrival of Ramírez de Fuenleal.

88. See, for example, *HGI*, 2:611–620 (decade III, bk. 10, chaps. 7–10), where he lists the decrees promulgated by the monarchy in 1526.

adopted easily to Christianity, attend to their religious obligations, and obey the priests who treat them kindly."[89] Yet for all of these efforts to highlight the monarchy's missionary zeal, Herrera had no intention of writing a full-blown ecclesiastical history of the Indies, a task that several of his successors in the office of cronista mayor undertook (see below). Rather, his method was to provide the proofs necessary to document that the policies of the monarchy, notwithstanding the allegations of its critics, were full in compliance with the requirements established by the Alexandrine bulls of donation.

Herrera's approach to the much-disputed issue of Spain's property rights (*dominium rerum*) in the Indies was much the same. Since he was primarily a humanist without much of a legal background, Herrera left the heavy lifting on this issue to jurists such as Antonio León Pinelo and Juan de Solórzano Pereira, two of his successors in the office of cronista mayor (see Chapter 6). However, he was fully prepared to address the pros and cons of the encomienda, a controversial subject that Oviedo and other historians took pains to avoid; Herrera dealt with it toward the end of the eighth decade of his history, the last he wrote. Ever the royalist, he supported the monarchy's decision (as part of the New Laws of the Indies) in 1542 to suspend the practice of granting encomiendas in perpetuity to individual conquistadors, even though he recognized that this prohibition helped spark a decade of bloody civil war in Peru. His narrative of this conflict, presented in decades VII and VIII, focused on the misdeeds of two of its leaders, Gonzalo Pizarro and Francisco de Carvajal, both of whom appear as murderous soldiers of fortune whose personal ambitions were directly at odds with a monarchy concerned with the promotion of "good government," both spiritual and temporal.[90] Yet as he began to write about this rather painful chapter in the history of the Spanish New World, Herrera, echoing Tacitus, assumed the persona of a Neo-Stoic narrator who recognized that even when writing about evil, important lessons could be learned:

> I wish that this history could address battles between states, sieges of fortresses and cities, [grand] stratagems and the kind of military events that happen in just wars . . . because these are the kinds of things readers like and which give them pleasure. It would be much better accepted and received if it did. But this [history] is one of many acts of disloyalty, disobedience, cruel homicides with infinite robberies, and other crimes. . . . [Yet] the memory of such events can be beneficial,

---

89. *HGI*, 2:353–354 (decade III, bk. 5, chap 10).
90. For Herrera's view of Pizarro, see *HGI*, 4:217 (decade VII, bk. 7, chap. 20); and 4:268 (decade VII, bk. 7, chap. 268). The civil wars in Peru occupy much of decades VII and VIII.

inasmuch as posterity abhors such works and it is thus likely to foster fidelity, constancy, fortitude and the other virtues that make men great.[91]

Herrera narrated these abuses in excruciating detail and ended the narration by addressing their perceived cause: the encomienda and the monarch's decision, in 1543, to abolish the granting of such privileges for more than a single lifetime. Individual encomenderos, he noted, were "avaricious" and unlikely to do anything to except exploit the natives under their control. Yet he was also prepared to present the arguments of those who believed that perpetual encomiendas were both necessary and beneficial. He managed this by citing a document of several Peruvian conquistadors who claimed that they merited it on account of the many services that they rendered the monarchy together with the "blood they had shed" in the discovery and conquest of the Indies.[92] Herrera recognized that heroic actions of this kind merited some form of compensation, and this view helps to explain why he devoted so much of his narrative to describing the sacrifices and struggles of those conquistadors who helped with the "pacification" of such "barbarous peoples." Yet Herrera's sympathies lay elsewhere. As a royalist, he argued that the monarchy, in keeping with the jurisdictional privileges originally granted to it by the papacy, had the greater obligation to defend the natives' natural liberty, protect them from exploitation, and see to their instruction in matters of faith. On this issue, Herrera sounded more like Fray Bartolomé de Las Casas than an official apologist of Spain's record of achievement in the New World, but after weighing the documentary evidence before him, he seemingly convinced himself that the monarchy's imperium over the Indies was not only righteous but just.[93]

This issue aside, what is perhaps the most original aspect of the *Historia general* was Herrera's decision to open each of his eight decades with an engraved frontispiece that summarized, albeit in comic-strip format, the narrative his readers were about to engage. Each frontispiece included a series of portraits depicting the main protagonists of his story, together with others illustrating the "hechos" or important events about which he wrote. Etched by a certain Juan Peyrou, these frontispieces appear to have been planned and then paid for by Herrera, although he was subsequently reimbursed by the king for these and other out-of-pocket expenses associated with the book's printing.[94]

91. *HGI*, 4:9 (decade VII, bk. 1, chap. 1).
92. *HGI*, 4:664 (decade VIII, bk. 10, chap. 18).
93. *HGI*, 4:666 (decade VIII, bk. 10, chap.19).
94. For the relevant documents, see Toribio Medina, *Biblioteca Hispano-américana*, 2:11; *Codindias*, 165, 174–175, 179; and Pérez Pastor, *Noticias y documentos*, 1:144 (for contracts associated with the printing of the *Historia general*); and AHPM: leg. 2754, fol. 605. Also useful is Cummins, "De Bry and Herrera."

The frontispiece that preceded the opening "description" highlighted the preconquest Indies and includes a somewhat schematic—remember Philip II's ideas about secrecy—map of the Americas, both north and south.[95] The same frontispiece emphasized the "barbaric" original state of the Indies by way of a series of small illustrations featuring effigies of various Aztec deities, including Huitzolopuchtil, god of war. Also included was a portrait of Acamapich, identified (erroneously) as the first "king of Mexico," and a stepped pyramid accompanied by the inscription "the design of the temple of the Indians of New Spain." At the bottom is a portrait of the author, labeled "Antonio de Herrera, coronista de s[u].m[ajestad]. natural de Cuellar."

The next frontispiece, which opened the first decade of the conquest, featured medallion portraits of Ferdinand and Isabella and of Christopher Columbus and his brother Bartolomé. The smaller vignettes and their accompanying labels constituted, in miniature, a pictorial introduction to the following narrative. They included a glimpse of Columbus's ships leaving the port of Palos "to discover," another of the "discovery of the Lucayo Islands, the first ones found in the Indies," of the construction of the settlement called La Navidad and Columbus bidding farewell to King Guanacanagaru prior to his return to Spain to announce his discoveries to Europe, and so forth.

The frontispieces introducing subsequent decades follow a similar format; each was intended to provide a visual key to the main topics and personalities that Herrera was about to address. Those of decades II and III, for example, contrast depictions of Aztec gods and religious practices and a map of the island city of Tenochtitlán with a portrait of Cortés, scenes from the conquest of New Spain, and a map of the new city constructed on top of the ruins of the Aztec capital. Later ones feature medallions with schematic portraits of the Inca rulers of Peru, depictions of battles associated with the conquest of Peru, the civil wars that ensued, and portraits of those officials who, according to Herrera, labored to bring good governance to the Indies. Yet these frontispieces did more than provide a visual résumé of the history that Herrera wrote. They were also designed to offer readers yet another level of documentary "proof" of the authoritative character of Herrera's text. That the illustrations were taken seriously is attested by the complaints of one outraged reader, the count of Puñonrostro, who in 1601 objected both to manner in which Herrera related Pedrarías Dávila's execution of the famous explorer Núñez de Balboa in 1518 and to the vignette depicting this incident. In this instance, Herrera removed the offending illustration but re-

95. *HGI*, 1:127.

frained from altering his text or his criticisms of Pedrarías Dávila on the grounds that to do so would be to admit that his history was not sufficiently authoritative, thus rendering it susceptible to further revisions that would ultimately prove detrimental to the interests and reputation of the Spanish Crown.[96]

Whatever Herrera's merits as a historian, the *Historia general*, if not exactly a best seller, traveled far and wide. Published intermittently over the course of more than ten years, it found its way into university circles in Spain. Copies also turned up in Mexico City. Heinrich Martin, alias Enrico Martínez, referred to Herrera (at least to the first volume) in his *Reportorio de los tiempos* (Mexico City, 1606), and from other sources we know that copies soon appeared in a variety of private libraries both in New Spain and in Peru.[97] In addition, the book's geographical instruction, known as the "Descripción de las Indias," was rapidly translated into French, German, and Latin and later into both English and Dutch.[98]

The *Historia general* is not without defects, as some of its first readers were quick to point out. Among these was Herrera's apparent failure to address the history of the Canaries, and another was the quality of the maps that formed part of his geographical "description" of the New World.[99] More serious was his failure to balance information gleaned from Spanish sources with that provided by indigenous writers, an omission highlighted by Fray Juan Antonio de Torquemada, a Franciscan author whose *Monarquía Indiana* (written ca. 1610) used native texts to fashion a more balanced account of the conquest of Mexico than the one offered by Herrera.[100] Torquemada accused Herrera of failing to consult the writings of Fray Bernardino de Sahagún, Fray Jerónimo de Mendieta, and other Franciscans

---

96. Some of the papers relating to this exchange are available in *Codindias*, 37:75–237. I am currently preparing a monograph on this lawsuit and the issues it raised.

97. For Martin's citations of Herrera's book, see Martínez, *Reportorio de los tiempos*, 223–224, 249, 264, 362, tratado 2, chap 24, p. 25. For Peru, see Paéz Guibovich, "La cultura libresca," where Herrera's history turned up alongside works by Ortelius and João de Barros in the library of the Portuguese converso merchant Manual Bautista Pérez; and Hampe Martínez, *Bibliotecas privadas en el mundo colonial*. The best overall introduction to book trade between Spain and America remains Carlos González Sánchez, *Los mundos del libro*.

98. The publishing history of the *Historia general* may be found in Cuesta Domingo, *Antonio de Herrera*, 61–64, 72–78.

99. With respect to the Canaries, see *HGI*, 4:5, where Herrera claims that the history of these islands rightfully belongs in the history of Castile, not the Indies. He subsequently addressed the history of the Canaries at the request of the future Philip IV. See BNE: Ms. 3011, "Varios epístolas y discursos y tractados de Antonio de Herrera," which includes his "Discurso y tratado del descubrimiento de las Islas de Canaria y las diferencias que sobre ella hubo entre castellanos y portugueses." Herrera's response to the quality of his maps may be found in *HGI*, 4:435, letter to Francisco de Texeda, where he claims that a "junta de cosmógrafos" had approved the maps but admits that they were imperfectly reproduced by an engraver ("artifice"), who should have been "more skilled and interested" ("más primo y curioso").

100. For these criticisms, see Fray Juan de Torquemada, *Primera parte de . . . Monarquía Indiana*, bk. 4, chap. 13, p. 379. This work first appeared in 1615.

who worked with indigenous sources. In Torquemada's view, their writings would have provided Herrera with a different perspective on the conquest of Mexico.[101] Herrera refuted these accusations with the claim that he had in fact consulted these and similar sources but, in keeping with the overall scheme of the *Historia general*, had used them for other purposes. He also took a shot at Torquemada by suggesting that this friar, rather than writing about Aztec customs, ought to have focused instead on the evangelization of the New World.[102]

Herrera's response to Torquemada was somewhat unfair. To be sure, he emphasized the monarchy's efforts to promote the spread of the divine cult, but aside from one or two examples, he did little to document the activities of individual missionaries. Partly, this was a matter of personal preference. In the sixteenth century the proper subjects for secular history were war and politics, and this was particularly true for Herrera, a humanist scholar whose notion of history was much influenced by Tacitus and his insistence that historians write about "weighty and remarkable occurrences." In contrast, ecclesiastical history tended to be the work of specialists, especially churchmen. Thus, when Herrera set out to write about the history of Spaniards in the New World, he gravitated toward momentous discoveries, pitched battles, and singular voyages, as opposed to efforts to catechize natives or to build churches and monasteries.[103] This lacuna is one that his immediate successors in the office of cronista mayor recognized as a glaring omission in the *Historia general*, one that they endeavored to correct. However, the only one who actually succeeded in this enterprise was Gil González Dávila,[104] a Jesuit whose *Teatro eclesiástico de la primitiva iglesia de Indias* (Madrid, 1649–1655) focused on "the deeds of the Catholic Faith, the immortal memory of its true triumphs, the glories of its divine victories won with the powerful arms of the Lord of the Armies in the New World of

---

101. Ibid., pp. 379–380. For Herrera's response, see *HGI*, 3:605 (decade VI, bk. 3, chap. 19), where he described the authors cited by Torquemada (they included Fray Andrés de Olmos, Fray Bernardino de Sahagún, and Fray Jerónimo de Mendieta) as authors "que no tienen autoridad," a phrase that refers to the fact that their books, not having been officially approved for publication and then printed, lacked "authority."

102. *HGI*, 4:275 (decade VII, bk. 9, chap. 7). Having related the story of the success of one friar in converting a *cacique* to Christianity, Herrera, targeting Torquemada, writes: "Sería más proprio de los religiosos tratar de ellos, que escribir monarquías indianas."

103. The first to write a *historia sacra* that pertained to the Indies was Dávila Padilla, *Historia de la fundación y discurso*, a history of the Dominican order in New Spain. Had he consulted it, Herrera might have gleaned valuable information about the monasteries the Dominicans had established (sixty-six by Padilla's account) but if Herrera was aware of this book, he failed to draw upon Padilla's findings.

104. González Dávila was appointed cronista mayor on 21 October 1641. Cf. AGI IG: leg. 762. His predecessor, Tomás Tamayo de Vargas, also set out to write the ecclesiastical history of the Indies but never achieved much other than sending a series of questionnaires to New World bishops.

the Indies, where the ignorance of idolatry was the absolute ruler of its crowns and kingdoms."[105]

Church history aside, perhaps the most glaring defect of Herrera's history, and certainly the one that most puzzles modern scholars, is its abrupt, seemingly inconclusive ending, in the middle of the eighth decade, in 1554.[106] At the start of decade VII, in a letter directed to the president of the Council of the Indies, don Luis de Velasco, Herrera explained that after this year, which marked the end of the civil wars in Peru, the history of the Indies was difficult to write using the same annalistic form he had previously employed. Without saying so directly, Herrera was suggesting that starting in 1554, following the heroic age of discovery and conquest of the Indies, events there became more routine and less suitable as subjects for the kind of grand history Herrera preferred. He also informed Velasco that many of the events that occurred in the Indies after 1554 were incorporated into his world history, a work he considered as the continuation of the *Historia general*. Finally, he blamed his critics, and especially the "rumors" (*murmuraciones*) that had caused him to get tired of working and lose all interest in continuing with the project.[107] Herrera was referring here to various court intrigues that, starting in 1609, led to his arrest, humiliation, and exile from the royal court in Madrid. As we shall see, these intrigues prompted him to destroy his papers and then, in an effort to restore his reputation, rush the concluding volume of the *Historia general* into print before ending its eighth and final decade.

The Politics of History at the Court of Philip III

Following his appointment as cronista mayor in 1596, Herrera emerged as the most influential chronicler in the monarchy's employ. His influence stemmed initially from the support he received from several of Philip II's most trusted advisers and, later, from the king himself. Secondarily, it came his offices: that of cronista mayor de las Indias; then, starting in 1598, cronista del rey; and starting in 1605, another appointment as royal secretary, a position that gave him virtually unrestricted access to important state papers and documents.

Herrera's influence also came from his writing, and especially his Polybean

---

105. González Dávila, *Teatro eclésiastico*, 1:59.
106. Later critics faulted Herrera for relying too heavily on "cartas misivas de los particulares." See Meléndez, *Tesoros verdaderos de las Yndias*, vol. 2, prologue. Meléndez considered such letters to be unreliable ("pocos verdicas") as compared with royal laws and decrees.
107. *HGI*, 4:5.

view of history as a "guide for action," a concept he wove into his histories and then subsequently expanded upon in his essays, especially his *Discurso y tratado de que el medio de la historia es suficiente para adquirir la prudencia,* which was written for the benefit of Philip III's successor, the young Philip IV. Here he explained that the historian's chief obligation was to offer princes sound and useful advice. "Simple narration," he opined, "is not enough." Herrera also explained that historians had the responsibility to offer judgments from which any reader could draw useful conclusions, or what he described as "precepts for . . . the governance of individuals, cities and entire kingdoms." To do this effectively, Herrera recommended that historians avoid the florid rhetoric characteristic of humanist history and employ instead a "pure, clean style." Finally, he advised historians to avoid hearsay and the commonplace rumors spread by the "vulgo" and rely instead on state papers and documents, a position that echoed one that he, together with Garibay, had previously expressed in the traça prepared for Philip II.[108]

Central to Herrera's thinking on this issue was his notion that history should be chiefly deployed to promote the "bien público," or public good, a term he related both to the monarchy and to the collective interests of the Spanish nation. On this point, Herrera's ideas approximated those of Fray Juan de la Puente, another royal chronicler (appointed in 1605). Puente likened his office to that of a press secretary (of the kind attached in modern times to the offices of presidents and prime ministers around the world), one whose responsibility was to "publicize the good deeds of the king and his vassals" in ways that offered "apologies and defenses as opposed to the simple narrations of events."[109] Such an argument, reminiscent of Botero's *Ragion di stato,* is also one used by Herrera when he suggested that monarchs, for the benefit of the republic, should reward those of his vassals who demonstrated "heroic virtue," whether in peace or in war.

As these recommendations suggest, Herrera had distanced himself from the older, Renaissance ideas that regarded history as a liberal art that was preferably practiced in isolated, quiet places where its humanist practitioners had both the time and the tranquility to craft independent judgments about the past. History for Herrera had little to do with *otium.* Rather, it was action, involvement, part of the *vita activa e civile,* a discipline inseparable from the hubbub of the court. Herrera further believed that historians, especially those writing about contempo-

---

108. BNE: Ms. 3011, "Varios Epístolas y Discursos y Tractados de Antonio de Herrera," fol. 153.
109. Puente, *Tomo primero de la conveniencia,* 2, 5.

rary subjects, needed administrative experience, arguing that "if those who write histories were experienced in governing the world, as opposed to having only attended lectures in schools and studying bundled up in rooms and isolated cells, there would not be so many errors."[110] For this same reason, he expected that historians should assist in the formulation of policy, both domestic and foreign; when writing his world history, he went so far as to express veiled criticisms of certain measures associated with the duke of Lerma, Philip III's powerful favorite. Among the things he criticized were the reasons adduced to justify the transfer of the monarchy's capital from Madrid to Valladolid in 1601; the 1609 edict expelling the *moriscos* from Spain (it was too cruel, in his view); and the government's failure to maintain the integrity of the empire, or what Herrera called the "conservation of the kingdoms of Spain," which was possibly a reference to the monarch's decision to sign a truce with the Dutch in 1609.[111] These criticisms, as will be seen below, did little to ingratiate Herrera with the duke of Lerma and seemed to contribute directly to his arrest and imprisonment in 1609.

As it happened, Herrera was a historian who practiced what he preached: he regularly drafted policy statements, or *memoriales*, that were addressed to the king and recommended specific action on a variety of issues. His first known memorial, dating from 1583, dealt with local issues: Madrid's wood supply and the indecency of having a wooden bread stall in the city's main square.[112] Later came others on fortifications and the kingdom's defense—here he was able to draw on his prior experience with his former employer, the viceroy Vespasiano Gonzaga Colonna—as well as foreign affairs, especially Spain's ongoing conflicts in northern Italy, a region in which he had particular expertise. Cartography also fell within his ken, as in 1601, when he advised Philip III on the correct placement of the Line of Demarcation separating Spanish and Portuguese territories in the western Pacific.[113] On this occasion he specifically criticized João Bautista La-

110. Herrera y Tordesillas, *HGM*, 1:282. Herrera's position on this issue was diametrically opposed to that of the contemporary Aragonese chronicler Lupercio Leonardo de Argensola, who believed that good history required a considerable investment of both effort and time, or as he expressed it: "To write hurriedly, without reflection and without diction and style is better suited to [the writers of] news sheets and novels than to historians." See Leonardo de Argensola, *Obras sueltas*, 1:370.

111. See Herrera, *HGM*, 2:744, where he comments negatively on the Christians' cruel treatment of the *moriscos* in Granada; 2:454, where he discusses Philip II's decision to make Madrid the permanent seat of the royal court; and 2:568, where he uses the phrase "conservación de los reynos de España" with reference to the Indies and Philip II's pledge that "q en ningun tiempo del mundo enagenaría él, ni sus herederos ni sucesores los dichos Reynos y Provincias y Islas no los apartarían de la corona real de Castilla y de León."

112. Herrera's suggestions about the city's wheat supply and surrounding woods may be found in IVDJ: Envio 21n735, memo dated 7 November 1583.

113. For Herrera's cartographical opinions, see Kagan, "*Arcana Imperii*," 52–53.

vanha's map of the "carrera de las Indias Occidentales," which in his view favored Portuguese interests as opposed to those of Castile.[114]

Herrera's *Discursos y tratados,* a series of essays drafted over the course of more than twenty years, offers additional insights into his interests and concerns. Together the essays suggest that Herrera fancied himself as something of a one-man political think tank, capable of offering opinions on issues as diverse as the legitimacy of Spain's title to the Canary Islands; the advisability of having foreigners, such as Alessandro Farnese and Ambroglio Spinola, serve as captains and generals in the king's army (Herrera's answer was yes); and, with specific reference to the ill-advised invasion of Muscovy by the Polish monarch Stephen Bathory in 1609, the necessity for princes to think twice and use prudence before engaging in "new, foreign wars." This last was presumably written around 1621, a moment when Philip IV and his chief minister, the count-duke of Olivares, were contemplating the end of the Twelve Years Truce with the Dutch.[115] Finally, in one of his later essays, written to coincide with Olivares's policy of reducing unnecessary expenditures in Madrid, Herrera, echoing the Neo-Stoic arguments associated with such authors as Justus Lipsius, suggested that the decline of nations was inextricably linked with excesses in luxury and wealth. In all, these papers and reports reflect Herrera's lifelong determination to remain a player in the conduct of matters of government and state.

Herrera took full advantage, then, of the multiple offices he held. As cronista mayor de las Indias, one of his obligations was to review and censor historical works pertaining to the Indies prior to publication. As earlier seen in his condemnation of Lope de Vega's *Dragontea,* Herrera used this power to become the de facto arbiter of any history remotely connected to the Spanish New World. He used his appointment as cronista del rey in similar ways, promoting publication of histories of which he approved. High on his list, for example, were Fray Prudencio de Sandoval's *History of the Emperor Charles V* (1604) and Luis de Guzmán's detailed account of the first Jesuit missions in China and Japan.[116] Occasionally, Herrera was also asked to pass judgment on books in other disciplines, as on 20 July 1604, when the Council of Castile asked him to review a manuscript by a certain Miguel de Cervantes Saavedra that bore the title *El ingenioso hidalgo don Quixote de la Mancha.* Herrera spent the rest of the summer with this manu-

---

114. For Herrera's criticisms, see BL Add. 26, 425, fol. 264, Antonio de Herrera, *Memorial a S.M. para la Junta de Portugal,* Villacastín, 1 January 1601.
115. Herrera dedicated this *discurso* to Pedro de Toledo, marquis of Villafranca, a member of the Council of State.
116. I refer to Guzmán, *Historia de las misiones.*

script and on 20 September reported that "the public will find it both pleasing and entertaining." Four days later the council approved publication of what became the most influential work of literature to emerge from Spain's Golden Age.[117] Herrera did not hesitate to censor those works he considered inferior, though, and in general he had a reputation for being a stern and unforgiving critic. As late as 1620, for example, when his influence was already on the wane, the duke of Sessa expressed concern upon learning that the Council of Castile had given the manuscript copy of Juan de Vera y Figueroa's *El embajador* to Herrera to evaluate before issuing a publication license. In a letter to the author, Sessa warned that Herrera's "critical eye (circumspeción zemirda) is such that he is not content with anyone except himself. I know that he is such an arrogant genius that it bothers him that not every history book comes out of his study."[118]

The moniker "arrogant genius" is apt. Herrera sincerely believed that the office of royal chronicler endowed him with authority and influence that ordinary historians lacked. While other writers struggled to get their hands on documents and firsthand reports, Herrera was able to draw on the secrets of Simancas and other royal archives to order to endow his histories with the necessary documentary weight. He also was quick to criticize those historians who failed to support their arguments with documentary proofs; and one of his targets was the Dominican historian Fray Juan de Torquemada.[119] At the same time, his handling of the historical record sparked numerous complaints. I have already made reference to those of the count of Puñonrostro, but this irate nobleman was so incensed by the *Décadas* that he went so far as to initiate a lawsuit, challenging the documentary basis, that is, the "facts," of Herrera's account of the actions of the count's paternal grandfather, Pedrarias Dávila, in Castillo de Oro (Panama) in 1516. The suit, a Bleak House–like affair that lasted almost a decade, charged Herrera with libel, but the nobleman lost the suit; the king's magistrates decided in Herrera's favor.[120]

Part 1 of Herrera's *Historia general del mundo*, published in 1601, was even more controversial, especially in Aragon, where members of the Diputación objected to the book's account of the revolt known as the "alteraciones" of 1590–1591. This uprising began when the Inquisitors of Zaragoza, acting on the orders of Philip II, arrested the fugitive royal secretary, Antonio Pérez, in apparent violation of traditional liberties, known as *fueros*, that offered residents of the

---

117. See Bouza Álvarez, "El primer lector de Cervantes."
118. BL Add. 28, 348, fol. 131, undated letter.
119. For Herrera's comments on Torquemada, see *HGI*, 3:604 (decade VI, bk. 3, chap. 19).
120. Documents pertaining to the lawsuit are included in the *Codindias*, 37.

kingdom of Aragon certain exemptions from royal justice. The circumstances surrounding the incident are complicated, but the arrest served as a catalyst for a popular uprising, Pérez's escape from prison, and finally a full-scale uprising that ended only after the arrival of a powerful royal army sent from Madrid.[121]

Key aspects of this uprising are still in dispute, and to this day, historians are divided in their opinions about the cause of the rebellion, the extent to which it represented a direct challenge to royal authority, and whether Philip II was justified in dispatching an army to suppress it. But Herrera's opinion on these and other matters was unequivocal. In keeping with the obligations attached to his office, he adopted a wholly absolutist perspective, defending the king's actions while criticizing the unlawful behavior of the Aragonese. Nor did Herrera express much sympathy for the Aragonese *fueros,* laws that he regarded as an unnecessary check on the royal prerogative, or what he termed "la majestad real." "Princes," he wrote, "give the laws and orders to the kingdom, not the kingdom to the prince."[122] The kingdom's task as he saw it was "to obey," not "to order," and this absolutist premise colored practically the whole of Herrera's account of the revolt. He defended the monarchy's actions and criticized the Aragonese for infidelity, although he stopped short of accusing them of lèse majesté, which was considered a capital crime.

Even so, the Diputación took exception with Herrera's history of the uprising and instructed its own official chronicler, Lupercio Leonardo de Argensola, to prepare a counterhistory challenging the royal chronicler on issues of both interpretation and fact. This commission resulted in Argensola's *Información de los sucesos de Aragón de los años de 1590 y 1591,* a work the Diputación decided was too inflammatory to be published.[123] However, it adopted a different stance following the publication in 1612 of Herrera's *Tratado, relación y discurso histórico de los movimientos de Aragón . . . ,* which offered an expanded yet equally promonarchical account of the rebellion.[124] On this occasion the Diputación not only ordered the book's seizure but commissioned another Aragonese historian, Fray Martin Carillo, to write yet another history exposing Herrera's "fictions" and presenting the "official" Aragonese interpretation of the events of 1590–1591.[125]

---

121. The literature on this uprising is voluminous, and for readers of English it may be approached through Gil Pujol, "Aragonese Constitutionalism and Habsburg Rule." See also various publications by Gascón Pérez, among them his *Bibliografía crítica de la rebelión aragonesa;* and his more recent *Aragón en la monarquía de Felipe II.*
122. *HGM,* 1:286.
123. For this controversy, see Gil Pujol's introduction to Leonardo de Argensola, *Información de los sucesos de Aragón.*
124. I refer to Herrera y Tordesillas, *Tratado, relación y discurso.*
125. See BNE: Ms. 9824. The Diputación subsequently commissioned one of its members, Vicen-

Throughout this squabble, Herrera refused to back down. As the king's official chronicler, he firmly believed that his histories, grounded as they were upon original sources, would be understood as far more authoritative than those by other historians, especially those who happened to be Aragonese. On this score, Herrera was probably right. As a royal chronicler, Herrera's interpretation of particular individuals and events was "authorized" in ways that the work of other, nonofficial historians was not. Official history in this sense carried with it the power of the state, and Herrera's readiness to exploit this prerogative explains why individuals and institutions who took issue with his interpretation of history felt obliged—*pushed* may be a better term—to respond, either with criticisms, lawsuits, or in the case of Aragon, alternate, counterhistories of their own.

Many of the criticisms levied at Herrera were justified. Ambitious for both power and wealth, he regularly exploited the prerogatives attached to his offices, occasionally by bending or otherwise tinkering with his histories for personal gain. The best example of this practice occurred in 1607, when Herrera was preparing the third and last part of the *Historia general del mundo,* which dealt with the period from 1575 to 1598. Parts of this narrative necessarily touched on the activities of Alessandro Farnese, the brilliant commander who, acting in his capacity as captain general of the Army of Flanders, helped Philip II to maintain control over the southern part of the Netherlands in the teeth of the Dutch Revolt. Yet Farnese was also accused of having subverted Philip II's plans to invade England in 1588, and in writing his account of the Armada, Herrera contemplated introducing some comments along these lines, a possibility that upset Farnese's nephew, Duke Ranuncio I of Parma, who had learned about Herrera's intentions from a certain Juan Canobio, his personal agent in Madrid. Instructed to contact Herrera, Canobio soon informed the duke that Herrera did have in his possession certain embarrassing papers about Farnese that, if published, could be a "mortal spear (*saeta*) against Your Highness's honor." Negotiations began shortly thereafter. Herrera informed Canobio that other princes, including the grand duke of Tuscany, with their honor at risk, had offered to pay him as much as 1,000 ducats to alter the *Historia del mundo* in ways they approved. Surprised at the historian's audacity, Canobio referred to Herrera as nothing less than a "bestia" and determined that he would offer him no more than a "cortesia"—we would call it a bribe—worth 150 *scudi,* a considerably lesser amount. What happened next is not entirely clear, but when, in 1612 part 3 of the *Historia* appeared, its representation

---

cio Blasco de Lanuza, to write yet another history of this same event. This resulted in his *Historias eclesiásticas y seculares de Aragon.*

of Farnese was wholly favorable.[126] Small wonder, then, that Herrera once told a friend that "the chronicler's ink had served him very well." He did not mention it on this occasion, but this same ink also enabled him to purchase a comfortable house in the very center of Madrid, as well as other property and rents.[127]

Over time such venality did little to enhance Herrera's reputation, but what really worked to his disadvantage, and nearly cost him his job, was his failure to ingratiate himself with Francisco Gómez de Sandoval, duke of Lerma, the most powerful minister at the court of Philip III.[128] In his role as the king's *privado*, or favorite, Lerma was especially skilled at arranging for the appointment of family and friends to influential posts as a way of creating a court faction, or *camarilla*, that could assist him with the business of the running the monarchy's affairs.[129] This patronage included the office of royal chronicler, and as early as 1599, Lerma managed to have one of his relatives, Fray Prudencio de Sandoval, appointed to this office. Herrera seemingly got on with Sandoval, whose work he approved of, but he was decidedly less enthusiastic about the appointment (in 1603) of Fray Atanasio de Lobera, a historian from León,[130] and especially that of Fray Juan de la Puente, a theologian whose qualifications for the office of royal chronicler rested principally on his personal ties to Lerma and other members of the Sandoval family. For Herrera, these appointments represented concrete demonstrations of the growing influence of Lerma over the conduct of royal affairs. They also threatened to undermine his own power and influence, and this fact helps to explain why, shortly after la Puente's appointment in 1605, Herrera referred to himself, somewhat operatically, as "el coronista infelice"[131] and in 1606 filled his letters with woeful remarks about how the monarchy was being run into the ground. "This world," he lamented, "is getting worse by the day while the evil of men is growing."[132]

In the meantime, Herrera's relations with Lerma went from bad to worse, and in 1607 the royal favorite, partly in an effort to isolate Herrera and render him

---

126. Cf. Pérez Bustamante, *El cronista Antonio de Herrera*.
127. AHN Cons, leg. 36, 211, no. 15, letter of Herrera to Almirante, dated 11 April 1609.
128. RAH: Ms. Salazar y Castro, A79, fol. 236, 7 VII 1606. See also AHN Cons, leg. 44, exp. 177, document dated 7 November 1605, which includes Herrera's petition asking to be appointed to the office of royal secretary.
129. Lerma and his policies are best approached through Feros, *Kingship and Favoritism in the Spain of Philip III*. See also Williams, *The Great Favorite*.
130. See BNE: Ms. 1753, fol. 49. Lobera, author of *Grandezas de la muy antigua e insigne ciudad*, had expressed interest in continuing the *Crónica general* where Morales had left off, for the purpose of perpetuating the memory of the "great and glorious deeds of the Spanish nation." Although he received an appointment as cronista del rey, the promised history never materialized.
131. RAH: Ms. Salazar y Castro 9/79, Herrera to Gondomar, 12 July 1606, fols. 332–334.
132. Ibid. In this same volume (fols. 236–238), see the letter dated 7 July 1606.

redundant, recommended that the king appoint a new kind of superchronicler, or *cronista general*. The idea for such an office had originated with the count of Gondomar, who was then serving as the king's representative (*corregidor*) in Valladolid; he strongly believed that history, as a discipline, should be subservient to the state. In a letter directed to both Lerma and the king, Gondomar suggested that such a "general chronicler" was necessary in order to bring an end to "the multitude of dis-organized books being printed and published, [many of which] deceive the nation and are notable only for omissions and faults." He continued by suggesting that this official be given the authority to inspect all history books in circulation and determine those that needed to be either censored or suppressed, and be provided the resources to support publication of new histories judged meritorious. Using language reminiscent of Botero, Gondomar concluded that this new chronicler would be able to guarantee that "the heroic and illustrious deeds attendant to Your Majesty's royal person, and those of the valor and loyalty of your vassals, remain in perpetual memory, for the honor of our nation, and universal example for everyone."[133]

Lerma's response to these suggestions was to arrange for the appointment in 1608 of Pedro de Valencia (1555–1620) to the new office of "cronista general de estos reinos y de las Indias." Valencia, a humanist who spent much of his time in the Extremaduran town of Zafra, was not much of a historian, but when it came to matters of policy, it appears that he and Lerma were on the same page. Valencia's favorite aphorism, "No parecer sino ser," which translates roughly as "reality before reputation," was one that Lerma, with his interest in ending Spain's costly foreign wars, could easily have adopted as his own.[134] Even more importantly, Valencia had the support of Lerma's son-in-law, the count of Lemos, president of the Council of the Indies. Lemos openly supported Valencia's appointment as cronista general, whereas Herrera's supporters, including the count of Miranda, president of the Royal Council, did not. In the end the two factions reached a compromise when the king, in appointing Valencia, agreed to drop the word *general* from his title.[135] Yet Valencia's annual salary, one thousand ducats, was more than double Herrera's. In addition, the new chronicler was to receive seven hundred ducats as a pension for his children and to help him defray his expenses at court.[136] To make matters worse for Herrera and essentially relegate him to the

---

133. Cited in Sarmiento de Acuña, *Cinco cartas político-literarias*, 116.
134. Valencia first used this aphorism in his 1596 treatise, *Academica sive de iudicio erga veram*. See Gómez Canseco, *El humanismo despues de 1600*, 246; and Valencia, *Academica*.
135. For this appointment, see Paniagua Pérez, "Pedro de Valencia."
136. AGI IG: leg. 752, p. 5 October 1616.

sidelines of history-writing at the Spanish court, Valencia was commissioned to write a history of the reigning monarch, Philip III, and for this purpose he was granted permission to consult documents stored in the royal archive at Simancas. He was also instructed to add to the chronicle of the Indies by writing about Spain's wars with the Araucanian Indians in Chile, a commission clearly intended to demonstrate to Herrera that his services as cronista mayor were no longer necessary.[137]

Dueling Chroniclers

In the chess game of court politics, the power and prerogatives that the monarchy invested in Valencia signaled an important change in the state of the cronista mayor. Suddenly, Valencia was in and Herrera was out, relegated to the outer circles of the royal court. Herrera's newly diminished status also helps to explain his decision to join the court faction opposed to the duke of Lerma. A prominent member of this faction was Francisco de Mendoza, admiral of Aragon, who, as a brother of the duke of Infantado, belonged to one of the most powerful noble houses in Spain. An outspoken critic of Lerma and his policies, the admiral ran afoul of the royal favorite as early as 1606.[138] The following year the admiral hatched a poorly executed plot to unseat the royal favorite and a few of his most prominent henchmen, but the conspiracy was discovered in December 1607 after authorities entered his house and discovered certain papers that criticized the way the monarchy was being run. The search also turned up letters from Herrera containing "words and things prejudicial to and against the service of His Majesty." By May 1608, the admiral was imprisoned and charged with the crime of lèse majesté.[139] A month later Herrera found himself under house arrest, with two guards posted at the door. At this point, determined to destroy any evidence that might be used against him, Herrera burned most of his papers and notes, informing one of his friends, "I really did it. I burned all my papers. . . . I determined to do so, having decided that if the king orders me to write some-

---

137. For the commission to write the history of Philip III, see Morocho Gayo, "Una historia de Felipe III." The permission for Valencia to use Simancas may be found in AGS Est: leg. 1494, unfol., "Consulta del Comendador Mayor de León [Don Juan de Idiáquez] sobre la conveniencia de autorizar al cronista Pedro de Valencia el acceso a la documentación de Simancas, para elaborar la historia de Felipe III." I owe this reference to the kindness of Geoffrey Parker. As for the history of the Indies, Valencia's first task was to conduct a new geographical survey intended to supplement the *relaciones geográficas* previously collected by López de Velasco. Although the survey was never completed, some of the reports he collected are published in Pedro de Valencia, *Relaciones de Indias*, in *Obras completas*, vol. 5.
138. The only study of this incident is Rodríguez Villa, "Don Francisco de Mendoza."
139. For the admiral's arrest on 20 May 1609, see Cabrera de Córdoba, *Relaciones*, 370.

thing, His Majesty will give me the necessary papers to do so."[140] These remarks were probably exaggerated, since Herrera continued to write, but they may well explain why so little of his personal—and apparently incriminating—correspondence no longer survives.

Whatever papers Herrera destroyed, his ploy failed to prevent the start of criminal proceedings against him. The trial began in November 1609, with the royal prosecutor accusing Herrera not only of having insulted the king and his ministers but also of having revealed state secrets to persons living abroad. Several of these charges stuck, and Herrera was punished by having his offices suspended and his salaries put on hold; he was also exiled from Madrid and the court.[141]

At this point Herrera set out to repair his reputation, mainly by doing what he did best: writing history. The second edition of his book defending the monarchy's prerogatives in the duchy of Milan had recently appeared, and while living in exile, mainly in the city of Guadalajara, Herrera worked on the second and last part of the *Historia general del mundo*, which was published in 1612. He also succeeded in finishing the closing decades of the *Historia general de las Indias*, which, as noted earlier, carried the narrative forward to 1554, the year that effectively marked the reestablishment of royal power in Peru. However, he wrote the last decades somewhat hurriedly and clearly did so in the hope of restoring his tarnished reputation as a historian. Such, it seems, was the purpose of the letter, addressed to Philip III, included at the opening of decade V. The letter is undated but apparently was written in 1614. It begins with the phrase "Many are the reasons to write history." Some historians, he observes, do it simply to ingratiate themselves with the persons whose deeds they relate. Others write to demonstrate their "eloquence" and make themselves famous, while others want to draw attention to events in which they had a part. But there are other historians who write only for reasons of "utility" and to make known what is otherwise secret "so that the truth can be revealed." Herrera, as might be expected, included himself among this last group and continued by reminding the king that his father, Philip II, had personally commissioned him to write this history of the Indies in order to reveal the "errors" of others and that the "true light" of Spanish accomplishments there could be known. He also suggested that the king, should he ever have time to read this history, would find it useful because it was "a mir-

---

140. BR: Ms. II-2144, document 230, Herrera to Diego Sarmiento de Acuña, 10 September 1609.
141. Cabrera de Córdoba reports that Herrera was imprisoned "por escribirse con él [the Almirante] y con algunos amigos de Milan, de donde se ha sabido el duque de Lerma que deicn que esta muy ofendido." Cabrera de Córdoba, *Relaciones*, 379.

ror of prudence" as well as a guide to "good government" and the "establishment and conservation of the new republic that his predecessors had created in the New World."[142]

Whether Philip III took the time to read this letter is unknown. But these additions to the general history enabled Herrera's friends in Madrid—they included Juan de Idiáquez, then one of the most senior members of the Council of State; the count of Miranda, who was the president of the Royal Council of Castile and a ranking member of the king's household; and the count of Gondomar, soon to be named Philip III's ambassador at the Court of St James—to convince the king, if not Lerma, that Herrera deserved a royal pardon. The king agreed. By the end of 1614, after an absence of almost three years, Herrera was back in Madrid and had his old offices returned and back salary paid. The king also rewarded with him with a *merced* worth one thousand ducats, and the following year the closing decades of the *Historia general* finally appeared in print.

The book's publication speaks directly to Herrera's tenacity. It was also part of his campaign to remind Philip III of how much he, as cronista mayor de las Indias, was able to accomplish in comparison to Pedro de Valencia, who, after five years as cronista general, had failed to write anything pertaining to the "war in Chile." This subject was one that Valencia steadfastly refused to write, and Herrera, as part of a studied campaign to embarrass his rival, forwarded a petition to the Council of the Indies in which he explained that in the course of twenty years of service as royal chronicler, he had done more, written more, and published far more than any of his predecessors in the office. Then, much like a disgruntled university professor who feels cheated by his dean, Herrera noted that despite all this productivity, the Crown had failed to reward him adequately. To prove his point, Herrera forwarded to the council a list of royal chroniclers that started with Pulgar, Nebrija, and Galíndez de Carvajal and enumerated the many grants and gifts that successive monarchs had given their royal chroniclers even though they had written far less than he. The petition ended with a reference to Valencia and the claim that this chronicler, though handsomely compensated, "has not written or published any part of a history."[143]

The council responded by advising Philip III that his veteran councillor deserved a grant of four hundred ducats, but it is not clear whether the king ever approved this reward. Later that same year, Herrera, tired of playing second fiddle to Valencia, it seems, asked for and received a four-year leave of absence (with

---

142. *HGI*, 3:150, letter to Philip III.
143. See AGI IG: leg. 652, memorial dated 22 May 1615.

pay), which freed him from his obligation as cronista mayor to advance the history of the Indies.[144] In the meantime, the council asked Valencia to explain himself, and he responded with the excuse that if he were to write about the war in Chile, he risked not only "offending persons of quality" but also "defaming the Spanish nation" because of his obligation, as a committed humanist, to make reference to the "cruelties and injustices committed there." Valencia also feared that if he wrote this history as he should, "foreign nations" would use it against Spain. He ended his letter by suggesting that "it was not convenient to provide any more information about this war than what was written about it," a reference to accounts by Alonso de Ercilla, José de Acosta, and several unpublished *relaciones* relating Spain's ongoing efforts to "pacify" the Araucanians.[145]

Valencia's intransigence on this issue reflected Bodin's idea that historians interested in writing good history should avoid writing about current and recent events, but it did little to endear Valencia to the council, many of whose members, supporters of Herrera, had never warmed to Valencia's appointment. The council's next move was to inform the king that the office of general chronicler required Valencia to "continue writing the general history of the Indies with the greatest precision and truth possible." It also declined to accept Valencia's rationale for refusing to write this history on the grounds that "the excuses he offers for not writing this history cannot and should not be accepted. . . . A prudent writer should know how to write [history] without separating himself from the truth and also without causing unnecessary scandal or rumor."[146] Finally, if Valencia refused to relent, the council recommended that his salary as chronicler ought to be suspended. This measure was one that Philip III refused to endorse, and the king's decision to ignore the council's recommendations enabled Valencia to hang on to his job, and his salary, for another four years—he died in 1620—without advancing the general history he was commissioned to write.

Herrera's Later Years

Although Herrera had just turned seventy, Valencia's death offered the aging chronicler a new lease on life. Herrera also benefitted from a new political climate occasioned by the accession of a new monarch, Philip IV, in 1621. Lerma, and Philip III, had been strong advocates of making peace with Spain's enemies, notably the Dutch, a policy that did not sit well with Herrera. In contrast, the

144. The relevant document is cited in Morocho Gayo, "Una historia de Felipe III," 1148.
145. AGI IG: leg. 752, 17 September 1616.
146. Ibid.

policies of the new royal favorite, Gaspar de Guzmán, count (later count-duke) of Olivares, reflected his own belief that the only way for the monarchy—and Spain—to strengthen its international reputation was to adopt a hard line against Protestant forces that threatened its interests, whether in Netherlands, the Mediterranean, or the New World. Growing tensions in northern Italy, especially the Valtelline, a strategically important Swiss valley to the north of Milan, also played into Herrera's hands. The population of the valley was predominantly Catholic, its overlords Protestant, and the relationship between the two parties was far from peaceful. In addition, the French were known to have designs on the valley, the Venetians as well, and to prevent the possibility of an invasion, the duke of Feria, the Spanish governor of Milan, occupied the Valtelline in July 1620, quickly establishing a series of armed garrisons to protect the valley's inhabitants and forestall any external attack. Another potential flashpoint was the small marquisate of Monferrato, which was coveted by Charles-Emmanuel, duke of Savoy. These and other disputes provided Herrera the opportunity to return to the political fray and demonstrate that his mastery of the region's complex history was second to none. He also saw them as an opportunity to offer suggestions as to what policies the monarchy might adopt.

Herrera first went public with his thoughts on this subject in May 1621, when he was summoned to the meeting of the Cortes of Castile in Madrid and asked to present his analysis of the situation in the Valtelline. Herrera responded with a capsule history of recent events in the region, emphasizing the extent to which Protestants, known as the *grisons*, were oppressing the local Catholics and forcing the monarchy to spend vast sums (150,000 ducats per month, according to Herrera's calculations) to guard against a possible attack on Milan. Echoing arguments he had expressed in his histories, Herrera warned that "the intent of the enemies of our Holy Catholic Faith is to rob and steal, as well as to find a way to introduce their false opinions which we have so far guarded successfully against, with strongly guarded frontiers . . . galleys and ships."[147] Pointing, moreover, to recent successes of the Army of Flanders in the Netherlands, he recommended that the king should do even more to defend the Valtelline.

Herrera expounded upon these ideas in a book—his last—with the inordinately lengthy title of *Comentarios de los hechos de los españoles, franceses y venecianos en Italia y de otra republicas, principes y capitranes famosos italianos desde el año de 1281 hasta el de 1559*. Completed in 1621 but not published until 1624, just a

---

147. As cited in Danvila y Collado, "Nuevos datos," 499. Herrera addressed the Cortes in May 1623 and again in February 1623.

year before his death, the volume was pointedly dedicated to Olivares. This history, his first in almost a decade, offered a somewhat sketchy account of Italian history from the Sicilian Vespers (1282) through to the Treaty of Cateau-Cambresís (1559). But Herrera, politic as ever, chose these dates carefully (even though he got that of the Sicilian Vespers wrong.) The first marked the beginning of the Sicilian revolt to expel Charles of Anjou, the Angevin ruler who, with papal connivance, took control of the island in 1266. The second marked the treaty that put a temporary end to efforts by France's Valois kings to become masters of northern Italy. The narrative, such as it was, connecting these dates emphasized that the French had invaded Italy on eight different occasions, but according to Herrera, every invasion had been successfully repulsed, generally with help from Spain, as in 1559 when Philip II, having defeated the French at St. Quentin, enabled Italy to live in peace and without fear from further French attack.

Herrera's history did not explicitly address the prevailing strategic situation in Italy, but he clearly understood the extent to which a resurgent France threatened the Italian *pax hispanica* originally imposed by the emperor Charles V. In this respect, his account of Italy was less a history than a policy statement or position paper designed to provide Philip IV and Olivares with the historical background needed to justify sending additional troops to Milan. They responded by rewarding Herrera with a lucrative new office, a secretaryship attached to the royal commission on mining, which enabled him to pay some of his debts. It is also worth noting that Herrera's reading of the strategic situation in northern Italy was prescient. In 1624 a combined French-Savoyard army crossed the Alps, invaded Monferrato, and then used it as stronghold to threaten not only the Valtelline but Spain's ally the Republic of Genoa as well. Olivares took up this challenge by sending additional troops to Milan, but in doing so he initiated a wider conflict now known as the War of the Mantuan Succession (1628–1631), in which Spanish forces successfully fought to expel French soldiers from Italian soil. Historians are rarely prophets, but on this occasion, Herrera, with a lifetime of experience behind him, proved clairvoyant. Occasionally, historians get it right.

On balance, Herrera's career is best described as that of an activist. As a historian, he was not especially innovative nor original, and reading his unadorned prose is definitely something of a slog. Yet plain prose was part of Herrera's rhetorical strategy; it was meant to impress upon readers the essential truthfulness of his narrative. Herrera was equally determined to reach a broad audience, which accounts for his decision to write in the vernacular. As this audience was primarily home grown, he constructed his histories to convince Spanish readers that their future as a nation rested upon on the monarchy's willingness to uphold its sacred mission to promote good government and defend the Catholic faith. Moreover, Herrera took his job seriously, considering it both an honor and a duty to write history in support of his *patria* and his prince. His contemporaries Francis Bacon and Paolo Sarpi had similar ideas, but given the depth of his commitment to official history, Herrera did far more than others to transform Clio, history's cherished muse, into a servant of the state.

CHAPTER SIX

"To Mortify Our Enemies"
History and Propaganda at the Court of Philip IV

Opinion holds the key to reputation.
—Lope de Vega, *El rey don Pedro en Madrid* (1626?)

It is difficult to write about contemporaries; all men commit errors, and few, after having done them, want to hear anything more about them. Better then to praise these men, or keep quiet.
—Baltasar Gracián, *Agudeza y el arte del ingenio* (1648)

We already know princes and potentates in our century who, bribing their historians and even foreign ones, rent praises and purchase encomia, in order to obtain . . . the reputation they cannot achieve with their struggles and virtues.
—José Pellicer de Ossau y Tovar, *Epitome de la historia universal* (1638)

In 1628, shortly after Louis XIII had honored him with the title of *historiographe de France*, Charles Sorel announced his idea for a new history of the French monarchy in his *Avertissement sur l'histoire de la monarchie française*. A former novelist, Sorel explained that he wanted this history to be popular and "agréable," and he proposed to achieve a broad readership by writing with clarity and simplicity and avoiding the lengthy harangues and Greek citations characteristic of humanist history. He would also have none of the "chicaneries" and fascination with court gossip he associated with previous histories of the

---

Epigraphs: Lope de Vega, *El rey don Pedro en Madrid y infanzón de Ilescas*, edited by Carol Bingham Kirby (Kassel, Germany, 2003), 145 (*Jornada* 1, line 168); Baltasar Gracián, *Agudeza*, in *Obras completas*, 510; José de Pellicer Ossau y Tovar, "*Epitome de la historia universal*," BNE: Ms. 2066, 148v.

monarchy. Rather, he would emphasize only the "glorious actions" of its rulers in both peace and war.[1]

When Sorel's proposed history appeared the following year as *Histoire de la monarchie française*, it was far from a popular success. However, the "agreeable" history he wanted to produce was precisely the kind of history that appealed to Spain's new monarch, Philip IV (1621–1665), but with an important difference. Whereas Sorel wrote a history that spanned the whole of the French monarchy, Philip IV's understanding of history was more closely aligned with the more utilitarian or politic history embraced by his father, Philip III, a ruler known to have "read history and meditated about it, as if it were essential for governing well, recognizing that it was teacher of human life, a guide to understanding, and an inspiration for learning about the customs and inclinations of foreigners, as well as to defend himself against them."[2] The new monarch's historical preferences also reflected those of his tutors and advisers, especially Gaspar de Guzmán, the count (later count-duke) of Olivares who, as the royal favorite, or *privado*, exercised enormous influence over Philip IV and his policies throughout the first half of the king's long reign. Olivares's understanding of history was particularly pragmatic, and as this chapter explores, the royal favorite rarely hesitated to treat Clio as if her only task was to promote the reputation of Spain's Habsburg monarchy, both at home and abroad.[3]

The count-duke's—and Philip IV's—interest in history with a political edge formed part of a larger political program predicated on the concept of *conservación*, the need to maintain the Catholic Monarchy's power and prestige as a political actor. *Conservación* as then understood derived primarily from the idea of prudence as formulated by Justus Lipsius, the Neo-Stoic writer whose works were especially influential in Spain at the start of the seventeenth century. Different monarchs, however, interpreted *conservación* in different ways. For Philip III, and Lerma, it meant ending the wars they had inherited from Philip II, a policy that culminated in the Twelve Years Truce with the Dutch in 1609. For Philip IV, and Olivares, it entailed policies of economic and social reform that were coupled, somewhat uncomfortably, with a foreign policy predicated on "just wars"—first in the Low Countries, then Italy and Germany—fought to defend Philip IV's territorial inheritance, to defend Catholicism, and also to bolster the king's reputation as Europe's most powerful monarch. Translated into history, *conservación*

---

1. My understanding of Sorel rests primarily upon Ranum, *Artisans of Glory*, 129–147; along with Roy, *La vie et les oeuvres de Charles Sorel*, 329–344.
2. Novoa, *Memorias*, lx:29.
3. *HGM*, vol. 2, *dedicatoria* to the count of Miranda.

implied support for writers prepared to produce narratives, official histories, specifically tailored to Luis Cabrera de Córdoba's idea that "the purpose of history is the public good." "Public" in this instance was defined in the Aristotelian sense as the business of government, or what Spaniards in the seventeenth century were beginning to equate with the "estado," or state.[4]

As a member of the "generation that had read Botero," Cabrera de Córdoba derived his thoughts on the political importance of history partly from the *Ragion di stato*. They can also be traced to Francesco Patrizi, a sixteenth-century Italian writer who measured history's importance chiefly in terms of its political utility; to Machiavelli, who argued that history was valuable only insofar as it provided lessons for rulership; and ultimately to Polybius and his idea of history as a "guide for action." In this respect, Cabrera de Córdoba, along with his contemporary Herrera y Tordesillas, espoused an understanding of history that approximated the particular kind of politic history associated with such writers as Francis Bacon in England and J. A de Thou in France, both of whom envisioned history as a discipline meant to offer insights into political issues of contemporary concern. As Jacob Soll has observed, Thou regarded history as an instrument of peace and thus wrote his multivolume *History of Our Time* (1605–1609) with an eye toward rallying support, both Catholic and Protestant, for the monarchy of Henry IV following a half century of religious division and murderous civil war.[5] In contrast, Bacon advocated that James I sponsor a new history that, starting with the Wars of the Roses, would document Britain's progress toward unification and, though he did not say so directly, presumably end with the manner in which the first Stuart monarch had succeeded in bring this union about.[6] Bacon struck a similar theme in his *History of the Reign of Henry VII* (1622), a work dedicated to the prince of Wales in the hope that the future Charles I might learn from the policies the first Tudor had used to unite a kingdom divided by factions and war.

Not all seventeenth-century historians were as politic in their interests as Bacon. Yet the first half of the century marks a moment in which politic history flourished as never before, owing to the patronage and support it received from such rulers as James I, Louis XIII, and the Grand Dukes of Tuscany, as well as Philip IV. For the historians involved in this enterprise, the trick in crafting such

---

4. Cabrera de Córdoba, *De historia*, bk. 1, discurso 9, p. 35.

5. Soll, *Publishing the Prince*, 42–43. Despite Thou's good intentions, the monarchy withdrew its support for his history and successfully lobbied the papacy to have it placed on the *Index of Prohibited Books*. The book's publishing history is the subject of Kinser, *The Historical Works of Jacques-Auguste De Thou*.

6. See Bacon, *The Advancement of Learning*, 2:89. Bacon's historical writings may be approached through the introduction to his *The History of the Reign of Henry VII*.

narratives was, in keeping with the guidelines of "perfect history," to convince readers of the irrefutable logic of the argument before them. One of the best manuals for writing this kind of history was Cabrera de Córdoba's *De historia* (1611), which advised writers in princely service not to "invent their material" but rather to treat the historical record with "prudence and eloquence" and then shape it as a "sculptor takes a stone, polishes it, and then uses both imagination and art to mold into it into a pleasing shape."[7] The idea, in short, was to persuade the reader as to the essential verisimilitude of the material before him or her even though it had been ingeniously molded in ways that best served the interest of the state. Hence Fray Juan de la Puente's definition of the office of royal chronicler as "la boca de la república," the "voice" or "spokesman" of the state."[8]

Puente's definition raises the issue of the extent to which official history sought to influence public opinion, or, following Jürgen Habermas, the "discursive space" commonly equated with "civil society," the famous public sphere, where individuals could freely discuss a variety of religious and political ideas.[9] As is well known, Habermas equated this discursive space with "bourgeois society," especially the coffee houses, debating societies, and salons of eighteenth-century London and Paris. He further that argued that whatever discursive space existed in previous epochs was dominated by princely propaganda. Recent scholarship, however, suggests otherwise, inasmuch as the seventeenth century, especially in cities such as London and Paris, marked the appearance of news sheets, of which only a handful were directly controlled by the state.[10] It is now also understood that the "public" in these cities were not just passive recipients of information but also producers, actors who voiced their own opinions and used both pamphlets and engravings to influence monarchical policy.[11]

A similar situation obtained in seventeenth-century Madrid, where, despite inquisitorial oversight, there existed a flourishing arena for the *arbitrista*, the writer of *arbitrios* or opinion pieces. Such writings, akin to legal briefs, were generally addressed in the form of memoranda (*memoriales*) to the monarch and were intended both to influence and effect changes in royal policy.[12] This same material also found its way into increasing numbers of pamphlets, news sheets, and justificatory tracts (known alternately as *relaciones, avisos,* and *manifiestos*),

7. Cabrera de Córdoba, *De historia*, bk. 1, discurso 11, p. 46.
8. Puente, *Tomo primero de la conveniencia*, 2.
9. Habermas, *The Structural Transformation of the Public Sphere*.
10. The international dimensions of this information explosion is examined in Dooley and Baron, *The Politics of Information*.
11. For French pamphlets, see Sawyer, *Pamphlet Propaganda;* and Duccini, *Faire voire, faire croire*. For English pamphleteering, see Cogswell, "The Politics of Propaganda."
12. See Vilar Berrogain, *Literatura y economia*.

which, starting in the 1620s, circulated in increasing numbers both in manuscript and in print.[13] Many of these *relaciones* were critical of the person and the policies of the royal favorite, the count-duke of Olivares, and to keep a lid on such publications in 1627 the monarchy issued a decree specifically prohibiting the printing of any news sheet or pamphlet, especially those relating to "matters of state," that had not been personally approved by a member of the Royal Council of Castile.[14] Olivares subsequently used this decree to imprison Quevedo and other political enemies, but determined authors (and printers) got around the law either by ignoring it or by allowing their work to circulate in manuscript.[15] As a result the decree had to be reissued on several occasions, but its very existence speaks not only to the importance the monarchy accorded to public opinion but also its fear of the potential dangers posed by the random and unregulated circulation of information.[16] At the same time, historians recognized the growing importance of this public by writing in the vernacular instead of Latin. One author who made this choice was the Dominican scholar Fray Juan de la Puente, who wrote a history arguing for the superiority of Spain's Catholic Monarch to all other European princes in Castilian so as to reach a broad audience.[17]

This same arena, what one prominent historian of seventeenth-century Britain referred to as the "political nation," was precisely where public opinion during the seventeenth century was shaped.[18] It is difficult to pinpoint the moment when rulers came to recognize that the successful implementation of policy, whether national or international, was a matter of give and take, one that depended on a measure of popular consent to the extent that court factions were placated, national assemblies cowed, and influential ministers brought into line. But to venture a guess, that moment was closely linked to the outbreak, starting in 1619, of the Thirty Years War, a conflict that, owing in part to the sheer number of different princes involved, triggered a pamphlet war of truly international and unprecedented dimensions. This war of words began in 1620 with the appearance of the pamphlet *Altera secretissima instructio*. Prepared by the imperial chan-

---

13. On public opinion and its importance in seventeenth-century Spain, cf. Maravall, *Culture of the Baroque*, 97–98; and Ettinghausen, "Politics and the Press in Spain." For individual news sheets, see *Gacetas y nuevas de la corte de España; Gaceta Nueva, 1661–1663*; and Almansa y Mendoza, *Obra periodística*.

14. Cf. Domínguez Ortiz, "La censura de obras históricas," 115; and Elliott, "Power and Propaganda."

15. One chronicler, Matías de Novoa, did just this with his *Memorias*, which were openly critical of the count-duke and, if published, would almost certainly have led to his arrest.

16. For censorship in seventeenth-century France, see Soman, "Press, Pulpit, and Censorship in France"; and Klaits, *Printed Propaganda under Louis XIV*, esp. chap. 2.

17. Puente, *Tomo primero de la conveniencia*, 15.

18. See Plumb, *The Growth of Political Stability in England*, 27.

cery in Vienna, it suggested that the newly elected king of Bohemia, a Protestant, was about to sign a treaty allowing the Ottomans to take possession of most of eastern Europe. Contestant pamphlets soon followed, and it was not long before rulers across Europe embraced the politics of misinformation by sponsoring, both directly and indirectly, the publication of news sheets, propagandistic pamphlets, and engravings that defended their interests while attacking those of their enemies.[19] One of the few who argued for caution in the midst of this propaganda war was Paolo Sarpi, the official historian of the Republic of Venice. Sarpi advised his government that the best way to defend the interests of the republic was to take the high ground and either remain silent, so as not to appear overly defensive, or to respond in a more measured way via a well-written history, preferably one written by a sympathetic foreigner rather than one who was native born. For Sarpi, therefore, history and politics were essentially one.[20]

Politic history thus belonged to, and was indeed a product of, a broad and ever-widening discursive space populated by competing and often contradictory points of view. In such a climate, few histories went unanswered, leading to a kind of tit-for-tat history that contributed to what Jacob Soll, with reference to early-seventeenth-century France, has aptly called "an arms race of criticism and attacks" based on competing historical texts.[21] But what Soll overlooked was that this arms race was not constrained by national frontiers. Tit-for-tat history played out on an international stage, involving competing systems of religious beliefs, different state actors, multiple reading publics, and overlapping narratives offering alternate and often opposing interpretations of similar happenings and events.[22]

In such a world, contemporary history acquired new meaning and importance. Knowledge of ancient history remained de rigueur, but already in the 1580s even as learned a humanist as Montaigne questioned the relevance of ancient experience to the present; his, after all, was a new world, with new continents and peoples that the ancients were not aware of.[23] Similar questions about the "utility" of ancient history can be found in the work of Francis Bacon and Richard Burton in England, as well as in Juan Antonio de Vera y Figueroa's widely read diplomatic

19. See Dooley and Baron, *The Politics of Information*, together with such more focused studies as Elliott and Brown, *A Palace for a King*; Callard, *Le prince et la république*; and Burke, *The Fabrication of Louis XIV*.
20. For Sarpi's ideas about propaganda, see his "Del confutar scritture malediche." Of related interest is Vivi, "Paolo Sarpi and the Uses of Information."
21. Soll, *Publishing the Prince*, 41.
22. For this world of competing narratives, and Spain's role within it, see Schmidt, *Spanische Univerisalmonarchie*. Also useful is Malcolm, *Reason of State, Propaganda, and the Thirty Years' War*.
23. Cf. Bouwsma, *Waning of the Renaissance*, 57.

treatise *The Ambassador* (1620), which recommended that would-be statesmen would find it much more useful to read the histories of "our time" than those of "past centuries."[24] History was also politicized, becoming a matter of state policy, and was even militarized to the extent that it was not unusual to refer to history as a weapon, usually a lance or spear, to be deployed in accordance with particular interests and concerns. Evidence for this move—what I call history's "political turn"—can be found across Europe: in the Netherlands, where in 1601 the States General of Holland commissioned its official historian, Hugo Grotius, to write a series of histories that have been likened to "legal briefs";[25] in England, where James I attempted (albeit unsuccessfully) to create a new office of historiographer royal for the purpose of writing a new history of Great Britain that he could approve; in France, where Cardinal Richelieu, starting in the 1620s, created a *cabinet d'histoire,* whose members were expected to prepare both pamphlets and histories in support of state policy; and in Spain, where, as previously noted, international debates over the monarchy's policies contributed directly to Philip II's decision to harness the power of history to that of state. As a ruler whose admiration for his grandfather was profound, Philip IV could be expected to look upon history in a similar way.

Philip IV and History

In keeping with what was already family tradition, Philip IV's introduction to history began early, probably at the age of seven, when Galcerán Albanell was appointed to serve as "maestro de príncipe."[26] While it remains uncertain what kind of history this "caballero de Barcelona" taught the young prince, instruction in this subject definitely got under way in 1613, when Philip III appointed the Portuguese chronicler and cosmographer João Bautista Lavanha (1555–1624) as "maestro de matemáticas del príncipe."[27] Lavanha promptly prepared several textbooks, including one on cosmography and another on geography, so organized as to help the prince to get a grip on the global reach of the monarchy he was soon to inherit. Lavanha also presented Philip with a historical atlas incorporating

24. Vera y Figueroa, *El Enbajador,* discurso 1, 91v.
25. Blanc, "Hugo Grotius."
26. Cf. Cabrera de Córdoba, *Relaciones,* 469, where Galcerán is described as "muy docto en letras hiumans." Philip IV's education is examined in Hoffman-Strock, "Carved on Rings and Painted in Pictures."
27. For Lavanha's biography, see Cortesão, *Portugaliae Monumenta Cartographica,* 4:63–70. Pérez Pastor, *Bibliografía madrileña,* 2:320. The chronicler Matías de Novoa referred to Lavanha as an "autor científico y sin duda abonado." See *Codoin,* 61:116.

maps of his kingdoms, genealogies of the House of Habsburg, and a synopsis of his own, still unfinished, manuscript on the monarchy's history.[28] The atlas is no longer extant, but if it was like all the other textbooks that Lavanha prepared, it articulated a utilitarian notion of knowledge that integrated the study of history, geography, and natural phenomena with the conduct of human affairs. Lavanha thus anticipated by several years Cabrera de Córdoba's suggestion that the prince "should read histories, as these contain so much of what is necessary both to live well and to rule, together with geography, and state papers."[29]

For Philip, introduction to the world of kingship began in 1614 when he was presented with an "army" of toy soldiers. The gift of Ambrosio Spinola, Spain's captain general in the Netherlands, this army consisted of wooden soldiers "six fingers high" as well as horses, artillery pieces, models of fortresses, and more. Philip's reaction to this gift is not recorded, but five years later his "army" was laid out on a special cork-surfaced platform (or "tablado") so as to introduce the prince to various aspects of the "art of war": battle formation, the management and defense of military encampments, and the complexities of siege warfare. The *tablado* also included cubbyholes and shelves to store various charts, atlases, and maps.[30]

This *tablado* and its army were simply one element in a special "camarín" or small gallery that Lavanha created for the prince in Madrid's royal palace, the Alcázar, at the very top of the tower known alternatively as Torre Alta or Torre Dorada. Details are few, but Lavanha, anticipating Bacon's imagined "House of Solomon" by several years, conceived and organized the *camarín* as a place of universal but practical learning, a space where Philip could acquire the knowledge necessary to govern an empire that was global in scope. By 1621, the year in which Philip became king, this gallery already contained a small "cabinet of wonders" filled with "natural rarities from all over the world"; a map room that, in addition to the items stored in the *tablado*, contained sea charts of both the Atlantic and the Pacific oceans (the work of Lavanha?); a map of China "made by them"; "a map of the Indies made by the Indians themselves"; and a genealogical

---

28. Juan Baptista Lavaña, "Abregé de la geographie et de l'histoire d' Espagne," BNF: Mss. Espagnols, 131. Dedicated "al Príncipe N.S." and dated San Lorenzo el Real, 18 August 1616, as cited in Bibliothèque Nationale (France), Département des manuscrits, *Catalogue des manuscrits espagnols et des manuscrits portugais* (Paris, 1892), 43. Lavanha noted that he had prepared this synopsis especially for the prince "en quanto no se estampa el libro de descripción i historia de los grandes reinos i estados de que la monarchia de España se constituie."

29. Luís Cabrera de Córdoba, *Considerando la educación de su Alteza* (1618), as cited in Bouza Álvarez, *El libro y el cetro*, 30.

30. Sáenz de Miera, "Lo raro del orbe," 279. According to Echevarria Bacigalupe, *Alberto Struzzi*, 18, the army was destroyed in a fire in the royal palace in 1884. This "army" was first described in *Imago militae auspiciis Ambrosii Spinolae*, a rare pamphlet I have not had the opportunity to consult.

tree of the House of Austria, almost certainly one of several that Lavanha had previously prepared for Philip III.[31]

This same gallery, which was situated directly above the office in which Philip IV ordinarily dispatched business, also housed the king's private library. According to one observer, the young monarch was "so interested in books that, at the beginning of his reign, he ordered the creation of this library as he was not content with the one in El Escorial; he wanted to be able to consult it daily."[32] The exact date of this library's creation remains uncertain, but Lavanha almost certainly had a hand in its creation, because both its contents and its organization reflected his ideas about the need for princes to relate different branches of learning to the business of state. Control of the library, however, soon passed to the royal favorite Olivares, who assumed full responsibility for the king's education following the death of Lavanha in 1624. A bibliophile in his own right, Olivares possessed one of the largest and most important collections of printed books and manuscripts in Spain, outside of the royal library at El Escorial, and he still had the time to purchase more even as he immersed himself in the business of state. Olivares's personal librarian, Francisco de Rioja (1583–1659), served also as the king's librarian and, starting in 1621, held the office of royal chronicler as well.[33] Olivares was therefore uniquely positioned to determine the contents of the king's personal library, and according to Fernando Bouza, the boundary separating the king's personal library from that of the count-duke was never clearly drawn. In fact, Olivares regularly used the king's library as if it were his own, and there is at least one instance in which, with help from Rioja, books from the king's collection found their way into the count-duke's, then housed in Loeches, a small town near Madrid.[34]

When first cataloged by Rioja in 1637, this library contained 2,244 books housed in forty cabinets, one for "cosmography, geography and topography" and others for "government and state," "agriculture," "music," "books of devotion and piety," and so forth. History books accounted for 36 percent of the books housed in the library. These were stored in seventeen different cabinets, subdivided by themes.

31. Sáenz de Miera, "Lo raro del orbe," 279.
32. Cited in Bouza Álvarez, *Del escribano a la biblioteca*, 131n22.
33. Elliott and de la Peña, *Memoriales y cartas*, 1:185. For Rioja's appointment as royal chronicler on 10 July 1621, see AHN Cons, lib. 513, fol. 96v.
34. Writing in 1639, the Aragonese chronicler Andrés de Uztárroz claimed that in 1626, during the course of a visit to Zaragoza, the count-duke sought to "enriquecer su biblioteca" with manuscripts belonging to Jerónimo Zurita that were then housed in that city's Carthusian monastery ("De este lugar los sacó el conde-duque"). Cf. BNE: Ms. 8389, fol. 170, Uztárroz to Tamayo de Vargas, 14 March 1639. For Olivares's library, see Andrés, "Historia de la biblioteca del Conde-Duque"; and his "Biblioteca selecta del Conde-Duque."

Books in King Philip IV's Library

World histories	8
Histories of Spain and Castile	53
Histories of cities and bishoprics of Spain	36
Histories of the kingdoms of Aragon, Valencia, Catalonia, Cerdegne, Mallorca and Menorca, Navarre, and Vizcaya	44
History of the Kingdom of Portugal and its India, China, Japan, Philippines, and Ethiopia possessions	77
Histories of the West Indies	31
Histories of Africa and Ethiopia	26
Histories of Persia	11
Histories of Poland, Muscovy, Bohemia, Hungary, Transylvania, Denmark, and Sweden	15
Histories of England and Scotland	15
French histories	39
Italian histories	132
History and wars of Flanders and Germany in Italian and Castilian	33
Nobility and lineages of Spain and other places	32
History of important persons	53
Military orders and [the order of] The Golden Fleece	24
Greek historians in translation	30
Latin historians, translated into romance [Castilian], Italian, and French	34
Ecclesiastical history	115
Total	808

Source: Adapted from Bouza, *El libro y el cetro*.

That more than one-third of the royal library was devoted to history was not unusual. William Bouwsma has argued that the seventeenth century marked a sharp decline in historical consciousness, but the contents of this library, and of other collections dating from the period, suggest that Spain was not part of this trend.[35] To be sure, the king's private library, if judged by European standards, was not especially large—the library of the French historian de Thou contained more than ten thousand volumes—but given the scope and geographical range of its contents, it is perhaps best described as a private library (or *bibliotheca selecta*) that bordered on what historians of libraries call a *bibliotheca universalis*. But the collection still had limitations. Although it incorporated such books as Franchi de Conestaggio's history of the war in Flanders, a volume that Spanish censors had previously banned, works by George Buchanan, Francis Hotman, and a host of other Protestant historians were conspicuously absent, meaning that the histories in his library offered Philip IV an almost uniformly Catholic vision of the world. As Spain's Catholic Monarch, Philip IV was expected to fight heretics but refrain from reading what these same heretics wrote about Europe's recent past.

How many of these books did Philip actually read? And, equally important,

---

35. Bouwsma, *Waning of the Renaissance*, 198–214.

how did he read them? Montaigne used his famous library—also housed in a tower—as a place of seclusion, an idyllic retreat.[36] In contrast, Philip's IV's library was more of a practical resource, and together with the cartographic materials housed in the *tablado*, it served as a database to be consulted for information and ideas relevant to formulating policy, planning strategy, and the everyday business of running a monarchy as large as his own. Olivares certainly used the library in this way when, shortly after learning about the revolt of Portugal in December 1640, he and some advisers climbed the Torre Alta to consult not only a map of Portugal but also various histories for insights into the legal basis of Spain's claim to the Portuguese crown. They also looked at Franchi di Conestaggio's previously banned *Union of Spain and Portugal*, for information about the military tactics used by Philip II to pacify that kingdom in 1580–1581, evidently expecting to repeat his success.[37] Presumably Philip IV used the library in a similarly utilitarian fashion, although one chronicler, Matías de Novoa, no friend of the count-duke, faulted the royal favorite for encouraging the king to read history simply for pleasure. "What is the point of liking, even reading histories," asked Novoa, "if we do not take out of the utility and benefit, and living examples that influence us together with the knowledge to foresee risks and dangers and thus to avoid them?"[38]

This comment was somewhat unfair. Philip IV was something of an intellectual lightweight, but he knew his history, and in 1627 one of his secretaries reported that he was "accustomed to read histories of Castile and foreign countries every night."[39] Moreover, the king acknowledged his love of the subject in a short autobiographical sketch that he wrote around 1633. "Reading histories," he claimed, helped satisfy his desire to learn about the world. "These [works]," he added, echoing some of the basic ideas of politic history, "are a true school in which a Prince or King will find examples to follow, events worthy of note, and the ways to rule a Monarchy successfully."[40] He then listed many of the histories he had read: chronicles of Castile and its monarchs, starting with Ferdinand III and concluding with the history of the emperor, "my great-grandfather"; Mariana's *Historia general de España*; histories of Flanders, France, Germany, and the Indies;

---

36. For Montaigne's library as a retreat, see Adi Ophir, "A Place of Knowledge Re-Created: The Library of Michel de Montaigne," *Science in Context* 4, no. 1 (1991): 163–189.
37. "Memorias de Matías de Novoa," *Codoin*, 80:396–397.
38. Novoa, *Historia de Felipe IV*, 282. On this occasion, Novoa noted that the king was reading Commines and Guicciardini. I am grateful to Prof. Bouza for bringing this citation to my attention.
39. Antonio de Mendoza, as cited in *Catálogo de los manuscritos que pertenecieron a Pascual de Gayangos existentes hoy en la Biblioteca Nacional*, edited by Pedro Roca (Madrid, 1904), 210–211.
40. Cf. Philip IV, "Autosemblanza de Felipe IV," 232–233.

the Jesuit Pedro de Ribadeneyra's history of the Armada; and various Roman histories (he specifically mentioned those by Sallust, Livy, Lucan, and Tacitus, all of which could be found in his library).

In the same document the king confessed that he read some histories "more for entertainment than for any other reason," noting that they offered a "diversion" from the "endless work and obligations" associated with kingship. In this respect, Novoa's above-mentioned comment was correct, and in keeping with the then current idea of using history as "a guide for action," the king acknowledged that he read in search of "noticias de provecho" (utilitarian advice) and other information that individuals "occupying the position I hold" might find of use.[41] Even then, he expressed disappointment in the kind of *noticias* that history, especially ancient and medieval history, was able to offer. "I was not really happy with these histories because it strikes me that they dealt with past times. It is necessary to read those that deal with the present," he said, echoing Vera y Figueroa's recommendation about the need for statesmen to read contemporary history. In the end, however, the king concluded that the best way to obtain the *noticias* he was after was through experience: "In the seventh year of my reign [1627], I decided, in order to achieve what I had set out to do, to dispatch personally (without even the assistance of a secretary to read them to me) all of the memoranda [*consultas*] related to government and appointments."[42] In doing so, Philip confessed that he was modeling himself on "the most prudent prince who had ever lived," his grandfather, Philip II, a ruler whose history he is likely to have approached either through the work of Luis Cabrera de Córdoba or though Lorenzo Van der Hamen y León's *Don Felipe el Prudente*, a short, popular biography that was published in 1625.[43]

As Philip dipped into this administrative routine, Olivares advised that "the art of government" also required knowledge of foreign languages, especially Italian, and suggested that one way to gain such knowledge was to translate portions of Guicciardini's *History of Italy*, notably books 8 and 9, into Castilian. For Philip, Guicciardini was "the most elegant, concise, pleasing, and powerful ["de gran nervio"] historian one could read," but the decision to translate only books 8 and 9, which focused on the efforts of France's Valois kings to control northern Italy, was politically motivated: it was meant to provide the young monarch with the background to understand the ongoing crisis in the Valtelline.[44] Philip later ex-

---

41. Ibid.
42. Ibid., 233. Translation in Elliott, *Count-Duke of Olivares*, 318.
43. The royal library in the Torre Alta included Cabrera de Córdoba, *Historia de Felipe II*; along with the biography by Van der Hamen.
44. Philip IV, "Autosemblanza de Felipe IV," 235. The idea of this translation has been attributed to the count-duke, but it could also have easily come from Vera y Figueroa's *El Enbajador*, a book that

plained, "I was also inspired to select this section, because it appeared as if the events it examined seem similar to those of today, especially with respect to wars, alliances, and other happenings in Europe during the first twelve years of my reign." He also believed that his translation one day might benefit his own son, Baltasar Carlos, then age four. All this, he added, "convinced me to undertake this translation, which offers very useful lessons that will benefit future generations and especially my descendants, [who will be] charged with the universal government of these kingdoms and the various states that comprise this Monarchy."[45]

These statements offer invaluable, almost unique insights into historical consciousness of a seventeenth-century prince. They also indicate that by 1633, the year of this "autobiography," Philip IV had a clear understanding of the kind of history he preferred. Pleasure and relaxation aside, he was on the lookout for histories that related past events to what he called "el presente" and, like his father, sought to link history, as Lavanha first taught him, to "the art of governance."

Philip's present-minded, utilitarian vision of history manifested itself in various ways. Initially in 1623, the young monarch had Juan de Mariana update his *Historia general de España* with an addendum covering the period from 1516 to 1621, the latter marking the first year of Philip's reign.[46] That same year the king, believing that Philip III's untimely death had robbed him of the opportunity to benefit from his father's example and experience with "the business of the monarchy," ordered Gil González Dávila, a royal chronicler since 1617, to write a history of Philip III's reign.[47] Dutifully Dávila complied, completing this history sometime before 1625, but at this point the manuscript went underground, with copies circulating, in clandestine fashion, in and around the court. Even the king, who had his own copy, was said to keep it a secret ("la tiene oculta").[48] The best explanation for the book's disappearance and failure to get into print stems from González Dávila's suggestion that Philip IV, unlike his father, should rule independently and without a favorite. "The king of such an extended monarchy," wrote Dávila, "has to have many ministers, because just as the rivers that lead to

---

figured in Torre Alta and where Philip could read, with specific reference to Guicciardini, that "the recent histories of Italy are without any doubt filled with most useful examples." Discurso 1, 91v–93.

45. Philip IV, "Autosemblanza de Felipe IV," 235. For insights into Philip IV's thinking about history, see Stradling: *Philip IV and the Government of Spain*, 63, 309–312.

46. The king reportedly offered Mariana a gift of fifteen hundred ducats "para imprimir la historia de España, que tiene muy añadida." Cf. Almansa y Mendoza, *Obra periodística*, 247.

47. Philip IV, "Autosemblanza de Felipe IV," 232. Philip III had appointed González Dávila cronista del rey with the understanding that he was to write an ecclesiastical history of Castile. Cf. Agustín Millares Carlos, *Tres estudios biobibliográficos* (Maracaibo, 1941), 117–192.

48. On the "secrecy" surrounding Dávila's book, see Guadalajara y Xavier, *Quinta parte de la historia pontifical*, 416; and especially AGS: Estado leg. 8814, Lorenzo Van der Hamen y León to the marquis of Villena, Madrid, 19 December 1628.

the sea are many, if everyone is obliged to pass through the same door, confusion and complaints are inevitable."[49]

These comments were clearly directed at Olivares, the minister whom González Dávila later described as the worst royal favorite among the nineteen he was able to find in Castile's long history.[50] Olivares's personal opinion of González Dávila remains unknown, but the royal favorite was almost certainly responsible for squashing publication of his history of Philip III. At the same time, and in recognition of Philip IV's interest in his father's accomplishments, Olivares is likely to have been the driving force behind the publication of *Eternidad del rey don Felipe III . . . el Piadoso,* a rather saccharine biography that came from the pen of Ana de Castro Egas, a learned but somewhat obscure female courtier who steered clear of the issue of royal favorites and focused instead on Philip III's virtues, representing him in traditional fashion as the ideal prince, an *exemplum* that Philip IV could do well to emulate.[51] In 1637, when Francisco de Rioja inventoried Philip IV's library, Castro Egas's biography was there, but the history by González Dávila was not.

An oversight? Or, as is much more likely, a calculated "disappearance" of a controversial text? What is certain is that during the years of his *privança*, which lasted from 1621 until 1643, Olivares effectively assumed control of the writing along with the publishing of history at the Spanish court. For this reason, it is almost impossible to separate the king's utilitarian understanding of history from that of his *privado,* who used history—and historians—in a particularly politic way.

"Mortify Our Enemies"

In October 1634 Spain's Council of State interrupted its ordinary activities to discuss the current state of historical writing in Spain. Such a discussion was not unprecedented, but it speaks directly to the importance that Spain's monarchy

---

49. González Dávila, *Historia de . . . Felipe III,* 41. The printed version of González Dávila's history, dating from 1770, suggests that the author revised this manuscript after he first presented it to Philip III as it includes references to the year 1633 (p. 209) and 1656 (p. 262).
50. Cf. BNE: Ms. 8389, "Cartas del Maestro Gil González de Avila . . . al Dr. Juan Francisco Andrés de Uztárroz," fol. 36 (letter of 14 February 1643); and fol. 38 (letter of 21 February 1643), where Dávila remarks that Olivares has committed more crimes than all of the other *privados*—he counted a total of nineteen—in Spain's history. Dávila also made critical comments about royal favorites in other histories, notably his *Historia de la vida y hechos del rey Henrique Terecero.* The best assessment of González Dávila as a historian is Cuart Moner's introduction to González Dávila's *Historia de las antigüedades de Salamanca.*
51. I refer to Castro Egas, *Eternidad del rey don Felipe III,* which was dedicated to Philip IV's younger brother Cardinal-Infante Ferdinand. Egas Castro awaits detailed study, but she may be approached through Cruz, "Gender and Class."

accorded an instrument of statecraft. On this occasion, the council's debate over history, and the lack thereof, was prompted by a request from the imperial ambassador Franz Cristoph Khevenhüller, count of Frankenburg (1578–1650), for permission to consult the papers and documents stored in the royal archive in Simancas. The count explained that he needed access to this collection because the emperor Ferdinand II (r. 1619–1637) had commissioned him to write a history of the empire's ongoing wars against Protestants. This history, later published (in twelve volumes) as the *Annales Ferdinandei,* was still in progress,[52] but the ambassador provided the council a *librillo,* a kind of outline or synopsis of what he was going to write. Ordinarily, Simancas was out of bounds for all but a handful of royal officials, but this request, coming from a diplomat closely allied with the monarchy, demanded attention. It also piqued the interest of Olivares, who intervened in the discussion with the remark: "Truly our faults are many, but none more serious than how little we attend to the writing of history. His Majesty should promptly consider ordering someone to write it, either one of his chroniclers or some other individual capable of doing it. And perhaps, if it is not too much of an inconvenience, the Count of Frankenburg might give the king something of what he has written about recent important events."[53]

Olivares continued by referring to a recently published polemic urging Philip IV to ally with the emperor and make common cause against the French, who had recently forged a series of defensive alliances with Protestant rulers fighting Ferdinand II. The author of this polemic, Juan Adam de la Parra, an inquisitor in Murcia, had painted a dire picture of French ambitions, emphasizing the longstanding designs of the French monarchy on the imperial crown. He even suggested that Philip IV, together with the emperor, should invade France in a defensive war designed to protect their common interests in both northern Italy and Germany.[54] Olivares, no friend of the French, was sympathetic to this argument, but for the moment he decided that a war of words would suffice. He therefore suggested that the council consider the possibility of having Parra, along with two or three other historians, compose a "worthy history . . . that could mortify the enemies of this Crown," and especially the French.[55] He imagined this history as a

---

52. Cristoph, *Annales Fernandini*.
53. AGS Est: leg. 2335, consulta, 27 October 1634, as cited in Elliott and de la Peña, *Memoriales y cartas,* 2:185.
54. Adam de la Parra, *Conspiración herético-cristianísima*. Similar arguments were made by Faria de Guzmán in his "Apologia en defensa," although this author went so far as to claim that the French throne rightly belonged to Philip IV "por linea de los condes de Habsburgo." Faria dedicated this polemic, dated 4 July 1634, to Olivares as well as Philip IV. According to Elliott, *Count-Duke of Olivares,* 615, Faria, a native of Granada, was serving as the head of the king's intelligence service.
55. See above, note 53.

weapon, a *saeta,* or sharp spear, capable of doing considerable damage in what soon mushroomed into a propaganda war directed at his French counterpart, Cardinal Richelieu, who, according to Parra, was responsible for having transformed Louis XIII into a "cruel enemy of the Roman church."[56]

This propaganda war, launched with equal intensity on both sides of the Pyrenees, is the subject of an excellent book by José María Jover Zamora, first published in 1949.[57] As Jover Zamora explains, Richelieu took the lead in this battle, since he was able to call upon the *chercheurs savants* already attached to his *cabinet de presse* to unleash a battery of pamphlets, engravings, even full-scale histories designed to marshal public support for his decision, on 1 April 1635, to declare war on Spain. Olivares responded with his own, somewhat hastily assembled junta or committee of historians. John Elliott, in his now-classic biography of the count-duke, dates this junta to June 1635, when Olivares informed the Council of State of the urgent need to counter the French with "a paper or general letter" addressed to the princes of Europe and the pope, and also *manifiestos* (pamphlets) to be scattered through France.[58] Yet new evidence suggests that the junta met as early as 24 April 1635 to prepare the "worthy history" that Olivares had suggested the previous year, in this instance one expressly designed to "demonstrate to the world the rationale underscoring His Majesty's actions and also to respond to the calumnies and false imputations fabricated by the French."[59]

The junta, dominated by the favorite's friends and protégés, had as its secretary Francisco de Calatayud, who had previously served the *privado* on various committees pertaining to education and culture. The junta also included Alonso Guillén de la Carrera, a jurist with expertise in Italian affairs,[60] Jusepe de Nápoles (d. 1642), a high-ranking member of the Council of Italy, Juan de Palafox y Mendoza, who represented the Council of the Indies, and Juan Adam de la Parra, whose anti-French polemic had so impressed Olivares that he had the inquisitor brought from Murcia to Madrid.

On April 24 these officials met, possibly in Olivares's private office, to outline the history they had been commissioned to write. Parra's polemic, together with Frankenburg's history, provided the junta with the language and some of the material for this history, which was intended to cover the period from 1624 (the

---

56. Adam de la Parra, *Conspiración herético-cristianísima,* xx.
57. Jover Zamora, *1635.*
58. Cf. Elliott, *Count-Duke of Olivares,* 489.
59. BR: Ms. II/1451, "Papeles de historia del reinado de Phelipe IV," fol. 19. Headed by Francisco de Calatayud, the junta, packed with Olivares's loyalists, included Adam de la Parra, Juan de Palafox y Mendoza, and Jusepe de Nápoles. This junta and its activities await detailed study.
60. Guillén de la Carrera headed the monarchy's governing council in Milan before his appointment to the Council of Italy in 1627.

start of the War of the Mantuan Succession) to 1635 and France's unilateral declaration of war against Spain. Another source was the treatise "On Italian Liberty" that Diego de Saavedra Fajardo had secretly prepared for Olivares in 1633 in an effort to counter the growing French threat to Spanish interests in Italy. Saavedra specifically tailored this treatise to expose the "calumnies" in French foreign policy, and in a letter to Olivares he suggested that it would be useful to any historian in his employ.[61] Armed with this and other sources, the junta also decided that once its members had completed their assignment, the finished history, pending Olivares's approval, was to be translated and printed in several languages—Spanish, French, Italian, and Latin—so that it could be "spread and distributed everywhere" in a concerted effort to drum up support for Spain and its policies.

The Junta de Cronistas was the seventeenth-century equivalent of the historiographical workshops organized by Alfonso X, the Catholic Monarchs, and Charles V. But whereas those earlier workshops reported directly to the monarch, the junta was essentially a private affair directed entirely by Olivares, an arrangement comparable to Richelieu's *cabinet de presse*. In both instances, the monarchy's official chroniclers played only a secondary role. Richelieu, for example, staffed his cabinet with individuals he could trust, and he even required Scipion Dupleix, "the king's private historian" (*historiographe privé de Sa Majesté*) to present drafts of his histories to him for approval.[62]

Whether the count-duke was fully apprised of the inner workings of Richelieu's press cabinet is not altogether clear, but he was surely aware that the cardinal, starting in the 1620s, used such publications as the *Mercure de France* to help sell his policies to a public suspicious of his growing influence over Louis XIII. Olivares did not go so far as to establish a journal or newspaper of his own, although he regularly called on the services of writers such as Francisco de Quevedo to influence public opinion by writing pamphlets supporting his policies (see below).[63] Quevedo, in fact, helped launch the propaganda war with France during the summer of 1635 with two broadsides designed to whip up Spanish support for the struggle against France. The first, an open letter to Louis XIII, accused the French king of divine lèse majesté ("lesa majestad divina") for having caused injury to God with his unjust decision to declare war on Spain, thereby

---

61. For this treatise (now lost) and Saavedra's letter, dated 20 April 1633, see Aldea Vaquero, *España y Europa*, 1:43.

62. For Richelieu's use of history and his relationship with Dupleix, see Church, *Richelieu and Reason of State*, 461–474; Orest Ranum, "Richelieu, l'histoire et les historiographes," in *Richelieu et la culture* (Paris, 1987), 125–137.

63. Cf. Elliott, "Quevedo and the Count-Duke of Olivares."

disrupting the peace. The second revolved around the discussions of a team of anatomists gathered in the famed faculty of medicine of the French university of Montpellier to inspect the inside of Cardinal Richelieu's skull. Together they determined that Louis XIII's favorite suffered from "morbio regio," or "royal disease," an ailment that had led him to usurp royal power and "vomit forth orders assaulting both provinces and families."[64]

Olivares also resembled Richelieu in that, with the exception of Rioja, who served as royal chronicler from 1621 until 1625, he regularly bypassed the monarchy's official chroniclers for writers he could trust. As noted above, his relationship with González Dávila was rocky to say the least. Nor did the count-duke evince much interest in the king's other chronicler, Tomás Tamayo de Vargas (1589–1641). Appointed cronista del rey following Herrera's death in 1625, Tamayo was known as something of a dilettante; he dabbled in subjects that ranged from antiquarian studies to biography to the controversial "false chronicles" relating to the early Christian history of Spain (see Chapter 7).[65] Tamayo's interest in these chronicles did little to endear him to Rioja, whose opinion of the new chronicler matched that of the Sevillian artist Francisco Pacheco, who described Tamayo as "without much substance, although fairly learned and skilled in the ways of the court."[66] Olivares's opinion of Tamayo was much the same, and in fact the only time he called upon this chronicler's services was in 1626 when he recruited him to write a *relación* commemorating the successful recapture of the Brazilian port of Bahía from the Dutch the previous year.[67] Otherwise, Olivares kept Tamayo at arm's length, having nothing to do, for example, with his "Junta de libros," a bibliographical compendium intended to demonstrate the depth and

---

64. Quevedo, *Obras completas*, 3: 267–315 for "Carta al serenísimo, muy alto y muy poderoso Luis XIII, rey cristianismo de Francia," and 3: 317–345 for "Visita y anatomia de la cabeza del Cardenal Armando de Richelieu."

65. For his defense of the false chronicles, see Tamayo de Vargas, *Defensa de Flavio Lucio Dextro*. Tamayo's biography—and bibliography—may be approached through Joseph Antonio Alvárez de Toledo, *Hijos de Madrid* . . . (Madrid, 1789; facsimile ed., Madrid, 1973), 4:341–347; see also Pérez Bustamante, *Antonio de Alcedo y su memoria*. Alcedo reports that Tamayo, before his appointment as royal chronicler in 1625, served as secretary of the Spanish embassy in Rome and subsequently as tutor and secretary for the count-duke's nephew, Cardinal Enrique de Guzmán. He was named cronista mayor de las Indias in 1634.

66. As cited in Marcelino Menéndez Pelayo, "Vida y escritos de Rodrigo Caro," in *Estudio de crítica literaria* (Madrid, 1894), 2:171.

67. This commission resulted in Tamayo de Vargas, *Restuaración de la ciudad del Salvador*. Antonio Moreno Vilches, in a letter dated 12 November 1625, stated that Tamayo, having been ordered to write this report, took especial care with it "por ser la primera cosa que escribe con título de cronista." See BCC: Ms. 58-1-9, Cartas y papeles de Rodrigo Caro, vol. 2, fol. 321. Once printed, Tamayo's report helped inspire a play by Lope de Vega, together with Juan Bautista Maino's painting *Surrender of the Dutch at Bahía de Todos los Santos*, one of twelve battle paintings especially commissioned by Olivares for the Hall of Realms in the Buen Retiro. Cf. Elliott and Brown, *A Palace for a King*, 171.

breadth of Spanish scholarship.[68] He also ignored Tamayo's efforts in 1629 to persuade the Cortes of Castile to create a special fund to support the publication of the work of such earlier Spanish chroniclers as Pérez de Guzmán, Pulgar, Valera, and Galíndez de Carvajal.[69] At the same time, Tamayo kept his distance from the royal favorite and from the kind of politic history that Olivares commissioned the Junta de Cronistas to write. Rather, he fancied his independence as royal chronicler, proudly announcing at one moment that his sole obligation was "to tell the truth" (*decir verdades*).[70]

But *verdades* of the kind that Tamayo envisioned did not mesh with the kind of history that Olivares wanted the members of the Junta de Cronistas to write. Their job: to bend, or at least deform, the historical record for propagandistic aims. These writers thus approximated what the noted Jesuit writer Baltasar Gracián sarcastically referred to as *plumas teñidas,* hired or rented pens, that is, individuals who put their talents and their genius at the service of a particular individual or cause. Richelieu employed a host of such writers—Père Joseph, the jurist Jacques Cassan, and historians such as La Mothe le Vayer—whereas Olivares regularly called upon the services of a such talented writers as Francisco de Quevedo and Diego de Saavedra Fajardo, together with many other publicists whose work is discussed below.[71] In Madrid, as in Paris, political exigencies not only determined the kind of history being written but also the creation of new, streamlined publicity agencies capable of producing "history on demand."

Such was the charge of the Junta de Cronistas, which got to work at the end of April 1635, or shortly after copies of Richelieu's *Manifeste* declaring war on Spain arrived in Madrid. In one of its first meetings, individual members offered suggestions about the history they were to write. The basic idea was simple: blame the

---

68. Cf. Tamayo de Vargas, *Junta de libros*. This bibliographic compendium of Spanish writers represented a revision of Andreas Schottus, *Hispana ilustrata* (Frankfurt, 1607).

69. BL: 1322.l.3 (26), printed pamphlet beginning: "Don Thomás Tamaio de Vargas, Chronista del Rei, nuestro señor, deseoso de dar a V.S. motivo para sea benemerito desta Monarchia . . ." See also BNE: Ms. 1750, fols. 357–358. Tamayo's petition can also be found in *ACC:* 48, 323–327.

70. BNE: Ms. 5782, fols. 49–52, letter of Tomás Tamayo de Vargas, 18 August 1639. For further insights into Tamayo's historical standards, see his *censura* Pedro Suárez de Castro's history of noble lineages from the town of Pedraza as recorded in AHN Cons 7155, año 1635, n. 5. There he expressed the general proposition that histories could only redound to "el crédito de la nación" if they contained sound "doctrine."

71. Cf. Elliott, *Count-Duke of Olivares*. Other writers in Olivares's circle included Juan Pablo Mártir Rizo (see Civil, "Vies d'hommes illustres et modèle politique"); Faria de Guzmán, whose contribution to Olivares's propaganda war was his *Apologia en defensa,* referring to France's long-standing "emulación" of the House of Austria and its territorial ambitions as opposed to Spain, which was interested solely in "la *conservación*" of its monarchy and "sosiego de la republica cristiana" (fol. 104); the Sevillian poet Juan de Jáuregui (1583–1641), who wrote another pamphlet attacking the policies of Richelieu (cf. Jáuregui, *Memorial*); and Juan Ruiz de Laguna, a member of the Council of Italy, who wrote *Compendio historial,* a lengthy defense of Philip IV's claims in northern Italy.

current hostilities wholly on France, Richelieu in particular. Guillén de la Carrera, for example, convinced fellow junta members that this history should not even attempt to defame either the character or personal judgment of Louis XIII, because Richelieu was certain to respond in kind and do needless damage to the reputation of Philip IV. Better, he argued, to make Richelieu the scapegoat, and in doing so appeal to those Frenchmen who were opposed to the cardinal's policies and who resented his undue influence over the king (he was right in thinking that opposition to Richelieu was considerable). Using language reminiscent of Olivares's notion of history as a weapon, Guillén maintained that this history's prime purpose was

> To stir up the French nation and place in front of them, as if in a mirror, the miseries and calamities they suffer as a direct of the result of the high taxes imposed on them [by Richelieu] for such deplorable ends as propagating heresy and oppressing religion, all to the detriment of the French name. [They must also be persuaded] to feel that Cardinal Richelieu has, for his own personal interests and in violation of the confidence [*grazia e sinceridad*] the kingdom has accorded him, signed treaties with sectarians and Protestants in Sweden, Germany and Flanders . . . that will only result in the end and extinction of the True Faith.

In addition, by targeting Richelieu, Guillén de la Carrera sought to convince his readers that this minister's nefarious influence had led Louis XIII to institute policies that "devastated his kingdom, saddened his people, opposed its nobility, . . . insulted his mother [Marie d'Medici], imprisoned his brother [Gaston d'Orléans], divided and disrupted the entire royal line, and even defamed his own royal name by having made himself into a protector of heretics and an oppressor of the Catholic Religion."[72]

The junta's other members agreed to this line of argument, but Jusepe de Nápoles intervened by raising an issue that Guillén had overlooked: the papacy's tacit complicity with France. Starting in the 1620s, Pope Urban VIII had allied himself more closely with France than Spain, and he later gave tacit approval to Richelieu's efforts to undermine Spanish influence in Germany. The junta's collective instinct was to attack the papacy as forcefully as it did France, but Jusepe de Nápoles, drawing on his experience in Italian affairs, urged caution. "The greater glory of God," he argued, required the junta not to write anything that would malign either "the vicar of Christ or the Apostolic See," inasmuch as the Protestants ("heretics" in his language) were likely to turn around and appropriate these

---

72. BR: Ms. II/1451, "Papeles de historia del reinado de Phelipe IV," 8v–9.

arguments for their own. Better, he advised, "to preserve the papacy's "authority and esteem" and "dissimulate ... burying and hiding the scandalous actions of the Pontiff." He therefore suggested that blame for the Franco-Papal alliance should be placed squarely on the shoulders of the papal legate in Paris, Giovanni Francesco di Bagno, a cardinal known for his hostility to Spain.[73] The other members of the junta concurred without dissent.

In the seventeenth century, the great age of Christian "reason of state," political thinkers had little positive to say about dissimulation. In Spanish, even the words, *disimular, dissimulación,* suggested dishonesty, immorality, even *malicia* or evil.[74] For this reason "dissimulation" was a term that even experienced statesmen were reluctant to employ. Jusepe, however, was probably referring to the allied concept of "honest dissimulation," a concept associated with the Neapolitan philosopher Torquatto Acetto (1598–1641), which allowed for "lying" under circumstances in which it could prove beneficial to the wider interests of the state.[75] With reference to the proposed history, dissimulation would have entailed the suppression of facts and selective use (or "spin") of evidence for the purpose of creating a narrative that would lead, ineluctably, toward a predetermined, wholly unequivocal reading of the past. In this respect, Jusepe's and the junta's concept of history approximated Olivares's notion of what a "worthy history" should be: an instrument or, better, a weapon, to be used to "mortify Spain's enemies," that is, to shape public opinion in his favor and rally support for his policies, especially at home.

Such, for example, was the aim of the pictorial history of the Thirty Years War that was commissioned, largely at the initiative of the count-duke, for the large ceremonial space now known as the Salón de los Reinos (or Hall of Realms). The artwork served as the centerpiece of the new royal palace, Buen Retiro, which was inaugurated during the spring of 1635.[76] France had recently declared war on Spain, and Philip IV's prospects for victory in the conflict appeared increasingly dim, but this history, centered on a series of twelve battle paintings by such noted Spanish artists as Diego de Velázquez, Francisco de Zurbarán, and Juan Bautista Maino, offered a wholly triumphal, and in this sense "official" or one-sided, account of the war that highlighted the monarchy's moments of victory and

---

73. BR: Ms. II/1451, fol. 15. Nápoles's ideas about not alienating the pope were wholly in line with those of the count-duke. Cf. Elliott, *Count-Duke of Olivares,* 428.

74. See Covarrubias Orozco, *Tesoro de la lengua castellana o española,* 478.

75. Accetto published his treatise *Della diussimulazione onesta* in 1641. For more on "honest dissimulation," see Villari, *Elogio della disimulazione.*

76. For the construction and decoration of the Hall of Realms, see Elliott and Brown, *A Palace for a King,* 149–202.

ignored its defeats. As history, the pictures also conformed to the king's notion that the best history was contemporary history that conveyed useful messages and ideas, in this instance, a view of the monarchy's involvement in the war as a "just" and wholly "defensive" enterprise undertaken solely for the purpose of defeating the enemies of the Roman Catholic Church. Toward this end the pictures celebrated Philip IV together with other members of the royal family, and one of the paintings, Maino's rendition of the combined Luso-Hispanic naval victory over the Dutch in the port of Bahía in Brazil, went as far as to represent Olivares as one of the chief architects of the victory on display. At the same time, and as I have argued elsewhere, these paintings appear to have been designed to win the support of Castile's powerful aristocracy, many of whose members were staunchly opposed to both the policies and the person of the count-duke.[77]

The count-duke's quest to win public support for his policies also underscores the history that the Junta de Cronistas was planning at the moment when the pictures in the Hall of Realms first went on display. Although ostensibly addressed to what the junta referred to as the "French nation," this "worthy history" was designed to open another front in the monarchy's war with France. In this instance, the war would be fought with words as opposed to bullets and steel. In the end, the junta, for reasons yet to be discovered, never completed this history, although its key arguments were summarized by Guillén de la Carrera in his *Manifiesto de España y Francia*, a capsule history of Franco-Spanish relations that Olivares used in June 1635 to compose Philip IV's statement announcing "a defensive, holy, and religious war" against France.[78] The junta's history was intended to be openly polemical and designed to "stir up" public opinion by impugning Richelieu in language that was deliberately provocative, even inflammatory. In contrast, Guillén, a jurist by training, couched the *Manifiesto*, a document written solely for internal use, in the cool, dispassionate, and unadorned language of a legal brief as he documented, on a case-by-case basis, those instances in which the French, in both northern Italy and the Rhineland, had broken international treaties and violated Spain's territorial rights. Also listed were the occasions on which Louis XIII, "to the ruin of his crown" and to the detriment of the Catholic religion, forged military alliances not only with Protestants, both Swedish and Dutch, but with "the Turk" and Muslim rulers in North Africa. The evidence he presented was one-sided and necessarily selective, as Guillén composed a carefully constructed narrative that presented a *casus*

---

77. See Kagan, "Imágenes y política en la corte de Felipe IV."
78. Elliott, *Count-Duke of Olivares*, 490.

belli from which only one conclusion could emerge: that France was an "aggressor" whose offenses and provocations were so many and so unjust that His Catholic Majesty had no alternative except to defend the "security of his estates and vassals."[79]

Organized in this way, the *Manifiesto* never considered the reasons why Louis XIII, whose forces had previously grappled with Spanish troops in northern Italy during the course of the Mantuan War, had declared war on Spain. Guillén, however, had little interest in offering a balanced assessment of relations between the two powers; his main concern was to structure his argument in such a way as to convince those among Philip IV's councillors who questioned the wisdom of a "hot war" with France that conflict was not only necessary but legitimate. In this sense the *Manifiesto* mimicked, albeit in miniature, what Olivares had envisioned as "worthy" or politic history that led toward a single, certain, predetermined, and impeccably argued narrative that accorded perfectly with the relevant facts. This history, moreover, was to reflect Olivares's broad vision of Spain's monarchy as a supranational entity whose interests rose above what he perceived as the narrow (in his language, "national") concerns of Catalonia, Aragon, Portugal, and the monarchy's other constituent parts. Olivares first articulated this vision of a more unified monarchy in 1625 in his "Union of Arms."[80] His "worthy history" rested on similar principles, and this helps to explain why he steered clear of the king's official chroniclers, many of whom harbored "national" allegiances of the kind he abhorred. Better to entrust this and other histories to "hired pens," publicists whom he could trust.

Hired Pens I: Juan Antonio de Vera y Figueroa

These "hired pens" constituted a diverse group: jurists, dramatists, painters, poets, historians; the only common denominator was a sense of personal commitment to the count-duke. To be sure, some of these pens proved more loyal than others. Quevedo, for example, moved in and out of Olivares's circle before his imprisonment in 1639, allegedly for having "spoke ill of the government" and allied himself with France.[81] In contrast, Francisco de Rioja never abandoned his patron: he not only accompanied Olivares into exile following the favorite's fall from power in 1641 but helped him prepare his *Nicandro*, an autobiographical work written to refute the many charges that had been leveled against him.

79. Cited in Jover Zamora, *1635*, 253.
80. For the "Union of Arms," see Elliott and de la Peña, *Memoriales y cartas*, 1:173–181.
81. José de Pellicer, *Avisos*, as cited in Elliott, *Count-Duke of Olivares*, 553.

Almost equally loyal was Juan Antonio de Vera y Figueroa (1583–1658), whose commitment to the person and policies of the count-duke never flagged. Grandson of Luis de Avila y Zúñiga, the historian who wrote about Charles V's wars in Germany, Vera y Figueroa, a lesser nobleman from Extremadura, first befriended Olivares in Seville before the publication, in 1620, of Vera y Figueroa's *The Ambassador*, a handbook expressly written for aspiring statesmen, among whom the author was one. Modeled on Lipsius's famous *Book of Politics*, this volume, using a mixture of maxims and historical *exemplae* to offer advice on topics ranging from modes of comportment to forms of address, offered a series of diplomatic dos and don'ts. It even weighed in on the somewhat touchy subject of secrecy, as well as those occasions upon which ambassadors—and their princes—might engage in a bit of "honest" dissimulation. These features transformed *The Ambassador* into a volume no diplomat could do without. It also won praise from that rather harsh critic Baltasar Gracián, who praised the author for his "learned erudition" and "the sharpness of his mind."[82]

Gracián also acclaimed Vera y Figueroa's later writings, a series of "politic" histories designed to offer examples in good governance, as "stores of wisdom, or to say it another way, dense jumbles stacked with sayings, maxims, and worthwhile advice."[83] The first of these histories, dating from 1622, transformed the life and deeds of Emperor Charles V into a textbook on leadership in a time of war.[84] Pointedly dedicated to the emperor's namesake, the *infante* Carlos, younger brother of Philip IV, this history was also used by Vera y Figueroa to express support for Olivares, his friend and soon-to-be patron. In his history of Charles V, Prudencio de Sandoval, in an effort to enjoin Philip III on the importance of personal rule, criticized Charles V for his dependency on his favorite, the lord of Chièvres. In contrast, Vera y Figueroa, mindful of the criticisms already being launched at Olivares, defended Chièvres and, by implication, Olivares, by claiming that most of the evils attributed to Chièvres resulted from the envy of courtiers resentful of his influence upon Charles V.[85] Vera y Figueroa also engaged in a bit of overt flattery by singling out the bravery of Olivares's grandfather in his account of the emperor's expedition to Tunis in 1635.[86] More importantly, by representing Charles V as a *roi de guerre*, a monarch whose military victories were the source of Habsburg grandeur, he seemingly lent his support to Olivares's deci-

82. Gracián, *Agudeza*, 490.
83. Ibid.
84. Vera y Figueroa, *Epitome*.
85. Ibid., 28–29. My argument here follows that of Fernández-Daza Álvarez, *El primer conde de la Roca*, 417.
86. Cf. Vera y Figueroa, *Epitome*, 70.

sion, in 1621, to persuade Philip IV to end the Twelve Year's Truce and declare war against the Dutch.

Vera y Figueroa's effort to bolster the reputation of the count-duke was his "Fragmentos históricos de la vida de don Gaspar de Guzmán, Conde de Olivares...," the first installment of what he envisioned as a full-fledged biography of his patron and friend.[87] Begun around 1626 in an effort to counter what he described as the "mortal hatred" ("odio mortal") the count-duke had engendered, this biography provoked controversy even before its completion ca. 1633. One cleric, for example, reminded Vera y Figueroa that "truth" was impossible to achieve for historians who set out to write about persons still alive, but Vera y Figueroa demurred, first by pointing to such precedents as the history that his grandfather wrote on behalf of Charles V, then with the old saw, drawn from the "arts of history" genre, that eyewitness evidence of the kind that he could provide would ensure both the accuracy and the veracity of his account.[88]

Despite such pretenses to verisimilitude, *Fragmentos históricos* was precisely the kind of biography, more panegyric than history, that "hired pens" were expected to write. As Gracián warned, "it is difficult it is to write about the living. All men commit errors, but few, having made mistakes, want to hear about them; better to praise them or keep quiet."[89] In effect, Vera y Figueroa followed Gracián's advice: his intention was to immortalize the count-duke even though his ministerial career was still *in media res*. "History is written," Vera y Figueroa observed, "to guarantee the living the truth about themselves," as well as to protect them from unnecessary criticism and injuries.[90] Toward this end he refuted, one by one, the various criticisms—avarice, self-interest, corruption—that had been levied against Olivares, and to substantiate this argument the *Fragmentos* included transcriptions of relevant letters and documents. The end result was a portrait of a minister who attended tirelessly to his obligations, surrounded himself by persons "free of all ambition and suspicion ... dedicated to the service of the king and the public good"; and who selflessly dedicated himself to the well-being, even the health, of Philip IV.[91] "No ruler," it concluded, "has been better served and in so many things by his *privado*, and his ministers, than Philip IV."[92]

Vera y Figueroa's reward for this biography was a noble title, *conde de la Roca*,

---

87. See Vera y Figueroa, "Fragmentos históricos." This work was first printed, in French, in 1673.
88. Vera y Figueroa's defense of his decision to write a biography of a living person may be found in BL Add., 18.289, fols. 127–132v, "Discurso del Conde de la Roca para el Maestro Fray Basilio de León sobre los fragmentos q escrivió de la vida del Conde de Olivares."
89. Gracián, *Agudeza*, 510.
90. "Discurso del Conde de la Roca," fol. 130.
91. Vera y Figueroa, "Fragmentos históricos," 2:250.
92. Ibid., 2:214.

together with an appointment as ambassador to Venice, one of the most honored and important offices in the Spanish diplomatic corps. But even while living abroad, he remained one of the count-duke's most faithful publicists, publishing a series of pamphlets that attacked French foreign policy,[93] along with his *Il milgior giglio di Francia* (1640), a politic history that used the famed thirteenth-century French ruler Louis IX, "Saint Louis," to criticize Philip IV's archenemy Louis XIII. Vera y Figueroa managed his comparison by casting Louis IX as a peace-loving monarch who ruled without ambitious favorites and cared little about expanding the territories under his control.[94] He also presented Saint Louis as a ruler wholly dedicated to the welfare of his vassals and the defense of the Church. The contrast with Louis XIII could not have been more obvious, and to give this history a ring of objectivity, Vera y Figueroa wrote it using a pseudonym, Notoniano Vadin, and falsified the book's title page by pretending that it was printed in Lyon when, in fact, he had it privately printed in Venice for distribution abroad.

Vera y Figueroa used this same formula, that of using the past to write about the present, in *El Rey don Pedro Defendido* (Madrid, 1647), his last effort to rehabilitate the reputation of the count-duke. Following the count-duke's fall from power in 1643, Madrid's bookstalls overflowed with pamphlets outlining his personal failings and political miscalculations. Olivares's response to these criticisms was *El Nicandro*, whereas Vera y Figueroa's initially took the form of a pamphlet printed in Milan,[95] and subsequently his *Pedro Defendido*, in which he sought to refute the arguments of those critics who suggested that the uprisings in Catalonia and Portugal had begun with the king's misplaced trust in the count-duke. Using the much-maligned fourteenth-century Castilian monarch Pedro I as a foil for Philip IV, Vera y Figueroa offered a revisionist reading that represented Pedro as a dedicated, hard-working, and principled ruler whose detractors—here he was thinking mainly of Pedro López de Ayala—unfairly branded him with the sobriquet "the Cruel." Vera y Figueroa explained that Pedro, like Philip, lived in difficult and dangerous times and, again like Philip, had assumed the throne at the age of sixteen, a situation that necessarily led to dependency on a favorite and eventually to the enmities and accusations that resulted in the unfortunate nick-

---

93. I refer to *Al Pio, al Grande, al Beatissimo Padre Urban Octavo*. It has been suggested that he used the Italian pseudonym because of the pamphlet's violent criticisms of the pope. See Church, *Richelieu and Reason of State*, 373n218.

94. I refer to Vera y Figueroa, *Il miglior giglio de Francia*, which subsequently appeared both in Spanish and in French. On the "political" themes woven into the biography, see Fernández-Daza Álvarez, *El primer conde de la Roca*, 474–481.

95. I refer to Vera y Figueroa, *Manifiesto*.

name that López de Ayala had coined. In this way Vera y Figueroa magically transformed Pedro "the Cruel" into Pedro "the Just," and in doing so invited his readers to reassess the achievements of Olivares along with the king to whose service the count-duke had dedicated his life.

Hired Pens II: Gonzalo Céspedes y Meneses

If Vera y Figueroa was a writer who took certain liberties with the historical record in order to offer a wholly positive reading of Olivares's historical record, Gonzalo (1585–1638) went even further, as he was fully prepared to reinvent history for political ends. As a writer, in fact, Céspedes y Meneses best epitomizes that category of historian that Gracián sardonically labeled "journalists and reporters, superficial and mechanical, lacking in both judgment and elevation of mind."[96]

Céspedes y Meneses was a *madrileño* by birth. His literary career began in 1615 with a story of the turbulent love life of "Gerardo, the Spaniard," a work one of its readers, an inquisitor, labeled "obscene."[97] In this instance, art imitated life, inasmuch as Céspedes, if not exactly obscene, became embroiled in a series of turbulent love affairs, one of which landed him in prison; another resulted in exile, starting in 1619, from the kingdom of Castile.

Taking refuge in Aragon, Céspedes, a writer previously known for fiction, transformed himself into a historian and embarked, somewhat opportunistically, on a brief, "apologetic" history of the Aragonese uprising of 1590–1591, which he cobbled together by borrowing freely from the work of other historians who had addressed the same event. In his preface Céspedes explained that Castilian historians who have written about the *alteraciones*—here he was thinking of both Antonio de Herrera y Tordesillas and Luis Cabrera de Córdoba—had deliberately "sullied" Aragon's "honor and reputation." Yet he also faulted Vicencio Blasco de Lanuza, the historian especially selected by the Diputación to respond to these histories, for having written a history that was slanted too far in the other direction as result of an excess of patriotic zeal. Céspedes asserted that his narrative, in comparison, would strictly adhere to what he called "the truth."

As it turned out, Céspedes's understanding of truth caused an uproar (some said a riot) immediately following the publication of the *Historia apologética* in Zaragoza in 1622. At issue was Céspedes's suggestion that the only persons to

---

96. See Gracián, *Criticón*, in *Obras completas*, 2:151.
97. AHN Inq., leg. 4467/40, "Censuras de libro historia apologetica del reino de Aragón . . ." For Céspedes's biography, I have principally relied upon the introduction to Céspedes y Meneses, *Historias pelegrinas y ejemplares*.

blame for the *alteraciones* were members of the *vulgo*, his term for the artisans and laborers who constituted the working classes of the kingdom's capital, Zaragoza. As he saw it, these workers, acting irrationally, solely upon the basis of rumors and without sufficient cause, sparked the uprising despite efforts of local notables to restrain them. Other historians had deployed similar arguments to write the histories of previous uprisings in Spanish history, but Céspedes on this occasion used the tactic specifically to win both the support and patronage of the Diputación.

But if such was his plan, it backfired from the very moment the book appeared in print. Blasco de Lanuza openly denounced it as fraudulent history, whereas the Diputación, far from rewarding its author for rescuing the kingdom's reputation, prohibited the book within the confines of the kingdom of Aragon.[98] The book's reception in Castile was equally hostile. There the Inquisition, objecting to Céspedes's injudicious use of language, labeled it "scandalous" and recommended that the Council of Castile immediately have it withdrawn it from circulation.[99] The council did just this in 1625, by which time Céspedes, having essentially been run out of Zaragoza, sought refuge in Lisbon, where, in an effort to repair his damaged reputation, he started work on an even more delicate subject: a history of the reigning monarch, Philip IV.

At the time, the young monarch, only four years into his reign, had no history he could call his own, a lacuna that Céspedes, sensing a hole in the market, rightly set out to fill. To do so, he turned to the popular press, especially the *relaciones* and *gacetas*, the majority of which, much like today's *Hola, People Weekly*, and similarly gossipy magazines, engaged readers with reports of natural disasters, shipwrecks, royal marriages, and war. As Gracián surmised, such reports figured prominently in part 1 of Céspedes's *Historia de don Felipe IIII, Rey de las Españas* (Lisbon, 1631), a history that, given the nature of the author's sources, necessarily focused less on the person and policies of the monarch than upon the major military victories—Bahia, Breda, and Cadiz—of his reign. However, by attributing each of these victories to what he described as the "indefatigable zeal" of the count-duke, it was clear that Céspedes tailored the history to capture the interest, together with the patronage, of the royal favorite. Toward the end he credited Olivares for having ended the "declinación" in Spanish power initiated by the

---

98. Céspedes y Meneses, *Historia apologética*, 315.

99. For these criticisms, see AHN Inq., leg. 4467/40, "Censura del libro Historia apologética..." Among the many things the inquisitorial censor found objectionable in the book were Céspedes's references to Ferdinand the Catholic as "el más santo" and "infallible" with reference to the works of men (as opposed to God and the papacy.)

duke of Lerma's readiness to sign peace treaties with heretics, and then he celebrated the count-duke's success in bringing to Spain "a felicitous conjunction of Mars and Mercury" that had resulted in a "new golden age of arms and letters."[100] He even defended the count-duke's double program of reform at home and war abroad and did so, as he put it, "without any better title than being a Spaniard and Castilian."

One gets the point. This cocktail of adulation and patriotism did not make for good history. Indeed, when the book first arrived in Madrid, it received a decidedly chilly reception from the royal chronicler Tamayo de Vargas, who criticized the author for his fatuous sources, "indecent style," "affected words," faulty Latin, and more.[101] However, the book pleased the royal favorite, and in less than a year Céspedes received a ticket back to Madrid together with the opportunity to enlist in the propaganda war the count-duke had recently initiated to defend the policies that had resulted in open war with France.

Compared to Adam de la Parra and Guillén de la Carrera, Céspedes had a decidedly minor role in this war of words, but he played it well. His main contribution, *Francia engañada, Francia respondida* (Caller [Zaragoza], 1635), was a short book, published under his old pseudonym of Gerardo Hispano, but one driven by the same kind of chauvinism he had manifested in his history of Philip IV.[102] Anxious to compare Spain, as a nation, with France, Céspedes, conveniently forgetting about al-Andalus, concluded that the former was not only thoroughly Christian but also noble, honorable, temperate, and just, whereas France was ambitious, heretical, "inexorably cruel," and perfidious. He also represented France as a nation whose monarchy had been usurped by an ambitious, amoral, and tyrannical minister, Cardinal Richelieu, who had perfidiously allied himself with heretics, both Swedish and Dutch, at the expense of Spain, the empire, and the Catholic Church. Compared with the cool, legalistic language of Guillén de la Carrera's *manifiesto*, Céspedes's was passionate and so peppered with digressions and pious invocations that one twentieth-century Spanish scholar rightly characterized it with the phrase "disorder; always disorder. Disorder and passion."[103] True enough. But is this how *Francia engañada* was read when it first appeared? Polemic, after all, is meant to inspire more than inform.

---

100. Céspedes y Meneses, *Historia apologética*, 581–582. Céspedes does not use the term *annus mirabilis* but rather "tales sucesos que tuvo España en este año [de 1625] por la bondad grande de Dios," and he refers to the "avisos" of the count-duke. See Céspedes y Meneses, *Historia de don Felipe IIII*, 546.

101. For these criticisms, see Pérez Pastor, *Bibliografía madrileña*, 3:53–59. Tamayo's critique, dated 28 August 1634, prevented Céspedes from publishing an expanded version of this book in Madrid that same year.

102. Bouza, *El libro y el cetro*, 24, notes that Céspedes was paid one thousand ducats for this work.

103. Jover Zamora, *1635*, 97.

Who read this kind of history, especially since it was printed only in Spanish, as opposed to French? This question applies equally well to the other *manifiestos* written in behalf of the count-duke, but because existing studies of these polemics have attended more to matters of ideology and politics than to audience, answers are few. The Junta de Cronistas had clearly envisioned an international audience, as it planned to have its history translated into several languages. The books and pamphlets composed by Olivares's other publicists were all in Spanish, though, and only rarely were they read beyond Spain's frontiers. One of these publicists, José de Pellicer (see below) boasted that his *Defensa de España contra las calumnias de Francia*, found its way to Paris, where it was publicly burned by order of the Parlement on 3 March 1637. This claim, like so much of what Pellicer wrote, is likely to be apocryphal.[104]

But even if it was true, the primary readership for such polemics was international only to the extent that it extended to foreign diplomats and spies resident in Madrid who then forwarded copies—or, more commonly, translated summaries of the contents—to their respective capitals abroad. Such were the channels through which the French pamphlet *Manifeste du roi coincernant les justes causes que le roi a eues de déclarer la guerre à l'Espagne*, a product of Richelieu's propaganda machine, found its way to Madrid, where it prompted an immediate response from several members of the Junta de Cronistas. Otherwise the primary audience for these pamphlets was domestic; Céspedes's *Francia engañada*, for example, targeted specifically those noblemen and courtiers who had marched out of Madrid in 1635 to demonstrate their opposition to the policies of the count-duke.[105] From this perspective, the passion and unalloyed patriotism unleashed by Céspedes y Meneses seemingly represented an effort to persuade these nobles to return.

Hired Pens III: Virgilio Malvezzi

Compared to Céspedes, who was little more than a hack, Virgilio Malvezzi (1595–1654) was an accomplished scholar with an international reputation when he entered the service of the count-duke. A minor Bolognese nobleman with the title

---

104. Pellicer claimed that he found a reference to this book-burning in chapter 38 of Dr. Malavite's *Pro Pace Sanncienda*, but there is no record of either of this author or this title in the online catalogs of the Bibliotheque de France. One anonymous Spanish polemic critical of Richelieu that definitely found its way to Paris may be consulted in the Bibliothèque Nationale de France: Ms. Rothchild 1518.A.15. Judging solely from its hyperbolic prose, this work is likely to have been the work of Pellicer.

105. For aristocratic dissatisfaction with Olivares, see Stradling, *Philip IV and the Government of Spain*, 151–171. Firsthand testimony to Olivares's difficulties with the powerful House of Alba and other grandees may be found in "Cartas de algunos PP. de la Companía de Jesús entre los años 1634 y 1648," *MHE* 13:79, 105–106; and Barberini, *El diario*, 307.

of marquess, Malvezzi in the course of the 1620s won international acclaim first for his commentaries on Tacitus, then for a pair of aphoristic treatises entitled *Romulo* and *Tarquino*,[106] which offered advice on topics ranging from "honest dissimulation" to proper behavior at court.[107] Nowadays, Malvezzi's convoluted syntax and superrefined vocabulary is best categorized as baroque, but it was much appreciated by his contemporaries, notably Gracián, who described his prose as "ponderous," in the sense of weighty and informed. Gracián also judged Malvezzi to be a first-class writer who combined the "pedagogic style of philosophers with the critical style of historians, which together make for an admirable mix: a Seneca who writes history, and the Valerius who writes philosophy."[108]

For his part, Malvezzi, along with many other Italians of his era, was eager to enter the service of the king of Spain. Already in the 1620s Malvezzi had contacted the duke of Feria, the Spanish governor of Milan, to sound out the possibility of some kind of appointment, and when, in 1634, he dedicated his *David perseguitto*, another book of aphorisms, to Philip IV, it was clear that he wanted to move from Bologna to Madrid. At this point, Malvezzi befriended Vera y Figueroa, then serving as Spain's ambassador in Venice, who suggested that if Malvezzi wanted to enter Philip's service, he should undertake a history of the count-duke disguised as a treatise on royal favorites. Cognizant of the criticism his *Fragmentos históricos* had sparked, Vera y Figueroa suggested that a history of Olivares would carry greater weight, particularly in Spain, if it came from the pen of a foreigner as opposed to that of a Spaniard. "No one," he wrote, "is a prophet in their own country . . . [and] plants born in Bologna will certainly flourish in Spain."[109] He consequently supplied Malvezzi with the historical material ("lo istorial") necessary to write what became this author's *Ritratto del privato político cristiano*, a thinly veiled eulogy of Olivares that appeared in Bologna in 1635.[110]

These efforts paid off. Called to Spain the following year, Malvezzi arrived in Madrid in July 1636 and was warmly received by the count-duke. Malvezzi reports that within a week of his arrival in the city, he was riding in Olivares's coach when the minister offered him the "task of writing His Majesty's history" in exchange for a stipend worth up to up to 4,500 *scudi* (ca. 3,000 ducats) a year—a figure at

---

106. I refer to Malvezzi, *Disscorsi sopra Cornelio Tacito;* his *Romulo;* and his *Tarquino superbo.*
107. Malvezzi is best approached through Belligni, *Lo scacco della prudenza;* and Bulletta, *Virgilio Malvezzi.* His historical writings are addressed in Colomer, "Esplicar los grandes hechos de vuestra majestad."
108. Gracián, *Agudeza,* lxii, 509–510.
109. Citations from a letter Vera y Figueroa wrote to a friend, possibly Luigi Manzini, in 1630. Cf. Bulletta, *Virgilio Malvezzi,* 32–33. The translations are my own. Malvezzi's relationship with Vera y Figueroa is examined in Colomer, "El Conde de la Roca."
110. Cf. Malvezzi, *Il ritratto del privato politico christiano.*

least ten times the salary paid to the king's official chroniclers—plus lodging. In addition, Olivares promised to supply him all the papers he would need to write such a work. The offer was too good to refuse, and Malvezzi, as he later informed a friend, plunged headlong into this history, managing to complete the first volume (out of a projected seven) within a year and a half, mainly by "sleeping only a few hours at night and also working during the day, so much so that in a very brief time I lost not only my complexion but also my appetite—eating only once a day, and this at night, and then only some broth and bread and three ounces or so of chopped up meat, and not drinking very much either."[111]

Such energy is evident throughout Malvezzi's history, which centered on the opening years of Philip's reign. Like Vera y Figueroa, who was evidently the inspiration for this project, Malvezzi was cognizant of the dangers that the writing of contemporary history entailed, yet he stood firm in the belief that historians who wrote about "things done in their own time" deserved greater credit than those who wrote of "things done in the past."[112] Echoing Tacitus, he also justified this enterprise by explaining that the events of his own era were far too important to be left for future historians to write: "The history that I am writing is tragic, by its individuals; horrible for its events; frightening for what is going on. Princes exiled, disinherited, killed; foreign wars, civil wars, mixed wars . . . battles won, battles lost. Cities besieged, defended, destroyed. Treaties broken, sacrileges, deceits, treasons; brother against brothers, sons against mothers, subjects against lords; friends turned into enemies; hunger, plague, fires, earthquakes, shipwrecks; and if man against man were not enough, it seems that all the elements have united to destroy nature."[113] As for the danger of adulation, one of the principal risks this kind of history was thought to entail, Malvezzi announced that Philip IV was so virtuous that he had no need to resort either to artifice, to hide his shortcomings, or flattery, to magnify the importance of his deeds. "This monarchy," he insisted, "does not have any secrets about trying to dominate [the world]; it does not hide in corners, nor does it employ any artifice [*arte*] except to live without it." Epideictic rhetoric of this sort is of course endemic to official history, both present and past, and in this instance Malvezzi used it to represent Philip IV as a "príncipe cristiano," motivated solely by religion, as opposed to a "príncipe político"—read Louis XIII—motivated solely by political and territorial concerns.[114]

---

111. Malvezzi, *Lettere a Fabio Chigi*, 143.
112. Malvezzi, *Discourse upon Tacitus*, 76–77.
113. Ibid., 2. Tacitus, *Annals*, I, 2, had noted that he was writing about a period that "abounded in disasters, was pitiless in battles, riven by discord, and cruel even in peace."
114. Cf. Malvezzi, *Historia de los primeros años*.

Nor, in writing this history, did Malvezzi ever lose sight of Olivares, whom he often referred to, in Mafia-esque language, as "father, patron and friend" ("padre, padrone y amico"). His loyalty to the royal favorite surfaced toward the very start of his *Philip IV*, where he reflected upon the institution of the *privanza* in ways expressly designed to deflect the many criticisms of the count-duke. Pointing to such "fallen" favorites as Lerma, Malvezzi recognized that bad favorites far outnumbered the good but still argued that favorites were indispensable for good governance: "*Privanza* is necessary. The prince cannot do everything, and there are many things he should not do. A large extended monarchy cannot be governed without entrusting great authority in a single minister. The [prince] who divides it, makes many errors; the palace becomes a battleground; the kingdom is divided into factions; he hears only rumors; he sees only ministers filled with envy, which causes problems; everything is confusion."[115]

Malvezzi's position on favorites was very different from that of the king's official chronicler, Gil González Dávila, whose thoughts on this issue can be found earlier in this chapter. But they meshed neatly with the view of the count-duke, and presumably that of Philip IV. Also approved by the count-duke and the king was the manner in which Malvezzi planned to write the rest of the king's history. The first volume, completed sometime before the end of 1637, covered the first decade of Philip IV's reign, roughly the period between 1621 and 1632. Starting with the events of 1633, however, Malvezzi, changed format and elected to continue the history by writing annual installments, or *relaciones*. Traditionally, the task of writing these annual *relaciones* fell to the cronistas del rey, but Philip IV was so taken with Malvezzi that he issued an order that the Italian was the only historian allowed to write his history. We know about this from Fulvio Testi, a Modenese poet resident in Madrid, who, with reference to a document shown him by Malvezzi, reported:

> His Majesty has given the signor Marquess Virgilio Malvezzi the honor of an appointment to the Council of State here in Madrid, together with others in the Council of State in Naples and in Milan, as well as an *encomienda* worth 300 *ducatoni* of silver. On the other side, His Majesty, in his own handwriting, declared that he was prepared to present him with many more rewards, and that he already decided in his heart to give him an ambassadorship and other positions of confidence, concluding that he wanted no other historian to write about his life and achievements except for the Marquess.[116]

115. Ibid., 24.
116. Letter dated Madrid, 30 May 1639, as cited in Bulletta, *Virgilio Malvezzi*, 41.

The source of such esteem is difficult to determine, since the first part of Malvezzi's history of Philip IV never got into print.[117] As for the annual *relaciones*, only one, entitled *La Libra*, which surveyed events of 1638, had appeared, written in Italian, and then under the anagrammatic pseudonym of Grivilio Vezzalmi!

Why Malvezzi resorted to this kind of subterfuge remains unclear, although it was possibly connected to the manner in which he narrated that year's most newsworthy event: Spain's hard-fought and ultimately successful defense of the frontier fortress of Fuenterrabia. French troops had crossed into Spain in July 1638 and laid siege to Fuenterrabia by both land and sea. At the time Olivares was busy in Madrid, and though he purportedly wanted to rush to the front and personally direct the stronghold's defense, the king refused to allow him to go. Other noblemen, however, went in his place, notably the admiral of Castile, whose forces, after almost three months of touch-and-go fighting, successfully broke the siege the following September.

A notable triumph? No. But when Malvezzi wrote *La Libra*, he deliberately ignored the contributions of the admiral and the other Spanish generals and credited the victory to Olivares along with the king.[118] No surprise, then, that the admiral branded *La Libra* as nothing less than a "pack of lies."[119] Yet Malvezzi was undeterred. As the personal historian of both the king and the count-duke (he did not become an "official" historian until 1645), Malvezzi could not be bothered with the admiral; his primary aim was to magnify the importance of both the monarch and the *privado* at a moment when Spain's military prospects were teetering on the edge of defeat.[120] In 1639, for example, Philip's Army of Flanders suffered several major reverses and the monarchy's treasury was practically empty, yet in his *relación* relating to this year, Malvezzi, cognizant of his duties as

---

117. Malvezzi sent this volume to a printer in 1640, but it was never published, possibly for reasons connected to the outbreak of revolts in both Catalonia and Portugal.

118. Malvezzi, *La Libra;* as well as his *Relaciones de sucesos*. At the time this battle was being fought, Olivares ordered Juan de Palafox y Mendoza, a former member of the Junta de Cronistas, to write yet another account of the siege. Cf. Pellicer, *Avisos*, 1:8, entry for 17 May 1639: "Deseando el Conde-Duque q salga la historia de Fuenterrabia, del año de 38, ha dado orden a Don Juan Palafox y Mendoza, del consejo de indias, para que la acabe, y se ha retirado a una aldea a hacerlo." Pellicer was undoubtedly referring not to an original history of the siege but rather a Spanish translation of *La Libra*, which was published later that year.

119. BNE: Ms. 18.660, no. 4, "Respuesta a un libro intitulado Libra de Marques Virgilio Malvezzi, sobre el suceso de Fuenterrabia, año de 1638."

120. It should be noted that the admiral had his own supporters, among them the playwright Pedro Calderón de la Barca, who wrote a panegyric in his behalf. Cf. Wilson, "Calderón y Fuenterrabia."

an official publicist of the monarchy, likened it to "an athletic body, so healthy that its growth is the source of envy and dangerous jealousies."[121]

For an official (or, in this case, semiofficial) historian, such rhetoric was not only necessary but expected. To do otherwise, that is, to admit to weakness, was unthinkable. It follows that Philip IV, true to his promises, appointed Malvezzi as his ambassador to the Court of St. James and in 1640 ordered him to London to negotiate an anti-Dutch alliance with Charles I. The embassy failed, and for a time Malvezzi went to Brussels, where he served as adviser to Cardinal-Infante Ferdinand but maintained a regular correspondence with the count-duke following the latter's fall from power and exile from Madrid.[122] He returned to Madrid in 1643, presumably to continue work on his history, but by this time the energy he had previously invested in the project had waned. Malvezzi managed a short summary of events relating to 1640, but this year was Spain's *annus horribilis*, marked by revolts in Catalonia and Portugal, and the report never found its way into print.

In 1645, about the time of Olivares's death, Malvezzi left Spain and returned to Italy, taking up residence in his native Bologna. Once there, he returned to a subject reminiscent of his youth: ancient history in the guise of an advice book, in this instance a double volume dedicated both to Alcibiades, the Athenian statesman known for his aggressive foreign policy, and Coriolanus, the Roman aristocrat who, according to Plutarch, was unfairly judged by the Roman tribunes and exiled for his sins. Malvezzi's choice of these two figures was by no means accidental, since both, though in markedly different ways, served as simulacra for Olivares, his former friend and *padrone* whose *fama* he was determined to defend.

Hired Pens IV: Pellicer

The defense of the count-duke's *fama* also figured centrally in the work of the last, and possibly the most controversial, of Olivares's publicists, José Pellicer de Ossau y Tovar (1602–1679). Born Aragonese but a long time resident of Madrid, Pellicer was the quintessential hired pen, a writer fully prepared to twist the historical record, even to invent sources, for both political and personal gain. He was also the most ambitious of all Olivares's publicists and in the course of his life published several "bibliotecas," detailed lists of his publications and other achievements. Pellicer envisioned these lists as testaments to his scholarly impor-

---

121. Malvezzi, *Relaciones de sucesos*, 4. This pamphlet is cataloged in the BNE as Varios Especiales 59/1, with the title *Sucesos principales de la monarquía de España en el año de 1639* (Madrid, 1640).

122. For this correspondence, see Colomer, *"La Carta del Desprezio de la Dignidad."*

tance, yet upon close inspection much of the information they included, if not patently false, was inflated.[123] He pretended, for example, to hold a law degree from Salamanca but did not; to have published more than three thousand *pliegos* or pamphlets, a number no bibliographer has ever been able to verify; and to have written fifty-eight books—again, a number impossible to verify.

No surprise, then, that starting already in his lifetime, Pellicer's scholarship provoked controversy. Gracián rightly described him as "erudite and inventive."[124] Others regarded him as a plagiarist, among them the royal chronicler Tamayo de Vargas, who called Pellicer a "mojuelo," or fibber. Tamayo also rebuked Pellicer for his "chronistería," an untranslatable but decidedly derogatory term that underscored the latter's eagerness to puff up his reputation by claiming to be the official chronicler of this agency or that.[125] In 1629, for example, the Cortes de Castile appointed Pellicer, together with three other writers, "coronista del reino."[126] The position was purely honorific, offering neither salary nor emoluments of any sort, but Pellicer regularly referred to himself by this title and proudly included it in his *bibliotecas* and on the title pages of everything he published, apparently in the expectation that it would enhance his reputation and, more concretely, sell more books. In 1636 Pellicer also claimed the title of *coronista del reino de Aragon*, even though Francisco Jiménez de Urrea was already in this post, and two years later Pellicer started calling himself *coronista de Su Majestad en los reinos de Castilla y Aragón*, an office that did not exist. Later, he referred to himself by the title, again apocryphal, of "cronista mayor de España," chief chronicler of Spain.[127]

Pellicer was born in Zaragoza in 1602, and his early life and education are shrouded in obscurity. What is certain is that he was a skilled linguist, schooled in Latin, Greek, Hebrew, Italian, and French, and a gifted if somewhat pretentious writer. He first made a name (and a living) for himself as a poet, though he sparked an uproar when he dared criticize such established poets as Luís de Góngora. He then turned to history and in 1629 embarked on an ambitious general history of Spain that he envisioned as a replacement for Mariana's. Pellicer's large family, however, required him to abandon this project and to eke out a living on Madrid's grub street, churning out pamphlets and *pliegos* on subjects that

123. I refer to Pellicer de Ossau y Tovar, *Biblioteca*. I used BNE, shelfmark 2/68197.
124. Gracián, *Agudeza*, xix, 324.
125. For these comments, see BNE: Ms. 8389, fol. 166, Tamayo de Vargas to Andrés de Uztárroz, 1 February 1639.
126. ACC, 48:285, where Pellicer is referred to as don Joseph de Salas y Tovar. Others accorded this honorific were Fray Marcelo Antonio de Carvajal, Francisco de Morovelli, and Fernán Gutiérrez de Eraso.
127. See the title page of Pellicer, *El lirio*.

ranged from the historical importance of Santiago, Spain's patron saint, to the war with France.[128] He also earned money as a genealogist, mainly by "inventing" family histories for noblemen in a search of a lengthy and unblemished genealogy free from either Jewish or Moorish blood.[129] He did the same for the monarchy, and in one pamphlet that challenged the legitimacy of France's Salic Law, he endeavored to prove that Philip IV was a direct descendant of Charlemagne and therefore the rightful heir to the kingdom of France.

As this project suggests, Pellicer's scholarship was not always sound, but he was far better than his critics allowed, and even his most panegyrical and pedantic works, while challenging to read, reveal his command of history, poetry, and the arts. All this is evident in his first verifiable publication, *El Fénix y su historia natural* (Madrid, 1630), his response to the *Catholique d'estat* (1625), an anti-Habsburg treatise written by Richelieu's pamphleteers at the time of the War of the Mantuan Succession, which argued that the French monarchy had traditionally done far more to support the Catholic Church than its treacherous neighbor to the south.[130] Pellicer's *Fénix* argued the opposite. It also maintained that France, for political reasons, allied with heretics, whereas Spain, true to its historical commitment to Catholicism, did not, an argument that anticipated one used by Olivares in his 1635 pamphlet war with France.

The *Fénix* was clearly written in the expectation of royal patronage, but as Pellicer discovered, this was not easy to obtain. For one thing, he had numerous enemies, many of whom hated him for his earlier criticisms of Góngora. Further complications arose in 1635, when after killing a young man who reportedly refused to marry his daughter, Pellicer was a fugitive from justice for over nine years. He led a somewhat clandestine existence, drifting in and out of Madrid, until he finally received a royal pardon in June 1644.[131]

Yet for all his personal difficulties, and possibly on account of them, Pellicer was extraordinarily prolific, writing books and pamphlets purposely crafted to capture the attention of the king and the count-duke. One of the first was *El anfiteatro del*

---

128. Many of these pamphlets are gathered in the volume BNE: 2/34594.
129. For a partial list of these genealogies, see Pellicer, *Biblioteca*. See also BNE: 3/60605, a volume entitled *Varios tratados*, by Joseph Pellicer de Ossau i Tovar, which includes a genealogy of the House of Avellañeda (1667) and another of the House of Sarmiento de Villamayor (1663).
130. For more on this pamphlet, see Church, *Richelieu and Reason of State*, 128–147.
131. For the murder, see *Gacetas y nuevas de la corte de España*, 375: "noticias que Joseph Pellicer poeta y don Antonio, su hermano, a media noche mataron a don Diego de Atiença, edad de veinte i dos porque no se quiso casar con hija de don Joseph Pellicer." For his pardon, see Pellicer, *Avisos*, 1:520, entry for 21 June 1644: "Ayer, Lunes, 20 deste, se vio en la Sala, en Definitiva, la Causa de Don Joseph Pellicer de Tovar, Cronista Mayor de Su Majestad, sobre la Muerte de Don Diego de Santander, por la qual ha estado ausente I retrahído nueve años i medio, por querella del padre del Difunto."

Felipe el Grande (1631), an avowedly panegyrical account of Philip IV's bravura performance in a bullfight held in Madrid. Next came his *Templo de la fama, alcáçar de la fortuna*, a paean to the person and policies of the count-duke, and it was apparently this treatise that gave Pellicer what he most wanted: the opportunity to serve as a publicist of the royal favorite's propaganda war against France.[132]

The extent of Pellicer's contributions to this war of words remains somewhat uncertain, partly because he was in the habit of attributing to himself treatises signed by others. He claims, for example, to have ghostwritten Adam de la Parra's *Conspiración herético-crisitiana*, but his claim is clearly false.[133] The originality of his polemic *La defensa de España contra las calumnias de Francia* (1635) is also in doubt, inasmuch as Pellicer specialized in reworking the texts of other authors, in this instance Guillén de la Carrerra, and then claiming them as his own. Even so, it appears that Olivares arranged to have this pamphlet printed in Venice for further distribution in both Italy and France. In it, Pellicer expressed outrage at what he described as the hundreds of anti-Spanish "libels" sponsored by Richelieu. "I am very bothered," he wrote, "by these French writers who, hating our nation and wishing to only magnify their Princes, publish things that should never be said, even about private individuals." Pellicer continued by launching a somewhat disingenuous attack on "politic history," that is, precisely the kind of history favored by the count-duke. "In our own century," he wrote, "we have seen princes and potentates who, by bribing their own as well as foreign historians, rent praise and buy encomia in an effort to achieve the fame that their own efforts and virtues do not merit and which would otherwise escape them."[134] That, of course, was precisely the kind of history in which Pellicer specialized, although he justified his own work on the grounds that his monarch's and his nation's grandeur was such that anyone who addressed these subjects responsibly had no need to resort to either chicanery or exaggeration. In other words, his pen was not for rent.

Similar rhetoric pervades Pellicer's other polemics, many of which were written under the auspices of the count-duke. They included—the list is long—*La Astrea Sáfica* (1635), a short panegyrical history of Philip IV that included an attack on Richelieu as well as praise for the count-duke;[135] *El mármol triunfal* (1638), which touted Spain's victory at Fuenterrabia; *El embaxador chimérico* (1638), Pelli-

---

132. In 1635, Pellicer also contributed a "panegírico" to a collection of verses published to commemorate the inauguration of the Buen Retiro, the king's new pleasure palace located on the eastern edge of Madrid. The volume, dedicated to the count-duke, was Covarrubias y Leiva, *Elogios al Palacio Real*.

133. Pellicer, *Biblioteca*, 27v–28.

134. Pellicer de Ossau y Tovar, *La defensa de España*, 128. For this work, see Soledad Arredondo, "Literatura polémica e reescritura en 1635."

135. On this treatise, see Martín Polin, "Pellicer de Ossau," which refers to the second, 1641 edition of *La Astrea Sáfica*.

cer's translation, adaptation, and reformulation of Mathieu des Morgues's *L'ambassadeur chimérique*, a bitingly satirical attack on Richelieu and his anti-Spanish policies;[136] *El anti-católico de estado y lágrimas de Europa* (1639), yet another response to Richelieu's *Catholique d'estat* and one in which he boasted that his earlier *Defensa de España* "was publicly burned in Paris, to my great honor"; *La exortación de la paz* (1639), another polemic aimed at Richelieu; and *La fama austriaca* (1641), written "against Scipion Dupleix, chronicler of France" and in praise of the many virtues, both personal and political, of Philip IV's chief ally, Emperor Ferdinand II.[137] In addition, Pellicer demonstrated his personal commitment to Olivares in his *Constancia cristiana en el Válido* (1638), a treatise that defended the count-duke at a moment when complaints about the royal favorite were on the rise.

In the end, loyalty of this kind brought its rewards. As early as 1636, there was talk of an appointment as royal chronicler, and in 1639 a rumor surfaced that Pellicer was to be named "historian of Spain," a kind of superchronicler similar to the position occupied by Pedro de Valencia under Philip III. The rumor, given Philip IV's outspoken support for Malvezzi, was surely false, but it apparently persuaded Pellicer to begin his famous *Avisos,* a daily chronicle of happenings at the royal court that was meant to serve as the basis for his long-planned history of Philip IV.[138] Finally, in October 1640, Pellicer got what he wanted: an appointment as *cronista mayor de los reinos de Aragon,* and then another office, that of *cronista mayor de Aragon,* which was especially created by Olivares in order to enlist Pellicer's services in the propaganda campaign he directed at the Catalans, whose revolt against the monarchy had begun several months before.[139] This campaign also led to the creation of a new Junta de Cronistas consisting of two others of Olivares's loyalists, Adam de la Parra and Francisco de Rioja, together with Pellicer.

The junta's first order of business was to draft replies to *Proclamación católica,* a manifesto published by the city government of Barcelona that justified the rebellion by listing the many occasions upon which Philip IV, as count of Bar-

---

136. Morgues, a member of the *devot* party, was staunchly opposed to Richelieu and his anti-Spanish policies. For more on Pellicer's rewriting of Morgues, see Soledad Arredondo, "La guerre franco-espagnole de 1635."

137. Pellicer catalogs his work in his "Carta a Nicolás Antonio" (BNE: Ms. 11.262, no. 17); and in his *Biblioteca.*

138. For this project, see Clare, "L'Espagne au quotidien dans les *Avisos* de José Pellicer."

139. The office of *cronista de los reinos de Aragón,* previously held by Bartolomé Leonardo de Argensola, had been vacant since 1631. Pellicer's appointment as *cronista mayor de Aragón* subsequently put him at odds with the *cronista del reino de Aragón,* whose incumbent was traditionally appointed by the Diputación.

celona, had failed to protect the Catalans in violation of their *furs*, the traditional liberties and rights he had sworn to uphold.[140] Following the game plan outlined by the Junta de Cronistas Olivares had created in 1635, the new one orchestrated a coordinated response accusing the Catalans of lèse majesté. Parra was first off the mark with *Súplica de Tortosa* (1640), which challenged the legitimacy of the revolt largely on political and religious grounds, whereas Rioja's reply was *Aristarco, o censura de la proclamación Católica* (1641), which invoked the work of the ancient Greek astronomer Aristarchus to attack the historical basis of the principality's feudal rights and to defend the doctrine of royal absolutism in Catalonia itself.[141]

Pellicer's contribution to this new war of words was *La idea del principado de Catalunya* (1642), a historical treatise that harked back to the eighth century to challenge the legitimacy of the *furs* and to forestall the possibility that Louis XIII might seek to take advantage of Spanish weakness to annex portions of Catalonia to France. Such fears were real. As early as 1627 the French monarch had ordered a jurist, Jacques Cassan, to research French claims not only to Catalonia but also to other Spanish territories, including Milan, Aragon, Navarre, Portugal, even Castile itself. But what had previously appeared as mere pretense became a reality once Louis XIII, during the spring of 1642, joined French troops preparing to besiege the city of Perpignan, then part of Catalonia.[142] Pellicer's *Idea* refuted the legitimacy of these claims by noting acerbically that "only in the reign of Louis XIII . . . has this cadaver of rights been disinterred from history, when before it was little more ashes."[143] In addition, he attempted to turn the tables on Cassan with a genealogy demonstrating that the French crown legitimately belonged to the king of Spain.[144]

Other parts of *La idea* dealt more specifically with the history of Catalonia and sought to "unmask" ["desenmascarar"] the legitimacy of the principality's fundamental laws, the basis of which was a feudal (or pactist) notion of government enshrined in the eleventh-century law code known as the *Usatges* of Barcelona,

---

140. The *Proclamación*, printed in October 1640, is generally attributed to the Augustinian friar Gaspar Sala. For a general introduction to recent literature pertaining to the *Proclamación* and other political pamphlets generated by Catalan revolt, see Bouza Álvarez, "Gramática de la crisis."

141. For these treatises, see Soledad Arredondo, "Noticia de la *Súplica de Tortosa*." Pellicer had nothing but praise for the *Súplica*: "The book is absolutely beautiful and well-written. . . . It is very timely, true, and meets all of the objections of the members of the Consell de Cent." *Avisos*, 1:255, entry for 7 July 1641.

142. For this commission, see Church, *Richelieu and Reason of State*, 360. The book in question was Cassan, *La Recherche des droicts du Roy et de la Couronne de France*.

143. Pellicer, *La idea del principado de Catalunya*, 293.

144. Pellicer based this claim upon the illegitimacy of France's Salic Law, which denied women the right of inheritance.

which had traditionally set limits on the powers of the counts of Barcelona. Pellicer took the position that these laws were essentially meaningless, inasmuch as the Catalans, starting with the conquest of the Spanish march by Charlemagne's generals in the eighth century, were "vassals by right of conquest, not of a pact." He therefore argued that the *furs* were essentially meaningless and concluded that the "movedores" of the rebellion, having allied with France, were guilty of the capital crime of lèse majesté. In addition, Pellicer, in a move used by official historians, impugned the historical veracity of the *Proclamación católica* with the charge that the sources used by its reputed author, Fray Gaspar Sala, were invented out of whole cloth.[145]

As history, *La idea* was specious, its arguments and evidence flawed, but in the prologue Pellicer insisted: "This is not a panegyric. It is a narration sewn together with sources, new and old, that do not allow for anything more than a literal interpretation. . . . History, as it is a fact, does not allow for subtle interpretations [*delicacedzas*] allowed in other arts and sciences."[146] And even though he claimed to be writing objective history, "free of passion and hate," he cobbled together a powerful statement in defense of Philip IV's regalist rights over Catalonia. His timing, moreover, was impeccable. Printed in Antwerp on 1 June 1642, *La idea* offered the king the arguments needed to defend his claim to the principality and to oppose France's claims at the precise moment when his armies were making preparations to invade Catalonia and put an end to the revolt.[147] Equally importantly, by invoking the importance of what he called "la gran monarchía de España," Pellicer openly expressed support of Olivares and his long-standing efforts to integrate the monarchy's different Iberian kingdoms into a more unified whole.

Recent critical discussion of *La idea* tends to dismiss it as nothing more than propaganda written in the teeth of a revolt, but for Pellicer it was but one piece in a larger historical enterprise intended to strip away what he described as the "flood

---

145. Cf. Pellicer de Ossau y Tovar, *Anales de la historia*, 301, where Pellicer criticized Sala for his "execrable método, en ofensa de la majestad real, de los primeros ministros, de la verdad, de la causa pública, con tanto escándalo de la crisitiandad."

146. Pellicer, *La idea del principado de Catalunya*, "Al que leyere" (To the reader), n.p.: "Este no es panegírico. . . . Es una narración tejida de testimonios antiguos y modernos que no admiten más interpretación que el sentido literal. . . . La historia, como es hecho, no admite delicadezas que son propias de otras artes o ciencias, donde la delegadeza del ingenio suele convencer al menos sutil, aunque esté de parte de lo cierto."

147. Scholarship on *La idea* may be approached through Soledad Arredondo, "Entre polémica e historia." Note that Pellicer wrote a similar pamphlet following the revolt of the Kingdom of Portugal against Philip IV. See Bouza, *Papeles y opinión*, 162–163.

of fables that have served to sink the histories of Spain."¹⁴⁸ This enterprise began, or so he claimed, in 1628, when he first outlined a monumental history of Spain that was to run from antiquity to his own day. At that moment, Pellicer still defended the veracity of the "false chronicles" that documented Santiago's original mission to Spain in 37 CE and his subsequent burial in Galicia (see Chapter 7). Pellicer subsequently changed his mind about these chronicles and about the authenticity of various Carolingian cartularies and other documents that Catalan chroniclers had used to justify the historical basis of the *furs*. Jesús Villanueva López has suggested that this change of heart derived from Pellicer's growing commitment to what came to be called "critical" history freed of the myths and stories that had figured in Spain's national history since the Middle Ages.¹⁴⁹ However, Pellicer's change of heart, which dates to the mid-1630s, is more likely to have been connected to his quest for royal patronage, since it reflected his recognition that Francisco de Rioja and other writers closely connected to the count-duke had soured on the "false chronicles," together with those scholars such as Tamayo de Vargas who continued to defend them.¹⁵⁰

Pellicer, in this respect, was an opportunist, yet his rejection of the false chronicles was in line with his emergent vision of himself as Spain's national historian, one who identified closely with the monarchy and whose interests transcended the narrow patriotic ambitions of "the particular chroniclers of each individual kingdom."¹⁵¹ For Pellicer, these chroniclers, having privileged political expediency over accuracy, found themselves predisposed to accept the validity of any source, however dubious, so long as it set limits the authority of the Crown. Pellicer's use of history was equally politic, but from his perspective nothing associated with the monarchy could be either deceitful or wrong. His interest in purifying Spain's history thus had less to do with his avowed interest in writing critical history than with a political agenda that paralleled and in some ways anticipated the efforts of Etienne Baluze, Jean Mabillon, and other historians aligned with the French monarchy to document the origins of the Gallican church.¹⁵² In comparison, Pellicer's aim was to strengthen the Habsburg monarchy by demonstrating the importance and continuity of unchecked monarchical authority in Spain since the time of the Goths. He further believed that a broader "general" as opposed to

---

148. Pellicer, *Anales de la historia*, 328.
149. Villanueva López, *Política y discurso histórico*.
150. For Rioja's attack on Dextro, see Chapter 7.
151. Pellicer, *Anales de la historia*, 180.
152. For the efforts of these French scholars, see Soll, "The Antiquary and the Information State."

"particular" history would best serve "the public good," a term he equated with "God, the king, the republic, my country, and the century in which I have lived, and perhaps those of the future as well."[153]

Such was the underlying theme of Pellicer's proposed national history, a new *historia pro patria*, which, as it developed, was divided into two parts, the first dealing with Spain's ancient history through the era of the Goths and the second starting in 711 CE at the start of the Reconquest. Neither, judged by the standards of the eighteenth century, offered an especially critical approach to the history of the Spanish past, partly because Pellicer, in addition to challenging the authenticity of historical sources he did not approve, was fully prepared to invent others that he did. A good demonstration of Pellicer's bifurcated method may be found in the first part of his history, *Aparato de la monarquía antigua de las Españas* (1673), where he rejected as false the list of Spain's "primitive" kings previously invented by Annius di Viterbo, only to replace them by a new list of sixty equally imaginary monarchs that one astute contemporary dismissed as little more than a "pack of lies."[154]

Just as Mariana had embraced the king list of Annius in order to demonstrate both the antiquity and the universality of the monarchy within the whole of the Iberian peninsula, the defense of the institution of the monarchy was central to the *Aparato*. It also appeared in the second part of this history, which was published posthumously in 1681 as *Anales de la monarquía de España después de su pérdida*. Once again, Pellicer's stated purpose was to exorcize from Spain's history "the evil of the fabricators of the false chronicles," and in order to establish the veracity of his own narrative, he listed his sources, both printed and manuscript. Furthermore, in an effort to generate support for his larger monarchical project, he challenged the historicity of the myths surrounding the laws and liberties of Spain's constituent parts, among them Aragon's Laws of Sobrarbe, the Catalan *usatges*, and the liberties of Vizcaya, which, according to medieval legend, originated from an oath taken at the ninth-century battle of Arigorriaga.[155] Pellicer had few qualms about inventing new myths of his own, however, and among the most important was the eighth-century pledge by nobles from Asturias, Galicia, Ara-

---

153. See Arco y Garay, *La erudución española*, 2:706, letter of 6 May 1651; and Pellicer, *Anales de la historia*, 304.

154. Ibáñez de Segovia, *Noticia y juicio*, 242.

155. This battle, which pitted Vizcayans against the king of Asturias and León, resulted in a victory for the former. Afterward, the military chiefs of Vizcaya gathered to elect their first *señor*, establishing a tradition of elected lordship that curtailed the powers of the lord of Vizcaya even when passed to the kings of Castile and León. For more on this battle and the attendant myths, see Bazán, "La historiografía medieval de Vizcaya."

gon, and Catalonia to grant King Pelayo the unrestricted authority to issue laws and decrees. For Pellicer, this pledge created what he called the "fundamental law of the Spanish monarchy," which, in his view, trumped all subsequent efforts to limit the exercise of monarchical authority throughout the "Spains."[156]

Pellicer the critic; Pellicer the mythographer. As a historian Pellicer was both, but his commitment to the monarchy and its history was such that what others saw as flaws in his scholarship does not appear to have cost him any sleep. What is certain is that Pellicer's enemies far outnumbered his friends. Some took issue with his criticisms of the false chronicles, others with his readiness to lard Spain's history with new myths of his own. And he seemed to be universally detested in both Aragon and Catalonia for his attempt to define Spain as a single "nation" embodied in the monarchy.[157] In addition, his unbridled ambition, his "chronistería," and his eagerness to exploit the positions he held for personal gain sparked the resentment of his contemporaries, including those who were otherwise sympathetic with his regalist ideas. Everyone was against Pellicer, it seems, except for Olivares and, even more importantly, Philip IV.

Official History after Olivares

Within two years of the count-duke's disgrace in 1643, Philip IV had a new favorite, Luis Méndez de Haro; yet this "change of ministers"—the phrase is Pellicer's—did little to alter the king's ideas about history. With revolts in Catalonia and Portugal complicating his continuing efforts to defeat the Dutch, Philip went on the defensive. Politically, he opted for continuity over change and, with respect to history, tightened censorship so much that it seemed that all history was to become a state monopoly, the work of writers who enjoyed royal protection and support.

This policy, as noted earlier in this study, was nothing new. It had its roots in Galíndez de Carvajal's suggestion to Charles V that history was best entrusted to chroniclers attached to the royal court. The count of Gondomar had made a similar proposal to Philip III, and in 1614 the Council of State seriously debated a proposal restricting the writing of history to the chroniclers appointed by the

---

156. Pellicer, *Anales de la historia*, 1:110. See also López Villanueva, *Política y discurso histórico*, 208.
157. Pellicer's idea of Spain as a single "nation" derived in part from Mariana but also from López Madera, *Excelencias de la monarchía y reyno de España*. It was also predicated on the notion of the Spanish nation as an abstract theological entity. For more on this concept, see Botella Ordiñas, "Monarquía de España." I am grateful to Dr. Botella Ordiñas for sending me a copy of this dissertation and to the anonymous reviewer who first brought it to my attention.

king.[158] Such a measure, if enacted, would have been impossible to enforce. Owing to the composite nature of Spain's monarchy, each of its constituent kingdoms, in addition to having its own official chroniclers, retained the right to authorize the publication of books within its own borders. In 1546 Charles V required authors seeking to have their books printed in Castile first to obtain a publishing license from the Council of Castile, but because this council's regulatory authority applied only to the kingdom of Castile, the measure did nothing to prevent authors from having their books printed in Aragon, where the Diputación reserved this power, let alone in Portugal, Naples, Flanders, or Milan, where censorship remained in the hands of local as opposed to royal officials. Céspedes y Meneses took advantage of this particular loophole when, in 1631, he published the first part of his history of Philip IV in Lisbon rather than in Madrid, where the Council of Castile had effectively banned his work.

Philip IV had also to contend with the fact that his historical agenda did not necessarily coincide with that of local governing authorities. In Aragon, for example, the Diputación regularly financed publication of books relating to the *alteraciones* that would otherwise have been banned in Madrid; among them was Vicencio Blasco de Lanuza's *Historias eclesiásticas y seculares de Aragón*. Disputes over this and similar histories eventually led to a royal decree, promulgated in 1637, ordering the Council of Aragon not to authorize the publication of any "history or *relación*" without the king's personal consent.[159]

The monarchy's worries about history, especially that of the Indies, surfaced again in 1638 when Juan de Solórzano Pereira, a distinguished jurist then serving as a member of the Council of the Indies, petitioned for a license to publish the second volume of *De Indiarum jure*, a work of legal history expressly written to legitimate Spain's presence in the New World.[160] In part 1 of this history, published in 1629, Solórzano had focused on the monarchy's efforts to comply with the papal bulls of donation in order to prove, largely on the basis of laws and ordinances the monarchy had issued, that the charges of misconduct and cruelty leveled by such "heretics" as Ralegh, Purchas, and De Bry were calumnies without any basis in fact.

In his second volume, Solórzano turned away from the bulls of donation to

---

158. For this debate, see AGS Est: leg. 1874, papel de Juan Pablo Bonet, 2 September 1614.
159. RAH: Salazar y Castro Ms. K 17, decree dated El Pardo, 6 February 1637. This decree was reissued in January 1645.
160. Much of what follows is based on AGS Est: leg. 2660. For Solórzano, see García Hernán, *Consejero de ambos mundos*, although this otherwise important study omits reference to the controversy over the publication of part 2 of *De Indiarum jure*.

argue that the monarchy's imperium derived from the right of "just occupation" that the initial discovery of the Indies had conferred. He also contended that Spain's presence there was consistent with the monarchy's continuing determination to defend the native population and to attend to their conversion to Christianity and a more civilized form of life. As proof, he included the texts of relevant laws and decrees designed to protect native rights, together with others intended to punish individual Spaniards accused of enslaving natives or mistreating them in a particularly cruel or inhuman fashion.

Ordinarily the task of monitoring the publication of books relating to the Indies belonged to the Council of the Indies, along with the cronista mayor de las Indias. In this instance, however, the Council of State, the body with overall responsibility for managing the monarchy's foreign affairs, arrogated for itself the decision to determine whether Solórzano's treatise merited publication. Its members subsequently asked Jusepe de Nápoles to review the volume and offer his advice. In a report dated 22 March 1638, Nápoles praised the book for its "sound organization, clarity, Christianity, and zeal," and Solórzano for his "learning and erudition," but he argued strongly against publication on the grounds that the author went too far in his efforts to document "the great repression and continuous vexations in the way Spaniards treat the Indians, the unjustness of this mistreatment, together with the avarice and greed motivating such actions." Such material, he added, "will provide the enemies and rivals of the Crown" with new source material to attack it. Worse, it would allow them "to resuscitate the old debate that the conquest [of the Indies] emanated entirely from self-interest as opposed to [Christian] zeal." The report ended with a detailed accounting of those sections of the book that required change; for example, it called for the removal of references to laws ordering officials not to mistreat the natives, because these, in Nápoles's opinion, served only to draw attention to "the negligence of these officials, the lack of obedience, the avarice and greed of the Spaniards, which is exactly what the rivals and enemies of the monarchy need for their political aspirations and designs and which they can also use to provoke discord in the Indies."[161]

A more succinct summary of the aims and intentions of official history would be hard to find, and when the Council of State got around to debating this report, it decided to censor the volume along the lines Nápoles had suggested. Solórzano's book appeared in 1639, albeit with the offending sections removed, its publication seemingly timed to coincide with a royal decree in which Philip IV

---

161. Quotations from the report are included in AGS Est: leg. 2660.

announced the "liberty of the Indians" and prohibited Spaniards from requiring them to perform forced labor of any sort.[162]

That Solórzano's book triggered such debate within the highest circles of the monarchy underscores the importance that its policymakers accorded to the writing of history. This book was also important because of fears that, if published unaltered, it might rekindle the old, sixteenth-century debate over the Indies, providing new ammunition the English and the Dutch could use to justify their own growing presence in the New World. At the same time, the council recognized that when it came to history, political considerations, or what it understood as "reason of state," took precedence. Better, therefore, to dissimulate than to run the risk of printing a history that could be used "against the nation."

Such was a policy that Philip IV embraced as his own, especially during the 1640s when supporters of the rebellions in both Catalonia and Portugal published histories justifying the reasons for breaking with the monarchy in Madrid. As noted earlier, the count-duke's initial response to these publications was to counter them with histories of his own.[163] In 1645, however, Philip IV adopted a more programmatic response to these histories when he issued a royal decree ordering both the Council of Aragon and the Council of Castile not to authorize the printing of any history touching on matters of government and war without the express permission of the Council of State. That this decree had to be reissued in January 1651 underscores its ineffectiveness, but this did little to deter Philip, who, like most other seventeenth-century princes, was determined to control the way in which history, especially his history, was written. A month later, in fact, the king, referring to the "many and grave problems" caused by histories and *relaciones* that were being printed in Granada without official license, instructed royal officials in that city to enforce existing laws relating to "the said books, news sheets, and other historical materials given their importance for the good governance of our kingdoms."[164]

It is not clear which publications had occasioned this particular decree, al-

---

162. One councillor, the marquis of Santa Cruz, suggested that the book should not be published and recommended that it be put way for safekeeping in either the royal archive at Simancas or the one attached to the Council of the Indies.

163. The count-duke adopted a similar policy with respect to Portugal, commissioning a series of books defending the historical basis of Spain's right to the Portuguese throne. I refer to Adam de la Parra, *Apologético contra el tirano y rebelde vergüenza y conjurados;* and Caramuel y Lobowitz, *Respuesta al manfiesto del reino de Portugal*. Caramuel wrote this treatise in Flanders while serving as an adviser to Cardinal Infante Ferdinand. He was also the author of *Philippus prudens*, a treatise defending Spain's rights in Portugal. The Portuguese responded with treatises by Antonio Sousa Maceda, Fernández de Villarroel, and various histories by Francisco Manoel de Melo, which argued the opposite. See, for example, Melo, *Epánafora de varias historias portuguesas*.

164. Domínguez Ortiz, "La censura de obra históricas," 116–117.

though it was subsequently invoked whenever the Council of State felt it necessary to censor a history it did not approve.[165] At issue here was the king's historical legacy, his *fama* or *reputación*, which seemingly preoccupied the aging monarch more and more. Philip IV spelled out his thoughts on this issue in a lengthy memo he directed to the Council of Castile in 1661, which included the statement, "It is my royal duty to maintain the justice of all my rights in the public credit.... I have been aware for many years that writers of foreign and ill-disposed nations constantly publish accounts of my kingdoms and policies which are set very far from the truth of events."[166]

But who was to write a history promoting the king's reputation at a time when his fortunes were demonstrably on the wane? Traditionally, the task of writing histories of this kind fell to the royal chroniclers, but following Malvezzi's death in 1647, none of the historians named to these offices, not even Pellicer, seemed prepared to write the kind of *historia pro persona* that Philip envisioned. There was one volunteer, Juan Antonio Calderón, a royal judge in Granada, who, in 1654, announced that he was prepared to write a nine-volume history of Philip's reign, but this truly monumental project, however well-intentioned, never very got far.[167] At this juncture the king turned to Francisco Ramos del Manzano, a legal humanist he had recently appointed to the Council of Castile.[168] Ramos del Manzano had long advocated a historical approach to the study of law, but he had never written any history, let alone a politic history of the kind the king clearly sought. The king thus drafted a memo outlining, in fairly precise terms, exactly the kind of history he wanted:

> [It will be] a history of the various ways in which God has been pleased to test these kingdoms during forty years.... Of a war of twenty-five continuous years with the major powers of Europe by sea and land, and within Spain of the rebellions of Catalonia and Portugal, until God should be willing to grant us our desired aim of peace.

---

165. One such history was Mascarenhas's *Campaña de Portugal*. The council objected to this publication on the grounds that it contained information useful to Spain's enemies, especially the English, and ordered that the publication be withdrawn from circulation and censored. For this incident, see Cid, "Pleitos de historiadores y confrontaciones literarias."

166. As cited in Stradling, *Philip IV and the Government of Spain*, 32.

167. On this project, see Calderón, *Memorial y discurso histórico-jurídico-político;* and his "Memorial q dió a la Magestad Cathólica," fols. 134–141v. Calderón's working title for this history was the somewhat pompous *Compendio universal histórico-jurídico-político-chronológico-genealógico de la Cathólica Monarquía España en las cuatro partes del mundo*. In writing it, Calderón changed the name America to Ferisabelica, and offered documentation to prove that Philip IV was the direct descendant of the Merovingians and therefore the legitimate ruler of France.

168. Cf. Peset and Marzal, "Humanismo jurídico tardío en Salamanca." Following Philip IV's death in 1665, Ramos del Manzano was named president of the Council of the Indies (1674), then president of the Council of Castile (1677). In 1669 he was also appointed tutor (or *ayo*) of the prince of Austrias, the future Charles II.

It must be written with sincerity, especially as regards the true intentions of the subjects who have served me with such value and devotion throughout these tribulations, and in a manner which will expose and obliterate the false impressions made on the understanding of this and future ages by the malignity of other writers.[169]

Ramos del Manzano's mission was clear, but it was one that he, like Ginés de Sepúlveda, Pedro de Valencia, and other humanists whose notion of history had less to do with Machiavelli than Cicero, was unable to complete. Whether he did anything to advance this history remains uncertain, but Philip IV's death in 1665 effectively brought the project to an end.

For one distinguished scholar, William Bouwsma, official history of the kind discussed in this chapter marked the "end of the Renaissance," because it arose at the end of the era in which a concern for writing objective or disinterested history gave way to politic history, or what he called "histories . . . subordinated to interested and barely disguised motives."[170] Bouwsma exaggerated the extent to which Renaissance historians were disinterested, but he is by no means the only scholar to underscore the shortcomings associated with the kind of politic history sponsored by Philip IV and the other European princes of his day. Other critics have also faulted official history for compromising the historian's freedom of expression and for its apparent repudiation of the fundamental tenets of the "perfect" history espoused by Bodin, Cabrera de Córdoba, and other contributors to the *ars historicae* genre. But whatever its defects, it is easy to forget that official history was not necessarily inferior history; many of the writers who volunteered to defend the persona and policies of their princes did so with all of the ingredients that the "artists of history" considered necessary for good history: erudition, sound judgment, elegant style, and documentary proofs. Furthermore, it is important to recognize that politic history of the kind demanded by Philip IV reflected not only the growing importance that seventeenth-century rulers attached to public opinion but also history's ability to communicate with that public and get the monarchs' message across.

More immediately, official history was something that no seventeenth-century ruler, no matter how powerful, could neglect. That arch salesman of absolute

---

169. As cited in Stradling, *Philip IV and the Government of Spain*, 312, Philip IV to Juan de Oyenguren, 9 May 1661. On this occasion the king also instructed his royal secretaries to provide Ramos with copies of documents that he might need for this work.

170. Bouwsma, *Waning of the Renaissance*, 214. The same sentiments may be found in Cochrane, *Historians and Historiography*, 479–494.

monarchy, Louis XIV, fully integrated history into the business of state and in the course of his reign employed the services of more than twenty *historiographes*.[171] Their task: create the image of a ruler whose "glory" embodied the spirit and power of the kingdom over which he ruled. Louis also emulated Emperor Charles V by having both artists and historians accompany him into battle and then by writing *mémoires* of his own.[172]

Philip IV was never so ambitious, if only because his glory, starting with the crisis of the 1640s, steadily lost much of its glow. For Louis XIV, moreover, history represented the essence of power. For Philip, it offered the illusion of power, the means though which he hoped to preserve his reputation for posterity. Such concerns, of course, are emblematic of the Baroque, an age in which appearance seemingly counted for more than substance and reputation more than reality, or, as Gracián advised, "The greater part of ruling is to dissimulate."[173] A Spanish courtier of this same era was somewhat more direct, stating that the purpose of official history was simply to "make the bad, good, and the good even better."[174] So it was with Philip IV and the somewhat diminished monarchy over which he ended his rule.

171. On this topic, see Burke, *The Fabrication of Louis XIV*; and Marin, *Portrait of the King*, 39–69.
172. I refer to Louis XIV, *Mémoires*. On these mémoires, see Abraham, "L'histoire, c'est moi."
173. Cited in Stradling, *Philip IV and the Government of Spain*, 63.
174. Roxas in the prologue of Martyr Rizo, *Historia de la vida de Mécenas*.

CHAPTER SEVEN

Critical History or Official History?

> Rest assured, there have never been more nor more heroic deeds than those the Spaniards have achieved. But the Spaniards have written about them poorly. Most of their histories are little more than bacon fat that in two bites cloys the senses.
> —Baltasar Gracián, *El Criticón* (1657)

> [The king] should have historians whose writings are validated by nothing except his royal authority and protection. These are to commemorate in perpetuity a record of the past that inspires good will, represses passions, and improves the effects [of good government].
> —Pedro de la Puente, *Los soldados en la guardia* (1657)

At the close of the seventeenth century, official history, in Spain at least, was nearing the end of what had been an extraordinarily successful run. Starting in the thirteenth century with the workshops of Alfonso X, it had taken many different forms: sprawling general histories centered on both the Reconquest of Spain and the conquest of the New World; biographies highlighting the *res gestae* of individual rulers; pamphlets touting the benefits of specific monarchical programs; and more. But whatever its subject, official history, whether as *historia pro persona* or *historia pro patria*, drew much of its energy and inspiration from the "politics of reputation," the monarchs' ongoing efforts to enhance their image, and ultimately their powers, through various media. Toward this end successive rulers assembled teams of artists, architects, and humanist advisers, together with clusters of chroniclers prepared to write narratives both long and short representing the rulers' interests and concerns.

Concurrently, these same chroniclers created, again starting in the Middle

---

Epigraphs: Baltasar Gracián, *El Criticón*, in *Obras Completas*, edited by Manuel Arroyo Stephen (1651; Madrid, 1993), 1:593; Puente, *Los soldados en la guardia*, 233.

Ages, a model of kingship that coupled the idea of territorial expansion with religion. Other rulers, as far back as Egypt's pharaohs, had also justified dominion over conquered territories on spiritual grounds, but in Castile, as well as in Aragon, this model helped fuel the struggle to restore Hispania to Christianity, along with the octane necessary to launch an overseas expansion that culminated in the discovery and conquest of the New World. In later centuries the same model allowed Spain's Habsburg dynasty to link the defense of their possessions in northern Europe, the Low Countries in particular, to the defense of religion and the church.

The role of written history in this enterprise cannot be underestimated, because the chroniclers' task was essentially to reach a domestic audience who needed to learn about, identify with, and ultimately celebrate the manifold benefits—honor, glory, wealth, and renown—that conquest would bring. Nebrija was right, therefore, to encourage Ferdinand and Isabella to have their history written not in Latin but in Castilian, inasmuch as this language was certain to offer their vassals a better understanding of and thus a stake in the global imperium they were eager to construct.

By the reign of Charles II (1665–1700), however, even the most ardent advocates of expansion recognized that the cost of maintaining imperium on a global basis was beginning to outweigh its benefits. Already in 1619, Sancho de Moncada, a leading *arbitrista,* advised that "conquest of remote nations in the Indies and the conservation of the royal patrimony in the kingdoms of Naples, and Sicily and the duchy of Milan, and the state of Flanders, have been a natural cancer in the body of Spain," the very source of what many of his contemporaries feared was its imminent "declinación."[1] Despite such warnings, the Habsburg monarchy, both in Europe and in the Americas, remained a formidable power, but a fatal combination of economic weakness and lackluster leadership at home and imperial overstretch abroad led gradually but inexorably to what Charles II, on his death bed, referred to as "diminution," that is, the dismemberment of the monarchy that Moncada had previously referred to as "decline."[2] Actual diminution began in 1640, the year marked by revolts in Catalonia, then Portugal, which achieved its independence in 1668 following a war hard-fought on several fronts. Diminution also entailed the loss of the northern Netherlands (in 1648), the island of Jamaica to the English (in 1655), and the western part of Hispaniola to the French, starting in 1664. It also manifested itself in the monarchy's failure to

---

1. Cited in Pagden, "Heeding Heraclites," 320.
2. William Coxe, England's ambassador in Madrid, as cited in Lynch, *Bourbon Spain,* 23.

provide adequately for the defense of its other colonies, rendering them vulnerable to the depredations of such notorious pirates as Henry Morgan, and the monarchy's inability to maintain its commercial monopoly in the Indies. With Spain's weakened economy unable to supply much-needed manufactured goods and other commodities, merchants in Mexico, Peru, and other parts of the Indies turned to Dutch, English, and French traders who could do so. In the process smuggling became a way of life; handsomely bribed or otherwise well-remunerated royal officials looked the other way as English cloths and French clocks found their way into the markets of Lima, Mexico City, and other New World cities. The gradual separation of the colonies from Spain had begun.

For all their historical importance, these developments attracted little notice in Madrid, where the monarchy, already "diminished" by the loss of the northern Netherlands and Portugal, seemed powerless even to institute the reforms necessary to give Spain's domestic economy a much-needed boost, let alone deal with external challenges. Paralysis was particularly acute during the regency (1665–1675) of the queen mother Mariana of Austria, a turbulent era marked by domestic unrest and the forced surrender of the Franche-Comté to France following the disastrous performance of Spanish forces in the War of Devolution (1667–1668). This downward spiral soon ended, but owing to the severe physical limitations of Charles II, who remained feeble, chronically ill, and often incapable of personal rule,[3] effective control of the government passed into the hands of noble factions more interested in self-enrichment than administrative and economic reform.

The worst was yet to come. Starting in the 1690s when news leaked out that the sickly monarch was incapable of siring an heir, the issue of succession dominated court politics in Madrid. Would the next king be Philip of Anjou, grandson of Louis XIV and his Spanish wife, María Teresa? Or the Habsburg pretender Charles, archduke of Austria? In November 1700 Charles II opted for Philip, a decision that triggered the global conflict known as the War of the Spanish Succession (1702–1713). Europe's newest major power brokers—the Dutch and the English supporting Charles, and Louis XIV backing his grandson—took sides in an effort to determine Spain's dynastic future. The war ended with a compromise, the Treaty of Utrecht (1713) allowing Philip V to retain both Spain and its American dominions at the cost of surrendering Flanders, Spain's one remaining possession in northern Europe, along with Milan, Naples, and Sicily. Another small but strategically and symbolically important loss was Gibraltar, which had been

---

3. For a recent reassessment of the reign of Charles II, see Storrs, *The Resilience of the Spanish Monarchy*.

occupied by the English since 1704 and which represented the end of Hispania, the territorially united Catholic monarchy that Philip V's Spanish ancestors had fought to create. Utrecht in this sense spelled out plainly what was already evident during the reign of Charles II, namely that Spain's once-mighty monarchy had lost the ability to maintain the integrity of an empire that had required centuries to construct. How then were the king's chroniclers to write the history of the monarchy in the throes of the diminution that Charles II, in a rare moment of lucidity, so rightly feared?

Further complicating the answer to this question was Charles II's apparent inability to articulate the kind of history he wanted his chroniclers to write. Each of his Habsburg ancestors, with the possible exception of Philip III, had evinced clear ideas about history, whether in the guise of *historia pro persona, historia pro patria,* or the kind of propagandistic history promoted by his father, Philip IV. In comparison, Charles II never expressed much interest in history, even though, starting around age seven, he had been encouraged by his tutor, Francisco Ramos del Manzano, to read about the achievements of his ancestors in the hope that they would inspire him to perform equally momentous deeds.[4]

Whether Charles, who had learning difficulties, read any of these histories remains in doubt. The king liked hunting, court masques, and theater but had only limited intellectual interests and certainly nothing to compare with those of his older bastard brother Juan José de Austria, who was known for his support of the *novatores,* a group of scholars seeking to introduce new methods of critical historical inquiry and scholarship into Spain (see below). Charles, however, had no such associations, and among all his favorites—and he ruled through several— only one, the count of Oropesa, Manuel Joaquín Álvarez de Toledo, took much interest in the arts. Even Oropesa was a far cry from his French counterpart, Jean Baptiste Colbert, who transformed Louis XIV's chroniclers into veritable "artisans of glory" whose histories celebrated the king's victories, ignored his defeats, and represented the monarch as a vital, animating force, the epitome of France itself.[5] Nothing remotely similar existed at the court of Charles II, even though the offices of royal chronicler remained on the books. As a result the importance of these positions gradually atrophied as they evolved, slowly but surely, into sinecures whose incumbents owed less to the monarch than to the minister who helped to secure their appointment.

---

4. For the king's learning difficulties, as well as the educational program laid out for him by his tutor, see Maura Gamazo, *Carlos II y su corte,* 2:76; and Martínez Ruiz, "Francisco Ramos del Manzano."

5. Cf. Ranum, *Artisans of Glory.*

Critical History or Official History? 255

Traditionally, the cronistas del rey, almost by definition, enjoyed a close, sometimes quite personal relationship with the rulers they served. Queen Isabella's chroniclers often served as her personal secretaries, and Charles V, despite all his travels, maintained close ties with each of his "imperial" chroniclers. Similarly, Philip II regularly closeted himself with his chroniclers—remember his conversation with Herrera y Tordesillas at the Escorial—to discuss the histories he expected them to write. In the seventeenth century, however, the ties that had previously connected kings to their chroniclers weakened as a series of royal favorites, starting with the duke of Lerma, came to the fore. In the process, the office of royal chronicler was "privatized," one might even say hijacked, as these ministers promoted chroniclers who served their particular interests rather than those of the Crown. The first instance of this occurred in 1608, when Lerma engineered the appointment of Pedro de Valencia as cronista general as part of a scheme designed to weaken the influence of Herrera y Tordesillas over history-writing at the court of Philip III. Further privatization occurred under Olivares, who began his *privança* by having his friend Francisco de Rioja named royal chronicler even though he had never applied for the job. Olivares then, in the 1630s, created a kitchen cabinet of historians, the Junta de Cronistas, for what amounted to a personal vendetta directed at his arch rival Richelieu. This junta, together with the one created in 1640 to fight the supporters of the Catalan revolt, effectively rendered the king's official chroniclers redundant. In addition, many of the prerogatives previously attached to their offices, including the all-important task of serving as the kingdom's historical watchdog, passed to other agencies, including the Council of State.

The next step was to create offices of *cronista ad honorem,* an honorific title that carried with it the right to become cronista del rey, with pay and other emoluments, whenever a vacancy should occur. The first documented appointment of this kind occurred in 1670, when Queen Mariana, serving as regent, appointed a relatively obscure Benedictine monk, Francisco de Sota, cronista ad honorem.[6] Sota waited nine years to become titular chronicler, using this time to write *Chrónica de los príncipes de Asturias y Cantabria* (1681), a spurious history that traced the origins of the prince of Asturias to a certain Astur, son of the great

---

6. Sota's appointment was not unprecedented. Ambrosio de Morales had served Philip II in a purely honorary capacity for more than a decade (see Chapter 3). Starting in the 1620s, the Cortes of Castile also granted the honorary title of cronista de reino to a number of writers, including José de Pellicer. The Cortes apparently invented this title as a way of asserting its independence during the *privança* of the count-duke, but in every instance the initiative for these appointments derived from writers eager to add a bit of luster to their name.

Egyptian pharaoh Osiris, who, for reasons left unexplained, had emigrated to the north of Spain.[7]

More needs to be learned about the mechanisms through which Sota, Pedro Fernández de Pulgar, and other honorary chroniclers obtained their appointments, but their appearance was a sure sign that the ties that traditionally linked kings with their chroniclers were beginning to erode. The administrative counterpart of these honorary chroniclers was the so-called officials of *capa y espada,* or nobles who, starting in the reign of Philip III, found their way into the highest echelons of the royal administration at the behest of the king's favorites and other powerful ministers. *Capa y espada* appointments also symbolized the extent to which different court factions were able to appropriate the resources of the monarchy as their own. So it was with the honorary chroniclers, whose personal ties with the monarch, as opposed to individual ministers, were practically nil, a separation that diminished the chroniclers' importance and prestige. At the start of the eighteenth century, Luis de Salazar y Castro (see below) was briefly able to arrest this development, but over the long run the distance separating the king from his chroniclers contributed directly to the suppression of these offices of royal chronicler during the reign of Philip V. In the short run, though, it allowed the king's chroniclers a measure of independence that their predecessors rarely enjoyed, essentially freeing them from the burden of writing histories expressly tailored to meet the policy requirements of the king. In the process *historia pro persona* diminished and *historia pro patria,* with *patria* increasingly identified with that new, supranational entity known as Spain, came to the fore.

Novatores, the "False Chronicles," and the Rebirth of National History

Of key importance in this development was the emergence, starting in the 1670s, of the *novatores,* or innovators. The novatores were a loosely connected group of scholars who traced Spain's economic and political difficulties to the failure of their countrymen to embrace the new modes of scientific and philosophical thinking associated with such intellectual luminaries as Bacon, Grotius, and Descartes. Novatores were equally concerned with what they regarded as the backwardness of

---

7. Sota, *Chrónica de los príncipes de Asturias y Cantabria,* note to reader. Sota conceived of this history as a continuation of Diego de Saavedra Fajardo's widely acclaimed *Corona gótica, castellana y austriaca* (1646). In contrast, the royal censors who approved Sota's book for publication felt obliged to admit that "it says nothing that is new."

historical writing in Spain. Of particular concern here was myth-history of the kind propagated by the false chronicles, a peculiar feature of seventeenth-century Spanish historiography that deserves brief examination here.

The first of these "false chronicles" was attributed to Beroso and crafted at the close of the fifteenth century by Giovanni Nanni. It subsequently influenced such otherwise reputable historians as Ocampo, Morales, and Mariana.[8] Even more popular, starting early in the seventeenth century, was the chronicle attributed to the fifth-century writer Flavius Lucius Dextrus (Flavio Lucio Dextro in Spanish) but fabricated ca. 1594 by the Jesuit scholar Jerónimo Román de la Higuera (1538–1611) as part of a wider search for new documentary sources relating to the early history of Christianity in Spain.[9] The search for traces of paleo-Christianity in Spain had actually begun in the 1570s when Philip II sent Ambrosio de Morales on a series of "literary voyages" to various monasteries in search of old manuscripts. Philip subsequently initiated attempts to recover the relics of early Spanish martyrs, an effort that included the repatriation of the remains of San Eugenio and Santa Leocadia. In addition, the prudent king supported the efforts of García de Loaysa to locate information pertaining to the origins of the church in Toledo, Spain's primatial see. Loaysa's collaborators on this project included a trio of Jesuit scholars: Mariana, who was commissioned to prepare an edition of works by Saint Ildefonso, the seventh-century bishop famous for his belief in the doctrine of the Immaculate Conception of the Virgin Mary; Andreas Schottus (b. André Schott, Antwerp, 1552–1629), who later edited *Hispania illustrata* (Frankfurt, 1608), a four-volume collection of Spanish scholarship that included the first printed edition of Lucas de Tuy's *Chronicon Mundi;* and Román de la Higuera, an antiquarian interested in writing a history of the Toledan church with an eye toward defending its position as Spain's primatial see. Additional impetus for the recovery of new historical sources came from Cesare Baronio's *Martyrology* (1586) and, starting in 1588, his *Annales Ecclesiastici*, both of which questioned the historicity of the legends surrounding the arrival of Jesus's brother St. James the Greater in Spain and the apostle's subsequent burial in Galicia at a place that later came to be known as Santiago de Compostela. By the eighth century, Santiago had emerged as one of the cornerstones of Spanish Catholicism, but Baronio sug-

---

8. See Chapter 3.
9. The classic study of the false chronicles remains Godoy Alcántara, in *Historia crítica*. See also Kendrick, *Saint James in Spain*, 116–136; Caro Baroja, *Las falsificaciones de la historia;* and now Olds, "The False Chronicles." The search for traces of paleo-Christianity in sixteenth-century Spain is outlined in Harris, *From Muslim to Christian Granada*, esp. chap. 2.

gested that the stories surrounding Santiago could not be proven, casting doubt on the authenticity of his cult.[10]

In Spain, the monarchy, together with influential members of the clergy, rejected these allegations as false. Baronio's assertions, they claimed, were politically motivated and predicated upon the cardinal's well-known opposition to the Spanish presence in both Naples and Milan. Baronio, moreover, helped fuel an outburst of "pious nationalism," which manifested in different ways.[11] It contributed, for example, to the appearance of number of histories emphasizing the sacred, universal quality of both Spain and its monarchy, among them such monuments as Pedro Salazar de Mendoza's *Monarchía de España,* Gregorio López Madera's *Excelencias de la Monarchía y Reino de España* (1597), and Fray Juan de la Puente's *Dos Monarchias* (1602), a book aimed at proving "the superiority of our Catholic monarchs to that of other princes of Europe" as measured in terms of both its antiquity and its commitment to the Christian religion.[12] Pious nationalism also helped trigger a series of spectacular archaeological finds that supposedly attested to the physical presence of Santiago in Spain. Among the first and most important of these "finds" was the discovery of a series of lead boxes, the famous *plomos* of Sacromonte, between 1595 and 1599 in Granada. These boxes reportedly contained first-century inscriptions—in Latin, Castilian, and Arabic—listing the names of Santiago's first disciples, among them San Cecilio, who was consecrated as the first bishop of Granada before his martyrdom ca. 70 CE.[13]

The *plomos* sparked controversy almost as soon as they were unearthed. Benito Arias Montano, Pedro de Valencia, and other leading Spanish humanists suggested, quite rightly, that the documents in question had to be fakes on purely linguistic grounds, because not only was the Latin faulty but, even more importantly, neither Castilian nor Arabic existed as languages in the time of Saint James. But a number of powerful clerics, including the archbishop of Seville, argued in favor of their authenticity, initiating a protracted debate that was not settled until the mid-seventeenth century, when the papacy officially declared the *plomos* to be fakes.

Equally imaginative, and no less controversial, was Román de la Higuera's

---

10. For Baronio, see Wright, *Federico Borromeo and Baronius;* Pullapilly, *Caesar Baronius;* and Zen, *Baronio storico.*
11. For more on this topic, see Botella Ordiñas, "Monarquía de España."
12. Puente, *Tomo primero de la convenencía.*
13. The *plomos* are best approached through Harris, *From Muslim to Christian Granada;* and Barrios Aguilera and García-Arenal, *Los plomos de Sacromonte.* See also the studies assembled in *Al-Qantara* 24 (2003): 295–573.

"discovery" of fragments of a long-lost world chronicle attributed to Dextro, and its continuation by Máximo, a seventh-century bishop of Zaragoza; Luitprando, an early bishop of Cremona, in northern Italy; and, finally, Julián Perez, who was known to have been a parish priest in Toledo during the eleventh century. Of the three, the fragments—known collectively as the *cronicones*—by Dextro were by far the most important because they offered detailed information pinpointing the date of Santiago's arrival in Spain—37 CE—and the cities where he preached. In 1595 Higuera began distributing different copies of these manuscripts to various scholars and friends. Some, notably Mariana, rejected the chronicles in question as "false, fabricated, not credible."[14] Others proved more receptive, and of these none were more outspoken than the constable of Castile, Juan Fernández de Velasco, an important member of the Council of State. In an impassioned address delivered to the Cortes of Castile in 1603, Velasco drew upon Dextro to defend the legend of Santiago and to criticize "certain individuals [Baronio?] who some call wise, but who for political reasons have argued that it was false."[15] In comparison, the royal chronicler Fray Juan de la Puente, having cited Dextro to document Spain's early conversion to Christianity, did not hesitate to speak of Baronio as "a wise man, of great erudition, and admirable diligence in church history, but one ignorant of events in our Catholic nation."[16]

In the meanwhile Higuera drew upon Dextro to write an ecclesiastical history of Toledo, and one can imagine that he had "invented" Dextro with this history in mind.[17] Printing the history, however, was no easy matter. Higuera was a quarrelsome individual whose relations with Antonio Marcén, the Jesuit Provincial in Toledo, were anything but peaceful. Marcén, moreover, attempted to prevent its publication on the grounds that it touched upon issues related only tangentially to the history of the Toledan church. It was therefore in violation of the prescriptions of Claudio Aquaviva, who, starting with his appointment as general of the Society of Jesus in 1588, sought to prevent members of his order from publishing any history that fell outside the confines of *historia sacra*. Marcén consequently ordered Higuera to stop work on the history, but Higuera appealed to his friends on Toledo's municipal council, which, in a meeting held on 11 November 1595, voted to write a letter highlighting the importance of the history for Toledo and specifi-

---

14. As cited in Antonio, *Censura de historias fabulosas*, 672, letter of P. Thomas de León, S.J., to Gaspar Ibáñez de Segovia, 1 September 1668. Leon was quoting a letter (now lost) that Mariana had written in 1616.
15. Godoy Alcántara, *Historia crítica*, 171.
16. Puente, *Tomo primero de la convenencía*, 17.
17. Cf. Román de la Higuera, "Historia eclesiástica."

cally asking Marcén that Higuera be given "permission to continue with his history until it is finished and published."[18] Marcén eventually relented, but in the end, apparently because of lack of funds, Higuera's *Historia eclesiástica de Toledo* went unpublished and remains so today.[19]

Higuera had no better luck getting the *cronicones* into print. The many criticisms these chronicles spawned led the Jesuit Provincial to steer away from the project. The order also had Higuera transferred out of Toledo to a series of smaller Jesuit houses in New Castile, where, presumably, he would be kept busy with teaching and other duties. Higuera, however, was not one to give up without a fight. In a somewhat unusual move, he protested his order's actions in a petition addressed to the Inquisition that faulted the general of his order for blocking the publication of "certain books that, in my opinion, are in the service of God and which will also add luster to my nation as well as the history of Toledo."[20] This protest went nowhere, but Higuera kept busy by preparing various copies of the *cronicones* and sending them only to persons he could trust. One of the few individuals to receive a complete copy of the chronicle attributed to Dextro was Fray Diego Murillo, an Aragonese scholar who used Dextro to write a sacred history of Zaragoza that defended the tradition of Santiago's arrival in the city as well as the apostle's hand in the foundation of its fabled Marian sanctuary, Nuestra Señora del Pilar.[21]

The upshot was a growing demand for the chronicles' entire text. Copies produced copies, but even these remained in short supply until well after Higuera's death in 1611. The first printed edition of Dextro, dated 1619, was the work of Fray Juan Calderón, a Franciscan who obtained a copy of the manuscript from Diego Murillo and succeeded in getting the book approved for publication in Zaragoza, where censorship was relatively lax.[22] Rodrigo Caro, a leading antiquarian in Seville, soon produced another edition, and his enthusiasm for the text was apparently such that he convinced Francisco de Rioja to draw upon Dextro to write a treatise in support of the doctrine of the Immaculate Conception shortly before

---

18. For this petition, see AMT: lib. 366 (Libro de Jurados), entry for 4 November 1595.
19. Several manuscript copies of this history exist. See especially Román de la Higuera, "Historia eclesiástica," BNE: Mss. 1285–1296. For more on Higuera's troubles, see Martínez de la Escalera, "Jerónimo de la Higuera"; Martínez Gil, "Religión e identidad"; and especially Olds, "The False Chronicles," 101–170.
20. As cited in Olavide, "La inquisición, la Companía de Jesús, y el padre Jerónimo Román," 116. For the background to this protest and its relation to ongoing tensions between Acquaviva and a group of disgruntled Spanish Jesuits known as the "memorialistas," see Astraín, *Historia de la Companía de Jesús*, 3:207–694; and, much more succinctly, Olds, "The False Chronicles," 125–144.
21. Cf. Murillo, *Fundación milagrosa*. Murillo described Higuera as a "persona muy docta y en materia de antiguedades, uno de los mas inteligentes de España."
22. The book was printed as *Fragmentum Chronici*.

his appointment as royal chronicler in 1621.[23] Rioja later changed his mind about Dextro, joining a small band of scholars determined to "destroy Dextro,"[24] but these critics did not have much of an audience, especially after the publication of Tomás Tamayo de Vargas's *Defensa de Flavio Lucio Dextro* in 1624. In this influential book Tamayo, who was soon named royal chronicler, described Dextro as one of Spain's hidden "marvels" and announced that anyone who read the chronicle could possibly reach the conclusion that Dextro was a modern "invention."[25] From this moment on, what critics labeled a "delirium" for Dextro led scholars throughout the peninsula—local Baronios in the language of Simon Ditchfield—to mine this chronicle for the documentation they needed to write, and in many cases, rewrite, the histories of their cities, their churches, even Spain itself.[26] The result: a wave of new histories, both local and national, that used Dextro to offer another layer of "proof," in this case historical, to what so many Spaniards already took as a matter of faith, namely, their nation's privileged place in God's great design.[27]

Yet Dextro was not enough, and before long the mushrooming popularity of this chronicle inspired other scholars to invent chronicles of their own. One of the first to do so was José de Pellicer, whose *Cronicón de San Servando* figured centrally in his *Anales*. Another was the Catalan scholar Joan Gaspar Roig i Jalpi, author of a chronicle attributed to Liberato, a seventh-century Catalan monk whose papers he supposedly discovered in the monastery of Santa María de Ripoll.[28] But the most ambitious of all the so-called false chronicles was the one confected by the Benedictine scholar Antonio de Nobis, a.k.a. Antonio de Lupián Zapata, and attributed to a certain Hauberto Hispalense, a tenth-century Mozarab Christian from Seville. This chronicle, in addition to indicating the exact month and day of the Creation, claimed that Adam and Eve were Spain's first monarchs, instead of Tubal, grandson of Noah, or as Pellicer argued, Tharsis, Tubal's nephew.[29]

23. Caro's edition appeared as *Flavii Lucii Dextri Omninodae historiae*.
24. BCC: Ms. 58-1-9, "Cartas y Papeles de Rodrigo Caro, vol. 2," fol. 311, Antonio Moreno Vilches to Caro, 13 July 1628, where Antonio notes that Francisco de Rioja and the Sevillian canon, Alonso de la Serna, have joined forces to "derribar a Dextro." The letter is also cited in Antonio Sánchez y Sánchez Castañer, *Rodrigo Caro: Estudio biográfico y crítico* (Sevilla, 1914), 31. The anti-Dextro faction also included the Toledan historian Pedro Salazar de Mendoza, who claimed that it was a "novedad" that was "invented" by "alguno moderno." For Rioja's change of mind about Dextro, see Godoy Alcántara, *Historia crítica*, 262–264.
25. Tamayo de Vargas, *Defensa de Flavio Lucio Dextro*, 94.
26. See Ditchfield, *Liturgy, Sanctity, and History*, 285.
27. Among the new "national" histories that used the pseudo-Dextro were Maldonado, *Crónica universal;* and Cepeda, *Resumpta historial*. For the local histories, see Kagan, "Clio and the Crown"; and Olds, "The False Chronicles," 219–273.
28. For Liberato, see Godoy Alcántara, *Historia crítica*, 294–296; this author also notes that Roig i Jalpi wrote a history of Catalonia that he passed off as the work of the fifteenth-century scholar Mossen Nernat de Boades. For Pellicer, see Chapter 6 of the current volume.
29. Cf. Pellicer de Ossau y Tovar, *Población y lengua primitiva de España*, xviii.

Although it strikes some of today's readers as absurd, the debate over the identity of Spain's first ruler stemmed from the widespread notion that a kingdom, together with the nation that went with it, constituted a human community based on descent from an ancient, generally mythic ruler, preferably one closely related to Noah. For example, Gomer, his grandson, was claimed for Britain and Ashkenaz, the son of Gomer, for the Germanic peoples of Europe. Alternates included Aeneas for Rome; Brutus, son of Aeneas for England; Francus, son of Hector, for France; Lusus, son of Bacchus, for Portugal; and for Spain, Tubal, Tharsis, or some other contender.[30] These same rulers were also thought to endow their descendants with certain character traits—courage, constancy, industry, piety, and so on—that imparted to each nation an identity that was uniquely its own. Determining the name of a nation's founder, however, proved difficult, especially in the absence of sources. For this reason chronicles of the kind invented by Nobis were important. It also helps to explain why the chronicle attributed to Hauberto gained widespread notoriety following its publication, in 1667, by another Benedictine, Fray Gregorio Argaiz, in his best-selling *Población eclesiástica de España*, another myth-history that defended the veracity of Spain's founding myths, including the arrival of Santiago, the nation's precocious conversion to Christianity, and even the monarchy's claims to world dominion during an era otherwise marked by economic crisis and imperial retreat. It was easy, therefore, for the false chronicles to worm their way into the very fabric of Spain's history.[31]

Yet for all their popularity, and in large part because of it, starting in the 1660s there emerged a new generation of scholars, now known as the novatores, who declared open war on the "fictions and fables" these chronicles had spawned. The novatores also set out to write what they perceived as Spain's national history along new, more critical lines in the belief that pious nationalism of the kind that helped spawn the "false chronicles" had done serious damage to Spain's reputation abroad.[32]

---

30. The abundant literature on the medieval and early modern idea of nation as a community of descent may be approached through Kidd, *British Identities before Nationalism*, esp. 9–72; and Hastings, *The Construction of Nationality*. For Spain, see Botella Ordiñas, "Los novatores y el origen de España"; and Fernández Albadalejo, *Materia de España*. For nationalism as a political program, Bell, *The Cult of the Nation in France*, is indispensable.

31. Cf. Argaiz, *Población eclesiástica de España*. The book was reprinted in 1668 and again in 1669. The role of the Benedictine Order in the creation and dissemination of the false chronicles may be approached through Dubuis, "Les bénédictines d'Espagne." For the influence of the false chronicles on the writing of local history in seventeenth-century Spain, see Aranda Pérez, "Autobiografías urbanas."

32. The novator movement can be approached through the many works of Mestre Sanchis, including his *Humanistas, políticos e ilustrados*.

Methodological inspiration for this new wave of patriotic histories came from various sources, none more important than the somewhat belated arrival in Spain of the critical methods of legal humanist scholarship, *mos gallicus,* which entailed a return to the original sources and the careful collation, compilation, editing, and comparison of texts. Among the first jurists to introduce this line of legal thinking into Spanish universities was Francisco Ramos del Manzano, professor of civil law at Salamanca and the instructor of such notable novatores as Nicolás Antonio. Although Ramos del Manzano was himself not much of a historian—remember that he was reluctant to write the history Philip IV asked him to write—he was influential in encouraging other scholars to use archival sources to correct the legends and half-truths spawned by the false chronicles and by such older histories as Alfonso X's *Estoria de Espanna.*[33]

Further inspiration for the novatores came from Flanders and the cluster of Jesuits who, starting in the seventeenth century, edited the monumental work of hagiography known as the *Acta sanctorum.* Known as Bollandists (after Jean Bolland, the editor of the first volume), these scholars, following in the footsteps of Baronio, set out to examine the reliability of textual sources purporting to attest to the antiquity of certain monasteries as well as the historicity of Catholicism's martyrs and saints. One of the most influential and prolific scholars involved in this project was Father Daniel van Papenbroeck (1628–1714), who, as he put it, dedicated his life to "the distinction between true and false in old parchments."[34] Papenbroeck met Nicolás Antonio in Rome during the 1660s and in 1669 began regular correspondence with Gaspar Ibáñez de Segovia (1628–1708), marqués de Mondéjar, arguably the first Spanish scholar to mount a sustained attack on the false chronicles and erase them from Spain's historical map.[35]

Mondéjar's siege began in 1666 with his *Discurso histórico sobre el patronato de San Fructos en Segovia,* a book aimed at a certain clergy in Segovia who, having read Dextro, sought to replace Saint Fructos, the city's traditional patron saint, with San Hierotheo, a first-century martyr who was supposedly a direct disciple of Santiago. Hierotheo's supporters counterattacked in the form of Gregorio Argaiz's *Corona real de España por España, fundada en los créditos de los muertos y vida de San Hiereoteo* (1668), a work that impugned Mondéjar's attack on Dextro as

---

33. For his biography, see Alonso Pérez, "Vida y obra del doctor Francisco Ramos del Manzano"; and Alonso Romero, "Ius comune y derecho patrio."
34. As cited in Hiatt, *The Making of Medieval Forgeries,* 181.
35. For this correspondence, cf. Vilaplana Montes, "Correspondencia de Papebroch." Mondéjar still awaits a biographer. The best account of his life remains that of Álvarez y Baena, *Hijos ilustres de Madrid,* 2:304–312. See also Arzipe, "Don Gaspar Ibáñez de Segovia," and Díaz Esteban, "Unamujer orientalista."

nothing less than an insult to "the grandeur of Spain's monarchy."[36] News of this battle traveled far and wide, and when it reached Antwerp, Papenbroeck took time out from editing chores to write Mondéjar and encourage him to prepare a frontal attack on all of the "new fictions" in order to safeguard the study of Spanish antiquity. This suggestion prompted Mondéjar's *Disertaciones eclesiásticas* (1671), which castigated the false chronicles as nothing less than a "monstrous jumble of stupidities" and a "troop of fictions" that constituted a "stain" on the history of Spain, "my nation."[37]

Although this attack continued in most of his later writings, Mondéjar's interest in promoting critical scholarship had its limits; he lacked the courage to challenge the historicity of such key legends as those surrounding Santiago, Spain's patron saint.[38] At one point he even wrote an "apology in defense of the tradition of Santiago in Spain." Another of his international correspondents, Etienne Baluze (1630–1715), the distinguished medievalist who served as *bibliothecaire* of Jean-Baptiste Colbert, attempted to dissuade him from writing this treatise on the grounds that "[Santiago's] history is now suspect among most all scholars, and anyone who intends to defend it as true is undertaking a work filled with danger and risk."[39] Baluze was of course right, but Mondéjar persevered and in 1682 published his *Predicación de Santiago en España*, a work that he justified with the claim that it was based wholly on such reputable scholars as Isidore of Seville, as opposed to Dextro.[40] Notwithstanding this lapsus, Mondéjar continued his correspondence not only with Papenbroeck but also with Baluze, regularly supplying the latter with Spanish books for the library this French scholar was compiling for Colbert. In exchange, Baluze sent Mondéjar copies of the *Journal des Savants* together with books by J. B. Bosquet, Jean Mabillon, and Pierre Marca, all of which enabled the Segovian and his fellow novatores to keep abreast of the latest trends in French historical scholarship.[41]

The key meeting place for the novatores and their allies was Mondéjar's house in Madrid, which, starting around 1680, served as the site for a weekly *tertulia*, the Spanish equivalent of a salon. Fueled by cups of steaming hot chocolate, the New

---

36. See Ibáñez de Segovia, *Discurso histórico;* and Argaiz, *Corona real de España por España*, prologue.
37. Ibáñez de Segovia, *Disertaciones eclesiásticas*, "To the Reader" and p. 407.
38. On the ability of Mondéjar and other novators to challenge these myths, see Rey Castelao, *La historiografía del voto de Santiago*.
39. For this exchange, cf. Morel-Fatio, "Cartas eruditas del marqués de Mondéjar y Etienne Baluze."
40. Ibáñez de Segovia, *Predicación de Santiago en España*.
41. For this exchange, see Morel-Fatio, "Cartas eruditas del marqués de Mondéjar y Etienne Baluze." For Mondéjar's library, see Andrés, "La bibliofilia del marqués de Mondéjar."

World stimulant that was then all the rage in Madrid, the *tertulias* addressed a rainbow of historical and philosophical issues, although the main topic for discussion was how best to liberate Spain's history from the tyranny of the false chronicles. In addition to Ramos del Manzano, participants included several of this jurist's disciples, notably Juan Lucás Cortés and Nicolás Antonio (1617–1684), both of whom were Sevillians by birth and students of Manzano at Salamanca.[42] Both were among the most learned individuals of their day. Cortés was a ranking government official with a particular interest in legal history, whereas Antonio had also spent a number of years working as the secretary to the Spanish embassy in Rome, where, in addition to assembling a library said to contain more than thirty thousand volumes, he came into direct contact with Papenbroeck and other *bollandistes*. It was also in Rome that Antonio published the first volume of his *Bibliotheca Hispania*, a critical bibliography of two millennia of Spanish literary scholarship that remains invaluable today.[43] In the course of preparing this volume, Antonio read the chronicle attributed to Hauberto, a work he judged to be worthy of "the comedies of Lope de Vega," but nothing more.[44] Called back to Madrid in 1678, Antonio continued with his *Bibliotheca* in addition to writing his *Censura de historias falsas*, which, as its title suggests, sought to undermine the credibility of the false chronicles with evidence documenting their authorship and the extent to which they contradicted other, more reliable historical sources.[45]

Mondéjar's *tertulias* also attracted a trio of scholars—Pedro Abarca, Antonio de Solís, and Luis de Salazar y Castro—who managed to secure much-valued appointments to the office of cronista del rey. Their historiographical interests went in different directions (Solís, for example, wrote primarily about the Indies, while Abarca and Salazar y Castro gravitated toward Spain), but their epistemological and methodological agendas were essentially in tune with those of the marquess.[46] As a result, all used their offices, albeit in differing ways, to advance the cause of critical history and demonstrate that Spain, despite its reputation as an intellectual backwater, boasted scholarship equal to that of its imperial rivals to the north.

---

42. Cortés may be approached through González de San Segundo, "Juan Lucás Cortés"; and Andrés, "Un erudito y bibliofilo español olvidado." The Council of Castile commissioned Cortés to prepare a new, corrected edition of Ocampo's *Crónica general*, a project he never completed.

43. It is now available as Antonio, *Biblioteca hispana antigua*; and Antonio, *Biblioteca antigua nueva*.

44. Antonio to Juan Lucás Cortés, Rome, 1 July 1664, in Mayáns y Siscar, *Cartas de don Nicolás Antonio*, 25.

45. See Antonio, *Censura de historias fabulosas*.

46. For an insightful examination of the historical methodology employed by the novatores, see Botella Ordiñas, "Los novatores y el origen de España."

Pedro Abarca

I begin with Pedro Abarca (1619–1697) because he is a historian about whom little is known except that he was a native of Aragon, a Jesuit (after 1641), and the first scholar to occupy the chair in Jesuit theology founded by Queen Mariana de Austria at the University of Salamanca in 1671.[47] Plagued with ill health, Abarca retired from active teaching in 1678, at which point he decided to try his hand at history. Four years later he published part 1 of his *Los reyes de Aragón en anales históricos*, a work that led to an appointment as cronista del rey.

The reasons for Abarca's historical turn remain somewhat vague, although his books suggest that it was prompted by a combination of historiographical and political concerns. Historiography weighed in with Abarca's apparent dissatisfaction with those historians whose work was tainted by the false chronicles (here he was undoubtedly thinking of Joan Gaspar Roig i Jalpi), sources that Abarca dismissed as detrimental to both "the honor of history" and the "peace of historians."[48] At the same time, Abarca's interest in history represented his personal effort to heal some of the wounds opened by the Catalan Revolt of 1640, an agenda he shared with José Pellicer (see Chapter 6), whom he succeeded as cronista del rey. Like Pellicer, Abarca aimed at integrating the history of both Catalonia and Aragon into Spain's larger history rather than treating it, *pace* the official Aragonese chroniclers appointed by the Diputación in Zaragoza, as a "national" history standing apart from, and often in opposition to, that of Castile.

Abarca's integrationist agenda is apparent throughout his work, especially his *anales*,[49] which were modeled on the earlier ones by Zurita and were intended to place Aragon's history on a firm documentary basis by removing from its list of kings a series of eighth- and ninth-century rulers whose existence could not be verified in the available sources. By this measure, Abarca expressed his commitment to critical history. He also supported his findings with references to cartularies and other manuscripts he consulted in various archives, especially the one belonging to the Benedictine monastery of San Juan de la Peña, near the Aragonese city of Jaca. Abarca was not so much of a revisionist, however, as to remove from his king list such legendary figures as Alarico I, who supposedly ruled over Aragon at the start of the ninth century. Abarca justified this decision by resorting to an argument based on the then-current idea of probabilism, a variant of Pyrrhonism that emphasized that carefully reasoned conjecture offered a certain,

---

47. For his biography, cf. Esperabé Arteaga, *Historia de la universidad de Salamanca*, 2:544–545.
48. Abarca, *Los reyes de Aragón en anales históricos*, 1:43.
49. The second volume appeared in 1682, two years after his appointment as royal chronicler.

and from his perspective wholly acceptable, measure of verisimilitude ("lo verosímil" in Abarca's vocabulary) as opposed to absolute truth (la verdad). Probabilism, as Eva Botella Ordiñas has argued, was among the chief doctrines that defined the early novator movement in Spain as well as one that aligned such scholars as Mondéjar and Abarca with other "moderate skeptics," including their contemporaries Leibiniz and Locke.[50]

Abarca's commitment to probabilism, however, was increasingly tempered by the emergent methods of critical scholarship associated with the French Benedictine scholar Jean Mabillon (1632–1707). Like Papenbroeck, Mabillon believed that historians had an obligation to distinguish between verifiable documents and those known to be false. But whereas Papenbroeck had not developed any particular method for determining which documents were genuine, Mabillon did exactly this in his influential *De re diplomatica* (1681), a hefty, six-volume treatise that instructed historians how to examine paper, paleography, writing styles, seals, and the like to help determine the dating and authenticity of a particular source. Mabillon further believed that historians could arrive at a certain degree of historical certainty (or proof) providing they based their arguments on the judicious and reasoned use of authentic documents.[51] Mabillon's influence is especially noticeable in the second part of the *Anales* (1684), which was apparently written after Abarca took up residence in Madrid and joined in the *tertulias* held Mondéjar's house. In this volume, a history of the Aragonese monarchy from the twelfth century through to the end of fifteenth, Abarca provided detailed references to archival sources he cited together with an appendix that transcribed in toto many of the documents he had consulted, clearly a practice inspired by Mabillon.

Yet for all of Abarca's interest in this kind of critical scholarship, he remained, at bottom, an official historian interested in defending the history of the *patria* to which he owed allegiance. It follows that he ended this book with a rousing account of Ferdinand II, the Aragonese monarch whose marriage to Isabella of Castilla marked the beginning of the unified Catholic monarchy over which Charles II still ruled. Abarca further aligned himself with tradition in his representation of Ferdinand as the ruler who best epitomized Spain's enduring commitment to the defense of the Catholic Church. He also objected to the widely held seventeenth-century interpretation of Ferdinand as a quasi-Machiavellian ruler. He cited J.-A. de Thou's *Universal History*, which, as read by Abarca, referred to Ferdinand as "an intelligent but badly-intentioned king who treated both piety

50. Botella Ordiñas, "Los novatores y el origen de España."
51. My understanding of Mabillon derives mainly from Grell, *L'histoire entre érudtion et philosophie*, esp. 72–79; Pocock, *Barbarism and Religion*, 1:141–161; and Hiatt, *Making of Medieval Forgeries*, 181–187.

and religion as little more than lovely disguises for interests of state." For Abarca, such comments were nothing short of malicious calumnies that he felt obliged, given the responsibilities attached to his office, to refute by underscoring Ferdinand's role in the establishment of the Inquisition, the reform of Spain's religious orders, and the 1492 order expelling the Jews from the kingdoms of Spain. He ended this line of argument with the trenchant remark that "[Ferdinand] never used religion for the state, but used the state for religion."[52] In keeping, therefore, with the work of earlier royal chroniclers, Abarca's defense of both Spain and its monarchs rested firmly on religious grounds.

Antonio de Solís: A New Kind of Official History

The same orientation marked Antonio de Solís y Ribadeneyra (1610–1686), arguably the most literary and talented of all the royal chroniclers appointed by Charles II.[53] A native of Alcalá de Henares, a university town just east of Madrid, Solís left his birthplace to study law at the University of Salamanca, and it was there that he embarked on a moderately successful although not especially lucrative literary career, later continued in Madrid, as a poet and playwright. Madrid, however, was far more expensive than Salamanca, and to help make ends meet, in 1636 Solís accepted a position as the personal secretary of the young count of Oropesa, Duarte Alvárez de Toledo y Portugal, a high-ranking nobleman who, following the fall of Olivares in 1643, emerged as one of the leading ministers of Philip IV. With Oropesa's support, the king appointed Solís to the office of royal secretary in 1651 and in 1655 to another secretarial office attached to the Council of State. Somewhat more of a surprise—and again Oropesa's influence can be detected—was Solís's appointment in 1661 as cronista mayor de las Indias, a position for which he was seemingly unprepared. This nomination prompted one leading member of the Council of State, Jerónimo de Mascareñas, who was himself a historian, to complain to Philip IV that "his [Solís's] knowledge of history is extremely limited, and it is quite unnatural for anyone to ascend from writing jokes for comedies, which is his profession, to the position of chronicler of such an important monarch."[54] Still, the appointment stuck and Solís soon received instructions to continue the general history of the Indies that was begun by Herrera y Tordesillas but abandoned by his immediate successors, none of whom

---

52. Abarca, *Los reyes de Aragón en anales históricos*, 2:418v.
53. The classic biography of Solís, Arocena's *Antonio de Solís*, can now be supplemented with Serralta, "Nueva biografía de Antonio de Solís."
54. Cited in Cid, "Pleitos de historiadores y confrataciones literarias," 146.

had expressed any interest in writing what was described as a "labyrinth" from which there was no escape.[55]

As it turned out, Solís's opinion of the general history was much the same. He applauded Herrera y Tordesillas for having entered into this labyrinth but recognized that such a history demanded far too much in the way of synthesis and that it had necessarily required Herrera to switch rapidly from one topic to the next, undermining what Solís called the "comfort and clarity" of his argument. For his own history, Solís decided that it was next to impossible to cram an "infinity of minor enterprises" into a single narrative, especially one dealing with the Indies, since it incorporated the histories of "two great monarchies [the Spanish, and from 1580 to 1640, that of Portugal], many provinces, innumerable islands, different conquests, different conquistadores," and more.[56] So as to avoid the labyrinthine character of general history, and presumably add to the comfort and clarity of his own work, Solís embarked on a "particular" history focused on the conquest of Mexico, albeit with the excuse that the Indies contained only three "great histories," namely, those of Columbus, Cortés, and Pizarro.

Of these "great histories," Solís gravitated toward that of Cortés, a figure he saw as the quintessential conquistador. For Solís, Cortés was a true *milites christiana*, who combined pious chivalry with the courtly virtues—taste, elegance, sympathy, and especially prudence—that Solís had read about in Baltasar Gracián's treatise *El héroe* of 1647.[57] Solís also anticipated the work of the nineteenth-century American historian William Hickling Prescott, by envisioning Cortés's achievement as worthy of epic, one that harked back to what he would have seen as one of the most glorious moments in Spain's history and certainly one that offered his Spanish readers some respite from a troubled era of imperial retrenchment marked by what he tersely characterized as "misery, bankruptcies . . . and thieves."[58] Solís may also have imagined Cortés as the antithesis of the reigning monarch, Charles II. The latter was weak and mentally and physically deficient, the former a quasi-superman whom he presented as the "principal hero" in the first part (published in 1685) of his *Historia de la conquista de Mexico*.[59]

Solís's decision to abandon the general history and write solely about Cortés ruffled the Council of the Indies, some of whose members accused him of "negli-

---

55. Solís's immediate successor in the office of cronista mayor was the jurist Antonio de León Pinelo, who, in lieu of advancing the *historia general*, opted to prepare an administrative handbook for the use of the Council of the Indies. He was unable to complete this handbook by the time of his death, but an outline of its contents may be found in his *Política de las grandezas*.
56. Citations from Solís, *Historia*, bk. 1, chap. 1, pp. 5–6.
57. Arocena, *Antonio de Solís*, 195.
58. Mayáns y Siscar, *Cartas de don Nicolás Antonio*, 77.
59. Solís, *Historia*, bk.1, chap. 2, p. 5.

gence." They also rebuked him for failing to write the "histories, flyers, reports, memorials, letters and other books and papers" his office required.[60] These criticisms were only partially justified, inasmuch as he did write several reports dealing with the famous line of demarcation that separated Spanish holdings in the Americas from those of Portugal. Nevertheless, the council's criticisms could explain his decision to transform what he originally conceived as an epic history into something that more closely approximated a work of official history bent on defending the legitimacy of Spain's presence in the New World. By the end of the seventeenth century the "controversy of the Indies" that originally prompted Philip II to sponsor the *historia general* was definitely on the wane, but that controversy was by no means forgotten, especially at time when Europe's northern powers had already entered what was previously an exclusively Spanish lake. The Indies, moreover, had replaced Flanders as the new symbolic centerpiece of the Habsburg imperium, the new hub around which Spain's empire would revolve, not to mention an important source of silver and other wealth. In this respect, Spain and the Indies were one, and the importance the monarchy accorded the Indies does much to explain why Solís, echoing Herrera y Tordesillas, used the preface of his history to castigate "foreign historians" who had obscured or at least misrepresented the magnitude and importance of Spain's many achievements in the New World. "They [the foreign historians]," he affirmed with a burst of patriotic pride, "cannot tolerate the glory of our nation."[61]

To drive this point home, Solís juxtaposed contrasting accounts of the famous (or, for some, infamous) "massacre of Cholula," which occurred in 1519, when Cortés and his army, having recently allied with the Tlaxcalans, were marching toward Tenochititlán. Having arrived in Cholula, Cortés, fearing a possible betrayal, had his troops ambush the city's *caciques* and allowed his Tlaxcalan allies to lay waste to the town. Martyr and López de Gómara had both airbrushed this incident, whereas Ginés de Sepúlveda had interpreted it as a divinely ordained punishment for treason. In contrast, Benzoni and other foreign historians attributed Cholula and similar massacres to the cruelty of the Spaniards and their irrepressible thirst for gold. Solís disagreed and shot back with the charge that these foreign writers had failed to recognize the great service that Spaniards had performed by opening "the pathway for [the spread of] religion" in the Indies.[62] And while he confessed that the conquest of Mexico included "actions worthy of

60. Mayáns y Siscar, *Cartas de don Nicolás Antonio*, 66.
61. Solís, Historia, "A los que leyeron."
62. Solís, *Historia*, bk. 3, chap. 7, pp. 206–207.

criticism," such actions did not occur at Cholula, where, in his telling, whatever the Spaniards did was in keeping with divine sanction and intended only to punish the natives for their "malicia" and "inhumanidad."[63]

Solís's refusal to criticize Cortés was, of course, in keeping with the kind of self-serving history expected of those writers who served in the office of cronista mayor. Yet Solís seemed convinced that his account was wholly accurate, since his methodology, following Ramos del Manzano's critical methods of legal scholarship as well as those associated with Mabillon, entailed the careful comparison and cross-checking of existing accounts of the conquest, verification of the facts, and the rectification of any possible "discordances" or "divergences" between them. From a modern perspective, this process was flawed because Solís was highly selective in his choice of possible sources, studiously ignoring, for example, any work, printed or manuscript, that would have enabled him to appreciate the conquest as seen from the native point of view.[64] In this sense Solís's understanding of history was a far cry from that of Lorenzo Boturini, the eighteenth-century Italian antiquarian and collector whose projected "critical" history of Mexico rested primarily on indigenous sources.[65] Solís was content to juggle available Spanish sources, which, apart from the original *relaciónes* of Cortés, included works by López de Gómara (totally unreliable, according to Solís), Las Casas ("untrustworthy"), Díaz de Castillo (flawed by "jealousy and ambition"), and Herrera y Tordesillas, a historian whose scholarly pretensions he regarded as "dangerous" because this author's frequent references to Tacitus distracted the reader and obscured the magnitude of Cortés's achievement.[66]

Whatever its flaws, Solís's history was (and remains) a landmark achievement. Nicolás Antonio, reviewing the book for the Council of the Indies, congratulated the author for his erudition and style and for having produced a true "theater" of history. In another prepublication review, the marqués de Mondéjar praised Solís for his careful attention to topographical detail and for including ethnographical material that would enable readers to understand why Mexico's "bellicose nations" suffered defeat at the hands of Cortés.[67] But what really impressed Mondé-

63. Ibid., bk. 4, chap. 12, p. 349.
64. Arocena, *Antonio de Solís*, 146n38, offers a listing of the available sources that Solís ignored.
65. I refer to Boturini, *Idea de una nueva historia*. For more on Boturini and this history, see Jorge Cañizares-Esguerra, *How to Write the History of the New World*.
66. Solís, *Historia*, bk. 4, chap. 11, p. 387. He also faulted Herrera for relying too much on Bernal Díaz de Castillo, whose chronicle of the conquest he did not trust.
67. For Antonio's comments, see Mayáns y Siscar, *Cartas de don Nicolás Antonio*, 42. For Mondéjar's, see Solís, *Historia*, "Censura del excellentissimo señor don Gaspar de Mendoza Albañez de Segovia," n.p.

jar was Solís's success in larding his account of the conquest with "robust and solid maxims" that seventeenth-century readers accustomed to defining history as branch of rhetoric expected historians to provide.[68]

Among these maxims, and certainly the ones that reflected the interests of Mondéjar and other novatores, were those connected to Solís's effort to relate the conquest as a quintessentially human achievement as opposed to one providentially ordained. Herrera y Tordesillas had moved cautiously in this direction, but Solís went further, granting humans—Spaniards in this instance—a degree of agency in the movement of history that they had previously lacked. Courage, constancy, and the ability to gain the confidence of his soldiers: these were the principal ingredients that led Cortés to victory, rather than miracles worked from on high. Solís, of course, stopped short of denying Providence the power to intervene in human affairs; this was something that few seventeenth-century scholars, with the possible exception of Spinoza, dared even to contemplate. Solís did, however, express skepticism about the role of extraterrestrial forces in shaping the conquest, notably in his account of the battle against the Tabascans, where he questioned López de Gómara's assertion that the Spanish marched to victory only after the figure of Santiago, astride a white horse, had appeared miraculously in the sky:

> Some write that in the middle of this battle the Apostle Santiago, mounted on a white horse, appeared, fighting on the side of the Spaniards, and they add that Hernán Cortés, faithful in his devotion, attributed this help to the Apostle Saint Peter. But Bernal Díaz del Castillo steadfastly denies this miracle, saying that he did not see it nor did any of his fellow soldiers ever talk to him abut it. It is an excess of piety to attribute solely to Heaven unexpected happenings or unlikely events. I confess that I am not inclined toward this kind of explanation, and that whenever an extraordinary happening does occur, I am inclined in the first instance to attribute it to natural causes. But it is certain that those who read the History of the Indies will find there many truths that appear to be exaggerations, and many events that, in order to render them believable, were described as miraculous.[69]

Such observations—and they occur more than once—are worthy of Voltaire and other Enlightenment historians, who were prepared to distance the Divine from the everyday play of human events. In addition, Solís's favorable account of Aztec civil society, especially the Aztecs' laws, system of justice, educational institutions, and calendrical system, placed him alongside Boturini and other

---

68. Solís, *Historia*, "Censura."
69. Ibid., bk. 1, chap. 19, p. 74.

eighteenth-century historians whose sympathy toward indigenous society contrasted sharply with those historians who had previously written about the New World. Nevertheless, Solís still managed to represent the conquest of Mexico as an epic battle of good and evil, with God (and Spain) on one side, the Devil (and the Aztecs) on the other. To do otherwise would have risked running afoul of the Inquisition. It was surely to avoid censorship that Solís dismissed native religious practices as "an abominable mixture of all kinds of errors and atrocities" rather than discussing them in any detail.[70] As for justifying the conquest, Solís managed this by portraying Moctezuma as a tyrant who oppressed his people, an argument common to apologists of empire since the time of the Egyptians. In this instance, however, it enabled Solís to cast the Spaniards in the role of liberators whose primary motive in conquering Mexico was to free its oppressed inhabitants from the yoke of injustice.

Combined with his admirable narrative skills, Solís's defense of Spain's imperium does much to explain why the *Historia* received an overwhelmingly positive reception after its initial printing in Madrid in 1685. The reaction was such that Solís, in a letter to his friend Juan Lucás Cortés, boasted that his book was "the talk of the town." Yet like many historians whose books receive critical acclaim, Solís worried about slow sales (by his count, only 150 copies during the first year) and attributed this to "the shortage of money and the lack of people in Madrid who have more than two *reales* to their name."[71] A second, posthumous edition appeared 1691, the same year a French translation was issued in Paris. There, too, it sold briskly—five editions in less than a year—and in the course of the eighteenth century, the *Historia de la conquista de México,* reprinted in almost forty editions in French, Spanish, Italian, English, and even Danish, was by far the most widely read history of the Spanish New World. Solís had his critics, none harsher than Francisco Xavier Clavijero (1731–1787), the Jesuit Creole who dismissed the book as "more panegyric than history."[72] Even so, Solís's history remained the definitive study of both Cortés and the conquest of Mexico until the appearance of Prescott's *History of the Conquest of Mexico* in 1843.

Luis de Salazar y Castro: Constructing the Nation

The one other member of Mondéjar's circle to become a royal chronicler was Luis de Salazar y Castro (1658–1734), the preeminent Spanish genealogist and histo-

---

70. Ibid., bk. 3, chap. 27, p. 292.
71. Mayáns y Siscar, *Cartas de don Nicolás Antonio,* 88.
72. Francisco Xavier Clavijero, *Storia antica del messico,* as cited in Arocena, *Antonio de Solís,* 265.

rian of his age. A native of Valladolid in Old Castile, Salazar y Castro was already well known for his genealogical interests when, ca. 1680, he moved to Madrid.[73] Once there, he participated in the tertulias held in Mondéjar's house, and in 1685 he assumed the office of cronista del rey. Other honors soon followed, and in 1688 with the publication of his *Advertencias históricas,* a critical account of recent scholarship on the history of medieval Spain, Salazar y Castro bolstered his reputation as a historian receptive to the critical methods pioneered by Mabillon, entailing the careful transcription of archival documents. Salazar y Castro did the same with Spanish genealogy, in the belief that this important subject had been needlessly tarnished by the "carelessness" of other scholars, especially Pellicer. "No writer in Spain's history," he observed, "did more to disturb the dead than don Joseph Pellicer."[74]

Salazar y Castro's greatest wish, however, was to write the definitive history of Castile's royal house. Toward this end he assembled a horde of genealogical materials that later entered the collections of Spain's Royal Academy of History, where it is still known as the Colección de don Luis Salazar y Castro.[75] But the energy that Salazar y Castro invested in his genealogical researches left little time for other subjects, especially the "chronicle of the Indies," a subject that his 1698 appointment as cronista mayor de las Indias specifically required him to address. In 1711, for example, the Council of the Indies rebuked Salazar for his failure to write about the "events of the Indies," and even voted to dock his pay unless he did. Salazar's somewhat lame response was to claim that the council, in addition to failing to give him explicit instructions about this history, had neglected to provide him with the papers necessary to write it.[76]

Salazar y Castro's apparent lack of interest in the "events of the Indies" was more than simply a matter of personal preference. Solís excepted, few of the other early novatores expressed much interest in the history of the Indies. It was subject seemingly removed from their major concern, the liberation of Spain's national

---

73. At the moment of his appointment as cronista mayor, Salazar y Castro's genealogical publications included *Catálogo historial genealógico; Historia genealógica de la Casa de Silva;* and *Historia genealógica de la Casa de Lara.* Another publication was his *Advertencias históricas,* a critical account of recent scholarship on Spain's medieval history. Salazar y Castro recounts his own bibliography in his *Biblioteca Genealógico,* a compilation of Spanish genealogists that he completed ca. 1702. Cf. Soria Mesa, *La biblioteca genealógica de don Luís de Salazar y Castro.*

74. Cf. Salazar y Castro, *Carta del maestro de niños,* 44.

75. This collection can be approached through the *Indice de la colección Don Luis Salazar y Castro.*

76. For this incident, see RAH: leg. 9, documents 24–31; and Navas Rodríguez, *Reformismo ilustrado y americanismo,* 505. Salazar y Castro's predecessor as cronista mayor was Pedro Fernández de Pulgar, a historian whose additions to the general history were so riddled with errors that the Council of the Indies refused to grant him the publication traditionally accorded historians who occupied the office of cronista mayor. They remain unpublished, and largely unstudied, even today. See BNE: Mss. 2796–2799, Pedro Fernández de Pulgar, "Historia general de las Indias." See also BR: Ms. II, 2528.

history from the myths and legends associated with the false chronicles. So it was with Salazar y Castro, who dedicated his career to stripping from Castile's historical record the "stories, rumors, and fabrications" that detracted from the "greater honor of my nation."[77] At the same time, in conjunction with the fact that he served as both cronista del rey and cronista mayor de las Indias, Salazar y Castro fancied himself as the monarchy's principal historical adviser, a position that harked back to the position of superchronicler that Gondomar had recommended to the duke of Lerma during the reign of Philip III. In addition, his determination to protect the prerogatives attached to his offices does much to explain why Salazar y Castro rarely had anything positive to say about his fellow historians, especially those who dared to write about subjects close to his own.

The historian, and fellow novator, who bore the brunt of these attacks was a certain Juan de Ferreras (1652–1735), a theologian whom Philip V appointed to head the newly reorganized royal library in 1716.[78] Ferreras was in the midst of a massive revisionist general history of Spain that he intended to replace that of Mariana, a work the novatores praised for its "beauty and style" but criticized for its author's failure to investigate the accuracy of his sources.[79] As a disciple of Mondéjar, Ferreras, together with Salazar y Castro, was outspoken in his criticism of the "fables and fictions" he believed to have obscured Spain's history to the point where "foreigners joke about us and laugh."[80] He was also an ardent positivist, arguing in favor of what he called "the strength of the negative argument in history," the idea that the absence of contemporary or near-documentary proofs negated the historicity of past events.[81] When it came to Spain, however, Ferreras, like his mentor, prevaricated, adopting the kind of conjectural arguments that Abarca had deployed. On the one hand he defended the historicity of Tubal, Spain's legendary first monarch, together with the arrival of Santiago. On the other he questioned the legends surrounding the foundation of the important Marian sanctuary of Nuestra Señora de Pilar, a position that sparked a full-blown political scandal that ended only when Philip V issued a royal decree ordering

---

77. Salazar y Castro, *Advertencias históricas*, prologue. Despite this commitment, the eighteenth-century Valencian humanist Gregorio Mayáns y Siscar rebuked Salazar y Castro for his ignorance ("he did not know Latin, nor philosophy, nor any science") and his readiness to criticize the work of his fellow novators, notably Mondéjar and Nicolás Antonio. For these criticisms, see Mestre Sanchis, "*Historiografía,*" 830.

78. Philip V established the Biblioteca Real in 1712. Gabriel Alvarez de Toledo (appointed 1712) was the first to occupy the office of *bibliotecario mayor*. Ferreras was his successor. For a capsule of this library, and its first directors, see www.patrimonionacional.es/presenta/servicio/biblio.htm (accessed 24 October 2008).

79. Ibáñez de Segovia, *Advertencias a la historia del P. Juan de Mariana*.

80. Ferreras, *Synopsis histórica chronológica de España*, 1:2.

81. Cited in Mestre Sanchis, "*Historiografía,*" 839.

Ferreras to excise the offending portions of his history.[82] The king's Jesuit confessor, Pere Daubenton, is generally credited with engineering this decree, but Salazar y Castro played his part with a series of polemics attacking Ferreras for the inconsistency and inadequacy of his scholarship, his failure to consult archival sources, and finally the theologian's inability to "read gothic or ancient script."[83]

Jealousy? No doubt. Yet it is worth remembering that in keeping with the offices he occupied, Salazar y Castro's historiographical agenda was not necessarily his own. In his *Advertencias históricas*, published three years after he assumed the office of cronista del rey, he acknowledged that royal chroniclers, unlike other historians, were not independent actors, free to write what they wished.[84] Rather, they were beholden to their superiors and generally subject to whatever whims and desires that came into their heads. Chroniclers were further expected to write about important current events, and this surely accounts for the short history he wrote in conjunction with the marriage of Charles II to the German princess María Anna of Neuberg, explaining why the noble houses of Austria and Bavaria ought to be linked.[85]

Nor was Salazar y Castro in a position to steer clear of the great debate created by Charles II's apparent inability to sire an heir. The stakes involved in this debate were enormous, as it entailed the succession to the monarchy's many kingdoms, both in Europe and in the New World. Who would prevail? The French pretender, Philip of Anjou? Or his Habsburg rival, Archduke Charles of Austria? Under these circumstances the writing of history, especially genealogical history, Salazar y Castro's avowed specialty, more than an antiquarian pastime, was a matter of pressing political importance. In this respect, Salazar y Castro's genealogical researches spoke to the future as much as the past.

It is not altogether clear when Salazar y Castro first decided to cast his lot with Philip de Anjou, but he certainly did so by the time the eighteen-year-old king arrived in Madrid in 1701. Almost immediately the new monarch turned to his royal chronicler for both information and advice. Great Britain's ambassador, William Coxe, reported that Louis XIV had previously instructed his grandson, "You are going to reign over the greatest monarchy in the world. And over a people who have been ever distinguished for their honour and loyalty. I recommend that you love them and gain their affection by the mildness of your government."[86] It

---

82. On this issue, ibid., 831–832; and Pérez Magallón, *Construyendo la modernidad*, 171.
83. Salazar y Castro, *La crisis ferrerica*, 5.
84. Salazar y Castro, *Advertencias históricas*, 156.
85. Cf. Salazar y Castro, *Reflexión histórica*.
86. Coxe, *Memoirs of the Kings of Spain*, 1:7.

follows that Philip, desperate to learn about whom he should love, and how, ordered Salazar y Castro to write several works relating to the Spanish nobility, a group without whose assistance he could not begin to consolidate his government or defeat the forces, both domestic and foreign, that had allied with the archduke. Salazar y Castro soon produced a treatise comparing the rights and privileges of the French aristocracy, the fabled *ducs et pars*, with their Spanish equivalent, the haughty *grandes*, and shortly thereafter another outlining the ranks and privileges of members of the Spanish royal household.[87] Next came an alphabetical *nobilario* with the names of the kingdom's leading noblemen, the dates when their titles were originally conferred, their privileges, the location of their estates, their incomes, and the like.[88] This valuable treatise was soon followed by a history of Castile's royal house that Salazar y Castro cobbled together for the use of both the king and his ministers, the majority of whom at this point were French.[89] It is not clear how these genealogies were actually used, but in providing this kind of information, Salazar y Castro helped to solidify his position at court. Mnemosyne, the incarnation of memory, Salazar y Castro was definitely not, but his extensive knowledge of both Spain and its history constituted a treasure that the new monarch and his ministers were anxious to exploit. Philip also turned to Salazar to write a genealogical history of the Farnese family on the verge of his marriage with Isabel Farnese in 1714. The Farnese, as one of Italy's most distinguished noble houses, hardly needed any introduction, but Philip apparently looked to this history as another means to consolidate his rule. Initially, Salazar appears to have reluctant to accept the assignment because he was unable to consult the original documents—or what he called "instrumentos"—needed to craft such a history, but eventually he created a sumptuous volume, written in Spanish, that incorporated a series of elaborate genealogical trees expressly designed to demonstrate the antiquity and manifold accomplishments of the Farnese and, equally importantly, that family's long-standing alliance with Spain.[90]

Through these histories—and there were more—Salazar y Castro demonstrated his personal allegiance to Philip and the nation that the new monarch was setting out to construct. State-building began with the decrees of the Nueva Planta (1707–1715), a series of administrative and legal reforms that constituted the

87. I refer to Salazar y Castro, "Memorial sobre la igualdad"; and "Memorias históricas."
88. BNE: Ms. 10660: "Casas ylustres de España hasta el año 1702."
89. In his *Biblioteca genealógica*, 112, Salazar y Castro refers to his *Historia genealógica de la Casa Real de Castilla*, but this manuscript is apparently lost.
90. Cf. Salazar y Castro, *Indice de las glorias de la casa Farnese*. The work was originally completed in 1715, and as Salazar y Castro explains in the prologue, he entitled it "Indice" as opposed to a "Historia," with the latter's attendant suggestions of accuracy and truth, because of his inability to consult original documents relating to the Farnese clan.

foundation of the French-style, centralized monarchy that Philip envisioned. In addition to reorganizing the governing councils in Madrid, the Nueva Planta entailed the creation of a network of intendants, together with the abolition of the laws and governing institutions of Aragon and Catalonia; and in conjunction with these changes, it appears that Philip V aimed at recreating the Hispania of the Visigoths in the guise of a new nation, *el reino de España,* that would supersede and replace the older kingdoms and nations into which, starting in the eighth century, Spain was divided. The new Spain, however, also called for a new kind of a national history, and Philip V began moving toward the creation of such a history in 1709 when he decreed the imminent suppression of the office of cronista del reino de Aragón and that of the chronicler appointed by Barcelona's municipal government, the *consell de cent.* By this action, the king announced his intention to create a common (or Spanish) historical heritage meant to transcend those imparted by the "particular" histories crafted by chroniclers loyal to Castile, Aragon, Valencia, and the other *patrias* that had traditionally taken precedence over that larger, more abstract entity known as Spain. Their replacement? A new general history whose subject was to be the new "super-*patria*" (*patria gorda* in colloquial Spanish), the united "kingdom of Spain."[91]

The idea of writing such a history was, of course, nothing new. Alfonso X, in his *Estoria de Espanna,* and Mariana, in his general history of 1592, had had similar intentions. Olivares had also envisioned a broader national history when he contemplated the appointment of Pellicer as cronista general de España. Such was also the agenda of the royal librarian Juan de Ferreras (1652–1735), who, despite a hail of criticism from Salazar y Castro, managed to write (and to publish) the sprawling nineteen-volume, grandiosely entitled *Synopsis histórica chronológica de España,* which offered a wholly new and synthetic approach to Spain's complex past. Philip V carried this agenda one step further by announcing the end of such offices as the cronista del reino de Aragón. The next step: to suppress the remaining offices of royal chronicler, which, in view of their traditional charge to write the ruler's personal history as opposed to that of the kingdom at large, appeared expendable. The king's next move was to replace these offices with a new "national" agency, the Real Academia de la Historia, whose chief responsibility was to write a history commensurate with the new nation that the monarchy endeavored to construct.

---

91. For the juridical and political concepts Nueva Planta entailed, see Fernández de Albadalejo, *Fragmentos de monarquía,* 353–380.

Ilustrar la Patria

This transition, from chronicler to academy, began shortly after the death of Salazar y Castro in 1734. Four years later Philip V authorized the creation of the Real Academia de la Historia, which was modeled on France's L'Académie Royale des Inscriptions et Belles-Lettres, an institution that had been founded in 1663 with help from Colbert. It also derived from the new Real Academia Española that the king had created in 1723 for the purpose of promoting the Spanish language. The new academy would have similar responsibilities with respect to history.

As is now known, the new academy was the brainchild of a small group of scholars, *madrileños* mostly, who, starting in 1735, outlined plans for a "universal academy" intended to advance the entire gamut of the arts and sciences in Spain. Such in fact was precisely the kind of institution that the king, in a decree of 18 April 1736, agreed to support. But three days later, in the academy's first meeting, Agustín de Montiano y Luyando, the first director, and the other charter members voted to narrow their horizons and transform the universal academy into one concerned only with history, and then only that of Spain.[92]

The next challenge was to sharpen and define the academy's mission. From the outset the members agreed that their primary task was to rewrite Spain's history in accordance with the critical methods of the novatores and "to exile the fables introduced by ignorance and malice, and to increase knowledge of many things either obscured by antiquity or which carelessness has left undiscovered."[93] But how was this to be done? Initially the idea was to compile a *Diccionario histórico crítico universal de España*, a kind of historical encyclopedia modeled on Louis Moréri's *Le grand dictionaire historique* (first edition published in Lyon in 1674) and Pierre Bayle's *Dictionaire historique et critique* (1697) but with a difference. These dictionaries, as their titles suggest, shared a broad agenda to advance learning on numerous fronts, whereas the *Diccionario histórico* sought only to "to purify and to cleanse our Spain from the fables that detract from it, and to document it with more useful information."[94] Montiano, acting in his capacity as director, subsequently presented this project to the monarch, and his response,

---

92. For the politics and personalities involved in the academy's creation, see Navas Rodríguez, *Reformismo ilustrado y americanismo;* and Velasco Moreno, *La Real Academia*.

93. From a royal privilege, dated Aranjuez, 18 April 1738, as reproduced in Sempere y Guarinos, *Ensayo de una biblioteca española*, 64–65. Similar language appears in a statement, dated 17 June 1738, which reads, "el cultivo de la historia para purificar y limpiar de nuestra España de las fábulas que la deslucen, e ilustrarla con las noticias, que parezcan mas provechosos." *Fastos de la Real Academia* 1 (1739): 52.

94. Sempere y Guarinos, *Ensayo de una biblioteca española*, 65.

drafted in October 1744, was favorable. He not only sanctioned the idea of such a dictionary but agreed to support it by suppressing his "general and particular chroniclers" and transferring the annual income attached to these offices, a total of approximately sixteen thousand ducats, into the new academy's budget.[95]

Despite such support, the new academy's first task, in addition to developing a outline for the proposed dictionary, was to create a journal, *Fastos de la Real Academia*, that was inaugurated in 1744. Its publication, however, was suspended after only three issues, partly for financial reasons (not until 1796 did the academy start printing annual *memorias*, a journal that continues today). The lack of a journal did not necessarily mean that the academicians were idle. Starting as early as 1739, the academy sponsored a series of *disertaciones*—in the sense of lectures or talks—on various subjects related to the historical dictionary it had been commissioned to write. They were presented mainly by the academicians themselves, although by no means exclusively. One of the first, offered by one of the country's leading naturalists, Francisco Fernández de Navarrete, addressed "the character of the Spanish" and argued that nations, like people, have their distinctive qualities and characteristics. Such a theory was by no means new, but in keeping with the general drift of national philosophy in the eighteenth century, Fernández de Naverrete stated that these national traits had less to do with mythical founders than with a combination of climate and other natural forces. He also used this lecture to refute the ideas of several foreign scholars—mentioned specifically were Pierre d'Avity, Paulo Merula, and Pierre Martin La Martinière—whose understanding of the Spanish character differed radically from his own.[96] Other lecturers expounded on such issues as "whether mythology is part of history, and how it can be understood," "the first inhabitant of Spain," "the *patria* of the emperors Trajan, Hadrian, and Theodosius," and "the government of the Romans in Spain."[97]

As for the dictionary, quibbles over its contents disrupted progress from the very start. In the sixteenth century Philip II had warned about the dangers of "history by committee," and in this case the Prudent King proved prophetic: it took more than thirty years for the academy's members to decide on a definitive

---

95. The plan that Montiano presented to Philip V specifically noted that the proposed dictionary was intended to "remove all of the fables of the fictions that have unfortunately complicated our history, and offer a more exact chronology and also provide more accurate geographical information, both ancient and modern, that have been much wanted until now but never written." Navas Rodríguez, *Reformismo ilustrado y americanismo*, 511.

96. Fernández de Navarrete, "Sobre el caracter de los españoles." This lecture, delivered on 16 March 1739, subsequently appeared in *Fastos de la Real Academia*, 1:127–219.

97. For these disertaciones, cf. *Fastos de la Real Academia*; and *Memorias de la real academia de la Historia*.

outline for this important work. On a more positive note, the academy succeeded in organizing a series of "literary voyages," modeled on those of Ambrosio de Morales, which enabled interested members to consult manuscripts and other materials relevant to the dictionary in various repositories across Spain. The first such voyage, in 1751, was not especially ambitious; it entailed little more than a trip to the Escorial library and a search for documents needed to verify the chronology of the Goths, an important yet hardly innovative topic. Other voyages ventured farther afield: one went to La Mancha and the small town of Uclés to consult the archives of Spain's military orders, another to Toledo and the rich archives of that city's cathedral, again for the purpose of checking materials relating to the Goths. More innovative were the "voyages" of Luis José Velázquez de Velasco, marqués de Valdeflores (1722–1772), an antiquarian scholar who figured among the academy's charter members. In 1752, Valdeflores received permission to go to the Extremaduran city of Mérida in search of Roman medals and bas-reliefs, and this trip was such a success that he subsequently obtained permission to go to Salamanca to hunt for monuments and inscriptions along the Roman road known as the *camino de plata*, as well as to Málaga, his native town, in search of more.[98]

These journeys, the equivalent of today's "fact-finding missions," provided Valdeflores, arguably the most prolific, and most published, of the academy's founding members, to gather material for a series of important publications on Spanish antiquities.[99] At the same time, these trips familiarized academy members with both the importance and the rigors of archival and archaeological research. They also served to add new documentary materials—the cornerstone of critical history—to the academy's collections, and by the end of the century, in addition to assembling an important collection of books and manuscripts, the academy had established a *cabinet des antiquités* for purposes of study and research.

Toward a New Kind of History

Despite these successes, the academy's historical dictionary, its original raison d'être, remained on hold until 1764. In that year Montiano, the academy's first director, retired. Replacing him was the eminent and energetic Pedro Rodríguez de Campomanes (1723–1803), a noted *ilustrado* and a leading exponent of En-

---

98. Upon his return from Extremadura, Velázquez de Velasco described his findings in his *Informe a la Real Academia de la Historia*.
99. His publications include *Ensayo sobre los alphabetos*; *Anales de la nación española*; and *Colección de los documentos contemporaneos de España*.

lightenment thought in Spain. At this point the academy shifted into high gear. Campomanes's pet project was the historical dictionary, and to move it along he added substantially to the academy's collection of medals and coins; initiated plans for a monumental catalog of inscriptions in Greek, Latin, and Arabic; and launched a series of related publishing ventures that included a guide to Spanish paleography, the works of Juan Ginés de Sepúlveda, and a series of medieval chronicles, all with an eye toward creating the raw material out of which a new national history might be constructed.[100]

Notwithstanding these projects—and there were more—Campomanes also proved instrumental in persuading the academy's members to exercise the powers of censorship previously granted to them by the monarchy in their capacity as the new guardians of the Spanish past. The Inquisition still continued to monitor publications deemed detrimental either to religion or to the interests of the Catholic Church, but the brand of censorship proposed by Campomanes was more in keeping with Enlightenment ideas about the need for improvement, both individual and collective. He consequently suggested that the academy should prevent publication only of histories judged to be patently inferior (evidently those still inspired by the false chronicles) and those that failed to "improve the education of individuals, to enrich the nation, and to secure the public happiness."[101]

Another of Campomanes's initiatives was to persuade members of the academy to embrace the history of the Indies even though this subject was tangential to their original mission of removing the "stain" of the false chronicles from Spain's national history. Starting in the sixteenth century with the creation of the office of cronista mayor de las Indias, the monarchy had treated the history of the Indies as a separate chapter in its history, one not directly related to Spain's national chronicle. Campomanes thought otherwise, and in many respects his idea of integrating these separate histories into a single master narrative of Spanish accomplishment mirrored the efforts of the Bourbon monarchy, especially during the reign of Charles III (r. 1759–1788), to institute the administrative and economic reforms necessary to further the integration of metropolitan Spain with its colonies overseas. The Indies, in short, constituted a subject that the academy could no longer ignore.

That the academy took on this project is a history in itself, fraught with political infighting reminiscent of the fifteenth century and the struggle over which chronicler was best qualified to shape the historical memory of Henry IV. In this

---

100. A list of these projects may be found in Castañeda y Alcocer, *La Real Academia de la Historia*.
101. For Campomanes's, and the academy's, discussion of censorship, see Velasco Moreno, *La Real Academia*, 242–268.

instance, the struggle began in 1755 when King Ferdinand VI, following the death of Fray Martín Sarmiento, the last cronista mayor de las Indies, transferred both the assets and the obligations of this office to the academy. Henceforward, the academy, much like the chroniclers of old, had the power to censor, before publication, any written work relating to the history of the New World. Equally importantly, the king saddled this council with the task of writing, even rewriting, the general history of the Indies begun by Antonio de Herrera y Tordesillas under the auspices of Philip II.

What followed, as a number of scholars have ably explained, was a protracted debate over the direction this history should take.[102] The debate was less about methodology (it was virtually agreed that this history, in keeping with the standards of critical history, was to be grounded on original documents and reports) than about what kind of history the academy was to write. A geographical history, focused on the changing disposition—and relationships—between climate and peoples? A civil history dealing primarily with matters of governance? A philosophical history, which evaluated Spain's achievement in the Americas and its impact on the lives of the native peoples? Or a purely utilitarian history, a kind of history-cum-administrative handbook (*informe* in Spanish) that offered the monarchy the information it needed to govern, and profit from, its possessions in the New World?

By all appearances, the academy was unable to resolve this dilemma even though it appointed three of its members to decide on a plan. But as the academicians quibbled, the monarchy, which was now in the hands of Charles III, acted on its own. In 1764, the year in which Campomanes assumed the academy's directorship, Charles III, following a scheme previously outlined by Manuel Pablo de Salcedo, *fiscal* of the Council of the Indies, ordered that this history should combine a civil with a natural history of the New World.

Campomanes, however, had other ideas, partly because he was anxious to maintain the independence of the institution over which he now held sway. Following suggestions previously put forward by the Milanese scholar Lorenzo Boturini in his *Idea de una nueva historia de las Indias* of 1746, the newly installed director believed that the history should be essentially a philosophical inquiry that addressed such issues as the reasons why Spain, as a nation, set out on a path that culminated in the discovery and conquest of the New World, the status of native American cultures at the time of "discovery," and the veracity of the ideas of such

---

102. I refer here to Gerbi, *The Dispute of the New World;* Cañizares-Esguerra, *How to Write the History of the New World;* and Bas Martín, *El cosmógrafo e historiador Juan Bautista Muñoz.*

foreign scholars as the count of Buffon and Cornelius de Pauw about the extent to which the climate and physical conditions of the Indies necessarily led to the degeneration of the animal species, humans included, residing in that part of the globe.[103] Campomanes also believed that the proposed history needed to incorporate indigenous sources as opposed to the Spanish-language documents and chronicles that successive cronistas mayores de las Indias, starting with López de Velasco in 1571, had collected for purposes of writing the *Historia general*.[104] Toward this end Campomanes also arranged to have Boturini's papers, together with his fabled collection of New World artifacts, brought to Madrid and deposited in the collections of the academy.

But who was to write this history? Campomanes's preferred candidate was Antonio de Ulloa (1716–1795), a naval officer whose knowledge of the Indies was second to none.[105] But when, in 1766, Ulloa declined this offer, Campomanes was hard-pressed to find a volunteer, especially among members of the academy, few members of which were prepared, or even willing, to undertake a project that was somewhat tangential to the historical dictionary they were originally expected to write. Complicating the issue still further was the appearance, in relatively quick succession, of two broadly philosophical histories of the Indies that were sharply critical of Spain's achievement in the New World. The first was Abbé Raynal's wildly popular *L'histoire philosophique et politique des Européens dans les deux indes* (1770), which argued that Spain, far from contributing anything positive either to America's economy or to the welfare of its inhabitants, had done just the opposite owing to the cruelties of its soldiers, the ignorance of its missionaries, and the tyrannical nature of its government. The second was William Robertson's *History of America* (1777), which, though somewhat more moderate in its criticisms, still took the position that Spain's faulty economic policies had done little to advance either its economy or that of its colonies.

As might be expected, such criticisms prompted some Spaniards, notably the ex-Jesuit Catalan writer Joan, a.k.a. Juan Nuix, to write patriotic treatises defending Spain's record in the Americas.[106] Campomanes's response, especially with

---

103. The count of Buffon, a.k.a. Georges-Louis Leclerc, espoused his ideas on the degeneration of the animal species in his *Histoire naturelle, générale et particulière;* Pauw extended this argument to include America's natives in his *Recherches philosophiques sur les Américains*.

104. Boturini, *Idea de una nueva historia*.

105. Together with Jorge Juan, Ulloa authored the *Relación histórica del viaje hecho*, an important travelogue–cum–natural history of South America. Ulloa also wrote *Noticias secretas de América*, an administrative handbook that remained in manuscript until its belated publication (in London) in 1826. He had also formulated a plan for the history of the Indies, but in 1766 he elected to become governor of Louisiana in lieu of dedicating himself to scholarship.

106. Nuix's response was *Reflessione imparziale, sopra la humanitá degli spagnoli en la India*, first

respect to Robertson, was somewhat more nuanced. He admired the Scotsman for his scholarship and overall philosophical approach to the past, and for this reason he took steps not only to have Robertson's history translated into Spanish but also to have Robertson named a "corresponding member" of the Academy.[107] At the same time, in view of the many criticisms that Robertson and Raynal had levied against Spain, Campomanes set out to convince Charles III that the best way to respond to these allegations was to have the academy assume full responsibility for a new and presumably equally philosophical history of the Indies that he, as director of the academy, would supervise. Thus, in December 1777, Campomanes wrote to the monarch suggesting that the academy, in accordance with the responsibilities entrusted to it as cronista mayor de las Indias, should be authorized to undertake such a work.

But just as Campomanes offered this suggestion, he had to contend with other historians whose vision of the history of America was decidedly less philosophical than his own. Among these the most influential was Juan Bautista Muñoz (1745– 1799), a theologian from Valencia who, despite his lack of cartographical and mathematical training, was appointed (admittedly with the help of some powerful friends in Madrid) to the office of royal cosmographer of the Indies in 1770.[108] Muñoz soon befriended Charles III's first minister, José de Moñino y Redondo, count of Floridablanca, along with José Bernardo de Gálvez, Charles III's powerful secretary of the Indies. In 1778 these two ministers clashed with Campomanes over the issue of whether the Council of the Indies should agree to the publication of Guevara's translation of Robertson's history of America. The warning shot came in November 1778, when, in reference to both this translation and the new history that the academy wanted to write, Gálvez urged Campomanes that this new work had to "vindicate the truth of history," defend "the honor of the nation, the justice of the conquest, the governance of the Americas, and the reputation of its conquistadors," and "impugn all that which is against and offensive to our

---

published (in Venice) in 1780 and subsequently in Spanish translation in 1782 as *Reflexiones imparciales sobre la humanidad de los españoles en las Indias*. In this work Nuix defended the "humanity" of Spain's achievement in the Americas, partly by alleging that the English and other European powers, in their overseas adventures, were as cruel as the Spaniards, if not more so, but far less candid in admitting that any wrongdoing had occurred. For more on Nuix, see Tietz, "Las 'Reflexiones imparciales' de Juan Nuix."

107. See Bas Martín, *El cosmógrafo e historiador Juan Bautista Muñoz*, 71. Ramón Guevara Vasconcelos was the academician entrusted with the translation of Robertson's book.

108. Ibid., 56–58. According to Bas Martín, the chief architect of Muñoz's appointment was Francisco Pérez Bayer, a fellow *valenciano* and a confidante of Charles III. As noted above (Chapter 4) the office of royal cosmographer of the Indies was created in 1571. Philip IV, however, attached it to the Jesuit Colegio Imperial in Madrid. It was subsequently vacated following the expulsion of the Jesuits from Spain and its dominions in 1767. Muñoz took possession of the office in November 1770.

national annals."[109] A month later, Gálvez's, and presumably the monarch's, position on this issue had hardened. Gálvez therefore wrote to Campomanes to inform him that the king, in addition to blocking the publication of Guevara's translation of Robertson and preventing the circulation of the English original in territories under Spanish dominion, had also commissioned another historian—as it turned out, Muñoz—to write a history of America designed to "counter the false charges of Robertson and vindicate the Spanish Crown's true rights in the conquest and possession of the New World."[110] The actual commission for this history came from Floridablanca, who enjoined Muñoz to write what he conceived as little more than another "politic" history designed, much as Herrera's had been at the close of the sixteenth century, to counter those "foreigners who generally incriminate Spain's mode of procedure, diminishing the merit of our discoveries, obscuring the glory of our heroes, and censuring the most providential and beneficial intentions of our sovereigns."[111] To respond to these accusations and, equally importantly, to defend Spain's national honor, Floridablanca urged Muñoz to search out and utilize all the documents he needed to write the "true"—that is, official—history of the New World.

The assignment was an old one, seemingly taken from the play book of Philip II, but it was approved by Charles III, and by 1779 Muñoz, who had successfully managed to retrain himself as a cosmographer-cum-chronicler in the tradition of López de Velasco, immediately got to work. He began by rummaging through various documentary collections in Madrid, and in 1781, with assistance from Gálvez, Muñoz received blanket permission to visit Simancas and other royal archives and to copy whatever documents he needed.

So began a ten-year project that took Muñoz to the far reaches of the peninsula in search of sources relevant to his project. Starting in 1781, he also lobbied for the creation of a new archive, independent of Simancas, that would be devoted exclusively to the affairs of the Indies.[112] Muñoz argued that the contents of this new collection, to be housed in Seville and renamed the Archivo de Indias, once they were carefully analyzed, would further serve to legitimate Spanish achievements in the New World. The proposed archive ran up against Campomanes's own

---

109. Gálvez to Campomanes, 26 November 1778, as cited in Rodríguez Campomanes, *Pedro Rodríguez Campomanes*, 1:39.
110. Ibid., 1:40, Gálvez to Campomanes, 23 December 1778.
111. Cited in Bas Martín, *El cosmógrafo e historiador Juan Bautista Muñoz*, 95. Floridablanca was certainly aware of Raynal's *L'histoire philosophique et politique*, inasmuch as Robertson's *History of America* had only just appeared.
112. For this project, see Bas Martín, *Juan Bautista Muñoz*.

plans to centralize these very same papers in the Royal Academy of History, but this was a fight that Campomanes, who had by now fallen out with both Floridablanca and Gálvez, was going to lose; the transfer of documents from Simancas to Seville began in 1784. The next blow to the academy's director occurred in 1789 when Gálvez, in conjunction with Floridablanca, arranged for a royal order requiring the academy to allow Muñoz unbridled access to the its documentary collections together with the right to copy whatever materials he wished. In addition, Charles III ordered the academy to admit Muñoz as one of its members.

At this point, the battle between Campomanes and Muñoz was only *in media res*. Muñoz organized his history of the Indies as a tripartite work; the first part dealt with the era of the Catholic Monarchs, the second with Charles V, and a third with Philip II and his successors. Yet the only part of this history Muñoz was able to finish, *Historia del nuevo-mundo: Parte 1*, focused on the early voyages of Columbus, and even then it stopped in 1498, just short of the mariner's arrest and eventual disgrace. It also took the form of an essay, and, curiously for an author who pointedly informed his readers that he had scoured numerous "archives, offices, and libraries" in order to write it,[113] the volume lacked the supporting documentation of the kind that Floridablanca, in his original commission, had admonished him to include. While elegantly written and meant to address such broader issues as the extent to which Columbus's achievement shifted Europe's geopolitical focus toward the Atlantic and the New World, the volume offered little more than a quasi-panegyrical account of Columbus that had more in common with the history Solís had written in behalf of Cortés than with the kind of critical-cum-philosophical history that Campomanes and other members of the academy had embraced. Muñoz, moreover, sounded very much like Herrera in his description of the New World as a Spanish "field of glory" and by commenting on the jealousies occasioned when other European nations learned about what Spaniards had accomplished through their "valor, genius, and religious zeal."[114]

Muñoz completed the manuscript of this history in October 1791, but in order to have it published, he needed to secure the approval of the academy, which, in its capacity as cronista mayor, still possessed the authority to pass on the suitability of any history related to the New World. What happened next amounted to an imperial storm that lasted almost two years and ended only when Campomanes,

---

113. Muñoz. *Historia del Nuevo-Mundo*, 24.
114. Ibid., 25.

having been essentially outmaneuvered by Gálvez and his allies, resigned from his directorship after the academy, and then the Council of the Indies, decided to approve Muñoz's *Historia del nuevo-mundo* for publication.

The details surrounding the incident, along with the arguments put forward both for and against Muñoz's book, are the subject of Jorge Cañizares-Esguerra's *How to Write the History of the New World*.[115] Within the context of this present study, Muñoz's triumph suggests that when it came to history, what Charles III and his *ilustrado* ministers wanted was less a critical, or even philosophical history than an official history that organized the available evidence, both primary and secondary, in ways that suited the monarchy's political interests and concerns. The same incident further underscores the extent to which responsibility for writing the monarchy's history, formerly the exclusive preserve of the king's official chroniclers, had passed to other officials, in this instance to a powerful minister who was close to the king. This book, then, has come full circle. Official history ended where it began, with authors whose authority ultimately depended upon their ability to gain the confidence of whatever ruler they served.

Predictably, the reception of Muñoz's account of Columbus was mixed. The harshest criticism did not come from the academy, which was effectively silenced following Campomanes's resignation from the directorship in 1793 and his replacement by the duke of Almodóvar, a well-known supporter of Muñoz. Rather it came from an outsider, Francisco Javier Iturri, a Creole historian who rightly targeted the book's factual errors, Muñoz's lack of firsthand knowledge of the Indies, and especially his failure to deal adequately with Amerindian history. "Prejudice and self-interest," he opined, marred the entire book.[116]

That Muñoz's history should stir up such emotions was far from unique, inasmuch as the faults outlined by Iturri resonate with those incurred by virtually all of the official histories outlined in this book. To be sure, the strengths and the weaknesses of Muñoz's history are best understood within the particular historiographical context in which it was produced, but the criticisms it engendered suggests that by the end of the eighteenth century state-sponsored history had evolved into a dinosaur ill-equipped to survive in an era marked by revolution and open dissent.

Despite this change in climate, the dinosaur refused to die. In July 1812, in the teeth of a bloody struggle to end the Napoleonic regime of Joseph I, ruler of Spain since 1808, Antonio de Alcedo, a member of the Royal Academy of History,

---

115. Cf. Cañizares-Esguerra, *How to Write the History of the New World*, 196–201. The pioneering study of this incident was Fernández Duro, "Juan Bautista Muñoz."
116. Cañizares-Esguerra, *How to Write the History of the New World*, 198–201.

harangued his fellow academicians with a *memoria* outlining yet another scheme for a monumental, wholly comprehensive history of the Spanish New World. Alcedo's credentials for orchestrating such a project were impeccable. Born a Creole (in Quito) and educated in the New World, Alcedo (1735–1812) was already well known for a dictionary of the Americas predicated upon the Enlightenment ideal of "useful knowledge." "Commerce," in his view, had sparked growing interest in the history of the Indies, but the difficulties imposed by a "universal history" that encompassed the region's natural, civil, political, and ecclesiastical history had required him to "reduce it to the form of a dictionary."[117] Yet the possibility of writing such a history never left his head, and with this end in mind Alcedo compiled a bibliography of Americana that, in addition to histories and travel accounts by European authors, included "three hundred Indian volumes," possibly manuscripts from Boturini's collection that he had consulted in the academy's library in Madrid.[118] Subsequently, the controversy surrounding the publication of Muñoz's book on Columbus strengthened his resolve to have the Royal Academy fulfill its "obligation" as cronista mayor de las Indias and complete what Herrera y Tordesillas had begun. Yet by the time Alcedo finally managed to organize his project and announce it, his grandiose scheme for writing the history of the New World proved no more manageable than any of those previously recommended to the academy. Within a few months Alcedo, age seventy-seven, was dead, and the dinosaur of the *Historia general de las Indias occidentales* all but extinct.[119]

117. Cf. Alcedo, *The Geographical and Historical Dictionary*, 1. The dictionary was published originally as *Diccionario geográfico-histórico de las Indias Occidentales o América*.
118. For this bibliography and its history, see Onís, "Alcedo's *Biblioteca Americana*." The *Biblioteca* was first printed as Alcedo, *Biblioteca Americana*.
119. Cf. Pérez-Bustamante, *Antonio de Alcedo y su "memoria."*

CONCLUSION

Rethinking Official History

> What you have not published you can destroy; the word once sent forth can never come back.
>
> —Horace, *Ars poetica*

I have done little in the preceding chapters to offer a complete survey of Spanish historiography during the centuries covered in this book. Official historians of the kind I examine represent but a tiny percentage of Spain's important but still somewhat understudied community of historians. Starting already in the fourteenth century, historians who worked independently, without benefit of royal patronage, far outnumbered those who had such patronage. In many instances, moreover, these historians were more imaginative and original than those whose work I have surveyed.

One example is Luis Cabrera de Córdoba (1559–1629), a writer whose history of Philip II, first published in 1619, was far superior to anything produced by his contemporary Antonio de Herrera y Tordesillas. Cabrera's history remains essential reading for anyone seriously interested in learning about either the person of this monarch or the inner workings of his government. Born in 1559, Cabrera spent most of his life in royal service, first as a spy (a "roving ambassador") for Philip II, then as a guard at El Escorial, then as a member of the household of Margaret of Austria, queen of Philip III. Having been appointed a *familiar* by the Inquisition in 1621, he died in quasi-retirement in 1626.

Cabrera's intimate knowledge of palace life is reflected on almost every page of his history, which exudes the "I was there" quality reminiscent of the chronicles composed by López de Ayala at the close of the fourteenth century but absent from most of Herrera's histories, which were based primarily on documents and

---

Epigraph: Horace, *Ars Poetica*, translated by H. Ruston Fairclough (Cambridge, MA, 1991), lines 391–393.

material found in the royal archives. Cabrera was also an exacting critic, who rarely hesitated to criticize historians whose work he considered deficient; Herrera was a favorite target. He resembled Herrera, though, in that he was unable to keep his grievances to himself. Both shared a common antipathy to Philip III's favorite, the duke of Lerma. As noted earlier, Herrera's animosity toward Lerma led to his arrest and subsequent exile from Madrid in 1609. In comparison, Cabrera was on the outs with the royal favorite as early as 1602, when he was arrested and exiled from the court for having the temerity to attack one of Lerma's lackeys with a sword.[1]

Despite this incident, Cabrera managed to secure a royal pardon and went on to complete his history, its original title "Philip II: A Perfect King," by around 1610. The following year Philip III issued a license approving the manuscript's publication on the grounds that it "says less about the king's deeds than the reasons why they were done." History of this kind resembled that of such giants of Renaissance historiography as Francesco Guicciardini, but in this instance the king also congratulated Cabrera for having transformed his account of Philip's *gestae* into a textbook that "explained how a prince can become perfect within the limits of human nature, all this in imitation of Xenophon in his Cyropedia."[2]

As the first published history devoted exclusively to the reign of Philip II, Cabrera's work justly deserved such praise. But Philip III, possibly because of opposition from Lerma, offered Cabrera nothing in the way of a publication subsidy. As a result it took another nine years, and a grant from the Castilian Cortes, for Cabrera to get his book into print. Even then, only part 1 of this history, dedicated to the period between 1527 (the year of Philip's birth) and 1583, was actually published.[3] Part 2, which examined the remainder of Philip's reign, necessarily touched on the still hot-button issue of the Aragonese *alteraciones* of 1591–1592. Aragon's Diputación had previously voiced its objections to Herrera's treatment of this same event, and now its members had Cabrera in their sights. No matter that Cabrera lacked the authority accorded by the office of cronista del rey. He was still a Castilian, and from the Diputación's perspective, his account of the uprising was unnecessarily tendentious and contrary to the honor and reputa-

---

1. García López, "Sobre la historiografia en tiempos de Felipe II."
2. ANT: Secc. Osuna, 455/1, fol. 85, license dated 13 February 1611. This *legajo* offers a wealth of material relating to Cabrera's life. See Martínez Bara, "Los Cabrera de Córdoba," 202–233.
3. The most complete edition is Cabrera de Córdoba, *Historia de Felipe II*. In addition to the valuable introduction to this edition, Cabrera de Córdoba's historical scholarship may be approached through Harry Sieber, "Teoría y práctica del discurso historiográfico: 'Felipe II, Rey de España' (Historia escrita por Luís Cabrera de Córdoba)," *Edad de Oro* 18 (1999): 207–218.

tion of Aragon. Leading the attack was Bartolomé Leonardo de Argensola, an official Aragonese chronicler, who claimed that Cabrera's account was so biased, so misinformed, so scandalous that it teetered on the edge of blasphemy. Cabrera, he further alleged, was "very poorly informed" about the incident in addition to being a scholar with a penchant for "exaggerated affronts" and transforming "individual into collective guilt." Such failings, he wrote, "are not signs of a good historian."[4]

The next blow to Cabrera occurred the following year in the course of the monarchy's search to appoint a new royal chronicler. The search for this chronicler had actually begun in May 1620, when the Cámara de Castilla, the royal agency nominally in charge of such appointments, invited interested individuals to submit their résumés. By January 1621, a total of eleven applications had been received, including, as noted in the Introduction to this volume, one from Lope de Vega, the famous writer who expressed "his long-standing desire and willingness to enter His Majesty's service." Another long shot for the position was Lope de Deza, a jurist whose treatise *Gobierno político de la agricultura* (1618) had advocated that the monarchy could improve its balance sheet by discouraging emigration to the Americas and encouraging peasants to remain on the land. But perhaps the most unusual application came from Francisco de Arce, a scribe who earned additional money working in as *confitero* (pastry chef) in the royal kitchens in Madrid. Arce imaginatively proposed that all the applicants for the position should be asked to submit to the Cámara a history of "the birth, death and miracles of San Isidro Labrador," Madrid's patron saint. The one judged to have written the best history should get the job.[5] Needless to say, the Cámara, like most other governmental agencies in seventeenth-century Europe, was not ready to entertain this kind of open competition for an official post.

Of the four historians who applied for the position, Cabrera was arguably the best qualified and by far the best known. The others included the Dominican historian and inquisitor Fray Jaime Bleda, who had recently published a chronicle celebrating the monarchy's 1609 decision to expel the *moriscos*, remnants of the peninsula's former Muslim population, from its Iberian kingdoms; Luis Tribaldos de Toledo, a professor of rhetoric whose one published poem, *Ibérica epaenensis*, honored the Canary Islands; and Dr. Tomás Tamayo de Vargas, then barely

---

4. RAH: Ms. 9/489, fols. 57, 60. This manuscript includes Bartolomé Leonardo de Argensola's annotated manuscript copy of part 2 of Cabrera de Córdoba's history of Philip II.

5. Papers relating to this concurso are located in AGS: Cámara de Castilla, leg. 1111n17. These are published in García Oro and Portela Silva, "Felipe III y sus cronistas."

twenty years old, whose only publication was a treatise defending the veracity of Mariana's *Historia general*. In comparison, Cabrera, in addition to his history of Philip II, could point to his *De historia* (1611), along with his outline of a planned history of the reign of Philip III.

When the members of the Cámara finally got around to making their decision, early in 1621, Cabrera lost out. The office went to Francisco de Rioja, who had never actually applied for the position but who enjoyed the trust and confidence of the new royal favorite, Gaspar de Guzmán, count of Olivares. At first glance, Cabrera's bid failed because he lacked pull at court. But a closer look suggests that factors of more strictly historiographical character may have played their part.

Today's scholars celebrate Cabrera's history of Philip II because it is a true insider's history, one brimming with details and insights found nowhere else. It is also appreciated for Cabrera's interpretative skills, his reflections on causality, and, as Philip III suggested, the author's success in transforming history into a primer for kingship. In its own day, however, the candor of Cabrera's approach sparked criticism almost as soon as the book appeared. The details he offered about factional infighting struck some readers as excessive. In addition, his penetrating analyses of royal decision-making had a whiff of Machiavellianism about them in that they suggested that factors other than religion and service to God may have influenced the formulation of policy at Philip's court. One influential reader who garnered such an impression of Cabrera's history was Antonio de Mendoza, royal secretary to Philip IV. About 1624, in conjunction with a treatise he prepared on the history of Spain's nobility for the benefit of the young king, Mendoza offered a quick review of the many Spanish historians whose work touched on this important subject. Mendoza praised Cabrera as a "man of genius and good judgment," but he also went out of his way to castigate him for the mistake of entering into the "the most intricate details of palace secrets." These, Mendoza suggested, "should have been emended, shortened to tid-bits, or removed."[6]

Mendoza's judgment of Cabrera is revealing. His opinions of Spain's other historians—his list begins in the fifteenth century and ends with Mariana—are equally important as they underscore the changing criteria through which both history and historians are judged. Today's heroes often turn out to be yesterday's goats. The reverse is also true: Mendoza placed Diego Enríquez del Castillo, the vernacular chronicler best remembered for the loss of his notes and his passion-

---

6. Mendoza, "Tratado de los titulos y grandes de España," fol. 73v.

ate defense of King Henry IV, on a par with his rival chronicler Alonso de Palencia, the humanist whose elegant Latin history is currently regarded as one of the finest examples of Renaissance historiography in Spain.

Changing ideas about good history also apply to the work of the official historians surveyed in this book. By today's standards, many of these writers were hacks, scholars lacking in both originality and imagination. Others wrote history commensurate with the highest standards of "perfect history." Yet, as noted in the Introduction, the work of official historians is still categorized as lying somewhere between the polemical (at best) and the mendacious (at worst). Most of today's critics of official history, if pushed, would agree with Franchi di Conestaggio's candid assessment of the individuals responsible for such works as historians who were "commissioned to lie."

In history, as in life, one's person's lie is another's truth. Official historians obtained their position through trust, and it was that trust, coming from the prince or someone close to the prince, that granted authority to their work. That is why few official chroniclers forgot to make reference to their office on the title page of their books, as Pellicer was careful to do. The trust placed in them, and the title that went with it, subsequently metamorphosed into authorial authority and ultimately into truthfulness, especially in the minds of those readers—"the local" in Bernard Williams's spatial formulation of truth[7]—who were already well disposed toward the prince or dynasty the historian in question happened to serve. For this reason, the count of la Roca, in a letter directed to a nephew residing in Peru who was anxious to be granted certain honors back in Madrid, informed his young relative that the only way to "make himself immortal" (*perpetuarse*) was through writing and books. The city of Troy, the count observed, is remembered only in the books, and the same applied to such heroes as Alexander the Great. The count continued by suggesting that his nephew "should try to become friends with historians and those who write genealogies." At the same time, however, he warned that he should do this prudently lest he be judged "vain or ambitious."[8]

Sound advice. As noted earlier, this count, one of the most trusted "hired pens" in the service of Olivares and Philip IV, recognized that history had power, especially what today's political scientists refer to as "soft" power, namely the ability to cajole, convince, influence, and persuade. But where did this power

---

7. Williams, *Truth and Truthfulness*, 54.
8. Juan de Vera y Figueroa to his nephew Juan de Vera, a colonel in Cuzco, dated 10 October 1636, as printed in *Epistolario español*, 71. The nephew had asked his uncle how best to a secure a *hábito* or membership in one of the prestigious military orders, an honor that only the king could bestow.

reach? Whom did it influence? As noted in previous chapters of this book, Spain's official historians tended to write in the vernacular rather than Latin, the international language of scholarship (the same holds true for those in the service of Louis XIV and other European princes). They did so intentionally because they were primarily interested in addressing a local audience, the vassals of their prince, even as they attacked foreigners and other gainsayers for disparaging both their country and their king.

Many members of this target audience had already pledged their loyalty to the prince and his policies. Presumably, they did not need much convincing. But others harbored suspicions of both him and his ministers; still others questioned the wisdom of royal policy on any number of issues, especially those involving taxation and war; and given the importance, especially starting in the seventeenth century, of the emergent court of public opinion, these individuals needed to be brought into the king's camp. There were of course many ways in which this could be done. Honors and titles could serve the purpose, offices as well, and there is little doubt that the royal "magnificent fountain" of favor overflowed as rulers sought to bolster their support.[9] History constituted another important lure, especially when it was written in ways designed to offer vassals an opportunity to "perpetuarse," by granting them an honored place in their kingdom's history. Already in the sixteenth century, João de Barros, royal chronicler to John III of Portugal, made certain to include the "gloriosos feitos" of those Portuguese engaged in the conquest of both Asia and Africa for purposes of posterity.[10] Such was also one of the principal aims of the battle paintings celebrating victorious Spanish captains that Philip IV put on display in the Buen Retiro palace in 1635, and it helps to account, too, for the Spanish monarchy's enduring interest in *historia pro patria*. Whether dedicated to recounting the deeds of the Reconquest, triumphs in Europe, or the conquest of the New World, "national" history was the favored vehicle through which the *fama* of those vassals who served their princes was best preserved. Monuments were erected for a similar purpose, but they were not considered nearly as durable as histories. Only these, it was said, could withstand the ravages of time. Fernando del Pulgar asserted as much in his comments quoted at the beginning of Chapter 1.

Despite such advantages, only rarely was official history perfect history, and there were always critics ready to disparage a chronicler's handling of his sources, his selective use of evidence, or his ability to turn a good phrase. Antonio de

---

9. Sieber, "The Magnificent Foundation."
10. Barros, *Asia*, prologue. This work was first printed in 1552.

Mendoza, for example, criticized Herrera's lack of eloquence while praising him as both "serious and well-informed" ("harto noticiosa y grave").[11] But none of Herrera's critics, and they were many, ever impugned his commitment and loyalty to his monarch. Put simply, Herrera was a historian who merited trust, and even at the start of the nineteenth century, Antonio de Alcedo observed that Herrera's history of the Indies had "always been regarded as the fountain of truth for the deeds of Spaniards in those regions."[12]

Other, more distant readers were not so easily persuaded. Was Herrera's history necessarily more truthful than others, especially those with direct experience in the New World? The truthfulness of history is a huge subject about which philosophers continually wrangle, and certainly one that I am ill equipped to resolve. What is certain is that truth, if defined as factual accuracy, does not come easy, especially in those contexts in which documented "facts" are relatively few and the veracity of eyewitness reports difficult to check. As previously noted, Thucydides confronted a similar situation at the outset of his history of the Peloponnesian War, where he admitted that "truth" was never "easy to discover." He thus fell back to the position that the truthfulness of history lay in its utility, initially for contemporaries, the "immediate public," and equally importantly, for future readers as well.

So it is with the official histories and chronicles this study has surveyed. Whatever their flaws, they represent narratives that were read and used in many different ways. For Thevet, the French geographer, Oviedo's history of the Indies constituted a veritable encyclopedia that rendered the "conquest [of the Indies] easy to grasp." His contemporary the French humanist Louis le Roy interpreted Martyr's and Oviedo's histories as testaments to the "industry" of the Castilians.[13] Las Casas, in contrast, read both of these authors far more critically and then responded with a counterhistory that provided another, far less heroic account of the Spanish conquest of the New World. Meanwhile, English readers, starting with Hakluyt, looked at these same histories as guides to action and subsequently used them to persuade their fellow countrymen to embark on glorious imperial adventures of their own. Ralegh read the histories in a similar fashion, only to be caught out when, in 1616, the Spanish ambassador in London used Herrera's world history to snare the English adventurer in a trap of his own making. Shortly thereafter, the Amsterdam printer Michael Colijn published translations of Her-

---

11. Mendoza, "Tratado de los titulos y grandes de España," fol. 73v.
12. Pérez-Bustamante, *Antonio de Alcedo y su "memoria,"* 25.
13. Le Roy, *De la vicissitude ou variété*, 99. For Thevet, see Chapter 5, note 12.

rera's *Descripción de las Indias* in Dutch, French, and Latin, all in one year. Why he did so is not entirely clear, but this three-part project was almost certainly the brainchild of one of the directors of the Dutch West India Company, possibly Johannes de Laet, inasmuch as the *Descripción,* especially its maps, offered Dutch merchants a valuable guide to the geography of the Indies and, more importantly, riches that they hoped to exploit for their own benefit.[14]

Even in the eighteenth century, when other scholars began to write the history of the New World, Herrera's history continued to exercise a powerful pull on the European imagination. Translated into several languages, it remained an essential building block for anyone interested in writing about the Spanish New World. To begin with, it provided a valuable time line that helped orient the work of such Spanish scholars as Solórzano, Solís, and finally Muñoz, along with a string of Creole historians who, writing in the Americas, sought to document the achievements of their predecessors in the conquest and settlement of the New World. In addition, Herrera was essential reading for foreign scholars interested in the Americas. His work figures prominently, for example, in Louis Moréri's *Grand dictionaire historique,* in Voltaire's writings about the Indies, and later in the histories of Robertson and Raynal, both of whom used and interpreted Herrera for philosophical purposes of their own.[15] Starting with the decision of the Real Academia de la Historia in 1780 to publish Ginés de Sepúlveda's history of the New World, this situation gradually changed, as documents pertaining to the histories of the Indies were, for the first time in history, pushed into print. Previously these documents, classified under the rubric *arcana imperii,* had represented the stuff of official history, the sources that Herrera used to assert that his histories were truthful while others were false. Now, for reasons partially connected with the loss of its colonies in the Americas, the Spanish government released its hold over the documents, allowing them to enter the public domain for interpretation and review. The first of the resulting documentary collections was Martín Fernández de Navarrete's *Colección de los viajes y descubrimientos que hicieron por mar los españoles desde fines del siglo xv, con varios documentos inéditos concernientes á la historia de la marina castellana y de los establecimientos españoles en*

---

14. The translation into Latin (*Novus orbis sive Descriptio Indiae Occidentalis* [Amsterdam, 1622]) was the work of the famed Dutch humanist Gaspar Barlaeus. For these translations, see Cuesta Domingo, *Antonio de Herrera y su obra,* 76–77.

15. For Voltaire's (mainly critical) remarks about both Spain and its colonies in the Americas, see Salvio, "Voltaire and Spain." For Moréri, see Moréri, *Le grand dictionaire historique,* 1:353, s.v. "l'Amérique." For Raynal and Robertson, see above, Chapter 7. Note that this list of eighteenth-century scholars who made use of Herrera is not meant to be exhaustive.

las Indias, the first volume of which appeared in 1825. That same year an American writer, Washington Irving, then on a visit to Spain, made use of this new collection to write his pioneering *A History of the Life and Voyages of Christopher Columbus*, first published in 1828. Two years later another North American, Obadiah Rich, a book dealer (and former diplomat) residing in London, gained access to the collections at Simancas for the purpose of completing his *Biblioteca Americana Nova*, one of the first bibliographies of Americana to appear in print. The breakthrough in Spanish historical writing occurred in 1836, when Spain's first liberal government officially opened the doors of its once-secret archives in Simancas and Seville to the general public. Others soon followed, and at one point the government, echoing the positivist mantra cherished by Leopold van Ranke and so many other nineteenth-century historians, proudly announced that "without documents to check [the veracity] of history, there is no glory for the nation."[16] Only then were historians, regardless of nationality, able to judge the extent to which Herrera and other official historians had distorted the historical record. Henceforward, Herrera's record of Spanish accomplishment in the Indies was less a "fountain of truth" than a first draft whose thoroughness historians, with help from the archives, were in a position to verify, essentially subjecting it to the process of checking and cross-checking of evidence that Thucydides recognized as essential to the establishment of historical truth.

But whether it is in reference to Spain's conquest of the Indies or some other important historical event, the establishment of what approximates objective truth is elusive. It is also adversarial in that it resembles the manner in which the truth surrounding a crime or conflict is established in a court of law. In that arena, lawyers, each armed with evidence supporting his or her interpretation, do battle with one another, hammering away at both the reliability and the relevance of the facts presented by the opposing side. Ultimately it is left to a judge or a jury to decide which of the competing narratives best approximates the truth. A similar logic applies to history. Writing in 1788, Juan Pablo Forner, a Spanish jurist with an interest in history, looked wistfully back at the reign of Philip II, an era that he regarded as "the most glorious in our history because this monarch had the singular good sense to appoint skilled historians." He then added that "the king knew how to make certain that the skills of these historians did not remain sterile." The secret? The king, in addition to having his own royal chroniclers, had others in each of his many kingdoms, and according to Forner, "this rivalry

---

16. As cited in Peiró Martín, *Los guardianes de la historia*, 43.

popularized the cultivation of history and at the same time assured the truth of each of these narratives." Competition, rivalry, exchange. According to Forner— and I think this Spanish thinker got it right—these ingredients are essential not only for good history but for history perceived to be true.[17]

As I suggested in the Introduction, this adversarial legal framework is possibly the best way to understand the work of official historians, whether in the context of sixteenth-century Spain and such works as Herrera's *Historia general* or in that of the early twenty-first century, when on 30 June 2008 the U.S. Army published what is being called the "official" history of the opening years (2003–2005) of the invasion of the Islamic Republic of Iraq by the United States.[18] In many respects, these two histories, though separated by space, time, and culture have much in common. Both are counterhistories, intended to refute other, nonofficial histories dealing with the same event. Therefore they offer a narrative in which certain facts are included, while others, allegedly for reasons of state security, are either omitted or downplayed as irrelevant. With reference to the official history of Iraq, it is too early to say with any certainty what the response will be, but if my experience with Herrera's history provides a basis of comparison, other historians, like dueling lawyers, will challenge the veracity of the military's interpretation either by marshaling new facts or by resurrecting those that the army's historians, having previously submitted their manuscripts for review by superiors, were obliged to leave out. I am no prophet, nor in a position to venture a guess at how long this twenty-first-century version of tit-for-tat history is likely to last, but I can imagine that sooner or later readers, following the examples of jurors in a court of law, will finally decide which of these narratives best approximates the truth of what happened in Iraq in the turbulent years between 2003 and 2005.

From this perspective, official history of the kind examined here acquires both a stature and importance far greater than its critics have allowed. History, as I understand it, is a process. It entails constant wrangling, histories and counterhistories, checking and cross-checking of relevant facts, and the continual discovery of new sources and relevant information. History in this sense is a field in motion, constantly changing and regularly subject to revision and review before any general agreement on what approximates truth can be established. Such a process rarely occurs overnight. It is invariably protracted. Even then, other readings are always possible, challenging consensus interpretations of historical truth.

---

17. Forner, "Discurso sobre la historia de España," 65, 99.
18. I refer to *On Point II, Transition to the New Campaign.*

If I have learned anything in the course of this inquiry, it is that official history, even when marmorealized, is essential to this process of historical give and take. As a genre, its defects are numerous, its practitioners sometimes flawed. Yet this particular iteration of Clio retains its utility, and, if nothing else, helps move us along the twisting road toward histories that, as Cicero would have it, illuminate only the truth.

SELECTED BIBLIOGRAPHY

Primary Sources

Abarca, Pedro. *Los reyes de Aragón en anales históricos.* Madrid, 1678–1682.
Accetto, Torquato. *Della dissimulazione onesta.* 1641. Reprint, edited by Salvatore Silvano Negro. Torino, 1997.
Acosta, José de. *Historia natural y moral de las Indias.* Edited by José Alcina Franch. Madrid, 1987.
Adam de la Parra, Juan. *Apologético contra el tirano y rebelde vergüenza y conjurados: Arzobispo de Lisboa y sus parciales: En respuesta a los doce fundamentos del Padre Mascareñas.* Zaragoza, 1642.
———. *Conspiración herético-cristianísima.* Translated by Angeles Roda Aguirre, with a prologue by Joaquín de Entrambasguas. Madrid, 1943.
Adriani, Giovanni Battista. *Istorie de'suoi tempi.* Florence, 1583.
Advertencias que los catolicos de Inglaterra escrivieron a los Catolicos de Francia, tocantes a las presentes reboluciones, y cerco de Paris. Translated by Antonio de Herrera y Tordesillas. Zaragoza, 1592.
Alcedo, Antonio de. *Biblioteca Americana.* Edited by Jorge A. Garcés. Quito, 1965.
———. *The Geographical and Historical Dictionary of America and the West Indies.* Translated by G. A. Thompson. London, 1812. Published originally as *Diccionario geográfico-histórico de las Indias Occidentales o América,* 5 vols. (Madrid, 1786–1789).
Alfonso X El Sabio. *General Estoria, Primera Parte.* Edited by Pedro Sánchez-Prieto Borja. Madrid, 2001.
———. *Primera crónica general de España.* Edited by Ramón Menéndez Pidal. Madrid, 1955.
Almansa y Mendoza, Andrés. *Obra periodística.* Edited by Henry Ettinghausen and Manuel Borrego. Madrid, 2001.
Álvarez, Vicente. *Relation du beau voyage que fit aux Pays-Bas en 1548 le prince Philippe d'Espagne.* Edited by M.-T. Dovilée. Brussels, 1964.
Álvarez y Baena, José Antonio. *Hijos ilustres de Madrid.* Madrid, 1789. Facsimile edition, 4 vols., Madrid, 1973.
Andrada, Francisco de. *Crónica de D. João III.* Edited by M. Lopes de Almeida. Porto, 1976.

Andrés de Uztárroz, Juan, and Diego D. Dormer, eds. *Progresos de la historia de Aragón.* Zaragoza, 1680, 1878.
Antonio, Nicolás. *Biblioteca antigua nueva.* Madrid, 1999.
———. *Biblioteca hispana antigua.* Madrid, 1998.
———. *Censura de historias fabulosas, obra póstuma de Nicolás Antonio.* Edited by Gregorio Mayàns i Siscàr. 1742. Madrid, 1999.
Argaiz, Fray Gregorio. *Corona real de España por España, fundada en los créditos de los muertos y vida de San Hyerotheo.* Madrid, 1668.
———. *Población eclesiástica de España.* Madrid, 1667.
Ávila y Zúñiga, Luis de. *Comentarios ... de la guerra de Alemania hecha por Carlos V (1546–1547).* Salamanca, 1549.
Avisos de la Biblioteca Real de Madrid. Accessible at www.patrimonionacional.es/real biblioteca/avisos3202.htm.
Ayora, Gonzalo de. "Cartas de Gonzalo de Ayora." In *Epistolario Español,* edited by Eugenio de Ochoa. *BAE* 13. Madrid, 1850.
Aytta, Wigle van. *Mémoires de Viglius et d'Hopperus sur le commencement des troubles de Pays Bas.* Brussels, 1858.
Bacon, Francis. *The Advancement of Learning and the New Atlantis.* Oxford, 1974.
———. *The History of the Reign of Henry VII.* 1622. Edited by Brian Vickers. Cambridge, 1998.
Barberini, Franceso. *El diario del viaje de España del cardenal Francesco Barberini escrito por Casiano del Pozzo.* Edited by A. Anselmi. Aranjuez (Madrid), 2004.
Barros, João de. *Asia: Dos feitos que os portuguese fizeram no descobrimento e conquista dos mares e terras do Orient, Primera parte.* 1552. Edited by Hernan Cedad. Lisboa, 1945.
Beltrán de Heredia, Vicente. *Cartulario de la Universidad de Salamanca.* 6 vols. Salamanca, 1970–1973.
Benzoni, Girolamo. *La historia del nuevo mundo.* Translated by Marisa Vannini de Gerulewicz. Caracas, 1967.
Beuter, Pere Antóni. *Primera part de la historia de Valencia.* Valencia, 1538.
Blasco de Lanuza, Vicencio. *Historias eclesiásticas y seculares de Aragón.* Zaragoza, 1617.
Bodin, Jean. *Method for the Easy Comprehension of History.* Translated by Beatrice Reynolds. New York, 1965.
Botero, Giovanni. *The Reason of State.* Translated by P. J. and D. P. Waley. London, 1956.
Boturini, Lorenzo. *Idea de una nueva historia general de la América septentrional.* Madrid, 1746.
Brantôme, Pierre de Bourdielle, seigneur de. *Oeuvres complètes de Pierre de Bourdielle, seigneur de Brantôme.* Edited by Ludovic Lalanne. Paris, 1866.
Brito, Frey Bernardo de. *Elogios dos Reis de Portugal.* Lisbon, 1603.
———. *Monarchia Lusitana.* 2 vols. Lisbon, 1609.
Bruto, Giovanni Michale. *De Rebus Carolus V Caesare Romanorum imperatore gestis.* Antwerp, 1555.
Busto, Bernabé de. *Geschichte des Schmalkaldischen Krieges.* Edited by Otto Adalbert and Graf von Looz-Corswaren. Burg, 1938.
———. *Introductiones gramáticas, breves e compendiosas.* Salamanca, 1533.

Cabrera de Córdoba, Luis. *De historia para entenderla y escribirla.* 1611. Edited by Santiago Montero Díaz. Madrid, 1948.

——. *Historia de Felipe II, Rey de España.* Madrid, 1619. Edited by José Martínez Millán and Carlos Javier de Carlos Morales. 3 vols. Valladolid, 1998.

——. *Relaciones de las cosas sucedidas en la corte de España desde 1599 hasta 1604.* Valladolid, 1997.

Calderón, Juan. *Fragmentum Chronici, sive Omnimodae historiae Flavii Lucii Dextri Barcinonensis, cum chronico Marci Maximi, & additionibus Sancti Braulionis, & etiam Helecae episcoporum caesaraugustanorum . . . labore P.Fr. Ioannis Calderon, Franciscanae familiae.* Zaragoza, 1619.

Calderón, Juan Alonso. *Compendio universal histórico-jurídico-político-chronológico-genealógico de la Cathólica Monarquía España en las cuatro partes del mundo.* Madrid, 1651.

——. "Memorial q dió a la Magestad Cathólica del Rey N. S. don Phelipe IV el Doctor Juan Alonso Calderón . . . referido a lo que ha escrito en cuatro tomos y trienta libros del Compendio dela Monarquía Catholica de España." BL Add.: 10,252.

——. *Memorial y discurso histórico-jurídico-político q dió a su Magestad . . . don Phelipe Quarto.* . . . Madrid, 1659.

Calvete de Estrella, Juan Cristóbal. *De rebus indicis de Calvete de Estrella.* Translated by José López de Toro. Madrid, 1950.

——. *El felicíssimo viaje del muy alto y muy poderoso príncipe don Felipe.* 1552. Edited by Paloma Cuenca. Madrid, 2001.

——. *Rerum a Carolo V Caesare Augusto in Africa bello gestarum Commentarii.* Antwerp, 1555.

Campana, Cesare. *Compendio histórico, delle guerre ultimamente sucesse tra christiani & turchi . . . fino al presente anno MDXCVII.* Venice, 1597.

——. *La vita del catholico e invittissimo don Filippo Secondo di Austria, re delle Spagna.* Vicenza, 1605–1608.

Capella Galeazzo, Flavio. *De rebus nuper in Italia gestis.* Nuremberg, 1532. Translated into Spanish as *Historia de las cosas que han passado en Italia desde el año MDXXI . . . hasta el año XXX* (Valencia, 1536).

Caramuel y Lobowitz, Juan de. *Philippus prudens Caroli V Imp.* Antwerp, 1639.

——. *Respuesta al manfiesto del reino de Portugal.* Antwerp, 1642.

Carbonell, Pere Miquel. *Cròniques d'Espanya.* Edited by D. Augustí Alcoberro. Barcelona, 1997.

Carrillo de Huete, Pedro. *Crónica del halconero de Juan II.* Edited by Juan de Mata Carriazo. Madrid, 1946.

Cartagena, Alfonso de. *Anacephaleosis.* Edited and translated by Yolanda Espinosa Fernández. Madrid, 1989.

——. "Discurso de . . . sobre la precedencia del rey católico sobre el de Inglaterra en el Concilio de Basilea." In *Prosistas castellanas del siglo XV,* edited by Mario Penna, BAE 119. Madrid, 1959.

"Cartas de algunos PP. de la Compañía de Jesús sobre los sucesos de la monarquia entre los años de 1634 y 1648." *MHE,* vols. 13–19. Madrid, 1861–1865.

Cartas recibidas de España por Francisco Cervantes de Salazar (1569–1574). Edited by Agustín Millares Carlos. Mexico City, 1946.

Casas, Bartolomé de las. *Historia de las Indias*. Edited by Lewis Hanke and Agustín Millares Carlo. Mexico City, 1965.

———. *A Short Account of the Destruction of the Indies*. Translated by Nigel Griffen. London, 1992.

Cassan, Jacques. *La Recherche des droicts du Roy et de la Couronne de France: Sur les Royaumes, Duches, Comtez, et Villes et Pais occupez par les Princes estrangers*. . . . Paris, 1632.

Castro Egas, Ana de. *Eternidad del rey don Felipe III N.S. el Piadoso, Discurso de su vida y santas costumbres*. Madrid, 1629.

Catálogo de consultas del Consejo de Indias, 1521–1591. Edited by Antonio Heredia Herrera. Madrid, 1983.

Catálogo de los manuscritos que pertenecieron a Pascual de Gayangos existentes hoy en la Biblioteca Nacional. Edited by Pedro Roca. Madrid, 1904.

Cátedra, Pedro M. *La historiografía en verso en la época de los Reyes Católicos: Juan Barba y su Consolatoria de Castilla*. Salamanca, 1989.

Cepeda, Fray Francisco de. *Resumpta historial de España, desde el deluvio hasta el año de 1642*. Madrid, 1643.

Céspedes y Meneses, Gonzalo. *Historia apologética en los sucesos del reyno de Aragón y su ciudad de Zaragoza, años de 91 y 92, y relaciones fieles de la verdad que hasta aora manzillaron diveros escritores*. Zaragoza, 1622.

———. *Historia de don Felipe IIII, Rey de las Españas*. Lisbon, 1631.

———. *Historias pelegrinas y ejemplares*. Edited by Yves-René Fonquerne. Madrid, 1980.

Chastellain, Georges. *Oeuvres de Georges Chastellain*. Edited by Keryn de Lettenhove. Brussels, 1863.

Chronicle of Alfonso X. Translated by Shelby Thacker and José Escobar. Lexington, KY, 2002.

Cieza de León, Pedro. *Obras completas*. 3 vols. Edited by C. Saenz de Santa María. Madrid, 1985.

Colección de documentos inéditos relativos al descubrimiento, conquista y organización de las Indias. Madrid, 1823. Facsimile edition, Nendelen, 1967.

Comines, Philippe de. *Las memorias de los hechos y empresas de Luis undecimo y Carlos octavo, reyes de Francia*. 2 vols. Antwerp, 1643.

Conestaggio, Girolamo Franchi di. *Dell'unione del regno di Portogallo alla Corona di Castiglia*. Genoa, 1585; Florence, 1642. Translated as *The Historie of the Uniting of the Kingdom of Portugal to the Crowne of Castile* (London, 1600).

Conquerors and Chroniclers of Early Medieval Spain. Edited by Kenneth Baxter Wolf. Liverpool, 1990.

Corpus documental de Carlos V. Edited by Manuel Fernández Álvarez. 5 vols. Salamanca, 1979.

Correia Montenegro, Manuel. *Historia de los reyes, señorias y emperadores de España*. Salamanca, 1608.

Cortes de los antiguos reinos de Castilla y León. 7 vols. Madrid, 1861–1903.

Covarrubias Orozco, Sebastián de. *Tesoro de la lengua castellana o española*. 1611. Madrid, 1979.

Covarrubias y Leiva, Diego de. *Elogios al Palacio Real del Buen Retiro.* 1635. Facsimile edition, Valencia, 1949.
Coxe, William. *Memoirs of the Kings of Spain of the House of Bourbon.* 3 vols. London, 1812.
Cristoph, Franz. *Annales Fernandini.* 12 vols. Leipzig, 1721–1726.
Crónica de Alfonso III. Edited by Antonio Ubieto Arteta. Valencia, 1961.
Crónica del rey don Alfonso X. Edited by Cayetano Rosell, *BAE* 66. Madrid, 1875.
Crónica incompleta de los Reyes Católicos (1469–1478). Edited by Julio Puyol. Madrid, 1934.
Crónicas de los reyes de Castilla. Edited by Cayetano Rosell. *BAE* 66, 68, 70. Madrid, 1875–1878.
Crónicas de Perú. Edited by Juan Pérez de Tudela Bueso. *BAE* 164–168. Madrid, 1963–1965.
Dávila Padilla, Fray Agustín de. *Historia de la fundación y discurso de la provincia de Santiago de Mexico, de la orden de predicadores, por las vidas de sus varones insignes, y casos notables de Nueva España.* Madrid, 1596.
Desclot, Bernat. *Crónica.* Barcelona, 1949–1951.
Deza, Lope de. *Gobierno político de la agricultura.* Madrid, 1618.
Documentos inéditos para la historia de España. Edited by Jacobo Fitz-James Stuart y Falcó, duque de Alva. 13 vols. Madrid, 1936–1957.
Documentos relativos a Pedro de la Gasca y a Goinzalo Pizarro. Edited by Juan Perez de Tudela Bueso. *Archivo Documental Español* 21. Madrid, 1944.
Dolce, Ludovico. *Vita dell'invitiss. e gloriosiss. imperador Carlos Quinto.* Venice, 1561.
Enríquez del Castillo, Diego. *Crónica de Enrique IV.* Edited by Aureliano Sanchez Martín. Valladolid, 1994.
Epistolario de Juan Ginés de Sepúlveda. Edited by Ángel Losada. Madrid, 1979.
Epistolario Español. Edited by Eugenio de Ochoa. *BAE* 62. Madrid, 1870.
Erasmus, Desiderius. *Education of a Christian Prince.* Edited by Lester K. Born. New York, 1936.
Escavias, Pedro de. *Hechos del condestable don Miguel Lúcas de Iranzo (crónica del siglo XV).* Edited by Juan de Mata Carriazo. Madrid, 1940.
———. *Reportorio de Principes de España.* Edited by Michel Garca. Jaen, 1972.
Faria de Guzmán, Marcelino. *Apologia en defensa desta Monarchia y la casa de Austria para el desengaño de los potentados de Europa y satifacción de los políticos destos tiempos* (4 July 1634). BNE: Ms. 1185.
Fastos de la Real Academia Española de la Historia. 3 vols. Madrid, 1739–1741.
Fernández de Navarrete, Fernando. "Sobre el caracter de los españoles." In *Fastos de la Real Academia Española de la Historia,* 1 (1739).
Fernández de Navarrete, Martín. *Colección de los viajes y descubrimientos que hicieron por mar los españoles desde fines del siglo XV, con varios documentos inéditos concernientes á la historia de la marina castellana y de los establecimientos españoles en las Indias.* 5 vols. 2nd ed. Madrid, 1829–1859.
Fernández de Oviedo, Gonzalo. *Catálogo de los reyes de España.* Biblioteca de San Lorenzo del Escorial: Ms. H-I-7.
———. *Historia general y natural de las Indias.* Edited by Juan Pérez de Tudela Bueso. *BAE* 117–121. Madrid, 1959.
———. *Libro de la cámara real del príncipe Don Juan.* Madrid, 1880.

———. *Las memorias de Gonzalo Fernández de Oviedo*. Edited by Juan Bautista Avalle-Arce. 2 vols. Chapel Hill, NC, 1974.
———. *Writing from the Edge of the World: The Memoirs of Darién, 1514–1517*. Edited and translated by G. F. Dille. Tuscaloosa, AL, 2006.
Fernández de Pulgar, Pedro. "Historia general de las Indias." BNE: Mss. 2796–99.
Ferreras, Juan de. *Synopsis histórica chronológica de España*. 16 vols. Madrid, 1700–1727.
Forner, Juan Pablo. "Discurso sobre la historia de España." 1788. In his *Discurso sobre el modo de escribir y mejorar la historia de España*, edited by François López. Barcelona, 1973.
Gaceta Nueva, 1661–1663. Edited by E. Varela Hervias. Madrid, 1960.
Gacetas y nuevas de la corte de España desde el año 1600 en adelante. Edited by Gerónimo Gascón de Torquemada. Madrid, 1991.
Galíndez de Carvajal, Lorenzo. "Anales breves del reinado de los Reyes Católicos don Fernando y doña Isabel. . . ." In *Codoin* 18: 227–423.
———. "La chrónica y hechos acontecidos en el reinado del . . . rey don Enrique 4." In *Estudios sobre la "Crónica de Enrique IV" del Doctor Galíndez de Carvajal*, edited by Juan Torres Fontes. Madrid, 1946.
———. "Generaciones, semblanzas é obras de . . . don Enrique el Tercero é don Juan el Segundo. . . ." In *Crónicas de los reyes de Castilla*, edited by Cayetano Rosell. Madrid, 1877.
———. *Memorial o registro breve de los Reyes Católicos*. Edited by Juan Carretero Zamora. Segovia, 1991.
———. "Memorial y registro breve de los lugares donde el Rey y Reina Católicos, nuestros Señores, estuvieron cada año desde el de 1468. . . ." In *Codoin* 18: 237–246.
———. "Prefación en la crónica del rey don Juan el Segundo." In *Crónicas de los reyes de Castilla*, BAE 68. Madrid, 1875–1878.
Garibay y Zamalloa, Esteban de. *Los cuarenta libros del compendio historial de España*. 1628. Facsimile edition, Lejona, Vizcaya, 1986.
———. *Discurso de mi vida*. Edited by Jesús Moya. Bilbao, 1999.
———. *Los XL libros d'el compendio historial de las chrónicas de España*. Antwerp, 1571.
———. *Illustraciones genealógicas de los Cathólicos reyes de las Españas, y de los Christianíssimos de Francia, y de los Emperadores de Constantinopla, hasta el Cathólico Rey nuestro señor Don Philipe el II, y sus sereníssimos hijos*. Madrid, 1596.
———. *Letreros e insignias reales de todos los sereníssimos reyes de Oviedo, León y Castila para la sala real de los alcaçares de Segovia, ordenandos por mandado del Cathólico Rey, nuestro señor, Don Felipe el II . . . por Esteban de Garibay su chronista*. 1593. Facsimile edition, edited by Fernando Collar de Cáceres, Segovia, 1993.
———. *Memorias de Garibay*. Edited by Pascual Gayangos. MHE 7. Madrid, 1854. Also published as Esteban de Garibay y Zamalloa, *Discursos de mi vida*, edited by Jesús Moya (Bilbao, 1999).
Gentile, Fray Bernardo de. *Carmen ad Carolum quintum Caesarum*. BNE: Ms. 10019.
Giovio, Paolo. *Commentario de le cose de' Turchi*. Edited by Lara Michelacci. Bologna, 2005.
———. *Historiarum sui temporis*. Florence, 1550–1552.

———. *Lettere*. Edited by Giuseppe Guido Ferrero. Rome, 1956–1958.
González Dávila, Gil. "Cartas del Maestro Gil González de Avila . . . al Dr. Juan Francisco Andrés de Uztárroz." BNE: Ms. 8389.
———. *Historia de . . . Felipe III*. Madrid, 1770.
———. *Historia de las antigüedades de Salamanca*. 1606. Edited by Baltasar Cuart Moner. Salamanca, 1994.
———. *Historia de la vida y hechos del rey Henrique Terecero de Castilla*. Madrid, 1638.
———. *Teatro eclesiástico de la primitiva iglesia de Indias Occidentales*. Madrid, 1649–1655. Edited by Jesús Paniagua Pérez and María Isabel Viforcos Marinas. 2 vols. León, 2004.
González de Mendoza, Juan. *Historia de las cosas mas notables, ritos y costumbres del gran reyno de China*. 1585. Edited by Félix García. Madrid, 1944.
Gracián, Baltasar. *Obras completas*. Edited by Arturo del Hoyo. Madrid, 1960.
Gran Crónica de Alfonso XI. Edited by Diego Catalán. Madrid, 1976.
Guadalajara, Antonio Trillo de. *Historia de la rebelión y guerras de Flandes*. Madrid, 1592.
Guadalajara y Xavier, Marcos de. *Quinta parte de la historia pontifical y cathólica*. Madrid, 1630.
Guazzo, Marco. *Historie di tutte le cose degne di memoria quai del anno MDXXIIII sino a questo presente sono accorse nella Italia, nella Provenza, nella Franza*. . . . Venice, 1540.
Guzmán, Luis de. *Historia de las misiones que han hecho los religiosos de la Compañía de Jesús para predicar el santo evangelio . . . en la India oriental y en los reinos de la China y Japón*. Alcalá de Henares, 1601.
Haedo, Diego de. *Topografía e historia general de Argel*. Valladolid, 1612.
Hakluyt, Richard. "Dedication of Peter Martyr." In Hakluyt's *Original Writings and Correspondence*.
———. *Original Writings and Correspondence of the Two Richard Hakluyts*. Edited by E. G. R. Taylor. Nendeln, 1967.
Hamen y León, Lorenzo van der. *Don Felipe el Prudente*. Madrid, 1625.
Hernández, Francisco. *The Mexican Treasury: The Writings of Francisco Hernández*. Edited by Simon Varey. Stanford, CA, 2000.
Herrera y Tordesillas, Antonio de. *Cinco libros de la historia de Portugal y la conquista de las islas de los Azores*. Madrid, 1591.
———. *Comentarios de las alteraciones de Flandes*. Madrid, 1600.
———. *Discursos morales, políticos é históricos*. Madrid, 1804.
———. *Historia de los sucesos de Francia desde el año 1585, que comenzó la liga católica, hasta el fin de 1594*. Madrid, 1598.
———. *Historia de lo sucedido en Escocia y Inglaterra, en treinta e quatro años en que vivió María Estuardo, reyna de Escocia*. Madrid, 1589.
———. *Historia general del mundo de XLVI años del tiempo de Felipe II, el prudente, desde el año de 1554 hasta el de 1598*. 3 vols. Madrid, 1601–1612.
———. *Información en hecho y relación de lo que pasó a Milan*. Madrid, 1598.
———. *Tratado, relación y discurso histórico de los movimientos de Aragón*. Madrid, 1612.
———. "Varios Epístolas y Discursos y Tractados de Antonio de Herrera." BNE: Ms. 3011.

Ibáñez de Segovia, Gaspar. *Advertencias a la historia del P. Juan de Mariana*. Madrid, 1795.

———. *Discurso histórico por el patronato de San Frutos contra la supuesta cathedra de San Hierotheo en Segovia*. Zaragoza, 1666.

———. *Disertaciones eclesiásticas por el honor de los antiguos titulares contra las ficciones modernas*. Zaragoza, 1671.

———. *Noticia y juicio de los mas principales historiadores de España*. Madrid, 1795.

———. *Predicación de Santiago en España*. Zaragoza, 1682.

Indice de la colección Don Luis Salazar y Castro. Edited by Antonio de Vargas-Zapata y Monteros de Espinosa. 48 vols. Madrid, 1949–1979.

Isidore of Seville. *History of the Goths, Vandals, and Suevi*. Translated by Guido Donini and Gordon B. Ford Jr. Leiden, 1970.

Jáuregui, Juan de. *Memorial al rey . . . ilustra la singular onra de España, aprueba, la modestia en los escritos contra Francia*. Madrid? 1635? (See BNE: R/22160[3]).

Jiménez de Quesada, Gonzalo. *El Antijovio*. Edited by Rafael Torres Quintero. Bogota, 1952.

Jover Zamora, José María. *1635: Historia de una polémica y semblanza de una generación*. Madrid, 1949. Facsimile edition, Madrid, 2003.

Laval, A. de. *L'historical des rois non-catholiques sur un roi antichristianne et la resistance continuelle des catholiques*. Lyon, 1592.

Leclerc, Georges-Louis. *Histoire naturelle, générale et particulière*. 36 vols. Paris, 1749–1778.

Leonardo de Argensola, Bartolomé y Leonardo. *Obras sueltas*. Edited by Conde de la Viñaza. 2 vols. Madrid, 1889.

Leonardo de Argensola, Lupercio. *Información de los sucesos de Aragón de los años de 1590 y 1591*. Edited by Xavier Gil Pujol. Zaragoza, 1991.

León Pinelo, Antonio de. *Política de las grandezas y govierno supremo y real consejo de las Indias*. N.p., n.d. [1658?]. Accessible at BL: 8155.c.45.

———. *Recopilación de las Indias*. Edited by Ismael Sánchez Bella. 3 vols. Mexico City, 1992.

Le Roy, Louis. *De la vicissitude ou variété des choses en l'univers*. 1575. Paris, 1577.

Lettres sur la vie intérieure de Charles V écrites par Guillaume van Mâle. Edited by Fréderique A. F. T. de Reiffenberg. Brussels, 1843.

Libro copiador del Cristóbal Colon: Correspondencia inédita con los reyes católicos sobre los viajes a América. Edited by Antonio Rumeu de Armas. 2 vols. Madrid, 1989.

Lipsius, Justus. *Sixe Books of Politickes, or Civil Discourse*. Translated by William Jones. London, 1594.

———. *Politica: Six Books of Politics or Political Instruction*. Edited and translated by Jan Waszink. Assen, Netherlands, 2004.

Lobera, Atanasio de. *Grandezas de la muy antigua e insigne ciudad y iglesia de León y su iglesia*. Valladolid, 1597. Facsimile edition, León, 1987.

López de Ayala, Pedro. *Las Décadas de Tito Livio*. Edited by Curt J. Witten. Barcelona, 1982.

López de Gómara, Francisco. *The Annals of the Emperor Charles V*. Edited by Roger B. Merriman. Oxford, 1912.

———. *Historia de la conquista de Nueva España*. Edited by José Luis de Rojas. Madrid, 2000.

———. *Historia general de las indias y vida de Hernán Cortés*. Edited by Jorge Gurria Lacrox. Caracas, 1979.

López de Velasco, Juan. *Geografía y descripción universal de las Indias.* BAE 248. Madrid, 1971.
———. *Ortografía y pronunciación castellana.* Burgos, 1560.
López Madera, Gregorio. *Excelencias de la monarchía y reyno de España.* Madrid, 1625.
Louis XIV, king of France. *Mémoires.* Edited by Jean Longnon. Paris, 1933.
Lucae Tudensis. *Chronicon mundi.* Edited by Emma Falque. Turnhout, 2003.
——— (Lucas, Obispo de Tuy). *Crónica de España.* Translated by Julio Puyol. Madrid, 1926.
Maldonado, Fray Alonso. *Crónica universal de todas las naciones y tiempos.* Madrid, 1624.
Malvezzi, Virgilio. *Discourse upon Tacitus.* Translated by Sir Richard Baker. London, 1642.
———. *Disscorsi sopra Cornelio Tacito.* Venetia, 1622.
———. *Historia de los primeros años del reinado de Felipe IV.* Edited by D. L. Shaw. London, 1986.
———. *Lettere a Fabio Chigi.* Edited by Maria Caterina Crisafulli. Fasano, 1990.
———. *La Libra.* Pamplona, 1639.
———. *Relaciones de sucesos.* Torino, 1638.
———. *Il ritratto del privato politico christiano.* 1635. Edited by Maria Luisa Doglio. Palermo, 1993.
———. *Romulo.* Bologna, 1629.
———. *Tarquino superbo.* Bologna, 1632.
Mar de historias. Edited by Andrea Zinato. Padova, 1999.
Mariana, Juan de. *De rege et regis institione libri III.* Toledo, 1599; Aalen, 1969. Translated into Spanish as *La dignidad del rey y la educación del rey,* edited by L. Sánchez Agesta (Madrid, 1981). Translated into English by G. A. Moore as *The King and the Education of the King* (Chevy Chase, MD, 1948).
———. *Historiae de rebus Hispaniae.* Toledo, 1592.
———. *Historia general de España.* In *Obras completas de Juan de Mariana,* BAE 30–31. Madrid, 1950.
Marineo Sículo, Lucio. *De rebus hispaniae.* Alcalá de Henares, 1530.
Martin, Heinrich, alias Enrico Martínez. *Reportorio de los tiempos e historia natural de Nueva España.* Mexico City, 1606. Edited by Francisco de la Maza. Mexico City, 1998.
Mártir de Anglería, Pedro. *Décadas del Nuevo Mundo.* Madrid, 1989.
Martyr Rizo, Juan Pablo. *Historia de la vida de Mécenas* Edited by Antonio de Roxas. Madrid, 1626.
Mascarenhas, Jerónimo de. *Campaña de Portugal por la parte de Extremadura año de 1662.* Madrid, 1662.
Mayáns y Siscar, Gregorio, ed. *Cartas de don Nicolás Antonio y de don Antonio de Solís.* Lyon, 1755.
Mayerne, Lewis Turquet de. *General Historie of Spain.* London, 1612.
Meléndez, Fray Juan. *Tesorosos verdaderos de las Yndias.* Rome, 1681.
Melo, Francisco Manoel de. *Epanáfora de varias historias portuguesas.* Edited by Josel Serrão. Lisbon, 1977.
Memorias de la real academia de la Historia. Madrid, 1796.
Mendoza, Antonio de. "Tratado de los titulos y grandes de España," BL Eg. 2061.

Mendoza, Bernardino de. *Comentarios de don Bernardino de Mendoza de lo sucedido en las guerras de los Payses Baxos, desde el año de 1567 hasta de 1577*. Madrid, 1592. Edited by Cayetano Rosell. *BAE* 21. Madrid, 1852.

Mexía, Pedro de. *Historia del Emperador Carlos V*. Edited by J. De Mata Carriazo. Madrid, 1945.

———. *Silva de varia lección*. Edited by Antonio Castro. Madrid, 1989.

Minadoi, Giovanni Tomasso. *Historia della gverra fra Tvrchi, et Persiana . . . cominciando dall'anno MDLXXVII*. Rome, 1587. Translated into Spanish by Antonio de Herrera y Tordesillas as *Historia de la guerra entre Turcos y Persianos*. Madrid, 1588.

Montaigne, Michel de. *Complete Works of Michel de Montaigne*. Edited by Donald Frame. Stanford, CA, 1957.

Morales, Ambrosio de. *Antigüedades de las ciudades de España*. Madrid, 1792; facsimile ed., Valencia, 2001.

———. *Los cinco libros postreros de la coronica general de España*. Córdoba, 1586.

———. *La coronica general de España*. 2 vols. Alcalá de Henares, 1578.

———. *Los otros dos libros de la coronica general de España*. Alcalá de Henares, 1577.

———. *Viage santo de . . . por orden del rey don Phelipe II a los reinos de León y Galicia y Principado de Asturias para reconocer las relíquias de los santos, sepulchros reales y libros manuscritos de las cathedrales y monasterios*. Madrid, 1765. Facsimile edition, Oviedo, 1985.

Moréri, Louis. *Le grand dictionaire historique*. 6 vols. Paris, 1732.

Morgues, Matthieu des. *L'Ambassadeur Chimérique*. Translated into Spanish by José Pellicer de Ossau y Tovar as *El embaxador chimérico*. 1638.

Muñoz, Andrés. *Viaje de Felipe II a Inglaterra*. Edited by Pascual Gayangos. Madrid, 1877.

Muñoz, Juan Bautista. *Historia del Nuevo-Mundo*. Madrid, 1793.

Muntaner, Ramón. *Crónica*. Translated by J. F. G. Vidal Jové. Madrid, 1970.

Murillo, Fray Diego de. *Fundación milagrosa de la capilla angélica de la Madre de Dios de Pilar y excelencias de Zaragoza*. Barcelona, 1616.

Navarra, Pedro de. *Diálogos para la eternidad del alma*. Tolosa, 1566.

Nebrija, Elio Antonio de. *Gramática de la lengua castellana*. Edited by Antonio Quilis. Madrid, 1992.

———. *Guerra de Granada (De bello granatensis)*. Edited and translated by María Luis Arribas. Madrid, 1990.

———. *Historia de la guerra de Navarra (De bello navarriense)*. Edited by Duque de Alba. Translated by José López de Toro. Madrid, 1953.

Nebrija historiador. Edited and translated by Virginia Bonmatí and Felicidad Álvarez. Lebrija, Seville, 1992.

Nieremberg, Juan Eusebio. *En la corona virtuosa*. Madrid, 1642.

Novoa, Matías de. *Historia de Felipe IV, rey de España*. In *Codoin* 69. Madrid.

———. *Memorias*. In *Codoin* 80. Madrid.

Nuix, Juan. *Reflessione imparziale sopra la humanitá degli spagnoli en la India*. Venice, 1780. Translated into Spanish as *Reflexiones imparciales sobre la humanidad de los españoles en las Indias*. 1782.

Núñes do Lião, Duarte. *Primera parte das chronicas dos reis de Portugal*. Lisbon, 1600.

O'Callaghan, Joseph F., ed. *The Latin Chronicles of the Kings of Castile*. Tempe, AZ, 2002.

Ocampo, Florián de. *Coronica general de España*. 10 vols. Madrid, 1791–1792.

———. *Las cuatro partes enteras de la Crónica de España que mando componer el Serenissimo rey don Alfonso llamado Sabio*. Zamora, 1541.

Padilla, Lorenzo de. *Libro pimero de las antiguedades de España*. Edited by Jose Pellicer de Ossau y Tovar. Valencia, 1669.

Páez de Castro, Juan. "Apuntes históricos del Dr. Páez de Castro." Biblioteca de San Lorenzo del Escorial: Ms. &.III.10.

———. "De las cosas necesarias para escribir la historia." *Ciudad de Dios* 28 (1892): 601–610; 29 (1892): 27–37.

———. "Memorial del Dr. Juan Páez de Castro, dado al rey Phelippe II al principio de su reinado." *RABM* 9 (1883): 165–178.

Palencia, Alonso [Fernández] de. *Crónica de Enrique IV*. Edited by A. Paz y Melia, *BAE*: vols. 257, 258, 167. Madrid, 1973–1975.

———. *Gesta Hispaniensia Ex Annalibus Svorvm Diervum Collecta*. Edited and translated by Brian Tate and Jeremy Lawrance. Madrid, 1998.

Papiers d'état du Cardenal de Granvelle. Edited by Charles Weiss. Paris, 1842.

Pauw, Cornelius de. *Recherches philosophiques sur les Américains, ou Mémoires intéressants pour servir à l'Histoire de l'Espèce Humaine*. London, 1771.

Pedro IV, king of Aragon. *The Chronicle of San Juan de la Peña*. Edited and translated by Lynn H. Nelson. Philadelphia, 1991.

Pellicer de Ossau y Tovar, José. *Anales de la historia de la monarquía de España despus de su perdida*. Edited by Miguel Pellicer de Ossau y Tovar. Madrid, 1681.

———. *Anfiteatro de Felipe el Grande*. Madrid, 1631. Facsimile edition, Cieza (Murcia), 1974.

———. *El Anti-católico de estado y lágrimas de Europa*. Barcelona, 1639.

———. *La Astrea Sáfica*. 2nd ed. Zaragoza, 1641.

———. *Avisos*. Edited by Jean-Claude Chevallier and Lucien Clare. 2 vols. Paris, 2002.

———. *Biblioteca formada de los libros i obras públicas por Joseph Pellicer de Ossau y Tovar*. Valencia, 1671.

———. *Constancia cristiana necessaria en el Válido*. (1638). Valencia, 1998. Microform.

———. *La defensa de España*. Madrid, 1635.

———. *La fama austriaca*. Barcelona, 1641.

———. *La idea del principado de Catalunya*. Antwerp, 1642.

———. *El lirio, hymen nupcial-genealógico, en las reales bodas de los reyes . . . [Don Carlos Segundo, con Doña Maria Luisa de Borbon]*. Madrid, 1680.

———. *Población y lengua primitiva de España*. Valencia, 1672.

———. *Templo de la fama, alcáçar de la fortuna: Dedicado a las acciones de Don Gaspar de Guzmán, Conde Duque de Olivares*. BNE: Ms. 2237, fols. 116–135.

———. *Varios tratados* (1667). BNE: 3/60605.

Pérez, Antonio. *Relaciones y Cartas*. Edited by A. Alvar Ezquerra. Madrid, 1986.

Pérez de Guzmán, Fernán. *Crónica de Juan II*. Edited by Cayetano Rosell, *BAE* 68. Madrid, 1875–1878.

———. *Pen Portraits of Illustrious Castilians*. Translated by Marie Gillette and Loretta Zehngut. Washington, DC, 2003.

Pérez de Oliva, Fernán. *Historia de la inuención de las Yndias.* Edited by José Juan Arrom. Bogotá, 1965.

Philip IV, king of Spain. "Autosemblanza de Felipe IV." In *Cartas de sor María de Ágreda de Jesús y de Felipe IV,* edited by Carlos Seco Serrano, *BAE* 109:231–236. Madrid, 1958.

Porreño, Baltasar. *Dichos y hechos del señor rey don Felipe II el prudente.* Cuenca, 1621. Madrid, 1942.

Pozzo, Casiano del. *El diario de viaje de España del cardenal Francesco Barberini escrito por Casiano del Pozzo.* Edited by A. Anselmi. Aranjuez (Madrid), 2004.

Public Record Office, Great Britain. *Calendar of State Papers and Manuscripts.* Venetian, 1592–1603. Edited by Horatio F. Brown. London, 1897.

Puente, Juan de la. *Tomo primero de la conveniencia de las dos Monarquias Catolicas, la de la iglesia romana y la del Imperio Español, y defensa de la precedencia de los Reyes Católicos de España a todos los reyes del mundo.* Madrid en la Imprenta Real, 1612.

Puente, Pedro de la. *Los soldados en la guardia.* 1657. Edited by Fernando Chavarría Múgica. Madrid, 2006.

Pulgar, Fernando del. *Claros varones de Castilla.* Edited by Robert Brian Tate. Oxford, 1971.

———. *Crónica de los Reyes Católicos.* Edited by Juan Mata Carriazo. Madrid, 1943.

———. *Letras.* Edited by J. Domínguez Bordona. Madrid, 1929. Translated in *Isabel la Católica, Queen of Castile: Critical Essays,* ed. David Boruchoff. London, 2003.

Quevedo, Francisco de. *Obras completas en prosa.* Edited by Alfonso Rey. 3 vols. Madrid, 2003.

Quintilian. *Institutio Oratoria.* Translated by H. E. Butler. Cambridge, MA, 1958–1960.

Raleigh, Walter. *History of the World.* 1614. Edited by C. A. Patrides. London, 1971.

———. *The Letters of Sir Walter Raleigh.* Edited by Agnes Latham and Joyce Youngs. Exeter, 1999.

Ramusio, Gian Battista. *Navigatione e viaggi.* 3 vols. Amsterdam, 1967–1970.

Raynal, Abbé. *L'histoire philosophique et politique des Européens dans les deux indes.* 1st ed. 4 vols. Amsterdam, 1770.

Recopilación de leyes de los reynos de las Indias. Madrid, 1943.

Ribadeneyra, Pedro de. "Carta . . . sobre las causas de la pérdida de la Armada." In *Historias de la Contrareforma,* by Pedro de Ribadeneyra, 1:351–352. Madrid, 1945.

———. *Vida de San Francisco de Borja, que fue duque de Gandía.* Madrid, 1592.

Rioja, Francisco de. *Aristarco o censura de la proclamación católica de los catalanes.* 1640.

———. *Flavii Lucii Dextri Omninodae historiae, quae extant fragmenta, cum Chronico M. Maximi et Helecae ac Braulionis, notis Ruedrici Cari Baeticis illustrata.* Seville, 1627.

Robertson, William. *History of America.* Edinburgh, 1777.

Rodríguez Campomanes, Pedro. *Pedro Rodríguez Campomanes. Epistolario (1778–1802).* Edited by Jerónimo Herrera Navarro. Madrid, 2004.

Rodríguez de Cuenca, Juan. *Sumario de los reyes de Castilla.* Edited by Eugenio de Laguno Amirola. Valencia, 1971.

Román, Fray Jerónimo. *Chronica dela orden de los Ermitaños del glorioso P. Santo Agustín.* Salamanca, 1569.

———. *Repúblicas del Mundo.* Madrid, 1575.

Román de la Higuera, Jerónimo. "Historia eclesiástica de la ciudad imperial de Toledo." 8 vols. BNE: Mss. 1285–1293.

Ruiz de Laguna, Juan. *Compendio historial de los progresos dela ciudad de Placencia en Lombarida, y de los señores que han dominado desde su fundación hasta los tiempos del rey don Phelipe IV de Grande, N.S.* Madrid, 1637.

Saavedra Fajardo, Diego de. *Obras completas.* Madrid, 1946.

Sala, Gaspar. *Proclamación católica.* October, 1640.

Salazar, Pedro de. *Coronica de nuestro invictissimo emperador Carlos quinto.* Seville, 1552.

Salazar y Castro, Luis de. *Advertencias históricas sobre las obras de algunos doctos escritores modernos.* Madrid, 1688.

——. *Biblioteca Genealógico.* ca. 1702.

——. *Carta del maestro de niños a don Gabriel Alvárez de Toledo, primer bibliotecario del rey.* Zaragoza, 1713.

——. "Casas ylustres de España hasta el año 1702." BNE: Ms. 10660.

——. *Catálogo historial genealógico de los señores y condes de la casa y villa de Fernán Núñez, desde la conquista de Córdoba, año de 1236, haste ésto de 1682.* Madrid, 1682.

——. *La crisis ferrerica.* Zaragoza, 1720.

——. *Historia genealógica de la Casa de Lara.* Madrid, 1696.

——. *Historia genealógica de la Casa de Silva.* Madrid, 1685.

——. *Indice de las glorias de la casa Farnese, que consagra a la augusta reyna de las españas, doña Isabel Farnese,* 2 vols. Madrid, 1716. Facsimile edition. Ollobarren (Navarra), 1997.

——. "Memorial sobre la igualdad de los duques pares de Francia con los grandes de España." 1701. BNE: Ms. 13189.

——. "Memorias históricas de los grandes oficiales de la Corona." 1701. BNE: Ms. 9905.

——. *Reflexión histórica sobre los matrimonios de las casa de Austria y Baveria.* Madrid, 1689.

Sandoval, Fray Prudencio de. *Historia de la vida y hechos del emperador Carlos V.* Edited by Carlos Seco Serrano. *BAE* 80–82. Madrid, 1955.

San José, Jerónimo de. *Genio de la Historia (1651).* Edited by Higinio de Santa Teresa. Vitoria, 1957.

Sansovino, Francesco. *Dell' historia universale dell' origine et imperio de Turchi.* Venice, 1561.

Santa Cruz, Alonso de. *Crónica del Emperador Carlos V.* 5 vols. Madrid, 1920.

Sarmiento de Acuña, Diego. *Cinco cartas político-literarias de Diego Sarmiento de Acuña, primer Conde de Gondomar, embajador á la corte de Inglaterra, 1613–1622.* Edited by Pascual de Gayangos. Madrid, 1869.

Sarpi, Paolo. "Del confutar scritture maledíche." In *Opere,* by Paolo Sarpi, edited by Gaetano and Luisa Cozzi, 1170–1180. Milan-Naples, 1969.

Sempere y Guarinos, Juan. *Ensayo de una biblioteca española de los mejores escritores del reynado de Carlos III.* Madrid, 1969.

Sepúlveda, Juan Ginés de. *Del Nuevo Mundo.* Vol. 11 of his *Obras completas.* Edited by Luis Rivera García. Pozoblanco. 2005.

——. *Epistolario.* Vol. 9, parts 1–2, of his *Obras completas.* Edited by Ignacio J. García Pinilla and Julián Solana Pujalte. Pozoblanco, 2007.

———. *Historia de Carlos V.* Vols. 1, 2, and 10 of his *Obras completas.* Edited by F. Rodríguez Pelegrina. Pozoblanco, 1995–2003.

———. *Historia de Felipe II.* Vol. 4 of his *Obras completas.* Edited by B. Pozuelo Calero. Pozoblanco, 1998.

Snouckhaert, Willem. *De republica, vita, moribus, gestis, fama, religione sanctitate, Imperatoris, Caesaris, Augusti, Quinti, Caroli, Maximi, Monarchae libri septem.* Ghent, 1559.

Solís, Antonio de. *Historia de la conquista de Mexico.* 1685. Facsimile reproduction of the 9th ed. Brussels, 1705. Mexico City, 1988.

Solórzano Pereira, Juan de. *De Indiarum jure.* 3 vols. Madrid, 1994–2001.

Sota, Francisco de. *Chronica de los príncipes de Asturias y Cantabria.* Madrid, 1681.

Tamayo de Vargas, Tomás. "Don Thomás Tamaio de Vargas, Chonista del Rei, nuestro señor, deseoso de dar a V.S. motivo para sea benemerito desta Monarchia. . . ." BL: 1322.l.3 (26).

———. *En Defensa de Flavio Lucio Dextro.* Madrid, 1624.

———. *Junta de libros.* Edited by Belen Álvarez García. Madrid, 2007.

———. "Junta de libros: La mayor que España ha visito en su lengua hasta el año de 1624." BNE: Ms. 9752.

———. *Restauración de la ciudad del Salvador, i Bahía de Todos los sanctos en la provincia de Brazil.* Madrid, 1628.

Tarafa, Francesc. *De origine ac rebus gestis Regum Hispaniae.* Antwerp, 1553.

Thou, Jacques-Auguste de. *Historiam sui temporis.* 3 vols. Paris, 1604–1609.

Thucydides. *History of the Peloponnesian War.*

Tomich, Pere. *Histories e conquestes dels reys d'Arago e comtes de Catalunya.* Valencia, 1970.

Torquemada, Fray Juan de. *Primera parte de los veinte i un libros de . . . la Monarquía Indiana.* 1615. Madrid, 1723.

Ulloa, Alfonso de. *Vita dell' invitissimo imperator Carlo V.* Venice, 1560.

Ulloa, Antonio de. *Noticias secretas de América.* London, 1826.

Ulloa, Antonio de, and Jorge Juan. *Relación histórica del viaje hecho de orden de su Majestad a la América Meridional.* Madrid, 1748.

Valdés, Alonso de. *Relación de las nuevas de Italia. . . .* Madrid, 1881.

Valencia, Pedro de. *Academica: Sive deidicio ergaverum.* Edited and translated by José Oroz Retata. Badajoz, 1987.

———. *Obras completas.* Edited by Pedro Morocho Gayo. León, 1993.

Valera, Diego de. *Crónica anónima de Enrique IV de Castilla 1454–1474 (Cronica castelana).* Edited by María Olar Sánches-Parra. 2 vols. Madrid, 1991.

———. *Crónica de los Reyes Católicos.* Edited by Juan de Mata Carriazo. Madrid, 1927.

———. *Memorial de diversas hazañas.* Edited by Juan de Mata Carriazo. Madrid, 1941.

Valla, Lorenzo. *Historia de Fernando de Aragón.* Edited by Santiago López Moreda. Madrid, 2002.

———. *Opera Omnia.* Edited by Eugenio Garin. Torino, 1962.

Vandenesse, Jean. *Journal des voyages du Philippe II.* In *Collections des voyages des souverains des Pays-Bas,* edited by L. P. Gachard. 4 vols. Brussels, 1882.

Vaseus, Johannes. *Chronicon Rerum Memorabilium Hispaniae.* Salamanca, 1552.

Vega, Garcilaso de la. *Royal Commentaries of the Incas.* Translated by Harold V. Livermore. 2 vols. Austin, TX, 1966.

Vega, Hernando de. "Noticia de lo que paso en Africa con Hrdo de Vega." BRME: Ms. U-II-3.

Velázquez de Velasco, Luis José, Marqués de Valdeflores. *Anales de la nación española desde el tiempo de los romanos hasta la entrada as los romanos.* Málaga, 1759.

——. *Colección de los documentos contemporaneos de España desde el tiempo más remoto hasta el año de 1516.* Madrid, 1765.

——. *Ensayo sobre los alphabetos de la letras desconocidas que se encuentran en la más antiguas medallas.* Madrid, 1752.

——. *Informe a la Real Academia de la Historia sobre su viaje a Extremadura entre 1752 y 1753.* Available at www.cervantesvirtual.com/servlet/SirveObras/12715733118055996964 3624/p0000001.htm#I_0_ (accessed 17 March 2008).

Vera y Figueroa, Juan Antonio. "Discurso del Conde de la Roca para el Maestro Fray Basilio de León sobre los fragmentos q escrivió de la vida del Conde de Olivares." BL Add. 18.289, fols. 127–132v.

——. *El Enbajador.* Madrid, 1620, 1947.

——. *Epitome de la vida y hechos del invicto emperador Carlos V.* Madrid, 1622.

——. "Fragmentos históricos de la vida de don Gaspar de Guzmán." 1673. In *Semanario Erudito,* edited by Antonio de Valladares de Sotomayor, 2:145–296. Madrid, 1787.

——. *Manifiesto para que lo sea una verdad indubitable.* Milan, 1644.

——. *Il miglior giglio di Francia.* Lyon, 1640.

——. *El Rey don Pedro Defendido.* Madrid, 1647.

Verzosa, Juan de. *Anales del reinado de Felipe II.* Edited by José María Maestre Maestre. Madrid, 2002.

——. *Epístolas.* Edited by Eduardo del Pino González. Alcañiz, 2006.

"Vida y obra del doctor D. Lorenzo Galíndez de Carvajal del Consejo y Cámara de los señores Reyes Católicos, D Fernando y doña Isabel y doña Juana y don Carlos, su hija y su nieto." In *Codoin,* 20:279–406.

Vitoria, Francisco de. *Poltical Writings.* Edited by Anthony Pagden and Jeremy Lawrence. Cambridge, 1991.

Vives, Juan-Luis. *Obras completas.* Edited and translated by Lorenzo Riber. 2 vols. Madrid, 1947–1948.

Wheare, Deagoreaus. *Order and method of Reading Histories.* London, 1685.

William of Orange. *The Apologie of... against the Proclamation of the King of Spain.* Edited by H. Wansink. Leiden, 1969.

Ximénez de Rada, Rodrigo. *Historia de los hechos de España.* Translated by Juan Fernández Valverde. Madrid, 1989.

Zurita, Jerónimo de. *Correción y enmienda de las crónicas de Pedro I.* Zaragoza, 1683.

Secondary Sources

Abraham, Claude. "L'histoire, c'est moi." *Romanistische Zeitschrift für Literaraturgeschichte.* 13 (1989): 246–258.

Adorno, Rolena. "Censorship and Its Evasion: Jerónimo Román and Bartolomé de las Casas." *Hispania* 75 (October 1992): 812–887.

———. "Sobre censura y su evasión: Un caso transatlántico del siglo XVI." In *Grafías del imaginario: Representaciones culturales es España y Amércia (siglos XVI–XVIII)*, edited by Carlos Alberto González Sánchez and Enriqueta Vila Vilar, 13–52. Mexico City, 2003.

Agnew, Michael. "*Evangelista temporal:* The Limits of Historiographical Discourse in Juan de Flores's Royal Chronicle." In Gwara, *Juan de Flores*, 11–47.

Aldea Vaquero, Quintín. *España y Europa: Correspondencia de Diego Saavedra Fajardo*. Madrid, 1986.

Alfonso Antón, Isabel. "Judicial Rhetoric and Political Legitimation in Medieval León-Castile." in *Building Legitimacy: Political Discourse and Forms of Legitimacy in Medieval Europe*, edited by Isabel Alfonso Antón, Hugh N. Kennedy, and Julip Escalar, 51–87. Leiden, 2004.

Alonso Pérez, Mariano. "Vida y obra del doctor Francisco Ramos del Manzano, eximio romanista de la ínclita Universidad de Salamanca." In *Estudios en homenaje al profesor Juan Iglesias*, edited by Jaime Roset Esteve, 1:21–47. Salamanca, 1988.

Alonso Romero, María Paz. "Ius comune y derecho patrio en la Universidad de Salamanca durante los siglos modernos: Trayectoria docente y métodos de enseñanza de Antonio Pichardo Vinuesa, Juan Solórzano Pereira, Francisco Ramos del Manzano, y José Fernández de Retes." In *El decrecho y los juristas en Salamanca (siglos XVI–XX)*, edited by Eugenia Torijano Pérez, Salustiano de Dios, and Javier Miguel-Motta, 43–148. Salamanca, 2004.

Alvar Ezquerra, Alfredo. "Sobre la historiografía castellana." *Torre de los Lujanes* 32 (1996): 89–106.

Amelang, James. *Flight of Icarus: Artisan Autobiography in Early Modern Europe*. Stanford, CA, 1998.

Anderson, Benedict. *Imagined Communities: Reflections on the Origin and Spread of Nationalism*. New York, 1991.

Andrés, Gregorio de. "La bibliofilia del marqués de Mondéjar y su biblioteca manuscrita." In *Primeras Jornadas de Bibliografía*, 583–602. Madrid, 1977.

———. "Biblioteca selecta del Conde-Duque D. Gaspar de Guzmán." *Cuadernos para investigación de la literature hispánica* 21 (1996): 115–142.

———. "Un erudito y bibliofilo español olvidado: Juan Lucás Cortés (1624–1701)." *RABM* 81 (1978): 3–72.

———. "Historia de la biblioteca del Conde-Duque de Olivares y descripción de sus códices." *Cuadernos bibliográficos* 28 (1972): 131–142; 30 (1973): 5–73.

———. "31 Cartas inéditas de Juan Páez de Castro, cronista de Carlos V." *BRAH* 168 (1971): 516–571.

Antolín, Fray Guillermo. "Inventario de los papeles del cronista Esteban de Garibay." *Boletín de la Real Academia de la Historia* 89 (1926): 15–26.

Appleby, Joyce, Lynn Hunt, and Margaret Jacob. *Telling the Truth about History*. New York, 1994.

Aranda Pérez, Francisco José. "'*Autobiografías urbanas*': Historias, mitomanía y falsificación en el mundo urbano hispánico de la Edad Moderna." In *El poder en Europa y América: Mitos, tópicos, y realidades,* edited by Ernesto García Fernández, 141–168. Bilbao, 2001.

Arco y Garay, Ricardo. *La erudución española en el siglo XVII.* Madrid, 1950.

Arocena, Luis A. *Antonio de Solís, cronista indiano.* Buenos Aires, 1963.

Arróniz, Othón. "Alfonso de Ulloa: Servidor de Don Juan Hurtado de Mendoza." *Bulletin Hispanique* 70 (1968): 437–457.

Arzipe, Victor. "Don Gaspar Ibáñez de Segovia, marqués de Mondéjar, 'Rey y Príncipe de la Erudición de España': Un novator de la segunda mitad del siglo xvii." In *Estudios de filología y retórica en homenaje a Luisa López Grigera,* 31–43. Bilbao, 2000.

Assman, Jan. *The Mind of Egypt: History and Meaning in the Time of the Pharaohs.* Translated by Andrew Jenkins. New York, 2002.

Astraín, Antonio. *Historia de la Companía de Jesús en la asistencia de España.* 6 vols. Madrid, 1602–1620.

Avalle-Arce, Juan Bautista. *El Cronista Pedro de Escavias: Una vida del siglo XV.* Chapel Hill, NC, 1972.

Bahrani, Zainab. "Assault and Abduction: The Fate of the Royal Image in the Ancient Near East." *Art History* 18 (1995): 363–382.

Barrios Aguilera, Manuel, and Mercedes García-Arenal, eds. *Los plomos de Sacramonte.* Madrid, 2006.

Bas Martín, Nicolás. *El cosmógrafo e historiador Juan Bautista Muñoz.* Valencia, 2002.

———. *Juan Bautista Muñoz (1745–1799) y la fundación del Archivo General de las Indias.* Valencia, 2000.

Bataillon, Marcel. "Hernán Cortés, autor prohibido." In *Libro jubilar de Alfonso Reyes.* Mexico City, 1959.

Baudot, Georges. *Utopia and History in Mexico: The First Chronicles of Mexican Civilization (1520–1569).* Translated by Bernard R. Ortiz de Montellano. Boulder, CO, 1995.

Bautista Pérez, Manual, and T. Hampe Martínez. *Bibliotecas privadas en el mundo colonial: La difusión de los libros e ideas en el virreinato del Perú, siglos xvi–xvii.* Frankfurt am Main; Madrid, 1996.

Bazán, Iñaki. "La historiografía medieval de Vizcaya y su influencia en la obra de Garibay." In *El historiador Esteban de Garibay,* edited by Iñaki Bazán, 75–122. Donostia, 2001.

Beasley, William G., and Edwin G. Pulleyblank, eds. *Historians of China and Japan.* Oxford, 1961.

Bell, David A. *The Cult of the Nation in France: Inventing Nationalism, 1680–1800.* Cambridge, MA, 2001.

Belligni, Eleonora. *Lo scacco della prudenza: Precettistica politica ed esperienza storica en Virgilio Malvezzi.* Firenze, 1999.

Bermejo Cabrero, José Luis. "Origines del oficio de cronista real." *Hispania* 40 (1980): 396–409.

Berthe, Jean-Pierre. "Juan López de Velasco (ca. 1530–1598)." *Relaciones* 75 (1998): 143–172.

Bireley, Robert. *The Counter Reformation Prince: Anti-Machiavellianism or Catholic Statecraft in Early Modern Europe.* Chapel Hill, NC, 1990.

Blanc, Jan. "Hugo Grotius, historiographe des Batavaes au XVIIe siècle." In Grell, *Les historiographes en Europe de la fin du Moyen Age à la Révolution*, 297–313.
Bochi, Patricia A. "Death by Drama: The Ritual of Damnatio Memoriae in Ancient Egypt." *Götinger Miszellen* 171 (1999): 73–86.
Boruchoff, David A. "Historiography with License: Isabel, the Catholic Monarch, and the Kingdom of Gold." In *Isabel la Católica, Queen of Castile: Critical Essays*, edited by David A. Boruchoff. New York, 2003.
Botella Ordiñas, Eva. "Monarquía de España: Discurso teológico, 1590–1685." Ph.D. diss, Universidad Autónoma de Madrid, 2006.
———. "Los novatores y el origen de España: El vocabulario hispano de probabilidad y la renovación del método histórico en tiempos de Carlos II." *Obradoiro de Historia* (Santiago de Compostela) 14 (2005): 39–64.
Bouwsma, William J. *The Waning of the Renaissance, 1550–1640*. New Haven, CT, 2000.
Bouza Álvarez, Fernando J. *Del escribano a la biblioteca: La civilización escrita europea en la alta edad moderna (siglos XV–XVII)*. Madrid, 1992.
———. "Gramática de la crisis: Una nota sobre la historiografía del 1640 hispánico entre 1940 y 1990." *Cuadernos de historia moderna* 11 (1991): 223–246.
———. "Guardar papeles—y quemarlos—en tiempos de Felipe II: La documentación de Juan de Zúñiga: Un capítulo para la historia del Fondo Altamira (I)." *Reales sitios* 23 (1996).
———. *El libro y el cetro: La biblioteca de Felipe IV en la torre alta del alcázar de Madrid*. Salamanca, 2005.
———. "La majestad de Felipe II: La construcción del mito real." In *La corte de Felipe II*, edited by José Martínez Millán, 37–72. Madrid, 1994.
———. "Monarchie en lettres d'imprimerie: Typographie et propagande au temps de Philippe II." *Revue d'histoire moderne et contemporaine* 41 (April–June 1994): 206–220.
———. *Papeles y opinión: Políticas de publicación en el siglo de oro*. Madrid, 2008.
———. "Para no olvidar y para hacerlo: La conservación de la memoria a comienzos de la edad moderna." In *A história: Entre memoria e invenção*, edited by Pedro Cardim. Lisbon, 1998.
———. *Portugal no tempo dos Filipes: Política, cultura, representações (1580–1668)*. Lisbon, 2000.
———. "El primer lector de Cervantes." *ABC.es*, 19 April 2008, no. 846.
Boyd, Carolyn P. *Historia Patria: Politics, History, and National Identity in Spain, 1875–1975*. Princeton, NJ, 1997.
Brandi, Karl. *The Emperor Charles V*. London, 1939.
Braun, Harald E. "Conscience, Counsel, and Theocracy at the Spanish Habsburg Court." In *Contexts of Conscience in Early Modern Europe, 1500–1700*, edited by Edward Vallance and Harald Braun, 56–66. Houndsmill, 2004.
———. *Juan de Mariana and Early Modern Political Thought*. Aldershot, 2007.
Braxton Ross, W., Jr. "Giovani Colonna: Historian of Avignon." *Speculum* 45 (October 1970): 533–563.
Brook, Timothy. "Censorship in Eighteenth-Century China: A View from the Book Trade." *Canadian Journal of History* 22 (August 1988): 177–198.

Bryce, Trevor. *The Kingdom of the Hittites*. Oxford, 2005.
Bulletta, Silvia. *Virgilio Malvezzi e la storiografia classica*. Milan, 1995.
Burke, Peter. *The Fabrication of Louis XIV*. New Haven, CT, 1992.
———. "Presenting and Representing Charles V." In *Charles V 1500–1558 and His Time*, edited by Hugo Soly. Antwerp, 1999.
Bury, J. B. *The Ancient Greek Historians*. London, 1909.
Bustamante, Jesús. "El conocimiento como necesidad de estado: Las encuestas oficiales sobre Nueva España durante el reinado de Carlos V." *Revista de Indias* 60 (2000): 34–55.
Bustos Guadaño, María del Mar de. "La crónica del Ocampo y la tradición Alfonsí en el siglo XVI." In Fernández-Ordoñez, *Alfonso X el Sabio y las crónicas de España*, 187–217.
Cabañas Agrela, Miguel, ed. *Bernardino de Mendoza, un escritor soldado al servicio de la monarquía católica (1540–1604)*. Guadalajara, 2001.
Callard, Caroline. *Le prince et la république: Histoire, pouvoir et société dans la Florence des Médicis au XVIIème siècle*. Paris, 2007.
Cañizares-Esguerra, Jorge. *How to Write the History of the New World*. Stanford, CA, 1998.
Carbia, Rómulo. *La crónica oficial de las Indias Occidentales*. Buenos Aires, 1940.
Cardenas y Vicent, Vicente de. *Carlos de Habsburgo en Yuste*. Madrid, 1984.
Carman, Glen. "The Voices of the Conquerer in López de Gómara's *Historia de la Conquista de México*." *Journal of Hispanic Philology* 16 (1992): 223–236.
Caro Baroja, Julio. *Las falsificaciones de la historia*. Barcelona, 1992.
Carrasco Manchado, Ana Isabel. "Discurso político y propaganda en la corte de los Reyes Católicos: Resultados de una primera investigación (1474–1482)." *En la España medieval* 25 (2002): 299–379.
Carrillo Castillo, Jesús María. "The *Historia general y natural de las Indias* by Gonzalo Fernández de Oviedo." *Huntington Library Quarterly* 65 (2002): 321–344.
———. *Naturaleza e imperio: La representación de la naturaleza en la 'Historia general y natural de las Indias' de Gonzalo Fernández de Oviedo*. Madrid, 2004.
Castañeda y Alcocer, Vicente. *La Real Academia de la Historia*. Madrid, 1930.
Castro, M. de. "Las ideas políticas y la formación del príncipe en el 'De preconiis Hispanie' de Fr. Juan Gil de Zamora." *Hispania* (Madrid) 22 (1962): 507–541.
Castro Diaz, Antonio. *Los "Coloquios" de Pedro Mexía*. Sevilla, 1977.
Cat, E. *Essai sur la vie et les ouvrages du chroniquer Gonzalo de Ayora*. Paris, 1890.
Catalan, Diego. *De la silva textual al taller historiográfica Alfonsí*. Madrid, 1997.
Checa Cremades, Fernando. *Carlos V y la imagen del héroe en el Renacimiento*. Madrid, 1987.
———. *Felipe II: Mécenas de las artes*. Madrid, 1993.
Church, William F. *Richelieu and Reason of State*. Princeton, NJ, 1973.
Cid, Jesús-Antonio. "Pleitos de historiadores y confrontaciones literarias: Antonio de Solís contra Jerónimo Mascareñas (1662–1663)." In *Homenaje a Elena Càtena*, 137–162, Madrid, 2001.
Cirot, Georges. *Mariana historien*. Bordeaux, 1904.
———. "Quelques lettres de Mariana et nouveaux documents sur son procès." *Bulletin Hispanique* 19 (1917): 1–25.
Civil, Pierre. "Culture et histoire: Galeries de portraits et 'hommes illustres' dans l'Espagne

de la deuxième moitié du XVIe siècle." *Mélanges de la Casa de Velázquez* 26, no. 2 (1990): 5–32.

———. "Vies d'hommes illustres et modèle politique: Les discourses biographiques de Juan Pablo Mártir Rizo (1625–1633)." In *Littérature et politique en Espagne aux siècles d'or,* edited by Jean-Pierre Etienvre, 363–375. Paris, 1998.

Clare, Lucien. "L'Espagne au quotidien dans les *Avisos* de José Pellicer: Littérature, histoire ou politique." In *Littérature et politique en Espagne aux siècles d'or,* edited by Jean-Pierre Etienvre, 179–193. Paris, 1998.

Clavería, Carlos. *Le Chevalier Délibéré de Olivier de la Marche y sus versiones españolas del siglo XVI.* Zaragoza, 1950.

Cochrane, Eric. *Historians and Historiography in the Italian Renaissance.* Chicago, 1981.

Cogswell, Thomas. "The Politics of Propaganda: Charles I and the People in the 1620s." *Journal of British Studies* 29 (July 1990): 187–215.

Colomer, José Luis. "*La Carta del Desprezio de la Dignidad:* Una epístola consolatoria inédita de Virgilio Malvezzi al Conde-Duque de Olivares." In *Littérature et politique en Espagne aux siècles d'or,* edited by Jean-Pierre Etienvre, 375–391. Paris, 1998.

———. "El Conde de la Roca y el marqués Virgilio Malvezzi: Dos diplomáticos panegiristas del conde duque de Olivares." In *'Por discreto y por amigo': Mélanges offerts à Jean Canavaggio,* 513–534. Madrid, 2005.

———. "'Esplicar los grandes hechos de vuestra majestad': Virgilio Malvezzi historien de Phelippe IV." In *Repubblica e virtù: Piensiero politico e Monarchia Cattolica fra XVI e XVII secolo,* 45–76. Rome, 1995.

Coroleu, Alejandro. "Humanismo en España." In *Introducción al humanismo renacentista,* edited by Jill Kraye and Carlos Clavería, 295–330. Cambridge, 1998.

Cortesão, Armando. *Portugaliae Monumenta Cartographica.* 6 vols. Lisbon, 1960-.

Costes, René. "Pedro Mexía, Chroniste de Charles-Quint." *Bulletin Hispanique* 22 (1920): 1–36, 256–266.

Courcelles, Dominique. *Écrire l'histoire: Écrire des histoires dans le monde hispanique.* Paris, 2008.

Cruz, Anne J. "Gender and Class as Challenges for Feminist Biographies in Early Modern Spain." Accessible at www.gc.maricopa.edu/laberinto/2002/cruz.htm.

Cuart Moner, Baltasar. "Estudio histórico." In *Obras completas,* by Juan Ginés de Sepúlveda, edited by E. Rodríguez Peregrina. Pozoblanco, 1995.

———. "La historiografía áulica en la primera mitad del siglo xvi: Los cronistas del emperador." In *Antonio de Nebrija: Edad Media y Renacimiento,* edited by Carmen Codoñer and J. A. González Iglesias, 39–58. Salamanca, 1994.

———. "Juan Ginés de Sepúlveda, cronista del Emperador." In *Carlos V y la quiebra del humanisimo político en Europa,* edited by José Martínez Millán, 3:342–367. Madrid, 2001.

Cuesta Domingo, Mariano. *Antonio de Herrera y su obra.* Segovia, 1998.

Cummins, Tom. "De Bry and Herrera: 'Aguas Negras' or the Hundred Years War over an Image of America." In *XVII Coloquio Internacional de Historia del arte: Arte, historia e identidad en America: Visiones Comparativas,* 1:17–31. Mexico City, 1994.

Danvila y Collado, Manuel. "Nuevos datos para escribir la historia de las Cortes de Castilla en el reinado de Felipe IV." *BRAH* 15 (1889): 385–433, 497–542.

De la Campa della Gavela, Mariano, and Lola Montero Reguera. "El mundo del libro desde las escrituras públicas notariales: Baltasar Gutiérrez." *Edad de Oro* 17 (1998): 9–17.
Detienne, Marcial. *Les maîtres de la verité dans les grèc archaique.* Paris, 1967.
Deyermond, Alan, ed. *Historical Literature in Medieval Iberia.* London, 1996.
Díaz Esteban, Fernando. "Una mujer orientalista del siglo XVII: la duquesa de Aveiro." *BRAH* 204 (2007): 171–198.
Díaz Gito, Manuel Antonio. "Un epigrama y una carta del humanista Calvete de Estrella." In *Humanismo y pervivencia del mundo clásico: Homenaje al Profesor Luis Gil,* 2:1335–1342. Cádiz, 1997.
Ditchfield, Simon. *Liturgy, Sanctity, and History in Tridentine Italy.* Cambridge, 1995.
Domínguez Ortiz, Antonio. "La censura de obras históricas en el siglo XVII español." *Chronica nova* 9 (1991): 113–121.
———. "Un testimonio de protesta social a fines del reinado de Felipe II." In *Homenaje a Pedro Saínz Rodríguez,* 3:219–226. Madrid, 1986.
Dooley, Brandon, and Sabrina Baron, eds. *The Politics of Information in Early Modern Europe.* London, 2001.
Dubuis, M. "Les bénédictines d'Espagne devant les fausses chroniques." In *Practiques et concepts de l'histoire en Europe XVIe–XVIIIe siècles,* edited by Chantal Grell and Jean-Michel Dufays, 97–111. Paris, 1990.
Duccini, Helene. *Faire voire, faire croire: L'opinion publique sous Louis III.* Paris, 2003.
Dyer, N. J. "Alfonsine Historiography: The Literary Narrative." In *Emperor of Culture: Alfonso X the Learned of Castile and His Thirteenth-Century Renaissance,* edited by R. T. Burns, 141–158. Philadelphia, 1990.
Echevarria Bacigalupe, M. A. *Alberto Struzzi: Un precursor barroco del capitalismo laboral.* Leuven, 1995.
Edouard, Sylvène. "Enquête hagiographique et mythification historique: Le 'saint voyage' d'Ambrosio de Morales (1572)." *Melanges de la Casa de Velazquez* 33, no. 2 (2003): 33–60.
Elliott, John H. *The Count-Duke of Olivares: The Statesman in an Age of Decline.* New Haven, CT, 1986.
———. "A Europe of Composite Monarchies." *Past and Present* 137 (1992): 48–71.
———. "Power and Propaganda in the Spain of Philip IV." In *Rites of Power: Symbolism, Ritual, and Politics since the Middle Ages,* edited by Sean Wilentz, 146–173. Philadelphia, 1985.
———. "Quevedo and the Count-Duke of Olivares." In *Spain and Its World,* by John H. Elliott, 189–209. New Haven, CT, 1989.
Elliott, John H., and Jonathan Brown. *A Palace for a King.* New Haven, CT, 2005.
Elliott, John H., and José F. de la Peña. *Memoriales y cartas del Conde Duque de Olivares.* 2 vols. Madrid, 1981.
Elliot van Liere, Katherine. "The Missionary and the Moorslayer: James the Apostle in Spanish Historiography from Isidore of Seville to Ambrosio de Morales." *Viator* 37 (2006): 519–543.
———. "'Shared Studies Foster Friendship': Humanism and History in Spain." In *The Renaissance World,* edited by John Jeffries Martin, 242–261. New York, 2007.

Esperabé Arteaga, Enrique. *Historia de la universidad de Salamanca*. 2 vols. Salamanca, 1917.

Estepa, Carlos. "The Strengthening of Royal Power in Castile under Alfonso XI." In *Building Legitimacy: Political Discourse and Forms of Legitimacy in Medieval Europe*, edited by Isabel Alfonso Antón, Hugh N. Kennedy, and Julip Escalar, 179–222. Leiden, 2004.

Ettinghausen, Henry. "Politics and the Press in Spain." In Dooley and Baron, *The Politics of Information in Early Modern Europe*, 199–215.

Fenster, Thelma, and Vacvid Lors Smail, eds. *Fama: The Politics of Talk and Reputation in Medieval Europe*. Ithaca, NY, 2003.

Fernández Albadalejo, Pablo. *Fragmentos de monarquía: Trabajos de historia política*. Madrid, 1992.

———. *Materia de España: Cultura política e identitad en la España moderna*. Madrid, 2007.

Fernández Álvarez, Manuel. "Las 'memorias' de Carlos V." *Hispania* 18 (1958): 690–718.

Fernández-Daza Álvarez, Carmen. *El primer conde de la Roca*. Mérida, 1995.

Fernández Duro, Cesare. "Don Juan Bautista Muñoz: Censura por la Aacademia de su 'Historia del Nuevo Mundo.'" *BRAH* 42 (1903): 5–59.

Fernández-Ordoñez, Inés, ed. *Alfonso X el Sabio y las crónicas de España*. Valladolid, 2000.

Feros, Antonio. *Kingship and Favoritism in the Spain of Philip III, 1598–1621*. Cambridge, 2000.

Flood, Finnbarr Barry. "Between Cult and Culture: Bamiyan, Islamic Iconoclasm, and the Museum." *Art Bulletin* 84 (December 2002): 641–659.

Flowers, Harriet. *The Art of Forgetting: Disgrace and Oblivion in Roman Political Culture*. Chapel Hill, NC, 2006.

Foronda, François. "Le prince, le palais et la ville: Ségovie ou le visage du tyrant dans la Castille du XVe siècle." *Revue historique* 603 (2003): 521–541.

Fraker, Charles F. *The Shape of History: Studies in the Historiography of Alfonso el Sabio*. Ann Arbor, MI, 1991.

Franklin, Julian. *Jean Bodin and the Sixteenth-Century Revolution in the Methodology of Law and History*. New York, 1963.

Freide, Juan. "La censura española del siglo XVI y los libros de la historia de América." *Revista de historia de América* 47 (1959): 45–94.

Gachard, Louis-Prosper. *La bibliothèque nationale de Paris*. Brussels, 1875.

———. *Retraite et mort de Charles-Quint au monastère de Yuste: Lettres inédites*. Brussels, 1854.

García Carcel, Ricardo, ed. *La construcción de las historias de España*. Madrid, 2004.

———. *La leyenda negra: Historia y opinión*. Madrid, 1992.

García Fuentes, José María. "Bernabé de Busto, cronista de Carlos V." In *Carlos V: Europeísmo y Universalidad*, edited by J. L. Castellano Castellano and F. Sánchez-Montes González, 1:177–194. Madrid, 2001.

García Hernán, Enrique. *Consejero de ambos mundos: Vida y obra de Juan de Solórzano Pereira (1575–1655)*. Madrid, 2007.

———. "Construcción de las historias de España en los siglos XVII y XVIII." In García Carcel, *La construcción de las historias de España*, 127–193.

———. "La iglesia de Santiago de los Españoles en Roma: Trayectoria de una institución." *Anthologica annua* 42 (1995): 307–314.

García López, Aurelio. "Sobre la historiografia en tiempos de Felipe II: La vida y obra de Luis Cabrera de Córdoba." In Martínez Millán, *Felipe II (1527–1598)*, 4:217–234.

García Oro, José, and María José Portela Silva. "Felipe III y sus cronistas, Candidaturas y méritos." In *Universitas: Homenaje a Antonio Eiras Roel*, edited by C. Fernández Cortizo, D. L. González Lopo, and E. Martínez Rodríguez, 1:255–279. Santiago de Compostela, 2002.

———. *La monarquía y los libros*. Alcalá de Henares, 1999.

Gascón Pérez, Jesús. *Aragón en la monarquía de Felipe II*. 2 vols. Zaragoza, 2007.

———. *Bibliografía crítica de la rebelión aragonesa de 1591*. Zaragoza, 1995.

Gerbi, Antonello. *The Dispute of the New World: The History of a Polemic, 1750–1900*. Translated by Jeremy Meyle. Pittsburgh, 1973.

Gil Pujol, Xavier. "Aragonese Constitutionalism and Habsburg Rule: The Varying Meanings of Liberty." in *Spain, Europe, and the Atlantic World*, edited by Richard L. Kagan and Geoffrey Parker, 160–187. Cambridge, 1995.

———. "Las fuerzas del rey: La generación que leyó a Botero." In *Le forze del principe*, edited by Mario Rizzo, José Javier Ruiz Ibañez, and Gaetano Sabatini, 2:969–1022. Murcia, 2004.

Gimeno Pascual, Helena. *Historia de la investigación epigráfica en España en los siglos XVI y XVII a la luz del recuperado manuscrito del Conde de Guimerá*. Zaragoza, 1997.

Godoy Alcántara, José. *Historia crítica de los falsos cronicones*. Madrid, 1868.

Gómez Canseco, Luis. *El humanismo despues de 1600: Pedro de Valencia*. Seville, 1993.

Gómez Redondo, Fernando. "La construcción del modelo de la crónica real." In Fernández-Ordoñez, *Alfonso X el Sabio y las cronicas de España*, 133–158.

———. "De la crónica general a la real." In *La historia alfonsí: El modelo y sus destinos (siglos XIII–XV)*, 95–123. Madrid, 2000.

———. *Historia de la prosa medieval castellana*. Vol. 2. Madrid, 1999.

———. "Historiografía medieval: Constantes evolutivas de un género." *Anuario de estudios medievales* 19 (1989): 3–15.

González-Casanoves, Robert J. *Imperial Histories from Alfonso X to Inca Garcilasso*. Potomac, MD, 1997.

González de San Segundo, Miguel Angel. "Juan Lucás Cortés (1624–1701): Notas sobre su origen familiar y actividad profesional." *Anuario de historia del derecho español* 71 (2001): 575–584.

González Jiménez, Manuel. *Alfonso X*. Madrid, 1993.

González Palencia, Ángel. *Don Luis de Zúñiga y Avila*. Madrid, 1932.

———. "Polémica entre Pedro Mantuano y Tomás Tamayo de Vargas, con motivo de la 'Historia' del Padre Mariana." *BRAH* 84 (1924): 331–351.

González Sánchez, Carlos Alberto. *Los mundos del libro*. Seville, 2001.

Gonzalo Sánchez-Molero, José Luis. *El aprendizaje cortesano de Felipe II, 1527–1546*. Madrid, 1999.

———. *El César y los libros: un viaje a través de las lecturas del Emperador desde Gante a Yuste*. Cáceres, 2009.

———. *El erasmismo y la educación de Felipe II (1527–1557)*. Madrid, 2003.

Grafton, Anthony. *Defenders of the Text: The Traditions of Scholarship in an Age of Science, 1450–1800*. Cambridge, MA, 1991.

———. *What Was History? The Art of History in Early Modern Europe*. Cambridge, 2007.
Grell, Chantalle. *L'histoire entre érudition et philosophie: Etude sur la conaissance historique à l'âge des Lumiéres*. Paris, 1993.
———, ed. *Les historiographes en Europe de la fin du Moyen Age à la Révolution*. Paris, 2006.
Grendler, Paul. "Francesco Sansovino and Italian Popular History." *Studies in the Renaissance* 16 (1969): 139–180.
Guenée, Bernard. *Histoire et culture historique dans l'occident médiéval*. Paris, 1980.
———. *Politique et histoire au Moyen Age*. Paris, 1981.
Gwara, Joseph J. "The Identity of Juan de Flores: The Evidence of the *Crónica Incompleta* de los Reyes Católicos." *Journal of Hispanic Philology* 11 (1987): 104–129.
———, ed. *Juan de Flores: Four Studies*. Papers of the Medieval Hispanic Research Seminar, 49. London, 2005.
Habermas, Jürgen. *The Structural Transformation of the Public Sphere*. Cambridge, MA, 1989. Originally published as *Strukturwandel der Offentlichkeit* (Neuwied, 1962).
Haebler, Konrad. *Bibliografia ibérica del siglo XV*. Leipzig, 1903.
Halbwachs, Maurice. *On Collective Memory*. Translated by Lewis A. Coser. Chicago, 1992.
Hampe Martínez, T. *Bibliotecas privadas en el mundo colonial: La difusion de los libros e ideas en el virreinato del Perú, siglos XVI–XVII*. Frankfurt am Main; Madrid, 1996.
Hanke, Lewis. *Spanish Struggle for Justice in the Conquest of America*. Philadelphia, 1949.
Harlow, V. T. *Raleigh's Last Voyage*. London, 1932.
Harris, A. Katie. *From Muslim to Christian Granada: Inventing a City's Past in Early Modern Spain*. Baltimore, MD, 2007.
Hastings, Adrian. *The Construction of Nationality*. Cambridge, 1997.
Hay, Denys. "The Historiographers Royal in England and Scotland." *Scottish Historical Review* 30 (1951): 15–29.
Headley, John M. "The Habsburg World Empire and the Revival of Gihibellinism." In *Theories of Empire, 1450–1800*, edited by David Armitage, 45–79. Ashgate, 1998.
———. "Rhetoric and Reality: Messianic, Humanist, and Civilian Themes in the Imperial Ethos of Gattinara." In *Prophetic Rome in the High Renaissance Period*, edited by Marjorie Reeves, 241–269. Oxford, 1992.
Hernández González, M. I. *El taller historiográfico: Cartas de relación de la conquista de Oran (1509) y textos afines*. London, 1997.
Hiatt, Alfred. *The Making of Medieval Forgeries*. London, 2004.
Hillgarth, J. N. "Spanish Historiography and Iberian Reality." *History and Theory* 24 (February 1985): 23–43.
Historia de la historiografía española. Edited by José Andrés-Gallego. Madrid, 1999.
Hoffman-Strock, Martha K. "'Carved on Rings and Painted in Pictures': The Education and Formation of the Spanish Royal Family, 1601–1634." Ph.D. diss., Yale University, 1996.
Horn, Hendrik J. *Jan Cornelisz Vermeyen, Painter of Charles V and His Conquest of Tunis: Paintings, Etchings, Drawings, Cartoons, and Tapestries*. Doornspijk, 1989.
Huppert, George. *The Idea of Perfect History: Historical Erudition and Historical Philosophy in Renaissance France*. Urbana, IL, 1970.
Ianziti, Gary. "Bruni on Writing History." *Renaissance Quarterly* 51 (1998): 367–391.

———. *Humanistic Historiography under the Sforzas: Politics and Propaganda in Fifteenth-Century Milan*. Oxford, 1988.
Imágenes históricos de Felipe II. Edited by Alfredo Alvar Esquerra. Madrid, 1999.
Jameson, A. K. "Lope de Vega's *La Dragontea:* History and Literary Sources." *Hispanic Review* 6 (1936): 104–119.
Johannesson, Kurt. "The Renaissance of the Goths in Sixteenth-Century Sweden." In *Johannes and Olaus Magnus as Politicians and Historians*, edited by J. Larson. Berkeley, CA, 1991.
Johnston, Kevin. "Broken Fingers: Classic Maya Scribe Capture and Polity Consolidation." *Antiquity* 75, no. 288 (2001): 373–378.
Jones, Joseph R. "Fragments of Antonio de Guevara's Lost Chronicle." *Studies in Philology* 63 (1966): 30–50.
Kagan, Richard L. "*Arcana Imperii:* Mapas, Sabiduría y Poder a la corte de Felipe IV." In *El atlas del rey planeta*, edited by Fernando Marías and Felipe Pereda, 49–70. Madrid, 2002.
———. "Clio and the Crown: Writing History in Habsburg Spain." In *Spain, Europe, and the Atlantic World*, edited by Richard L. Kagan and Geoffrey Parker. Cambridge, 1995.
———. "The Emperor and His Chroniclers." In *Carolus Imperator*, edited by Pedro Navascués Palacio. Madrid, 1999.
———. "Felipe II: El hombre y la imagen." In *Felipe II y el arte de su tiempo*, 457–474. Madrid, 1998.
———. "Imágenes y política en la corte de Felipe IV: Nuevas perspectivas sobre el Salón de Reinos." In *La historia imaginada: Construcciones visuales del pasado en la edad moderna*, edited by Joan Lluis Palos and Diana Carrió-Invernizzi, 101–119. Madrid, 2008.
———. *Lucrecia's Dreams: Politics and Prophecy in Sixteenth-Century Spain*. Berkeley, CA, 1990.
———. "Philip II, History, and the Cronistas del Rey." In *Philippus II Rex*, edited by Pedro Navascués Palacio, 19–29. Madrid, 1998.
———. "Philip II and the Art of the Cityscape." In *Art and History*, edited by Robert I. Rotberg and Theodore K. Rabb, 115–136. Cambridge, 1988.
———. *El rey recatado: Felipe II, la historia, y los cronistas del rey*. Valladolid, 2004.
———, ed. *Spanish Cities of the Golden Age: The Views of Anton van den Wyngaerde*. Berkeley, CA, 1989.
———. *Urban Images of the Hispanic World, 1493–1793*. New Haven, CT, 2000.
Kamen, Henry. *Philip of Spain*. London, 1997.
Kantorowicz, Ernst H. *The King's Two Bodies: A Study in Medieval Political Theology*. Princeton, NJ, 1957.
Kelley, Donald R. *The Beginning of Ideology: Consciousness and Society in the French Reformation*. Cambridge, 1981.
———. "Johann Sleidan and the Origins of History as a Profession." *Journal of Modern History* 52 (December 1980): 573–598.
Kendrick. T. D. *Saint James in Spain*. London, 1960.
Kidd, Colin. *British Identities before Nationalism*. Cambridge, 1999.

Kinser, Samuel. *The Historical Works of Jacques-Auguste De Thou*. The Hague, 1966.
Klaits, Joseph. *Printed Propaganda under Louis XIV: Absolute Monarchy and Public Opinion*. Princeton, NJ, 1976.
Kusche, Maria. *Retratos y retratadores: Alonso Sánchez Coello y sus competidores*. . . . Madrid, 2003.
Lazure, Guy. "Possessing the Sacred: Monarchy and Identity in Philip II's Relic Collection at the Escorial." *Renaissance Quarterly* 60 (2007): 58–93.
———. "To Dare Fame: Constructing a Cultural Elite in Sixteenth-Century Seville." Ph.D. diss., Johns Hopkins University, 2003.
Levillier, Roberto. *Francisco de Toledo*. Buenos Aires, 1935.
Levin, Michael. *Agents of Empire: Spanish Ambassadors in Sixteenth-Century Italy*. Ithaca, NY, 2005.
Levy, J. *Tudor Historical Thought*. San Marino, CA, 1967.
Lewy, Gunter. *Constitutionalism and Statecraft during the Golden Age of Spain: A Study of the Political Philosophy of Juan de Mariana*. Geneva, 1960.
Lida de Malkiel, Maria Rosa. *La idea de la fama en la edad media castellana*. Mexico City, 1948.
Linehan, Peter J. *History and Historians of Medieval Spain*. Oxford, 1993.
López de Toro, José. "Los 'anales' de Juan Verzosa." *BRAH* 150 (1950): 91–122.
———. *Epístolas de Juan Verzosa*. Madrid, 1945.
López Piñero, José María. *El Códice Pomar (ca. 1590): El interés de Felipe II por la historia natural y la expedición de Hernández a América*. Valencia. 1991.
Losada, Ángel. *Juan Ginés de Sepúlveda a través de su epistolario y nuevos documentos*. Madrid, 1973.
Lowenthal, David. *The Past Is a Foreign Country*. Cambridge, 1985.
"Lucas de Tuy: Chroniquer, hagiographe, théologian." In *Cahiers de Linguistique et Civilisation Hispaniques Médiévals* 24 (2001).
Lupher, David. *Romans in a New World: Classical Models in Sixteenth-Century Spanish America*. Ann Arbor, MI, 2003.
Lynch, John. *Bourbon Spain*. Oxford, 1989.
Maestre Maestre, J. M. "La divinatio in scribende historia de Nebrija." *Euphrosyne* 23 (1995): 141–173.
Malcolm, Noel. *Reason of State, Propaganda, and the Thirty Years' War: An Unknown Translation by Thomas Hobbes*. Oxford, 2007.
Maltby, William. *The Black Legend in England: The Development of Anti-Spanish Sentiment, 1558–1660*. Durham, NC, 1971.
Manuppella, Giaccinto. "Girolamo de Franchi Conestaggio." In *Miscelânea de estudos em honra do Prof. Hernâni Cidade*, 216–287. Lisbon, 1957.
Maravall, José Antonio. "El concepto de monarquía en la edad media española." In *Estudios de historia del pensamiento español*, 1:59–77. Madrid, 1999.
———. *Culture of the Baroque*. Translated by Terry Cochran. Minneapolis, 1986.
March, José M. *Niñez y juventud de Felipe II*. Madrid, 1941–1942.
Marin, Louis. *Portrait of the King*. Translated by Martha M. Houle. Minneapolis, 1988.
Martin, Georges. "Alphonse X et le pouvoir historiographique." In *L'histoire et les nouveaux publics dans l'Espagne médiévale*, edited by Jean-Philippe Genet. Paris, 1997.

Martínez Bara, José Antonio. "Los Cabrera de Córdoba, Felipe II y El Escorial." *RABM* 71 (1963): 202–233.
Martínez de la Escalera, José. "Jerónimo de la Higuera, S.J., falsos cronicones, historia de Toledo, culto de San Tirso." In *Tolède et l'expansion urbaine en Espagne (1450–1650)*, 67–97. Madrid, 1991.
Martínez Gil, Fernando. "Historia y cohesión urbana: La escuela historiográfica toledana del Siglo de Oro." In *Ensayos humanísticos: Homenaje al profesor Luis Lorente Toledo*, edited by Rafael Villena Espinosa. Cuenca, 1997.
———. "Religión e identidad urbana en el arzobisopado de Toledo (siglos xvi–xvii)." In *Religiosidad popular y modelos de identidad en España y América*, edited by Juan Carlos Vuzuete Mendoza and Palma Martínez-Burgos García. Cuenca, 2000.
Martínez Millán, José, ed. *Felipe II (1527–1598): Europa y la monarquía católica*. Madrid, 1998.
Martínez Ruiz, Adolfo. "Francisco Ramos del Manzano y la educación de Carlos II." *Chronica nova* 12 (1981): 127–133.
Martín Polin, Raquel. "Pellicer de Ossau: Una visión de la monarquía católica en torno a 1640." *Espacio, tiempo, forma* 4 (2000): 133–164.
Maura Gamazo, Gabriel, duke of Maura. *Carlos II y su corte*. 2 vols. Madrid, 1911–1915.
Menéndez Pidal, Gonzalo. "Cómo trabajaron las escuelas alfonsíes." *Nueva revista de filología hispánica* 5 (1951): 367–379.
Mesnard, Pierre. "L'expérience politique de Charles Quint et les enseignements d'Erasme." In *Fêtes et cérémonies au temps de Charles Quint*, edited by Jean Jacquot, 45–66. Paris, 1975.
Mestre Sanchis, Antonio. "Historiografía." In *Historia literaria de España en el siglo XVIII*, edited by F. Aguilar Piñal, 815–882. Madrid, 1996.
———. *Humanistas, políticos e ilustrados*. Alicante, 2002.
Millares Carlos, Agustín. *Tres estudios biobibliográficos*. Maracaibo, 1941.
Montero Reguera, Lola, and Mariano de la Campa della Gavela. "El mundo del libro desde las escrituras públicas notariales: Baltasar Gutiérrez." *Edad de oro* 17 (1998): 9–17.
Morel-Fatio, Alfred. "Cartas eruditas del marqués de Mondéjar y Etienne Baluze (1679–1690)." In *Homenaje a Meléndez y Pelayo*, 1:1–39. Madrid, 1899.
———. "El cronista Antonio de Herrera y el Archiduque Alberto." *RABM* 12 (1905).
———. *Historiographie de Charles-Quint*. Paris, 1913.
Moreno Espinosa, Gerardo. *Don Carlos: El príncipe de la leyanda negra*. Madrid, 2006.
Moreno Gallego, Valentín. "Juan de Mariana ante la imprenta de Luis Sánchez: El *textus receptus* de la Historia General de España." *Bulletin Hispanique* 110 (June 2008): 111–144.
Morocho Gayo, Gaspar. "Una historia de Felipe III escrita por Pedro de Valencia." In *Homenaje al Profesor Juan Torres Fonts*, 2:1141–1151. Murcia, 1987.
Moya, Jesús. *Esteban de Garibay: Un guipuzcano en la corte del rey Felipe*. Bilbao, 1999.
———. "Garibay, historiador vasco." *Cuadernos hispanoamericanos* 533–534 (1994): 163–187.
Myers, Kathleen Ann. *Fernández de Oviedo's Chronicle of America: A New History for a New World*. Austin, TX, 2007.

Navas Rodríguez, María Teresa. *Reformismo ilustrado y americanismo: La Real Academia de la Historia, 1735–1792*. Madrid, 1989.

Novick, Peter. *That Noble Dream: The "Objectivity" Question and the American Historical Profession*. Cambridge, 1988.

O'Callaghan, Joseph. *The Learned King: The Reign of Alfonso X of Castile*. Philadelphia, 1993.

Olavide, Ignacio. "La inquisición, la Companía de Jesús, y el padre Jerónimo Román." *BRAH* 42 (1903): 107–119.

Olds, Katherine B. "'The False Chronicles' in Early Modern Spain: Forgery, Tradition, and the Invention of Texts and Relics, 1595–c. 1670." Ph.D. diss., Princeton University, 2008.

Olschki, L. "Hernan Perez de Oliva's 'Ystoria de Colon.'" *Hispanic American Historical Review* 23, no. 2 (1943): 165–196.

Onís, José de. "Alcedo's *Biblioteca Americana*." *HAHR* 31 (1971): 530–541.

On Point II, The Transition to the New Campaign: The United States Army in Operation Iraqi Freedom, May, 2003–January, 2005. Washington, DC, 2008.

Orgel, Stephen. *The Illusion of Power: Political Theater in the English Rennaisance*. Berkeley, CA, 1975.

Paéz Guibovich, Pedro. "La cultura libresca de un converso procesado por la Inquisición de Lima." *Historia y cultura* 20 (1990): 133–160.

Pagden, Anthony. "Heeding Heraclites: Empire and Its Discontents, 1619–1812." In *Spain, Europe, and the Atlantic World*, edited by Richard L. Kagan and Geoffrey Parker. Cambridge, 1995.

——. *Lords of all the World: Ideologies of Empire in Spain, Britain, and France, c. 1500–c. 1800*. New Haven, CT, 1998.

——. *Spanish Imperialism and the Political Imagination*. New Haven, CT, 1990.

Paniagua Pérez, Jesús. "Pedro de Valencia, cronista e historiógrafo oficial de las Indias (1607–1620)." *Anuario de estudios atlánticos* 53 (1996): 231–249.

Parker, Geoffrey. "Maps and Ministers: The Spanish Habsburgs." In *Monarchs, Ministers, and Maps*, edited by David Buisseret, 124–152. Chicago, 1992.

Paz y Melia, A. *El cronista Alonso de Palencia*. Madrid, 1914.

Peiró Martín, Ignacio. *Los guardianes de la historia: La historiografía académica de la Restauración*. Zaragoza, 1995.

Peña y Camara, José de la. "Un cronista desconocido de Carlos V. El humanista siciliano Fray Bernardo Gentile, O.P." *Hispania* 4 (1944): 536–568.

Pérez Bustamante, Ciriaco. *Antonio de Alcedo y su "memoria" para la continuación de las "Décadas" de Herrera*. Madrid, 1968.

——. *El cronista Antonio de Herrera y la Historia de Alejandro Farnese*. Madrid, 1933.

Pérez Magallón, Jesús. *Construyendo la modernidad: La cultura española en el tiempo de los novatores (1675–1725)*. Madrid, 2002.

Pérez Pastor, Cristóbal. *Bibliografía madrileña*. Madrid, 1917. Pamplona, 2000.

——. "Cronistas del emperador Carlos V." *BRAH* 22 (1893): 420–427.

——. *Noticias y documentos relativos a la historia y literatura españolas*. 4 vols. Madrid, 1910.

Peset, Mariano, and Pascual Marzal. "Humanismo jurídico tardío en Salamanca." *Studia histórica* (Salamanca) 14 (1996): 63–83.

Philips, Carla Rahn. "Visualizing *Imperium:* The Virgin of the Seafarers and Spain's Self-Image in the Sixteenth Century." *Renaissance Quarterly* 58 (2005): 815–856.
Plaza, Ángel de la. *Archivo General de Simancas: Guía del Investigador.* Madrid, 1962.
Plumb, J. H. *The Growth of Political Stability in England, 1675–1725.* London, 1967.
Pocock, J. G. A. *Barbarism and Religion.* Cambridge, 1999-.
Portuondo, Maria M. *Secret Science: Spanish Cosmography and the New World.* Chicago, 2009.
Pozuelo Calero, Bartolomé. "Propaganda y crítica en la *Historia de Carlos V* de Juan Ginés de Sepúlveda." *Cademas Renascens* (Alcañiz-Cádiz) 1 (2000): 299–309.
Les princes et l'histoire du XIVe au XVIIIe siécle. Edited by Chantall Grell, Werner Paravicini, and Jürgen Vos. Bonn, 1998.
Pullapilly, Cyriac K. *Caesar Baronius: Counter-Reformation Historian.* South Bend, IN, 1985.
Quinn, David B. *Set Faire for Roanoke.* Chapel Hill, NC, 1980.
Quint, David. *Epic and Empire: Politics and Generic Form from Virgil to Milton.* Princeton, NJ, 1993.
Ramos Pérez, Demetrio. *La primera noticia de América.* Valladolid, 1986.
Ramos Santana, Carmen. "Una biografía desconocida de Lucio Marineo Sículo: El Ms. 9/5962 de la Real Academia de la Historia." *Cademus Renascens* 1 (2000): 311–329.
Ranum, Orest. *Artisans of Glory: Writers and Historical Thought in Seventeenth-Century France.* Chapel Hill, NC, 1980.
Rashed, Abdur. "The Treatment of History by Muslim Historians in Mughal Official and Biographical Works." In *Historical Writing of the Peoples of Asia,* vol. 1, *Historians of India, Pakistan, and Ceylon,* edited by C. H. Philips, 139–151. London, 1961.
Redondo, Augustín. *Antonio de Guevara (1480?–1545) et l'Espagne de son temps.* Geneva, 1976.
———. "Exaltación de España y preocupaciones pedagógicas alrededor de 1580: Las reformas preconoizadas por Juan López de Velasco, cronista y cosmógrafo de Felipe II." In Martínez Millán, *Felipe II (1527–1598),* 4:425–436.
Rey Castelao, Ofelia. *La historiografía del voto de Santiago: Recopilación crítica de una polémica histórica.* Santiago de Compostela, 1985.
Rodríguez de Diego, José Luis. "La formación del Archivo de Simancas en el siglo XVI: Función y orden interno." In *El libro antiguo español,* vol. 4, *Coleccionismo y bibliotecas: Siglos XV–XVIII,* edited by M. L. López Vidriero and P. M. Cátedra, 519–557. Salamanca, 1998.
———, ed. *Instrucción para el gobierno del Archivo de Simancas (año 1588).* Madrid, 1989.
Rodríguez de Gracia, Hilario. "Contratos de impresión suscritos por Juan de Mariana, Alonso de Villegas, y Francisco de Pisa." *Hispania Sacra* 55 (2003): 51–84.
Rodríguez Peregrina, Elena. "Juan Ginés de Sepúlveda, un historiador al servicio de Carlos V." In *Actas del Congreso Internacional sobre el V Centenario del nacimiento de Dr. Juan Ginés de Sepúlveda,* 107–127. Córdoba, 1993.
Rodríguez Villa, A. "Don Francisco de Mendoza, Almirante de Aragon." In *Homenaje á Menéndez y Pelayo,* 2:487–610. Madrid, 1899.
Rosenthal, Earl J. "The Invention of the Columnar Device of the Emperor Charles V at the

Court of Burgundy in Flanders in 1519." *Journal of the Warburg and Courtauld Institutes* 36 (1973): 199–230.

———. "*Plus Ultra, Non Plus Ultra*, and the Columnar Device of Emperor Charles V." *Journal of the Warburg and Courtauld Institutes* 34 (1971): 204–228.

Roy, Emile. *La vie et les oeuvres de Charles Sorel (1602–1674)*. Paris, 1891.

Ruiz, Teófilo F. "Unsacred Monarchy: The Kings of Castile in the Late Middle Ages." In *Rites of Power: Symbolism, Ritual, and Politics since the Middle Ages*, edited by Sean Wilentz, 109–144. Philadelphia, 1985.

Ruiz García, Elisa. "El poder de la escritura y la escritura del poder." In *Orígenes de la monarquía hispánica: Propaganda y legitmación (ca. 1400–1520)*, edited by José Manuel Nieto Soria. Madrid, 1999.

Ruiz Pérez, Pedro. *Fernán Pérez de Oliva y la crisis del renacimiento*. Córdoba, 1997.

Ruiz Povedano, José María. "El Doctor Lorenzo Galíndez de Carvajal, hombre de negocios en el reino de Granada." *Baetica* 3 (1980): 167–184.

Rummel, Erika. "Marineo Sículo: A Protagonist of Humanism in Spain," *Renaissance Quarterly* 50 (Autumn 1997): 701–722.

Sáenz de Miera, Jesús. "Lo raro del orbe: Objetos de arte y maravillas en el Alcázar de Madrid." In *El Real Alcázar de Madrid*, edited by Fernando Checa, 264–287. Madrid, 1994.

Salvador Martinez, H. *Alfonso X, el Sabio*. Madrid, 2003.

Salvio, Alfonso de. "Voltaire and Spain." *Hispania* 7 (1924): 69–110, 157–164.

Samson, Alexander. "Florián de Ocampo, Castilian Chronicler and Habsburg Propagandist: Rhetoric, Myth, and Genealogy in the Historiography of Early Modern Spain." *Forum for Modern Language Studies* 42 (2006): 339–354.

Sánchez Alonso, Benito. *Historia de la historoiografía española*. 3 vols. Madrid, 1941–1950.

———. "Nebrija, historiador." *Revista filología española* 29 (1945): 129–152.

Sánchez Jiménez, Antonio. "'Muy contrario a la verdad': Los documentos del Archivo General de las Indias sobre *La Dragontea* y la polémica entre Lope y Antonio de Herrera." *Bulletin of Spanish Studies* 85 (July 2008): 569–579.

Sánchez Madrid, Sebastián. *Arqueología y humanismo: Ambrosio de Morales*. Córdoba, 2002.

Saslow, Edward L. "Dryden as Historiographer Royal, and the Authorship of 'His Majesties Declaration Defended.'" *Modern Philology* 75 (1978): 261–273.

Sawyer, Jeffrey K. *Pamphlet Propaganda, Faction Politics, and the Public Sphere in Early Seventeenth-Century France*. Berkeley, CA, 1991.

Schmidt, Benjamin. *Innocence Abroad: The Dutch Imagination and the New World, 1570–1670*. Cambridge, 2001.

Schmidt, Peer. *Spanische Universalmonarchie oder "teutsche Libertet": Das spanische Imperium in der Propaganda des Dreissigjahrigen Krieges*. Stuttgart, 2001.

Serralta, F. "Nueva biografía de Antonio de Solís y Rivadeneyra." *Criticón* 34 (1986): 51–157.

Shapiro, Barbara J. *A Culture of Fact: England, 1550–1720*. Ithaca, NY, 2000.

Sieber, Harry. "The Magnificent Foundation: Literary Patronage at the Court of Philip III." *Cervantes* 18, no. 2 (1998): 85–116.

Sima, Qian. *The Records of the Grand Historian*. Translated by Burton Watson. New York, 2003.

———. *Records of the Grand Historian: Qin Dynasty*. Translated by Burton Watson. Hong Kong, 1993.
Skovgaard-Petersen, Karen. "The Literary Feud between Denmark and Sweden in the Sixteenth and Seventeenth Centuries and the Development of Danish Historical Scholarship." In *Renaissance Culture in Context: Theory and Practice*, edited by Jean R. Brink and William F. Gentrup, 114–120. Aldershot, 1993.
Socarrás, Cayetano J. *Alfonso X of Castile: A Study on Imperialistic Frustration*. Barcelona, 1976.
Soledad Arredondo, María. "Entre polémica e historia, o 'Pellicer y Tovar,' *Idea de Principado de Cataluña* (1642) de José Pellicer y Tovar." In *Homenaje a Elena Catena*, 47–62. Madrid, 2001.
———. "La guerre franco-espagnole de 1635 et l'intertextualité des polémistes: Les 'Ambassadeurs' de Mathieu de Morgues et de José Pellicer." In *Devis d'Amitié: Mélanges en l'honneur de Nicole Cazauran*, 887–900. Paris, 2002.
———. "Literatura polémica e reescritura en 1635: *Defensa de España contra las calumnias de Francia* de José Pellicer." *Criticon* 79 (2000): 47–64.
———. "Noticia de la *Súplica de Tortosa* (1640), atribuida al Inquisidor Juan Adam de la Parra." *Cuadernos de historia moderna* 22 (1999): 139–156.
Soll, Jacob. "The Antiquary and the Information State: Colbert's Archives, Secret Histories, and the Affair of the *Régale*." *French Historical Studies* 31, no. 1 (2008): 1–26.
———. *Publishing the Prince: History, Reading, and the Birth of Political Criticism*. Ann Arbor, MI, 2005.
Soman, Alfred. "Press, Pulpit, and Censorship in France before Richelieu." *Proceedings of the American Philosophical Society* 120 (1976): 439–463.
Soons, Alan. *Juan de Mariana*. Boston, 1982.
Soria Mesa, Enrique. *La biblioteca genealógica de don Luís de Salazar y Castro*. Córdoba, 1997.
Spiegel, Gabrielle M. *The Chronicle Tradition of Saint-Denis: A Survey*. Brookline, MA, 1978.
———. *Romancing the Past: The Rise of Vernacular Prose Historiography in Thirteenth-Century France*. Berkeley, CA, 1993.
Stebbing, William. *Sir Walter Raleigh: A Biography*. Oxford, 1899.
Steffen, Sarmiento Hans. "Anotaciones a la historia indica del Capt. Pedro Sarmiento de Gamboa." *Anales de la universidad de Santiago de Chile* 129 (1911).
Stenhouse, William. *Reading Inscriptions and Writing Ancient History: Historical Scholarship in the Late Renaissance*. London, 2005.
———. "Thomas Dempster, Royal Historian to James I, and Classical Scholarship in Early Stuart England." *Sixteenth-Century Journal* 35 (2004): 395–410.
Storrs, Christopher. *The Resilience of the Spanish Monarchy, 1665–1700*. Oxford, 2006.
Stradling, R. A. *Philip IV and the Government of Spain, 1621–1665*. Cambridge, 1988.
Strauss, Gerald. *Historian in an Age of Crisis: The Life and Work of Johannes Aventinus, 1477–1534*. Cambridge, MA, 1963.
Suárez Fernández, Luis. *El canciller Pedro López de Ayala y su tiempo, 1332–1407*. Vitoria, 1962.
Subrahmanyam, Sanjay. "On World Historians in the Sixteenth Century." *Representations* 91 (2005): 26–57.

Tang, Frank. "De 'sterke' König: Juan Gil de Zamora en zijn vorstenspiegel." *Theoretische Geschiedenis* 21 (1994): 385–403.

Tanner, Marie. *The Last Descendant of Aeneas: The Hapsburgs and the Mythic Image of the Emperor.* New Haven, CT, 1993.

Tate, Robert B. "Nebrija, historiador." In *Ensayos sobre la historiografía peninsular del siglo XV,* by Robert B. Tate, translated by Jesús Díaz, 183–212. Madrid, 1970.

———. "The Official Chronicler in the Fifteenth Century: A Brief Survey of Western Europe." *Nottingham Medieval Studies* 41 (1997): 157–185.

———. "The Re-Writing of the Historical Past—Hispania et Europa." In *L'histoire et les nouveaux publics dans l'Europe médiévale (XIIIe–XVe siècles),* edited by Jean-Philippe Genet, 241–257. Madrid, 1997.

———. "Sancho de Nebrija y su antología historiográfica." *Insula* 551 (November 1992): 17–19.

Tietz, Manfred. "Las 'Reflexiones imparciales' de Juan Nuix y Perpiñá (1740–1793): El 'saber americanista' de los jesuitas y 'las trampas de la fe.'" In *Las Jesuitas españolas expulsos: Su imagen y su contribución al saber sobre el mundo hispánico en la Europa del siglo XVIII,* edited by Manfred Tietz, 611–644. Frankfurt am Main; Madrid, 2001.

Toribio Medina, José. *Biblioteca Hispano-américana (1493–1810).* 2 vols. Santiago de Chile, 1898–1900.

Torres Fontes, J., ed. *Estudios sobre la 'Crónica de Enrique IV' de Dr. Galíndez de Carvajal.* Murcia, 1946.

Torres Revelló, José. *El libro, la imprenta y el periodísmo en América durante la dominación española.* Buenos Aires, 1940.

Tracy, James D. *Holland under Habsburg Rule, 1506–1566.* Berkeley, CA, 1990.

Trevelyan, Raleigh. *Sir Walter Raleigh.* London, 2002.

Trevor-Roper, Hugh. *Queen Elizabeth's First Historian.* London, 1971.

Turner, Daymond. "Forgotten Treasure from the Indies: The Illustrations and Drawings of Fernández de Oviedo." *Huntington Library Quarterly* 48 (1985): 1–46.

Twitchett, Denis. *The Writing of Official History under the T'ang.* Cambridge, 1992.

Varey, Simon, Rafael Chrabrán, and Doron Weiner. *Searching for the Secrets of Nature: The Life and Works of Dr. Francisco Hernández.* Stanford, CA, 2000.

Velasco Moreno, Eva. *La Real Academia de la Historia en el siglo XVIII.* Madrid, 2000.

Vicente Maroto, M. I., and M. Esteban Piñeiro. *Aspectos de la ciencia aplicada en la España del Siglo de Oro.* Valladolid, 1991.

Vilaplana Montes, María Asunción. "Correspondencia de Papebroch con el Marqués de Mondéjar." *Hispania sacra* 25 (1972): 293–349.

Vilar Berrogain, Jean. *Literatura y economia: La figura satírica del arbitrista en el siglo de oro.* Madrid, 1973.

Villanueva López, Jesús. *Política y discurso histórico en la España del siglo XVII: Las polémicas sobre los orígenes medievales de Cataluña.* Alicante, 2004.

Villari, Rosario. *Elogio della disimulazione: La lotta politica nel Seicento.* Rome, 1987.

Villarroel, Fidel. *Fray Jerónimo Román, Historia de Siglo de Oro.* Zamora, 1974.

Vivi, Felippo di. "Paolo Sarpi and the Uses of Information." In *News Networks in Seventeenth-Century Britain and Europe,* edited by Joad Raymond, 35–49. London, 2006.

Vogelstein, Ingeborg Berlin. *Johann Sleidan's Commentaries: Vantage Point of a Second Generation Lutheran.* New York, 1986.
Voigt, Georg. *Die Geschichtschreibung über den Zug Karls V gegen Tunis.* Lepizig, 1874.
Völkel, Markus. *Geschichtes-schreibung.* Cologne, 2006.
Wade, Majorie D. "The Education of the Prince: A Mirror of Reality in Maxmilian's *Weisskunig.*" Ph.D. diss., University of Michigan, 1974.
Wagner, Klaus. "Legajos y otras aficiones del inquisidor Andrés Gascó." *BRAH* 176 (1979): 149–185.
Wallace-Hadrill, Andrew. *Suetonius: The Scholar and His Caesars.* New Haven, CT, 1983.
Weinberg, B. *A History of Literary Criticism in the Italian Renaissance.* Chicago, 1966.
Wilkinson, Endymion. *Chinese History: A Manual.* Cambridge, 2000.
Williams, Bernard. *Truth and Truthfulness: An Essay in Genealogy.* Princeton, NJ, 2002.
Williams, Patrick. *The Great Favorite: The Duke of Lerma and the Court and Government of Philip III, 1598–1621.* Manchester, 2006.
Wilson, E. M. "Calderón y Funtearrabia: El 'Panegírico' al Almirante de Castilla." *Boletín de la Real Academia Española* 49 (1969): 253–278.
Woodhall, Joanna " 'His Majesty's Most Majestic Room': The Division of Sovereign Identity in Philip II of Spain's Lost Portrait Gallery at El Pardo." *Nederlands Kunsthistorisch Jaarboek* 46 (1995): 52–103.
Woodhead, Christine. "An Experiment in Official Historiography: The Post of Sehnameçi in the Ottoman Empire, c. 1555–1605." *Wiener Zeitschrift für die Kunde des Morgenlandes* 75 (1983): 157–182.
Woolf, Stuart. *The Idea of History in Early Stuart England.* Toronto, 1990.
Wright, A. D. *Federico Borromeo and Baronius: A Turning-Point in the Development of the Counter-Reformation Church.* Reading, 1974.
Wright, Elizabeth R. "Epic and Archive: Lope de Vega, Francis Drake, and the Council of the Indies." *Calíope* 3, no. 2 (1997): 37–55.
———. *Pilgrimage to Patronage: Lope de Vega and the Court of Philip III.* Lewisberg, PA, 2001.
Yoyette, Jean. "Le martelage des noms royaux éthiopiens par Psammétique II." *Revue d'egyptologie* 8 (1951): 215–239.
Zagorin, Perez. *Ways of Lying: Dissimulation, Persecution, and Conformity in Early Modern Europe.* Cambridge, MA, 1990.
Zen, Stefano. *Baronio storico.* Naples, 1985.
Zimmermann, T. C. Price. *Paolo Giovio: The Historian and the Crisis of Sixteenth-Century Italy.* Princeton, NJ, 1995.
———. "The Publication of Paolo Giovio's Histories: Charles V and the Revision of Book XXXIV." *La bibliofilia* 7 (1972): 49–90.

INDEX

Abarca, Pedro, *cronista del rey*, 265, 266–268, 275
Acetto, Torquatto, 221
Acosta, José de, *Historia natural y moral de las Indias*, 171–172
Adam de la Parra, Juan, 215–216, 239; *Conspiración herético-cristiana*, 238; *Súplica de Tortosa*, 240
Adriani, Giovanni Battista, 130
Agrippa, Heinrich Cornelius, 67
Aguado, Fray Pedro de, *Recopilación historial*, 169–170
Albert, Archduke of Austria, 147
Albuquerque, Duke of, Gabriel de la Cueva, 135
Alcedo, Antonio de, 288–289, 296
Alcocer, Pedro de, ix
Alfonso, Prince of Castile-León, 38
Alfonso III, chronicle of, 20
Alfonso V, King of Portugal, 9–10
Alfonso VI, King of León, 20–21
Alfonso VII, King of Castile-León, 19
Alfonso X, King of Castile-León, 21–27, 149; chronicles of, 22–27, 32; *Estoria de Espanna*, 23, 32, 63–64, 107, 278; historiographical workshop of, 24–25, 51; *Siete Partidas*, 25–26, 30
Alfonso XI, King of Castile-León, 28, 31, 34
Almodóvar, Duke of, 288
Alvaro de Luna, 41–42
Anderson, Benedict, 119
Andrade, Francisco de, *cronista-mor*, 132
Annius of Viterbo. *See* Nanni, Giovanni
Antiquarians, in Spain, 111–112, 281
Antonelli, Giovanni Battista, 147

Antonio, Nicolás, 263, 265, 271–272
Aquaviva, Claudio, 259
Aragón: *alteraciones* of, 129, 189, 227; chroniclers of, 239, 266–267, 278; *Diputación*, historical policies of, 189–190, 227–228, 266; history writing in, 30, 49, 104–105, 190
Arbitristas, 204, 252
Arce, Francisco de, 292
Argaiz, Fray Gregorio, 262–263
Argote de Molina, Gonzalo, 112
Arías de Loyola, Juan, *cronista mayor de las Indias*, 171
Arias Montano, Benito, 112, 258
Arredondo, Fray Gonzalo de, 63
Augustine, Saint, 5, 85
Autobiographies, early modern attitudes toward, 58
Aventinus, Joahnnes, 108
Avila y Zuñiga, Luis de, 67, 68, 87–89, 224; *Commentarios de . . . la guerra de Alemania hecha de Carlos V*, 68, 82–83
Ayala, Diego de, 104, 133
Ayora, Gonzalo de, *cronista del rey*, 52–53
Aytta, Wigle (or Vigilius) van, 99

Bacon, Francis, 173, 200, 206; *History of the Reign of Henry VII*, 203; "House of Solomon," 208
Baluze, Etienne, 242, 264
Barbarini, Matteo, 94
Baronio, Cesare, 257–258
Barros, João de, *cronista-mor*, 4, 295
Baudoin, François, 103
Bayle, Pierre, 279

Beltrán de la Cueva, Juan, 44
Bembo, Pietro, 4
Benzoni, Girolamo, 161, 270
Bernáldez, Andrés, 48
Beuter, Pere Antoni, 105
Biography, early modern ideas about, 94–95
Blasco de Lanuza, Vicencio, historian of Aragon, 227–228
Bleda, Fray Jaime, 292
Bodin, Jean, 66, 88, 102
Bolland, Jean, 263
Borja, Francisco de, 58
Botella Ordiñas, Eva, 267
Botero, Giovanni, 124–126, 137; *Le relationi vniversali*, 145
Boturini, Lorenzo, 271–272, 283–284, 289
Bouwsma, William, 249
Brito, Bernardo de, *cronista-mor*, 132–133
Bruni, Leonardo, 107
Bruto, Giovanni Michele, 91
Buchanan, George, 10, 137
Burke, Peter, 61
Burton, Richard, 206
Busto, Bernarbé de, *cronista del rey*, 80–81

Cabeza de Vaca, Alvar Núñez, 102
Cabrera de Córdoba, Luis, 102, 290–293; *De historia*, 98, 204, 227, 249; ideas about history, 140, 203, 208
Calatayud, Francisco de, 216
Calderón, Fray Juan, 260
Calderón, Juan Antonio, 248
Calvete de Estrella, Juan Cristóbal, 99, 133, 170
Camden, William, 10
Campomanes, Pedro Rodríguez de, 281–288
Cañizares-Esguerra, Jorge, 288
Cano, Melchor, 4–5, 152
Canobio, Juan, 191
Capello, Galeazzo, 78
Carbonell, Pere Miguel, 49
Carillo, Fray Martín, 190
Carillo Castillo, Jesés, 156
Carillo Huete, Pedro, 42
Caro, Rodrigo, 260
Carvajal, Bernardino de, 49
Castro Egas, Ana de, 214
Catholic Monarchs: attitudes toward history, 49–53; and Bulls of Donation, 151–152; and historiographical workshop, 51; use of print by, 47. *See also* Ferdinand II; Isabella I
Cervantes de Salazar, Francisco, 167; *Crónica de Nueva España*, 174–175
Cervantes Saavedra, Miguel de, 188
Céspedes y Meneses, Gonzalo, 227–230, 245; *Francia engañada, Francia respondida*, 229–230; *Historia apologética de Aragón*, 227; and *Historia de . . . Felipe IV*, 229
Chacón, Pedro, 112
Charlemagne, 8, 29, 126
Charles II, King of Spain, 252–255, 269, 276
Charles III, King of Spain, 282–283, 285–286
Charles V, Holy Roman Emperor, 56; and architecture, 62; attitudes toward history, 63, 64, 66; biographies of, 91–93; concern over his reputation, 61–63, 68, 80; education of, 59–61; and Paolo Giovio, 73–74, 79–80, 87–89; and the imperial chronicle, 67, 80, 90–91; *Memorias*, 57–58, 68, 85–90, 98
Charles IX, King of France, 107
Chastelain, George, 4, 59, 62
Chile, histories of, 196–197
Chinchón, Count of, 127, 134
Cicero, 4, 31, 76, 139, 300
Cieza de León, Pedro, *Crónica de Peru*, 163, 165
Cirot, Georges, 119
Clavijero, Francisco Xavier, 273
Colbert, Jean-Baptiste, 254, 264
Columbus, Christopher, 51–52, 182
Commines, Philippe de, 4
Conestaggio, Girolamo Franchi di, 131, 135; *Dell'unione del regno di Portogallo alla corona di Castigli*, 131–132, 211
Cortés, Hérnan, 158, 159, 168, 269–270, 272
Cortés, Juan Lucás, 265
Cortes of Castille, and history, 63–64, 70
Cosimo II de' Medici, Grand Duke of Tuscany, 87–88
Coxe, William, 276
Cromberger, Juan, 154
cronista ad honorem, 255–256
cronista del rey (court chronicler), 8–10, 17–18, 28, 69, 255; offices suppressed, 278
cronista mayor de las Indias, 151–162; office transferred to Royal Academy of History, 283
Croy, Guillaume de, Lord of Chièvres, 59, 61
Cuart, Baltasar, 77, 91

Daubenton, Pere, 276
Dávila, Pedrarías, 182–183, 189
De Bry, Theodore, 151
Dempster, Thomas, 10
Desclot, Bernart, 30
Detienne, Marcel, 31
Dextro, Flavius Lucius, 258–261
Deza, Lope de, 292
Díaz de Casillo, Bernal, 271–272
Díaz de Vivar, Rodrigo ("El Cid"), 27
Dolce, Ludovico, 85, 92
Dupleix, Scipion, 4

Elizabeth I, Queen of England, 10, 48, 107; as described by Herrera y Tordesillas, 137
Elliott, John, 216
Emilio, Paulo, 107
Enrique II, King of Castile-León, 36
Enrique III, King of Castile-León, 28
Enríquez del Castillo, Diego, *cronista del rey*, 37, 40–41, 43, 293; papers siezed, 38–39; praise for Henry IV, 44
Erasmus, Desiderius, 60
Escavias, Pedro de, 42–43
Esquivel, Pedro de, 97

"False chronicles," 257–262; repudiated, 263, 274–275
Farnese, Alessandro, 191
Farnese, Isabel, Queen of Spain, 277
Ferdinand II, King of Aragon, 10, 14, 17, 46–56, 267; and *cronistas del rey*, 47–51; use of history by, 48–49. *See also* Catholic Monarchs
Ferdinand III, King of Castile-León, 21, 27
Ferdinand VI, King of Spain, 283
Fernández de Córdoba, Gonzalo ("Gran Capitan"), 71
Fernández de Navarrete, Francisco, 280
Fernández de Navarrete, Martín, 297
Fernández de Oviedo, Gonzalo, 55, 57, 68, 296; bid for office of *cronista del rey*, 69–70; *Catálogo de los reyes de España*, 70; *Historia general y natural de las Indias*, 69–70, 154–160
Fernández de Palencia, Diego, historian of Peru, 169
Fernández de Pulgar, Pedro, *cronista mayor de las Indias* and *cronista del rey*, 256, 274n

Fernández de Velasco, Pedro, constable of Castile, 122
Fernández Franco, Juan, 112
Ferrer, Pedro, 121
Ferreras, Juan de, 275–276, 278
Flores, Juan de, *cronista del rey*, 7, 46–47, 68; bias toward Isabella, 48
Floridablanca, Count of, José de Moñino y Redondo, 285
Foglietta, Uberto, 99
Forner, Juan Pablo, 298
Francis I, King of France, 71
Frankenburg, Count of. *See* Khevenhüller, Franz Cristoph
Fresneda, Fray Bernardo de, 100, 164

Galíndez de Carvajal, Lorenzo, 53–56; ideas about history, 64–66, 88, 91
Gálvez, José Bernardo de, 285–287
García de Santa María, Alvar, 42
Garibay y Zamalloa, Esteban de, *cronista del rey*, 115–117; *Compendio historial*, 115–116, 118, 122; as historian of Philip II, 133–134; *Illustraciones genealógicas*, 134–135; outline for history of Philip II's reign, 139–144
Gasca, Pedro de la, 170
Gattinara, Mercurino Arborio di, 61, 67, 69, 70, 90
Gentile, Bernardo de, *cronista del rey*, 70–71
Geoffrey of Monmouth, 28–29, 107
Gil de Zamora, Juan, 23
Gil Pujol, Xavier, 126
Ginés de Sepúlveda, Juan, *cronista del rey*, 4, 7, 152–153, 164, 270, 282, 297; attitudes toward history, 76–78; *Democrates segundus*, 153; history of Charles V, 77–79; history of the New World, 78, 100, 164; history of Philip II, 100–101; and Bartolomé de Las Casas, 76; and Philip II, 100–102; as royal chronicler, 75–79
Giovio, Paolo, 73–74, 79–80; *Historiarum sui temporis*, 74, 87–89; reputation of, 103
Giustiniani, Pietro, 130
Gondomar, Count of, Diego Sarmiento de Acuña, 1–3, 196; ideas about history, 193, 244
Gonzaga Colonna, Vespasiano, 129, 135–136, 187
González, Fernán, Count of Castile, 27

González Dávila, Gil, *cronista mayor de las Indias*, 184, 218, 233; *Historia de . . . Felipe III*, 213–214; *Teatro de . . . Indias*, 184
Gracián, Antonio, 106
Gracián, Baltasar, 13, 251; *Agudeza . . .*, 201, 224–225; *El héroe*, 269
Grafton, Anthony, 4, 5, 173
Grandes chroniques de France, 22–24
Granvelle, Antoine Perrenot de, 67, 82, 87–88
Grotius, Hugo, 4, 132, 207
Guazzo, Marco, 78
Guevara, Fray Antonio de, *cronista del rey*, 70–73
Guicciardini, Francesco, 89, 151, 291; translated by Philip IV, 212
Guillén de la Carrera, Alonso, 216; and Junta de Cronistas, 220, 229; and *Manifiesto de España . . .*, 222–223
Guzmán, Gaspar de, Count-Duke of Olivares, 13, 188, 198, 209, 211, 255, 293; attitude toward history, 202, 212–214, 223; and *conservación*, 202; and education of Philip IV, 212–213; and Gil González Dávila, 213–214, 217; and Junta de Cronistas, 216–219; propaganda war with France, 215–217, 220, 222–223; and Juan Antonio de Vera y Figueroa, 224–226
Guzmán, Luis de, historian of China and Japan, 188

Habermas, Jürgen, 204
Haillan, Bernard Girard du, 107
Hakluyt, Richard, 151–152, 296
Henry IV, King of Castile-León, 37–38, 41–42; disparaged by Alonso de Palencia, 44
Hernández, Francisco, 166
Herrera y Tordesillas, Antonio de, *cronista mayor de las Indias* and *cronista del rey*, 3, 15, 121, 126, 227, 255, 269, 271–272, 296–298; and Aragon, 189–191; arrest of, 194–195; as censor, 172, 174–175, 188; censors Cervantes' *Don Quixote*, 188; censors Lope de Vega, 172; characterization of Philip II, 146–147; and Conde-Duque de Olivares, 199; as *cronista mayor de las Indias*, 129, 171–185; defense of empire by, 176–180, 190; and Duke of Lerma, 192–193, 194; early career of, 125, 135–139; essays of, 186, 188; and Flanders, 198; and Fray Juan Antonio de Torquemada, 183–184; ideas about history, 185–189, 195; and Italy, 198–199; and Philip III, 195–196; reputation of, 190–191, 195; and Pedro de Valencia, 194–197; and Vespasiano Gonzaga Colonna, 129; working methods, 173–175
Herrera y Tordesillas, Antonio de, works of: *Cinco libros de la historia de Portugal . . .*, 136; *Comentarios de los hechos de los españoles, franceses y venecianos en Italia*, 198–199; *Descripción de las Indias*, 182, 297; *Historia de . . . Francia*, 138; *Historia general . . . del mar océano*, 172, 177–178, 181–183, 195, 299; *Historia general del mundo . . .*, 130, 135, 139, 144–149, 189, 195; and history of England, 137; and history of French Wars of Religion, 138; translation of Botero, 126, 137
Historia per persona, 27, 33, 35, 48, 55, 64; defined, 14
Historia pro patria, 27, 32–33, 35, 55, 64, 104, 243; defined, 14
Historia sacra, in Spain, 259–262
History: and "culture of facts," 29–31; as *fama*, 40–41; "general," 145; "particular," 146, 278; "politic," 206; power of, 3; sacred, 5; and truth, 5–6
History, official: in antiquity, 8, 12; in Asia, 10–11, 12; Chinese, 10–12; Danish, 108; defined, 3–7; and Iraq War, 299; Italian, 107, 262; Mayan, 11; in medieval period, 8; in Ottoman empire, 11; Portuguese, 9–10, 126; in Sweden, 108; use of vernacular in, 23–24; uses of, 3
History, official, English, 10, 28–29, 107, 171; royal support for, 203
History, official, French, 28–29, 107, 262; and Louis XIV, 250, 253; royal support for, 203
History, official, Spanish, 3, 5, 28–29; accounts of discovery and conquest of New World, 15; imperialist ideology in, 25–26; imperial template in, 20; in medieval period, 16–56; and political turn, 207, 221–222; and public opinion, 204–205; reassessment of, 290–300; sacred, 18–20, 23, 111, 257–258, 261–262
Horace, 290
Hurtado de Mendoza, Diego, 112
Hurtado de Mendoza, Juan, 82

Idiáquez, Juan de, 127, 129–130; as patron of Herrera y Tordesillas, 135, 196
Indies: histories of, 15, 176–179, 269–273, 274,

283–289, 296–298; Mexico, 174, 179–180, 183; and New Granada, 168–170; Peru, 159–160, 163, 165, 169; Spanish title to, 151–153, 270
Irving, Washington, 298
Isabella I, Queen of Castile-León, 7, 10, 13–14, 38, 46–56; and *cronistas del rey*, 47–48; praised by Palencia, 44; proclamation as queen, 47. *See also* Catholic Monarchs
Isidore of Seville, 18–20, 110
Iturri, Francisco Javier, 288

James I, King of England, 1–2, 10
Jaume I, King of Aragon, 21, 24, 57
Jover Zamora, José María, 216
Juana, "la Betraneja," 44
Juan I, King of Castile-León, 28
Juan II, King of Aragon, 48–49
Juan II, King of Castile-León, 41

Kelley, Donald, 4
Khevenhüller, Franz Cristoph, Count of Frankenburg, 215

Laet, Johannes de, 297
La Marche, Olivier de, 59–60, 62
Las Casas, Bartolomé de, 157, 271, 296; *Brevísima relación de la destrucción de las Indias*, 100, 153, 160–162; *Historia general del Nuevo Mundo*, 164
Lavanha, João Bautista: as *cosmógrafo-mór*, 132, 187; as tutor to Philip IV, 207–209
Le Challeux, Nicolas, 161
Lemos, Count of, 193
Leonardo de Argensola, Bartolomé, *cronista del reino de Aragón*, 292
Leonardo de Argensola, Lupercio, *cronista del reino de Aragón*, 190
Leoni, Leone, 82
León Pinelo, Antonio, *cronista mayor de las Indias*, 180, 269n
Lerma, Duke of, Francisco Gómez de Sandoval, 187, 196, 255, 291; historical interests of, 192–193
Le Roy, Louis, 296
Lettenhove, Kervyn de, 90
Lipsius, Justus, 124–125, 202
Loaysa Girón, García de, 117, 120, 257

Lobera, Fray Atanasio de, *cronista del rey*, 192
López de Ayala, Pedro, 34–37, 290
López de Gómara, Francisco, 92, 158–160, 270–271; *Historia general de las Indias y conquista de México*, 158–160
López de Velasco, Juan, *cronista y cosmógrafo mayor de las Indias*, 126–127, 150, 162–171; attitudes toward history, 126–127; censorship of history, 168–169; *Geografía y descripción universal de las Indias*, 167
López Madera, Gregorio, 238
Louis VI, King of France, 28
Louis IX, King of France, 24, 226
Louis XIII, King of France, 201, 216–217, 220, 232; as critiqued by Malvezzi, 226
Louis XIV, 250, 253
Lowenthal, David, 14
Lucas of Tuy, 21, 23
Lyschander, C. C., 108

Mabillon, Jean, 242, 267, 269, 271
Magnus, Johannes, 108
Maino, Juan Bautista, 221
Malvezzi, Virgilio, *cronista del rey*, 1, 230–235; and *relaciones*, 233–234
Mantuano, Pedro, 122
Manuel, Juan, 34
Marcén, Antonio, 259–260
Margaret of Austria, Queen of Spain, 67
María Ana of Neuberg, Queen of Spain, 276
Mariana, Juan de, 213, 257, 259; *Historia General de España*, 117–123, 213
Mariana of Austria, Queen-regent of Spain, 253, 255, 266
Marliani, Luigi, 61
Martin, Heinrich (a.k.a. Enrico Martínez), 183
Martínez de Siliceo, Juan, 98
Martyr, Peter (Pietro Martire d'Anghiera), *cronista del rey*, 66, 163; *De orbe novo*, 69, 153–154
Mary of Burgundy, 67–68, 82
Mary Stuart, Queen of Scotland, 137
Mascareñas, Jerónimo de, 268
Maximilian I, Holy Roman Emperor, 57
Mayerne de Tourquet, Louis, *Histoire general de l'Espagne*, 128
Mena, Juan de, *cronista del rey*, 42
Méndez de Haro, Luis, 245

Mendoza, Antonio de, 293–294, 296
Mendoza, Francisco de, Admiral of Aragon, 194
Mendoza, Juan Hurtado de, 80
Mexía, Pedro, *cronista del rey*, 80, 81, 89; *Historia del emperador Carlos V*, 82–84; *Historia imperial y caesarea*, 81
Mexico: conquest of, 159; historians writing about, 153, 159–160; official chronicler of, 167. *See also* Cortés, Hernán
Miranda, Count of, 196
Moncado, Sancho de, 252
Mondejár, marqués de, Gaspar Ibáñez de Segovia, 263–264, 267, 271
Monmouth, Geoffrey of, 23, 29, 107
Montaigne, Michel de, 89, 124, 206
Montiano y Luyando, Agustín, 279, 281
Mora, Count of. *See* Rojas, Pedro de
Morales, Ambrosio de, *cronista del rey*, 109–114; and *La coronica general de España*, 112–114; ideas about El Escorial, 110; "literary voyages of," 110–111, 257, 280; and Spanish antiquities, 111–112
Moréri, Louis, 279, 297
Moura, Cristóbal de, 116, 127, 131; and Garibay, 134
Munater, Ramón, 30
Muñoz, Juan Bautista, *cosmográfo real de las Indias*, 285–289, 297; *Historia del nuevo-mundo*, 287–289
Murillo, Fray Diego, 260

Nanni, Giovanni, (a.k.a. Annius of Viterbo), 49, 121, 243, 257
Nápoles, Jusepe de, 216, 220–221, 246
Nebrija, Antonio de, 16–18, 55; as *cronista del rey*, 17–18, 47
News and news gathering, 204–205
New Spain. *See* Mexico
Nobís, Antonio de (a.k.a. Antonio de Lupián Zapata), 261
Novatores, 256, 263
Novoa, Matías de, 211
Nuix, Joan, 284
Núñes de Lião, Duarte, 132
Núñez de Guzmán, Ramiro, 57

Ocampo, Florián de, *cronista del rey*, 64, 70, 80; and *La coronica general de España*, 61, 102, 104–105

Olivares, Count-Duke of. *See* Guzmán, Gaspar de
Onderíz, Pedro Ambrosio de, *cosmógrafo mayor de las Indias*, 171
Orgel, Stephen, 3
Orley, Bernard van, 71
Oropesa, Count of, Duarte Alvarez de Toledo, 268
Oropesa, Count of, Manuel Joaquin Alvarez de Toledo, 254
Ovando, Juan de, 162

Pacheco, Francisco, 218
Páez de Castro, Juan, *cronista del rey*, 90–91, 97–98; on history, 96; and Philip II, 102–104
Pagden, Anthony, 152
Palafox y Mendoza, Juan de, 216
Palencia, Alonso de, *cronista del rey*, 38–39, 47, 50, 294; *Gesta Hispanensia*, 43–44
Pamphlets, 205–206
Papenbroeck, Daniel van, 263, 265, 267
Parma, Duke of. *See* Ranuncio I
Patrizi, Francesco, 203
Pedro I, King of Castile-León, 35, 36
Pedro III, King of Aragon, 30
Pedro IV, King of Aragon, 48
Pelayo, 19
Pellicer de Ossau y Tovar, José, *coronista del reino*, 201, 235–244, 266, 274, 294; *Cronicón de San Servando*, 261; as *cronista mayor de los reinos de Aragón*, 239; *Defensa de España*, 230; *El Fénix y su historia natural*, 237; and *historia pro patria*, 242–243; *La idea del principado de Catalunya*, 240–241; *Templo de la fama* . . . , 238
Pérez, Antonio, 129, 146, 189
Pérez de Guzmán, Fernán, 39, 42, 66
Pérez de Oliva, Fernán, 111–112
Peru: conquest of, 159, historians writing about, 159–160, 163, 165, 169
Philip II, King of Spain, ix–x; and annexation of Portugal, 130–131; attitudes toward biography, 94–95, 98–100; attitudes toward history, 92–93, 98, 150–151, 280, 291–292; bans use of term "conquest," 170; and censorship of historical documents, 160, 163–165; and creation of archives, 97, 104; education of, 101–

102; and El Escorial, 97; and Paolo Giovio, 73–74, 79, 87–88; historical preferences of, 78, 102–103, 104, 106–107, 132, 257; and history of the Indies, 130, 159–162, 163, 165; and history of Portugal, 130–132; and history of Spain, 109, 130; and maps, 97; and Juan de Mariana, 117, 119–120; reputation of, 129

Philip III, King of Spain, 6; attitudes toward history, 202; education of, 81

Philip IV, King of Spain, 8, 13; attitudes toward history, 202, 207, 211–213; and Buen Retiro palace, 221–222, 295; and censorship of history, 244–248; and court chroniclers, 8; education of, 207–209; history paintings and, 221–222, 295; library of, 209–211

Philip V, King of Spain, 253–254, 275; and creation of royal academies, 279; governmental reforms of, 277–278

Pisa, Francisco de, ix

Pizarro, Francisco, 159

Pizarro, Gonzalo, 180

Pole, Reginald, 77

Polybius, 186

Ponce de León, Pedro, 111

Porreño, Baltasar, 94

Prescott, William Hickling, 269, 273

Puente, Fray Juan de la, *cronista del rey*, 6, 186, 192, 205, 258; and definition of royal chronicler, 204

Puente, Pedro de la, 251

Pulgar, Fernando del, *cronista del rey*, 16, 47, 50–51, 295

Puñonrostro, Count of, 182, 189

Purchas, Samuel, 1

Quevedo, Francisco de, 217, 219, 223

Quint, David, 6

Racine, Jean, 4

Ralegh, Walter, 1–2, 15, 296; *History of the World*, 145

Ramírez de Fuenleal, Sebastián, 179

Ramos del Manzano, Francisco, 254, 263, 265, 269, 271; and history of Philip IV, 248

Ranuncio I, Duke of Parma, 191

Raynal, Abbé, 284–285

Real Academia de la Historia, 14, 274; creation of, 278–279; *Fastos*, 280; title of *cronista mayor de las Indias* transferred to, 283; work of, 279–281, 297

Real Academia Española, 279

Relaciones geográficas, 97, 166

"Republic of letters," Spanish, 111

Ribera, Hernando de, 53

Rich, Obadiah, 298

Richelieu, Cardinal-Duc de, Armand Jean du Plessis Richelieu, 207, 217–220

Rioja, Francisco de, *cronista del rey*, 218, 223, 239, 255, 293; *Aristarco*, 240; and "false chronicles," 260–261; as royal librarian, 209, 214

Robertson, William, 284–286

Roca, Count of. *See* Vera y Figueroa, Juan Antonio de

Roig i Jalpi, Joan Gaspar, 261, 266

Rojas, Pedro de, Count of Mora, x

Román, Fray Jerónimo, 168

Román de la Higuera, Jerónimo, 257–259, 260

Saavedra Fajardo, Diego de, 217, 219

Sacramonte, *plomos* of, 258

Sahagún, Fray Bernardino de, 163–164, 179

Salazar de Mendoza, Pedro, 258

Salazar y Castro, Luis de, *cronista del rey* and *cronista mayor de las Indias*, 7, 167, 256, 265, 273–279

Salcedo, Manuel Pablo de, 283

Sallust, 140

Sánchez Alonso, Benito, 15

Sánchez de Arevalo, Rodrigo, 108

Sánchez de Valladolid, Fernán, 28, 31–35

Sancho IV, King of Castile-León, 25–26, 28

Sandoval, Fray Prudencio de, *cronista del rey*, 73, 192; *Historia de . . . Carlos V*, 93, 188, 224

Sansovino, Francesco, 92

Santa Cruz, Alonso de, 73, 92

Santiago (St. James the Apostle) and Spain, 112–113; defense of legends surrounding, 257–259, 264

Sarmiento, Fray Martin, *cronista mayor de las Indias*, 283

Sarmiento de Gamboa, Pedro, *Historia de las Incas*, 165

Sarpi, Pietro, 4, 200

Schott, André (Andreas Schottus), 257

Sebastian, King of Portugal, 130
Sessa, Duke of, 189
Sforza, Francesco, 9
Shapiro, Barbara, 29
Sículo, Lucio Marineo, 17, 49, 105
Siliceo, Juan Martínez de, 98
Simancas, royal archive of, 97, 104, 298
Sleidan, John, 78, 89
Snouckhaert, Willem, 91
Solís y Ribadeneyra, Antonio de, *cronista mayor de las Indias*, 265–268, 297; *Historia de la conquista de México*, 269–273
Soll, Jacob, 206
Solórzano Pereira, Juan de, *cronista mayor de las Indias*, 180, 245–247, 297; *De Indiarum jure*, 245–246
Soranzo, Francesco, 94–95
Sorel, Charles, 201–202
Sota, Francisco de, *cronista del rey*, 255–256
Spiegel, Gabrielle, 23–24, 29
Spinola, Ambrosio, 208

Tacitus, 180, 184, 232
Tamayo de Vargas, Tomás, *cronista mayor de las Indias*, 218–219, 292; criticisms of *Céspedes y Meneses*, 229; *Defensa de Flavio Lucio Dextro*, 261
Tarafa, Francesco, 108
Thevet, André, 155, 296
Thirty Years War, battle paintings of, 221–222
Thou, J.-A. de, 173, 267; *Historiam sui temporis*, 203; library of, 210
Thucydides, 5, 31, 296, 298
Toledo, Francisco de, Viceroy of Peru, 165
Torquemada, Fray Juan Antonio de, 183–184; *Monarquía Indiana*, 183
Tribaldos de Toledo, Luis, *cronista mayor de las Indias*, 292
Tubal, 23, 261, 262, 275
Tuy, Lucas of, 21

Ulloa, Alfonso de, 91
Ulloa, Antonio de, 284

Vagad, Fray Gauberto Fabricio de, 49, 105
Valdés, Alfonso de, 71
Valencia, Pedro de, *cronista general*, 7, 193, 255, 258; and Duke of Lerma, 193, 194; and Antonio de Herrera y Tordesillas, 194–199
Valera, Diego de, 45–46
Valla, Lorenzo, 9
Van der Hamen y León, Lorenzo, 212
Varchi, Benedetto, 89
Vaseaus, Johannes, 108
Vega, Lope de, 8, 265, 292; *La Dragontea*, 172; *El Rey don Pedro*, 201
Velasco, Juan Fernández de, 259
Velasco, Luis de, 185
Velasco, Luis José Velázquez de, marqués de Valdeflores, 281
Velázquez, Diego de, 221
Vera y Figueroa, Juan Antonio de, 206, 212, 223–22, 294; *El Embajador*, 207, 224; *Fragmentos históricos de . . . Gaspar de Guzmán . . .*, 225; letters to Malvezzi, 231; *Il milgior giglio di Francia*, 226; *El Rey don Pedro Defendido*, 226
Vergil, Polydore, 107
Verzosa, Juan de, 112
Villanueva López, Jesús, 242
Viperano, Giovanni Antonio, 95
Vitoria, Francisco de, 152
Vives, Juan Luis, 6
Voltaire, 4, 272, 297

William, Prince of Orange, 128
Williams, Bernard, 5, 294
Wyngaerde, Anton van den, 97

Xenophon, 8, 291
Ximénez de Rada, Rodrigo, 21–23, 108

Zayas, Gabriel de, 114
Zúñiga, Juan de, 99
Zurara, Gomes Eanes de, *cronista-mor*, 4, 9
Zurita, Jerónimo de, *cronista del reino de Aragón*, 4, 102, 104; *Anales de la Corona de Aragón*, 105–106; as royal secretary, 106

Library of Congress Cataloging-in-Publication Data
Kagan, Richard L., 1943–
Clio and the crown : the politics of history in medieval and early modern Spain.
    p. cm.
Includes bibliographical references and index.
ISBN-13: 978-0-8018-9294-3 (hardcover : alk. paper)
ISBN-10: 0-8018-9294-5 (hardcover : alk. paper)
1. Spain—History—711–1516—Historiography. 2. Spain—History—16th century—Historiography. 3. Spain—History—17th century—Historiography. 4. Spain—History—18th century—Historiography. I. Title.
    DP97.6.K34 2009
    946.0072—dc22   2008042178

A catalog record for this book is available from the British Library.